Language,
Rhetoric
and
Idea

Language,
Rhetoric and Idea

Edited by

Louis E. Glorfeld
Northern Illinois University

Tom E. Kakonis
Wisconsin State University, Whitewater

James C. Wilcox
Northern Illinois University

Charles E. Merrill Books, Inc.
Columbus, Ohio

Library of Congress Catalog Number: 67-21600

1 2 3 4 5 6 7 8 9 10 11 12 13—75 74 73 72 71 70 69 68 67

Tom Kakonis wishes to express his appreciation to the administration of Wisconsin State University at Whitewater for the time and support granted for the completion of this book.

Printed in the United States of America

PREFACE

At a time when freshman composition texts are pouring off the presses it is never easy to justify the addition of yet another to that apparently endless parade. Nevertheless, we believe that while this book adds nothing new to the much-dissected subject matter of the composition course, it is unique in its conception of including under one cover all the areas of study essential to the student of writing. As the title implies, *Language, Rhetoric and Idea* is divided into three units, each of which can be studied independently of the others (even though the latter two are arranged in close conjunction). However, it is our feeling that one section leads logically into the next; that a knowledge of language is the basis for the understanding of the principles of rhetoric and the development of individual style; and that, ultimately, every writer who aspires to any degree of intellectual excellence must exercise that knowledge and style on challenging ideas. Our assumption is that by embracing all phases of the typical composition course this book provides a unified approach to the total subject.

The first section is predicated on the belief that an understanding of the elements of language is as fundamental a discipline for the novice writer as anatomy is for the medical student. To this end the essays selected touch on a number of significant aspects of language, from its origin and development to the most recent techniques of syntactic description. This very diversity suggests the intention: to introduce the student to the manifold possibilities of language both as a medium of thought and a means of communication and expression. Thus the essays were chosen primarily for their informational qualities rather than for any stylistic or rhetorical virtues they may possess.

The second section deals with the subject of rhetoric, for if language provides the writer with the needed raw material, a mastery of rhetoric supplies the shaping tools. Yet to study these tools in a vacuum can be not only tedious business but questionable pedagogy as well. Therefore, each essay that defines and elaborates a rhetorical principle is followed by another that fully demonstrates the successful working out of that particular principle (and, of course, many others) in a piece of prose. These latter essays have been selected with an eye to "content"; that is, the ideas discussed are relevant to any student regardless of his field and as such furnish a thought-provoking basis for discussion and writing.

The essays on rhetoric were chosen to illustrate the principal topics of that extensive study, and while only modern treatments of those topics are used they are so ordered as to fall into a sequence patterned loosely on classical rhetoric.

The final section consists of ten essays the instructor may use as he will. He may employ them as further examples of rhetorical techniques, as illustrations of specific problems in language, or simply as issues to be analyzed in writing assignments of his choice. The issues are fundamental ones. In each case they are treated by both a contemporary figure and a writer of long established reputation. A comparison of style and attitude will offer interesting insights on several levels.

Our guiding purpose, then, is threefold: awareness of language, dexterity in its use, and thoughtful handling of complex ideas. The questions at the end of the essays in parts one and two are intended for review and discussion of the material, and theme topics, where included, are suggested to assure close reading and to stimulate further research. The sections on rhetoric and idea are unified in that the latter is keyed to the former, and the discussion questions and theme topics overlap to provide a balanced approach to both units.

CONTENTS

Part One

LANGUAGE

Introduction 3

A Model of the
Communication Process   *David Berlo*   6

Linguistics and the
Social Sciences   *John B. Carroll*   22

Science and Linguistics   *Benjamin Lee Whorf*   51

The Development of Language   *L. M. Myers*   65

Revolution in Grammar   *W. Nelson Francis*   77

The Patterns of Grammar   *L. M. Myers*   98

Theories of English Grammar   *Wayne O'Neil* 111

Transformational Grammar:
An Introduction   *Andrew MacLeish* 122

Linguistics and Teaching
Introductory Literature   *Seymour Chatman* 135

A Not Disinterested/Uninterested
Note on the New Dictionary   *Howard K. Battles* 144

Right vs. Wrong   *Robert A. Hall, Jr.* 152

Part Two

RHETORIC AND IDEA

Introduction

Rhetoric: Its Function and Its Scope *Donald Bryant* 177

Organization:

Organizing the Composition   *Robert Penn Warren and Cleanth Brooks* 212

Are Colleges Killing Education?   *Oscar Handlin* 224

Description:

Description   *Richard E: Hughes and P. Albert Duhamel* 237

The Gray Beginnings   *Rachel Carson* 254

Definition:

Definition   *Leo Rockas* 268

Liberals and Conservatives   *Laurence Sears* 278

Comparison and Contrast:

Logical Order: Comparison and Contrast   *James W. Johnson* 292

The Crisis of American Masculinity   *Arthur Schlesinger* 302

Logic:

Persuasion by Logical Argument   *Newman and Genevieve Birk* 314

In Favor of Capital Punishment   *Jaques Barzun* 330

Analogy:

Analogy: This is Like That   *Manuel Bilsky* 344

Civilization on Trial   *Arnold J. Toynbee* 350

Rhetoric of the Sentence:
  Rhetoric and Emphasis: Differences
    in Sentences   *John E. Jordan* 364
  The Hard Kind of Patriotism   *Adlai E. Stevenson* 388

Style:
                                John Halverson and
  Structure in Style   *Mason Cooley* 398
  Why I Am Not Going to
    the Moon   *Joseph Wood Krutch* 411

Part Three

ESSAYS FOR FURTHER ANALYSIS

The Uses of the Moon   *Arthur C. Clarke* 424

Of the Limits to the Authority of
  Society over the Individual   *John Stuart Mill* 436

Civil Disobedience   *Henry David Thoreau* 454

Inviting Communists to Speak
  at Colleges   *William F. Buckley, Jr.* 474

Learning vs. Invention   *Samuel Johnson* 481

The American Scholar   *Ralph Waldo Emerson* 485

Literature and Science   *Matthew Arnold* 502

An Argument Against Abolishing
  Christianity   *Jonathan Swift* 520

Man Against Darkness   *Walter T. Stace* 531

Aes Triplex   *Robert Louis Stevenson* 543

PART ONE

PART ONE

Language

Language is the highest and most complex form of human activity. Without it no education could be conducted, no scientific quest pursued, no cultural tradition passed from one generation to the next. Indeed, without language no civilization, as we understand that term, could possibly exist. Yet most people, because they get along reasonably well in their native tongue, tend to ignore language and, should they think of it at all, consider it to be as automatic and unconscious an activity as breathing. And the student is scarcely different from the rest of the population. He has for so long taken for granted the tool of language that he can quite legitimately ask: Why is language so complex? Why study it?

The answer to the former question will be found through the close reading and study of the essays in this unit. The steady and rapid growth of interest in linguistics during this century has doubtless been influenced by the analytic bent of our age. But whatever the reason for this burgeoning growth, the fact is that linguistics is now an established discipline, a discipline that is only beginning to discover the full extent of its own possibilities. The eleven essays included here will demonstrate how linguists are pushing back the frontiers of our knowledge about language and will introduce the reader to both the kind of research currently being done and its immense range.

The second question — why study language — is perhaps more immediately meaningful to the student. There are two answers to this question, and the first is purely practical. If language is the most fundamental tool of education, then it is safe to assume that greater facility with that tool will result in greater success with the subject matter itself. It makes no difference what that subject matter may be — science, business, history, the humanities — all must finally be communicated through oral and written expression.

And a knowledge of how language works, of its many nuances and ambiguities, will better equip the student to confront the difficult process of learning regardless of his special interest.

The study of language has a cultural value that is equally as important as the practical. Since it is essentially language that sets man apart from the lower animals, the study of this unique phenomenon leads to a deeper appreciation of the mystery of humanity. Literature, philosophy, the accumulated knowledge and traditions of the past are all transmitted through the ever-shifting medium of language; to understand something of that medium is to understand more of one's origin and behavior and aspirations. Again, the essays in this unit offer a glimpse of how we come to such an understanding and where, ultimately, it may lead us. Should that glimpse prove tantalizing, the essays themselves may serve as merely a springboard for the further exploration and research suggested in the discussion questions, writing topics, and bibliography.

Part One

Contents

Language

Introduction

A Model of the Communication
Process   *David Berlo* 6

Linguistics and the Social Sciences   *John B. Carroll* 22

Science and Linguistics   *Benjamin Lee Whorf* 51

The Development of the Language   *L. M. Myers* 65

Revolution in Grammar   *W. Nelson Francis* 77

The Patterns of Grammar   *L. M. Myers* 98

Theories of English Grammar   *Wayne O'Neil* 111

Transformational Grammar:
An Introduction   *Andrew MacLeish* 122

Linguistics and Teaching
Introductory Literature   *Seymour Chatman* 135

A Not Disinterested/Uninterested
Note on the New Dictionary   *Howard K. Battles* 144

Right vs. Wrong   *Robert A. Hall, Jr.* 152

5

Any student wishing to seem up-to-date can begin an essay with the words "In our modern fast-changing world . . ." and go on from there. Apparently, he has accepted the fact that his world is one of flux and fluidity. But has he? Usually, he has merely pinned a label reading "changeable" on his environment and then gone on to accept that environment as static and constant, and he acts as if it had meaning and value for all time. This type of person has usually accepted the reality of technological change (he watches television, whereas his father went to the movies), but his view of the world is still Newtonian.

Newtonian physics recognized a world of "things." A "thing" was supposed to have a real existence, independent of other "things" or their operations. This way of looking at the world was a comfortable one. It overlooked only two problems: 1) any "thing" cannot be examined except in relation to other "things" or happenings related to it; and 2) the development of better observational tools — microscopes, for instance — let us see that a "thing" was changing all the time, in relation to the environment and in relation to the observer, whose very observations often affected the "thing" under examination.

Obviously, a better way of looking at the world was needed. Scientists now see the world as process: everything consists of inter-relationships, and everything is in motion. The world is no longer a clearly defined metaphorical sausage that we can slice into handy divisions for examination in isolation. In this essay "A Model of the Communication Process," David Berlo defines the concept of "process" and illustrates how an understanding of this concept can aid in an objective discussion of the meaning and significance of communication.

For communication is itself a process. And when we examine communication, we encounter the same two problems we encounter when we examine any other process: 1) we must stop the process in order to examine it, and hence we distort the process; and 2) we must use language to describe the process, and language itself changes. Examining communication, or any process, then, is a slippery one, and our only hope (if there really is any) is for us to become as consciously aware as possible of that slipperiness.

6

A Model of the Communication Process

David Berlo

1   Every communication situation differs in some ways from every other one, yet we can attempt to isolate certain elements that all communication situations have in common. It is these ingredients and their interrelationships that we consider when we try to construct a general model of communication.

2   We attach the word "process" to our discussion of communication: The concept of process is itself complex. If we begin to discuss a model of the communication process without a common meaning for the word "process," our discussion might result in distorted views about communication.

THE CONCEPT OF PROCESS

3   At least one dictionary defines "process" as "any phenomenon which shows a continuous change in time," or "any continuous operation or treatment." Five hundred years before the birth of Christ, Heraclitus pointed out the importance of the concept of process when he stated that a man can never step in the same river twice; the man is different and so is the river. Thomas Wolfe's novel of the 1940's, *You Can't Go Home Again*, makes the same point.

4   If we accept the concept of process, we view events and relationships as dynamic, on-going, ever-changing, continuous. When we label something as a process, we also mean that it does not have *a* beginning, *an* end, a fixed sequence of events. It is not static, at rest. It is moving. The ingredients within a process interact; each affects all of the others.

5   The concept of process is inextricably woven into the contem-

porary view of science and physical reality. In fact, the development
of a process viewpoint in the physical sciences brought about one
of the twentieth-century revolutions that we mentioned earlier. If
we analyze the work of physical scientists up to and including Isaac
Newton, we do not find a comprehensive analysis of process. It
was believed that the world could be divided into "things" and
"processes." It was believed also that things *existed*, that they were
static entities, that their existence was independent of the existence
or operations of other "things."

6   The crisis and revolution in scientific philosophy brought about
by the work of Einstein, Russell, Whitehead, and others denied
both of these beliefs in two ways. First, the concept of relativity
suggested that any given object or event could only be analyzed or
described in light of other events that were related to it, other
operations involved in observing it. Second, the availability of more
powerful observational techniques led to the demonstration that
something as static or stable as a table, a chair, could be looked on
as a constantly changing phenomenon, acting upon and being acted
upon by all other objects in its environment, changing as the person
who observed it changes. The traditional division between things
was questioned. The traditional distinction between things and
processes was broken down. An entirely different way of looking at the world had to be developed — a process view of reality.

7   Communication theory reflects a process point of view. A communication theorist rejects the possibility that nature consists of
events or ingredients that are separable from all other events. He
argues that you cannot talk about *the* beginning or *the* end of
communication or say that a particular idea came from one specific
source, that communication occurs in only one way, and so on.

8   The basis for the concept of process is the belief that the structure of physical reality can not be *discovered* by man; it must be
created by man. In "constructing" reality, the theorist chooses to
organize his perceptions in one way or another. He may choose
to say that we can call certain things "elements" or "ingredients."
In doing this, he realizes that he has not discovered anything,
he has created a set of tools which may or may not be useful in
analyzing or describing the world. He recognizes that certain
things may precede others, but that in many cases the order of
precedence will vary from situation to situation. This is not to say
that we can place no order on events. The dynamic of process has
limitations; nevertheless, there is more than one dynamic that can
be developed for nearly any combination of events.

9   When we try to talk or write about a process, such as communi-

cation, we face at least two problems. First, we must arrest the dynamic of the process, in the same way that we arrest motion when we take a still picture with a camera. We can make useful observations from photographs, but we err if we forget that the camera is not a complete reproduction of the objects photographed. The interrelationships among elements are obliterated, the fluidity of motion, the dynamics, are arrested. The picture is a representation of the event, it is not the event. As Hayakawa has put it, the word is not the thing, it is merely a map that we can use to guide us in exploring the territories of the world.

10   A second problem in describing a process derives from the necessity of the use of language. Language itself, as used by people over time, is a process. It, too, is changing, on-going; however, the process quality of language is lost when we write it. Marks on paper are a recording of language, a picture of language. They are fixed, permanent, static. Even spoken language, over a short period of time, is relatively static.

11   In using language to describe a process, we must choose certain words, we must freeze the physical world in a certain way. Furthermore, we must put some words first, others last. Western languages go from left to right, top to bottom. All languages go from front to back, beginning to end —even though we are aware that the process we are describing may not have a left or right, a top and a bottom, a beginning and an end.

12   We have no alternative if we are to analyze and communicate about a process. The important point is that we must remember that we are not including everything in our discussion. The things we talk about do not have to exist in exactly the ways we talk about them, and they certainly do not have to operate in the order in which we talk about them. Objects which we separate may not always be separable, and they never operate independently—each affects and interacts with the others. This may appear obvious, but it is easy to overlook or forget the limitations that are necessarily placed on any discussion of a process.

13   To illustrate the point, let us take an example other than communication. Education is a process. In discussing education, we can list certain ingredients. We have students, teachers, books, classroom lectures, libraries, discussion, meditation, thought, etc. We can order the ingredients. We can say that, in education, a teacher lectures to students (50 minutes at a time, three days a week, for x years). We can say that a student reads books (6 books, 119 books, any number of books). We can say that the library has 100,000 volumes, or 1,000,000 volumes, or 6,000,000

volumes. We can say that students will hold *x* discussion sessions, spend *y* hours meditating, and write *z* papers or examinations.

14   When we put all this together, we can say that if all of these ingredients are available and have been used, the student has received "an education." We *can* say this, but if we do we have forgotten the concept of process, the dynamics of education. As any good cook knows, it is the mixing process, the blending, that makes a good cake; ingredients are necessary, but not sufficient.

15   For an example in the communication field, take the theatre. What is "theatre"? Again, we can list ingredients: a playwright, a play, directors, actors, stage hands, audiences, scenery, lighting, an auditorium. Add them, and the total is theatre? Definitely not. Again, it is the blending, the dynamic interrelationships among the ingredients developed in the process that determine whether we have what we would call "theatre."

16   We need to remember that the dynamic of movement which relates the ingredients is vital. The concept of dynamic also implies that factors that we may overlook in any single listing of the ingredients also determine what is produced.

17   The dynamic of theatre is in part related to whether the play is produced for an audience before or after they have eaten dinner, or whether they had a heavy or a light meal, whether they enjoyed it or disliked it. The dynamic of education is in part determined by whether the student has just come from another situation in which he learned something which still excites him or whether he is fresh and has an "uncluttered" mind, whether he is taking an elective course he chose himself or a required one, whether his classmates make comments which stimulate him, or whether he has only his own thinking to help him, and so on.

18   Much of the scientific research in communication attempts to isolate factors which do or do not make a difference in the development of the process. Obviously, all the ingredients have not been determined—in fact, there is considerable basis for doubt as to whether they ever will be determined.

19   In any case, we need constantly to remember that our discussion of a process is incomplete, with a forced order and possibly a distorted perspective. Discussion is useful, it can lead to greater insight about a process. But it is not a complete picture, it can never reproduce the process itself. We cannot list all the ingredients nor talk adequately about how they affect each other. We can provide some suggestions, some hints about both the ingredients and the dynamic of the process.

20   There have been approaches to analyzing communication that have not been process-oriented. Such approaches might be labeled

as " hypodermic needle" concepts of how communication works, or "click-click, push-pull" points of view. Such descriptions of communication are restricted to saying that first the communicator does A, then he does B, then C happens, and so on.

21   Much of the early discussion of the effects of the mass media of communication were of the "hypodermic-needle" variety. Critics as well as advocates of the print or electronic media (radio, TV) talked about how these media would affect the American public. Their concept of effects implied that a radio broadcast or a television program could be viewed as a hypodermic needle. If we would just stick these messages in the minds of the public, learning or entertainment or greater participation in civic affairs would be produced. The research conducted on the effects of the media indicates otherwise; whether or not these sources of communication are effective depends on a complex of factors, some of which the media can control and some of which they cannot.

22   Much of the debate over the effects of comic books on children, the effects of the movies, advertising, or political campaigns on the public is of this variety. Critics and commentators often overlook the effect of children on the contents of the comics, the effect of the public on movies, etc. It certainly is true that newspapers affect public opinion, but a process point of view argues that it is equally true that public opinion affects the newspapers.

23   With the concept of process established in our minds, we can profit from an analysis of the ingredients of communication, the elements that seem necessary (if not sufficient) for communication to occur. We want to look at elements such as *who* is communicating, *why* he is communicating, and *to whom* he is communicating. We want to look at communication behaviors: *messages* which are produced, *what* people are trying to communicate. We want to look at style, how people *treat* their messages. We want to examine the means of communication, the *channels* that people use to get their messages to their listeners, their readers. In short, we want to list the elements in the communication process that we must take into account when (a) we initiate communication, (b) we respond to communication, or (c) we serve as communication observers or analysts.

THE INGREDIENTS OF COMMUNICATION

24   The concern with communication has produced many attempts to develop models of the process—descriptions, listing of ingredients. Of course, these models differ. None can be said to be "right,"

or "true." Some may be more useful than others, some may correspond more than others to the current state of knowledge about communication.

25   In the *Rhetoric*, Aristotle said that we have to look at three communication ingredients; the speaker, the speech, and the audience. He meant that each of these elements is necessary to communication and that we can organize our study of the process under the three headings of (1) the person who speaks, (2) the speech that he produces, and (3) the person who listens.[1]

26   Most of our current communication models are similar to Aristotle's, though somewhat more complex. One of the most-used contemporary models was developed in 1947 by Claude Shannon, a mathematician, and explained to the nonmathematician by Warren Weaver.[2] Shannon and Weaver were not even talking about human communication. They were talking about electronic communication. In fact, Shannon worked for the Bell Telephone Laboratory. Yet behavioral scientists have found the Shannon-Weaver model useful in describing human communication.

27   The Shannon-Weaver model certainly is consistent with Aristotle's position. Shannon and Weaver said that the ingredients in communication include (1) a source, (2) a transmitter, (3) a signal, (4) a receiver, and (5) a destination. If we translate the source into the speaker, the signal into the speech, and the destination into the listener, we have the Aristotelian model, plus two added ingredients, a transmitter which sends out the source's message, and a receiver which catches the message for the destination.

28   There are other models of the communication process, developed by Schramm,[3] Westley and MacLean,[4] Fearing,[5] Johnson,[6] and others. A comparison will indicate the great similarities among them. They differ partly in terminology, partly in the addition or subtraction of one or two elements, partly in the differences in the point of view of the disciplines from which they emerged.

---

[1]W. Rhys Roberts, "Rhetorica," in *The Works of Aristotle* (W. D. Ross, ed.). Oxford University Press, 1946, Volume XI, p. 14.
[2]Claude Shannon and Warren Weaver, *The Mathematical Theory of Communication.* University of Illinois Press, 1949, p. 5.
[3]Wilbur Schramm, "How communication works," in *The Process and Effects of Mass Communication* (Wilbur Schramm, ed.). University of Illinois Press, 1954, pp. 3–26.
[4]Bruce Westley and Malcolm MacLean, Jr., "A conceptual model for communication research," *Journalism Quarterly,* 34:31–38, 1957.
[5]Franklin Fearing, "Toward a psychological theory of human communication," *Journal of Personality,* 22:71–78, 1953.
[6]Wendell Johnson, "The fateful process of Mister A talking to Mister B," in *How Successful Executives Handle People.* Harvard Business Review, 1953, p. 50.

29   In developing the model presented here, I have tried to be consistent with current theory and research in the behavioral sciences. It has been changed many times in the past few years, as a result of using it with students in the classroom, with adults in extension courses, and with workshops and seminars in industry, agriculture, and government. It is similar to other communication models and is presented only because people have found it a useful scheme for talking about communication in many different communication situations.

A COMMUNICATION MODEL

30   We can say that all human communication has some *source*, some person or group of persons with a purpose, a reason for engaging in communication. Given a source, with ideas, needs, intentions, information, and a purpose for communicating, a second ingredient is necessary. The purpose of the source has to be expressed in the form of a *message*. In human communication, a message is behavior available in physical form—the translation of ideas, purposes, and intentions into a code, a systematic set of symbols.

31   How do the source's purposes get translated into a code, a language? This requires a third communication ingredient, an *encoder*. The communication encoder is responsible for taking the ideas of the source and putting them in a code, expressing the source's purpose in the form of a message. In person-to-person communication, the encoding function is performed by the motor skills of the source —his vocal mechanisms (which produce the oral word, cries, musical notes, etc.), the muscle systems in the hand (which produce the written word, pictures, etc.), the muscle systems elsewhere in the body (which produce gestures of the face or arms, posture, etc.).

32   When we talk about more complex communication situations, we often separate the source from the encoder. For example, we can look at a sales manager as a source and his salesmen as encoders: people who produce messages for the consumer which translate the intentions or purposes of the manager.

33   For the present, we shall restrict our model to the minimum complexity. We have a communication source with purpose and an encoder who translates or expresses this purpose in the form of a message. We are ready for a fourth ingredient, the *channel*.

34   We can look at channels in several ways. Communication theory presents at least three meanings for the word "channel." For the

moment, it is enough to say that a channel is a medium, a carrier of messages. It is correct to say that messages can exist only in *some* channel; however, the *choice* of channels often is an important factor in the effectiveness of communication.

35   We have introduced a communication *source*, an *encoder*, a *message*, and a *channel*. If we stop here, no communication has taken place. For communication to occur ,there must be somebody at the other end of the channel. If we have a purpose, encode a message, and put it into one or another channel, we have done only part of the job. When we talk, somebody must listen; when we write, somebody must read. The person or persons at the other end can be called the communication *receiver*, the target of communication.

36   Communication sources and receivers must be similar systems. If they are not similar, communication cannot occur. We can go one step further and say that the source and the receiver may be (and often are) the same person; the source may communicate with himself—he listens to what he says, he reads what he writes, he thinks. In psychological terms, the source intends to produce a stimulus. The receiver responds to that stimulus if communication occurs; if he does not respond, communication has not occurred.

37   We now have all the basic communication ingredients except one. Just as a source needs an encoder to translate his purposes into a message, to express purpose in a code, the receiver needs a *decoder* to retranslate, to decode the message and put it into a form that the receiver can use. We said that in person-to-person communication the encoder would be the set of motor skills of the source. By the same token, we can look at the decoder as the set of sensory skills of the receiver. In one- or two-person communication situations, the decoder can be thought of as the senses.

38   These, then, are the ingredients that we will include in our discussion of a model of the communication process:

1. the communication source;
2. the encoder;
3. the message;
4. the channel;
5. the decoder;
6. the communication receiver.

39   We will mention many other communication factors; however, we will return to these six ingredients again and again, as we talk about communication at various levels of complexity.

The Parts of the Model

40   What do we mean by a source, an encoder, and so on? Our preliminary discussion has given us the beginnings of a meaning for each of these terms—but only the beginnings. At this point, precise definitions of each term might not be as useful as a set of examples which include all the ingredients.

41   Let us start with a common communication situation: two people talking. Suppose it is Friday morning. We find Joe and Mary in the local coffee shop. There is a picnic scheduled for Sunday afternoon. Suddenly, Joe realizes that Mary is *the* girl to take on the picnic. Joe decides to ask her for a Sunday afternoon date. Joe is now ready to act as a communication source—he has a purpose: to get Mary to agree to accompany him on Sunday. (He may have other purposes as well, but they are not our concern.)

42   Joe wants to produce a message. His central nervous system orders his speech mechanism to construct a message to express his purpose. The speech mechanism, serving as an encoder, produces the following message: "Mary, will you go to the picnic with me on Sunday?"

43   The message is transmitted via sound waves through air, so that Mary can receive it. This is the channel. Mary's hearing mechanism serves as a decoder. She hears Joe's message, decodes the message into a nervous impulse, and sends it to her central nervous system. Mary's central nervous system responds to the message. It decides that Friday is too late to ask for a Sunday date. Mary intends to refuse the date, and sends an order to her speech mechanism. The message is produced: "Thanks, Joe, but no thanks." Or something somewhat more polite.

44   This is a very elementary and oversimplified treatment of the nature of the communication process, but it includes, at least superficially, all six ingredients we have introduced. Let us try another example.

45   Take the communication situation in which you are now engaged: reading this chapter. In this communication situation, I served as the source. I had a purpose in producing this manuscript —this message. My writing mechanisms served as an encoder (of course, typewriters, typists, and printing presses also served as encoders). The message includes the words on this page, and the way that the words are arranged. The message is transmitted to you through the medium of a book, by means of light waves. Your eye is the decoder. It receives the message, decodes it, retranslates it into a nervous impulse, and sends it to your central nervous system.

Your central nervous system is the receiver. As you read, you will make responses to the book.

46   Let us take another example, and look at it more closely. Suppose Bill and John are at the dinner table. Bill has a problem. He is ready to eat a sandwich. He likes salt on a sandwich. The salt is at John's end of the table. Bill wants the salt. What does he do? He could reach from his end of the table to John's end and get the salt himself; however, this not only would be rude, it would be work. More likely, Bill asks John to pass the salt. Being a congenial sort of fellow, John passes Bill the salt. Bill puts it on his sandwich. All is well.

47   Again, what has happened, in terms of our communication model? Bill's central nervous system served as a communication source. He had a need, *salt on sandwich.* He had an intention, a purpose, to get John to pass him the salt. Bill relayed this purpose as a nervous impulse to his encoder, his speech mechanism. His encoder translated and expressed his purpose in code—English— and produced a message. The message: "Pass the salt, please."

48   Bill transmitted this message via sound waves, through the air, in such a way that John could receive the message. John's hearing mechanism caught the message, decoded it, and sent it on to John's central nervous system. John had meaning for the message, responded to it, and passed Bill the salt. Mission accomplished.

49   This is communication. These are elementary examples, but even here communication is quite complex. The process we have just described occurs in only a small fraction of the time it took to talk about it—and we oversimplified our description at that. What were some of the things that could have gone wrong?

50   Suppose Bill did not have a clear idea of his purpose. He knew he needed something for his sandwich but he did not know what he needed. How could he have instructed his encoder to transmit a message?

51   Suppose Bill did not like John, or thought that John was inferior to him. This information might get through to his encoder, and the message might come out something like "Hey, you, gimme the salt —now." John might pass the salt—or he might say, "Get it yourself."

52   Suppose Bill was a new clerk in the company, and John was a Vice-President. Bill might not feel that he should start any communication with John—and Bill eats a sandwich without salt.

53   Suppose wires get crossed between Bill's nervous system and his encoder, and he produces an embarrassing message such as "Sass me the palt." Suppose his encoder is deficient, and it substitutes an

"m" for an "s"; the message becomes "Pass me the malt." Either John gives Bill something Bill doesn't want or he doesn't give him anything at all.

54   Suppose the coffee shop is crowded and noisy. John does not hear Bill because the communication channel is overloaded. Result —John does not respond, and Bill never eats with John again. Finally, suppose John and Bill come from different cultures. In John's culture people do not eat salt on meat, or John might even disapprove of anyone using salt on meat. Result—he might not understand Bill, or he might not think as well of him.

55   These are only a few examples of the kinds of things that can go wrong, even in a simple two-person communication situation. You might like to return to our example of Joe asking Mary for a date or of your reading of this manuscript. What kinds of things could have happened at one or another stage of the process to cause those two communication situations to break down?

56   Our examples have been confined to relatively uncomplicated communication situations. The model is equally useful in describing the communication behavior of a complex organization. In such a situation, the encoding and decoding functions often are separable from source and receiver functions. Correspondingly, certain people in the organization occupy roles as both sources and receivers.

57   Take a large-city newspaper as an example. The operation of the newspaper involves a complex network of communication. The newspaper hires people whose prime job is decoding—reporters who observe one or more kinds of events in the world and relay them to the "central nervous system" of the paper, the "desk" or "slot" or central control office.

58   When these messages are received, some decision is reached by the editorial staff. As a result of these decisions, orders are given from the control desk to produce or not produce a given message in the paper. Again, the encoding function becomes specialized. The paper employs rewrite men, proofreaders, linotype operators, pressmen, delivery boys. They all are responsible for one or another part of the encoding and channeling functions, getting the message out of the control office on to the pages of the newspaper, and thence to a different set of receivers, the reading public.

59   The communication model can be used to describe the personal behavior of any member of the newspaper staff. At the same time, it can be applied at a different level of analysis, and used to describe the workings of the organization as a communication network.

60   Within the paper, elaborate subdivisions of communication responsibility are made. Some people decode only certain kinds of

messages: police work, society behavior, sports, etc. Others are assigned to a more general beat. Some people do not feed information into the paper, but are responsible solely for encoding messages which get this information back out. Still others neither decode nor encode (at the network analysis level), but are responsible for receiver-source behaviors; in other words, for making decisions about the messages they receive and giving orders about messages they want sent out.

61   The newspaper is one example of a communication network. Others might include the behaviors of any information organization, the operations of the Department of State, and the structure of a large industrial organization. Communication analysis can be performed on communicative institutions or on a specific person. The model is equally applicable to both. It represents a point of view, a way of looking at behavior, whether the behavior is individual or institutional.

62   The examples given have several implications for further discussion. One is the varying nature of communication purposes. To a large extent, the modern newspaper is not an "original" source of communication. It specializes in interpreting information it receives from one set of sources and transmitting this information, as interpreted, to another set of receivers. It works as an intermediary in communication.

63   At the same time, through the editorial page, the newspaper does originate messages, does transmit "original" information to its reading audience. It both originates and interprets. One of the canons of responsible journalism is the requirement that the newspaper keep these two functions separate—that it avoid originating material while pretending to be interpreting material received from outside its own system.

64   There are other examples of the originator-interpreter distinction. The New York Stock Exchange is a good illustration. The operation of the market can be analyzed as an intricate communication network, in which the behaviors allowed to people performing various roles are explicitly defined and rigorously enforced. Some brokers on the floor are primarily encoders. They transmit the intentions of the main office or of customers who may live far from the exchange itself. Other brokers are both encoders and decoders. They transmit their employer's purposes and decode messages from others about the state of the market, the price of a particular stock. They send these messages to their office, where a decision is made. Still others are allowed to make decisions by themselves. They may

buy or sell on their own initiative, for their firms or their personal holdings.

65   A second implication of the examples given concerns the way in which we should interpret the concepts of source, encoder, decoder, and receiver. These should not be viewed as separate things or entities or people. They are the names of behaviors which have to be performed for communication to occur. More than one person may be involved in the same behavior-form (multiple sources, encoders, etc.). One person may perform more than one set of behaviors. The same person may be both a source and a receiver, even simultaneously. The same person may—and usually does—both encode and decode messages. This illustrates the earlier point that the ingredients of communication, or of any process, are not separable, cannot be divided into independent or nonoverlapping entities.

66   The examples also can be used to illustrate the principle of relativity referred to earlier. At one level of analysis, we can describe a reporter as a decoder. At another, he is both a source and a receiver and performs both encoding and decoding behaviors. What we call him depends upon our own purposes, how we view him, in what context we place him, and so on.

67   Finally, the examples demonstrate the meaning of process, the interrelationship of the ingredients of communication. Within the newspaper, we cannot order communication events as (1) reporting, (2) decision-making by the central office on the value of messages received, (3) orders to put certain articles in the paper, and (4) encoding of those articles. It is hard to say which comes first.

68   Clearly, the reporter is affected by what he believes his editors want him to report, by the deadlines he faces in order to meet the requirements of the encoding process, etc. The central office is limited by what it receives from its reporters. It also is affected by what it believes to be the editorial policy of the publisher, his political beliefs, the space available in the paper, the time and costs of encoding, etc. And, of course, all employees are affected at all times by their assumptions as to the purposes of the reader who eventually will consume the paper. What they believe the reader wants affects what they report, what they interpret, and what they encode.

69   The communication of news is a process. All the ingredients of the process affect each other. A dynamic peculiar to that specific process is developed. A journalism student can quickly become

familiar with the ingredients of journalism: events, typewriters, articles, city desks, printing presses, distribution systems, etc. It is the dynamic which is hard to learn, and which usually has to be experienced before it is understood.

70   The ingredients discussed are essential to communication. Whether we talk about communication in terms of one person, two persons, or an institutional network, the functions labeled as source, encoder, decoder, and receiver have to be performed. Messages always are involved and must exist in some channel. How they go together, in what order, and with what kinds of interrelationships depend on the situation, the nature of the specific process under study, the dynamic developed.

71   It is useful to use these ingredients to talk about communication. It is dangerous to assume that one comes first, one last, or that they are independent of each other. This denies the concept of process, and communication is a process. The importance of process might best be typified by the traditional argument of the relative priority of chickens and eggs. One useful deterrent to forgetting about interrelationships within a process is to remember the following definition: a chicken is what an egg makes in order to reproduce itself.

QUESTIONS FOR STUDY

1. What differences in personality might you expect to find between the person who lives in a world of "things" and one who sees the world as "process"? What assumptions underlie each concept that might explain this difference?

2. In what ways do Aristotle's communication ingredients differ (other than in number of terms) from those of either Shannon or Weaver? Was Aristotle merely "bull-headed" or might there be practical reasons for his divisions?

3. The author gives us six ingredients of the communication process: the communication source, the encoder, the message, the channel, the decoder, the communication receiver. What part does each play in the communication process?

4. Can you see any paradox in dividing the communication process into six parts? Would it be less paradoxical if the process was divided into either four or eight parts?

5. The author claims that by seeing the world in terms of process we take into account the dynamics of that world. Does the author's account of this process seem very dynamic to you? What seems to be lacking?

6. At what point might feedback be expected to enter into the communication process? Why?

7. What part do you think the emotions might play in interrupting the communication process? Why do you think the author has not stressed the importance of the emotions?

8. What effect might slang or jargon have on the communication process?

9. Can you think of any instances when the purpose of the message might be the interruption of the communication process? Does the author's explanation take this factor into account? Explain.

A child misbehaves, and we wish to reprimand him. Since we speak English, we say "Be Good!" But the French say *"Soit sage!"* (Be wise, or be reasonable!) And the Germans say *Gehorche!* (Obey!) One misbehaving child, but three different responses, each response revealing something of the world of the person issuing the reprimand. And if each of our respondents offered us more language samples to examine, we could study each world in greater depth—because the language *is* the world. We strain the world through the sieve of our perceptions, and our perceptions are formed by the categories and classes that our language offers.

What better way, therefore, is there to examine the world we or others live in than through an examination of language? Once we accept this idea, we are in the company of Terence who said: *"Homo sum: humani nihil a me alienum puto."* (I am a man: I think naught that is human alien to me.) And nothing is more human than language, the most common denominator of all.

The study of language, then, can be a powerful tool in any of the social sciences. Each discipline, of necessity, blocks out a special area for examination; or rather, each discipline determines to examine the special area using specific observational techniques. But each discipline must also examine the language behavior within this special area if the examination is not to be superficial. This is why John B. Carroll, in his essay "Linguistics and the Social Sciences," can say: "Linguistics thus appears to have a bearing on all the social sciences which are concerned with studying the behaviour of groups or the behaviour of individuals in relation to these groups."

Linguistics and the Social Sciences

John B. Carroll

INTRODUCTION

1 Language is without doubt cultural in nature and determination. This is true whether one believes, with some, that language must be distinguished from culture, or, with others, that language is one major aspect of culture and hence is to be included in culture. Furthermore, it is true regardless of whether one considers linguistics primarily as a social science or as one of the humanistic studies. Controversies on such problems are mainly terminological; they do not obscure the important role which linguistics may play when applied to various social sciences.

2 For one thing, a language system may be regarded as a cultural "marker." Hence, as a guide in indicating the boundaries of a culture area or as an aid in tracing the spread of culture by migration and by cultural borrowing, linguistic facts are often far more reliable than other cultural markers, such as the tools used by a culture, or its style of architecture. Tools and styles of architecture are much more readily borrowed than certain aspects of language.

3 Moreover, the members of a culture are usually aware, consciously or unconsciously, of language as a cultural marker. In the United States, we are in the habit of identifying people with a "Southern accent" as belonging to a particular subculture; likewise, individuals in the educated classes are likely to identify persons with substandard speech as belonging to "inferior" social classes. When dialectal differences become the basis for invidious comparisons, their relevance in social interaction becomes painfully obvious.

Reprinted by permission of the publishers from John B. Carroll's, *The Study of Language*. Cambridge, Mass.: Harvard University Press, Copyright, 1953, by the President and Fellows of Harvard College.

4   Finally, it is overwhelmingly significant that every facet of a
language system contributes to the way in which a community uses
language in social control. Not only everyday conversation and
address but also all the varieties of mass communication, such as
propaganda and advertising, depend upon the precarious standards
of a common language system.

5   Linguistics thus appears to have a bearing on all the social
sciences which are concerned with studying the behavior of groups
or the behavior of individuals in relation to those groups. There
is even a possibility that linguistics may play a part in the solution
of certain social problems. If so, a new kind of applied science—
"language engineering," as it has recently been termed—may come
into being.

6   In this chapter we will consider the relations between linguistic
science, on the one hand, and anthropology, sociology, and social
psychology on the other. We will also attempt to sketch the possible implications of linguistic studies for certain problems of social
engineering, such as the resolution of problems caused by linguistic
diversity throughout the world and the adjustment of social conditions in communities where the folk language is not accorded
its proper status.

LINGUISTICS IN RELATION TO ANTHROPOLOGY

7   In anthropological literature, there are many expressions of confidence in the idea that there are intimate connections between
linguistics and ethnology.[1] Olmsted (1950) has sorted out some

---

[1]There are even suggestions that racial genetics and physical anthropology
may have a bearing on linguistic problems. Van Ginneken (1927), for example,
proposed that divergent phonetic changes in different subcultures might be
accounted for by hereditary factors. Luchsinger (1940) and Tarnóczy (1947)
are said to have established the genetic basis for individual differences in the
articulatory mechanism. The geneticist Darlington (1947) has discovered a
correlation between the frequency of genes for type-O blood in a culture and
the presence of what he calls TH sounds (including, apparently, [θ,ð, tʰ, dʰ,
tθ, dð] and similar sounds) in the language of the culture. He does not explain
how blood grouping could be conceived to have any effect on speech sounds,
but assumes that genetic factors in general could make for increased ease or
difficulty in the articulation of certain phonetic elements, and hence could lead
to preferences for the "easier" sounds. Darlington's results are sufficiently
striking to suggest that they could not have occurred by chance; however, they
could have occurred through the operation of a third variable, namely, the
parallel distribution of linguistic and cultural traits. It is also quite possible
that Darlington's classification of the phonetic data was too loose and hence
subject to unconscious manipulation on the part of the investigator.

of these connections in his survey of what he recognizes as "ethno-linguistics." He points out that ethnolinguistics has been understood in several senses, as referring to (*a*) the use, in ethnology, of findings in linguistics, (*b*) the use, in linguistics, of findings from ethnology, (*c*) the interchange between linguistics and ethnology of certain features of their respective methodologies, (*d*) studies of problems clearly requiring data from both ethnology and linguistics, and (*e*) an integrative approach in the social sciences made possible by the combined forces of ethnology and linguistics. It is wise to agree, as Olmsted seems to imply, that ethnolinguistics embraces all these things.

8　　The ethnologist, whose job is to describe the traits of a given culture, is under a routine obligation to list the language system or systems prevalent in the culture. Usually the ethnologist is not a technical linguist, but, depending upon the thoroughness with which he wishes to conduct his work, he may find it necessary to acquire at least some skill in speaking and understanding the language of the community whose culture he is studying. If the language has already been described by a linguist, the ethnologist is obviously benefited; if only in this trivial and operational sense, linguistic results can be applied in ethnology. Although ethnologists occasionally disparage the value of linguistic training, Sapir's remarks on the subject are convincing:

> Some day the attempt to master a primitive culture without the help of the language of its society will seem as amateurish as the labors of a historian who cannot handle the original documents of the civilization which he is describing (Mandelbaum, 1949, p. 162).

9　　The relevance of linguistics to ethnology goes far beyond the mere operational necessities mentioned in the last paragraph. In both the structural and the lexical and semantic aspects of a language system, there exist correlations with traits of the culture either as it exists at any given moment or as it has existed at some previous time. Linguistic expressions of kinship and social status[2]

---

[2]Various ethnolinguistic phenomena of this type have been surveyed by Thomas (1937, Chap. IV). Of particular interest is his account of how a Swedish personal pronoun fell from grace. The form *ni,* once a respectable form of address to the second person, acquired a pejorative connotation, with the result that a sentence like "Have you forgotten your cane?" had to be expressed by saying something like "Has Mr. Smith forgotten Mr. Smith's cane?" Circumlocution of this kind came to be so awkward that linguistic reformers seriously proposed that men of good will should wear buttons proclaiming *"Ni* is used here'!

systems readily afford examples of such correlations, and the use
of kinship nomenclature as a possible clue to the establishment of
linguistic families has been illustrated in a brief note by Kroeber
(1941). As to the general relations between linguistics and ethnology, Kroeber concludes:

> On the whole, it is evident that of the two disciplines ethnology is
> the one which is dependent on linguistics. But the relations are com-
> plex and now and then it is the linguist who can profit by what the
> anthropologist can tender him (1941).

10   Greenberg (1948) has pointed out that the complete description
of the semantic components of a language system is possible only
by reference to cultural facts. Thus, "careful compilation of a
lexicon is then a field in which the linguist and ethnologist can
fruitfully collaborate." Greenberg also makes the telling observation that the semantic analysis of a language should be of interest
to the ethnologist because "it presents him with a practically
exhaustive classification of the objects in the cultural universe of
the speakers." Of course one may raise a question whether the
semantic structure of a language (that is, the particular way in
which potential meanings are associated with particular linguistic
forms) does in fact yield information as to the "cultural universe
of the speakers." Perhaps there are nonlinguistic aspects of this
cultural universe, and perhaps it is not truly universal, but instead
varies somewhat from speaker to speaker. In any case, Greenberg's
hypothesis deserves attention; it seems to emphasize again the
notion of "labeling" which Dollard and Miller (1950) have made
much of in their discussion of psychological mechanisms in personality and psychotherapy.

11   Greenberg summarizes his rather theoretical paper as follows:

> The foregoing analysis ... suggests that linguistics and extralin-
> guistic segments of culture are intimately connected in a number of
> ways. The ethnologist may ... view each specimen of the informants'
> speech as an instance of verbal behavior revealing both cultural and
> personal aspects ... Altogether there is a rewarding field which awaits
> the linguistically oriented ethnologist and a mature science of culture
> is unlikely to emerge without the linguistic approach to culture having
> played a significant role (1948, p. 147).

12   An anthropologist who has found much profit in linguistic studies
is Clyde Kluckhohn. In his book on the Navaho Indians, written

in collaboration with Dorothea Leighton, he not only recommends that administrators, teachers, and missionaries who have to do with Navahos should "learn something about the salient features of the linguistic structure," but also affirms that "anyone who wants to understand the Navahos at all must know something about their language and the way in which it molds thought, interest, and attitudes" (Kluckhohn and Leighton, 1946, p. 184). Later, in speaking of failures of communication between the Navahos and the whites, he writes, "Even a few days of intelligent study will show that the lack of equivalence in Navaho and English is merely the outward expression of inward differences between two people in premises, in basic categories, in training in fundamental sensitivities, and in general view of the world" (p. 215). It will be obvious at once, even from these quotations and much more from an examination of Kluckhohn's chapter on "The Tongue of the People," that the relations between linguistics and ethnology do not manifest themselves necessarily only in trivial details like the manner in which members of the culture greet each other in the morning, but also with respect to the way in which a language system may reflect the world-view of a culture. Thus, what Kluckhohn is talking about is equivalent to no less than the *"Weltanschauung"* problem which has been delineated earlier in this report.

13   Ethnolinguistic investigations of the kind suggested by the more or less programmatic statements cited here have thus far not been undertaken in any thoroughgoing way. This is perhaps because such investigations would probably require extremely detailed and comprehensive linguistic analyses. For examples, the ethnolinguistic study of American speech would require penetrating analyses of dialectal variations, intonation patterns, and special features such as slang.

14   The well-known investigation of the language of gardening among the Trobriand Islanders by the anthropologist Bronislaw Malinowski (1935) was severely vitiated by the lack of *expertise* in linguistics and by the adoption of a number of questionable premises. Malinowski gained a reputation for the view that it is impossible to study the language of a community without knowing its culture — indeed, that if one desires to specify the meaning of an utterance one must refer to the total situational and cultural context of that utterance. From this it would appear that while ethnological data would be crucial in linguistics, the reverse would not be true. Malinowski was, in fact, strongly opposed to traditional linguistics with its alleged emphasis on the study of texts; he rejected the Saussurean distinction between language and speech,

and asserted that all study of speech necessarily leads immediately to sociological investigation (Malinowski, 1937). Nevertheless, in the work which he himself called his best effort, it is amply clear that he was at all points concerned with relations between ethnological observations and the kinds of data which would be studied by a descriptive linguist; if Malinowski had been a trained descriptive linguist, the linguistic facts would no doubt have had more compelling implications.[3]

LINGUISTICS AND CULTURAL HISTORY

15   In the study of cultural history, particularly the history of cultures whose beginnings are not recorded in their own written documents, linguistic results are almost indispensable before final

---

[3]Malinowski's objections to linguistic analysis were ill-founded. He confused different levels of analysis, appearing impatient to get to "sociological interpretations" before he had quite grasped the significance of the linguistic structure as such. His essentially antilinguistic position is belied by the fact that the major outlines of a language structure can emerge, through suitable techniques of analysis, even where only the barest reference is made to the specific nonlinguistic traits of the culture. His careless handling of linguistics is illustrated by his claim (1936) that primitive grammatical categories are less precise than those of civilized languages; this is patently an overstatement.

Malinowski's views on meaning are unanswerable because he established his own definition of meaning — but a definition which leads to a vicious particularism in which every utterance must be treated, as it were, by a clinical method which leaves no room for generalization. Furthermore, his insistent assertions about the importance of "situational context" do not, on scrutiny, turn out to have much heuristic value. The following is, I think, a fair example of his technique:

At one point in his *Coral Gardens and Their Magic* (1935, Vol. 2, p. 37), he makes much of the fact that a "literal rendering" of a certain utterance can be given a highly meaningful "free translation" only when one is aware of the "contextual specification of meaning." Thus, the "literal rendering"

       'Informant's father in child his he see'

becomes, surprisingly,

       'Molubabeba in his childhood witnessed a famine.'

This remarkable transformation becomes commonplace, even ridiculous, when we turn back to page 23 and find that the original utterance was a response to Malinowski's asking a group of informants whether any of them had experienced a bad famine. One of the informants had simply replied, in effect, "Molubabeba saw one in his childhood":

Molubabeba	*o*	*gwadi-la*	*i-gise*
(informant's father)	in	child his	he see

It is difficult to see how a descriptive linguist would have had any trouble with this; "contextual specification of meaning" prove to be little more than specification of grammatical antecedents and the satisfaction of mandatory linguistic rules in the language of translation. Note also that Malinowski's literal rendering was not really literal when it supplied "informant's father."

conclusions can be drawn. Several examples of such studies may be given.

16   If one is interested in the prehistory of Africa, one might turn to the work of the German scholar Carl Meinhof. In his book *Die Sprachen der Hamiten* (1912) he drew certain conclusions as to the prehistoric relationships between "Hamitic" tribes and the Bantus and Hottentots of South Africa. These conclusions were based on his idea that the language of the Hottentots showed certain resemblances to Hamitic languages such as Ethiopian. Present-day analysis, however, seems to show that Meinhof's theories are not tenable. Greenberg, at Columbia University, is now at work on a classification of African languages based on more modern techniques of linguistic analysis, and hopes to draw up alternative hypotheses as to the prehistory of cultures in Africa.

17   A similar task is being undertaken by Isidore Dyen at Yale University in connection with Malayo-Polynesian languages of the Pacific Ocean area. It is almost impossible to trace the various movements of various Pacific Ocean peoples before the advent of the white man on the basis of anthropological and ethnographic evidence alone. Dyen hopes that comparative linguistics will provide some key to this mass of confused material. Nevertheless, the case of the Malayo-Polynesian languages is one of those which Kroeber (1941) cites as illustrating the proposition that sometimes "anthropological factors have direct bearing on a broad problem of linguistic theory."

18   As a final case in point, the history of the westward migrations of the white man in North America seems to be a problem which cannot be solved entirely by reference to written historical documents. Nor can it be solved completely by references to such ethnographic factors as architectural styles, food habits, and the like. A number of linguists are engaged in developing the dialect geography of American English.[4] Quite apart from the intrinsic interest of such studies, they may very well have implications for the study of the migration of the white man in the pioneer days.

LINGUISTICS AND SOCIOLOGY

19   The subject matter of cultural anthropology overlaps with that of sociology to a considerable extent. Studies in cultural anthropology usually concern cultures other than our own, often the strange and unusual cultures of the so-called "primitive" parts of

---

[4]See reference to Kurath (1949) in Bibliography.

the world. Sociology, on the other hand, studies the interaction of social groups, usually in our own culture. Both of these disciplines are studying *culture*. Perhaps the only real distinction between the two disciplines is that sociology attempts to draw generalized inferences about the formation and interaction of social groups, inferences of presumed universality for all cultures, while cultural anthropology is interested primarily in the general traits and themes of particular cultures. (Even so, some anthropologists would raise objections to any such delimiting of their field of interest.)

20   It naturally follows that to the same extent that linguistics may have implications for cultural anthropology, it may also have implications for sociology. Such a conclusion seems to be accepted by many sociologists, at least in principle; the extent to which results of linguistic science can be applied to sociological problems in detail, however, remains almost completely unexplored.[5]

21   Several references may be cited for an interpretation of sociological phenomena in terms of language behavior. The philosophically inclined sociologist G. H. Mead, in *Mind, Self and Society* (1934), emphasized the role of language as a means of social control, for example, in developing a consciousness of the "generalized other" through a process of verbal role playing. Two recent textbooks in social psychology (Lindesmith and Strauss, 1949; Hartley and Hartley, 1952), are heavily weighted with an interpretation of social-psychological data by reference to verbal behavior. In my opinion, however, none of these works outlines the full scope of ways in which linguistic results might aid the study of social behavior. For example, the effect of dialect differences in marking various social groups is ignored, possibly because few concrete investigations of the problem have been attempted.

----

[5]In Odum's (1951) history of American sociology, one looks in vain for any reference to sociological studies of language. Linton, in his preface to *The Science of Man in the World Crisis* (a survey of the contributions of various social sciences), has this to say: "That linguistics ultimately will be of great value for the understanding of human behavior and especially of human thought processes can hardly be doubled. However, work along these lines has hardly begun and linguistics is still unable to make any great contribution toward the solution of our present problems" (1945), p. 8). One standard text in sociology which reveals an unusual awareness of the place of language and communication as a societal process is that of Lundberg (1939); however, it contains no citations of specific research in this area. The task of pointing out the detailed implications of linguistic phenomena in social processes has thus devolved mainly upon linguists and other students of language, such as Schlauch (1942, especially Chap. 10), Lewis (1947), and Bodmer (1944).

22   A linguist of my acquaintance suggested that an important addendum might have been made to Warner and Lunt's study of "Yankee City" (1941) by a consideration of the varieties of dialect to be found in the various social classes identified in this sociological survey. Allison Davis (1951) and his associates at the University of Chicago have thrown social class differences in verbal ability into sharp relief, but since these differences were measured almost exclusively in terms of vocabulary (that is, knowledge of lexical items), it now remains to describe the finer points of divergence. Although there has been considerable interest in developing dictionaries and glossaries of slang and underworld speech,[6] surprisingly little attention has been paid to linguistic variations within the normal range of the social class structure. This is perhaps due to the fact that the variations lie in subtler aspects, such as phonetic structure and intonation patterns, rather than in the more obvious vocabulary items.

23   Another line of study which remains almost completely unexplored, except by novelists and popular writers, is the matter of personal attitudes toward the speech characteristics of others. Such attitudes are undoubtedly relevant in connection with race prejudice. For example, a Negro who speaks with a New England accent (or with an Oxford accent) is likely to be viewed differently from one who speaks in a dialect of the South.

24   Outstanding among sociological studies for its attention to verbal behavior is the work of Bossard and his associates (1943, 1945, 1950) on family modes of expression. Bossard recorded and transcribed the dinner-table conversations of 51 families, seeking to establish dimensions of analysis. The finer details of the results have not been made available in published form, but Bossard reports that families tend to develop highly distinctive patterns of speech, not only in the content and function of table talk, but even in respect to special word meanings, idiomatic expressions, and pronunciation. There are even familial idiosyncrasies in gesture. His data give support to the notion of language as a social index of occupation, religion, and social class, and he emphasizes that "language comes in a peculiar way to serve as a symbol of home, family, class, state, status, and country."

---

[6]See, for example, Partridge's *Dictionary of Slang and Unconventional English* (1949) and *Dictionary of the Underworld; British and American; 16th-20th Centuries* (1950), or even a *Dictionary of American Underworld Lingo* compiled with the aid of former convicts (Goldin, O'Leary, and Lipsius, 1950). None of these works are by technical linguists.

LINGUISTICS AND THE STUDY OF
MASS COMMUNICATIONS

25   There is a rapidly growing field concerned with the study of
social attitudes and opinions and the effects of mass communications media such as propaganda and advertising.[7] The general
theory of mass communications has been discussed by various
writers. Harold Lasswell has put the matter in these terms: "The
study of diffusion and restriction processes [in society] calls for a
general theory of language as a factor in power. . . . When men want
power, they act according to their expectation of how to maximize
power. Hence *symbols* (*words and images*) *affect power as they
affect expectations of power*" (Lasswell *et al.*, 1949, pp. 18–19).

26   There are at least three points where linguistic studies (broadly
defined to include descriptive linguistics, psycholinguistics, etc.)
may have specific application in the area of mass communications.
All three involve the specification of what effect a given message is
likely to have upon a hearer or receiver of that message.

27   In the first place, the messages must often be analyzed in terms
of their purely formal characteristics; the mass communications
specialist should, ideally, be aware of the linguistic system within
which he is operating, particularly with respect to dialectal differences in the sounds and meanings of linguistic forms. The effect of
a radio transmission over the Voice of America in the Czech language, for example, depends partly upon the extent to which it
conforms in every subtle detail to the speech norms of its intended
audience.

28   Secondly, there is the operational problem of analyzing the
semantic content of messages; this step has come to be known as
content analysis. Lasswell's book on the language of politics (Lasswell *et al.*, 1949) is addressed primarily to the efficient accomplishment of reliable and valid content analyses. Content analysis
depends on the use of proper units of analysis; that is, the content
has to be reduced to a manageable number of mutually exclusive
categories. But what should these units be; and what rules should
govern? Admittedly the units should be recognizable, and the rules
should be explicitly formulated. Content analysts have experi-
mented with "rigid" schemes in which the analyst tries to get an

---

[7] A fairly recent reference guide to this field has been prepared by Smith,
Lasswell, and Casey (1946).

impression of semantic content regardless of the sign vehicles used. "Rigid" schemes give greater reliability but less validity than flexible schemes. It may be suggested that linguistic and psycholinguistic studies could aid in the formulation of more reliable and valid content-analysis categories. Linguistic analysis suggests the possibility of establishing categories based on form classes or substitution groups (for example, the range of ways in which a particular country could be referred to might be described in this way). Psycholinguistic analysis might suggest the units of selection in messages and better ways of gauging their semantic content.

29   A third potential application of linguistic studies in mass communications is in the conduct and analysis of public-opinion polls. One of the strategic problems in opinion polls is the formulation of the questions used in eliciting knowledge, opinion, and attitude on the part of the respondents. Pollsters have become keenly aware of the subtle changes in effect produced by seemingly inconsequential changes in the form of questions. One of them has written a book devoted to just this problem (Payne, 1951). For example, it makes a considerable difference whether one asks whether something *should* be done, *could* be done, or *might* be done. Asking the question "Where did you read that?" may elicit such diverse responses as "In the *New York Times*" or "At home in front of the fire." The question "Do you prefer A or B?" sometimes produces different statistics if changed to "Do you prefer B or A?" The way in which a question is intoned by a door-to-door interviewer is often an uncontrolled factor: "Why do you say THAT?" (with high stress on *that*) is quite different from "Why do you say that?" (with relatively even stress). The linguist, with his techniques of describing the precise formal content of messages, and the psycholinguist, with techniques of describing semantic contents and stimulus values of messages, can obviously make a contribution in public-opinion research. It is also possible that the mass statistics collected in this type of research, particularly where a split-ballot technique is used to investigate the role of different question formulations, will provide the psycholinguist with a rewarding set of material for study.

LANGUAGE ENGINEERING

30   In various parts of the world, either in particular cultural groups or in various aggregations of persons with special problems and interests, difficult and unfortunate situations exist for which the

remedy may possibly be an adjustment of certain language factors. Difficulties arise because people do not speak a common language, because they are illiterate, or because they regard certain languages as having an inferior or debased status. The idea that linguistics, in company with other sciences, might be able to resolve some of these difficulties has been given the name "language engineering." (The first public use of such a term in America, to the writer's knowledge, was in a paper read by G. A. Miller at the conference on Speech and Communication held at the Massachusetts Institute of Technology in June 1950.[8])

31   Actually, efforts in "language engineering" have been in progress for some time. The American Bible Society and other missionary organizations have long been interested in the problem of literacy, and have not failed to recognize the role that linguistics science can play in their work. It is of unusual interest to know that one large group of linguistic scientists, led by such men as Pike, Nida, and George Cowan, originally came to linguistics through their interest in the dissemination of the Gospel to underdeveloped areas of the world. These men, well recognized by their colleagues as thorough linguistic scientists, have organized training schools for the purpose of teaching missionaries the elements of linguistics.[9] As a result, there is an increasing number of individuals who are going out to all continents to study so-called primitive languages and to develop systems of writing which can be used in literacy programs.

32   Problems of language engineering are also met in the work of the United Nations Educational, Scientific, and Cultural Organization, particularly in its program of "fundamental education." The term "fundamental education" was adopted by UNESCO (1949) to refer to the kinds of education which are deemed urgently needed in the underdeveloped areas of the world — education in literacy, in the basic skills of productivity required to raise living standards, in health and sanitation, in recreation, and in basic civic duties. The relevance of linguistic science in implementing such a program has already been recognized by UNESCO.

33   There are four types of problems on which a linguistic scientist should be consulted in any program of fundamental education.

         1.   In many cases, it will be necessary for a linguistic expert to

---

[8]Miller's paper is now available in print (1950).
[9]A textbook of linguistics specially designed to meet the needs of missionaries has been prepared by Dean Pittman (1948). Its concluding chapters discuss methods of teaching natives to read and problems met in translating the Bible. See, however, a review of this book by Hodge (1950).

make a fairly thorough analysis of the native language which may be involved. This will be true even when there is some knowledge of the language available through materials prepared by non-specialists. A refined linguistic analysis will save much needless time and effort in connection with the other three problems discussed below.

2. It will frequently be necessary to develop a system of orthography for the language. Such an orthography must be constructed in the light of the phonemic system of the language as revealed by a linguistic analysis. Reading difficulties due to an inconsistent orthography, like that which exists in English, may just as well be circumvented at the outset. The linguist may on occasion be called upon to decide what kind of alphabet should be the basis of the system of writing. In this connection, a point which may perhaps too easily be neglected is that the orthography must be suitable for the making of dictionaries.

3. The advice of linguists must be sought if there arises a problem of the choice of a regional auxiliary language toward which major efforts in the literacy program will be directed.

4. The linguist may be able to offer valuable advice on methods of teaching literacy and on the preparation of instructional materials. The special virtue of the linguistic expert in this connection is that he is likely to have the most precise knowledge of what has to be taught — the language system and the orthography devised for committing it to writing. It is evident, however, that other specialists besides linguists have something to contribute to the success of literacy programs. Educational psychologists, for example, should be consulted on such problems as the sequencing of the instructional material and the establishment of desirable conditions of learning.

34   It is impossible and unnecessary to spell out here the enormous scope of the problems of language engineering when applied to the problem of literacy throughout the world or to international communication.[10] The mere mention of the linguistic situation in India, for example, where local dialects run into the hundreds, will immediately bring to mind the conviction that language engineering has wide application. Some scheme for the efficient collection of information about languages (such as Lounsbury's) is obviously

[10]One of the most active participants in world literacy programs has been Frank C. Laubach; he has published several books on his methods and experiences (1938, 1943).

pertinent to language-engineering programs. A large number of languages throughout the world remain to be described, and the manpower in linguistic science is not presently adequate to meet this task unless special ingenuity is displayed in the problem of collecting and analyzing field data. The support of such a program as Lounsbury's is especially attractive in view of the current aims of UNESCO. At the same time, these aims make urgent the necessity of developing a more adequate formulation of the problems of teaching the fundamental language arts.

35   The problem of an international auxiliary language is so complex that it deserves special attention and evaluation in this report. Before proceeding to that topic, however, it will be interesting to focus our attention on the rather special problem of language engineering which exists in certain communities.

36   The linguistic situation in Haiti will be our example. As it happens, this situation was investigated at first hand by the linguist R. A. Hall, Jr., under the sponsorship of UNESCO; the following remarks are based on the UNESCO monograph, "The Haiti Pilot Project — Phase One, 1947-1949," which describes UNESCO's experimental program designed to reduce illiteracy in a test area in Haiti, and which incorporates some of Hall's findings and conclusions (UNESCO, 1951).

37   French is the official language of Haiti, but it is used only in the upper classes. The language of the people is called Haitian Creole. It is a development from French, but it cannot be regarded simply as a dialect of French; instead, it is an entirely independent language, about as closely related to French as modern Italian is to Latin. Its phonetics and vocabulary are largely of French origin, but it possesses many features which show the influence of West African languages. Because of the lowly origins of Haitian Creole, it is widely regarded by Haitians as inferior to French, which is of course the language of official documents, newspapers, books, legal proceedings, and higher education. Even in the lower schools, there is an unrealistic attempt to teach French as if it were the native language.

38   In Haiti, therefore, language distinctions lead to an open cleavage between social classes. Members of the lower classes, in particular, are put at a disadvantage in business, trade, and law because they cannot speak, read, or write French. Nevertheless, proposals to make Haitian Creole the official language, or even to publish newspapers and books in Creole, have met with much opposition. The basic difficulty is one of social attitudes concerning the status

of Creole. Attempts to establish a reasonable system of spelling for Haitian Creole have met with scorn because the results do not look like French. A system of orthography originally introduced by the Rev. Ormond McConnel was endorsed by an expert in literacy campaigns, Dr. Frank C. Laubach, and subsequently, after 1943, given an official stamp of approval by the government. Vigorous efforts to accelerate the literacy program ensued but were slowed down by continuing opposition to the system, which was regarded in some quarters as "a wicked innovation threatening Haitian spiritual and political independence."

39   After the UNESCO pilot project was initiated in 1947, the question of orthography was again examined, because a final settlement of the issue was desirable before pouring efforts into the preparation of textbooks and other material. At this time the American linguist Dr. R. A. Hall, Jr. was called in. Upon making a thorough analysis of Haitian Creole, Hall concluded that the McConnel system was scientifically sound and wholly practical. Limited progress has now been made in preparing materials for the teaching of Haitian Creole. Further steps are being planned in order to provide a greater variety of literature in Creole, as well as to develop instructional materials for allowing pupils to pass easily from Creole to French. It is recognized that the ultimate aim of the literacy training must include the reading of French because of the established position of that language as one which links Haiti with an international culture.

40   In the situation we have described, the problem of the "language engineer" is twofold. First, there is a purely linguistic aspect in which scientific analyses of the languages involved had to be performed in order to make sound decisions as to what was to be done. Second, there is a psychological aspect, in that the unrealistic and emotionally toned attitudes of the populace must be changed if any real progress is to be made. The situation neatly illustrates the need for coöperative work by different kinds of social scientists.

THE PROBLEM OF AN INTERNATIONAL
AUXILIARY LANGUAGE

41   The problem of an international auxiliary language is charged with strong feelings and factional disputes. One runs the risk of making enemies, no matter what one says about it. It is, in any case, an extremely complex problem and any fair-minded observer must grant some validity to each of the several points of view.

42   There is dispute even on the question of whether there is any
need for an international auxiliary language, and if so, what value
it would have. The extreme point of view is held by those who claim
that the lack of an international auixiliary language is the chief
obstacle to the reduction of world tensions and the improvement
of mutual understanding among the peoples of the world. This view
can easily be refuted by the method of contrary cases. For example,
the adversaries in the American Civil War spoke the same language,
while the English and the French have long been at peace despite
language differences. The best argument for an international auxiliary language is to suggest its promise of greater convenience and
economy in the conduct of international trade and in the exchange
of information between nations. In his book *Cosmopolitan Conversation* (1933) Herbert Shenton describes the linguistic problems
of international conventions and urges the adoption of an international language at least for the purpose of such conventions. Rundle
(1946) has carefully studied the social and political difficulties
created by language barriers. Nevertheless, even if an international
language could be agreed upon by those most closely associated
with the various proposals, there would remain grave problems in
getting it accepted by the international public at large.

43   The problem of an international auxiliary language is not unlike
the problem of a United Nations organization. Whether it can exist
and continue to be accepted is a matter not so much of its own
internal structure as of the social pressures and forces which play
upon it. Of course, an international language should be as simple
as possible, but even an artificial language as relatively complex
as Esperanto has had considerable success. When and if the world
becomes ready for an international auxiliary language, the problem
of its selection and construction will be relatively simple, although
I believe that linguistic scientists should play a major role in the
enterprise. It is interesting that UNESCO seems to put its stamp
of approval on the idea of an auxiliary language: "The selection
of an auxiliary language with the widest possible field of usefulness
— a world language as against a purely local one — will therefore
commend itself" (UNESCO, 1949, p. 36).[11]

44   From one standpoint, there is no reason why there could not be
a single language which would be a world-wide *lingua franca*, in

---

[11]At a UNESCO-sponsored conference in Paris, it was proposed that French
and English be established as the two world auxiliary languages (Hart, 1947).

some future Utopian state of our civilization. Unfortunately, this seems to be one of the premises adopted by any imperialistic nation. This was true of ancient imperialism (Egyptian, Greek, Roman) as well as of modern imperialism (British, French, German, and now Russian). The first objection which any international auxiliary language proposal has to meet is that it may be a manifestation of somebody's imperialism.

45   Basic English, one of the major candidates for the status of an international language, walks right into this objection, on all four feet, we might say. Proponents of Basic English say that since English, especially as represented by its scientific vocabulary, is rapidly becoming the most widely used language in the world, it might easily form the basis for an international auxiliary language. Certainly Basic English has a distinct advantage in this regard. But speakers of some languages resist the notion that English, rather than their own language, should form the basis of an international tongue.

46   Most international languages which have been proposed have been based on the premise that a successful international language must be contrived from elements taken from the existing languages, particularly the more common and widely known languages.[12] These proposed international languages are often called "artificial" and have only a moderate resemblance to any natural language. An objective in the construction of an artificial language is to make maximal use of elements which are found in common among various natural languages. This objective was only partially realized in Esperanto, developed by the Pole Dr. Zamenhof in 1887, which to English speakers shows too many evidences of its having been based partly on languages of the Central European area. Nevertheless, for various reasons Esperanto has had the widest currency of any of the proposed artificial languages. A recent attempt to rationalize an artificial language by making maximal use of elements common to the most widely used natural languages is Interlingua, the work of the International Auxiliary Language Association of New York.[13] A sample of the most recent version of Interlingua is given below. In order to encourage the reader to

---

[12]Guérard (1922) has written a useful history of the international-language movement. Some contemporary viewpoints are described by Jacob (1947, 1948); see also a review by McQuown (1950).

[13]IALA has recently become affiliated with Barnard College as an Institute. An Interlingua dictionary has been published by IALA (1951), and also a grammar (Gode and Blair, 1951).

make his own translation, the English translation is presented at the end of this chapter.

> In le presente phase del evolution del lingua international, que es tanto necessari in nostre era de communication mundial, IALA crede que un dictionario del vocabulario international in forma general es essential por le futur disveloppamento del experimentation. Le Dictionario de IALA offere le vocabulos commun e indubitabilmente international, e sic pone les, como nunquam avante, al disposition del adherentes de omne linguas auxiliar basate super le idea fundamental que un lingua international existe potentialmente in linguas national.

47   If one should ask the question, there are interesting technical problems involved in the construction of an artificial language. Some linguistic scientists, notably Sapir (1925), have taken an interest in the problem, pointing out that some of the grammatical processes and categories to be found in exotic and unusual languages may be valuable in such an enterprise. Under the sponsorship of the International Auxiliary Language Association (IALA), Sapir, Swadesh, and Collinson contributed a number of monographs (Sapir, 1930, 1944; Sapir and Swadesh, 1932; Collinson, 1937) on several conceptual categories which were thought to be of interest in connection with an international auxiliary language. These monographs possess considerable intrinsic value, quite apart from the problem of an artificial language. If one really felt the need to contrive an entirely synthetic language, the attempt to utilize the full implications of linguistic science would be a thoroughly engaging task. It seems that at one time, say around 1935, this is what IALA set out to do. More recently, however, the direction of its work has turned toward the development of an auxiliary language which "should be composed of elements and features familiar to the largest possible number of people with different mother tongues" (IALA, 1945, p. 19). Trubetskoy (1939b) addressed himself to the problem of establishing for such a language a phonetic system which would contain the most common sounds of the languages of the world.

48   The interests of psychologists have also at times touched on the problem of an international language. Arsenian (1945) has reviewed some of the relevant psychological facts. At the request of IALA, E. L. Thorndike[14] studied the rate at which artificial languages like Esperanto and Ido could be learned by English-speaking pupils as

---

[14]The work was directed by Thorndike and carried out chiefly by Dr. Laura H. V. Kennon. The reference is cited under Division of Psychology, Institute of Educational Research, Teachers College, Columbia University (1933).

compared with natural languages like French, Spanish, and German. The results strongly favored the artificial languages. Whether similar results would be obtained with a different selection of the languages to be compared and with samples of learners composed of speakers of non-European languages, we do not know. Nevertheless, it is fair to make the guess that an artificial language would almost always be easier to learn than any natural language picked at random, whatever the language background of the learner.

49   The claim of Basic English as a possible international auxiliary language needs to be seriously examined, particularly since the British government recently threw its support to the idea. (This official recognition may turn out to be more of a hindrance than a help, because it has had the effect of identifying Basic English somewhat too closely with the interests of the British Commonwealth, thus adding fuel to the argument that Basic English is "just a form of Anglo-Saxon imperialism.") Basic English was developed by C. K. Ogden over a period of several years after the first appearance, in 1923, of Ogden and Richards's noteworthy work *The Meaning of Meaning* (1936). One of the major points made by Ogden and Richards in this book was that one way of indicating the meaning of a symbol is to give a definition of it by means of other symbols, preferably by means of a relatively small "defining vocabulary." Ogden must be accorded much honor for taking the trouble to act upon this suggestion, where many another philosopher would have been content merely with the vision that it *could* be acted upon. Ogden's project soon took the form of a major attempt to devise a limited form of language in which almost anything useful could be said and which at the same time would have a minimal vocabulary. After examining the vocabularies of several well-known languages, Ogden early came to the conclusion that English would be a suitable basis for the kind of language he had in mind. The final form of Basic English was first given to the public in 1930; there have been no official modifications in it since that time save the publication of special lists of auxiliary and scientific words useful in technical fields. The Basic word list consists of 850 words. A major simplification was achieved by the device of eliminating most English verbs and expressing verb concepts by the use of constructions involving an "operator"[15] with an

---

[15]The operators are *come, get, give, go, keep, let, make, put, seem, take, be, do, have, say, send, may, will*. It should be understood that these are used with their normal English inflections.

accompanying noun, adjective, adverb, preposition, or other "operator." For example, in Basic English one does not *compel* a person to do something; he *makes him do it.* The following is a sample passage in Basic English (Richards and Gibson, 1945, p. 7).

> Basic is a system of everyday English words used in the regular forms of normal English. It is a selection of those English words which — taken together and used as we are all using them all the time — will among them do the most work. It is the smallest number of English words with a general enough covering power, among them, to let a man say *almost everything* — to say it well enough for his general day-to-day purposes in all the range of his interests however wide — in business, trade, industry, science, medical work — in all the arts of living and in all the exchanges of knowledge, beliefs, opinion, views, and news which a general-purpose language has to take care of.

50   The standard references on Basic English are Ogden's *Basic English, A General Introduction with Rules and Grammar* (1930a), *The Basic Vocabulary, A Statistical Analysis, with Special Reference to Substitution and Translation* (1930b), *The Basic Dictionary* (1932), *The System of Basic English* (1934), and I. A. Richards' *Basic English and its Uses* (1943). Richards and Gibson have recently published a useful guide to Basic English, *Learning Basic English* (1945), designed for the speaker of English who wants to learn and teach Basic English. A number of books and articles in Basic English are available. Julia E. Johnsen has compiled a useful summary of information about Basic English, including excerpts from both favorable and unfavorable accounts (1944). Haber (1948) has enthusiastically suggested the establishment of a national institute of Basic English in America.

51   While a good many people endorse the idea of using a limited form of English as an international auxiliary language, there has been a continuing controversy as to whether Basic English is the best form of limited English. Fries and Traver, in *English Word Lists* (1940), approve the general structure of the Basic English vocabulary, but there have been outspoken critics of the system. West, Swensen, and others made a violent attack on Basic English in their monograph, *A Critical Examination of Basic English* (1934), prompting an equally violent rejoinder from Ogden in his *Counter-Offensive, An Exposure of Certain Misrepresentations of Basic English* (1935). Many criticisms of Basic English *as a system* have been unsound and misleading. To criticize the Basic English vocabulary on the ground that the 850 words contain thousands of different meanings is to ignore the fact that any similar number

of common English words, however chosen, will likewise contain a large number of meanings. In fact, it has been observed that in normal English there is a high correlation between the frequency of a word and the number of separate dictionary meanings associated with it. Some critics have asserted that Basic English falls far short of being truly simple because thousands of highly idiomatic expressions can be constructed from the 850-word vocabulary. This assertion fails to recognize the restrictions which have been placed upon the use of the vocabulary by Ogden himself. These critics also fail to remember that "idiomatic" expressions inevitably tend to develop even in constructed languages like Esperanto. *Fancy dress ball* is one poorly chosen example which has somehow gained currency among critics of Basic English. The facts of the matter are that *fancy* and *dress* are not in the Basic word list, and *ball* is explicitly restricted in its use to mean a spherical object.

52   Somewhat more cogent criticisms can be made of certain structural features of Basic English. For example, the rules of Basic English provide that derivatives in "-er," "-ing," "-ed" can be made from 300 nouns in the Basic vocabulary. The learner of Basic English has to learn which nouns these are. Actually, they happen to be the nouns which *as verbs* permit such derivatives in standard English. It will seem odd to most learners that these forms can be used as verbs in Basic English when they occur in participial or passive constructions, but not as active verbs. Since a great many non-English-speaking learners of Basic English have well-developed verb systems in their own languages, there is undoubtedly a temptation for them to use nonpermitted verbs in Basic.[16] Ogden's defense of Basic in this respect is not wholly convincing; he asserts that elimination of the verb system makes learning easier, but many persons feel that it actually compounds the learner's difficulty.

53   Nevertheless, these criticisms are not of crucial import. Let us grant that Basic English is a language system possessing a high degree of potential effectiveness in communication. If so, it can presumably be learned in the same way that other language systems are learned. It is true that Basic English will present some peculiar difficulties, not only because of its use of the phonology and orthography of normal English, but also because of some of its structural characteristics, acquired in the process of eliminating the verb. Furthermore, as anyone who tries to translate a passage into Basic English will soon discover, the conversion of a complex

---

[16]For a detailed discussion on this point, see Walsh (1933).

idea into Basic English calls for considerable ingenuity and a major intellectual exercise in semantics, even with the aid of the Basic English dictionary; there is some doubt whether Basic English could stand up as an international language if its use presented too much difficulty at the higher levels of discourse. It seems probable that the major languages of the world show many similarities in their selections of semantic content which are at variance with the semantic patterning of the Basic English vocabulary; if so, any international language with a vocabulary structured as in Basic English will have a somewhat lessened survival value.

54   Despite all these potential difficulties, however, Basic English continues to have wide appeal as a possible international language, especially if it is understood that Basic English would be regarded as a somewhat flexible and expandable medium of communication which would draw ever closer to a near-normal form of full English. There are grounds for believing that if Basic English were to be proposed as an international language to be officially approved by some international body possessing the requisite authority, the proposed initial form which the international language might take should indeed be considerably less limited and restrictive than Basic English in the form originally published by Ogden.[17] In this way account could be taken of the experience which has been gained in teaching Basic English — experience which indicates that a somewhat modified form of limited English is usually easier to learn than "pure Basic." The mere fact that Basic English as Ogden originally proposed it has a neatly self-contained definition vocabulary does not guarantee that it is ideally suited to use as an international language.

55   All these considerations will undoubtedly appear highly academic to many. In reply we can only reiterate the assertion made earlier in this section that the establishment and continued acceptance of an international auxiliary language is a matter connected not so much with the structure and characteristics of the language itself as with the social pressures and conditions which affect it.

SUMMARY

56   Linguistic scientists are becoming increasingly aware of the implications of their work for their sister sciences, sociology and anthropology. They have begun also to be impressed with the

[17]Already I. A. Richards (1942b) has used such a modified form of Basic in his translation of Plato's *Republic*.

possibilities of applying the techniques and results of linguistic science to the improvement and adjustment of social conditions. Some linguists have deplored the fact that while they themselves persist in writing treatises which are unintelligible to the layman, popular writers on language have had the courage, if not always the competence, to try to relate linguistic studies to the broader problems of society which alone can make such studies profitable and worthwhile.

This is the English translation of the passage in Interlingua on page 40:

In the present phase of evolution of the international language which is so necessary in our era of world-wide communication, IALA believes that a dictionary of the international vocabulary in a general form is essential for the further development of experimentation. The dictionary of IALA offers the words [which are] common and indisputably international, and thus places them, as never before, at the disposal of the adherents of all auxiliary languages [that are] based upon the fundamental idea that an international language exists potentially in the national languages.

Bibliographical References for *Linguistics and Social Sciences*

Arsenian, Seth (1945), "Bilingualism in the post-war world," *Psychological Bulletin* 42: 65-86.

Bodmer, Frederick (1944), *The Loom of Language* (Lancelot Hogben, ed.). New York: Norton. 692 p.

Bossard, James H. S. (1943), "Family table talk — an area for sociological study," *American Sociological Review* 8: 295-301.

_____ (1945), "Family modes of expression," *American Sociological Review* 10: 226-237.

_____ Eleanor S. Boll, and Winogene P. Sanger (1950), "Some neglected areas in family-life study," *Annals of the American Academy of Political and Social Science* 272: 68-76.

Collinson, William Edward (1937), "Indication; a study of demonstratives, articles, and other 'indicators,'" *Language Monographs,* No. 17. 128 p.

Darlington, Cyril P. (1947), "The genetic component of language," *Heredity, an International Journal of Genetics* 1: 268-286.

Davis, Allison, Kenneth Eells, Robert J. Havighurst, Virgil Herrick, and Ralph W. Tyler (1951), *Intelligence and Cultural Differences.* Chicago: University of Chicago Press. 396 p.

Division of Psychology, Institute of Educational Research, Teachers College, Columbia University (1933), *Language Learning; Summary of a Report to the International Auxiliary Language Association in the United States, Incorporated.* New York: Bureau of Publications, Teachers College, Columbia University. viii, 59 p.

Dollard, John, and Neal E. Miller (1950), *Personality and Psychotherapy; an Analysis in Terms of Learning, Thinking, and Culture.* New York: McGraw-Hill. xiii, 488 p.

Fries, Charles C., and Aileen A. Traver (1940), *English word Lists; A Study of their Adaptability for Instruction.* Washington, D. C.: American Council on Education. ix, 109 p.

Goldin, Hyman E., Frank O'Leary, and Morris Lipsius (eds.) (1951), *Dictionary of American Underworld Lingo.* New York: Twayne Publishers. 327 p.

Greenberg, Joseph H. (1948), "Linguistics and ethnology," *Southwestern Journal of Anthropology* 4: 140-147.

Guérard, Albert Léon (1922), *A Short History of the International Language Movement.* New York: Boni & Liveright. 268 p.

Haber, Tom Burns (1948), "The present status of Basic English in the United States," *Quarterly Journal of Speech* 34: 483-488.

Hart, Donn V. (1947), "UNESCO studies one-world language problems," *French Review* 21: 317-319.

Hartley, Eugene L., and Ruth E. Hartley (1952), *Fundamentals of Social Psychology.* New York: Knopf. 832 p.

Hodge, Carleton T. (1950), [Review of Pittman's *Practical Linguistics*], *Language* 26: 149-152.

International Auxiliary Language Association (1945), *General Report.* International Auxiliary Language Association, Suite 1808, 420 Lexington Avenue, New York 17, N. Y.

Jacob, H. (1947), *A Planned Auxiliary Language.* London: Dennis Dobson. 160 p.

———— (1948), *On Language Making.* London: Dennis Dobson. 16 p.

Johnsen, Julia E. (compiler) (1944), *Basic English.* New York: Wilson. 234 p. *(The Reference Shelf,* Vol. 17, No. 1.)

Kluckholn, Clyde, and Dorothea Leighton (1946), *The Navaho.* Cambridge: Harvard University Press. xx, 258 p.

Kroeber, A. L. (1941), "Some relations of linguistics and ethnology," *Language* 17: 287-291.

Kurath, Hans (1949), *A Word Geography of the Eastern United States.* Ann Arbor: University of Michigan Press. x, 88 p., 163 maps.

———— with Marcus L. Hansen, Julia Bloch, and Bernard Bloch (1939), *Handbook of the Linguistic Geography of New England.* Providence: Brown University. xii, 240 p.

Lasswell, Harold, Nathan Leites, *et al.* (1949), *Language of Politics: Studies in Quantitative Semantics.* New York: Stewart vii, 398 p.

Laubach, Frank C. (1938), *Toward a Literate World.* New York: Columbia University Press. 174 p.

——— (1943), *The Silent Billion Speak.* New York: Friendship Press. vi, 201 p.

Lewis, M. M. (1947), *Language in Society.* London: Nelson. vi, 249 p.

Lindersmith, A. R. and A. L. Strauss (1949), *Social Psychology.* New York: Dryden Press, xvi, 549 p.

Linton, Ralph (ed.) (1945), *The Science of Man in the World Crisis.* New York: Columbia Univ. Press. xiv, 532 p.

Luchsinger, R. (1940), "Die Sprache und Stimme von ein- und zwei-eiigen Zwillingen in Beziehungen zur Motorik und zum Erbcharakter," *Archiv der Julius Klaus Stiftung* 15: 461-527.

Lundberg, George A. (1939), *Foundations of Sociology.* New York: Macmillan. xx, 556 p.

Malinowski, Bronislaw (1935), *Coral Gardens and their Magic: A Study of the Methods of Tilling the Soil and of Agricultural Rites in the Trobriand Islanders.* London: Allen and Unwin. 2 vols.

——— (1936), "The problem of meaning in primitive languages," Supplement I, pp. 296-336 in Ogden and Richards, *The Meaning of Meaning,* 3rd edition. New York: Harcourt, Brace.

——— (1937), "The dilemma of contemporary linguistics" Review of M. M. Lewis's *Infant Speech, Nature* (London) 140: 172-3.

Mandelbaum, David G. (ed.) (1949), *Selected Writings of Edward Sapir in Language, Culture, and Personality.* Berkeley and Los Angeles: Univ. of California Press, xv, 617 p.

Mead, George H. (1934), *Mind, Self and Society from the Standpoint of a Social Behaviorist.* Ed. with an introduction by Charles W. Morris. Chicago: University of Chicago Press. xxxviii, 400 p.

Meinhof, Carl (1912), *Die Sprachen der Hamiten.* Hamburg: Friederichsen. xv, 256 p.

Miller, George A. (1950), "language engineering," *Journal of the Acoustical Society of America* 22: 720-725.

Odum, Howard W. (1951), *American Sociology: The Story of Sociology in the U.S. Through 1950.* New York: Longmans, Green. vi, 501 p.

Ogden, Charles K. (1930a), *Basic English; A General Introduction with Rules and Grammar.* London: K. Paul, Trench, Trubner. 100 p.

——— (1930b), *The Basic Vocabulary; A Statistical Analysis, with Special Reference to Substitution and Translation.* London: K. Paul, Trench, Trubner. 96 p.

———— (1932), *The Basic Dictionary, Being the 7,500 Most Useful Words with Their Equivalents in Basic English, for the use of Translators, Teachers, and Students.* London: K. Paul, Trench, Trubner. xx, 106 p.

———— (1934), *The System of Basic English.* N.Y.: Harcourt, Brace. ix, 322 p.

———— (1935), *Counter-Offensive; an Exposure of Certain Misrepresentations of Basic English.* Cambridge, England, and Peiping, China: The Orthological Institute.

———— and Ivor A. Richards (1936), *The Meaning of Meaning.* (3rd ed.) New York: Harcourt, Brace. xxii, 363 p.

Partridge, Eric (1949), *A Dictionary of Slang and Unconventional English.* (3rd ed.). London: Routledge & Kegan Paul. xvi, 1230 p.

———— (1950), *A Dictionary of the Underworld, British and American; Being the Vocabularies of Crooks, Criminals, Racketeers, Beggars, and Tramps; 16th-20th Centuries.* London: Routledge. xv, 804 p.

Payne, Stanley L. (1951), *The Art of Asking Questions.* Princeton: Princeton University Press. xiv, 249 p.

Pittman, Dean (1948), *Practical Linguistics.* Cleveland: Mid-Missions (314 Superior Avenue). xiii, 229 p.

Richards, Ivor A. (1942a), *How to Read a Page: A Course in Effective Reading, with an Introduction to a Hundred Great Words.* New York: Norton. 246 p.

———— (1943), *Basic English and its Uses.* New York: Norton. 143 p.

———— and Christine Gibson (1945), *Learning Basic English; A Practical Handbook for English-Speaking People.* New York: Norton, 116 p.

Rundle, Stanley (1946), *Language as a Social and Political Factor in Europe.* London: Faber & Faber. 207 p.

Sapir, Edward (1921), *Language; An Introduction To the Study of Speech.* New York: Harcourt, Brace. vii, 258 p.

———— (1930), "Totality," *Language Monographs,* no. 6. 28 p.

———— (1944), "Grading: a study in semantics," *Philosophy of Science* II: 93-116.

———— and Morris Swadesh (1932), "The expression of the ending-point relation in English, French, and German." *Language Monographs,* No. 10. 125.

Schlauch, Margaret (1942), *The Gift of Tongues.* New York: Modern Age Books. ix, 342 p.

Shenton, Herbert N. (1933), *Cosmopolitan Conversation; the Language Problems of International Conferences*. New York: Columbia Univ. Press. xviii, 803 p.

Smith, Bruce Lannes; Harold D. Lasswell, and Ralph D. Casey (1946), *Propaganda, Communication and Public Opinion; A Comprehensive Reference Guide*. Princeton: Princeton University Press. 442 p.

Tarnoczy, T. H. (1947), "Physical characteristics of speech sounds and some aspects of their anthropological relations," *Acta Anthropobiologica* (Budapest) I: 1-43.

Trager, George L. (1949), *The Field of Linguistics*. Norman, Okla.: Battenburg Press. 8 p.

Trubetskoy, N. S. (1939b), "Wie soll das Lautsystem einer kunstlichen internationalen Hilfsprache beschaffen sein?" *Travaux du Cercle Linguistique de Prague* 8: 5-21/

UNESCO (1949), *Fundamental Education; Description and Programme*. Paris: UNESCO Publication No. 363. 85 p.

_____ (1951), *The Haiti Pilot Project: Phase One*. Paris: UNESCO. 79 p.

Walsh, Chad (1933), "The verb system in Basic English," *American Speech* 8: 137-143.

Warner, W. L., and P. S. Lunt (1941), *The Social Life of a Modern Community*. New Haven: Yale Univ. Press. xx, 460 p.

West, Michael P., E. Swensen, and others (1934), *A Critical Examination of Basic English*. Toronto: University of Toronto Press. 53 p.

QUESTIONS FOR STUDY

1. The author states: "When dialectal differences become the basis for invidious comparisons, their relevance in social interaction becomes painfully obvious." Can you see how this statement might explain why upwardly mobile social groups are hypersensitive about their own language patterns as well as those of the larger group they have since left behind? How might it explain majority group attitudes toward emerging minority groups?

2. Why might a knowledge of linguistics be helpful to an ethnologist? How might an ethnologist use linguistics to explain the lack of communication between, say, a skilled auto mechanic and a woman who knows almost nothing about the inner workings of an automobile?

3. In what way might sociologists use the findings of linguistics to investigate class structure?

4. Carroll writes that linguistic studies have application to mass communications at three points. How do these points differ? At which point or points might the application of linguistic techniques be more valid? For those who have read J. D. Salinger's *Catcher in the Rye:* How much, or to what degree, is Holden Caulfield's world-view a product of mass communication? How is his world-view reflected in his language behavior?

5. Define "Language Engineering." What dangers are inherent in "Language Engineering" that is geared to changing the language patterns of lower-class elements in order to encourage the formation of middle-class language behavior?

6. How does Carroll expand his analogy between an international auxiliary language and a United Nations organization? How valid is the analogy? How might the rise of nationalism affect the acceptance of an auxiliary language? Which classes in a given country might be more favorably inclined toward accepting an auxiliary language? How might their acceptance of this auxiliary language be viewed by the others in the society?

7. What application might there be for linguistic studies by persons who are not specialists? Can you think of any groups of people who make use of linguistic techniques in their daily work without their being aware they are using anything other than common sense?

If you point out a butterfly to a Hopi Indian and ask its name, you will be told *masa'ytaka*. If you point to an airplane, you will again be told that it is called *masa'ytaka*. The reason for this is simple, as Benjamin Lee Whorf explains in his article "Science and Linguistics": "Hopi has a noun that covers every thing or being that flies, with the exception of birds, which class is denoted by another noun. The former noun may be said to denote the class FC-B — flying class minus bird. The Hopi actually call insect, airplane, and aviator all by the same word, and feel no difficulty about it." And lest we feel too upset by this state of affairs, keep in mind that the Eskimo might be equally upset by the manner in which we label so many varieties of winter precipitation *snow*.

To know that many cultures view reality in ways different from ours comes as a shock to most of us. To know that their views may sometimes be as consistent and reliable as ours, even though we have scientists and scholars, levels our egos and forces us into a humility that, Whorf points out, need not discourage us. He points to humility as an attribute "which accompanies the true scientific spirit" and to arrogance of the mind as that "which hinders real scientific curiosity and detachment."

51

Science and Linguistics

Benjamin Lee Whorf

1   Every normal person in the world, past infancy in years, can and does talk. By virtue of that fact, every person — civilized or un-civilized carries through life certain naive but deeply rooted ideas about talking and its relation to thinking. Because of their firm connection with speech habits that have become unconscious and automatic, these notions tend to be rather intolerant of opposition. They are by no means entirely personal and haphazard; their basis is definitely systematic, so that we are justified in calling them a system of natural logic — a term that seems to me preferable to the term common sense, often used for the same thing.

2   According to natural logic, the fact that every person has talked fluently since infancy makes every man his own authority on the process by which he formulates and communicates. He has merely to consult a common substratum of logic or reason which he and everyone else are supposed to possess. Natural logic says that talking is merely an incidental process concerned strictly with communication, not with formulation of ideas. Talking, or the use of language, is supposed only to "express" what is essentially already formulated nonlinguistically. Formulation is an independent process, called thought or thinking and is supposed to be largely indifferent to the nature of particular languages. Languages have grammars, which are assumed to be merely norms of conventional and social correctness, but the use of language is supposed to be guided not so much by them as by correct, rational, or intelligent *thinking*.

Reprinted from *Language, Thought & Reality* by Benjamin Lee Whorf by permission of The M.I.T. Press, Cambridge, Massachusetts. "Science and Linguistics," *The Technology Review*, April, 1940. Reprinted by permission of the author and *The Technology Review*.

3   Thought, in this view, does not depend on grammar but on laws of logic or reason which are supposed to be the same for all observers of the universe — to represent a rationale in the universe that can be "found" independently by all intelligent observers, whether they speak Chinese or Choctaw. In our own culture, the formulations of mathematics and of formal logic have acquired the reputation of dealing with this order of things, i.e., with the realm and laws of pure thought. Natural logic holds that different languages are essentially parallel methods for expressing this one-and-the-same rationale of thought and, hence, differ really in but minor ways which may seem important only because they are seen at close range. It holds that mathematics, symbolic logic, philosophy, and so on, are systems contrasted with language which deal directly with this realm of thought, not that they are themselves specialized extensions of language. The attitude of natural logic is well shown in an old quip about a German grammarian who devoted his whole

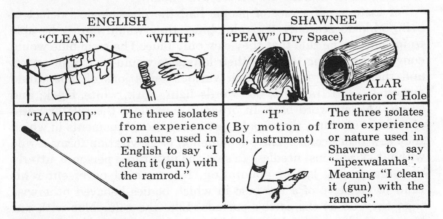

Figure 1.   *Languages dissect nature differently. The different isolates of meaning (thoughts) used by English and Shawnee in reporting the same experience, that of cleaning a gun by running the ramrod through it. The pronouns "I" and "it" are not shown by symbols, as they have the same meaning in each case. In Shawnee "ni-" equals "I"; "-a" equals "it."*

life to the study of the dative case. From the point of view of natural logic, the dative case and grammar in general are an extremely minor issue. A different attitude is said to have been held by the ancient Arabians: Two princes, so the story goes, quarreled over the honor of putting on the shoes of the most learned grammarian of the realm; whereupon their father, the caliph, is said to have remarked that it was the glory of his kingdom that great grammarians were honored even above kings.

4   The familiar saying that the exception proves the rule contains a good deal of wisdom, though from the standpoint of formal logic it became an absurdity as soon as "prove" no longer meant "put on trial." The old saw began to be profound psychology from the time it ceased to have standing in logic. What it might well suggest to us today is that if a rule has absolutely no exceptions, it is not recognized as a rule or as anything else; it is then part of the background of experience of which we tend to remain unconscious. Never having experienced anything in contrast to it, we cannot isolate it and formulate it as a rule until we so enlarge our experience and expand our base of reference that we encounter an interruption of its regularity. The situation is somewhat analogous to that of not missing the water till the well runs dry, or not realizing that we need air till we are choking.

5   For instance, if a race of people had the physiological defect of being able to see only the color blue, they would hardly be able to formulate the rule that they saw only blue. The term blue would convey no meaning to them, their language would lack color terms, and their words denoting their various sensations of blue would answer to, and translate, our words light, dark, white, black, and so on, not our word blue. In order to formulate the rule or norm of seeing only blue, they would need exceptional moments in which they saw other colors. The phenomenon of gravitation forms a rule without exceptions; needless to say, the untutored person is utterly unaware of any law of gravitation, for it would never enter his head to conceive of a universe in which bodies behaved otherwise than they do at the earth's surface. Like the color blue with our hypothetical race, the law of gravitation is a part of the untutored individual's background, not something he isolates from that background. The law could not be formulated until bodies that always fell were seen in terms of a wider astronomical world in which bodies moved in orbits or went this way and that.

6   Similarly, whenever we turn our heads, the image of the scene passes across our retinas exactly as it would if the scene turned around us. But this effect is background, and we do not recognize it; we do not see a room turn around us but are conscious only of having turned our heads in a stationary room. If we observe critically while turning the head or eyes quickly, we shall see no motion, it is true, yet a blurring of the scene between two clear views. Normally we are quite unconscious of this continual blurring

but seem to be looking about in an unblurred world. Whenever we walk past a tree or house, its image on the retina changes just as if the tree or house were turning on an axis; yet we do not see trees or houses turn as we travel about at ordinary speeds. Sometimes ill-fitting glasses will reveal queer movements in the scene as we look about, but normally we do not see the relative motion of the

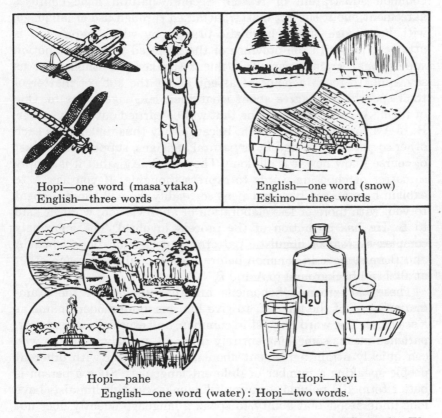

Hopi—one word (masa'ytaka)
English—three words

English—one word (snow)
Eskimo—three words

Hopi—pahe
English—one word (water) : Hopi—two words.

Hopi—keyi

Figure 2.   *Languages classify items of experience differently. The class corresponding to one word and one thought in language A may be regarded by language B as two or more classes corresponding to two or more words and thoughts.*

environment when we move; our psychic make-up is somehow adjusted to disregard whole realms of phenomena that are so all-pervasive as to be irrelevant to our daily lives and needs.

7   Natural logic contains two fallacies: First, it does not see that the phenomena of a language are to its own speakers largely of a background character and so are outside the critical consciousness

and control of the speaker who is expounding natural logic. Hence, when anyone, as a natural logician, is talking about reason, logic, and the laws of correct thinking, he is apt to be simply marching in step with purely grammatical facts that have somewhat of a background character in his own language or family of languages but are by no means universal in all languages and in no sense a common substratum of reason. Second, natural logic confuses agreement about subject matter, attained through use of language, with knowledge of the linguistic process by which agreement is attained; i.e., with the province of the despised (and to its notion superfluous) grammarian. Two fluent speakers, of English let us say, quickly reach a point of assent about the subject matter of their speech; they agree about what their language refers to. One of them, A, can give directions that will be carried out by the other, B, to A's complete satisfaction. Because they thus understand each other so perfectly, A and B, as natural logicians, suppose they must of course know how it is all done. They think, e.g., that it is simply a matter of choosing words to express thoughts. If you ask A to explain how he got B's agreement so readily, he will simply repeat to you, with more or less elaboration or abbreviation, what he said to B. He has no notion of the process involved. The amazingly complex system of linguistic patterns and classifications which A and B must have in common before they can adjust to each other at all, is all background to A and B.

8   These background phenomena are the province of the grammarian — or of the linguist, to give him his more modern name as a scientist. The word linguist in common, and especially newspaper, parlance means something entirely different, namely, a person who can quickly attain agreement about subject matter with different people speaking a number of different languages. Such a person is better termed a polyglot or a multilingual. Scientific linguists have long understood that ability to speak a language fluently does not necessarily confer a linguistic knowledge of it — i.e., understanding of its background phenomena and its systematic processes and structure — any more than ability to play a good game of billiards confers or requires any knowledge of the laws of mechanics that operate upon the billiard table.

9   The situation here is not unlike that in any other field of science. All real scientists have their eyes primarily on background phenomena that cut very little ice, as such, in our daily lives; and yet their studies have a way of bringing out a close relation between these unsuspected realms of fact and such decidedly foreground

activities as transporting goods, preparing food, treating the sick, or growing potatoes, which in time may become very much modified simply because of pure scientific investigation in no way concerned with these brute matters themselves. Linguistics is in quite similar case; the background phenomena with which it deals are involved in all our foreground activities of talking and of reaching agreement, in all reasoning and arguing of cases, in all law, arbitration, conciliation, contracts, treaties, public opinion, weighing of scientific theories, formulation of scientific results. Whenever agreement or assent is arrived at in human affairs, and whether or not mathematics or other specialized symbolisms are made part of the procedure, *this agreement is reached by linguistic processes, or else it is not reached.*

10   As we have seen, an overt knowledge of the linguistic processes by which agreement is attained is not necessary to reaching some sort of agreement, but it is certainly no bar thereto; the more complicated and difficult the matter, the more such knowledge is a distinct aid, till the point may be reached — I suspect the modern world has about arrived at it — when the knowledge becomes not only an aid but a necessity. The situation may be likened to that of navigation. Every boat that sails is in the lap of planetary forces; yet a boy can pilot his small craft around a harbor without benefit of geography, astronomy, mathematics, or international politics. To the captain of an ocean liner, however, some knowledge of all these subjects is essential.

11   When linguists became able to examine critically and scientifically a large number of languages of widely different patterns, their base of reference was expanded; they experienced an interruption of phenomena hitherto held universal, and a whole new order of significances came into their ken. It was found that the background linguistic system (in other words, the grammar) of each language is not merely a reproducing instrument for voicing ideas but rather is itself the shaper of ideas, the program and guide for the individual's mental activity, for his analysis of impressions, for his synthesis of his mental stock in trade. Formulation of ideas is not an independent process, strictly rational in the old sense, but is part of a particular grammar and differs, from slightly to greatly, as between different grammars. We dissect nature along lines laid down by our native languages. The categories and types that we isolate from the world of phenomena we do not find there because they stare every observer in the face; on the contrary, the world is presented in a kaleidoscopic flux of impressions which has to be

organized by our minds — and this means largely by the linguistic systems in our minds. We cut nature up, organize it into concepts, and ascribe significances as we do, largely because we are parties to an agreement to organize it in this way — an agreement that holds throughout our speech community and is codified in the

Objective Field	Speaker (Sender)	Hearer (Receiver)	Handling of Topic Running of Third Person
Situation 1a.			English ... "He is running."
			Hopi . . . "Wari", (running, statement of fact)
Situation 1b. Objective field blank devoid of running			English ... "He ran".
			Hopi . . . "Wari", (running, statement of fact)
Situation 2.			English ... "He is running"
			Hopi . . . "Wari", (running, statement of fact)
Situation 3. Objective field blank			English ... "He ran".
			Hopi . . . "Era wari", (running, statement of fact from memory)
Situation 4. Objective field blank			English ... "He will run".
			Hopi . . . "Warikni", (running, statement of expectation)
Situation 5. Objective field blank			English ... "He runs". (e.g. on the track team.)
			Hopi . . . "Warikngwe". (running, statement of law.)

Figure 3.   *Contrast between a "temporal" language (English) and a "timeless" language (Hopi). What are to English differences of time are to Hopi differences in the kind of validity.*

patterns of our language. The agreement is, of course, an implicit and unstated one, *but its terms are absolutely obligatory;* we cannot talk at all except by subscribing to the organization and classification of data which the agreement decrees.

12 The fact is very significant for modern science, for it means that no individual is free to describe nature with absolute impartiality but is constrained to certain modes of interpretation even while he thinks himself most free. The person most nearly free in such respects would be a linguist familiar with very many widely different linguistic systems. As yet no linguist is in even any such position. We are thus introduced to a new principle of relativity, which holds that all observers are not led by the same physical evidence to the same picture of the universe, unless their linguistic backgrounds are similar, or can in some way be calibrated.

13 This rather startling conclusion is not so apparent if we compare only our modern European languages, with perhaps Latin and Greek thrown in for good measure. Among these tongues there is a unanimity of major pattern which at first seems to bear out natural logic. But this unanimity exists only because these tongues are all Indo-European dialects cut to the same basic plan, being historically transmitted from what was long ago one speech community; because the modern dialects have long shared in building up a common culture; and because much of this culture, on the more intellectual side, is derived from the linguistic backgrounds of Latin and Greek. Thus this group of languages satisfies the special case of the clause beginning "unless" in the statement of the linguistic relativity principle at the end of the preceding paragraph. From this condition follows the unanimity of description of the world in the community of modern scientists. But it must be emphasized that "all modern Indo-European-speaking observers" is not the same thing as "all observers." That modern Chinese or Turkish scientists describe the world in the same terms as Western scientists means, of course, only that they have taken over bodily the entire Western system of rationalizations, not that they have corroborated that system from their native posts of observation.

14 When Semitic, Chinese, Tibetan, or African languages are contrasted with our own, the divergence in analysis of the world becomes more apparent; and when we bring in the native languages of the Americas, where speech communities for many millenniums have gone their ways independently of each other and of the Old World, the fact that languages dissect nature in many different ways becomes patent. The relativity of all conceptual systems, ours

included, and their dependence upon language stand revealed. That
American Indians speaking only their native tongues are never
called upon to act as scientific observers is in no wise to the point.
To exclude the evidence which their languages offer as to what
the human mind can do is like expecting botanists to study nothing
but food plants and hothouse roses and then tell us what the plant
world is like!

15   Let us consider a few examples. In English we divide most of our
words into two classes, which have different grammatical and
logical properties. Class 1 we call nouns, e.g., "house," "man";
Class 2, verbs, e.g., "hit," "run." Many words of one class can act
secondarily as of the other class, e.g., "a hit," "a run," or "to man"
the boat, but on the primary level the division between the classes
is absolute. Our language thus gives us a bipolar division of nature.
But nature herself is not thus polarized. If it be said that strike,
turn, run, are verbs because they denote temporary or short-lasting
events, i.e., actions, why then is fist a noun? It also is a temporary
event. Why are lightning, spark, wave, eddy, pulsation, flame,
storm, phase, cycle, spasm, noise, emotion, nouns? They are temporary events. If man and house are nouns because they are long-
lasting and stable events, i.e., things, what then are keep, adhere,
extend, project, continue, persist, grow, dwell, and so on, doing
among the verbs? If it be objected that possess, adhere, are verbs
because they are stable relationships rather than stable percepts,
why then should equilibrium, pressure, current, peace, group,
nation, society, tribe, sister, or any kinship term, be among the
nouns? It will be found that an "event" to *us* means "what our
language classes as a verb" or something analogized therefrom. And
it will be found that it is not possible to define event, thing, object,
relationship, and so on, from nature, but that to define them always
involves a circuitous return to the grammatical categories of the
definer's language.

16   In the Hopi language, lightning, wave, flame, meteor, puff of
smoke, pulsation, are verbs — events of necessarily brief duration
cannot be anything but verbs. Cloud and storm are at about the
lower limit of duration for nouns. Hopi, you see, actually has a
classification of events (or linguistic isolates) by duration type,
something strange to our modes of thought. On the other hand, in
Nootka, a language of Vancouver Island, all words seem to us to
be verbs, but really there are no Classes 1 and 2; we have, as it
were, a monistic view of nature that gives us only one class of word
for all kinds of events. "A house occurs" or "it houses" is the way
of saying "house," exactly like "a flame occurs" or "it burns."

These terms seem to us like verbs because they are inflected for durational and temporal nuances, so that the suffixes of the word for house event make it mean long-lasting house, temporary house, future house, house that used to be, what started out to be a house, and so on.

17   Hopi has a noun that covers every thing or being that flies, with the exception of birds, which class is denoted by another noun. The former noun may be said to denote the class FC — B — flying class minus bird. The Hopi actually call insect, airplane, and aviator all by the same word, and feel no difficulty about it. The situation, of course, decides any possible confusion among very disparate members of a broad linguistic class, such as this class FC — B. This class seems to us too large and inclusive, but so would our class "snow" to an Eskimo. We have the same word for falling snow, snow on the ground, snow packed hard like ice, slushy snow, wind-driven flying snow — whatever the situation may be. To an Eskimo, this all-inclusive word would be almost unthinkable; he would say that falling snow, slushy snow, and so on, are sensuously and operationally different, different things to contend with; he uses different words for them and for other kinds of snow. The Aztecs go even farther than we in the opposite direction, with cold, ice, and snow all represented by the same basic word with different terminations; ice is the noun form; cold, the adjectival form; and for snow, "ice mist."

18   What surprises most is to find that various grand generalizations of the Western world, such as time, velocity, and matter, are not essential to the construction of a consistent picture of the universe. The psychic experiences that we class under these headings are, of course, not destroyed; rather, categories derived from other kinds of experiences take over the rulership of the cosmology and seem to function just as well. Hopi may be called a timeless language. It recognizes psychological time, which is much like Bergson's "duration," but this "time" is quite unlike the mathematical time, T, used by our physicists. Among the peculiar properties of Hopi time are that it varies with each observer, does not permit of simultaneity, and has zero dimensions; i.e., it cannot be given a number greater than one. The Hopi do not say, "I stayed five days," but "I left on the fifth day." A word referring to this kind of time, like the word day, can have no plural. The puzzle picture (Fig. 3), will give mental exercise to anyone who would like to figure out how the Hopi verb gets along without tenses. Actually, the only practical use of our tenses, in one-verb sentences, is to distinguish among five typical situations, which are symbolized in

the picture. The timeless Hopi verb does not distinguish between the present, past, and future of the event itself but must always indicate what type of validity the *speaker* intends the statement to have: (a) report of an event (situations 1, 2, 3 in the picture); (b) expectation of an event (situation 4); (c) generalization or law about events (situation 5). Situation 1, where the speaker and listener are in contact with the same objective field, is divided by our language into the two conditions, 1*a*, and 1*b*, which it calls present and past, respectively. This division is unnecessary for a language which assures one that the statement is a report.

19   Hopi grammar, by means of its forms called aspects and modes, also makes it easy to distinguish between momentary, continued, and repeated occurrences, and to indicate the actual sequence of reported events. Thus the universe can be described without recourse to a concept of dimensional time. How would a physics constructed along these lines work, with no T (time) in its equations? Perfectly, as far as I can see, though of course it would require different ideology and perhaps different mathematics, Of course V (velocity) would have to go too. The Hopi language has no word really equivalent to our "speed" or "rapid." What translates these terms is usually a word meaning intense or very, accompanying any verb of motion. Here is a clew to the nature of our new physics. We may have to introduce a new term I, intensity. Every thing and event will have an I, whether we regard the thing or event as moving or as just enduring or being. Perhaps the I of an electric charge will turn out to be its voltage, or potential. We shall use clocks to measure some intensities, or, rather, some *relative* intensities, for the absolute intensity of anything will be meaningless. Our old friend acceleration will still be there but doubtless under a new name. We shall perhaps call it V, meaning not velocity but variation. Perhaps all growths and accumulations will be regarded as V's. We should not have the concept of rate in the temporal sense, since, like velocity, rate introduces a mathematical and linguistic time. Of course we know that all measurements are ratios, but the measurements of intensities made by comparison with the standard intensity of a clock or a planet we do not treat as ratios, any more than we so treat a distance made by comparison with a yardstick.

20   A scientist from another culture that used time and velocity would have great difficulty in getting us to understand these concepts. We should talk about the intensity of a chemical reaction; he would speak of its velocity or its rate, which words we should at

first think were simply words for intensity in his language. Likewise, he at first would think that intensity was simply our own word for velocity. At first we should agree, later we should begin to disagree, and it might dawn upon both sides that different systems of rationalization were being used. He would find it very hard to make us understand what he really meant by velocity of a chemical reaction. We should have no words that would fit. He would try to explain it by likening it to a running horse, to the difference between a good horse and a lazy horse. We should try to show him, with a superior laugh, that his analogy also was a matter of different intensities, aside from which there was little similarity between a horse and a chemical reaction in a beaker. We should point out that a running horse is moving relative to the ground, whereas the material in the beaker is at rest.

21   One significant contribution to science from the linguistic point of view may be the greater development of our sense of perspective. We shall no longer be able to see a few recent dialects of the Indo-European family, and the rationalizing techniques elaborated from their patterns, as the apex of the evolution of the human mind; nor their present wide spread as due to any survival from fitness or to anything but a few events of history — events that could be called fortunate only from the parochial point of view of the favored parties. They, and our own thought processes with them, can no longer be envisioned as spanning the gamut of reason and knowledge but only as one constellation in a galactic expanse. A fair realization of the incredible degree of diversity of linguistic system that ranges over the globe leaves one with an inescapable feeling that the human spirit is inconceivably old; that the few thousand years of history covered by our written records are no more than the thickness of a pencil mark on the scale that measures our past experience on this planet; that the events of these recent millenniums spell nothing in any evolutionary wise, that the race has taken no sudden spurt, achieved no commanding synthesis during recent millenniums, but has only played a little with a few of the linguistic formulations and views of nature bequeathed from an inexpressibly longer past. Yet neither this feeling nor the sense of precarious dependence of all we know upon linguistic tools which themselves are largely unknown need be discouraging to science but should, rather, foster that humility which accompanies the true scientific spirit, and thus forbid that arrogance of the mind which hinders real scientific curiosity and detachment.

QUESTIONS FOR STUDY

1. Whorf obviously looks down on those persons who believe that "Languages have grammars, which are assumed to be merely norms of conventional and social correctness . . ." Using your own school experiences as background, can you explain how an attitude toward language such as this might have arisen?

2. What is "natural logic"? How natural is it? In what ways does "natural logic" create a false dichotomy between thought and language? How are we being false to the reality of language if we say: "I knew the answer all the time, but I couldn't find the words to say"?

3. For those who have read *The Chairs* by Eugene Ionesco: What does this play seem to "say" about the effectiveness of language as a medium of communication?

4. Why do you think "our psychic make-up is somehow adjusted to disregard whole realms of phenomena that are so all-pervasive as to be irrelevant to our daily lives and needs"? What might happen to us if this were not so? Relate your answer to any feelings of uneasiness you might have about examining your own use of language.

5. What does Whorf mean when he says: "We dissect nature along lines laid down by our native language."? How is this statement in accord with Robert Frost's definition of poetry — "Poetry is what is lost in translation." In what ways might a given scientific terminology be a "foreign" language to you? (Those who have read C. P. Snow's *The Two Cultures* might be willing to discuss it in the light of the Whorf article.)

Charles Darwin is often accused of claiming that mankind is descended from the apes. What he actually claimed was that *both* mankind and the ape — somewhere in the distant past — probably shared a common ancestor. This is not much comfort to those who prefer to see man as only slightly lower than the angels, but quite sufficient for those who are content to view the world as process — evolutionary this time.

Similarly, and contrary to popular notions, the English language is not exactly descended solely from either French or German — although we can see strong traces of both these languages in English. But we can say that English *and* French *and* German — and many other languages besides — do have a common ancestor.

The history of the English language is much too complex to be covered in one brief essay. Nonetheless, L. M. Myers, in his article "The Development of the Language," traces some of the important and interesting stages in its development.

The Development of the Language

L. M. Myers

1   If you looked at the French and Italian words for *hundredcent* and *cento* respectively — you would easily guess that they are related, and they are. They both developed from the Latin word *centum*. And if you looked at the German word *hundert* you could recognize it as a close relative of the English word. You would be right again, but you could not prove it quite so easily, because we do not have any written records of the early form of Germanic from which modern English and German developed. We have to prove the relationship by other methods which are too complicated to go into here.

2   You would probably not guess that *hundred* and *centum* are also related; but if you happened to think of these two words along with *horn* and *corno, house* and *casa,* and various other pairs that begin with *h* in English and *c* in Italian, you might suspect that these resemblances were systematic, and that English is also related to Italian, although not nearly as closely as French is. Your suspicions would be justified. Experts can trace the relations among all four of these languages and a good many others. We can say roughly that French and Italian are sister languages, both born of Latin; that English and modern German are approximately second cousins; and that English and Italian are something like third cousins twice removed.

3   Nobody knows for sure how language began, or even whether it began just once or at a number of different times and places. What we do know is that some languages, as we have just seen, show evidence of a common origin, while others do not. If our written records went back a few thousand years further it is possible that

we might find signs of resemblance between the languages that we have just mentioned and Chinese or Arabic or Navajo. But if such resemblances ever existed, they disappeared a long time ago, and it seems most unlikely that we will ever find any evidence to prove them. We must therefore study them as separate families, though they may have had a common ancestor about which we now know nothing.

ORIGIN OF ENGLISH

4   English belongs, in a rather complicated way, to the Indo-European family, which includes most of the European languages and a few Asiatic ones. We do not know where the original speakers of the parent Indo-European language lived. Guesses about their homeland range all the way from northeastern Europe to central Asia. According to all the early records they were a tall, blond, and warlike people, with a good deal of energy and intelligence. In their native land they had developed neither writing nor cities, so there is not much evidence about how they lived when they were at home. But when they left home and went out in search of new lands — which they did in various waves from about 2500 B.C. to about 1000 B.C. — the Indo-Europeans seem to have been generally successful in conquering the countries they came to.

5   When a wave of them settled in a territory already crowded, they mixed with the original population. In time they lost their distinctive appearance by intermarrying with the earlier inhabitants, and sometimes they also gave up most of the features of their language. When a wave went to a more thinly settled territory, they naturally preserved their physical characteristics comparatively unchanged for a much longer time; and they were likely to preserve the distinctive features of their language also, though the two things did not always go together.

6   The Slavic and Celtic languages, as well as Indian, Persian, and some others, are of Indo-European origin, but the three branches with which English is most concerned are the Greek, Latin, and Germanic, particularly the last. All languages are changing to some extent all the time; and before the invention of writing they seem to have changed faster than they do now. Since the various waves left at different times, they were speaking noticeably different varieties of Indo-European at the times of their departure, and the further changes that took place after they left made their languages more and more unlike. As they split up and settled (more or less)

in different regions, the differences became so great that the Greeks, for instance, could not possibly understand the Germans; and a little later some of the Germans could not understand the others.

7   Old Germanic split into North, East, and West Germanic. West Germanic split into High and Low German. And Low German split into further dialects, including those of the Angles, Saxons, and Jutes. There were differences in pronunciation, and even in word endings, between these last three; but most of the root words were enough alike to be recognizable, and the three tribes seem to have had no great difficulty in understanding each other. About 450 A.D. members of all three tribes moved into what is now called England (from Angle-land), and began to take it over. It is at this time that we usually say the English language, as such, began.

8   It is worth noticing that even at the very beginning of English as a separate language there was no one simple standard. The Jutes undoubtedly thought that the Angles "talked funny," and vice versa. Efforts have been made for centuries to develop a set of standard practices, and there is much to be said in their favor; but they have never been quite successful, and they never will be. There is just no way to make millions of people talk exactly alike.

9   These early English settlers do not seem to have made much of an effort to understand the language of the Britons who lived in England (then called Britain) before they came. The Britons also spoke an Indo-European language, but it belonged to the Celtic rather than the Germanic branch, and was by now completely unrecognizable to the newcomers. The English added only a handful of Celtic words to their language — not nearly as many as the Americans later picked up from the Indians.

10   We can only guess about how the language would have developed if the descendants of these three tribes had been left to themselves. The fact is that two great invasions and a missionary movement changed the language enormously. The total result of these and other influences was that the English vocabulary became the largest and most complex in the world, and the grammar changed its emphasis from inflections (changes in the forms of words) to word-order.

THE SCANDINAVIAN INFLUENCE

11   Some three hundred years after the West Germanic tribes had settled in England, there was another wave of invasions, this time

by Scandinavians. In the history books these people are usually referred to as "Danes," but there were Swedes and Norwegians among them, and their speech was probably no more uniform than that of the first wave. The dialects they spoke belonged to the Northern rather than the Western division of Germanic. They differed rather more from the dialects of the Angles, Saxons, and Jutes than these differed from each other — roughly, about as much as Spanish differs from Italian. In spite of different habits of pronunciation, most of the root words were enough alike to be recognizable. The difficulty caused by differences in inflection was partly solved by dropping some of the inflections altogether and being broad-minded about the others. Spelling was not much of a problem, because most people could not read nor write; and those who could, spelled as they pleased. There were no dictionaries to prove them wrong.

12   Although these Danes moved in on the English, and for a time dominated them politically, their conquest was nothing like as thorough as that of the English over the Britons. After the early fighting the two peoples settled down together without much attention to their separate origins, and the languages mingled. On the whole, English rather than Danish characteristics won out; but many of the words were so much alike that it is impossible to say whether we owe our present forms to English or Danish origins, and occasionally the Danish forms drove out the English ones. Sometimes both forms remained, usually with a somewhat different meaning. Thus we have *shirt* and *skirt*, both of which originally meant a long, smock-like garment, although the English form has come to mean the upper part, and the Danish form the lower. Old English *rear* and Danish *raise* are another pair — sometimes interchangeable, sometimes not.

THE NORMAN CONQUEST

13   In 1066 the Normans conquered England. They, like the Danes, had originally come from Scandinavia. But they had settled in northern France, and for some undiscoverable reason had given up their own language and learned to speak a dialect of French. For several centuries Normans, and other Frenchmen that they invited in later, held most of the important positions in England, and it seemed quite possible that French would become the standard language of the country. But the bulk of the population were still English, and they were stubborner than their rulers. Most of them

never learned French, and eventually — though only after several
centuries — all the nobles and officials were using English.

14 It was not, however, the English of the days before the conquest.
A good many French words had gotten into the language; and
most of the inflections that had survived the Danish pressure had
dropped out, with a standard word-order making up for their loss.
We need not go into the argument about whether the new word-
order had to develop because the endings dropped out, or the endings disappeared because the new word-order made them unnecessary. The two changes took place together, and by the time of
Chaucer (died 1400) the language had become enough like Modern
English to be recognizable. The pronunciation was quite different
and the spelling was still catch-as-catch can; but a modern student
can get at least a general idea of Chaucer's meaning without special
training, while he can no more read Old English than he can
German or Latin, unless he has made a special study of it. Compare the two following passages:

> 1. Hwaet! We gardena   in geardagum
>   Theodcyningas   thrym gefrunon
> 2. Whan that Aprille with his shoures soote
>   The droghte of March hath perced to the roote

15 In the first two lines from *Beowulf* only *we* and *in* are readily
recognizable; while in the first two from Chaucer's *Canterbury
Tales,* only *soote* (sweet) offers much of a problem.

16 From Chaucer's time to our own the language has developed
with no outside pressure comparable to that of the Danish and
Norman invasions. Still more endings have disappeared, and there
have been other changes; but the greatest development has been in
the vocabulary. A considerable number of Chaucer's words have
dropped out of use, and a much greater number of new words have
been added. Some of these new words have been made by com-
pounding or otherwise modifying old ones, but most of them have
been borrowed from other languages, particularly Latin.

THE LATIN INFLUENCE

17 Even before they came to England our ancestors had picked up
a few Latin words; and they learned others from the Christian missionaries who began to convert them in the sixth century. These
early borrowings were taken directly into the spoken language, and
most of them have now changed so that their Latin origins are not

easy to recognize. *Street, wine, bishop, priest,* and *church* (the last three originally borrowed from Greek by the Romans) are examples.

18   After the Norman Conquest borrowings from Latin were enormously increased. French itself is directly descended from Latin, and we cannot always tell whether an English word came directly from Latin or through French. *Suspicion,* for instance, could have come into English by either route. But we do know that many words must have come straight from Latin, either because they don't occur in French or because their French forms are different. Scholars often could not find an English word for an idea they wished to express; and even if they could, they might think that a Latin word was more exact or more impressive.

19   English has also borrowed words from many other languages, particularly Greek, and is continuing to do so at present; but ever since the late Middle English period it has simply been a matter of helping ourselves, rather than yielding to pressure.

DEVELOPMENT OF A LITERARY STANDARD

20   The changes that took place in the language throughout the Old and Middle English periods were simply a natural development, unguided by any theory. Men talked more or less as their neighbors did, and anybody who wrote simply tried to indicate the sound of his speech on paper. There were no dictionaries, no grammars, and no printed books of any kind. As far as we know, very few people thought about the language at all; and most of those who did think about it seem to have considered it a crude and rather hopeless affair, unworthy of serious study. There were exceptions, of course, but they did not have much influence. Local differences were so great that a man trained in northern England would have serious difficulty reading a manuscript written in the southern part. However, the dialect of London had a certain prestige throughout the country; and although this dialect itself was by no means uniform, and changed with shifts in city population, it gradually came to be accepted as the standard. By the latter half of the fifteenth century it was quite generally used in writing throughout the country except in the extreme north. The introduction of printing in 1476, with London as the publishing center, greatly strengthened the influence of the London dialect. Strong local differences in spoken English remain to this day, especially among the less educated classes. But throughout the modern period written (or at least published) English has been surprisingly uniform.

EIGHTEENTH CENTURY MOVEMENT
TO REGULARIZE THE LANGUAGE

21   Until the eighteenth century the uniformity was the result of
social pressure rather than of educational theory. Early English
grammars (the first appeared in 1586) had been written either to
help foreigners learn English or to prepare English students for the
study of Latin grammar. On the whole these books neither had nor
were intended to have any influence on the use of English by native
speakers. It was not until about 1750 that there was any general
attempt to teach Englishmen systematically how to use their own
language.

22   It is too bad that this attempt was not postponed for a few more
generations. Since the really scientific study of various languages
had not yet begun, the eighteenth century grammarians had to
base their work on a set of theories that we now know are definitely
wrong. For one thing, they thought that grammar had an absolute
existence, and must therefore be the same in all languages. Since
they believed that this grammar was well preserved in Latin and
badly frayed in English, they often tried to reform a natural English expression on a Latin model.

23   For another thing, they thought that the simplifying of inflections, which had been going on for centuries, was decay instead of
progress. They could not do anything about the ones that had
already completely disappeared, but they did make a deliberate and
fairly successful effort to preserve those that were just disappearing.
We would not have so many irregular verbs today if they had just
let nature take its course.

24   Perhaps the most dangerous of their ideas was that they could
keep the language from ever changing any more. They argued that
Latin had remained unchanged for centuries, and they saw no
reason why English should not do the same. They failed to realize
that the only reason classical Latin had remained unchanged was
that the men who had written it had been dead for a long time.
There were still scholars — there are a few even today — who could
imitate classical Latin. But as a natural language for the people,
Latin had developed, in different areas, into Italian, French,
Spanish, and so forth. All of these languages, as well as English,
are still changing, and we have every reason to believe that they
will continue to change as long as they are used.

25   If these theories had merely been the bad guesses of a few
scholars, they would not have done much harm. But they became

the guiding principles in most schoolroom instruction just at the time when education was becoming general, and when the study of the English language was beginning to be recognized as an end in itself and not merely as a preliminary step to the study of Latin. As a result, during the two hundred years in which English has been seriously taught in our schools, it has been taught almost entirely on a set of theories which can now be proved wrong; and a great deal of the effort that has gone into teaching English has therefore been worse than wasted.

26   Since most students find it hard enough to learn English grammar without making comparisons with other languages, we need not go into a detailed explanation of why the eighteenth century theories were wrong. But very briefly (and you may skip this if you like) Latin is a *synthetic* language. That is, it is highly inflected, and the relations between words are shown primarily by their endings. Old English was also synthetic, but modern English has become an *analytical* language. Most of the endings have dropped off, and even those that remain are much less important than they used to be, since the relations between words are now shown largely by word-order and *function words*, such as connectives and auxiliary verbs. It is now rather generally held that the shift from a synthetic to an analytical structure is an improvement, but most eighteenth century grammarians considered it a calamity and tried to stop it.

27   One effect of this misdirected effort has been to interfere with the natural development of the language. By 1750 most of the Old English irregular verbs either had dropped out of use or had become regular: *help, holp* had become *help, helped; wash, wesh* had become *wash, washed*, etc. A number of others were in the process of making the same change: *blow, blew* to *blow, blowed; throw, threw* to *throw, throwed*; etc. We should probably still have some irregular verbs even if eighteenth century grammarians had not deliberately resisted this development, but there would certainly not be so many. Most of us probably have a feeling that such forms as *blowed* and *throwed* are intrinsically wrong; but our acceptance of *helped* and *washed* as correct shows that this is purely a matter of habit.

28   At the same time, many of those troublesome verbs like *sing* and *take*, which have separate forms for the past participle, were simplifying to a single past form. This change also was resisted on the theory that the small number of inflections was "the greatest defect in our language." The fact that only about forty of our verbs

now have these separate forms proves conclusively that we don't need them, and most of them would probably have disappeared by now if they had been allowed to depart in peace. But after two centuries of insistence on the importance of these unfortunate survivals, we may never get rid of them.

AFTER-EFFECTS OF EIGHTEENTH CENTURY GRAMMATICAL THEORIES

29   Of course the language continued to change in spite of all objections; and if the grammarians had done no more than slow up the rate of change it could be argued (although not proved) that their efforts had on the whole been useful. But they did something much worse than this. By insisting on rules which often had no foundation in the speech habits of the people, they converted "grammar" into an artificial and generally distasteful subject. When a Frenchman studies French grammar, he is learning how educated Frenchmen actually talk and write; and in his later life he can practice what he has learned in school with a comfortable assurance. But a good deal of what an Englishman or an American learns under the name of grammar has nothing to do with the use of our language; and a good deal more is in direct conflict with the actual practices of most educated people.

30   The result is that many Americans go through life feeling inadequate, even guilty, about their language habits. Even if they actually speak English very well, they seldom have the comfort of realizing it. They have been taught to believe in a mysterious "perfect English" which does not exist, and to regard it as highly important; but they have never had the structure of the language explained to them.

AMERICAN ENGLISH

31   In the early part of the seventeenth century, English settlers began to bring their language to America, and another series of changes began to take place. There were all sorts of new things, and eventually new ideas, to talk about; and the language had to be modified to meet the new circumstances. If the colonization had taken place a few centuries earlier, American might have become as different from English as French is from Italian.

32   But the English settlements occurred after the invention of printing, and continued through a period when the idea of educat-

ing everybody was making rapid progress. For a long time most of the books read in America came from England, and a surprising number of Americans read those books, in or out of school. Moreover, most of the colonists seem to have felt a strong tie with England. In this they were unlike their Anglo-Saxon ancestors, who apparently made a clean break with their continental homes.

33   Nevertheless, American English, particularly the spoken variety, developed a number of differences from the English of Britain. A good many Englishmen, and some Americans, used to condemn every such difference; and as recently as a generation ago it was not uncommon to hear all "Americanisms" condemned, even in America. It is now generally recognized in this country that we are not bound to the King's English, but have a full right to work out our own habits. Even a good many of the English are now willing to grant us this right; though many of them object strongly to the fact that Americanisms are now having an influence on British speech.

34   A list of the detailed differences would be long, but the theory that the American language is now essentially different from English does not hold up. It is often quite difficult to decide whether a book was written by an American or an Englishman. Even in speech it would be hard to prove that national differences are greater than some local differences in either country. On the whole, it now seems probable that the language habits of the two countries will grow more, rather than less, alike, although some differences will undoubtedly remain and others may develop.

35   It also seems probable that there will be narrow-minded and snobbish people in both countries for some time to come. But generally speaking, anybody who learns to speak and write the standard English of his own country, and to regard that of the other country as a legitimate variety with certain interesting differences, will have little trouble wherever he goes.

QUESTIONS FOR STUDY

1. Why might a careful study of the roots of English be a humbling experience for those who adhere to any mystique founded on race or language?

2. Discuss three specific early influences on English. Was it the natural superiority of these foreign influences that caused the native speakers to alter their own language habits, or was there some more practical reason for the influence of, say, Norman French?

3. Often the first contact foreign persons have with American English is through our literature. Can you think of any reasons why our literature might present a false picture of our language (not to mention our culture)? Relate your answer to the development of a literary standard in England from the 15th century onward.

4. What have been some of the "after-effects" of eighteenth century grammatical theories? Illustrate from your own school experiences. Do you see any hopeful signs on the grammatical horizon?

5. Can you think of any ways (from your own reading or experiences) in which American English differs from its British counterpart? Can you think of any influences that might tend either to lessen or to exaggerate these differences?

6. Can you think of any ways in which the present "youth culture" in this country can be regarded as a source of foreign words? Is this a legitimate source of new words? Explain.

This article by W. Nelson Francis, "Revolution in Grammar," signals the beginning of a widespread reappraisal—still going on—of English grammar. It makes a clear, objective case for a new approach to grammar, an approach that describes the language as it is rather than as it should be. It supplies facts to overcome opposition that traditionalists might have to linguistic grammar. In doing this, the author gives us easily understood terminology and definitions that foster precision of thought and promote insights into the workings of the language, as well as offering a means of describing this language system honestly. Francis gives the scientific study of language its just due and provides the impetus for investigation that only the lazy or closed mind can afford to ignore.

Revolution in Grammar

W. Nelson Francis

I

1   A long overdue revolution is at present taking place in the study of English grammar—a revolution as sweeping in its consequences as the Darwinian revolution in biology. It is the result of the application to English of methods of descriptive analysis originally developed for use with languages of primitive peoples. To anyone at all interested in language, it is challenging; to those concerned with the teaching of English (including parents), it presents the necessity of radically revising both the substance and the methods of their teaching.

2   A curious paradox exists in regard to grammar. On the one hand it is felt to be the dullest and driest of academic subjects, fit only for those in whose veins the red blood of life has long since turned to ink. On the other, it is a subject upon which people who would scorn to be professional grammarians hold very dogmatic opinions, which they will defend with considerable emotion. Much of this prejudice stems from the usual sources of prejudice—ignorance and confusion. Even highly educated people seldom have a clear idea of what grammarians do, and there is an unfortunate confusion about the meaning of the term "grammar" itself.

3   Hence it would be well to begin with definitions. What do people mean when they use the word "grammar"? Actually the word is

From *Quarterly Journal of Speech,* October 1954. Reprinted by permission of the Speech Association of America and the author.

"This article was written thirteen years ago. Since that time, further extensive changes, amounting in effect to another revolution, have taken place in the theory and description of English grammar. For this reason, many of the detailed statements in the article are out of date. But its underlying premises are still acceptable and sound."

used to refer to three different things, and much of the emotional thinking about matters grammatical arises from confusion among these different meanings.

4   The first thing we mean by "grammar" is "the set of formal patterns in which the words of a language are arranged in order to convey larger meanings." It is not necessary that we be able to discuss these patterns self-consciously in order to be able to use them. In fact, all speakers of a language above the age of five or six know how to use its complex forms of organization with considerable skill; in this sense of the word—call it "Grammar 1"— they are thoroughly familiar with its grammar.

5   The second meaning of "grammar"—call it "Grammar 2"—is "the branch of linguistic science which is concerned with the description, analysis, and formulization of formal language patterns." Just as gravity was in full operation before Newton's apple fell, so grammar in the first sense was in full operation before anyone formulated the first rule that began the history of grammar as a study.

6   The third sense in which people use the word "grammar" is "linguistic etiquette." This we may call "Grammar 3." The word in this sense is often coupled with a derogatory adjective: we say that the expression "he ain't here" is "bad grammar." What we mean is that such an expression is bad linguistic manners in certain circles. From the point of view of "Grammar 1" it is faultless; it conforms just as completely to the structural patterns of English as does "he isn't here." The trouble with it is like the trouble with Prince Hal in Shakespeare's play—it is "bad," not in itself, but in the company it keeps.

7   As has already been suggested, much confusion arises from mixing these meanings. One hears a good deal of criticism of teachers of English couched in such terms as "they don't teach grammar any more." Criticism of this sort is based on the wholly unproved assumption that teaching Grammar 2 will increase the student's proficiency in Grammar 1 or improve his manners in Grammar 3. Actually, the form of Grammar 2 which is usually taught is a very inaccurate and misleading analysis of the facts of Grammar 1; and it therefore is of highly questionable value in improving a person's ability to handle the structural patterns of his language. It is hardly reasonable to expect that teaching a person some inaccurate grammatical analysis will either improve the effectiveness of his assertions or teach him what expressions are acceptable to use in a given social context.

8   These, then, are the three meanings of "grammar": Grammar
1, a form of behavior; Grammar 2, a field of study, a science;
and Grammar 3, a branch of etiquette.

II

9   Grammarians have arrived at some basic principles of their
science, three of which are fundamental to this discussion. The
first is that a language constitutes a set of behavior patterns
common to the members of a given community. It is a part of
what the anthropologists call the culture of the community. Actually it has complex and intimate relationships with other phases
of culture such as myth and ritual. But for purposes of study
it may be dealt with as a separate set of phenomena that can be
objectively described and analyzed like any other universe of
facts. Specifically, its phenomena can be observed, recorded, classified, and compared; and general laws of their behavior can be
made by the same inductive process that is used to produce the
"laws" of physics, chemistry, and the other sciences.

10   A second important principle of linguistic science is that each
language or dialect has its own unique system of behavior patterns. Parts of this system may show similarities to parts of the
systems of other languages, particularly if those languages are
genetically related. But different languages solve the problems
of expression and communication in different ways, just as the
problems of movement through water are solved in different ways
by lobsters, fish, seals, and penguins. A couple of corollaries of
this principle are important. The first is that there is no such
thing as "universal grammar," or at least if there is, it is so
general and abstract as to be of little use. The second corollary
is that the grammar of each language must be made up on the
basis of a study of that particular language—a study that is free
from preconceived notions of what a language should contain and
how it should operate. The marine biologist does not criticize
the octopus for using jet-propulsion to get him through the water
instead of the methods of a self-respecting fish. Neither does the
linguistic scientist express alarm or distress when he finds a language that seems to get along quite well without any words that
correspond to what in English we call verbs.

11   A third principle on which linguistic science is based is that the
analysis and description of a given language must conform to the
requirements laid down for any satisfactory scientific theory.
These are (1) simplicity, (2) consistency, (3) completeness, and

(4) usefulness for predicting the behavior of phenomena not brought under immediate observation when the theory was formed. Linguistic scientists who have recently turned their attention to English have found that, judged by these criteria, the traditional grammar of English is unsatisfactory. It falls down badly on the first two requirements, being unduly complex and glaringly inconsistent within itself. It can be made to work, just as the Ptolemaic earth-centered astronomy can be, but at the cost of great elaboration and complication. The new grammar, like the Copernican sun-centered astronomy, solves the same problems with greater elegance, which is the scientist's word for the simplicity, compactness, and tidiness that characterize a satisfactory theory.

III

12 A brief look at the history of the traditional grammar of English will make apparent the reasons for its inadequacy. The study of English grammar is actually an outgrowth of the linguistic interest of the Renaissance. It was during the later Middle Ages and early Renaissance that the various vernacular languages of Europe came into their own. They began to be used for many kinds of writing which had previously always been done in Latin. As the vernaculars, in the hands of great writers like Dante and Chaucer, came of age as members of the linguistic family, a concomitant interest in their grammars arose. The earliest important English grammar was written by Shakespeare's contemporary, Ben Jonson.

13 It is important to observe that not only Ben Jonson himself but also those who followed him in the study of English grammar were men deeply learned in Latin and sometimes in Greek. For all their interest in English, they were conditioned from earliest school days to conceive of the classical languages as superior to the vernaculars. We still sometimes call the elementary school the "grammar school"; historically the term means the school where Latin grammar was taught. By the time the Renaissance or eighteenth-century scholar took his university degree, he was accustomed to use Latin as the normal means of communication with his fellow scholars. Dr. Samuel Johnson, for instance, who had only three years at the university and did not take a degree, wrote poetry in both Latin and Greek. Hence it was natural for these men to take Latin grammar as the norm, and to analyze English in terms of Latin. The grammarians of the seventeenth

and eighteenth centuries who formulated the traditional grammar
of English looked for the devices and distinctions of Latin grammar in English, and where they did not actually find them they
imagined or created them. Of course, since English is a member
of the Indo-European family of languages, to which Latin and
Greek also belong, it did have many grammatical elements in
common with them. But many of these had been obscured or
wholly lost as a result of the extensive changes that had taken
place in English—changes that the early grammarians inevitably
conceived of as degeneration. They felt that it was their function
to resist further change, if not to repair the damage already done.
So preoccupied were they with the grammar of Latin as the
ideal that they overlooked in large part the exceedingly complex
and delicate system that English had substituted for the Indo-
European grammar it had abandoned. Instead they stretched
unhappy English on the Procrustean bed of Latin. It is no wonder
that we commonly hear people say, "I didn't really understand
grammar until I began to study Latin." This is eloquent testimony
to the fact that the grammar "rules" of our present-day textbooks
are largely an inheritance from the Latin-based grammar of the
eighteenth century.

14   Meanwhile the extension of linguistic study beyond the Indo-
European and Semitic families began to reveal that there are
many different ways in which linguistic phenomena are organized
—in other words, many different kinds of grammar. The tone-
languages of the Orient and of North America, and the complex
agglutinative languages of Africa, among others, forced grammarians to abandon the idea of a universal or ideal grammar and to
direct their attention more closely to the individual systems employed by the multifarious languages of mankind. With the
growth and refinement of the scientific method and its application to the field of anthropology, language came under more rigorous scientific scrutiny. As with anthropology in general, linguistic
science at first concerned itself with the primitive. Finally, again
following the lead of anthropology, linguistics began to apply its
techniques to the old familiar tongues, among them English.
Accelerated by the practical need during World War II of teaching languages, including English, to large numbers in a short
time, research into the nature of English grammar has moved
rapidly in the last fifteen years. The definitive grammar of English is yet to be written, but the results so far achieved are
spectacular. It is now as unrealistic to teach "traditional" grammar of English as it is to teach "traditional" (i.e. pre-Darwinian)

biology or "traditional" (i.e. four-element) chemistry. Yet nearly all certified teachers of English on all levels are doing so. Here is a cultural lag of major proportions.

IV

15   Before we can proceed to a sketch of what the new grammar of English looks like, we must take account of a few more of the premises of linguistic science. They must be understood and accepted by anyone who wishes to understand the new grammar.

16   First, the spoken language is primary, at least for the original study of a language. In many of the primitive languages,[1] of course, where writing is unknown, the spoken language is the *only* form. This is in many ways an advantage to the linguist, because the written language may use conventions that obscure its basic structure. The reason for the primary importance of the spoken language is that language originates as speech, and most of the changes and innovations that occur in the history of a given language begin in the spoken tongue.

17   Secondly, we must take account of the concept of dialect. I suppose most laymen would define a dialect as "a corrupt form of a language spoken in a given region by people who don't know any better." This introduces moral judgments which are repulsive to the linguistic scholar. Let us approach the definition of a dialect from the more objective end, through the notion of a speech community. A speech community is merely a group of people who are in pretty constant intercommunication. There are various types of speech communities: local ones, like "the people who live in Tidewater Virginia"; class ones, like "the white-collar class"; occupational ones, like "doctors, nurses, and other people who work in hospitals"; social ones, like "clubwomen." In a sense, each of these has its own dialect. Each family may be said to have its own dialect; in fact, in so far as each of us has his own vocabulary and particular quirks of speech, each individual has his own dialect. Also, of course, in so far as he is a member of many speech communities, each individual is more or less master of many dialects and shifts easily and almost unconsciously from one to another as he shifts from one social environment to another.

---

[1]"Primitive languages" here is really an abbreviated statement for "languages used by peoples of relatively primitive culture"; it is not to be taken as implying anything simple or rudimentary about the languages themselves. Many languages included under the term, such as native languages of Africa and Mexico, exhibit grammatical complexities unknown to more "civilized" languages.

18   In the light of this concept of dialects, a language can be defined
as a group of dialects which have enough of their sound-system,
vocabulary, and grammar (Grammar 1, that is) in common to
permit their speakers to be mutually intelligible in the ordinary
affairs of life. It usually happens that one of the many dialects
that make up a language comes to have more prestige than the
others; in modern times it has usually been the dialect of the
middle-class residents of the capital, like Parisian French and
London English, which is so distinguished. This comes to be
thought of as the standard dialect; in fact, its speakers become
snobbish and succeed in establishing the belief that it is not a
dialect at all, but the only proper form of the language. This
causes the speakers of other dialects to become self-conscious
and ashamed of their speech, or else aggressive and jingoistic
about it—either of which is an acknowledgment of their feelings
of inferiority. Thus one of the duties of the educational system
comes to be that of teaching the standard dialect to all so as to
relieve them of feelings of inferiority, and thus relieve society
of linguistic neurotics. This is where Grammar 3, linguistic etiquette, comes into the picture.

19   A third premise arising from the two just discussed is that the
difference between the way educated people talk and the way
they write is a dialectal difference. The spread between these
two dialects may be very narrow, as in present-day America, or
very wide, as in Norway, where people often speak local Nor-
wegian dialects but write in the Dano-Norwegian *Riksmaal*. The
extreme is the use by writers of an entirely different language,
or at least an ancient and no longer spoken form of the language
—like Sanskrit in northern India or Latin in western Europe
during the later Middle Ages. A corollary of this premise is that
anyone setting out to write a grammar must know and make
clear whether he is dealing with the spoken or the written dialect.
Virtually all current English grammars deal with the written
language only; evidence for this is that their rules for the plurals
of nouns, for instance, are really spelling rules, which say nothing
about pronunciation.

20   This is not the place to go into any sort of detail about the
methods of analysis the linguistic scientist uses. Suffice it to say
that he begins by breaking up the flow of speech into minimum
sound-units, or phones, which he then groups into families called
phonemes, the minimum significant sound-units. Most languages
have from twenty to sixty of these. American English has forty-
one: nine vowels, twenty-four consonants, four degrees of stress,

and four levels of pitch. These phonemes group themselves into minimum meaningful units, called morphemes. These fall into two groups: free morphemes, those that can enter freely into many combinations with other free morphemes to make phrases and sentences; and bound morphemes, which are always found tied in a close and often indissoluble relationship with other bound or free morphemes. An example of a free morpheme is "dog"; an example of a bound morpheme is "un-" or "ex-". The linguist usually avoids talking about "words" because the term is very inexact. Is "instead of," for instance, to be considered one, two, or three words? This is purely a matter of opinion; but it is a matter of fact that it is made up of three morphemes.

21   In any case, our analysis has now brought the linguist to the point where he has some notion of the word-stock (he would call it the "lexicon") of his language. He must then go into the question of how the morphemes are grouped into meaningful utterances, which is the field of grammar proper. At this point in the analysis of English, as of many other languages, it becomes apparent that there are three bases upon which classification and analysis may be built: form, function, and meaning. For illustration let us take the word "boys" in the utterance "the boys are here." From the point of view of form, "boys" is a noun with the plural ending "s" (pronounced like "z"), preceded by the noun-determiner "the," and tied by concord to the verb "are," which it precedes. From the point of view of function, "boys" is the subject of the verb "are" and of the sentence. From the point of view of meaning, "boys" points out or names more than one of the male young of the human species, about whom an assertion is being made.

22   Of these three bases of classification, the one most amenable to objective description and analysis of a rigorously scientific sort is form. In fact, many conclusions about form can be drawn by a person unable to understand or speak the language. Next comes function. But except as it is revealed by form, function is dependent on knowing the meaning. In a telegraphic sentence like "ship sails today"[2] no one can say whether "ship" is the subject of sails" or an imperative verb with "sails" as its object until he knows what the sentence means. Most shaky of all bases for grammatical analysis is meaning. Attempts have been made to reduce the phenomena of meaning to objective description, but so far they have not succeeded very well. Meaning is such a subjective quality that it is

---

[2]This example is taken from C. C. Fries, *The Structure of English* (New York, 1952). p. 62. This important book will be discussed below.

usually omitted entirely from scientific description. The botanist
can describe the forms of plants and the functions of their various
parts, but he refuses to concern himself with their meaning. It
is left to the poet to find symbolic meaning in roses, violets, and
lilies.

23   At this point it is interesting to note that the traditional grammar of English bases some of its key concepts and definitions on
this very subjective and shaky foundation of meaning. A recent
English grammar defines a sentence as "a group of words which
expresses a complete thought through the use of a verb, called
its predicate, and a subject, consisting of a noun or pronoun about
which the verb has something to say."[3] But what is a complete
thought? Actually we do not identify sentences this way at all. If
someone says, "I don't know what to do," dropping his voice at
the end, and pauses, the hearer will know that it is quite safe
for him to make a comment without running the risk of interrupting an unfinished sentence. But if the speaker says the same words
and maintains a level pitch at the end, the polite listener will wait
for him to finish his sentence. The words are the same, the meaning
is the same; the only difference is a slight one in the pitch of the
final syllable—a purely formal distinction, which signals that the
first utterance is complete, a sentence, while the second is incomplete. In writing we would translate these signals into punctuation: a period or exclamation point at the end of the first, a comma
or dash at the end of the second. It is the form of the utterance,
not the completeness of the thought, that tells us whether it is a
whole sentence or only part of one.

24   Another favorite definition of the traditional grammar, also based
on meaning, is that of "noun" as "the name of a person, place,
or thing"; or, as the grammar just quoted has it, "the name of
anybody or anything, with or without life, and with or without
substance or form."[4] Yet we identify nouns, not by asking if they
name something, but by their positions in expressions and by the
formal marks they carry. In the sentence, "The slithy toves did
gyre and gimble in the wabe," any speaker of English knows that
"toves" and "wabe" are nouns, though he cannot tell what they
name, if indeed they name anything. How does he know? Actually
because they have certain formal marks, like their position in
relation to "the" as well as the whole arrangement of the sentence.

---

[3]Ralph B. Allen, *English Grammar* (New York, 1950), p. 187.
[4]*Ibid.,* p. 1.

We know from our practical knowledge of English grammar (Grammar 1), which we have had since before we went to school, that if we were to put meaningful words into this sentence, we would have to put nouns in place of "toves" and "wabe," giving something like "The slithy snakes did gyre and gimble in the wood." The pattern of the sentence simply will not allow us to say "The slithy arounds did gyre and gimble in the wooden."

25   One trouble with the traditional grammar, then, is that it relies heavily on the most subjective element in language; meaning. Another is that it shifts the ground of its classification and produces the elementary logical error of cross-division. A zoologist who divided animals into invertebrates, mammals, and beasts of burden would not get very far before running into trouble. Yet the traditional grammar is guilty of the same error when it defines three parts of speech on the basis of meaning (noun, verb, and interjection), four more on the basis of function (adjective, adverb, pronoun, conjunction), and one partly on function and partly on form (preposition). The result is that in such an expression as "a dog's life" there can be endless futile argument about whether "dog's" is a noun or an adjective. It is, of course, a noun from the point of view of form and an adjective from the point of view of function, and hence falls into both classes, just as a horse is both mammal and a beast of burden. No wonder students are bewildered in their attempts to master the traditional grammar. Their natural clearness of mind tells them that it is a crazy patchwork violating the elementary principles of logical thought.

V

26   If the traditional grammar is so bad, what does the new grammar offer in its place?

27   It offers a description, analysis, and set of definitions and formulas—rules, if you will—based firmly and consistently on the easiest, or at least the most objective, aspect of language, form. Experts can quibble over whether "dog's" in "a dog's life" is a noun or an adjective, but anyone can see that it is spelled with "'s" and hear that it ends with a "z" sound; likewise anyone can tell that it comes in the middle between "a" and "life." Furthermore he can tell that something important has happened if the expression is changed to "the dog's alive," "the live dogs," or "the dogs lived," even if he doesn't know what the words mean and has never heard of such functions as modifier, subject, or attributive genitive. He cannot, of course, get very far into his

analysis without either a knowledge of the language or access to someone with such knowledge. He will also need a minimum technical vocabulary describing grammatical functions. Just so the anatomist is better off for knowing physiology. But the grammarian, like the anatomist, must beware of allowing his preconceived notions to lead him into the error of interpreting before he describes —an error which often results in his finding only what he is looking for.

28   When the grammarian looks at English objectively, he finds that it conveys its meanings by two broad devices: the denotations and connotations of words separately considered, which the linguist calls "lexical meaning," and the significance of word-forms, word-groups, and arrangements apart from the lexical meanings of the words, which the linguist calls "structural meaning." The first of these is the domain of the lexicographer and the semanticist, and hence is not our present concern. The second, the structural meaning, is the business of the structural linguist, or grammarian. The importance of this second kind of meaning must be emphasized because it is often overlooked. The man in the street tends to think of the meaning of a sentence as being the aggregate of the dictionary meanings of the words that make it up; hence the widespread fallacy of literal translation—the feeling that if you take a French sentence and a French-English dictionary and write down the English equivalent of each French word you will come out with an intelligible English sentence. How ludicrous the results can be, anyone knows who is familiar with Mark Twain's retranslation from the French of his jumping frog story. One sentence reads, "Eh bien! I no saw not that that frog has nothing of better than each frog." Upon which Mark's comment is, "if that isn't grammar gone to seed, then I count myself no judge."[5]

29   The second point brought out by a formal analysis of English is that it uses four principal devices of form to signal structural meanings:

1. Word order—the sequence in which words and word-groups are arranged.
2. Function-words—words devoid of lexical meaning which indicate relationships among the meaningful words with which they appear.

---

[5]Mark Twain, "The Jumping Frog; the Original Story in English; the Retranslation Clawed Back from the French, into a Civilized Language Once More, by Patient and Unremunerated Toil," *1601 . . . and Sketches Old and New* (n.p., 1933), p. 50.

3. Inflections—alterations in the forms of words themselves to signal changes in meaning and relationship.

4. Formal contrasts—contrasts in the forms of words signaling greater differences in function and meaning. These could also be considered inflections, but it is more convenient for both the lexicographer and the grammarian to consider them separately.

30   Usually several of these are present in any utterance, but they can be separately illustrated by means of contrasting expressions involving minimum variation—the kind of controlled experiment used in the scientific laboratory.

31   To illustrate the structural meaning of word order, let us compare the two sentences "man bites dog" and "dog bites man." The words are identical in lexical meaning and in form; the only difference is in sequence. It is interesting to note that Latin expresses the difference between these two by changes in the form of the words, without necessarily altering the order: "homo canem mordet" or "hominem canis mordet." Latin grammar is worse than useless in understanding this point of English grammar.

32   Next, compare the sentences "the dog is the friend of man" and "any dog is a friend of that man." Here the words having lexical meaning are "dog," "is," "friend," and "man," which appear in the same form and the same order in both sentences. The formal differences between them are in the substitution of "any" and "a" for "the," and in the insertion of "that." These little words are function-words; they make quite a difference in the meanings of the two sentences, though it is virtually impossible to say what they mean in isolation.

33   Third, compare the sentences "the dog loves the man" and "the dogs loved the men." Here the words are the same, in the same order, with the same function-words in the same positions. But the forms of the three words having lexical meaning have been changed: "dog" to "dogs," "loves" to "loved," and "man" to "men." These changes are inflections. English has very few of them as compared with Greek, Latin, Russian, or even German. But it still uses them; about one word in four in an ordinary English sentence is inflected.

34   Fourth, consider the difference between "the dog's friend arrived" and "the dog's friendly arrival." Here the difference lies in the change of "friend" to "friendly," a formal alteration signaling a change of function from subject to modifier, and the change of "arrived" to "arrival," signaling a change of function from predicate to head-word in a noun-modifier group. These changes

are of the same formal nature as inflections, but because they produce words of different lexical meaning, classifiable as different parts of speech, it is better to call them formal contrasts than inflections. In other words, it is logically quite defensible to consider "love," "loves," "loving," and "loved" as the same word in differing aspects and to consider "friend," "friendly," "friendliness," "friendship," and "befriend" as different words related by formal and semantic similarities. But this is only a matter of convenience of analysis, which permits a more accurate description of English structure. In another language we might find that this kind of distinction is unnecessary but that some other distinction, unnecessary in English, is required. The categories of grammatical description are not sacrosanct; they are as much a part of man's organization of his observations as they are of the nature of things.

35   If we are considering the spoken variety of English, we must add a fifth device for indicating structural meaning — the various musical and rhythmic patterns which the linguist classifies under juncture, stress, and intonation. Consider the following pair of sentences:

> Alfred, the alligator is sick!
> Alfred the alligator is sick.

These are identical in the four respects discussed above — word order, function-words, inflections, and word-form. Yet they have markedly different meanings, as would be revealed by the intonation if they were spoken aloud. These differences in intonation are to a certain extent indicated in the written language by punctuation — that is, in fact, the primary function of punctuation.

VI

36   The examples so far given were chosen to illustrate in isolation the various kinds of structural devices in English grammar. Much more commonly the structural meaning of a given sentence is indicated by a combination of two or more of these devices: a sort of margin of safety which permits some of the devices to be missed or done away with without obscuring the structural meaning of the sentence, as indeed anyone knows who has ever written a telegram or a newspaper headline. On the other hand, sentences which do not have enough of these formal devices are inevitably ambiguous. Take the example already given, Fries's "ship sails today." This is ambiguous because there is nothing to indicate which of the first two words is performing a noun function and which a verb function.

If we mark the noun by putting the noun-determining function-word "the" in front of it, the ambiguity disappears; we have either "the ship sails today" or "ship the sails today." The ambiguity could just as well be resolved by using other devices: consider "ship sailed today," "ship to sail today," "ship sail today," "shipping sails today," "shipment of sails today," and so on. It is simply a question of having enough formal devices in the sentence to indicate its structural meaning clearly.

37   How powerful the structural meanings of English are is illustrated by so-called "nonsense." In English, nonsense as a literary form often consists of utterances that have a clear structural meaning but use words that either have no lexical meaning, or whose lexical meanings are inconsistent one with another. This will become apparent if we subject a rather famous bit of English nonsense to formal grammatical analysis:

All mimsy were the borogoves
And the mome raths outgrabe.

This passage consists of ten words, five of them words that should have lexical meaning but don't, one standard verb, and four function-words. In so far as it is possible to indicate its abstract structure, it would be this:

All ....y were the ....s
And the ...   ...s   ....

38   Although this is a relatively simple formal organization, it signals some rather complicated meanings. The first thing we observe is that the first line presents a conflict: word order seems to signal one thing, and inflections and function-words something else. Specifically, "mimsy" is in the position normally occupied by the subject, but we know that it is not the subject and that "borogoves" is. We know this because there is an inflectional tie between the form "were" and the "s" ending of "borogoves," because there is the noun-determiner "the" before it, and because the alternative candidate for subject, "mimsy," lacks both of these. It is true that "mimsy" does have the function-word "all" before it, which may indicate a noun; but when it does, the noun is either plural (in which case "mimsy" would most likely end in "s"), or else the noun is what grammarians call a mass-word (like "sugar," "coal," "snow"), in which case the verb would have to be "was," not "were." All these formal considerations are sufficient to counteract the effect of word order and show that the sentence is of the type

that may be represented thus:

All gloomy were the Democrats.

39   Actually there is one other possibility. If "mimsy" belongs to the small group of nouns which don't use "s" to make the plural, and if "borogoves" have been so implied (but not specifically mentioned) in the context as to justify its appearing with the determiner "the," the sentence would then belong to the following type:

[In the campaign for funds] all alumni were the canvassers.

[In the drought last summer] all cattle were the sufferers.

But the odds are so much against this that most of us would be prepared to fight for our belief that "borogoves" are things that can be named, and that at the time referred to they were in a complete state of "mimsyness."

40   Moving on to the second line, "And the mome raths outgrabe," the first thing we note is that the "And" signals another parallel assertion to follow. We are thus prepared to recognize from the noun-determiner "the," the plural inflection "s," and the particular positions of "mome" and outgrabe," as well as the continuing influence of the "were" of the preceding line, that we are dealing with a sentence of this pattern:

And the lone rats agreed.

41   The influence of the "were" is particularly important here; it guides us in selecting among several interpretations of the sentence. Specifically, it requires us to identify "outgrabe" as a verb in the past tense, and thus a "strong" or "irregular" verb, since it lacks the characteristic past-tense ending "d" or "ed." We do this in spite of the fact that there is another strong candidate for the position of verb: that is, "raths," which bears a regular verb inflection and could be tied with "mome" as its subject in the normal noun-verb relationship. In such a case we should have to recognize "outgrabe" as either an adverb of the kind not marked by the form-contrast ending "ly," and adjective, or the past participle of a strong verb. The sentence would then belong to one of the following types:

And the moon shines above.

And the man stays aloof.

And the fool seems outdone.

But we reject all of these — probably they don't even occur to us — because they all have verbs in the present tense, whereas the "were" of the first line combines with the "And" at the beginning of the second to set the whole in the past.

42   We might recognize one further possibility for the structural meaning of this second line, particularly in the verse context, since we are used to certain patterns in verse that do not often appear in speech or prose. The "were" of the first line could be understood as doing double duty, its ghost or echo appearing between "raths" and "outgrabe." Then we would have something like this:

All gloomy were the Democrats
And the home folks outraged.

But again the odds are pretty heavy against this. I for one am so sure that "outgrabe" is the past tense of a strong verb that I can give its present. In my dialect, at least, it is "outgribe."

43   The reader may not realize it, but in the last four paragraphs I have been discussing grammar from a purely formal point of view. I have not once called a word a noun because it names something (that is, I have not once resorted to meaning), nor have I called any word an adjective because it modifies a noun (that is, resorted to function). Instead I have been working on the opposite direction, from form toward function and meaning. I have used only criteria which are objectively observable, and I have assumed only a working knowledge of certain structural patterns and devices known to all speakers of English over the age of six. I did use some technical terms like "noun," "verb," and "tense," but only to save time; I could have got along without them.

44   If one clears his mind of the inconsistencies of the traditional grammar (not so easy a process as it might be), he can proceed with a similarly rigorous formal analysis of a sufficient number of representative utterances in English and come out with a descriptive grammar. This is just what Professor Fries did in gathering and studying the material for the analysis he presents in the remarkable book to which I have already referred, *The Structure of English*. What he actually did was to put a tape recorder into action and record about fifty hours of telephone conversation among the good citizens of Ann Arbor, Michigan. When this material was transcribed, it constituted about a quarter of a million words of perfectly natural speech by educated middle-class Americans. The details of his conclusions cannot be presented here, but they are sufficiently different from the usual grammar to be revolutionary. For instance, he recognizes only four parts of speech among the words with lexical meaning, roughly corresponding to what the traditional grammar calls substantives, verbs, adjectives, and adverbs, though to avoid preconceived notions from the traditional

grammar Fries calls them Class 1, Class 2, Class 3, and Class 4 words. To these he adds a relatively small group of function-words, 154 in his materials, which he divides into fifteen groups. These must be memorized by anyone learning the language; they are not subject to the same kind of general rules that govern the four parts of speech. Undoubtedly his conclusions will be developed and modified by himself and by other linguistic scholars, but for the present his book remains the most complete treatment extant of English grammar from the point of view of linguistic science.

VII

45   Two vital questions are raised by this revolution in grammar. The first is, "What is the value of this new system?" In the minds of many who ask it, the implication of this question is, "We have been getting along all these years with traditional grammar, so it can't be so very bad. Why should we go through the painful process of unlearning and relearning grammar just because linguistic scientists have concocted some new theories?"

46   The first answer to this question is the bravest and most honest. It is that the superseding of vague and sloppy thinking by clear and precise thinking is an exciting experience in and for itself. To acquire insight into the workings of a language, and to recognize the infinitely delicate system of relationship, balance, and interplay that constitutes its grammar, is to become closely acquainted with one of man's most miraculous creations, not unworthy to be set beside the equally beautiful organization of the physical universe. And to find that its most complex effects are produced by the multi-layered organization of relatively simple materials is to bring our thinking about language into accord with modern thought in other fields, which is more and more coming to emphasize the importance of organization — the fact that an organized whole is truly greater than the sum of all its parts.

47   There are other answers, more practical if less philosophically valid. It is too early to tell, but it seems probable that a realistic, scientific grammar should vastly facilitate the teaching of English, especially as a foreign language. Already results are showing here; it has been found that if intonation contours and other structural patterns are taught quite early, the student has a confidence that allows him to attempt to speak the language much sooner than he otherwise would.

48   The new grammar can also be of use in improving the native speaker's proficiency in handling the structural devices of his own

language. In other words, Grammar 2, if it is accurate and consistent, *can* be of use in improving skill in Grammar 1. An illustration is that famous bugaboo, the dangling participle. Consider a
specific instance of it, which once appeared on a college freshman's
theme, to the mingled delight and despair of the instructor:

Having eaten our lunch, the steamboat departed.

What is the trouble with this sentence? Clearly there must be something wrong with it, because it makes people laugh, although it
was not the intent of the writer to make them laugh. In other
words, it produces a completely wrong response, resulting in total
breakdown of communication. It is, in fact, "bad grammar" in a
much more serious way than are mere dialectal divergences like
"he ain't here" or "he never seen none," which produce social
reactions but communicate effectively. In the light of the new
grammar, the trouble with our dangling participle is that the form,
instead of leading to the meaning, is in conflict with it. Into the
position which, in this pattern, is reserved for the word naming
the eater of the lunch, the writer has inserted the word "steamboat." The resulting tug-of-war between form and meaning is only
momentary; meaning quickly wins out, simply because our common
sense tells us that steamboats don't eat lunches. But if the pull of
the lexical meaning is not given a good deal of help from common
sense, the form will conquer the meaning, or the two will remain in
ambiguous equilibrium — as, for instance, in "Having eaten our
lunch, the passengers boarded the steamboat." Writers will find it
easier to avoid such troubles if they know about the forms of English and are taught to use the form to convey the meaning, instead
of setting up tensions between form and meaning. This, of course, is
what English teachers are already trying to do. The new grammar
should be a better weapon in their arsenal than the traditional
grammar, since it is based on a clear understanding of the realities.

49   The second and more difficult question is, "How can the change
from one grammar to the other be effected?" Here we face obstacles
of a formidable nature. When we remember the controversies
attending on revolutionary changes in biology and astronomy, we
realize what a tenacious hold the race can maintain on anything it
has once learned, and the resistance it can offer to new ideas. And
remember that neither astronomy nor biology was taught in the
elementary schools. They were, in fact, rather specialized subjects
in advanced education. How then change grammar, which is taught
to everybody, from the fifth grade up through college. The vested
interest represented by thousands upon thousands of English and

Speech teachers who have learned the traditional grammar and taught it for many years is a conservative force comparable to those which keep us still using the chaotic system of English spelling and the unwieldy measuring system of inches and feet, pounds and ounces, quarts, bushels, and acres. Moreover, this army is constantly receiving new recruits. It is possible in my state to become certified to teach English in high school if one has had eighteen credit hours of college English — let us say two semesters of freshman composition (almost all of which is taught by people unfamiliar with the new grammar), two semesters of a survey course in English literature, one semester of Shakespeare, and one semester of the contemporary novel. And since hard-pressed school administrators feel that anyone who can speak English can in a pinch teach it, the result is that many people are called upon to teach grammar whose knowledge of the subject is totally inadequate.

50   There is, in other words, a battle ahead of the new grammar. It will have to fight not only the apathy of the general public but the ignorance and inertia of those who count themselves competent in the field of grammar. The battle is already on, in fact. Those who try to get the concepts of the new grammar introduced into the curriculum are tagged as "liberal" grammarians — the implication being, I suppose, that one has a free choice between liberal and "conservative" grammar, and that the liberals are a bit dangerous, perhaps even a touch subversive. They are accused of undermining standards, of holding that "any way of saying something is just as good as any other," of not teaching the fundamentals of good English. I trust that the readers of this article will see how unfounded these charges are. But the smear campaign is on. So far as I know, neither religion nor patriotism has yet been brought into it. When they are, Professor Fries will have to say to Socrates, Galileo, Darwin, Freud, and the other members of the honorable fraternity of the misunderstood, "Move over, gentlemen, and make room for me."

QUESTIONS FOR STUDY

1. What are the three "grammars" mentioned by Francis? How do they differ from one another? Which one is most likely to be stressed by concerned laymen? Explain. Which one is most important to you as a speaker of English? Explain. Which one would most likely be of interest to a professional linguist? Explain.

2. What basic principles are fundamental to the science of linguistics? How do these principles operate to clear up confusion concerning the traditional definition of grammar?

3. What are some of the weaknesses of traditional grammar? Illustrate from your own school experiences if possible.

4. How does Francis define language? How does language differ from dialect? Why is it likely that you know more dialects than languages? Can you think of any dialects that Francis hasn't mentioned? Francis speaks of writing as a dialect. Does this mean that there is only one written dialect? Explain.

5. What are the devices by which English signals form? Meaning? How does ambiguity occur in English?

6. What are the two main questions raised by the "revolution in grammar"? How might this "revolution" affect your school career? How might this "revolution" affect your role as a parent? How might this "revolution" affect your role as a businessman? Explain.

7. What forces are in operation that might overcome this "revolution"? If possible, illustrate from your own experiences, school and otherwise.

8. What role might mass communications play in this "revolution"? What might be the role of the publisher? What might be some less-than-respectable reasons for fostering a "revolution"?

Suppose this prefatory note were to begin as follows: *Please oggle this froob hunkily.* What might your reaction be? Would you cry in dismay, "What sort of foreign language is this?" Or would you say — looking at the words *Please* and *this* — "This sentence appears to be an English sentence, but it contains certain words that I am unfamiliar with."

If your answer is similar to the second one, then you are eligible for initiation into the ranks of structural linguists. For you are able to see that the word *please* usually precedes a verb, and with this knowledge you might insert the verb *read* (in the present tense) into the slot filled by the word *oggle.* With this substitution completed, we now have the sentence *Please read this froob hunkily.* Well, that's a little better, but what about the words *froob* and *hunkily?*

The word *froob* shouldn't give us too much trouble. We know that the word *this* usually comes before a noun. So we can guess that the word *froob* is a noun. And into the slot filled by *froob* we might now insert the noun *essay.* Now our sentence reads *Please read this essay hunkily.* Not too bad, except what exactly does *hunkily* mean?

We can't say for sure just what *hunkily* means, but we do know that it describes the manner in which we are supposed to read the essay. With this information plus the fact that *hunkily* ends in *-ly,* we can now guess that *hunkily* is an adverb. So into the slot filled by *hunkily* we might now insert the adverb *carefully.* Now the sentence reads *Please read this essay carefully.*

And that's a good piece of advice, because in this essay, "The Patterns of Grammar" by L. M. Myers, the author shows that you already know quite a bit about the way English sentences are put together. He indicates that even when you are quite young you already know how to indicate the various parts of speech and their functions on the bases of their endings and the way they pattern in sentences. In other words, this way of looking at language allows us to discuss the "structural meaning" of an English sentence.

The Patterns of Grammar

L. M. Myers

1   The very popular statement that "grammar is a lot of nonsense" contains a great deal of truth, though not quite in the way that is usually intended. Let's look at some nonsense and see what we can learn from it:

> The floog sirily mirlated naxes with a sool pern.

Since most of the words are strange we don't know exactly what this statement means, but we do know the following things:

1. Whatever happened, the *floog did it*.	Clue—	position
2. There was probably only one *floog*.	"	no -*s* ending
3. It was done to the *naxes*.	"	position
4. There was more than one *nax*.	"	-*es* ending
5. The action of *mirlating* is over.	"	-*ed* ending
6. *Sirily* tells something about how it was done.	"	-*ly* ending
7. *With a pern* tells more about how it was done.	"	word *with*
8. There was only one *pern*.	"	word *a*
9. *Sool* tells what kind of a pern it was.	"	position

2   We know these things because our language contains a system of patterns which convey what is called "structural meaning" almost without regard to the dictionary meanings of the particular words used. As the clues above indicate, the main elements in the patterns of written English are:

Word order, or relative *position*

Word form (usually, but not always, a matter of endings)

Function words like *a*, *the*, and *with*, which are more important

L. M. Myers, *Guide to American English*, Second Edition, © 1959. Reprinted by permission of Prentice-Hall, Inc., Englewood Cliffs, New Jersey.

for what they tell us about how other words are used than for exact meanings of their own

3   In spoken English at least three other elements called *pitch*, *stress*, and *juncture* must be recognized. These are to some extent implied in writing, but cannot be indicated as explicitly as the first three. We will therefore postpone discussing them until we have seen how the more obvious elements work.

4   It used to be believed that a language was made up simply of words, which had only to be arranged according to the logical rules of "universal grammar" in order to make good sentences. It is now recognized that there is no such thing as universal grammar. Each language has its own patterns as well as its own words, and these patterns are matters of habit rather than logic. We have been exposed to our own particular patterns of word form, word order, and function words for so long that we now react to them automatically even when they are filled with nonsense words. If there were just one dialect of English we could use them automatically, too, and not have to think about them. But most of us have grown up in such a confusing mixture of dialects that simple imitation is not enough. In order to speak and write with accuracy and confidence we have to make some sort of study of the competing patterns; and we'd better make the study systematic so that we'll know when we have covered the ground.

GRAMMATICAL POSITION

5   In analyzing our nonsense sentence we gave only one clue for each bit of information, as if the three elements of position, word form, and function words could be completely separated. Actually they cannot. For instance, grammatical position is not merely numerical position in a sentence but relative position; and we recognize it by considering word form and function words as well as word order. Take another look at the first four words of our sentence:

The floog sirily mirlated

We know that the *floog* did the *mirlating* — that it is what we call the subject — not by the fact that it is the second word in the sentence, but by taking all the following facts together:

1.   When we see a pattern like "The _____ _____ _____ed" we assume that the word ending in *-ed* is the verb, and that one of the two words between *the* and _____*ed* is the subject.

2. Since the word just before the verb ends in *-ly* it almost certainly tells something about the verb and therefore cannot be the subject.

3. Therefore the other possible word — *floog* — is the subject. (Notice that if the sentence had begun "The floog *siliry*" instead of "The floog *sirily*" we would take *siliry* to be the subject and *floog* to be an adjective modifying it.)

6　　It is obvious that the study of grammatical position could become a pretty complicated subject, but we don't have to go into it very deeply. To begin with we are interested only in the way it can help us to classify four important kinds of words.

THE KINDS OF WORDS

7　　We have to classify words in order to discuss them in groups. Even in the last section we had to use the terms *verb* and *adjective*, though we have not yet had time to define these; and if we couldn't say things like "the possessive form of a noun is always written with an apostrophe" it would take quite a while to cover the language. Unfortunately, nobody has ever found a perfect way to classify words in English. The two most obvious ways are by form and by meaning. If we base our classes on either one of these we run into trouble with the other; if we try to use both at once we get a complicated mess; and if we decide to have two separate classifications we find that they overlap so much that it is very difficult to keep them separate.

8　　As a compromise, not perfect but reasonably workable, we will use in this book a system based on three main principles:

1. We will use such familiar *single* terms as *noun* and *adjective* to designate the ways words and word-groups function in sentence patterns.

2. We will use such *double* terms as *inflected noun* or *regular noun* (which means "noun inflected in a certain way") to discuss forms and form changes.

3. We will not bother to classify a word at all unless we have a definite reason for doing so. And if a word happens to be both a noun (by use) and an inflected noun (by form) we will use whichever designation seems to be handiest at the time.

CLASSIFICATION BY POSITION

9　　We began this chapter by analyzing a sentence composed of three familiar words, *a*, *the*, and *with*, and six nonsense words, *floog*, *sirily, mirlated, naxes, sool,* and *pern.* We could of course make up any number of similar sentences; and if we made up, say, ten pages of them, we should discover the curious fact that all the nonsense words could be reasonably put into just four classes:

1. Words that pattern like *floog, naxes,* and *pern,* which can be called *nouns.*
2. Words that pattern like *mirlated,* which can be called *verbs.*
3. Words that pattern like *sool,* which can be called *adjectives.*
4. Words that pattern like *sirily,* which can be called *adverbs.*

10   The nucleus of an English sentence is a combination like *man is* or *girls sang* or *floog mirlated,* in which one word seems to name something and the other seems to say something about it—even if both words are nonsense or completely unknown. In such combinations we call the naming word the subject—and the kind of word that is or could easily be the subject we call a *noun.* The saying word we call the *verb.* Words that seem to describe nouns we call adjectives—*big* man, *young* girls, *sool* pern. And words that seem to describe verbs we call adverbs—*probably* was, *merrily* sang, *sirily* mirlated.

11   Far more than ninety-nine per cent of all the words in English fall into these four classes, and more are being added to them every year. They are therefore called open or unlimited classes. There is nothing surprising about seeing an unfamiliar word in a position that seems to indicate any one of these classes; and even if we are quite sure that the word has no real meaning we somehow feel that we know how it acts.

12   All the other kinds of words (which we will not classify just now) total only a few hundred all together, and no new ones are being added. We have to know these words individually to react to the patterns of our sentences; and if we replace them by nonsense words the patterns disappear. Let's try it:

Pra floog sirily mirlated naxes tran oc sool pern.

Possibly the successive endings *-ly, -ed,* and *-es* still suggest some meaning, but there is no longer a firm pattern for the sentence as a whole. Nonsense substitutes for *a, the,* and *with* won't work.

13   At first glance classification by position may seem a very roundabout way of getting at such familiar definitions as "a noun is a word used to name a person, place, thing, or idea," but it has its advantages. These familiar definitions work beautifully in selected sentences, but simply do not apply to the language as a whole unless we stretch them until they are practically meaningless. The

reason is that we do not always use the same grammatical patterns to express the same ideas, and it is silly to pretend that we do. Look at the following sentences:

> Sometimes he works and sometimes he loafs.
> His industry and laziness alternate.
> He is alternately industrious and lazy.
> He acts industriously and lazily by spells.

Each of these conveys the same basic information; but the contrast between his working and his loafing is shown in the first sentence by verbs, in the second by nouns, in the third by adjectives, and in the fourth by adverbs. There just is no fixed relation between the meaning conveyed and the grammatical pattern used to convey it; and since we are discussing grammar, not philosophy, we'd better depend on the perceptible patterns.

THE FORMS OF WORDS

14   The second element in our grammatical patterns is word form. Some words, like *always, into, must, tactics,* and *which,* have only one form; but most words have from two to five different forms called *inflections.* Inflected words fall into four groups, three of which may be divided into *regular* and *irregular* subgroups.

> *Inflected nouns*
>   *Regular:* boy, boy's, boys, boys'
>   *Irregular:* man, man's, men, men's
> *Inflected pronouns*
>   All *irregular:* I, me, my, mine, myself
> *Inflected verbs*
>   *Regular:* save, saves, saved, saving
>   *Irregular:* take, takes, took, taken, taking
> *Inflected adjectives*
>   *Regular:* big, bigger, biggest
>   *Irregular:* good, better, best

These are the only kinds of inflection in English. Such endings as *-al, -dom, -hood, -ic, -ish, -ize, -ly, -ment,* and *-ness* are considered to make different words rather than different forms of the same word. (It is much simpler to accept the fact that this is so than to try to decide whether it should be.) They are called derivational suffixes, and will not be discussed here.

15   There are many thousands of regular nouns and regular verbs, and both groups are still growing. Whenever we adopt a new noun

like *sputnik* everybody seems to assume at once that the only reasonable plural is *sputniks*, not *sputnak* or *sputniki*. In other words, we automatically treat it as a regular noun. And if we adopt a new verb, or make a new verb out of an old noun, we treat *it* as regular. As soon as we read that sputniks *orbit* we know that we can also say that they *orbited* or have *orbited*, not that they *orbat* or have *orbiten*. It is therefore only the regular nouns and verbs that are "open." There are about six hundred regular adjectives, and this class might be called "open at one end." Nobody knows why, but whenever we adopt a new two-syllable adjective ending in *-y*, such as *newsy* or *corny*, we give it the regular *-er* and *-est* endings. All other new adjectives are unchanging, and show degrees by *more* and *most*.

16   Nobody has much trouble with the spoken forms of these three regular groups, and the spelling of the written forms follows rather simple rules which will be given later. The four irregular groups are more difficult, since each word has to be learned individually. Fortunately these groups are much smaller than the regular ones, and are shrinking rather than growing.

17   Along with the four inflected groups we must consider one group of words that never change form but do have a characteristic form of their own—the *-ly* adverbs like *badly* and *wonderfully*. This is another open class; we feel free to add *-ly* to almost any adjective and thus make a new adverb, if we can find a use for it.

FUNCTION WORDS

18   Function words are words which are used to form grammatical patterns, and which cannot be changed without changing the patterns. Look at the following sentence:

The old man *had* cheerfully started *the* job *with a* sharp knife.

The words in ordinary type could be varied indefinitely without changing the pattern. We could find dozens of substitutes for *started* or *job*, and hundreds for each of the others. But if we change *the* to *an* or *had* to *has* or *with* to *on* we get a different pattern at once. *The* implies that you know which old man the sentence is about; *an* implies that you don't. *Had* puts the statement in a different time relation from *have*. And the things that you can reasonably do *on* a knife are quite different from those that you can do *with* it.

19   The difference between function words and others (sometimes called *content words*) are not absolutely sharp or reliable, and

you can argue with the statements in the preceding paragraph if you care to. But if we consider the distinction as a matter of convenience rather than of desperate doctrine, we will find it useful. Function words are used principally to make up grammatical patterns; content words are used to fill those patterns and give them specific meanings. You have to know the meanings of the content words in a particular sentence to understand that sentence; but you have to know the ways most function words are used to understand English at all.

20   It is reasonably easy to divide content words into four classes— nouns, verbs, adjectives, and adverbs. A satisfactory classification of function words is a good deal more difficult. For the moment we will merely indicate three principal types:

1. Auxiliary verbs, like those italicized in the following verb-phrases: *will* go, *could* eat, *has* been, *is* going, *must have* seen.
2. Connectives, including all prepositions (*to, from, with,* etc.) conjunctions (*and, because,* etc.), and many words often called adverbs and pronouns (*there, when, which,* etc.).
3. Certain special modifiers of the kinds sometimes called deter-miners (*a, the, those,* etc.) and qualifiers (*very, quite,* etc.).

THE PARTS OF SPEECH?

21   It may seem curious that we have discussed two different kinds of classification of words, one by function and one by form, without even mentioning the "parts of speech." But the fact is that the whole concept of parts of speech depends on a stable relation be-tween form and function which has almost disappeared in our language. The concept can, of course, still be applied to modern English, but it no longer seems to be really useful; and those people who insist most strongly that there *are* parts of speech disagree about whether it is the function classes or the form classes that deserve this name. And those who take form as the basis disagree about whether it is simply the form of the words or the form of the patterns in which the words are used that must be considered.

22   Since there is no discoverable way of settling this argument (or of stopping it, either) we will simply disregard it. Anybody can call anything he wants to the parts of speech. Meanwhile we will try to make it clear whenever we are talking about form rather than function or function rather than form. When the two overlap

(as they often do) we can use either set of terms as long as we don't over-generalize. Thus in the sentence "The best cost no more" we can say that *best* is an irregular adjective in form but a noun by function in this sentence; and we can call *cost* an irregular verb or simply the verb without much danger of misleading anybody.

CONVERSION BY SUFFIX

23   Earlier in the chapter we mentioned that endings other than inflections are called suffixes—for instance, *-dom*, *-ize*, *-ly*, and *-ment*. Suffixes are sometimes used to give words different meanings without changing their functional classification. Thus we have *gray* and *grayish*, both normally adjectives, and *man* and *manhood*, both normally nouns. More often suffixes convert words from one classification to another, as in the following examples:

> *Verbs to nouns:* appease-appeasement, serve-service
> *Adjectives to nouns:* free-freedom, happy-happiness
> *Nouns to verbs:* atom-atomize, gas-gasify
> *Adjectives to verbs:* dark-darken, tranquil-tranquilize
> *Nouns to adjectives:* child-childish, man-manly
> *Adjectives to adverbs:* glad-gladly, frantic-frantically

This kind of conversion is common in many languages, including Greek, Latin, and French, from which a great many English words come. It explains many of the related words in the language.

FUNCTIONAL SHIFT

24   Conversion of a word to a new function *without* the use of a suffix occurs much more often in English than in most other languages. This is known as *functional shift*, and it has gone so far as to make a single classification of words into parts of speech almost meaningless, as we have already suggested. The general tendency is to use any word in any way that is convenient and makes sense, without regard to its original classification. Thus we may use *work* as a noun (a *work* of art), a verb (they *work* hard), or an adjective (his *work* clothes). We cannot use it as a connective, not because of any grammatical rule, but simply because there is no way to do it. And nobody but a historian of the language has any reason to care about what its original part of speech may have been.

25   If a word shifts its function to that of a noun or a verb, it takes on the regular inflections of its new class. Thus the irregular noun *man* gives us the regular verb *to man*, with the forms *man, mans, manned, manning*. Likewise the irregular verb *to drink* gives us the regular noun *drink, drinks*. In other shifts of function no new inflections are needed.

REASON FOR FUNCTIONAL SHIFT

26   Quite obviously the underlying reason for functional shift is economy—either the use of a shorter word for a longer one or the use of a word instead of a phrase. Use of the plain form of a verb as a noun eliminates either the *-ing* inflectional ending (*talk* for *talking*) or a suffix (a *serve* for a *service* in tennis); and use of a noun as an adjective eliminates a suffix (*wool* clothes for *woolen* clothes, *atom* bomb for *atomic* bomb). On the other hand, use of an adjective as a noun often saves a word or more (*the poor* for *the poor people, the beautiful* for *that which is beautiful*). Verbs converted from nouns are particularly economical, though not always graceful. Thus *to requisition* stands for *to put in a requisition for, to contact* for *to get in touch with*.

27   When the two kinds of economy conflict, the one that makes the greater overall saving generally wins out—at least in circles where efficiency is more prized than grace. Thus *to certificate* is longer than *to certify*, but shorter than *to furnish with a certificate*. It is therefore often used when the certification consists of supplying a document rather than guaranteeing a statement.

LIMITS TO FUNCTIONAL SHIFT

28   The fact remains that many functional shifts that might well have taken place have not done so. Sometimes this is because a familiar word that makes a shift unnecessary is already available. Thus the verb *to man* makes it unnecessary to convert *boy, girl, or woman* into verbs. Juveniles or females can *man* a boat. Fifty years ago, when automobiles were still competing with carriages, we used *to auto* down to the beach, since *to drive* was not sufficiently specific, and any other available expression would have been longer. Now that carriages have practically disappeared the one-syllable verb *drive* clearly means to go by automobile. *To auto* is no longer economical, and there would not be enough saving in *to car* to make it worth while.

29   At other times we have simply failed to make a shift for no discoverable reason. Thus we say *to reward* and *a reward*, *to punish*
but *a punishment*. A noun *punish* may develop in the future, but
it has not yet done so. Moreover, some shifts that certainly have
developed are often condemned. That is, although the general
principle of functional shift is universally accepted, a few individual
shifts have become shibboleths. We often hear that *like* must never
be used as a conjunction, that *than* and *as* must never be used
as prepositions, and that *loan* and *contact* must never be used
as verbs.

30   To object to these uses on the basis of any grammatical theory
is simply silly. Thousands of other words have extended their
functions in exactly comparable ways, and there is not the slightest
reason why this handful should not do the same. If we must condemn such expressions we should do so by making the honest statement that there is a certain amount of prejudice against them—
just as there is now a prejudice against calling a man "a certain
party" or a woman "an elegant female"—though there is no doubt
whatever that *party* and *female* are, in other expressions, acceptable as nouns.

INTONATION PATTERNS

31   So far we have dealt only with those elements of our grammatical
patterns which are visible as well as audible. In spoken English at
least three other elements would be perceptible (though not necessarily recognizable by people without some training). These can
sometimes be suggested in writing, but cannot be indicated as
explicitly as the first three. Compare the two following sentences:

> Jack put salt in his coffee.
> Jack put salt in his *coffee?*

Since these are identical in all three of the elements so far discussed, many people would call them "the same sentence punc-
tuated in two different ways." But, intelligently read, they sound
different and they mean different things—which should be enough
to make them different sentences. The fact that the differences do
not appear as clearly in writing as they do in speech proves only
that our system of writing is imperfect—it indicates some differences less clearly than others. If you read both sentences aloud
carefully and naturally you will see that they vary in three ways:

1. The first syllable of *coffee* is pronounced more strongly in the
    second sentence than in the first. This is a difference in *stress*.

2. The same syllable is also pronounced on a higher musical tone in the second sentence. This is a difference in *pitch*.

3. At the end of the first sentence the voice comes down in pitch as it fades into silence. At the end of the second it does not. This is a difference in *juncture*. In order to make the comparison as simple as possible we have shown the difference in stress, pitch, and juncture only at the ends of the two sentences, but they occur throughout. Every syllable that is pronounced at all must be pronounced with some degree of stress and at some pitch; and whenever two successive words are not completely run together the transition between them can be called juncture. Thus *white house* has a kind of juncture not found in *Whitehouse;* the sort of pause often shown by a comma is a second kind; and the rising and falling tones as your voice fades off after different kinds of sentences are two others.

32   It is possible to indicate all these things consistently by a special system of writing—the stress by accent marks, the pitch by numbers, and the juncture by special symbols. Thus the second sentence might be written as follows:

$$^2\text{Jâck} + \text{pùt} + \text{sâlt} + \text{in} + \text{his} + {}^1\text{cóffee}^3 \uparrow$$

(It might also be indicated in several other ways.) This more complete system of writing is very useful for experts who wish to make a detailed analysis of our sound patterns, but it is a little cumbersome for ordinary use. Most of us would rather get along with just a few hints, such as the italicizing of *coffee* and the question mark at the end. Moreover, experts are still disagreeing about such questions as how many degrees of stress and pitch are significant, and how regular and dependable are our uses of these elements. We are not therefore going into these matters in much detail. But we should realize that the experts are right in principle —these elements are quite as real as the first three, and at least some of the time they are quite as important.

33   Stress, pitch, and juncture together make up *intonation*. Every spoken sentence must have its pattern of intonation; and every good written sentence at least suggests one. If you don't believe intonation is as real or as important as the other sounds, perhaps you can remember a time when you were seriously misquoted by somebody who claimed to be repeating exactly what you had said, and who did repeat the same words in the same order—but who changed the intonation pattern so as to give an entirely different meaning.

QUESTIONS FOR STUDY

1. Construct at least three different sentences out of the original elements *The floog sirily mirlated naxes with a sool pern.* How is it that we can substitute entire groups of words—such as *man with a yellow hat, dog whose paw had been hurt,* or *tickling in my throat*—for the single word *floog* in the original demonstration sentence?

2. Why is the conventional concept of parts of speech not really useful in a description of English? Where did this concept originate? Why was it used to describe the English language?

3. Why and how does Myers distinguish between "function in sentence patterns" and "forms and form changes"? What might happen if this distinction were not made? What is wrong with describing a given sentence as consisting of a noun, a verb, and an object?

4. What is the difference between "function words" and words which take inflections? Point out the two kinds of words in the original demonstration sentence. Indicate how a knowledge of the differences between these two types of words can aid you in making correct substitutions for the "nonsense" words.

5. What is "functional shift"? How is this concept useful in explaining the ease with which users of English can "coin" words? Why does the "functional shift" place even greater responsibility on those who use the English language?

6. What is the function of intonation in conveying meaning in English? Read the original demonstration sentence aloud twice, giving a different meaning to the sentence each time by changing your intonation pattern. In what ways does punctuation indicate an author's intended intonation?

Let us say (in the interest of introducing you painlessly to a sometimes complicated bit of business) that you are fascinated with rocket engines. And let us say that in the interest of science you wanted to test the rate of lift of a rocket when using one, two, three, or four engines. To do this, you will start a rocket while it has all four engines and then measure the rate of lift. After this, you will cut out one engine and start the rocket again, measure again, and so on.

If you merely take accurate measurements of the rates of lift accomplished, you will have achieved *observational accuracy*. If, on the other hand, you used these accurate measurements to predict just how far rockets in general could fly with a given number of engines, you have achieved *descriptive adequacy*. But if you could fit all of your information into a general theory of flight so as to be able to choose the "most explicit and most consistent way of describing" the observed phenomena of flying then you will have achieved *explanatory adequacy*.

In his essay "Theories of English Grammar," Wayne O'Neil examines the adequacy of three different types of grammar — structural, traditional, and transformational—and casts his vote for transformational grammar since it achieves *explanatory adequacy*. His discussion is of relevance to thinking about theories of grammar in general as well as to a central issue in the changing English curriculum: Which grammars should be taught in our schools?

Theories of English Grammar

Wayne O'Neil

1 . . . I want to discuss three theories of English grammar. Perhaps you are already familiar with one or more of them. But you may never have thought about how adequate they are as theories, about how accurately and consistently they describe the structure of English sentences. In the course of [my discussion] I will offer you some reasons for favoring one theory above the other two and then describe briefly the inner workings of the theory that I want to recommend. I will discuss the other two grammatical theories as if they were already clearly presented in school textbooks, but actually this is seldom the case. In the books that children are supposed to learn grammar from, there is a fair amount of important grammatical information, though often it is poorly organized. But unfortunately the books nearly always contain a great deal of other information as well. Some of it, like semantics, belongs in the English course. Much more of it, such as the art of telephoning and the way to address envelopes, simply is not legitimate matter for the English classroom, however broadly our subject is conceived. This irrelevant material obscures the grammatical information in the books and interferes with a clear and orderly discussion of English grammar.

2 It is not wrong for these books to contain important and relevant nongrammatical matter, such as semantics and dialect information; but it is wrong for them to present an ill-organized and imprecise theory of grammar, and wrong for them to pass semantic or cultural information off as grammar. [There is] a useful distinction between "grammar as theory" and "grammar as usage," two notions that have become semantically confused in the minds of many people—including teachers and textbook writers. Most

of the other matters that have infiltrated the school grammar books don't have the excuse of semantic confusion to justify them. Having said this much, I will simply ignore the potpourri generally available in school grammars and speak only of the theories that underlie the grammar that we find in them.

3   When all of the other matters are weeded out of the books, two basic theories of English grammar are left standing. "Structural" and "traditional" are the words most often used to label them. Only a very few of the available books (and these will be the more recent) are "structural" texts; nearly all the rest are "traditional" grammars. Besides these two theories (the structural and the traditional), there is a newer one, the "transformational." This is the theory that we will talk about for the greater part of this [essay.]

4   Now I want to discuss these three theories of English in such a way as to get at their adequacy as theories of English syntax: remember that it is with the syntax, the structure of English sentences, that we are primarily concerned.

5   We are talking in quite abstract terms now, of determining the adequacy of theories. Let's continue in this direction for a moment: this talk of theories is fascinating and important business. What do we ask of theories? We ask first of all that they be serious as well as successful, that they do not attempt to be successful at accomplishing trivial things. For example, I can promote a theory that all English sentences have either an even number of words or an odd number of words, and I can easily claim that the theory is a precise and accurate description of a fact about English sentences. But my opponents (and there would be a lot of them if I seriously tried to promote such a theory) could claim that my theory was neither serious nor insightful. It does no more than give a precise formulation to a totally trivial fact.

6   The three theories that we are discussing here are serious. But even serious theories can within their seriousness achieve higher or lower levels of adequacy. We can begin to get at some of the crucial differences in the adequacy of the three theories if we take a brief look at their systems of diagramming sentences. Let's take the sentence

(1) The wind blew out the candle yesterday.

and look at the kind of syntactic diagram that each theory would impose on the sentence.

7   The structural grammarian would break the sentence into its two major constituents, then each of these into its two major

parts, and so on relentlessly until the job was done and he had reached the ultimate constituents. For example, he would break (1) into "the wind" and "blew out the candle yesterday"; "the wind" into "the" and "wind"; and "blew out the candle yesterday" into "blew out the candle" and "yesterday." And so on. The chinese box diagram is a fair example of the structure he would assign the sentence:

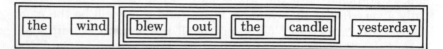

8   The diagramming of the traditional grammarian follows somewhat the same process although he indicates the dependencies between elements by angles and positions rather than boxes. He would also distort the natural word order to get at the modifying relationships that he felt to exist between the constituents of the sentence. The following is a fair example of a traditional grammarian's diagram of the sentence:

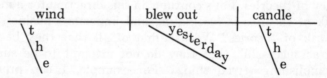

Notice that, unlike the structuralist who respects the order of elements in the particular sentence, the traditionalist feels compelled to reveal the *basic* relations by *rearranging* the constituents.

9   The transformational grammarian would be as relentlessly twofold as the structural grammarian with this particular sentence. But he would most generally represent the syntax of the sentence with a labelled "tree graph." It would look like this:

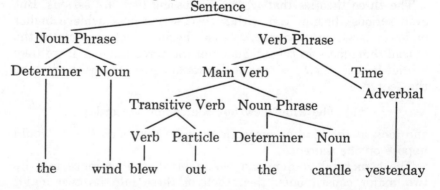

The tree graph preserves the given order of the particular sentence and indicates the relationship of constituent to constituent. It also explicitly labels the constituents. The labelling in structural and traditional diagrams is implicit only. But implicit labelling is not an irreparable fault, because the explicit labelling can easily be inferred from the diagrams. For example, in the traditional diagram adverbs are arranged below the verb; subject is divided from predicate by a long vertical line. And so on.

10   Let's now see what the three grammars would do with the following sentences in comparison with what they did with (1):

    (2) The wind blew the candle out yesterday.
    (3) Yesterday the wind blew out the candle.
    (4) Yesterday the wind blew the candle out.

It is in their handling of these sentences that we can see the crucial difference between the grammars, the one that separates them into increasingly superior levels of adequacy. The structural grammarian would say that each of these sentences is unique and so he would assign to each a unique visual representation in somewhat this manner:

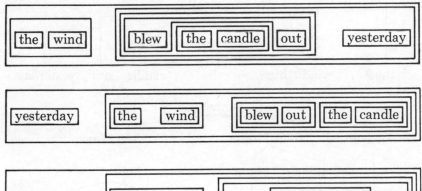

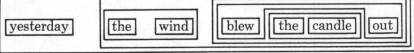

11   The structural grammarian catches what is certainly true about the four sentences: all are indeed different. His diagrams reveal this—but no more. The traditional grammarian, on the other hand, says that the four are in some way the same and gives the same diagram to all four sentences:

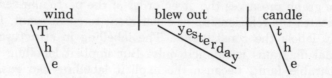

The distortion of word order that characterizes traditional diagrams now assumes importance, for the diagram though catching the underlying sameness of the four does not preserve the obvious differences. The traditional grammarian catches the similarity; the structuralist the difference.

12   The transformational grammarian, however, would try to catch both. He would assign to each sentence a unique and characteristic structure:

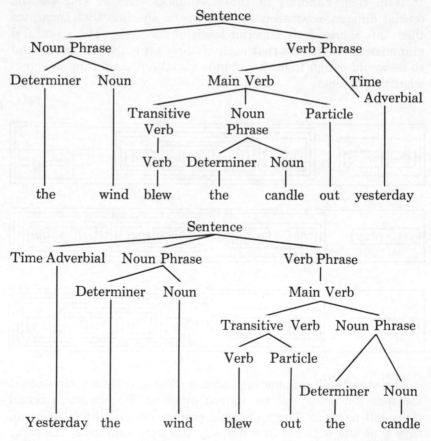

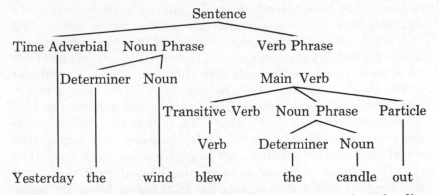

But he would not stop there. He would go on to say that the diagrams of (2)-(4) are derived from the diagram of (1) by very general changes that we will call "transformations." In this way he would not only say (what is true) that there are differences between the sentences; he would also say (what is also true) that the four are basically the same sentence. Finally he would provide a statement of the formal operations that are performed on the underlying structure of (1) to carry it into (2), (3), and (4). I would like to emphasize that the formal statement about the relationship of (1) and (2), for example, would be very general and necessary for an adequate discussion of English syntax. Not only would it get at the connection between (1) and (2), but it would also explain the syntactic peculiarities of such different sentences as

(5) He put out the cat
(6) He put him out.
(7) He gave me a book.
(8) He gave a book to me.

and many other sentences of the same general form.

13   Now which of these three theories is the most adequate? Let's consider an analogy from the history of astronomy. For over twenty years, Tycho Brahe, a Renaissance astronomer, made meticulous observations of Mars' position in the sky. Johannes Kepler, another astronomer of the period, was aware of Brahe's findings and was interested in discovering their significance. If Kepler had presented these observations, plus some few of his own, as a theory about Mars' location in the solar system, the theory would only have reached a level of *observational* adequacy. But Kepler wanted

to know more than this minimum; he wanted to know what shape the orbit was. So he asked what geometrical figure was implied by Tycho's observations. There were various possible answers, some simple geometric figures, some quite elaborate, some quite erratic— all of them totally reconcilable with the observations. And insofar as any one of these was totally reconcilable with the data, a theory that Mars' orbit was this or that figure would achieve the level of *descriptive* adequacy. By this I mean that the various points along the orbit would be predictable according to the geometric model that Kepler selected. But Kepler wanted even more than this. He wanted to choose from among these alternative theories the one that would best explain the facts about Mars. By trying to fit the geometric orbits that were descriptively possible within his more general theory of a sun-centered universe, Kepler found that the only possible and reasonable orbit for Mars was the per- fect ellipse. On the basis of a more general theory, then, Kepler was able to explain the best relationship between the data and only one geometric model. Kepler's theory about the orbit of Mars reached the highest level of adequacy—*explanatory* adequacy.

14   A scientist who presents important data accurately is merely *observing* adequately. To *describe* adequately he must see the implications of certain patterns in his data and generalize these in some relevant and significant way. To *explain* the data is to choose on the basis of a general theory the most explicit and most consistent way of describing.

15   The three theories of English syntax (structural, traditional, transformational) can be ranked on the same levels of adequacy. The structuralist, you will recall, made the observation that sen- tences that were different were to be diagrammed in a way that revealed that difference. Insofar as he satisfies this criterion, his grammar achieves the level of *observational* adequacy. The tradi- tionalist, trying to get at the feelings that speakers of the language have about the relatedness of sentences, describes the feelings by diagramming related sentences in a way that reveals their essential similarity. Insofar as he satisfies this criterion, his grammar reaches the level of *descriptive* adequacy. Actually he does not always satisfy the criterion; to give a simple example, he fails to catch the essential identity of the active and passive forms of a sentence:

   (9) The men chased the robber.
   (10) The robber was chased by the men.

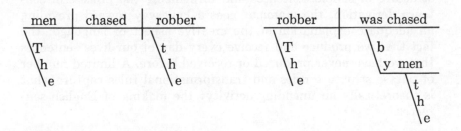

But even for all the many times that his diagramming is descriptively adequate, the traditional grammarian provides no more than a flat statement to the effect that some different sentences are the same. The transformational grammarian, trying to explicate the important regularities of the language, works from a general theory that allows him to choose the most precise and consistent explanation of the data. Insofar as he achieves this, his grammar reaches a level of *explanatory* adequacy.

16   The different levels of adequacy which the three grammars achieve mark a very important difference in the three. Structural grammars and traditional grammars are generally either incapable of noting the relationship that exists between obviously related sentences or unable to characterize the relationship. In contrast, transformational grammar is quite capable of assigning unique structures to unique sentences, of describing the underlying relationship of sentence to sentence, and of formalizing the relationship into a rule—that is, of explaining the relationship.

17   We have touched briefly on a very important kind of statement made in transformational grammar—the kind of statement that gives the grammar its name—the transformational *rules* that explain and characterize the process by which simple sentences become complex structures. . . .

18   So far we have spoken only of the rules that transform simple sentences into other kinds of sentences. We have said little about the structure of these simple sentences. We can think of the language as consisting of "kernel" sentences — simple, declarative, active sentences—and of "transformed" sentences. Rules called phrase structure rules try to specify the structure of the kernel sentences. They are the second kind of rule in our grammar. . . . The two kinds of rules that I have discussed lead to a more adequate theory of grammar than we have ever had. By explaining the

structure of simple sentences and formalizing the process of sentence derivation, the grammar goes a long way toward providing an adequate explanation of the creative aspect of language: the fact that we produce and receive every day of our lives sentences that we have never produced or received before. A limited number of phrase structure rules and transformational rules capture what is theoretically an unending activity: the making of English sentences.

QUESTIONS FOR STUDY

1. Why does O'Neil disapprove of the way most English textbooks treat grammar? Which materials is he willing to allow to remain? Why? Is he justified in this attitude? Which materials would he throw out? Why? Is he justified in this attitude? Which sort of materials did you spend most of your time with when you were in grade school? What effect did your study of English grammar have on your present ability to handle the language?

2. Why is it that the structural diagram of a group of similar English sentences reveals only differences? Why is it that the traditional diagram of a similar group of English sentences reveals only similarities?

3. Explain the apparent advantage of a "tree graph" over the traditional and structural diagrams. How might you argue with the person who puns: "I think that I shall never see,/a sentence ugly as a 'tree.' "?

4. What is the "essential identity" of active and passive sentences that the traditional grammarian fails to catch? Is structural grammar of any help at this point? How might transformational grammar provide a solution?

5. Define "kernel sentence" and give an example. Define "transformed sentence" and give an example. How does a "kernel sentence" become a "transformed sentence"?

6. Define observational, descriptive, and explanatory adequacy, illustrating your definitions with references to the three similar sentences on page 115.

7. Why will a knowledge of transformational grammar aid us in understanding "what is theoretically an unending activity: the making of English sentences"?

A FABLE

Once upon a time an Arabian Genie decided to open a little candy store in Brooklyn. He loved it, although sometimes he had trouble understanding the way the Brooklynites spoke the English language. One day a man walked into the store. "What can I do for you?" asked the genie. The man looked at the genie and replied "Make me a malted." So the genie waved his wand and said, "Okay, Poof! So now you're a malted."

In this little fable the Brooklynite made a terrible mistake. He used a single ambiguous surface structure, *Make me a malted*, to represent two possible deep structures: either *Make a malted for me* or *Make me into a malted*. Unfortunately, the genie thought the customer wanted to be turned into a malted and performed accordingly. Moral: misunderstanding can arise between speaker and listener when two or more possible choices are available in forming the deep structure of an utterance.

In this essay "Transformational Grammar: An Introduction" Andrew MacLeish takes the reader even further into the workings of a transformational grammar. He suggests some ways in which transformational grammar attains explanatory adequacy by moving from familiar ground (ambiguous statements, for instance, similar to those studied in conventional classroom grammar) to an understanding of the concepts underlying that familiar ground. He demonstrates how "Correctly-written generative and transformational rules . . . provide us with new insights into the operations of our language and consistently produce items that 'go together' grammatically."

Transformational Grammar:
An Introduction

Andrew MacLeish

1   In the last selection Wayne O'Neil clearly distinguished for us the differences among three of the grammatical theories that are of concern to anyone who thinks about the ways in which English syntax can be described. It now remains for us to learn something more about O'Neil's major concern, a transformational grammar.

2   In what is to follow, then, we are going to continue thinking about grammar in a way somewhat different from that to which we have become accustomed. This fact in itself should not be an obstacle to our understanding something about this interesting grammar, and, besides, this grammar is fun. Further, in some important ways transformational grammar tells us more about our language than does any other system of rules. But let's see for ourselves.

3   As we speak and write apparently endless varieties of English sentences we are, in reality, manipulating, in a very few ways, a finite number of basic sentence types. While this statement may appear strange at first, it is because of this fact that you yourself were able to learn all of your basic English by the time you were about four years old. What transformational grammar does is to make explicit to us these manipulations, or *operations* as we shall call them, as well as these basic sentence types. The basic sentence types are all varieties of what you know as the simple, active, declarative sentence. So there's no need to be afraid of them. But let's first examine the operations.

4   What are the operations that enable us to vary English sentence structure, and how many are there? There are five operations, ways in which we change English sentences.

Printed by permission of the author.

5   The first one we'll look at is probably the most powerful device we have in English for varying sentences: (1) *rearrangement* of the order of words. An example can be seen in the formulation of a question that demands an answer *yes* or *no*. Our understanding of this question is probably related to and conditioned by the simple, active, declarative sentence from which it is derived. From now on we'll call this simple, active, declarative sentence the *kernel sentence*, and the sentence resulting from a specific operation the *transformation*, or change, in the kernel sentence.

Kernel: John's going home.
Transformation: Is John going home?

The yes/no question transformation is, in part, the result of re-arranging the verb *is* (*'s*) from the position after the subject to the position before the subject.

6   (2) The next operation, *substitution*, is just as simple to understand:

Kernel: Mary kissed John.
Tranformation: She kissed him.

Here we substitute pronouns of the appropriate gender for proper nouns in the kernel sentence.

7   (3) *Conjoining* is merely the manner in which, for example, we make the familiar compound sentence. We join independent clauses by conjunctions:

Kernels: John swam.
Bill ran.
Transformation: John swam *and* Bill ran.

8   (4) *Addition* is the operation by which an element is added to the kernel sentence:

Kernel: Joe is a fool.
Transformation: Joe is an old fool.

Here, the adjective *old* is embedded into, or added to, the trans-formed sentence.

9   (5) Finally, there is *deletion* of sentence elements. This can be illustrated in the so-called short-answer in which the deleted portion of the predicate is in parenthesis. Let's remember that the question sentence has, of course, been transformed from a declarative sentence by rearrangement:

Kernel: You're going to New Jersey.
Question Transformation: Are you going to New Jersey?
Deletion Transformation: Yes, I am (going to New Jersey).

10   Now that we have examined the five operations of English, let's make some generalizations about transformational grammar and move on to examine them.

11   Noam Chomsky, one of the fathers of this grammar, wrote that it will "generate all and only the grammatical sentences of a language." This is a new concept of the function of a grammar and, besides, it's quite a big order for one set of rules. We'll suggest how this statement is true a bit later. Further, transformational grammar shows the relatedness and differences among sentences apparently different or alike in structure. O'Neil suggests this in his discussion of diagrams, and our look at operations also vaguely suggests it. We'll glance at this again later.

12   A transformational grammar is really two grammars which are closely related yet clearly distinguished in their functions. The first grammar is called a *generative grammar*, the second is the *transformational grammar*. Some people call this whole pot transformational-generative grammar, but we won't quibble about the terminology. The five operations which we have just described relate to the transformational portion of the grammar. It goes without saying that we must have basic sentences on which our five operations can be performed. Remember, we've called these the kernel sentences.

GENERATIVE GRAMMAR

13   The generative grammar produces these kernel sentences. We now entertain the relatively new notion of a grammar as a machine which generates, or produces, something. In some ways this grammar is analogous to a computer. It has an input of items and rules and an output, or result. The notion of grammatical rule is also new here. We are no longer confronted with the *prescriptive* rules of classroom grammar, rules that prescribe, or tell us, what we *must* do. The rules of the generative grammar are *descriptive;* they tell us what we *can* do without bringing in needless moral overtones and notions of right and wrong. They are called rewrite rules and look like this:

$$S \longrightarrow NP + VP$$

This merely means that any kernel sentence (S) can be rewritten ($\longrightarrow$) as a noun phrase (NP) plus a verb phrase (VP). This is another way of making the conventional statement that a sentence consists of a subject and a predicate:

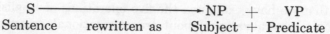

Sentence   rewritten as   Subject + Predicate

The next steps are to write rules which describe the various structures of noun phrases and, then, verb phrases. The result of this "generation," or rule writing, is a kernel sentence—the output of the grammatical machine. The process can be represented by what O'Neil calls the tree graph:

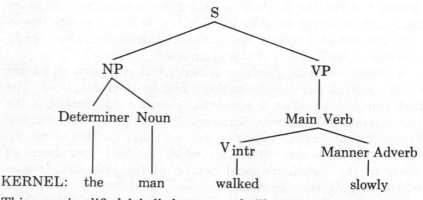

KERNEL: the   man   walked   slowly

This oversimplified labelled tree graph illustrates how the grammar produces, or generates, a kernel sentence.

14   And this seems like a lot of trouble just to "get to" a kernel sentence, doesn't it? Which brings us to the second, and most important, feature of the generative grammar. The word "generate" also means "select." Every native speaker of a language has within him a set of rules which enables him to produce infinite numbers of grammatical sentences. He also has rules for "selecting out", or rejecting, ungrammatical sentences, those not acceptable to him. Transformational grammar is an attempt to describe these rules that provide for grammatical sentences. This "providing for" is what is meant by *generating* grammatical sentences.

15   We initially provide for grammatical sentences by selecting subclasses of parts of speech, like nouns and verbs. Thus, there is the necessity for specific rules applied in a set order.

16   Our classroom grammar tells us, for example, that words of the class *noun* can be divided into four subclasses: proper and common, mass and count nouns. Insofar as this goes, our grammar is correct. But it does not even scratch the surface in describing the many subclasses of nouns that actually occur. This is so because the classroom grammar does not fully describe nouns in terms of such realities within our language as the different words and con-

structions that nouns "go with" when they occur in English sentences.

17   In other words, we must identify parts of speech not by reference to meaning in the world outside of language, but by reference to observable syntactic habits. For example, there is a class of nouns which can be either subject or object in sentences containing verbs such as *puzzle, provoke, frighten,* and *kill.* Consider the nouns in these sentences:

> The man puzzled the dog.
> The dog puzzled the man.
> Joe provoked his wife.
> His wife provoked Joe.

Then there is another class of nouns which can only be the subject of these verbs, not the object. We can't reverse the subject and object in these sentences:

> The bicycle puzzled the dog.
> The house provoked his wife.
> The gun killed the man.

18   We have here identified the conventional animate and inanimate nouns by understanding how they "go with" certain verbs, not by the fact that they refer to animate and inanimate items.

19   Let's see how a generative grammar can describe, and thus enable us to select, a few of some twenty subclasses of nouns. We'll use a tree graph representation, and the rules from which the tree is derived are listed. Brackets { } merely mean "you have to select one and only one of these numbered items."

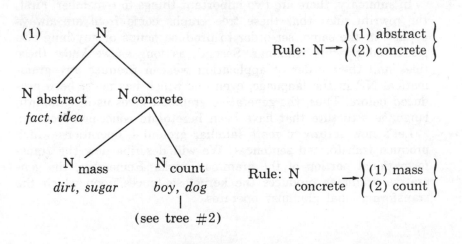

20   This means that the class *Noun* can initially be divided into
abstract and concrete nouns. Abstract nouns are incapable of
further subclassification except in a very complicated way so we
develop them no further. Concrete nouns can be subdivided into
the conventional classes of mass and count nouns. These subclasses, remember, are realistically differentiated from one another
on the bases of their syntactic habits. Now let's continue our tree
by showing a few subclasses of N_{count}.

(2)

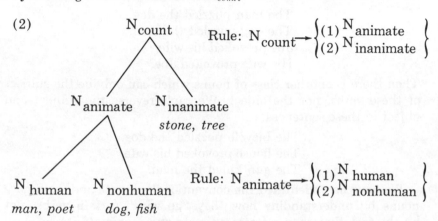

21   The N_{count} of tree #1 is expanded in tree #2 into animate and
inanimate nouns. Animate nouns can then be divided into nouns
naming humans and nouns naming nonhuman things and creatures.

22   This is enough to suggest the manner in which the generative
grammar selects subclasses of parts of speech and relates them
each to each.

23   In summary, there are two important things to remember. First,
the rewrite rules that these tree graphs come from are always
applied in the same, set order to produce nouns or anything else
generated by this grammar. Second, as long as we know these
rules and their order of application we can produce any grammatical NP in the language, even one which has never been produced before. Thus, the generative grammar gives us insights into
language structure that have been heretofore concealed from us.

24   Let's now return to more familiar ground — operations which
produce transformed sentences. We will describe how the transformational portion of the grammar works. Remember, the generative grammar produces the kernel sentences upon which the
transformational grammar operates.

SINGLE BASE TRANSFORMATIONS

25   There are two kinds of transformations: single base and double base. Single base transformations operate on one kernel sentence. Many single base transformations involve the first operation mentioned earlier, rearrangement. Let's look at the yes/no question transformation as an example of a single base transformation. Remember? It goes like this:

Kernel: The man can go.
Transformation: Can the man go?

What we see here, by recognizing the rearrangement, is the structural relationship between the question (transformed sentence) and the statement (kernel sentence) from which it is transformed.

26   Like the phrase structure rules of the generative grammar, transformational rules are expressed by formulae. In what follows we shall see that these rules which look so imposing need not terrify us. Actually, they are easy to understand. We will demonstrate that they are merely a way of making very precise statements concerning our intuitions about language structure.

27   Here is a simplified rule for the yes/no question transformation:

Noun Phrase + Tense + Modal + X ⟹ Tense + Modal + Noun Phrase + X

the man   + present + can + go ⟶ present + can + the man   + go

the man   can   go ⟹ can   the man   go

Like the rules of generative grammar, transformational rules have an input on the left of the arrow and an output on the right. We can call the input the kernel; the output is the transformed sentence. X stands for any element, in this case the verb *go*. Tense applies, in this case, to the modal auxiliary verb *can*. And the double-shafted arrow means "is transformed into." Thus, any time we have a kernel sentence with the structure

Noun Phrase + Tense + Modal + X

we can always produce a yes/no question by rearranging these kernel elements in the order

Tense + Modal + Noun Phrase + X

28   Now let's look at a single base transformation that involves more than one operation. The transformation from an active to a

passive sentence uses two operations: rearrangement and addition, plus one change necessitated by the addition.

Kernel: Tom gave Joe a book.

Transformation: Joe was given a book by Tom.

Here is a simplified version of the Passive Transformation Rule. The numbers under the structural elements are for clarification only; they aren't part of the rule. Don't be confused by the fact that transformationists find it useful to place *Tense* and *en* (which designates the past participle) before the verbs they go with.

$$NP_1 + Tense + V_{trans} + NP_2 + X = \!=\! \Rightarrow NP_2 + Tense + BE + en + V_{trans} + X + by + NP_1$$

①　　②　　③　④　⑤==▶④　②　+BE+en+③　⑤　+by+①

Tom　　gave　　Joe the book▶Joe　　was　given　the book by Tom

To produce a passive from this active sentence we perform the following rearrangement operations:

(1) Move NP_2, *Joe,* to the front of the sentence.

(2) Move NP_1, *Tom,* to the end of the sentence.

Then we make the following additions:

(3) Add the verb BE in the proper tense in the proper place, between NP_2 and the past participle of the transitive verb.

(4) Add the preposition *by* before NP_1.

and make the change in form of V_{trans} necessitated by the addition of BE:

(5) Change the V_{trans} to its "en form," the past participle: *given.* Isn't the formula showing structural change much simpler than the explanation?

29　　To sum it up: any time we have a kernel with the structure

$$NP_1 + Tense + V_{trans} + NP_2 + X$$

we can always transform it to a grammatical passive sentence by rearranging and adding in this way:

$$NP_2 + Tense + BE + en + V_{trans} + X + by + NP_1$$

DOUBLE BASE TRANSFORMATIONS

30　　Double base transformations expand English sentences from kernels like

      (1) Sue is a girl.

to

      (2) Sue is a girl who is lovely.

or

      (3) Sue is a lovely girl.

31   Actually, there is a wide range of double base transformations which combine operations in various ways to produce expanded and joined sentences. Let's look briefly at how we arrive at the expansions exemplified in sentences (2) and (3) above.

32   Since double base transformations operate on two kernels instead of one, it is convenient to label these kernels *consumer* and *source* sentences. The *consumer* sentence is the one which is finally transformed, or expanded, by receiving an element from the *source* sentence. The source sentence is, thus, *embedded* into the consumer, or, if you wish, added to it. Accordingly, to produce sentence (2) above we have, in general terms, the following operations:

Consumer: Sue is a girl.
Source: wh-the girl is lovely

wh-the girl merely means that later on we can substitute a *wh-word*, a relative pronoun like *who*, for *the girl*.

33   Since we wish to modify the noun *girl* in the consumer sentence, we embed (add) the source sentence into it:

Sue is a girl   *(wh-the girl is lovely)*
Consumer   Source

And, because the noun *girl* of the consumer is the same as the noun *girl* of the source, we substitute *who* for *wh-the girl* in the source sentence and come up with:

(2) Sue is a girl who is lovely.

34   A simplified rule to describe this relative clause transformation looks like this:

$$\left.\begin{array}{l} \textit{Consumer: } X + NP_1 \\ \textit{Source: } wh\text{-}NP_2 + Z \end{array}\right\} {=\!=\!=}\!\!\rightarrow X + NP_1 + wh\text{-}NP_2 + Z$$

where: X ----------→ Sue is
        NP_1 ----------→ a girl
        $wh\text{-}NP_2$ ----------→ wh-the girl, and later ------→ who
        Z ----------→ is lovely
Remember that ----------→ means "can be rewritten as."

35   Thus, given consumer and source sentences with structures such as those in the rule, we can always produce a sentence with a relative clause modifier after the final noun by arranging the elements as they are in the transformation above

$$X + NP_1 + wh\text{-}NP_2 + Z$$

Most of the time we can produce a sentence like (3):

Sue is a lovely girl.

by deleting *who is* in the source and moving the adjective *lovely* into position before the noun, in effect:

girl who is lovely ======► lovely girl

36   The question remains again: why do it this way? First, there are probably more adjectives and other kinds of noun modifiers that occur in the predicate position than in position before the noun. Thus, this may be the way in which our minds actually formulate utterances with pre-noun modifiers. Further, transformations assure that the proper things "go together".

37   Assume that we have a set of generative rules which assure proper reference of the relative pronouns *who, whom, which, that* to the human and nonhuman nouns they go with:

wh-Noun$_{human}$ --------► who, whom
Sue is a girl who is lovely

not

*Sue is a girl which is lovely
wh-Noun$_{nonhuman}$ ------► which, that
It's a stone which is big

not

*It's a stone who is big

The point is that we have a rule describing the fact that the real difference between *who* and *which* is that they occur, respectively, with human and nonhuman nouns.

38   Finally, examine the fact that it's probably simpler in many cases to understand what modifiers mean when they go with nouns by seeing the modifiers, first, in a predicate structure. The following transformed sentence has two meanings because of the ambiguilty of *scratching* in pre-noun position:

Joe hates scratching dogs.

39   The two meanings of *scratching* are clarified by putting the verb *scratch* in the predicate in two possible source sentences:

Consumer: Joe hates SOMETHING
Source #1: Joe scratches dogs
Source #2: Dogs scratch

40   Either of the two source sentences can be embedded in the consumer:

Embedment #1: Joe hates SOMETHING (Joe scratches dogs)
Source #1
Unambiguous Embedment Result: Joe hates to scratch dogs.
Embedment #2: Joe hates SOMETHING (Dogs scratch)
Source #2
Unambiguous Embedment Result: Joe hates dogs that scratch.

41   While we do not always need the clarification that the embedment process affords, it is useful to have it when we need it.

42   Correctly-written generative and transformational rules, then, provide us with new insights into the operations of our language and consistently produce items that "go together" grammatically. These two advantages are possessed by no other grammars.

QUESTIONS FOR STUDY

1. Examine the following five sentences in which the nouns are underlined:
   (a) He eats <u>sugar</u>.
   (b) Jane likes <u>dogs</u>.
   (c) A <u>man</u> is here.
   (d) I caught a <u>fish</u>.
   (e) He threw the <u>stone</u>.

   In what ways are the nouns similar? In what ways are they different? In what way or ways can an understanding of transformational grammar help you in explaining these differences?

2. Write examples in English of what the following rules produce:
   (a) S ———→NP + VP _____
   (b) NP———→Article + Noun _____
   (c) V ———→Auxiliary + Verb _____

3. Transform this kernel sentence

   Jane gave Jack a glance

   into a passive sentence using the Passive Transformation Rule.

4. What would be wrong with the rules of a generative grammar that produce *three dirt?*

5. With reference to pages 130-131 and page 124, write the consumer and source sentences which are necessary to produce:

   (a) John is a man who is tall.
   (b) Jack jumped and laughed.

6. Think about this sentence:

   Andy walks upstairs.

   How many possible meanings can we assign to this sentence? How can a knowledge of transformational grammar help us to avoid surface ambiguity such as this?

The instructions on the unannounced quiz were plain enough. You were to read the poem and then answer the questions dealing with the underlined portion of the poem. You were allowed to use a dictionary.

"Ozymandias" by Percy Bysshe Shelley

I met a traveler from an antique land
Who said: Two vast and trunkless legs of stone
Stand in the desert. Near them, on the sand,
Half sunk, a shattered visage lies, whose frown,
And wrinkled lip, and sneer of cold command,
Tell that its sculptor well those passions read
Which yet survive (stamped on these lifeless things),
The hand that mocked them and the heart that fed;
And on the pedestal these words appear:
"My name is Ozymandias, king of kings;
Look on my works, ye Mighty, and despair!"
Nothing beside remains. Round the decay
Of that colossal wreck, boundless and bare
The lone and level sands stretch far away.

Questions: 1) What does the word "mocked" mean?
2) To whom does "The hand that mocked them" belong?

To these questions you answered as follows: 1) The word "mocked" means "scorned" or "made fun of." 2) The person to whom "The hand that mocked them" belongs is Ozymandias, the king.

And of course, you were wrong both times. You thought you knew what the word "mocked" meant, so you did not look it up in your dictionary. If you had, you would have seen that the word "mocked" also meant "to copy or imitate." Had you known this meaning of "mocked," you probably would have realized that "The hand that mocked them" belonged to the sculptor (not the king) who used his talents to preserve Ozymandias' "sneer of cold command."

In this case, understanding poetry was not so much a matter of taste as it was a matter of making good use of materials available to all. In his essay "Linguistics and Teaching Introductory Literature," Seymour B. Chatman discusses how students of literature can, by the use of some simple linguistic principles, better understand the intended meaning of a poet. By using these principles, the student can bridge the gap between "lexicon" and "structure."

Linguistics and Teaching
Introductory Literature

Seymour Chatman

1   I assume that the purpose of introductory courses in English literature is to teach students how to read it. Yet many college students, in spite of the best intentions, never *do* learn to read the
masterpieces of our language with even elementary comprehension.
One reason for their failure is that the basic skill of interpretation
is all too easily assumed by the instructor, whose anxiety is to
prove the value of literature or whose scholarly interests may insulate him from the beginner's major problems. The kind of English which we want our students to learn to read differs strikingly
from the kind they are used to. For the first time, they must try
to make plain sense out of a dialect which is infinitely more subtle
in lexical distinction and more complex in structure than any they
have ever known; and there is no use in minimizing the size and
dangers of the linguistic gap that yawns before them.

2   The central problem in the teaching of literature is to bridge
the gap: to show students how to expand and refine their disturb-
ingly narrow grasp of potential structures, to develop a whole new
syntactic and lexical musculature for dealing with the complexities
of Milton, Shakespeare and Pope. One way to accomplish this is
to treat the text almost as if it were a foreign language (for it is
at least a foreign dialect), to be parsed and worked over until
pattern and meaning are learned and overlearned. All the devices
that linguistics has developed for teaching foreign languages might
be tried: substitution within a frame, imitative oral drill (with
particular attention to stress, pitch and juncture), restructuring
for analysis, expansion and omission, etc. Furthermore, the instructor must be aware at every moment of the specific linguistic complexities of the piece he is teaching in relation to the level of his

Reprinted by permission from *Language Learning,* 7.3-10 (1956-1957), and
the author.

class. This is as important to his immediate job as a knowledge of mythic patterns in the Modern English novel or what nasty fellows Elizabethan printers were. He must attempt—and it is a painful job—to uncover the multifoliate layers of his own literary sophistication and put himself in his students' position. He must realize that students are unable to move with the linguistic facility that he has developed in himself, that they are not alert to the lexical and structural possibilities of language and are quickly reduced to helplessness if the first meaning which comes to mind proves untenable. Nor are they willing to pore over a passage until it makes sense, because they know that more than poring will be needed to help *them*.

3   Let us consider three areas where linguistics might be helpful. I. Lexicon. We must be careful not to shrug our shoulders over the lexical problem and say 'It's all in the dictionary.' First of all, the facts of American college life are such that we cannot count on a student to *buy* a decent dictionary, let alone use one. This bit of student pathology, of course, is not our problem. What *is* disturbing is that even where a student shows a willingness to use the dictionary, it is all too clear that he often doesn't know *when*. Most students dutifully look up words that they don't 'know'; that is, *words that they've never seen before*. But it isn't the unusual word that causes the trouble. Even lazy students can be expected to look up 'incarnadine' and 'multitudinous' if threatened with quizzes. The real danger lies with relatively simple words that are known in one—but the wrong—definition. Not only doesn't the student understand the word, but far worse, he doesn't even *know* that he doesn't understand it. And the astonishment and disbelief in his eyes when you tell him that words *often* have more than one meaning. Here are a few rather obvious instances that have troubled my students:

I only hear

Its melancholy, long, withdrawing roar,
Retreating, to the breath
Of the night wind, down the vast edges drear
And naked *shingles* of the world.   (small beach stones)

From this descent

Celestial *virtues* rising will appear
More glorious than from no fall.   (angelic host)

. . . leaving the tumultuous throng,

To cut across the *reflex* of a star
That fled, and flying still before me, gleamed
Upon the glassy plain. . .   (reflection)

Love's not Time's fool, though rosy lips and cheeks
Within his bending sickle's *compass* come.   (range)

I sigh the lack of many a thing I sought
And with old woes new wail my *dear* time's waste.   (precious)

Becoming *aware* of a lexical difficulty is far more than half the
battle, for it is precisely the skill of recognition that students lack
so desperately. And it is obviously the teacher's affair, for even
the most heavily glossed text-book will not help students whose
real problem is that they refuse to admit that they do not 'know'
rather simple words. The teacher must demonstrate with semantic
exercises the perniciousness of taking the first meaning that comes
to mind if his students are ever to become competent and self-
dependent readers. Those students who have successfully studied
foreign languages will be the first to believe him; anyone who has
had to look up *facio* or *affaire* or *Bestimmung* a dozen times for
a dozen different contexts will readily accept the principle of
semantic diversity in English. It is the monolithic monolingual who
will be hardest to convince, just as he is the hardest to teach to
write decent compositions. This is basically a problem in sensitiz-
ing students to a higher degree of semantic awareness than they
have ever known, and they may offer fierce resistance. The whole
drift of their lives and the culture which nurtured them may go
against recognizing the possibility of finely wrought discrimination
of meaning. But it is a vital job of pedagogy and worthy of more
scientific interest among linguists than it has so far aroused.

4   II. Form-class identification. Separate from the lexical problem
(which is self-evident and a little removed from my major concerns) is the difficulty the beginner frequently encounters in
identifying a word's part-of-speech. Students are accustomed to
taking the path of least resistance: they only know how to identify
a word's structure in terms of its most *frequent* assignment, and
are reluctant to analyze the specific syntactic demands which the
environment makes upon it. For example:

The Sea of Faith
Was once, too, at the full, and *round* earth's shore
Lay like the folds of a bright girdle furled.

I have had all eighteen students in a class of eighteen tell me that
'round' is an adjective modifying 'shore'. The reason is obviously
quantitative: 'round' occurs far more frequently in their idiolects
as an adjective than as a preposition, and its occurrence immediately before 'earth' seems to have utterly incapacitated these
readers from making any other form-class identification. ('Full',

too, is easier for them to take as an adjective modifying 'earth' than as a nominal, the axis of 'at the . . .'.)

5 But we are more competent to handle this problem than the lexical problem, for we have the signals to help us. Rather than *tell* the student that 'round' should be taken as a preposition, we can make him *hear* his mistake. After convincing him that his reading is meaningless ('What then is the subject of "lay" ?'), we contrast his superfixes with our own.

His: The Sea of Faith
Was once, too | ²at the ³fûll and rôund eârth's shóre²

Lay like the folds of a bright girdle furled.

Ours: The Sea of Faith
Was once, too|²at the ³fúll¹# ²and roùnd êarth's
³shóre² |

Lay like the folds of a bright girdle furled.

The insertion of #between 'full' and 'round' and the substitution of tertiary for secondary on 'round' will be enough for three out of four students, simply because the signals are stronger than any abstract grammatical explanation could be.[1] (And, of course, if Smith's new syntactic views are correct, the phonological *is* the grammatical explanation.) The less astute fourth student will not understand the difference, but for non-linguistic reasons; either because he has never heard the expression 'at the full' before, or 'round' used as a preposition, but *not* because he is unprepared to interpret the comma as # and the tertiary on 'round' as the signal of a preposition.

Another example:

Me though just right, and the fixed laws of heaven,
Did first create your leader, next, free choice. . .

Most students take 'just right' to modify "me", thus tertiary on 'just' (and in some idiolects /jIst/ instead of jəst/), and secondary on 'right':

³Mé though jùst ríght²

But if forced to imitate another reading, many grasp the structure immediately:

---

[1] I use the Trager-Smith notation (*Outline of English Structure,* Norman: 1951) for stress, pitch and juncture. Pitch: levels 1, 2, 3, 4 (4 is highest); stress: / = primary, ∧ = secondary, \ = tertiary, no mark = weak; junctures; # = falling and fading, ‖ = rising, | = sustention. I do not mark plus-juncture.

³Mé¹|²thoùgh ³jûst ríght²|²and the ³fixed lâws of heáven²
('Although righteousness and heaven's laws first created me your
leader . . .')

Here are some other lines from the same passage:

> from this descent
> Celestial virtues rising will appear
> More glorious than from no fall.

Several students, after learning that 'virtues' refers to the fallen
host, took 'celestial virtues' as a vocative, and 'rising' as a gerund,
rather than as a post-positional participial modifier (with 'from
this descent' as adverbial object):

> ²from this de³scént³|
> ²Celêstial vír³tues||³rísing¹|²will appéar
> Mòre ³glórious ¹|² than from³ nó fâll¹#
> (And trust themselves to fear no second fate.)

('From this descent, O ye virtues, your rising will appear more
glorious than from no fall.') But this reading is only superficially
possible, for 'trust', then, has no subject. We ask them to imitate
the following:

> from ³this descént²|
> ²Ce³lêstial vírtues||rìsing²|²will ap³péar³|
> ³Môre glórious ²|² than from³ nó fâll²|

('Celestial virtues, rising from this descent, will appear more glorious than from no fall and will trust themselves to fear no second
fate.')

A final example; one student, reading it this way

> O bright-eyed Hope,²my ³môrbid fâncy chéer¹ #

wondered how Hope could be at the same time 'bright-eyed', 'fancy',
and 'morbid'. Her embarrassment knew no bounds when she heard
the following reading and immediately saw her error:

> O bright-eyed Hope, my ²mòrbid ³fáncy ¹|¹ chéer¹#

('O hope, please cheer up my morbid fancy'.)

6   III. Word Order. Word order is so vital in Modern English
structure that inversions² offer perhaps the most difficult syntactic
adjustment that a student has to make. What he needs is basically
a re-education in signalling potential. There is no use saying that
this comes with reading experience, because all too often even

---

²I use the term in the broad sense to mean any order of words not usual in
normal spoken English.

graduate students appear unable to parse locutions like Johnson's

> Behold surrounding kings their pow'r combine,
> And one capitulate and one resign;

Or Milton's

> to consult how we may best
> With what may be devis'd of honours new
> Receive him coming to receive from us
> Knee-tribute yet unpaid, prostration vile,
> Too much to one, but double how endur'd
> To one and to his image now proclaim'd?

7   Since inversions are easily analyzed and catalogued,[3] it is strange that no one has ever compiled a primer or drill-book to develop among novice readers the essential skill of interpreting them. It would seem that the very act of going through several examples of the same type would prove eminently useful as 'pattern practice'. An example is the difficult inversion of Object-Imperative (for Imperative-Object), which the tremendous pressures of the *usual* meaning of the NV pattern often lead students to interpret as Subject-Predicate, particularly where signals of potential subject-predicate agreement are lacking: 'Then, pilgrim, turn; thy cares forego' or 'Here subterranean works and cities see,' or 'Round my true heart thine arms entwine.' The student must be taught to search for *other* clues than he could normally count on; for example, in the Object-Imperative pattern, he could use previous straight-forward imperatives as a hint ('turn', in '. . . turn; they cares forego'), or quasi-imperative adverbials ('here . . .'). The important thing, however, as in all pattern practice, would be to set the model and then to fill it with numerous confirmatory examples.

8   Here are some of the kinds of poetic inversions that cause students trouble:

> SOV   Bright Thames the brightest beauties yield
> Prep SOV With hairy springes we the birds betray
> OSV   What though no credit doubting wits may give
> OVS   Among the Shepherd-grooms no mate/ Hath he
> SAuxOV Gums and pomatums shall his flight restrain
> SprepV Not fierce Othello in so loud a strain
>   Roared for the handkerchief that caused his pain

---

[3]The job has been done excellently by Mats Redin. *Word Order in English Verse From Pope of Sassoon* (Uppsala: Universiteits Arsskrift, II, 1925), from whom most of my examples are taken. I am grateful to Professor Josephine Miles for calling this study to my attention.

SVprepO   The God who darts around the world his rays
OConjSV   But fortune's gifts if each alike possessed
AdvSV   Unless aside thy purple had been thrown
AdvPrepVS Swift on his sooty pinions flits the gnome
SAuxPrepV There all the Learn'd shall at the labour
           stand
PrepImp   Hope humbly then; with trembling pinion soar
PrepP   A vile conceit in pompous words expressed
PrepInf   What moved my mind with youthful lords to
           roam
SPredNV   Some figures monstrous and mis-shaped appear.
           For I thy own dear mother am.
ObjCompOSV   Modes of Self-love the passions we may call
PrepN   O thou! Of Bu'ness the directing Soul.
NAdj   Not tyrants fierce that unrepenting die
AxisPrep   She talked and sung the words among.
           I went my work about. [4]

The teacher has no business assuming that his beginning students
have either the initiative or the ability to learn how to interpret
poetic inversions on their own. What they need is the same kind
of intensive drill that has proven so effective in foreign language
instruction—drill within the pattern, in this case with instances
drawn from all periods of English poetry. The alternative is a continuing incapacity to handle any other structure than SVO or its
standard variations—in short, incompetence as a reader of poetry.

9   It would be fatuous to suggest that all the problems of teaching
introductory literature can be solved by linguistics, for the obvious
reason that literature can never be defined in terms of language
alone. Obviously our methods do nothing to develop the vital poetic
prerequisites of emotional maturity, esthetic sensitivity, and general culture. Yet, as important as these qualities are, they do not
even *become* problems until the student has been successful in
piecing together the plain syntactic sense of a poem. Let us not
evade our linguistic responsibilities. Let us try to solve linguistic
problems with linguistic methods, and let the other things take
care of themselves.

---

[4]S = subject, O = object, V = verb, Prep = prepositional phrase, Conj. =
conjunction, Adv = adverb, P = participle, Inf = infinitive, Pred N = Predicate noun.

QUESTIONS FOR STUDY

1. What criticisms does Chatman make of the American student? Is the author justified in making these criticisms? If possible, refer to your own initial experiences with literature classes.

2. How is it possible for the dictionary to lead you astray? You might try looking up older meanings for words such as *cute*, *hussy*, and *fond*.

3. Describe the difference between lexical and structural criteria in literary interpretation. Refer to the various quoted passages in the essay.

4. What are the properties of word-use, according to Chatman, that cause difficulty? Illustrate from "Ozymandias" as well as from the essay itself.

5. What is meant by the "principle of semantic diversity in English"? Why might a student of foreign languages be more willing to accept the principle than a person who spoke only English?

6. Examining a poem of your own choice, show how lexical awareness, form class identification, stress and pitch, and word order analysis can be used to obtain a better understanding of a poet's meaning. (The sonnets of Shakespeare and the poems of John Donne are particularly good for this purpose. If you are interested in reading the work of a later poet, you might read some poems by either Robert Browning or Gerard Manley Hopkins.)

7. Try restructuring poetic inversions and transpositions in a few poems and explain how this restructuring helped you better understand meaning, if it did. What do you lose by restructuring poetic word-order?

Unthinkingly, the press photographer snaps away at the presidential candidate. Afterwards he notices that one of his shots shows Adlai Stevenson with his legs crossed. An ordinary photograph, except for one easily overlooked detail — Mr. Stevenson has a hole in the sole of his shoe.

The nation is amused by the photograph. The candidate himself treasures the pose. And the photographer is complimented on using photography to reveal still another side of a many-sided person. Almost no one says that the photograph should not have been printed. In these times no one claims that great men should only be revealed during formal state occasions. We wish to see our leaders and heroes as they really are, not as they would like to be or should be.

But we do not carry this attitude over when it comes to considering the language we use daily or the means we use to record that language. We want our language to be pure and uncorrupted. And we want the dictionary that records our language to serve as the preserver of that purity, to keep it undefiled.

When the Third Edition of *Webster's New International Dictionary* was published, it was said to have dropped all standards of right or wrong; slang was admitted into our midst indiscriminately; even *ain't* was, henceforth, to be permitted under certain circumstances.

Somehow, we have managed to survive. And somehow, teachers still have not given up notions of right and wrong. Then, what was the fight all about? Well, as a matter of fact, the fight is still going on, although there is a little more light than heat by now. In his essay "A Not Disinterested/Uninterested Note on the New Dictionary," Howard K. Battles discusses the controversy over *Webster's Third.* He does explain why certain people were so upset by the position taken by the dictionary's editors.

A Not Disinterested/Uninterested
Note on the New Dictionary

Howard K. Battles

1   It is a common and perhaps understandable weakness of those of us who labor anonymously in publishing offices to harbor secret dreams of notoriety. A few achieve this ambition by writing novels that expose the trade; others drift off into advertising. But for the hoard of editors who at one time or another worked on the staff of the Third Edition of *Webster's New International Dictionary* no special exertion seems necessary. Now, to have one's name listed in the front matter of such a book may seem a modest step away from anonymity, and so it would be under ordinary circumstances. But it appears that this new dictionary is generally regarded as an infernal machine for the subversion of the language. Indeed, a review in the *Atlantic*, not usually given to sensationalism, was entitled "Sabotage in Springfield." Those whose pleasure it is to ferret out subversion rarely stop short of finding out Those Responsible. Let those take comfort who may in the knowledge that few even among reviewers read the front matter of dictionaries. Who can rest easy having incurred the disfavor of both the New York *Times* and the Luce publications? Think of all those trained researchers accustomed to poking about in out-of-the-way places. Sooner or later, one of them will come upon us huddling between Preface and Outside Consultants and the game will be up. Others may do as they like. I'm for quiet surrender and a signed statement.

2   Although they vary in particulars, the hostile reviews of the Third Edition are unanimous in decrying the abdication of the Merriam editors from their role as Supreme Authority. It should be remembered that the claim of being the Supreme Authority originated with those who were out to sell dictionaries, not those

From *The English Leaflet* (Midwinter, 1962). Reprinted by permission of *The English Leaflet* and the author.

who made them. Lexicographers abandoned that claim long ago. By 1755, Dr. Johnson realized the futility of such authority:

> When we see men grow old and die at a certain time one after another, from century to century, we laugh at the elixir that promises to prolong life a thousand years; and with equal justice may the lexicographer be derided, who, being unable to produce no example of a nation that has preserved their words and phrases from mutability, shall imagine that his dictionaries can embalm his language, and secure it from corruption and decay, that it is in his power to change sublunary nature, or clear the world at once from folly, vanity, and affectation.

3   Still there exists an apparently unbridgeable gulf between the lexicographer's view of his work and that of the public he serves. The situation is almost unique. Obviously we don't know exactly what research chemists and higher mathematicians are about either; but to the extent that their work touches our lives at all, we form an idea of it which conforms, however crudely, to the facts. The fate of the lexicographer is less happy; he is bound to be misunderstood.

4   The reaction to the Third Edition is like that of a man who has employed a gardener for years with the most harmonious and satisfactory results. Then inexplicably he finds on visiting his garden that his roses are blighted, that weeds have been permitted to choke out flowers, and nature generally allowed to run riot. Naturally, he assumes his man has gone berserk. For the general reader of dictionaries does indeed think of lexicographers as custodians of the language. He expects them to protect it and to do what they can to eliminate impurities. But the editors of the Second Edition (1934) had a different view:

> In conformity with the traditional principle of the Merriam-Webster Dictionaries that definitions, to be adequate, must be written only after an analysis of citations, the definitions in this new edition are based on citations. . . . Since 1924 the editors have systematically reviewed chosen cross sections of contemporary printed materials, including many thousands of books, pamphlets, magazines, newspapers, catalogues, and learned, technical, and scientific periodicals.

5   Recognizing that "a dictionary so universally appealed to as a final authority must make accuracy its first objective," the editors of the Second Edition neatly duck all claims to infallibility. They base their claims to accuracy on the careful analysis of evidence — a million and a half or more citations from printed sources. The first few sentences of the following quotation (also from the Second Edition) help to define the modern lexicographer's notion of his function.

The entry, definition, and proper classification of selected nonstandard and substandard English words have been greatly extended in the New Edition. . . . With the growth in literacy of the past century, and the increase, in fiction and drama, in radio and motion picture, of the use of dialect, slang, and colloquial speech, it has become necessary for a general dictionary to record and interpret the vocabularies of geographical and occupational dialects, and of the livelier levels of the speech of the educated. The shifting status of many expressions in slang and colloquial speech has made it necessary to review and rejudge the status and validity of all such terms, whether newly collected or contained in former editions of this Dictionary. Slang terms and slang meanings of standard words have been entered only when there is evidence that the slang term has been in use for a considerable length of time, and when it has been used in a printed work which is likely to continue being read.

6   Under the general heading of abdication of authority, the editors of the Third Edition stand accused on the following counts: 1) They have admitted as entries "crude neologisms" and countless examples of "shabby diction." 2) They have further offended by quoting Jack Paar, Polly Adler, Art Linkletter, Dwight D. Eisenhower, and others whose achievements, however much they differ in other particulars, are not primarily literary. 3) They have ruthlessly deleted useful encyclopedic information (the fact that Mark Twain was an author; the names of Seven Wise Men of Greece). They have made the life of proofreaders and copy editors difficult, if not unbearable, by refusing to give absolute prescriptions for the use of capital letters, italics, and periods in abbreviations. The reaction of most reviewers to these acts of omission and commission is neatly summed up in the words of an editorial assistant on a distinguished magazine quoted in the *Atlantic* review: "Why have a Dictionary at all if anything goes?" (Capital *D* faithfully preserved.)

7   Well, it is something of an exaggeration to say that anything goes in the Third Edition. *One,* for example, is not given as a synonym for *two; war* does not turn out to mean *peace.* The countless divisions and subdivisions of senses reassure us that the customary distinctions in the meaning of words are still observed. But, of course, this is quibbling. We know perfectly well that the editorial assistant who said that was not thinking of meanings at all but those examples of "shabby diction" which are entered, often without a restrictive-usage label.

8   Now the specific criticisms set forth earlier can be answered. However, the answers will simply not be acceptable to people who

continue to take a different view of the function of a dictionary from that of the people who make the dictionary. The argument may be joined and even won, but that anguished cry cannot be stifled.

9   The dictionary may be viewed as a report on usage — not on the usage of the elite, but on the usage of all the people who speak English as their native tongue. It may be so viewed if one remembers the nature of the evidence on which it reports. The Second Edition of the *New International*, with its million and a half citations, and the Third Edition, with three times that many or more, are based on written language. While they provide respellings for pronunciation and have obvious applications for any kind of use, the definitions in the Third Edition — or any good dictionary for that matter — are, in fact, a record of the way in which words are used in print — where they come from, how they are spelled, what they have been used to mean. On the basis of such evidence, the dictionary editor may sometimes be able to assign, without qualification, the label *slang, nonstandard,* or *substandard* to the use of a particular word. But often, as the editors of the Third Edition point out, "There is no completely satisfactory objective test for slang, especially in application to a word out of context. No word is invariably slang, and many standard words can be given slang connotations or used so inappropriately as to become slang." If we bear in mind that the evidence on which the dictionary editor must base his decision is published material, in which, in general, slang and nonstandard forms are less likely to be found than in speech — that assistant on the distinguished magazine is not going to place them before his readers — we begin to see how difficult it is to legislate about language. If even a careful analysis of printed material does not yield criteria for hard and fast judgments about usage, what kind of sampling of the language would? No single book — no matter how many people work on it or how many citations they gather — can provide foolproof guides to using the language. The dictionary, then, records and reports. The enterprise is closer to the writing of history than it is to the writing of laws.

10   In their attempt to give an accurate report on the use of English words in print the editors of the Third Edition have had to find room for an impressive number of new words and meanings — 100,000 according to the advertising claims. These new entries are not exclusively slang words, scientific terms of recent vintage, or

such neologisms as *astronaut, sputnik,* or *countdown.* Such entries are there, to be sure, but the responsibility of a dictionary does not end with the definition of new words. The really impressive achievement of the Third Edition is much less obvious and indeed will probably not be fully appreciated until the book has been long in use. This achievement consists in the rewriting of all of the Second Edition entries with a view to making them precise, useful, and up to date. In many cases this process has resulted in further division into senses or in new boldface entries. A few samples will give a general idea of the kind of improvements made.

11   The Second Edition defines *Edwardian* as follows: "Of or pertaining to Edward;" (the Second Edition reader is accustomed to waiting patiently for information) "used specif. with reference to: a. Edward I of England. b. The reigns of the first three Edwards, as in relation to architectural styles. c. Edward VI, as in relation to reforms in the church. d. Edward VII, esp., in relation to literature during his reign (1901-10)."

12   The Third Edition editors, apparently having decided from their citations that senses a, b, and c, are not currently used except in contexts that made them completely self-explanatory, proceed to give the reader help where he needs it:

> **edwardian** . . . Of, relating to, or having the characteristics of the era of Edward VII of England (1901-10): as **a:** characterized by opulence and a complacent sense of material security **b:** marked by a socially analytical and critical frame of mind **c** *of clothing:* marked by the hourglass silhouette for women and the long narrow fitted suits for men that were popular during this period.

13   The following definitions of *detergent* illustrate the same kind of improvement:

> Second Edition:
> **detergent** . . . A cleansing agent, as water or soap; a medium to cleanse wounds, ulcers, etc.

> Third Edition:
> **detergent** . . . A cleansing agent: as **a:** soap **b:** an inorganic alkali, an alkaline salt (as a sodium phosphate or a sodium silicate), or a mixture of such compounds for use esp. in cleaning metals (as in dairy equipment) — called also *alkaline detergent* **c:** any of a large number of synthetic water-soluble or liquid organic surface-active agents for use in washing that resemble soaps in the ability to emulsify oils and hold dirt in suspension but differ in other respects (as in nonprecipitation of calcium and magnesium salts from hard

water and in chemical composition) ... d: an oil-soluble substance
that holds insoluble foreign matter in suspension and is used in
lubricating oils and dry-cleaning solvents.

14   For other instances of improved definitions, the reader may compare the Second Edition and Third Edition definitions of *melo-
drama, tragedy, effete,* and *plethora* (although if he reads on to
plethoric he may regret the loss of the domestic flavor of the Second
Edition's illustrative example: "a hamper grown *plethoric*"). A
random search will turn up countless additional examples.

15   It is in such matters of detail, whether they involve information
or ways of presenting it, that the achievements of the Third Edition should be measured. Whether one agrees that in all cases the
appropriate decision was made (maybe it would have been better
to enter those other senses of *Edwardian* after all; maybe it would
have been better to begin the entry with a capital letter instead
of labeling it *usu cap*), one must, I think, agree that a diligent
attempt was made to improve the quality of all definitions.

16   Of those who still object that such incidental gains in accuracy
and completeness are as nothing compared to the loss of an absolute authority, it must be asked whether we should be absolved
of having to make up our own minds about so important a matter
as the way in which we speak and write. In *American English in Its
Cultural Setting** Lloyd and Warfel counsel very well:

> Any influence that tries to set a book or a man up as an unquestionable
> authority is a hindrance to the full intellectual life; we ought to have
> such an ingrown alarm system to alert us as the scientist keeps always
> fully charged; his statements only hold for the evidence that has been
> observed. He leaves himself an out in case new evidence turns up. . . .

17   To those who are willing to find in it the information with which
to solve their language problems, not the solutions themselves, the
Third Edition has a good deal to offer.

---

*Alfred A. Knopf (New York, 1957), p. 467.

QUESTIONS FOR STUDY

1. Look up the terms *interested, uninterested,* and *disinterested* in *Webster's Third.* What is the probable reason (or reasons) the author titled his essay as he did?

2. How do the second and third editions differ? Have the editors of the third edition been false to linguistic principles? Explain.

3. How does the lexicographer's own conception of his function differ from the conception held by the general public? Can you offer any explanation of the general public's reaction to *Webster's Third?* How might you answer the negative criticism of *Webster's Third?*

4. Report on "Sabotage in Springfield" in *The Atlantic Monthly* (January, 1962) and on "The String Untuned" by Dwight McDonald in *The New Yorker* (March 10, 1962). Evaluate these criticisms of *Webster's Third* in the light of Battles' essay.

5. Those students who are interested in reading about the *Webster's Third* controversy at greater length should consult *Dictionaries and That Dictionary* by James Sledd (Scott, Foresman and Co.).

Those persons who were outraged at the editors of *Webster's Third* for being permissive in regard to English usage would, very likely, be somewhat upset after reading "Right vs. Wrong" by Robert A. Hall, Jr. The author — in a convincing, common-sense, and informal manner — presents the case for treating so-called "good English" as merely a prestige dialect used by certain dominant social classes. It is certainly an important dialect and very much worth learning.

Nevertheless, we all know that we have to vary our usage, depending on the social situation and the types of people we are speaking to. But in varying our usage, we still often feel vaguely uncomfortable. Somehow, we have sinned against linguistic purity. We have sacrificed our pure speech for mere communication.

After reading "Right Vs. Wrong," you should feel less inclined to do penance after saying "It is *me*" rather than "It is *I*." You might even feel a little more comfortable about your ability to handle the English language.

Right vs. Wrong

Robert A. Hall, Jr.

1 "How many of these frequent errors in English do YOU make?"
"Do YOU say KEW-pon for KOO-pon, ad-ver-TISE-ment for ad-VER-tise-ment, or AD-ult for ad-ULT?"
"Almost everybody makes these blunders in English: *between you and I, it's me, those kind of books.*"
"Even the greatest writers sin against the laws of grammar."

2 We have all seen advertisements in newspapers or magazines, with messages like those just quoted, implying to the reader "Shame on you if you are one of those who sin!" — and, of course, offering to teach him better. It is easy, on the one hand, to see that those who talk or advertise in this way and offer to cure our errors in pronunciation or grammar are simply appealing to our sense of insecurity with regard to our own speech. On the other hand, we must also admit that this sense of insecurity does exist, in almost all except those who are hardened against criticism and disapproval, and renders us easily susceptible to appeals of this kind. Our problem now is, to look at some of the ways in which we are supposed to be speaking wrongly, and to see whether there really exists a choice between "right" and "wrong", and, if so, what "right" and "wrong" consist of.

3 Our first approach may be made through very ordinary, everyday instances of "mistakes" like *I ain't, he don't, we seen him, you done it* or *hisn.* Most of us know that these are pretty widely condemned as "errors", when used instead of the corresponding *I am not* or *I'm not, he doesn't, we saw him, you did it, his.* But what is it that makes them "mistakes" or "errors"? If we drive through a traffic light, steal somebody's property, or kill someone, we know

From *Leave Your Language Alone,* Robert H. Hall, Jr., © 1960 by Doubleday & Company, Inc. Permission by author.

exactly what provides sanctions against these actions: the law of the land; and we know what will punish us if we disobey the law: the government. Is there any law of the land to set up rules about our speech, or any branch of the government that will enforce them? Obviously not. There are books that contain rules for speaking and writing, and there are people who will raise objections and criticise us if we fail to follow these rules; but those books and those people have no legal authority over us (outside of the rather special and limited situation in the schoolroom, where of course the teacher can give us a bad mark for not obeying the rules). Not only have they no legal authority, they have no authority whatsoever conferred on them by any power. Some countries, it is true, have had regulators of language with a kind of authority, such as the national Academies of France and Spain, which were set up by the king with the specific duty of "regulating and preserving the purity of the language". Even in those countries, very few people ever took the Academies' authority over language too seriously; but, technically speaking, their authority did exist in a way. But no such authority has ever existed in any English-speaking country, nor does it seem likely that speakers of English would ever be willing to accept the decrees of an Academy or similar institution, or of a Ministry of Education.

4   And yet, if we say *I ain't, you done it,* or *hisn,* we *are* likely to run into trouble. Trouble with whom? — with everybody? No. A foreigner using some completely abnormal turn of phrase, such as *this must we first do,* will confuse the ordinary speaker of English considerably, and will run no chance of finding anybody who would accept that as normal English. He would have trouble with everybody. But with *I ain't* and the like, some people would not be in the slightest upset; in fact, more than a few would find those "incorrect" forms more normal than the supposedly "correct" usage that they "ought" to be following themselves and insisting on in others. With some other people, however, our use of *he don't* and similar expressions may get us into more or less serious trouble. Our hearers may correct us on the spot, and tell us "Don't say *I ain't,* say *I'm not; not hisn,* but *his*"; or, even though they may not correct our usage then and there, they are nevertheless likely to hold it against us, and to allow it to determine their attitude toward us in one way or another. They may, perhaps, not consider us their social equals; they may not invite us to their home again; they may object to our marrying into their family; they may pick someone else, who says *I'm not* and *his,* to give a job or a promotion to; or some other form of unfavorable reaction

may result from our using a form or word which is the wrong one for the given situation.

5   Usually, we are told and we believe that "correctness" is a characteristic of educated, intelligent people, whereas "incorrectness" is the special quality of uneducated, ignorant, or stupid people. But notice that exactly the type of situation we described above, where someone arouses an unfavorable reaction because of his language, can arise from the use of "correct" speech where the hearer does not use that kind of speech, or has a prejudice or other objection against it. It can be just as much of a *faux pas* to say *I saw him*, where your hearer expects and wants *I seen him*, the other way around. One friend of mind found that, when he went to work in a Houston shipyard during the second World War, he was regarded as a snob for saying *those things* instead of *them things*, and he did not get full cooperation from his fellow-workers until he started to say *them things*. There are even some ways of speaking, some turns of expression, such as *am I not?*, which, no matter how "correct" they may be in theory, are just too artificial for almost any situation.

6   Notice also that the forms themselves are of equal worth as expressions of the ideas you are trying to communicate. *You done it* is just as good an expression of "doing" something, in past time, as *you did it*, and no present-day speaker of English will ever be confused as to what you mean. The same is true for *he don't* instead of *he doesn't*; for *we seen him* instead of *we saw him*; and for a host of others. In some cases, one might even argue that the "incorrect" form is actually somewhat preferable from the point of view of clarity or simplicity. The form *his*, in "correct" speech, is both an adjective (*his book*) and a pronoun (*that's his*); whereas the "incorrect" form *hisn* and the others parallel to it ending in *-n* (*hern, ourn, yourn, theirn*) are clearly marked, by their ending, as being possessive pronouns and nothing else. The argument runs similarly for *ain't*. To make the present-tense forms of the verb *be* negative, we must use, in "correct" speech, three different forms: *I'm not, he isn't, we (you, they) aren't;* whereas the "incorrect" *ain't* offers us one single form, exactly parallel to *can't, won't* or *don't*, and equally convenient. *He doesn't* instead of *he don't* is also an extra complication, seen to be needless when compared with *can't* or *won't*. We might make similar arguments in favor of other "incorrect" forms as well.

7   What is it, then, that makes some forms "incorrect" and others not? This is not a matter of legal or quasi-legal authority, as we have seen. It is not a matter of universal condemnation, nor yet

of incomprehensibility; in fact, some "incorrect" forms, as we have just pointed out, would be clearer or simpler than the corresponding "correct" forms. It all boils down, really, to a question of acceptability in certain classes of our society, in those classes which are socially dominant and which set the tone for others. Whether a form is accepted or rejected does not depend on its inherent merit nor yet on any official approval given it, but purely on whether its hearers like it or not — on whether they will react favorably or unfavorably towards a person they hear using it. "Correct" can only mean "socially acceptable", and apart from this has no meaning as applied to language.

8   The social acceptability, and hence "correctness", of any form or word is determined, not by reason or logic or merit, but solely by the hearer's emotional attitude towards it — and emotional attitudes naturally differ from person to person, from group to group, from social class to social class. Forms and words also change in social acceptability in the course of time: in the early seventeenth century, conservative speakers and purists objected violently to *ye* and *you*, used in speaking to one person, instead of the earlier *thou* and *thee*; and there must have been a time when *cows*, instead of the older plural *kine*, seemed an objectionable innovation.

9   Nevertheless, the difference in social acceptability between *I ain't* and *I am not*, between *hern* and *hers*, and so forth, is a real fact. If my child is likely to run into trouble later on for saying *I done it* or *hisn*, I will try to keep him from getting into the habit of using those forms which are actually not acceptable socially and which may cause others to react unfavorably towards him. But, if I am sensible about it, I will realize that the reason I want him to avoid these "incorrect" forms is not any inherent badness or evil character that they may have, but a purely practical consideration, that of their social acceptability. His choice of language will be used by others as a purely arbitrary means of classifying him socially among the sheep or the goats. All we need to do in the case of *I ain't*, etc., is to re-word the traditional instructions, and say that we avoid using such turns of speech, not because they are "bad" or "wrong" or "ungrammatical", but because they are socially unacceptable. Of course, as soon as people in any given group stop treating, say, *he don't* as socially unacceptable, it automatically becomes "correct".

10   There is a close parallel between acceptable usage in language and "correct" behavior in other social customs, such as personal

garb or table manners. What is it that makes it perfectly good
manners to eat some things, such as bread-and-jam, with the
fingers, and not others, like meat or vegetables? Certainly not the
decree of any official or self-appointed authority; and certainly not
any inherent feature or characteristic of what we eat or do not eat
with the fingers. Some things that we eat with our fingers are
much more messy than others that we would always take up with
knife and fork. Here again, it is social acceptability that determines
whether we may or may not eat a given item of food with our
fingers, or wear a four-in-hand tie with a tuxedo. This acceptability
varies from place to place, and from one period of time to another.
Thus, in England it is perfectly good manners to pile your peas
up on the back of your fork, using your knife as a pusher, and to
eat the peas from the back of the fork; but it is very much frowned
upon to keep changing the fork from the left hand to the right and
back again, as Americans normally do. And the permissibility of,
say, table behavior is constantly changing; for instance, I was
brought up always to eat bacon with knife and fork or in a
sandwich, whereas by now it has become much more widely
"correct" to eat it with the fingers.

11   For cases like those we have been discussing up to now, the
situation is clear: we will avoid forms like *I seen him, he don't*
because they are used as shibboleths, disregard of which may lead
to unfortunate results for us in our living and relations with others.
There are many instances, however, where reality and what we are
taught do not correspond as to the actual "correctness", the
actual acceptability, of what we are told to avoid. Take the case of
it's me. Grammarians tell us that a rule exists that "the verb *to be*
never takes a direct object", and that hence we must always say
it is I and never *it's me.* The rule itself is found in plenty of grammar books, but that is no guarantee of its accuracy or relevance;
in reality, this rule is meaningless as a statement of the facts of
English usage. It was taken over by English grammarians from
Latin grammar, where it is an accurate statement of the facts of
Latin usage: in Latin, you said *sum egō* "[it] am I", never *sum
mē* "[it] am me". The facts of actual acceptable usage in English
are quite different: we normally say, and have said for hundreds
of years, *it's me, it's us,* and so forth.

12   This is not merely an unsupported assertion on my part; statistical studies have been made which show *it's me* to be by far
the most frequent and normal usage in current English, as compared with *it is I.* Professor Charles C. Fries made a detailed study

of many such points that are often the objects of dispute and con-demnation, in his *American English Grammar*, by analyzing thou-sands of letters which had been written to the War Department by people of all levels of education and social standing. He found very clear documentary proof that many forms and many constructions that are often condemned are actually in perfectly good standing in the usage of educated persons, and hence by definition accept-able or "correct". He found, for instance, that it is normal to say *it's me, these kind of things, none of the children are here, every-body should take off their hat*, in standard English, and that there is no real difference in such respects between standard and vulgar speech. The story is told of a certain very puristic lady — let's call her Miss Fidditch — who was teaching her class very strictly to avoid *it's me:*

> Miss Fidditch: You must always say *it is I*. The inflexible rule of grammar is that the verb *to be* never takes a direct object.
> (A few minutes later:)
> Principal (outside the door, knocking): Who's there?
> Miss Fidditch: It's me — Miss Fidditch.

Miss Fidditch was right when she said *it's me*, naturally and norm-ally, in a give-and-take conversational situation and without reflect-ing; she was wrong when she tried to force on her class an artificial, unrealistic rule that applied to no one's, not even her own, usage in actual fact. And we all know the old story about the grammarian who said "Never use a preposition to end a sentence with."

13   We are often told that such-and-such a form or combination of forms is "in accordance with the rules of logic" which make other competing forms or combinations "illogical" and hence inadmis-sible. Such a rule as *"everyone* or *everybody* is singular and hence a word referring to it must be in the singular" is an instance of this, or the rule that "a double negative makes a positive" and that hence we mustn't say *I didn't see nobody* except when we really did see somebody. It is perfectly true that, in strictly ordered systems like mathematics or symbolic logic, a violation of the rules of discourse will introduce confusion and make a statement into its opposite or into something else from what was intended. The purists' error here lies in identifying language and logic, and expect-ing normal linguistic usage to be strictly logical. As a matter of fact, no language ever was strictly logical, nor can we make it so by preaching at its speakers. To begin with, we should have to

define what "logical" meant — and we would find that each different language would, from the outset, give its speakers different ideas as to what "logic" is. To us, for instance, it seems logical, and, in fact, inescapable to say *one book*, but *two books, three books, five books*, using the form *books* when we refer to more than one of them, and thus distinguishing between "one" and "more than one" or (to use the traditional grammatical terms) singular and plural. To someone brought up speaking Hungarian, that difference seems useful in general — a Hungarian will say *könyv* for "book" and *könyvek* for "books", with *-ek* indicating the plural for him just as *-s* does for us — but when he has a numeral to tell him how many books there are, he uses, not the plural, but the singular form of the word for "book". The Hungarian says *egy könyv* "one book", *két könyv* "two book", and likewise *három könyv* "three book", *öt könyv* "five book" and so forth. To him it seems silly, needless and illogical to say "five books" where the indication of plurality is already given by the number, so that "five book" will do just as well. Which is more logical, English or Hungarian, in this respect? One could argue both ways, and perhaps the Hungarian way of saying "two book, three book" might prove to be more strictly logical. It all depends on what you are brought up to say.

14   The same thing holds for such points as the "double negative", which many persons condemn violently — *I didn't see nobody* instead of *I didn't see anybody*. They tell us that "logically" a double negative makes a positive, and that therefore *I didn't see nobody* "really" means *I did see somebody*. Here again, our traditional grammar rule is based on Latin, as it is in so many other instances — as if the rules of Latin could be applied to English. In Latin, those who spoke it about the time of Caesar, Cicero and Augustus normally took a double negative to mean a positive. So for them, *non nihil* "not nothing" meant "something", and *non vidi neminem* "I didn't see nobody" could only have meant "I saw somebody". That was right, logical and natural *for them*, because that was the way they used Latin. But later, in the course of the centuries, those who spoke Latin and the Romance languages which developed out of Latin, got in the habit of using a double negative with *negative* meaning. In Spanish, for instance, it is downright incorrect (because nobody will accept it) to say such a thing as *ví a nadie* in the meaning of "I saw nobody". You *must* say *no ví a nadie*, literally "I didn't see nobody", with the two negatives *no* "not" and *nadie* "nobody", whenever *nadie* "nobody"

follows the verb; otherwise what you say is meaningless. It may be "illogical", and it may be "incorrect" from the point of view of Latin grammar; but in Spanish, French, and Italian, for instance, the requirement of a double negative is so absolute that no one would be able to get away with condemning it on the grounds of logic. The reason that the point can be raised at all in modern English is that we have a divided usage: in actual current speech, when there is no emphasis, a double negative and a single negative both have a negative meaning, and everybody will understand what we mean whether we say *I didn't see nobody* or *I saw nobody* or *I didn't see anybody*. But when we are putting emphasis on the verb or the pronoun, then *I DIDN'T see NObody* does have positive meaning, and would be normal as an answer, say, in contradiction to *You saw nobody*. The drift of our language is inevitably toward the use of the double negative; this is as normal and natural as anything else in English, and as logical in English as it is in Spanish and French.

15   Now with regard to this second group of "wrong" usages, the situation is essentially different from that of *ain't* and *hisn*. Such forms as *ain't* are both socially unacceptable and condemned by purists; whereas *it's me* and *those kind of things*, although grammarians may condemn them, are nevertheless in normal, everyday use by socially accepted people and hence are socially acceptable and by definition "correct". And when it comes to such pronunciations as KEW-pon, ad-ver-TISE-ment, AD-ult, the purists' condemnations are absolutely fanciful, without any rhyme or reason whatsoever. Both KEW-pon and KOO-pon, both ad-ver-TISE-ment and ad-VER-tise-ment, both AD-ult and ad-ULT are normal, regular, and acceptable variants; to call either member of these pairs "correct" and the other "incorrect" is quite arbitrary. Language is not an either-or proposition, in which no variation, no deviation from a strictly maintained party line is permissible; in many instances, such as those of *coupon* and *advertisement*, more than one alternative exists and both are equally acceptable or "correct".

16   Aside from these two types of "incorrectness" we have just discussed, there are other kinds of usage that are condemned, and (although this is not always realized) on somewhat different grounds. The largest group of forms of this sort are those which are under a social taboo of one kind or another. In our society, we tend to shy away from casual public discussion of certain topics,

particularly two: sexual reproduction and elimination of bodily waste; and we carry over our repugnance to terms which imply casual discussion of these subjects. This is of course a real repugnance with the classes of people who set the dominant tone of what is and what isn't acceptable in our society, and it establishes a taboo which absolutely *must* be observed on pain of very severe social sanctions: if you use the so-called "four-letter" or taboo words in mixed company in any except the lowest classes of society, you will immediately be subjected to extreme disapproval, condemnation and ostracism. But there are two things to be noticed about these taboos of decency, real as they are: 1) they are partial, and 2) they are relative, in that they are peculiar to our West European society.

17   On the first point, that these taboos are partial, note that I can use the terms *sexual reproduction* and *elimination of bodily waste*, as I did in the preceding paragraph, without fear of reproach or condemnation, although I would never wish or dare to use, in conversing, lecturing, or writing this book, the equivalent taboo words — words which most readers probably know as well as I do. It offends our sense of "decency" to discuss those subjects casually or to imply casual discussion of them; but it is acceptable to use more formal, learned terms that imply serious discussion on a scientific level. In the meanwhile, of course, the "four-letter" words go on in the normal, everyday usage of folk who are untroubled by social taboos, and are the only terms they know for the activities and body parts connected with sex and elimination. Many of us have doubtless heard the anecdote of the doctor who kept asking a constipated patient if he had *defecated,* and, always receiving the answer "No", kept prescribing more and more laxatives until he finally (and with considerable reluctance) used the taboo word, when he found out that his patient's intestines had nearly been ruined by the excessive purgation. The patient simply didn't know the fancy word *defecate,* and kept giving the answer "No", whereas he would have known and understood the "four-letter" word from the beginning. Which was more sensible — for the doctor to observe the taboo and ruin the patient's intestines, or to use the "four-letter" word at the start and get the result he was aiming at?

18   Such taboos, also, although certainly very real, are relative. Not all societies have the same taboos. Most societies do not have our feeling that sex and elimination are indecent; on the other hand, another society may taboo the mention of one's relatives, or of

dead people's names, or of certain game animals. With the Cree Indians, it is taboo to speak one's sister's name; the Cree will say that he "respects her too much", and he would feel as much repugnance towards mentioning her name as we would towards using a "four-letter" word. In some societies, especially in the islands of the Pacific, such taboos on one class of words or another have become very elaborate. We can imagine, for instance, a person from a society which tabooed the mention of one's relatives' names, as being highly shocked at such a comedy as *Charley's Aunt*, with its irreverent treatment of family relationships, whereas at the same time he might, without violating any of his society's taboos, sing his baby daughter a lullaby in which her sexual parts and their function were prominently mentioned. It would be extremely naive on our part to condemn such a person for not knowing the difference between decency and indecency: standards of decency, like other standards, are relative, not absolute, and no society can claim that its ideas of decency are right and all others wrong. So it is with our taboo words; they are condemned, it is true, and we would do extremely well to avoid using them in "decent" society; but the reason for avoiding them is, not that such words are inherently evil, but simply that they run counter to particular taboos of the dominant classes of our society.

19   Closely similar to the taboo on words that refer to sex and elimination is that on words that have a serious religious meaning, when they are used in any other connection: *Jesus, God, Christ, damn, hell* used as "swear-words". Here again, I can use any of these words in serious discussion: *Jesus Christ died to save us from damnation*, etc. But used frivolously, as in *Christ, am I tired!* or *Ouch! Damn it to hell!*, these words shock a great many of us. They used to shock still more people; in the 1880's, when Clarence Day Sr. was in the habit of saying *damn!* in the middle of the pastor's sermon and elsewhere, it was a serious breach of etiquette — and part of our amusement over his behavior in that respect comes from the difference in attitude between that day and this. Objectively speaking, *damn it!* is simply a succession of sounds that we use when we are angry, and even *damn you!* implies no desire on our part that the person or persons spoken to should literally roast in hell-fire for eternity, but simply that we're more or less irritated at them. The "badness" of swearwords of this kind comes from the fact that some people — people who are dominant in our society — are displeased by them and will act unfavorably towards people who use them.

20   Another objection that we often hear made against such a usage as *it's me* (instead of *it is I*) or *none of the boys are here* (instead of *none of the boys is here*) is that it is "ungrammatical" or that it does not "conform to the rules of grammar". The assumption involved here, whether we state it openly or not, is that there is such a thing as a body of rules, which are as fixed and unchangeable as the laws of the Medes and the Persians, which are called "grammar" and to which all language must conform or else be condemned as "ungrammatical". As a matter of fact, no such body of rules exists, or ever could exist. What passes for "grammar" in the usual textbook is really a conglomeration of rules, most of them taken from Latin grammars, some of them not, but often misstating the facts about English. We have already seen that the rule "the verb *to be* never takes a direct object" is a very good statement of the actual facts of Latin, but has no relation to the actual facts of English; and likewise for the double negative. Nor is there any reason why Latin should be taken as a model for all other languages, whether related or not. People used to think, and some still do, that Latin should be a universal model for language; the reason for this is that all during the Middle Ages in Western Europe, the language of learning and religion happened, through a historical accident, to be Latin. Educated people, just because they happened to get their education through Latin rather than through their native language, came to the conclusion that high intellectual activity and use of imitation of Latin were inseparable. We can easily see that such an idea was rather naive, and based on a false identification of two unrelated factors in the situation. Actually, Latin is just a language like any other, with its faults and shortcomings as well as its virtues, and its rules are far from being universally applicable. How would a speaker of Hungarian react to being told that he must say *három könyvek* "Three books" just because that is the way they say it in Latin or English or some other language?

21   Many other "grammar rules", although not derived from Latin grammar, are still quite inaccurate and unfounded: the best example of this is the "shall" and "will" rules that we are taught with regard to the future of English verbs. Most of us can never remember those rules, and are always uneasy about whether we are or are not making a mistake in their application: is it *I shall go* or *I will go, he should go* or *he would go*? We have been told that there is some difference in the meaning of each member of these pairs, that one of them indicates "determination" and the other "simple fu-

turity" — but which? As a matter of fact, there is no wonder that we can't remember — because such a distinction does not really exist: in normal speech we would usually say *I'll go, he'd go, we'll go.* Even with the full forms, there is no distinction in meaning, except the artificial distinction that we may have been taught to make. Where did the grammar books get this rule? A seventeenth-century English grammarian, one John Wallis, sitting in his study, dreamed the rule up, manufactured it out of whole cloth, and put it in his book; and later grammarians have copied and re-copied it, each from his predecessor. Its relation to the facts of the English language is completely null, and its origin classifies it among works of fiction rather than of science.

22   And even with rules that do state normal, current usage accurately — have they any authority beyond that of simple statements of fact? We have already seen that there is no legal sanction, not even any semi-legal academic backing, for any claim to "authority" in language and its use. Suppose that usage should change, and that what we now say universally (such as *he goes, she sings*) should go out of fashion and be replaced by some other usage which we now wouldn't accept (like *he go, she sing*). Would the old be "right" and the new be "wrong"? By no means; if people's habits and usage change, then there is no "authority", no law that can keep them from doing so, and the new is just as good as the old. Not necessarily better, of course: neither better nor worse, but just different. Some of us are inclined to think that because a habit, a custom, or a thing is old, it must necessarily be better than something new. This was the prevailing attitude all through ancient times and the Middle Ages, and has lasted even up to now in some matters like those of language; it is the only reason some grammarians have for preferring one usage to another.

23   Another norm that is often set up for deciding disputed points is the usage of great writers: do we find *it ain't, he don't* or split infinitives in great writers, men who must have had great knowledge of their own language in order to write their great books? First of all, though, we must ask *which* great writers — those of the present, or those of the past? Our choice is difficult here; if we go too far back, the literary language is obviously archaic, and nobody nowadays, not even the most conservative grammarian, would recommend every feature of Milton's or Dr. Johnson's prose for our modern usage. If we come too close to the present, it is hard to tell just who is a really great writer and who is not; and, even if we have our great writers picked out, we find that very often

they use freely the very forms we want to condemn, especially the more "realistic" writers like Steinbeck and Farrell. Then let's restrict our choice of great writers to, say, the late nineteenth and early twentieth century, so that they will fit what we want to prescribe. Even so, we find that their actual usage was considerably freer than we want to think. Hence the defensive accusations we often hear dogmatic purists make, that "even the greatest writers" make this, that or the other "mistake".

24   Furthermore, just how much bearing does great literature and its language have on normal everyday usage? That great literature gives us examples of the *artistic* use of language, we can easily grant; and that studying the way a Thomas Hardy or a Henry James has manipulated his language will be of use to us if we want to write literature — likewise granted. But such men as Hardy or James (to say nothing of authors like Carlyle or Meredith) are not typical, they are exceptional, in their language as in their content; and the very fact that they are exceptional disqualifies them as examples for everyday, normal, non-literary usage. Wouldn't it be nice if we all tried to talk like great literature in our daily contacts? It would be almost like trying to handle everyday affairs in the style of grand opera.

25   The entire attempt to set up absolute standards, rigid norms, for regulating people's language is destined to failure from the outset, because, as we have seen in this chapter, 1) there is no authority that has either the right or the ability to govern people's usage; and 2) such an authority, even when it has been set officially (as were the French and Spanish academies), can never find valid standards by which to govern usage. Logic, Latin grammar, the usage of literature, appeals to authority as such — none have any applicability. In our country, especially, attempts to prescribe rules, to set up a normative grammar, have been very widespread, and have battened on our insecurities, on our fears for our social standing in the face of linguistic shibboleths. But all such attempts have been, and will continue to be, failures.

26   Is there any definition at all that we can give for "good" language? Only, I think, something like this: "good" language is language which gets the desired effect with the least friction and difficulty for its user. That means, of course, that "good" language is going to vary with the situation it is used in. In elegant or puristically inclined society, "good" usage will include *it isn't he*, *he doesn't*, and also *this kind of people, it is I*, since those forms will get the best results in favor and compliance with what we

desire. In normal everyday situations with normal everyday people, *it isn't him, he don't, these kind of people, it's me* will be good usage, since ordinary people speak that way normally; and we won't be too worried about saying *damn!* unless our hearers have specific objections. With people who customarily say *it ain't him, he don't, we seen them, hisn,* those forms will be good usage, provided they serve to get results most effectively.

27   One type of confusion which often crops up at this point, and which we should be on our guard against, is that between language and style. We are often inclined to think that "correctness" is the same thing as good style, particularly in writing. Actually, the two are not the same, though the situation is parallel for both. "Good" style is simply that style of speaking or writing which is most effective under any given set of circumstances. When we speak of "good style", what we usually mean is clarity, absence of ambiguity, orderly structure, and the like — and these are, indeed, important in most situations. But they are not the same thing as type of language, and "good style" is possible in any dialect. Aesthetic considerations — whether a given way of expressing ourselves is pleasing or not to our listeners or readers — of course enter into the picture, too, with regard to "good" style. But all matters of aesthetics depend so much on individual preference, and differ so much not only from one language to another but from one speaker to another, that no one can presume to set up objective standards for them, nor legislate or make authoritative pronouncements on what is or is not pleasing to the ear or to the eye.

28   "Right" and "wrong", then, have no meaning, as applied to language, apart from the situations in which language is used. That is, by definition, we can never be wrong in our own language, when we use it as we have grown up speaking it, among our own family and friends. The ditch-digger who says *him and me ain't got none* and who uses swear-words and "four-letter" words freely is absolutely right — in his own language. His type of speech is not necessarily right for the language of other groups, just through the very fact that they speak differently. But when we condemn the ditch-digger's speech, we do so, not because of any inherent demerit of the way he talks, but because we take his speech as being characteristic of his social class. This factor in our speech attitudes is a relic from earlier, antidemocratic times, which accords very poorly with other aspects of our modern aspirations to true democracy.

29   When a person who has grown up using *him and me ain't got none* speaks in his normal, natural way and is told he is "wrong",

therefore, all that this really means is that he is using these forms in a situation where his usage would make things harder rather than easier for him. But most often — in fact, we can say usually — neither the person making the "error" nor the one criticizing him understands this. As a result, speakers who have not been brought up speaking "correctly" are made to feel inferior, and either have to make a strong (and often poorly guided) effort to change their habits of speech, or else take shelter behind defensive feelings of hostility, mockery, etc., towards the approved type of speech. Current prescriptions of "right" and "wrong" thus serve only to divide our society, and to increase further the split between upper and lower, favored and unfavored classes — just at the time when greater unity, not greater division, is our crying need.

30   In short: the entire structure of our notions about "correctness" and "right" vs. "wrong" in language is not only inaccurate, erroneous and useless; it is definitely harmful, and we would do well to outgrow it. When purists tell us that we are using "bad" or "incorrect" or "ungrammatical" language, they are simply telling us that what we say would not be acceptable in the upper social levels; sometimes they are right as to the facts of the case, and sometimes they are just talking through their hats. What our purists give us in the way of rules and laws to observe has no authority, no validity aside from their own preference, and is often based on specious pseudo-logic or on the structure of a distantly related language, Latin, which has no relevance to English. If an "error" or "mistake" is frequent, if almost everybody makes it, if it is found in even the greatest writers, then it is no error: as the great Byzantine emperor and law-codifier Justinian put it, *commūnis error facit iūs* — a mistake that everybody makes is no longer a mistake. We need to look at our language realistically, not feeling "inferior" about it and taking nobody's word as to its being "right" or "wrong". Often enough, we may find we need to change our usage, simply because social and financial success depends on some norm, and our speech is one of the things that will be used as a norm. In a situation like this, it is advisable to make the adjustment; but let's do so on the basis of the actual social acceptability of our speech, not because of the fanciful prescriptions of some normative grammarian or other pseudo-authority.

QUESTIONS FOR STUDY

1. According to the author, what makes some English forms correct and others not? Has the author overstated his case or not? Explain.

2. What determines social acceptability of any word or phrase? Illustrate from your own experience, both in class and out.

3. Why might it be a good idea to view "correctness" as a relative matter? What could happen if we do not?

4. Is there any danger at present that our American speech is becoming less democratic? Explain.

5. Why might it be useful to view class differences in speech in the same light as we do, say, the differences between the various Romance languages?

6. Why is it almost impossible to develop a useful standard of right and wrong in regard to language usage? Illustrate from your own experiences in various college classes.

7. Analyze Hall's argument that "the entire structure of our notions about 'correctness' and 'right vs. wrong' in language is ...inaccurate, erroneous and useless. . . ."

8. Why is it confusing to equate "language" with "style"?

A BEGINNING BIBLIOGRAPHY FOR READING ABOUT LANGUAGE

Articles

1. The files of *Elementary English* and *The English Journal*.
2. Articles chosen from the Bobbs-Merrill Reprint Series in Language and Linguistics. Write for free index to Bobbs-Merrill College Division, P.O. Box 558, Indianapolis, Indiana 46206.

Structural Grammar

1. Paul Roberts, *Patterns of English*. Harcourt, Brace & World, 1956.
2. W. Nelson Francis, *The Structure of American English*. Ronald Press, 1958.
3. Norman C. Stageberg, *An Introductory English Grammar*. Holt, Rinehart, & Winston, 1965.

Transformational Grammar

1. H.A. Gleason, Jr., *Linguistics and English Grammar*. Holt, Rinehart, & Winston, 1965.
2. Marshall L. Brown and Elmer White, *Introduction to Basic Sentences and Their Transforms*. Charles E. Merrill Books, Inc., 1966.
3. _____ , *Complex Transformations*. Charles E. Merrill Books, Inc., 1966.
4. Wayne A. O'Neil, *Kernels and Transformations: A Modern Grammar of English*. McGraw-Hill Book Company, 1965.
5. Paul Roberts, *English Sentences*. Harcourt, Brace & World, 1962.
6. _____, *English Syntax* (programmed). Harcourt, Brace & World, 1964.
7. Owen Thomas, *Transformational Grammar and the Teacher of English*. Holt, Rinehart, & Winston, 1965.

Anthologies of Readings

1. Harold B. Allen, *Reading in Applied Linguistics*. Appleton-Century, Croft, revised, 1964.
2. Wallace Anderson and Norman Stageberg, *Introductory Readings on Language*. Holt, Rinehart, & Winston, revised, 1966.

General Semantics

1. S.I. Hayakawa, *Language in Thought and Action*. Harcourt, Brace & World, 1963.

2. Louis B. Salomon, *Semantics and Common Sense*. Holt, Rinehart, & Winston, 1966.

3. Cleveland A. Thomas, *Language Power for Youth*. Appleton-Century, Crofts, 1955.

PART TWO

PART TWO

Rhetoric

Aristotle defined rhetoric as "the art of discovering all the possible means of persuasion on any subject whatsoever." Now this definition may appear to be rather sweeping, but in fact it implies certain limits beyond which rhetoric as independent study cannot go. For example, a knowledge of the techniques of persuasion will not supply any of the subject-matter information necessary for the close discussion of problems in a specific field such as science, politics or the arts. Without this information or with only a feeble grasp of it, the mastery of rhetoric alone would provide a hollow approach to any discussion; indeed, the term itself has quite undeservedly acquired the pejorative connotation of empty bombast. Let it be said then that rhetoric is not intended to train one as an expert in a particular discipline; what it can do is instill the habits of sound reasoning and clear expression and communication regardless of the discipline. In this unit we are restricting the definition even further to focus on written communication, though naturally many of the techniques described are pertinent to oral communication as well.

The student may wonder why the need for effective writing should concern him. It is unlikely he plans a career as a professional writer of any sort, and politics may seem equally remote from his own life. The college experience should soon dispel his notion that writing is not important to him, for the countless essay examinations, reports and papers required will make him painfully aware of the need to persuade readers of the logic and veracity of his thoughts on a variety of subjects. And it is a hard but inescapable fact that college is only the beginning of this need. Successful business and professional careers of all types demand an ability to communicate lucidly the ideas that of necessity originate from a broader knowledge of the subject. From the lowliest business correspondence to the most significant report on policy, this ability —or lack of it—marks the potential of the writer whose signature is found at the conclusion.

Happily, effective writing is a skill which can be learned. The rhetoric essays in this unit point out the means by which that skill is acquired. Following each is another essay which exemplifies a particular phase or element of rhetoric as used in practice. These selections, arbitrarily designated "content" essays, demonstrate how a writer can pragmatically apply rhetorical devices to persuade his reader to accept what he has to say. By reading these selections the student can see how a competent writer can mold and shape his ideas to present them to the best advantage. But it goes without saying that careful reading and analysis of other people's writing will not necessarily improve one's own; if it did, the process of learning to write would be immeasurably simplified. Consequently, the discussion questions and writing topics found at the end of each pair of essays have a threefold purpose: to insure understanding of the rhetorical principle at hand; to stimulate critical analysis of the use of that principle by a writer of recognized excellence; and, finally, to teach the novice to exercise the same discriminating use of the principle in his own work.

Rhetoric has never been easy to define, largely because of the imprecise and shifting meanings affixed to the word by individuals who use it in either a highly specialized or a grandly sweeping sense. In his essay "Rhetoric: Its Functions and Its Scopes," Donald Bryant limits his definition to, "the rationale of informative and suasory discourse," and he goes on to explain something of the history of the subject, its multifarious functions, and the areas in which it is a useful and workable means of discussing problems and arriving at decisions.

Part Two

Contents

Rhetoric and Idea

Introduction

Rhetoric: Its Function and Its Scope *Donald Bryant* 177

Organization:

Robert Penn Warren and
Organizing the Composition   *Cleanth Brooks* 212
Are Colleges Killing Education?   *Oscar Handlin* 224

Description:

Richard E. Hughes and
Description   *P. Albert Duhamel* 237
The Gray Beginnings   *Rachel Carson* 254

Definition:
Definition   *Leo Rockas* 268
Liberals and Conservatives   *Laurence Sears* 278

Comparison and Contrast:
Logical Order: Comparison
  and Contrast   *James W. Johnson* 292
The Crisis of American
  Masculinity   *Arthur Schlesinger* 302

175

Logic:
Persuasion by Logical
    Argument   *Newman and Genevieve Birk* 314
In Favor of Capital Punishment   *Jacques Barzun* 330

Analogy:
Analogy: This is Like That   *Manuel Bilsky* 344
Civilization on Trial   *Arnold J. Toynbee* 350

Rhetoric of the Sentence:
Rhetoric and Emphasis: Differences
    in Sentences   *John E. Jordan* 364
The Hard Kind of Patriotism   *Adlai E. Stevenson* 388

Style:
                    John Halverson and
Structure in Style   *Mason Cooley* 398
Why I Am not Going to
    the Moon   *Joseph Wood Krutch* 411

Rhetoric: Its Functions and Its Scope

Donald C. Bryant

1   When a certain not always ingenuous radio spokesman for one of our large industrial concerns some years ago sought to reassure his audience on the troublesome matter of propaganda, his comfort ran thus: Propaganda, after all, is only a word for anything one says for or against anything. Either everything, therefore, is propaganda, or nothing is propaganda; so why worry?

2   The more seriously I take this assignment from the Editor to reexplore for the *Quarterly Journal of Speech* (1953), the ground surveyed by Hudson and Wichelns thirty years ago, and since crossed and recrossed by many another, including myself,[1] the nearer I come to a position like our friend's conclusion on propaganda. When I remember Quintilian's *Institutes* at one extreme of time, and lose myself in Kenneth Burke's "new rhetoric" at the other, I am almost forced to the position that whatever we do or say or write, or even think, in explanation of anything, or in support, or in extenuation, or in despite of anything, evinces rhetorical symptoms. Hence, either everything worth mentioning is rhetorical, or nothing is; so let's talk about something encompassable — say logic, or semantics, or persuasion, or linguistics, or scientific method, or poetics, or social psychology, or advertising, or salesmanship, or public relations, or pedagogy, or politics, or psychiatry, or symbolics — or propaganda.

From *Quarterly Journal of Speech,* December, 1953. Reprinted with the permission of the Speech Association of America, and of the author.
[1]Hoyt H. Hudson, "The Field of Rhetoric," *OJSE,* IX (April, 1923), 167-180; Herbert A. Wichelns, "The Literary Criticism of Oratory," *Studies in Rhetoric and Public Speaking in Honor of James Albert Winans* (New York, 1925), pp. 181-216; Donald C. Bryant, "Some Problems of Scope and Method in Rhetorical Scholarship," *QJS,* XXIII (April, 1937), 182-188, and "Aspects of the Rhetorical Tradition," *QJS,* XXXVI (April and October, 1950), 169-176, 326-332.

3   But that is not the assignment Others have dealt with those subjects, and have given us such illuminating definitive essays as
"Speech as a Science" by Clarence Simon,[2] "The Spoken Word and
the Great Unsaid" by Wendell Johnson,[3] "General Semantics[1952]"
by Irving Lee,[4] and many other interpretive essays and *apologiae*
for the various branches of our curricula and for the multiform
captions in our departmental catalogues and organization charts.
Among these, "Rhetoric and Public Address" can hardly be thought
neglected over the years, at least in the *QJS* and *SM* [the *Quarterly
Journal of Speech* and *Speech Monographs*, eds.] But perhaps we
have assumed too quickly that rhetoric is now at last well understood. On the other hand, Hudson's "The Field of Rhetoric" may
be inaccessible or out of date, and Burke's "new rhetoric" too
cumbersome or recondite in statement, even after Marie Hoch-
muth's admirable exposition of it.[5] Even if all this be true, however,
one can hardly hope to clarify here what may remain obscure in
the work of thirty years — or twenty centuries; but in proper
humility, no doubt one can try. At least, common practice seems to
presume a restatement of most complex ideas about once in a
generation.

4   I shall not undertake to summarize Hudson's or Wichelns'
pioneer essays, relevant as they are to the central problem. They
and certain others like Hunt's "Plato and Aristotle on Rhetoric"[6]
are by now woven into the fabric of our scholarship. Nor shall I try
to duplicate the coverage of my two papers on "Aspects of the
Rhetorical Tradition." They can be easily reread by anyone
interested.

5   One further limitation upon the scope of this essay seems necessary: I shall not try to present a digest of rhetoric or even an
explanation of the main principles of rhetorical method. Those are
also easily available, from Aristotle's *Rhetoric* to the newest textbook in persuasion. Furthermore, I intend to discuss no particular
system of rhetoric, but the functions and scope which any system
will embrace.

CONFUSION IN MEANING OF "RHETORIC"

6   Very bothersome problems arise as soon as one attempts to define
rhetoric, problems that lead so quickly to hair-splitting on the one

---

[2]*QJS,* XXXVII (October, 1951), 281-298.
[3]*Ibid.* (December, 1951), 419-429.
[4]*QJS,* XXXVIII (February, 1952), 1-12.
[5]*Ibid.* (April, 1952), 133-144.
[6]*Studies . . . in Honor of James Albert Winans,* pp. 3-60.

hand or cosmic inclusiveness on the other, and to ethical or moral controversy, that the attempt usually ends in trifling with logomachies, gloss on Aristotle, or flat frustration. *Rhetoric* is a word in common parlance, as well as in technical use in the SAA and the Chicago school of literary critics. Hence we may presume it to have meanings which must be reckoned with, however vague, various, and disparate; for a word means what responsible users make it mean. Various as the meanings are, however, one occasionally encounters uses which seem little short of perverse, in persons who ought to know better. Not long since, a doctoral candidate in the classics, who had written as his dissertation a "rhetorical" analysis of one of St. Paul's sermons, was asked how Aristotle had defined rhetoric. Though the question, it would appear, was relevant, the candidate was unable to answer satisfactorily. Whereupon the questioner was taken firmly to task by one of his fellow examiners and was told that after all rhetoric could be adequately defined as a *way of saying something*. Now of course rhetoric may be so defined, as poetic may be defined, as a way of making something; but there is little intellectual profit in either definition.

7   Rhetoric also enjoys several other meanings which, though more common and less perverse, serve to make analysis of it difficult. In general these are the same meanings which Hudson reviewed thirty years ago: bombast; high-sounding words without content; oratorical falsification to hide meaning; sophistry; ornamentation and the study of figures of speech; most commonly among academic folk, Freshman English; and finally, least commonly of all, the whole art of spoken discourse, especially persuasive discourse. This last meaning has gained somewhat in currency in thirty years, especially among scholars in speech and renaissance literature.[7] During the same period the use of the term *rhetoric* (or the combinations *composition and rhetoric* and *grammar and rhetoric)* to label courses and textbooks in Freshman English has somewhat declined, and simultaneously the "rhetorical" content of them has declined also. The tendency now is to prefer just *Composition* or *English Composition*, or to resort to such loaded names as *Basic Writing, Effective Writing, Problems in Writing, Writing with a Purpose,* or *Communication and Analysis.*

---

[7]In his *The Ethics of Rhetoric* (Chicago: Henry Regnery, 1953), which has appeared since this article has been in proof, Richard M. Weaver of the College at the University of Chicago makes an interesting and useful effort to restore rhetoric to a central and respectable position among the arts of language and to assign it the function of giving effectiveness to truth.

8   In one of his early speeches, President Eisenhower declared that
we want action from the Russians, not rhetoric, as evidence of their
desire for peaceful settlement. Here is the common use of *rhetoric*
to mean empty language, or language used to deceive, without
honest intention behind it. Without question this use is in harmony
with the current climate of meaning where what our opponents say
is rhetoric, and what we say is something else. Hence our attempt
to define rhetoric leads almost at once into questions of morals and
ethics.

9   Rhetoric as figures of speech or artificial elegance of language is
also a healthy perennial, nurtured in literary scholarship and criticism as well as lay comment. Hence the second of the two meanings
of *rhetorical* in *Webster's New Collegiate Dictionary* is "emphasizing style, often at the expense of thought." Here we encounter a
second obscuring or limiting factor in our attempt at definition. We
are to describe rhetoric in terms of those *elements* of a verbal
composition for which it is to be held responsible. This mode of
procedure has always been attractive. It can produce interesting
and plausible conclusions, and it can be defended as schematically
satisfying and pedagogically convenient. Thus it proved in the
trivium of the middle ages and renaissance. If grammar has charge
of the correctness of discourse, and if logic has charge of the intellectual content, then it is natural to assign to rhetoric the management of the language of discourse (or the *elocutio*), and if we do
not include poetic in our system, the imaginative and emotional
content also.

10   Another definition in the *New Collegiate Dictionary* points to
the identification of rhetoric not with the elements of verbal composition but with the *forms* or *genres:* "The art of expressive speech
or of discourse, orig. of oratory, now esp. of literary composition;
esp., the art of writing well in prose, as disting. from versification
and elocution." This approach is promising and on the whole the
most popular through the ages. "Originally of oratory, now especially the art of writing well in prose—" this phrase does well enough
as a general description of the scope of rhetoric in ancient Greece,
as Baldwin has pointed out, when prose itself was virtually defined
as oratory and history, and when even history was composed largely
in the spirit of oratory. That is, rhetoric could be the art of prose
when prose was predominantly concerned with the intentional,
directional energizing of truth, of finding in any given situation all
the available means of persuasion, and of using as many of them as
good sense dictated.

11   Even then, however, the weakness of genres as the basis for constructing theories or writing handbooks was evident. What is the art of Plato's dialogues, which are in prose? or of Sappho's compositions, which are poems? Neither poetic nor rhetoric is adequate to either. The difficulty multiplies as variety in the kinds of compositions increases in Roman, renaissance, and modern times, and as print supplements — and often supplants — speech as the medium of verbal communication. As *poetic*, the art of imitation in language, became crystallized in Roman and renaissance learning as the theory and practice of the drama (especially tragedy) and the epic, so *rhetoric*, in Quintilian's and Cicero's theory the whole operative philosophy of civil leadership, showed in practice as the art of making winning speeches in the law courts, or later in public exhibitions. The very doctrine in rhetoric of the epideictic or ceremonial speech, as I shall show later, is excellent evidence of the weakness of the types or *genres* as the basis for definition.

12   All these meanings of rhetoric, in spite of their limitations, contribute something to the exposition of our subject, and the pursuit of each has yielded lucrative insights into the subject, or at least into the problem. Some of them, especially rhetoric as bombast, as excessive ornamentation, and as deceit, are evidence of the falling off of rhetoricians from time to time from the broad philosophy of the art which they inherited from the founders. For a redefinition, therefore, I know no better way of beginning than to return to that broad philosophy.

WORKING DEFINITION OF RHETORIC

13   First of all and primarily, therefore, I take rhetoric to be the *rationale of informative and suasory discourse*. All its other meanings are partial or morally-colored derivatives from that primary meaning. This rhetoric has been, at least since Aristotle; and at least since Aristotle there has existed a comprehensive, fundamental codification of its principles. It would be idolatrous to suggest that Aristotle uttered the first and last authentic words on rhetoric, or that his system is still adequate, or that it was completely satisfactory even for the Greeks of his day. Like his poetic theory, however, it enjoys unequalled scientific eminence in its field though it has sustained many additions and modifications through the centuries. Its limitations are historical rather than philosophical. Like the limitations of his poetic, the limitations of his rhetoric derive mainly from his failure to consider phenomena which had not

yet occurred and to make use of learnings which had not yet been developed.

14   Now as then, therefore, what Aristotle said of the nature and principles of public address, of the discovery of all the available means of persuasion in any given case, must stand as the broad background for any sensible rhetorical system. Much of Aristotle's formulation, even in detail, survives ungainsaid and can only be rearranged and paraphrased by subsequent writers. Again to cite a parallel with his poetic: though the relative importance of plot in drama has shifted radically since Aristotle, when good plots are made their excellences will still be best discovered by the application of Aristotle's criteria. Similarly, though modern psychology is very different from that of the Greeks, and doubtless more scientific, modern enlightenment has produced no new method of analyzing an audience which can replace Aristotle's.

15   Aristotle, however, identified rhetoric with persuasion. His chief interests lay in the speaking to popular audiences in the law court and in the legislative assembly, and his system of classification and analysis obviously was framed with those types of speaking as its principal object. Some means of persuasion, however, in spite of Aristotle's comprehensive definition, are not within the scope of rhetoric. Gold and guns, for example, are certainly persuasive, and the basic motives which make them persuasive, profit and self-preservation, may enter the field of rhetoric; but applied directly to the persons to be persuaded, guns and gold belong to commerce or coercion, not to rhetoric.

16   No more shall we admit the persuasive use of all symbols as belonging to rhetoric. Undoubtedly the persuasive force of pictures, colors, designs, non-language sounds such as fog horns and fire alarms, and all such devices of symbolic significance is great and useful. Traffic lights, however, are not normally agents of rhetorical influence. No more, in themselves, are elephants, donkeys, lions, illuminated bottles of whiskey, or animated packs of cigarettes. Their use has a kinship to rhetoric, and when they are organized in a matrix of verbal discourse, they become what Aristotle called the extrinsic or non-artistic means of persuasion. They are instruments of the wielder of public opinion, and they are staples of two techniques which must be recognized as strongly rhetorical — advertising and propaganda. Unless we are to claim practically all interhuman activity as the field of rhetoric, however, some limits must be admitted, even within the field of persuasion. True, in the "new rhetoric" of Kenneth Burke, where the utmost extension

rather than practical limit-setting is the aim, any manifestation of "identification," conscious or unconscious, is within rhetoric. Though the classic limitations of rhetoric are too narrow, others are too broad. Therefore I am assuming the traditional limitation to discourse.

17   Let us look now at Aristotle's apparent failure to include exposition as well as persuasion within rhetoric. Ancillary to persuasion, of course, exposition is clearly included. The idea of *demonstration*, the characteristic result of the logical mode, implies the most perfect exposition for audiences susceptible of reasoned instruction. Furthermore, another aspect of Aristotle's system admits exposition to independent status. At the expense of a slight venture into heresy (though I believe only a benign heresy) I suggest that any systematic construction of human phenomena, even Aristotle's, will either leave out something important and significant, or will include a category, however named, which is, in effect, "miscellaneous." That I think Aristotle did in discussing the rhetoric of the ceremonial or epideictic speech. The success of his categories, even so, is remarkable. The extension and effective application to the ceremonial speech in general of the principles of the persuasive speech whose end is active decision, provide very plausible coverage of that somewhat anomalous form. The three-fold, tripartite classification of speeches was too nearly perfect to abandon:

Forensic (time, past; ends, justice and injustice; means, accusation and defense.)

Epideictic (time, present; ends, honor and dishonor; means, praise and blame.)

Deliberative (time, future; ends, the expedient and inexpedient; means, exhortation and dehortation.)

When the problems of what to do with time-present in the system, and with Pericles' funeral oration among the observed phenomena had to be solved, the coincidence was too attractive to be resisted. It provided for a piece of practical realism which no system should be allowed to defeat. Through that adjustment Aristotle admitted within the scope of rhetoric the predominantly literary performance on the one hand and gave an opening on the other for the primarily informative and instructional as well as the demonstrative and exhibitionistic. Through this third category rhetoric embraces, in a persuasion-centered system, the *docere* and *delectare*, the teach and delight, of the Roman and renaissance rhetoric-poetic and permits them an independent status outside their strictly ancillary or instrumental functions in persuasion.

18   Aristotle's system, therefore, and his rationale of effective speaking comprehend with very little violence the art of the good man skilled in speaking of Cicero and Quintilian, or Baldwin's equation of rhetoric to the art of prose whose end is giving effectiveness to truth[8] — effectiveness considered in terms of what happens to an audience, usually a popular or lay audience as distinguished from the specialized or technical audience of the scientific or dialectical demonstration. This distinction, strictly speaking, is a practical rather than a logical limitation, a limitation of degree rather than kind. No matter what the audience, when the speaker evinces skill in getting into their minds, he evinces rhetorical skill.

19   If the breadth of scope which I have assigned to rhetoric is implicit in Aristotle's system, the basic delimitation of that scope finds early and explicit statement there. Rhetoric is not confined in application to any specific subjects which are exclusively its own. Rhetoric is method, not subject. But if it has no special subjects, neither are all subjects within its province. In its suasory phase, at least, rhetoric is concerned, said Aristotle, only with those questions about which men dispute, that is, with the contingent — that which is dependent in part upon factors which cannot be known for certain, that which can be otherwise. Men do not dispute about what is known or certainly knowable by them. Hence the characteristic concern of rhetoric is broadly with questions of justice and injustice, of the expedient and the inexpedient (of the desirable and undesirable, of the good and the bad), of praise and blame, or honor and dishonor.

20   To questions such as these and their almost infinite subsidiary questions, vital and perennial as they are in the practical operation of human society, the best answers can never be certain but only more or less probable. In reasoning about them, men at best must usually proceed from probable premise to probable conclusion, seldom from universal to universal. Hence Aristotle described the basic instrument of rhetoric, the enthymeme, as a kind of syllogism based on probabilities and signs.

21   Rhetoric, therefore, is distinguished from the other instrumental studies in its preoccupation with informed opinion rather than with scientific demonstration. It is the counterpart, said Aristotle, of dialectic. Strictly speaking, dialectic also may be said to attain only probability, not scientific certainty, like physics (and, perhaps, theology). The methodology, however, is the methodology of formal

---

[8]*Ancient Rhetoric and Poetic* (New York, 1924), p. 5.

logic and it deals in universals. Hence it arrives at a very high degree of probability, for it admits the debatable only in the assumption of its premises. Rhetoric, however, because it normally deals with matters of uncertainty for the benefit of popular audiences, must admit probability not only in its premises but in its method also. This is the ground upon which Plato first, and hundreds of critics since, have attacked rhetoric — that it deals with opinion rather than knowledge. This is the ground also from which certain scholars have argued,[9] after some of the mediaeval fathers, that rhetoric really deals, characteristically, not with genuine probability but only with adumbration and suggestion. It is, they say, distinguished from dialectic in *degree* of probability — dialectic very high, and rhetoric very low.

22   The epistemological question is interesting, and in a world of philosophers where only certain knowledge was ever called upon to decide questions of human behavior, it would be the central question. Rhetoric exists, however, because a world of certainty is not the world of human affairs. It exists because the world of human affairs is a world where there must be an alternative to certain knowledge on the one hand and pure chance or whimsey on the other. The alternative is informed opinion, the nearest approach to knowledge which the circumstances of decision in any given case will permit. The art, or science, or method whose realm this is, is rhetoric. Rhetoric, therefore, is the method, the strategy, the organon of the principles for deciding best the undecidable questions, for arriving at solutions of the unsolvable problems, for instituting method in those vital phases of human activity where no method is inherent in the total subject-matter of decision. The resolving of such problems is the province of the "Good man skilled in speaking." It always has been, and it is still. Of that there can be little question. And the comprehensive rationale of the functioning of that good man so far as he is skilled in speaking, so far as he is a wielder of public opinion, is rhetoric.

THE PROBLEMS OF VOCABULARY IN THIS ESSAY

23   Traditionally *rhetoric* and *oratory* have been the standard terms for the theory and the product. The *rhetor* was the speaker, the addresser of the public, or the teacher of speaking; the *rhetorician*,

---

[9]For example, Craig La Drière, "Rhetoric as 'Merely Verbal' Art," *English Institute Essays—1948,* ed. by D. A. Robertson, Jr. (New York, 1949), pp. 123-152.

the teacher of rhetoric or the formulator of the principles of rhetoric. Hence the special bias of the terms as I use them has been and probably still is oral. That is a practical bias and is not carelessly to be thrown away. From the beginning of publication in writing, however, essentially rhetorical performances, whether already spoken or to be spoken, have been committed to paper and circulated to be read rather than heard — from Isocrates' *Panathenaicus* or Christ's *Sermon on the Mount* to Eisenhower's message on the state of the nation. Furthermore, for centuries now, especially since the invention and cheapening of the art of printing, the agitator, the teacher, the preacher, the wielder of public opinion has used the press quite independently of the platform. Hence, obviously, rhetoric must be understood to be the rationale of informative and suasory discourse both spoken and written: of Milton's *Aeropagitica* as well as Cromwell's Address to the Rump Parliament; of John Wilkes' *North Briton* as well as Chatham's speech on the repeal of the Stamp Act; of Tom Paine's *Common Sense* as much as Patrick Henry's Address to the Virginia Assembly; of Swift's pamphlet on the *Conduct of the Allies* as well as Dr. Sacheverell's sermon on Passive Obedience; of George Sokolsky's syndicated columns in the press equally with Edward R. Murrow's radio commentaries or Kenneth McFarland's appearances before conventions of the Chambers of Commerce. I will use *rhetoric* and *rhetorical* with that breadth of scope.

24   Furthermore, the terms *orator* and *oratory* have taken on, like *rhetoric* itself, rather limited or distorted meanings, not entirely undeserved perhaps, which make them no longer suitable for the designation of even the normal *oral* rhetorical performance. *Practitioner of public address*, or some such hyphenated monstrosity as *speaker-writer*, might be used as a generic term for the product of rhetoric, but the disadvantages of such manipulations of vocabulary are obvious. I am using the terms *speech* and *speaker* for both written and oral performance and written and oral performer, unless the particular circumstances obviously imply one or the other. Likewise, in place of such a formula as *listener-reader*, I shall use *audience*, a usage not uncommon anyway.

25   One must face still another problem of vocabulary, that of the term *rhetoric* in the three distinguishable senses in which I use it: (1) as the rationale of informative and suasory discourse, a body of principle and precept for the creation and analysis of speeches; (2) as a quality which characterizes that kind of discourse and distinguishes it from other kinds; (3) as a study of the phenomenon

of informative and suasory discourse in the social context. Similarly, I fear, the term *rhetorician* will sometimes mean the formulator and philosopher of rhetorical theory; sometimes the teacher of the technique of discourse; sometimes the speaker with rhetorical intention; and finally the student or scholar whose concern is the literary or social or behavioral study of rhetoric. I have been tempted to invent terms to avoid certain of these ambiguities, such as *logology*, or even *rhetoristic* (parallel with *sophistic*), but the game would probably not be worth the candle.

26   In summary, rhetoric is the rationale of informative and suasory discourse, it operates chiefly in the areas of the contingent, its aim is the attainment of maximum probability as a basis for public decision, it is the organizing and animating principle of all subject-matters which have a relevant bearing on that decision. Now let us turn to the question of the subject-matters in which rhetoric most characteristically functions and of the relations it bears to special subject-matters.

SUBJECTS OF RHETORICAL DISCOURSE

27   Wrote Aristotle, "The most important subjects of general deliberation . . . are practically five, viz. finance, war and peace, the defense of the country, imports and exports, and legislation." This is still the basic list, though legislation now would be far more generally inclusive than it was to the Athenian assembly. In addition, within the scope of rhetorical discourse fall the subjects of forensic address — crime and its punishment and all the concerns of justice and injustice. Furthermore, the concerns of teaching, preaching — moral, intellectual, practical, and spiritual instruction and exhortation — and commercial exploitation, wherever the problems of adaptation of idea and information to the group mind are concerned, depend upon rhetorical skill for their fruition. Thus we are brought again to the position that the rhetorical factor is pervasive in the operative aspects of society.

28   Does this mean that the speaker must be a specialist in all subjects, as well as in rhetorical method? Cicero seemed willing to carry the demands thus far, at least in establishing his ideal orator; and this implication has been ridiculed from Plato onwards for the purpose of discrediting first the claims of the sophists and then all men "skilled in speaking." Plainly, in practice and in plausible human situations, the suggestion is absurd. Does the public speaker or the columnist or the agitator have to be a military

specialist in order rightly to urge peace or war? Does the citizen have to be a dentist and a chemist and a pathologist intelligently to advocate the use of fluorine in the municipal water supply? He does not become a specialist in these fields, of course, any more than the head of an industrial plant is the technical master of the specialties of all the men who serve under him. "He attempts to learn the authorities and sources of information in each, and to develop a method which he can apply to specific problems as they arise. He learns, in any given situation, what questions to ask and to answer. The peculiar contribution of the rhetorician is the discovery and use, to the common good, of those things which move men to [understanding and] action."[10] Looked at another way, the relation of rhetoric to the subject-matters of economics, or public health, or theology, or chemistry, or agriculture is like the relation of hydraulic engineering to water, under the specific circumstances in which the engineer is to construct his dam or his pumping station or his sewage system, and in view of the specific results he is to obtain. He develops a method for determining what questions to ask and answer from all that which can be known about water. If he is a good hydraulics engineer, he will see to it that his relevant knowledge is sound, as the good speaker will see to it that his relevant knowledge of hydraulic engineering is the best obtainable if he is to urge or oppose the building of a dam in the St. Lawrence River. If either is ignorant, or careless, or dishonest, he is culpable as a man and as a rhetorician or hydraulics engineer.

29   It was not the scientific chronologist, the astronomer Lord Macclesfield, who secured the adoption in England of the Gregorian calendar, thoroughly as he understood the subject in all its mathematical, astronomical, and chronometrical aspects. It was the Earl of Chesterfield, learning from the chronologist all that was essential to the particular situation, and knowing rhetoric and the British Parliament, who was able to impress upon his fellows not necessarily the validity of the calculations but the desirability and the feasibility of making a change. If the truth of scientific knowledge had been left to its own inherent force with Parliament, we would doubtless be many more days out of phase with the sun than England was in 1751. As Aristotle observed in his brief and basic justification of rhetoric, truth itself has a tendency to prevail over error; but in competition with error, where skillful men have an interest in making error prevail, truth needs the help of as attrac-

---

[10]Hudson, "Field of Rhetoric," *QJSE*, IX (April, 1923), 177.

tive and revealing a setting as possible. In the Kingdom of Heaven, truth may be its own sole advocate, but it needs mighty help if it is to survive in health among the nations on earth. As Fielding wrote of prudence in *Tom Jones:* "It is not enough that your designs, nay, that your actions, are intrinsically good; you must take care that they shall appear so. If your inside be never so beautiful, you must preserve a fair outside also. This must be constantly looked to."[11]

30   In this sense even honest rhetoric is fundamentally concerned with appearances, not to the disregard of realities as Plato and his successors have industriously charged, but to the enforcement of realities. Rhetoric at the command of honest men strives that what is desirable shall appear desirable, that what is vicious shall appear vicious. It intends that the true or probably true shall seem so, that the false or doubtful shall be vividly realized for what it is. A bridge or an automobile or a clothes-line must not only *be* strong but must *appear* to be so. This fact has been an obstacle to the use of many new structural materials. Accustomed to an older kind, we have been reluctant to accept the adequacy of a new, more fragile-seeming substance. Hence one important reason for surrounding steel columns with stone pillars is the necessity of making them seem as strong as their predecessors. Appearances, then, must be the concern of the wielder of public opinion, the rhetorician. Through ignorance or malice, to be sure, skill in establishing appearances may be applied to deceive. This is a grave peril which must be the concern of all men of good will. Knowledge of the devices of sophistry will always be acquired by those whose purposes are bad; ignorance of them will provide no defense for the rest. No great force can be used without hazard, or ignored without hazard. The force understood, rather than the force not understood, is likely to be the force controlled. That understanding is provided by rhetoric, the technique of discourse addressed to the enlightenment and persuasion of the generality of mankind—the basic instrument for the creation of informed public opinion and the consequent expedient public action.

OCCASIONS OF RHETORICAL DISCOURSE

31   Whether we will or no, we cannot escape rhetoric, either the doing or the being done to. We require it. As Edmund Burke wrote, "Men want reasons to reconcile their minds to what is done, as

---

[11]Book III, Chapter 7. Modern Library Ed., p. 97.

well as motives originally to act right."[12] Whether we seek advice
or give it, the nature of our talk, as being "addressed," and of the
talk of which we are the audience, as being addressed to us, neces-
sitates speaking the language of the audience or we had as well
not speak at all. That process is the core of rhetoric. It goes on
as genuinely, and is often managed as skillfully, over the frozen-
meats counter of the local supermarket as in the halls of Congress;
on the benches in front of the Boone County Court House on
Saturday afternoon before election as below the benches of the
Supreme Court the next Wednesday morning; around the table
where a new labor contract is being negotiated as in the pulpit
of Sainte-Marie de Chaillot where Bossuet is pronouncing the
funeral oration upon Henriette d'Angleterre; in the Petition from
Yorkshire to King George III for redress of grievances as in the
Communist Manifesto or the Declaration of Independence.

32   As we are teachers, and as we are taught, we are involved with
rhetoric. The success of the venture depends on a deliberate or
instinctive adjustment of idea-through-speaker-to-audience-in-a-
particular-situation. Pedagogy is the rhetoric of teaching, whether
formally in the classroom or the book, or informally in the many
incidental situations of our days and nights. The psychological
principle, for example, that we learn through association becomes
a rhetorical principle when we use it to connect one day's lesson
with what has gone before. It is the same principle by which
Burke attempted to establish in the minds of the House of Com-
mons the rights of American colonists when he identified the
colonists with Englishmen, whose rights were known.

33   As we are readers of newspapers and magazines and all such
information-giving and opinion-forming publications, and as we
write for them, we are receiving or initiating rhetorical discourse,
bad or good, effective or ineffective. The obligations of the journalist as investigator of the facts, as thinker about the facts, as discoverer of ideas and analyst and critic of ideas, are fundamental.
They demand all the knowledge and skill that the political, scientific, and technical studies can provide. The journalist's distinctive
job, however, is writing for his audience the highest grade of informative and suasory discourse that the conditions of his medium
will permit. Whether editorial writer, commentator, or plain news-
writer, reaching into his audience's mind is his problem. If the
people who buy the paper miss the import, the paper might as well
not be published. Call it *journalism* if you choose; it is the rhetoric

---

[12]*Correspondence* (1844), I, 217.

of the press: "it is always public opinion that the press seeks to change, one way or another, directly or indirectly."[13] Seldom can the journalist wait for the solution of a problem before getting into the fray, whether the question be a more efficient way of handling municipal finances or independence for India. He must know the right questions to ask and the bases for answering them with greatest probability for his audience now. That is his rhetorical knowledge.

34   The same is true of the radio and television news reporter, news analyst, and commentator. He must have rhetorical skill to survive in his occupation, and he must have knowledge and integrity if his effect is to be beneficial rather than destructive to informed public opinion. His staple, also, whether good or bad, is rhetoric. His efforts are aimed at the public mind and are significant only as they affect the public mind. If he is an honest rhetorician, he does not imply of most things, "It is so because," but only "I believe so because"; or "I recommend so because it seems probable where I cannot be sure." If he is tempted into exploiting the force of extravagant and authoritative assertion, his morals rather than his rhetoric have gone awry. Whether the use be honest or dishonest, the instrument is rhetoric.

35   It is obvious and commonplace that the agitator, the political speaker, the pamphleteer, the advocate, the preacher, the polemicist and apologist, the adviser of kings and princes, the teacher of statesmen, the reformer and counter-reformer, the fanatic in religion, diet, or economics, the mountebank and messiah, have enhanced the stature of a noble discourse or have exploited a degraded, shallow, and dishonest discourse. It matters not that we resort to exalted names for the one—eloquence, genius, philosophy, logic, discourse of reason; and for the other, labels of reproach and contempt—sophistry, glibness, demagoguery, chicanery, "rhetoric." That naming process itself is one of the most familiar techniques of rhetoric. The fact is that in their characteristic preoccupation with manipulating the public mind, they are one. They must not all be approved or emulated, but they must all be studied as highly significant social phenomena, lest we be ignorant of them, and hence powerless before them, for good or for ill.

36   Similarly, though perhaps not so easily acceptable into rhetoric, we must recognize most of what we know as advertising, salesmanship, propaganda, "public relations," and commercial, political,

---

[13]*The Press and Society: A Book of Readings,* ed. by George L. Bird and Frederic E. Merwin (New York, 1951), preface, p. iv.

and national "information" services. I shall have some special consideration to give to these later. At present I merely cite them as great users of rhetoric. In this day of press, radio, and television perhaps their rhetoric is that most continuously and ubiquitously at work on the public.

RELATIONS OF RHETORIC TO OTHER LEARNINGS

37   These, then, are fundamental rhetorical situations. In them human beings are so organizing language as to effect a change in the knowledge, the understanding, the ideas, the attitudes, or the behavior of other human beings. Furthermore, they are so organizing that language as to make the change as agreeable, as easy, as active, and as secure as possible—as the Roman rhetoric had it, to teach, to delight, and to move (or to bend). What makes a situation rhetorical is the focus upon accomplishing something predetermined and directional with an audience. To that end many knowledges and sciences, concerning both what is external to audiences and what applies to audiences themselves, may be involved, many of which I have discussed in a previous essay.[14] These knowledges, however, have to be organized, managed, given places in strategy and tactics, set into coordinated and harmonious movement towards the listener as the end, towards what happens to him and in him. In short, they have to be *put to use*, for, as Bacon said, studies themselves "teach not their own use; but that is a wisdom without them, and above them, won by observation." "Studies themselves do give forth directions too much at large, except they be bounded in by experience."[15] Rhetoric teaches their use towards a particular end. It is that "observation," that "experience" codified, given a rationale. Other learnings are chiefly concerned with the discovery of ideas and phenomena and of their relations to each other within more or less homogeneous and closed systems. Rhetoric is primarily concerned with the relations of ideas to the thoughts, feelings, motives, and behavior of men. Rhetoric as distinct from the learnings which it uses is dynamic; it is concerned with movement. It *does* rather than *is*. It is method rather than matter. It is chiefly involved with bringing about a condition, rather than discovering or testing a condition. Even psychology, which is more nearly the special province of rhetoric

---

[14]"Aspects of the Rhetorical Tradition" (1950), see above, note 1.
[15]"Of Studies."

than is any other study, is descriptive of conditions, but not of the uses of those conditions.

38   So far as it is method, rhetoric is like the established procedures of experimental science and like logic. As the method for solving problems of human action in the areas of the contingent and the probable, however, it does not enjoy a privilege which is at the same time the great virtue and the great limitation of science and logic—it cannot choose its problems in accordance with the current capacities of its method, or defer them until method is equal to the task. Rhetoric will postpone decision as long as feasible; indeed one of its most valuable uses in the hands of good men, is to prevent hasty and premature formulation of lines of conduct and decision. In this it is one with science—and good sense. But in human affairs, where the whole is usually greater than the most complete collection of the parts, decisions—makings up of the mind—cannot always wait until all the contingencies have been removed and solutions to problems have been tested in advance. Rhetoric, therefore, must take undemonstrable problems and do its best with them when decision is required. We must decide when the blockade is imposed whether to withdraw from Berlin or to undertake the air lift, not some time later when perhaps some of the contingencies may have been removed. And the making of the choice forever precludes trying out and testing the other possibilities under the circumstances which would have prevailed had we chosen differently at first. Likewise we must make a choice on the first Tuesday in November, whether we are scientifically sure or not. In each case, rhetoric, good or bad, must be the strategy of enlightening opinion for that choice.

39   To restate our central idea still another way: rhetoric, or the rhetorical, is the function in human affairs which governs and gives direction to that creative activity, that process of critical analysis, that branch of learning, which address themselves to the whole phenomenon of the designed use of language for the promulgation of information, ideas, and attitudes. Though it is instrumental in the discovery of ideas and information, its characteristic function is the publication, the publicizing, the humanizing, the animating of them for a realized and usually specific audience. At its best it seeks the "energizing of truth," in order to make "reason and the will of God prevail." But except in science, and no doubt theology, the promulgation of *truth*, sure or demonstrable, is out of the question. Normally the rhetorical function serves as high a degree of probability as the combination

of subject, audience, speaker, and occasion admits. Rhetoric may or may not be involved (though the speaker-writer must be) in the determination of the validity of the ideas being promulgated. Such determination will be the province in any given situation of philosophy, ethics, physics, economics, politics, eugenics, medicine, hydraulics, or bucolics. To rhetoric, however, and to no other rationale, belongs the efficiency—the validity if you will—of the relations in the idea-audience-speaker situation.

FUNCTIONING OF RHETORIC

40   We are ready now, perhaps, if we have not been ready much sooner, to proceed to the question of how rhetoric works, what it accomplishes in an audience. Speaking generally, we may say that the rhetorical function is the *function of adjusting ideas to people and people to ideas.* This process may be thought of as a continuum from the complete modification or accommodation of ideas to audiences (as is sometimes said, "telling people only what they want to hear") at the one extreme, to complete regeneration at the other (such perfect illumination that the "facts speak for themselves"). This continuum may, therefore, be said to have complete flattery (to use Plato's unflattering epithet) at one end and the Kingdom of Heaven at the other! Good rhetoric usually functions somewhere well in from the extremes. There, difficult and strange ideas have to be modified without being distorted or invalidated; and audiences have to be prepared through the mitigation of their prejudices, ignorance, and irrelevant sets of mind without being dispossessed of their judgments. The adjustment of ideas to people, for example, was being undertaken by the Earl of Chatham in his speech for the repeal of the Stamp Act, when he agreed that Parliament had legislative supremacy over the Colonies but that legislative supremacy did not include the right to tax without representation. And when Booker T. Washington assured the Southern white folk that they and the Negroes could be as separate as the fingers in social affairs and as united as the hand in economic, he was adjusting people to the idea of real freedom for his race.

41   The moral disturbances which rhetoric and rhetorical activity seem to breed do not usually result from this process of mutual accommodation itself. Most of them arise when the speaker tries so to adjust ideas to people that the ideas are basically falsified, or when he attempts so to adjust people to ideas as to deform or

anesthetize the people. Report has it that after Senator Hiram Johnson had campaigned through rural New England charging that England would have three votes to one for the United States in the League of Nations, he was taxed by a critic with misrepresenting the nature of the British Empire. One could not assume, so Johnson's critic declared, that Canada and South Africa would vote with England as a single bloc. "That may be," Johnson is said to have replied, "but New England farmers do not know the nature of the British Empire, and they do know common arithmetic." That is adjusting ideas to people so far as to falsify the basic idea. In the other direction, stimulating the "Red-menace-in-the-air-we-breathe" terror in order to adjust people to the idea of giving up their right of dissent is an effort to dispossess people of their judgments.

42   In terms of the old, but still convenient, faculty psychology, the terms in which rhetoric is most frequently attacked—reason, imagination, passions (emotions), judgment, will—rhetoric may still be described as the method of applying "reason to imagination for the better moving of the will." To complete our broad idea of the scope of rhetoric we should add "and the better clarification of the understanding." That is Francis Bacon's succinct statement of how rhetoric functions in the audience,[16] and it is still a good one. It establishes rhetoric squarely as an instrumental learning which manages the creative powers of the whole logical-psychological man toward a single dynamic end.

43   Rhetoric, therefore, has the greatest possible involvement with the logical and psychological studies. These learnings must be the core of the speaker's equipment. They are the *sine qua non* in the knowledge through which rhetoric must function. In the good rhetoric which Plato described in the *Phaedrus*, after knowledge of the truth, he saw the equipment of the rhetorically skilled man to consist in knowledge of the various possible kinds of arguments, knowledge of the various kinds of souls, and knowledge of which kinds of souls will be affected by which kinds of arguments—that is, knowledge of the rational processes and knowledge of the mutual adaptation of these processes to audiences. Furthermore, in the great counter-Platonic *Rhetoric* of Aristotle, the first Book is devoted chiefly to the rational processes of rhetoric, and the next Book is the first extant comprehensive treatise on individual and

---

[16]From *The Advancement of Learning*. See Karl R. Wallace, *Francis Bacon on Communication and Rhetoric* (Chapel Hill, 1943), p. 27.

group psychology. Likewise, in one of the best of the recent books on liberal education, which is, therefore, something like a basic statement on rhetoric, Hoyt Hudson sees the fundamental equipment of the liberally educated man to require three parts: the Arm of Information, the Arm of Operative Logic, and the Arm of Imagination.[17] Of these, in practical affairs, rhetoric is based on the second and third, and the first must be the starting place of the speaker in each particular situation.

44   Where in this pattern, then, does emotion come in, that famous roughneck who is said to spoil the rational life and vitiate the logic of behavior? As Hudson and many others have observed, and as Bacon knew well, emotion is a derivative of both reason and imagination. Love of truth and of the good life must be the results of any genuinely rational functioning, that is, of operative logic; and vivid realization of experience, which is imagination, can hardly occur without those strong emotional accompaniments which, in practice, have given rise to the identifying of emotion with imagination. This point seems hardly to need laboring over again. Hudson's book gives it adequate coverage, and I have summarized the traditional position of rhetoric and rhetoricians on it in the essay already mentioned.[18] The position is that a complete rhetoric, and that is the kind of rhetoric which we are discussing, knows the whole man and seeks to bring to bear the whole man in achieving its ends—what he is and what he thinks he is, what he believes and what he thinks he believes, what he wants and what he tells himself he wants. Towards its special ends, rhetoric recognizes the primacy of rational processes, their primacy in time as well as in importance, as Bacon's definition implies—applying reason to the imagination. Just so poetry recognizes the primacy for its purposes of the imagination. But rhetoric has always been akin to poetry—for long periods of history it has in fact annexed poetry—in its recognition of the honest and highly important power of imagination and of that emotion which does not supplant but supports reason, and sometimes even transcends it. Thus Sir Philip Sidney and most literary theorists of the renaissance attributed to poetry the distinctly rhetorical function of using imagination to create what might be called his-

---

[17]*Educating Liberally* (Stanford University, 1945), pp. 10 ff.
[18]Above, note 14.

torical fictions to give power and life to ideas. Rhetoric recognizes the strength of the fictions men live by, as well as those they live under;[19] and it aims to fortify the one and explode the other. Rhetoric aims at what is *worth doing*, what is *worth* trying. It is concerned with *values*, and values are established with the aid of imaginative realization, not through rational determination alone; and they gain their force through emotional animation.

45 We have observed that psychology, human nature, has been a staple of rhetorical learning through the ages. No doubt, therefore, scientific psychology will have more and more to contribute to modern rhetoric. The first notable attempt to ground rhetoric in a systematic modern psychology was made by George Campbell in his *Philosophy of Rhetoric* (1776), in which he stated as his purpose

> to exhibit . . . a tolerable sketch of the human mind; and, aided by the lights which the poet and the orator so amply furnish, to disclose its secret movements, tracing its principal channels of perception and action, as near as possible, to their source: and, on the other hand, from the science of human nature, to ascertain with greater precision, the radical principles of that art, whose object it is, by the use of language, to operate on the soul of the hearer, in the way of informing, convincing, pleasing, moving, or persuading.[20]

That same purpose governs our contemporary writers of treatises and textbooks on public speaking, argumentation, and persuasion, and most of them include as up-to-date a statement as possible of the psychological and the rational bases of rhetoric. It is a commonplace that of the studies recently come to new and promising maturity, psychology, especially social psychology, and cultural anthropology have much to teach modern rhetoric and to correct or reinterpret in traditional rhetoric. The same may be said of the various new ventures into the study of meaning, under the general head of semantics. How language *means* is obviously important to the rationale of informative and suasory discourse. Nevertheless, in spite of I. A. Richards' book,[21] the theory of meaning is not *the* philosophy of rhetoric, any more than is the psychology of percep-

---

[19]See the very relevant analysis of some of the fictions in the ideology of American business in C. Wright Mills, *White Collar* (New York, 1951), Ch. 3, "The Rhetoric of Competition."

[20]7th edn. (London, 1823), pp. vii-viii.

[21]*The Philosophy of Rhetoric* (New York, 1936).

tion. Rhetoric is the organizer of all such for the wielding of public opinion.

ADVERTISING, SALESMANSHIP, AND PROPAGANDA

46   Now that we have sketched the rhetorical process functioning at its best for the exposition and dissemination of ideas in the wielding of public opinion, with the ethical and pathetic modes of proof in ancillary relation to the logical, with the imagination aiding and reenforcing the rational, let us turn to some of the partial, incomplete, perhaps misused, rhetorics which I have already mentioned briefly.

47   It is axiomatic that men do not live by reason alone or even predominantly, though reason is such a highly prized commodity and stands in so high a repute even among the unreasoning and unreasonable, that men prefer to tell themselves and to be told that they make up their minds and determine their choices from reason and the facts. Intellectual activity, both learning and thinking, is so difficult that man tends to avoid it wherever possible. Hence education has almost always put its first efforts into cultivating the reasonable portion of the mind rather than the imaginative or emotional. Furthermore, the strength and accessibility of imaginative and emotional responses is so great in spite of education that though men seldom make effective reasonable decisions without the help of emotion, they often make, or appear to make, effective emotional decisions without the help of rational processes or the modification of reasonable consideration. Inevitably, therefore, the available reason in rhetorical situations will vary tremendously, and the assistance which imagination must provide towards the moving of the will must vary accordingly. Except in Swift's unexciting land of the Houyhnhnms, however, imagination will always be there.

48   Ever since men first began to weave the web of words to charm their fellows, they have known that some men can impose their wills on others through language in despite of reason. Almost as long, other men have deplored and feared this talent. If the talent were wholly a matter of divine gift and were wholly unexplainable, the only alternative to succumbing to the orator would be to kill him. In time it appeared, however, that this skill could be learned, in part at least, and could be analyzed. Thus if it were good, men could learn to develop it further; and if it were bad, they could be armed in some measure against it. Hence rhetoric, and hence

the partial rhetoric of anti-reason and pseudo-reason. And hence the appeal of such rhetorical eruptions as Aldous Huxley's total condemnation of oratory in *The Devils of Loudon*.[22] His indictment of public speakers is indeed skillful, and ought to be taken seriously. If the talent of his golden-voiced Grandiers be indeed magic, then we will have to agree that the fate of man before such wizards is hopeless. Rhetoric teaches, however, that the method and the power of this kind of discourse can be analyzed, at least in large part, and if its subtleties cannot be wholly *learned* by every ambitious speaker, the characteristics of its operation can be understood, and if understood, then controlled, for better or for worse.[23]

49   The oratory which Huxley would extirpate presents a rewarding approach to the rhetoric of advertising and propaganda, of which it is the historic prototype. In them the techniques of suggestion, reiteration, imaginative substitution, verbal irrelevance and indirection, and emotional and pseudological bullying have been developed beyond, one might hazard a guess, the fondest dreams of the sophists and the historic demagogues. This development does not represent a change in intention from them to our contemporaries, but an advance in knowledge and opportunity and media.

50   If you have a soap or a cigarette or a social order for quick, profitable sale, you do not neglect any method within your ethical system of making that sale. That is the paramount problem of the advertiser and the propagandist, and their solutions are very much alike. They are rhetorical solutions, at their best very carefully gauged to the mass audience, adapted to special audiences, and varying basically only as the initial sale or the permanent customer is the principal object. What advertising is in commerce, propaganda is in politics, especially international politics. Neither scorns reason or the likeness of reason, the rhetoric of information and logical argument, if the message and the audience seem to make that the best or only means to the sale. Neither, on the other hand, prefers that method to the shorter, quicker ways to unconsidered action. They concentrate — forcibly where possible, rhetorically where necessary—on the exclusion of competing ideas, on the short-circuiting or by-passing of informed judgment. By preference they do not seek to balance or overbalance alternative ideas or courses of action; they seek to obliterate them, to circumvent or subvert the rational processes which tend to make men weigh and

[22](New York, 1952), pp. 18-19.
[23]Observe the tradition of rhetoric as a systematic study, summarized in my "Aspects of Rhetorical Tradition," *QJS*, XXXVI (April, 1950), 169-172.

consider. As Adlai Stevenson said, slogans, the common staple of advertising and propaganda, "are normally designed to get action without reflection."

51   That advertising should enjoy a happier reputation than propaganda in a competitive, commercial-industrial nation such as the United States, which is only just now learning the term *psychological warfare*, is not to be wondered at. We do not have a public service institution for the defensive analysis of advertising, like the Institute of Propaganda Analysis, which assumed that propaganda is something from which we must learn to protect ourselves. The ethical superiority of our advertising is no doubt a compliment to our dominant business code—and to our laws. Still, if one wishes to know what the ungoverned rhetoric of advertising can be, he may get a suggestion by listening to some of what is beamed to us from certain radio stations south of the border.

52   The kinship of advertising and salesmanship, and their somewhat denatured relatives "public relations" and "promotion," to conventional public address, the established vehicle of rhetoric, may be embarrassing at times, but it must be acknowledged. The family resemblance is too strong to be ignored and too important to be denied. The omnipresence of the rhetoric of advertising, as I have suggested, gives it a standing which must be reckoned with, no matter what opinion the student of public address may hold of it. The rhetoric of public address, in this country at least, must function, whether or no, in a public mind which is steeped in the rhetoric of advertising, a rhetoric whose dominating principles must be recognized as adaptations of a portion of the fundamentals of any rhetoric. One need only compare a textbook or handbook of advertising methods with standard, conventional rhetorics—textbooks in public speaking and persuasion—especially in the handling of such topics as interest, suggestion, and motivation, to be convinced of the coincidence of method if not of philosophic outlook. Many times in adult evening classes in public speaking, have I heard speeches on the secrets of successful salesmanship, and as often have I found myself being offered a more or a less competent parody of certain portions of our textbook, which for some reason the student had omitted to read. Not by mere chance, one must confess, does the non-academic public take great interest in the four "miracle" courses to be found among the offerings of many universities — advertising, salesmanship, psychology, and effective speaking. Nor is it remarkable, though one may think it deplorable, that appearances of the officers of our national govern-

ment before the mass audience of the citizens are characteristic products of the country's leading advertising agencies.

53   Likewise propaganda and its brother "information" borrow and refine upon certain portions of rhetoric. No doubt it serves a useful purpose to identify propaganda with the vicious forces in the modern world, with the German Government of World War I and with the Nazi and Soviet totalitarianisms of the present time. At the same time, however, it would be the better part of wisdom to recognize that most of the major techniques of this propaganda are long-known rhetorical techniques gone wrong, that propaganda is not a new invention which we have no ready equipment for combatting, let alone fumigating and using for our honorable ends. The understanding of propaganda will be founded in the understanding of rhetoric first of all, whatever else may be necessary.[24] Both Ross Scanlan and Kenneth Burke have demonstrated the enlightenment which can come from the application of rhetorical criticism to both the internal and external propaganda of the Nazis;[25] and two articles by Scanlan and Henry C. Youngerman in the first issue of *Today's Speech* (April, 1953) are grounded on the assumption of a close kinship between rhetoric (or its corollary, "public address") and propaganda.[26] In fact, one of Scanlan's concluding statements indirectly makes both the identification and the basic distinction: "Today it is to be hoped that America will find means to match enemy propaganda in effectiveness without sacrificing the standards of morality and intellect that distinguish democracy from the totalitarian order."

RHETORIC AS A METHOD OF INQUIRY

54   More than once in the preceding pages I have in passing assigned to rhetoric a secondary function of the discovery of ideas, contributory to its prime function of the popularizing of ideas. That is the consequence of the division of *inventio*, the term applied in Roman rhetoric to the systematic investigative procedures by which rhetoric sought to turn up all the relevant arguments or

---

[24]See, for example, Everett L. Hunt, "Ancient Rhetoric and Modern Propaganda," *QJS,* XXXVII (April, 1951), 157-160.
[25]Burke, *The Philosophy of Literary Form* (1941), pp. 191-220; Scanlan, "The Nazi Party Speaker System, I & II," *SM,* XVI (August, 1949), 82-97, XVII (June, 1950), 134-148; "The Nazi Rhetorician," *QJS,* XXVII (December, 1951), 430-440.
[26]"Two Views of Propaganda," pp. 13-14; "Propaganda and Public Address," pp. 15-17.

considerations in any given situation. As part of *inventio,* for example, the elaborate doctrine of *status* was developed, through which by the application of analytical criteria it was possible to determine just what was the core, the central issue in any given case, just what had to be proved as a *sine qua non,* and where the lines of argument for proving it would lie if they were available. In general the division of *inventio* constituted a codification of the *topoi* or *places where arguments are to be found;* for instance, in *fact past, fact future, more and less, etc.* Rhetoric, thus, as we have said, provides scientific assistance to the speaker in discovering what questions to ask and how to go about answering them. It serves the speaker as laboratory procedures for analysis serve the chemist—by systematic inventory it enables him to determine with reasonable completeness what is present and what is absent in any given case.

55   We need not be surprised, therefore, that so useful a method tended to be incorporated into other arts and sciences where its original provenience was often forgotten. Historically, some of the studies to profit greatly from this borrowing from rhetoric have been the law, theology, logic, and poetic.[27] The Polandizing of rhetoric, one of the characteristic phenomena of its history, accounts in large part for the splinter meanings and the distortions which we have seen as typical of its current and historic significance. It has been the fate of rhetoric, the residual term, to be applied to the less intellectual segments of itself, while its central operating division, *inventio,* has been appropriated by the studies and sciences which rhetoric serves.

56   The functions of a complete rhetoric, however, have usually been operative under whatever temporary auspices as the whole art of discourse, even as they were in the renaissance tripartite grammar-logic-rhetoric. This splintering may go so far towards specialism, however, that the investigative function of rhetoric, the method of *inventio,* may be diverted from that to which it most properly applies. This diversion may very well be the tendency today, where a complete rhetoric hardly exists as a formal discipline except in those classically oriented courses in public speaking, debate, group discussion, argumentation, and persuasion whose central focus is

---

[27]See Richard McKeon, "Rhetoric in the Middle Ages," *Critics and Criticism, Ancient and Modern,* ed. R. S. Crane (Chicago, 1952), pp. 260-296, reprinted from *Speculum,* January, 1942; and Marvin T. Herrick, "The Place of Rhetoric in Poetic Theory," *QJS,* XXXVI (February, 1948), 1-22.

on *inventio*—the investigation and discovery of lines of argument and basic issues. Mostly rhetoric today survives, as we have seen, under other names and special applications in those specialties which contribute to it or draw upon it or appropriate selectively from its store of method—psychology, advertising, salesmanship, propaganda analysis, public opinion and social control, semantics, and that which is loosely called "research" in common parlance.

57   May I attempt in summary of this matter to bring rhetoric back to its essential investigative function, its function of discovery, by quoting from Isocrates, the Athenian politico-rhetorical philosopher, and from Edmund Burke, the eighteenth-century British statesman-orator? Wrote Isocrates in the *Antidosis*, "With this faculty we both contend against others on matters that are open to dispute and seek light for ourselves on things which are unknown; for the same arguments which we use in persuading others when we speak in public, we employ when we deliberate in our thoughts."[28] Twenty-two centuries later, the young Burke included in his notebook digest of the topics of rhetoric, which he headed "How to Argue," the following succinct, Baconian statement about the functions of *inventio:*

> To invent Arguments without a thorough knowledge of the Subject is clearly impossible. But the Art of Invention does two things—
> 1. It suggests to us more readily those Parts of our actual knowledge which may help towards illustrating the matter before us, &
> 2. It suggests to us heads of Examination which may lead, if pursued with effect into a knowledge of the Subject.
>
> So that the Art of Invention may properly be considered as the method of calling up what we do know, & investigating that of which we are ignorant.[29]

RHETORIC IN EDUCATION

58   If the burden of the preceding pages is not misplaced, the importance of rhetoric in the equipment of the well-educated member of society can hardly be in doubt. I am not inclined, therefore, especially in this journal, to offer to demonstrate the desirability of speech as an academic study. Our conventions and our journals

---

[28]*Isocrates,* trans. George Norlin (Loeb Classical Library, New York, 1929), II, 327.

[29]From an original manuscript among the Wentworth-Fitzwilliam papers in the Sheffield City Library, used with the kind permission of Earl Fitzwilliam and the trustees of the Fitzwilliam settled estates.

have been full of such demonstration for, lo, these thirty years.[30] If enlightened and responsible leaders with rhetorical knowledge and skill are not trained and nurtured, irresponsible demagogues will monopolize the power of rhetoric, will have things to themselves. If talk rather than take is to settle the course of our society, if ballots instead of bullets are to effect our choice of governors, if discourse rather than coercion is to prevail in the conduct of human affairs, it would seem like arrant folly to trust to chance that the right people shall be equipped offensively and defensively with a sound rationale of informative and suasory discourse.

59   In general education, especially, rhetoric would appear to deserve a place of uncommon importance. That is the burden of a recent article by Dean Hunt of Swarthmore. Rhetoric is the organon of the liberal studies, the formulation of the principles through which the educated man, the possessor of many specialties, attains effectiveness in society.[31] A complete rhetoric is a structure for the wholeness of the effective man, the aim of general education. But, as Dean Hunt concludes, the rhetorician himself must not become a technical specialist:

> He will keep his wholeness if he comes back again and again to Aristotle, but he must supplement those conceptions with what modern scientists have added to the mirror for man; he must illuminate the classical rhetoric with psychology, cultural anthropology, linguistics and semantics, special disciplines, perhaps, but disciplines in which he can lean heavily on interpreters who speak to others than their professional colleagues. Departments of speech which have emphasized training in rhetoric have a new opportunity to establish their place in general education. Their very claim to wholeness has been a source of distrust in an atmosphere of specialism. If now they can relate themselves to newer conceptions in the sciences, social sciences, and humanities, they can show that the ideal of the good man skilled in speaking is like the sea, ever changing and ever the same.[32]

60   So much for rhetoric in education as a study directed at the creation and at the analysis and criticism of informative and suasory discourse—at the ability, on the one hand, "to summon thought quickly and use it forcibly,"[33] and on the other to listen or read critically with the maximum application of analytical judgment.

---

[30]See, for example, one of the latest, W. N. Brigance, "General Education in an Industrial Free Society," *QJS*, XXXVIII (April, 1952), esp. p. 181.
[31]"Rhetoric and General Education," *QJS*, XXXV (October, 1949), 275, 277.
[32]*Ibid.*, 279.
[33]Harbert A. Wichelns, "Public Speaking and Dramatic Arts," in *On Going to College: A Symposium* (New York, Oxford University Press, 1938), p. 240.

61   Rhetoric would appear thus to be in certain senses a literary study, or as Wichelns wrote, at least "its tools are those of literature." It is a literary study as it is involved in the creative arts of language, of informing ideas. It is a literary study also as it contributes substantially to literary scholarship. Not only have literature and literary theory been persistently rhetorical for long periods—during much of the renaissance, for example, the seventeenth and eighteenth centuries in England, and for most of the short history of American literature—but writers and readers until fairly recently had been so generally educated in rhetoric that it provided the vocabulary and many of the concepts in terms of which much literature was both written and read. Clark's *Milton at St. Paul's School* may be cited as one conclusive demonstration of the importance of rhetoric in renaissance education and its importance in renaissance literature. This importance is now being recognized by literary scholars, and rhetoric is taking on considerable proportions in their studies, especially among those who are studying the renaissance. Myrick's study of Sir Philip Sidney as a literary craftsman,[34] for example, demonstrates how thoroughly Sidney was schooled in rhetoric and how carefully he constructed his defense of poetry on familiar rhetorical principles. If Myrick has been in error in his construction of the specific genealogy of Sidney's rhetoric, the fact of Sidney's rhetorical system is nevertheless in no doubt.

62   The plain truth is that whatever the inadequacies in specific cases of the analytical method ingrained in our educated ancestors, they *had* method, the method of formal rhetoric; whereas a general characteristic of our contemporary education is that it inculcates *no* method beyond a rather uncertain grammar and a few rules of paragraphing and bibliography. Rigidity of method is doubtless a grievous obstacle to the greatest fulfillment of genius in either belles lettres or public address; but the widespread impotence and ineptitude even of our best-educated fellows when faced with the problem of constructing or analyzing any but the most rudimentary expository or argumentative discourse, much less a complicated literary work, are surely worse. Rhetoric supplies the equipment for such practical endeavor in the promulgation of ideas, and twenty centuries have learned to use it to supplement and perfect chance and natural instinct.

63   That such method has at times become sterile or mechanical, that at other times it has been put to uses for which it was least

---

[34]Kenneth O. Myrick, *Sir Philip Sidney as a Literary Craftsman* (1935).

adapted is amusing, perhaps lamentable, but not surprising. The remote uses to which rhetorical methods of analysis and description have been put, in the absence of a more appropriate method, are well illustrated by the following passage from Sir John Hawkins' *History of Music*, first published in the late eighteenth century:

> The art of invention is made one of the heads among the precepts of rhetoric, to which music in this and sundry instances bears a near resemblance; the end of persuasion, or affecting the passions being common to both. This faculty consists in the enumeration of common places, which are revolved over in the mind, and requires both an ample store of knowledge in the subject upon which it is exercised, and a power of applying that knowledge as occasion may require. It differs from memory in this respect, that whereas memory does but recall to the mind the images or remembrance of things as they were first perceived, the faculty of invention divides complex ideas into those whereof they are composed, and recommends them again after different fashions, thereby creating variety of new objects and conceptions. Now, the greater the fund of knowledge above spoken of is, the greater is the source from whence the invention of the artist or composer is supplied; and the benefits thereof are seen in new combinations and phrases, capable of variety and permutation without end.[35]

From its lapses and wanderings, however, rhetoric when needed has almost always recovered its vitality and comprehensive scope, by reference to its classic sources. But that it should be ignored seems, as Dean Hunt suggests, hardly a compliment to education.

64   Rhetoric as a serious scholarly study I have treated in my former essay, and I shall not go over the same ground again. That there is a body of philosophy and principle worth scholarly effort in discovery, enlargement, and reinterpretation is beyond question, and fortunately more competent scholars each year are working at it. Rhetorical criticism and the study of rhetoric as a revealing social and cultural phenomenon are also gaining ground. New and interesting directions for research and these areas are being explored, or at least marked out; they are based on newly developed techniques and hitherto neglected kinds of data. One might mention, for example, those new approaches listed by Maloney:[36] the quantitative content analysis as developed by Lasswell; the qualitative

---

[35] (2 vols., London, 1875), I, xxv.
[36] "Some New Directions in Rhetorical Criticism," *Central States Speech Journal*, IV (February, 1953), 1-5.

content analysis as used by Lowenthal and Guterman; figurative analysis such as applied to Shakespeare by Caroline Spurgeon; and intonational analysis. Extensive and provocative suggestions are to be found in quantity in the text and bibliography of Brembeck and Howell's *Persuasion: A Means of Social Control*,[37] especially in Part VI. Lucrative also are the new attempts at the analysis of the rhetoric of historical movements, such as Griffin's study of the rhetoric of the anti-masonic movement and others under way within the Speech Association of America. Thonssen's review of recent rhetorical studies illustrates amply both the new and the traditional in rhetorical scholarship; and the section on rhetoric in the annual Haberman bibliography is convincing evidence of the vitality of current enterprise.[38]

65   Though new avenues, new techniques, new materials such as the foregoing are inviting to the increasing numbers of scholars whose interests and abilities — to say nothing of their necessities — lie in rhetorical research, especially those new directions which lead to rhetoric as a cultural, a sociological, a social-psychiatric phenomenon, the older literary-historical-political studies are still neither too complete nor too good. In any event, each new generation probably needs to interpret afresh much of the relevant history of thought, especially the thought of the people as distinguished from what is commonly considered the history of ideas. For this the scholarship of rhetoric seems particularly adapted. Towards this purpose, I find no need to relocate the field of rhetorical scholarship as envisioned by Hudson and Wichelns, nor to recant from the considerations which I outlined in the *QJS* in 1937.[39] One may find it reassuring to observe, however, that much which was asked for in those essays has since then been undertaken and often accomplished with considerable success. Especially is this true of the study of public address in its bulk and day-to-day manifestations: in the movement studies, the "case" studies, the sectional and regional studies, the studies of "debates" and "campaigns" such as the debates on the League of Nations and the campaigns for conservation.

66   There remains much to do, nevertheless, and much to re-do in the more familiar and conventional areas of research and interpretation. The editing and translation of rhetorical texts is still far

---

[37] (New York, 1952).
[38] "A Bibliography of Rhetoric and Public Address," ed. F. W. Haberman, formerly appearing annually in the *QJS*, latterly in *SM*.
[39] See above, note 1.

from complete or adequate. The canon of ancient rhetoric is, to be sure, in very good shape, and when Caplan's translation of the *Ad Herennium* is published in the Loeb Library there will hardly be a major deficiency. In post-classical, mediaeval, and renaissance rhetoric the situation is not so good, though it is improving. There are still too few works like Howell's *Rhetoric of Alcuin and Charlemagne* and Sister Therese Sullivan's commentary on the translation of the fourth book of St. Augustine's *De Doctrina*. Halm's *Rhetores Minores*, for example, is substantially unmolested so far.

67   English and continental rhetoric of the sixteenth, seventeenth, and eighteenth centuries is slowly appearing in modern editions by scholars who know rhetoric as the theory of public address. Our bibliographies show increasing numbers of these as doctoral dissertations, most of which, alas, seem to be abandoned almost as soon as finished. Only a few works of the sort, like Howell's *Fénelon*, represent mature, published work.

68   In the history and historical analysis of rhetoric, nothing of adequate range and scope yet exists. Thonssen and Baird's *Speech Criticism*, ambitious as it is, is only a beginning. The general history of rhetoric, and even most of the special histories, have yet to be written. Works now under way by Donald L. Clark and Wilbur S. Howell will make substantial contributions, but rhetoric from Corax to Whately needs far fuller and better treatment than it gets in the series of histories of criticism by the late J. W. H. Atkins.

69   Towards the study of the rhetorical principles and practice of individual speakers and writers the major part of our scholarly effort seems to have been directed. The convenience of this kind of study is beyond question and is hard to resist, either in public address or in literature. And this is as it should be. The tendency to write biographies of speakers, however, rather than rhetorico-critical studies of them, must be kept in check, or at least in proportion. Again for reasons of convenience, if not also of scholarly nationalism, the studies of American speakers are proportionately too numerous. British and foreign public address is still far too scantily noticed by competent rhetorical scholars.

RHETORIC AND POETIC

70   This would not be the place, I think, even if Professor Thonssen's review of rhetorical works were not appearing in this same issue of the *QJS*, for a survey of rhetorical scholarship. The preceding paragraphs are intended only as a token of decent respect to

accomplishment and progress in a discrete and important branch of humane scholarship. A further area where rhetorical scholarship may be very profitably pursued, however, perhaps deserves some special consideration.

71   Even if it were not for the contributions of Kenneth Burke, the study of rhetoric in literature and of the relation of the theory of rhetoric to the theory of poetic would be taking on renewed importance at the present time. The lively revival of rhetorical study in renaissance scholarship which I have mentioned is only one phase of the problem. A renewed or increased interest in satire, deriving in part, perhaps, from the excellent work which of late has been done on Swift, leads directly to rhetoric. The rhetorical mode is obviously at the center of satire, and any fundamental analysis of satire must depend upon the equipment for rhetorical analysis. Likewise a complete dramatic criticism must draw upon rhetoric, both practically and philosophically. The internal rhetoric of the drama was specifically recognized by Aristotle when he referred readers of the *Poetics* to the *Rhetoric* for coverage of the element of *dianoia*, for the analysis of speeches in which agents try to convince or persuade each other. What, however, is the external rhetoric of the drama? What is the drama intended to do to an audience? Herein lies the question of the province of poetic as opposed to the province of rhetoric. When Antony addresses the Roman citizens in *Julius Caesar*, the existence of an internal rhetoric in the play is clear enough; the relation between Antony and his stage audience is unmistakably rhetorical. But what of the relation between Antony and the audience in the pit, or the Antony-stage-audience combination and the audience in the pit? The more we speculate about the effect of a play or any literary work on an audience, the more we become involved in metaphysical questions in which rhetoric must be involved.

72   Much contemporary poetry or pseudo-poetry in any generation is rhetorical in the most obvious sense—in the same sense as the epideictic oration. It "pleases" largely by rhetorical means or methods. It "reminds" us of experience instead of "organizing" or "creating" experience. It appeals to our satisfaction with what we are used to; it convinces us that what *was* still may be as it was, that old formulas are pleasantest if not best. It is not so much concerned with pointing up the old elements in the new, even, as establishing the identity of the old and the contemporary. "What oft was thought, but ne'er so well expressed" is a distinctly rhetorical attainment, and it would not have occurred to Pope to

suppose that the poetic and the rhetorical were antithetical, if indeed they were separable. Though sporadically the effort of critics and theorists has been to keep *rhetoric* and *poetic* apart, the two rationales have had an irresistible tendency to come together, and their similarities may well be more important than their differences. When the forming of attitude is admitted into the province of rhetoric, then, to Kenneth Burke, rhetoric becomes a method for the analysis of even lyric poetry. Hence a frequent term in certain kinds of literary analysis now is *poetic-rhetoric*, as for example in the first two sentences in Ruth Wallerstein's analysis of two elegies: "I want this paper to consider two poems, John Donne's elegy on Prince Henry and Milton's *Lycidas*, in the light that is shed on them by seventeenth-century rhetoric-poetic as I understand it. Both the significance of that rhetoric and the test of my view of it will reside in its power to illuminate the poems."[40]

73   Undoubtedly there are basic differences between *poetic* and *rhetoric*, both practical and philosophical, and probably these differences lie both in the kind of method which is the proper concern of each and the kind of effect on audiences to the study of which each is devoted. The purely poetic seeks the creation or organization of imaginative experience, probably providing for reader or audience some kind of satisfying spiritual or emotional therapy. The rhetorical seeks a predetermined channeling of the audience's understanding or attitude. Poetry works by representation; rhetoric by instigation. The poetic is fulfilled in creation, the rhetorical in illumination. "An image," wrote Longinus, "has one purpose with the orators and another with the poets; . . . the design of the poetic image is enthralment, of the rhetorical, vivid description. Both, however, seek to stir the passions and the emotions. . . . In oratorical imagery its best feature is always its reality and truth."[41] Poetry, declared Sir Philip Sidney, cannot lie because it affirms nothing; it merely presents. Rhetoric not only presents but affirms. That is its characteristic. Both poetic and rhetoric attain their effects through language. If the poet's highest skill lies in his power to make language do what it has never done before, to force from words and the conjunction of words meanings which are new and unique, perhaps it is the highest skill of the speaker to use words in their accepted senses in such a way as to make them carry their traditional meanings with a vividness and effectiveness which they have never known before.

---

[40]"Rhetoric in the English Renaissance: Two Elegies," *English Institute Essays, 1948,* p. 153.
[41]Trans. Rhys Roberts, sec. 15.

SUMMARY

74   In brief we may assign to rhetoric a four-fold status. So far as
it is concerned with the management of discourse in specific situations for practical purposes, it is an instrumental discipline. It is
a literary study, involving linguistics, critical theory, and semantics
as it touches the art of informing ideas, and the functioning of
language. It is a philosophical study so far as it is concerned with
a method of investigation or inquiry. And finally, as it is akin to
politics, drawing upon psychology and sociology, rhetoric is a social
study, the study of a major force in the behavior of men in society.

Careful organization is the foundation for all effective writing. Without it, writing tends to wander aimlessly from one topic to the next, saying now too little, now too much, and never appearing to have any sense of direction or plan. Proper organization is achieved through an understanding and application of the principles of unity, coherence and emphasis. In this essay from the shorter edition of *Modern Rhetoric*, Cleanth Brooks and Robert Penn Warren define these three principles and demonstrate how they must be used in the shaping of an essay.

Organizing the Composition

Cleanth Brooks, Robert Penn Warren

1   The division into introduction, body, and conclusion, or, if you like, into beginning, middle, and end, is the natural sequential division of a piece of writing. It is the mode of organizing that naturally occurs to anyone who is getting down to the actual business of writing, whatever the topic. But there is another threefold set of terms that is also fundamental to any process of composition. They are *unity, coherence,* and *emphasis.*

2   Any sound piece of writing will exemplify these three principles, and a study of them is our first step toward understanding how to develop the main body of a discussion and how to relate it to the introduction and the conclusion.

UNITY

3   Any good piece of writing has unity. The fundamental interest, which determines the writer's subject, must permeate the whole composition. The composition must be *one* thing — not a hodgepodge.

4   Unity is not an arbitrary thing, a limitation imposed from the outside. It is simply an indication that the writer's mind can work systematically and can, therefore, arrive at a meaning. A unified composition indicates that the writer's ideas about his subject are unified, that he is not scatterbrained. But unity is not always easily achieved.

5   Suppose that you are given "Preparing for a Career" as a topic for a theme. After turning it over in your mind a few times, you realize that this topic includes too many possibilities to constitute

From *Modern Rhetoric,* Second Edition, by Cleanth Brooks and Robert Penn Warren, copyright, 1949, ©1958, by Harcourt, Brace & World, Inc.

a true subject. Therefore, your first step toward gaining unity is to limit and fix the subject. You bring your own interest to bear upon the topic. For example, you are a college freshman, and you are beginning to prepare for a career as a civil engineer. You decide, therefore, to call your theme: "Why I Wish To Be an Engineer." This title is more limited than the more general "Preparing for a Career," and it has the merit of drawing upon subject matter with regard to which you rightfully believe that you have some competence — the state of your mind.

6 The essay is to be short. You do not plan an elaborate introduction or conclusion. The introduction will simply make reference to your own experience with the subject. The conclusion can be a sentence or two in which you will reaffirm your main point, your choice of a career. Following is a theme such as you might write:

WHY I WISH TO BE AN ENGINEER

Choosing one's life work is about the most important decision that a person ever has to make. Many of my friends are still undecided about what they want to be. But my choice has been an easy one. For nearly as long as I can remember I have wanted to be an engineer.

I suppose that one reason why I want to be an engineer and have made my college plans in that direction is that my father is an engineer. He was a student here at the State University back in 1909-1914. He began his college career with the intention of being a doctor, but he soon changed his mind. He finished his course in 1914 and worked as a draftsman for two years in Chicago in an engineering firm. But World War I got him into the army, and he wound up a major in the Engineering Corps. His war experience was valuable to him in more ways than one, for he says it taught him how to deal with men of all kinds and to get work done under pressure. Also, it meant that he acquired a taste for action and adventure. After the war, he went to Mexico and worked on building a railroad in the mountains. He had many difficult construction problems to solve there. I was born in Mexico, and I was raised in a family where engineering was discussed all the time, for my mother was interested in my father's work.

There is a great future for an engineer in this country. It is true that during the depression many engineers were out of work, but that was true of many occupations and professions. Besides, many of the engineers out of work were not well trained to begin with. If you are really well trained and are willing to put out your best efforts, you can almost always get along. Engineering is especially important today, for we are in the midst of a great technological revolution which will mean the rebuilding of much of the industrial plant and the development of new transport facilities. There are also opportunities in land reclamation, the expansion of public works, and other long-range programs. This country is an engineer's paradise, for we are the most mechanical-minded people in the world. They say that industry is the great talent of America, and I see nothing to be ashamed of in that. Engineers make the world easier to live in for everyone. Think of the great bridges and dams, the highways and airports. What would we do without them?

I like a life of action, and that is another reason why I plan to be an engineer. My father had a very interesting life in Mexico. After five years there he went to Argentina. He had learned Spanish in Mexico and had made a name for himself there. So he got a good offer in Argentina. He sent my mother and me back to the United States until I grew up a little, but he came to see us at the end of the first year and took us back to Argentina with him. We lived there four years. Then he went to India and supervised the building of some bridges there. But he did not take us to India with him. He understood that the climate was too bad. And he was right, because he almost died there of dysentery. He never left America again, but his talk about his adventures gave me a desire for an active life, and he has never discouraged me.

I make my best marks in mathematics, which is the basis of engineering, and I think that a man should follow his best talent. I like other subjects, too—history, for instance, and I read a good many novels and stories. But I cannot see myself making a profession of any of these fields. Business would be too confining for me. I have an uncle who is a lawyer, and it seems to me that he never gets out of his office except to come home at night.

Taking everything together, I think that engineering is the right profession for me.

7   This theme has the unity of a true subject, but lacks the larger unity of good writing. When we examine the theme carefully, we can dig out the reasons for the student's choice of a career: family, the opportunity to make a good living, the appetite for action, and the aptitude for mathematics. These four reasons should give him the outline for his theme.

8   But he is constantly bringing in material which does not bear directly on the subject or which is developed without reference to the main line of interest. For instance, he is so much impressed with his father's life that he devotes far too much attention to it: most of the second and fourth paragraphs. For his purpose he needs to tell us only the barest facts about his father's career. The last part of the third paragraph, too, is not relevant. The writer may have two points here: that an engineer feels himself characteristically American and that the engineer has the sense of being a useful member of society. But he does not state these points,

and they are lost in his general remarks. If we get them at all, we get them by implication only. In the fifth paragraph, too, we find some irrelevant material: the reference to the writer's interest in history and fiction and the remark about his uncle's occupation. The writer has a main idea, but he does not stick to it.

COHERENCE

9   An effective discourse must have unity. It must also have coherence; that is, the elements of the discourse must stick together. This last comment may seem to be simply another way of saying that a discourse must have unity. Indeed, the failure of the student theme just discussed might be stated as a failure in coherence quite as accurately as a failure in unity; we have in effect pointed out how one part does not lead to the next, how the writer fails to develop needed linkages, and how he has pointlessly introduced items that he does not need and that do not tie into anything else. Unity and coherence are indeed ultimately related; and yet it is worth making a distinction between them. That distinction may be stated thus: When we speak of unity, we refer primarily to the relation of the materials to the subject. When we speak of coherence, we refer primarily to the organization of the materials so as to give a continuous *development* to the subject. A discourse that lacks coherence will, of course, seem to lack unity; for even though the individual parts are actually related to the subject, the incoherent author will have failed to demonstrate how they relate to each other and that they thus make up *one* discourse.

Coherence through over-all organization

10   There is no one principle by which the materials of a discourse are to be organized. Obviously, a principle of organization that is good for describing a woman's face would not be good for telling the story of a baseball game or a battle, or for arguing in favor of the abolition of Greek-letter fraternities, or for explaining the causes of the Russian Revolution. Different intentions demand different principles of organization. The basic intentions and some of the characteristic methods of organization, we shall study in subsequent chapters. Here we can content ourselves with the common-sense principle that one thing should lead to another.

11   Let us suppose that the student who wrote the essay entitled "Why I Wish To Be an Engineer" sets out to write another theme

and, in writing it, undertakes to pay special attention to the principles of unity and coherence. The topic "Interesting People" has been assigned to him, and, after some thought, he brings it down to a more limited and specific subject, something nearer to his special interests and experience and something nearer to a true subject. He decides to write about a member of the family that he knows intimately; his central idea will be to define his special admiration for that person. He will call his theme "The Person I Admire Most: Uncle Conroy."

12 But before starting to write the theme, the student does something else. He is determined to overcome his tendency to be scatterbrained; so he now jots down some of the points that he wants to make and tries to arrange them into a kind of sketch or outline. His outline looks something like this.

STATEMENT OF THE SUBJECT   Why I admire my Uncle Conroy

INTRODUCTION
I. My uncle as he now appears—apparent failure and real success
BODY
II. The background of my uncle's achievement
   A. His worldly success and ruin
   B. His illness and despair
III. The nature of my uncle's achievements
   A. His practical achievements
     1. Help with the children
     2. Help with my father's business
     3. Help with my mother's illness
   B. His achievement in self-control
     1. Naturalness of his actions
     2. Cheerfulness in the face of pain
   C. His greatest achievement, an example to others—the summary of his other achievements

CONCLUSION
IV. My uncle as a type of success and my admiration for him

13 The outline has narrowed the true subject to the uncle's success in life. The title of the theme thus could be, "Success and Uncle Conroy." Although the outline is relatively simple, it should be adequate for the subject.

14 Though not an end in itself, an outline is a help in the actual writing of a theme. It helps especially in solving the problem of unity and coherence, in indicating how the parts relate to the subject and hang together. An outline, however, need not be followed slavishly. In the process of writing, new thoughts may come, and

new material may be suggested. The writer should always be ready
to take advantage of these. He may have to stop writing and go
back to make a new outline, or he may be able to incorporate the
new thoughts or new material directly into the body of the theme.
In any event, it is a good idea to check the finished theme against
the original outline and, if necessary, make a new outline.

15   Actually, the student did not follow his outline slavishly in writing his theme about Uncle Conroy. Some of the ways in which he
departed from it we shall discuss a little later. But now let us look
at his theme. (Note that he has taken some care to make the introduction engage our interest in what is to come.)

SUCCESS AND UNCLE CONROY

I suppose that my Uncle Conroy is the person I admire most in the
world. This statement would probably seem strange to anyone who
happened to visit our home and see the old man sitting, hunched over
and shabbily dressed, at a corner of the hearth, not saying much. He
looks like the complete failure, and by ordinary standards he is. He
has no money. He has no children. He is old and sick, but he has made
his own kind of success, and I think he is happy.

At one time in his life he was a success by ordinary standards. He
was the son of a poor Methodist minister (my mother's father), but
he ran away from home in Illinois to Oklahoma, back in the days when
things were beginning to boom out there. He had a fine house in
Oklahoma City and a ranch. He was hail-fellow-well-met, and men and
women liked him. He was a sportsman, kept good horses, and took
long hunting trips to Mexico and Canada. Then one day, on his own
ranch, his horse stumbled in a gopher hole and threw him. He was
badly hurt and was in the hospital for many months. While he was
still in the hospital, the Depression came on. If he had been well and
able to take care of his affairs, he might have saved some of his money
from the crash. As it was, he lost everything. So he came back to Illinois, and my mother and father took him in.

It must have been an awful come-down for a man like that to be
living on charity. But the worst was yet to happen, for he developed
arthritis in a very painful form. I remember the first year or so, even
though I was a very small child. He even tried to commit suicide with
gas from the stove. But my mother saved him, and after that he began
to change.

The first thing was that he began to take an interest in us children.
He would read to us and talk to us. He helped us with our lessons.
That relieved mother a great deal and made her life easier. My father
was an insurance man and had a lot of paper work to do. It got so that
my uncle took an interest in that, and before long he was helping my

father by doing reports and writing letters. He helped my father tide over the bad time of the Depression. Then when my mother was ill for a long time, he learned to do some of the housework, as much as his strength would permit, and even dressed the two smaller children.

What he did was important, but more important was the way he did things. He was so natural about it. You never got the impression he was making any effort or sacrifice. We all got so we didn't notice what he did, and I am sure that that was what he wanted.

As I look back now, or when I go home and see Uncle Conroy, the biggest achievement, however, seems to be the kind of example he gave us all. He was often in pain, but he was always cheerful. If he felt too bad, he simply hid away from the family for a while in his room—what he called his "mope-room." He even made a joke out of that. And he didn't act like a man who had failed. He acted like a man who had found what he could do and was a success at it. And I think that he is a success. We all admire success, and that is why I admire my Uncle Conroy.

16   This theme is coherent. We can see how each section of it fits into the general pattern. The main business of the writer is to tell why he admires his uncle, but he does not immediately set up the reasons. First, by way of introduction, he gives a brief sketch of the man as he now appears—the man who is to be interpreted. The appearance of failure in contrast to the reality of success gives dramatic interest and excites the reader's curiosity.

17   In the second paragraph the writer tells of his uncle's days of outward success. This topic does not get into the theme merely because the uncle, as a matter of fact, had such success. Many things that happened to him are certainly omitted here. Instead, it gets in because the taste of worldly success makes more impressive the uncle's achievement in being able to shift his values in the face of adversity.

18   The third paragraph presents the despair of the uncle—a normal response to bankruptcy and illness. This topic has a place in the general organization, for it states the thing that the uncle must fight against.

19   The fourth, fifth, and sixth paragraphs define the nature of the uncle's achievement. The order here is one of ascending importance, toward a climax—the special practical things he did, the attitude he took toward the doing, the long-range effect of his example on others. The sixth paragraph not only states the uncle's most important achievement but serves as a kind of summary of the preceding material.

Coherence through local transitions

20   Thus far, we have been talking about what is involved in the
over-all organization of a piece of writing. But the question of local
transitions within the discourse is also extremely important. How
do we get from one section to another, one paragraph to another,
one sentence to another?

21   Obviously there must be an intrinsic continuity: What one section, paragraph, or sentence presents must bear some relation to
the whole subject and to what has just preceded. But even when
there is this intrinsic continuity, we may have to help the reader
by using certain devices of connection and transition, by giving him
links or signposts.

22   We can begin a section, paragraph, or sentence with some reference to what has gone before. The repetition or rephrasing of something in the preceding element will provide a link. For example,
let us look at the link that ties together the first and second paragraphs of the theme:

> . . . He is old and sick. But he has made *his own kind of success,* and
> I think he is happy.
>
> At one time of his life he was a *success by ordinary standards.* He
> was. . . .

23   The repetition of the word *success* (which points up the antithesis between "his own kind" and that according to "ordinary
standards") provides the link between the two paragraphs. But
pronouns and other words of reference (such as *such, similar, that,
these,* and so forth) may serve the same purpose. Notice, for
example, how paragraphs 4 and 5 of the theme are linked.

> . . . he *learned to do some of the housework* . . . and even *dressed*
> the two smaller children.
>
> *What he did* was important, but more important was the way he
> did things. . . .

24   Furthermore, there are words (though in this theme none are
used to connect paragraphs) the function of which is to indicate
specific relations: conjunctions, conjunctive adverbs, and some adverbs. These words say what they mean. *And, or, nor* establish a
coordinate connection. *But, however, nevertheless* establish a contrast. *So, therefore, consequently* establish a result. *Moreover* and
furthermore indicate additions or elaborations. *First, second, next,
last,* and so forth, indicate items in a series.

25   Another way to establish continuity is found in a large group
of more or less conventional phrases. Such phrases are also self-

explanatory: *in addition, as has been said, that is to say, that is, as a consequence, for example, for instance, as a result, on the contrary.*

26   None of these lists is complete. They are merely suggestive. But they may serve to indicate the function of such words and phrases so that the student can by his reading build up his own resources.

27   We must not use such transitional words and phrases unless they are necessary. They are not ornaments, and they impede the reader rather than help him if the sense is clear without them. Overuse of such expressions may, in fact, indicate a breakdown in the coherence of the composition.

EMPHASIS

28   A piece of writing may be unified and coherent and still not be effective if it does not observe the principle of *emphasis*. When this principle is properly observed, the intended scale of importance of elements in the discourse is clear to the reader. All cats are black in the dark, but all things should not look alike in the light of a reasonable writer's interest in his subject. To change our metaphor, there is a foreground and a background of interest, and the writer should be careful to place each item in its proper location. Like unity and coherence, emphasis is a principle of organization.

Emphasis by flat statement

29   How do we emphasize an element in a piece of writing?

30   The first and most obvious way is for the writer to state quite flatly his own view on the importance of a matter. If we turn back to the theme "The Person I Admire Most," we find that paragraphs 4, 5, and 6 represent a scale of importance.

> The first thing was that he began to take an interest in us children. . . .
> What he did was important, but *more important* was the way he did things. . . .
> As I look back now, or when I go home and see Uncle Conroy, the *biggest achievement,* however, seems to be the kind of example he gave us all. . . .

31   In depending on his own statement for emphasis the writer should remember that the actual content must justify the statement. Before he makes the statement, he must think through the subject and be sure that he really believes in his own statement.

Emphasis by position

32   A second way to emphasize is by position. "First or last" is a
fairly sound rule for emphasis by position. This rule corresponds
to two general methods for treating a subject. The main idea can
be presented and then discussed or proved, or discussion or proof
can lead up to the main idea. Ordinarily the second method is
better, and the end is the most emphatic position, for the last impression on a reader is what counts most. But some rather con-
ventionalized forms of writing, such as news stories, put the most
important material first. In any case, the middle is the least emphatic position.

Emphasis by proportion

33   Proportion in itself is a means of emphasis. The most important
topic in a discussion reasonably receives fullest treatment. This
principle, however, is more flexible than the preceding statement
would indicate. In some writings the last and most important topic
may have been so well prepared for by the foregoing discussion
that it does not require elaborate treatment. The writer must
decide each case on its own merits and be sure that he is not
indulging in elaboration merely for the sake of elaboration.

Other devices of emphasis

34   Flat statement, order of importance, proportion, and style are
major means of expressing emphasis, but there are certain minor
ones. For instance, repetition of an idea can give it prominence.
The danger here is that the repetition may become merely mechanical and therefore dull. To be effective, repetition must be combined
with some variety and some progression in the treatment of the
subject. Then there is the device of the short, isolated paragraph.
The idea set off by itself strikes the eye. But not all short paragraphs are in themselves emphatic. The content and the phrasing
of the short paragraph must make it appear worthy of the special
presentation. Obviously if many paragraphs are short, all emphasis
disappears.

Faulty devices of emphasis

35   Certain frequently occurring devices of emphasis are worse than
useless. Irresponsible exaggeration always repels the reader. Catch-

words and hackneyed phrases, such as *awfully, terribly, tremendously, the most wonderful thing I ever saw, you never saw anything like it, I can't begin to tell you,* make a claim on the reader's attention that he is rarely prepared to grant. Random underlining and italicizing and the use of capitals and exclamation points usually defeat their own purpose. Writers use these devices when they are not sure that what they have to say will stand on its own merits. To insist that what you have to say is important does not prove the point. As the writer, you must prove it.

36   In applying any of the means of emphasis the writer must first of all be sure that the thing emphasized is worth emphasizing. Common sense must help him here. Nothing else can.

The highly competitive atmosphere prevalent in American colleges today has affected adversely the broader aims and values of education. An archaic grading system tends to frustrate the student who is genuinely interested in education as a process of discovery as much as preparation for a career. Using the metaphor of the "race" for academic honors, Oscar Handlin demonstrates in his essay, "Are the Colleges Killing Education," how the present system leads to undue pressures, and stifles the aspirations of many of the best students.

Are the Colleges Killing Education?

Oscar Handlin

1   With the coming of spring, hysteria creeps across the campus. Tension mounts steadily, and even when it does not erupt in some overt form, it still disturbs the last two months of the college year. Now is the time when the steadily growing psychiatric staffs come into their own.

2   The young people who brood in their rooms, who forget to come down to the dining hall, and who burst out in fits of irrationality are not worrying about who will win the great game or who will come to the dance or be tapped for the fraternity. Joe College is dead, and his little anxieties are unrecognizably antique. His successors are immersed in their books and laboratories, and their concern is for the grade that an incomprehensible marking system will grind out for them.

3   Among the undergraduates, it is worst for the juniors. Most of the seniors are reconciled; they have by now amassed whatever capital they will possess and know it is too late to make serious changes. The sophomores are frenetically hopeful; despite the facts of the past, they feel they have a chance. The freshmen are still reeling from the shock of self-discovery but are not yet fully aware of what has hit them. The juniors are, and therefore the panic that all share to some extent is particularly intense among them.

4   The phenomenon is relatively recent, and it is not everywhere the same. Indeed, there may still be some refuge which is entirely unaffected, where college remains a place of learning, not a racetrack. But year by year the infection spreads, and it seems most virulent in the best institutions and among the best students.

5   The American college functions with a time-encrusted mechan-

ism, much of it immensely valuable because of the experience, tradition, and wisdom built into it. But some of its devices were designed for purposes long since forgotten. We do not question their presence; the grating noise they make seems a necessary part of the operation. Who can imagine that this is the sound of minds being crushed in a process that frustrates the whole educational enterprise?

6   Those great big beautiful A's so avidly sought, those little, miserly C's so often found, were meant for another time and another student body. They were the tools of the teacher in the day when the college was more a disciplinary than an educational institution. The miscellaneous lots of boys and young men who recited their lessons in the eighteenth- and nineteenth-century American college were indifferently prepared, only occasionally interested, and given to outbursts that took them altogether out of control. The instructor needed grades and fines and other punishments to keep them in hand.

7   The problems of discipline became less pressing when the college acquired its modern institutionalized form. The grading system nevertheless retained its importance. The curriculum was divided into blocks of courses, each worth a number of points, and an education was defined by the score that stood to the student's credit in the college accounting system. The grade then became critical, because it was evidence of the amount of learning deposited to his credit.

8   This pattern has persisted, although few remember what forces brought it into being. Yet no faculty would now maintain that education can be defined by a balance sheet of credits, or that the statistical magic that produces grade scores carried to the second decimal place is a reliable way of evaluating students.

9   Until recently the system was hardly effective enough to do much harm. A large percentage of the student body could afford to disregard it entirely. After the manner of the lads in Owen Wister's *Philosophy 5*, they looked down on the grinds and occupied themselves in their own ways. And the minority who were interested could study away to their hearts' content without the anxiety of involvement in a mass competition.

10   All that has now changed. The new students enter after a rigid selective process, they present few disciplinary problems, and they arrive after good and uniform preparation. The constant surveillance of their studies serves no useful function and only interferes with their education.

11   The trouble is that the students themselves do not know it. This generation has been so thoroughly harnessed to the treadmill of the examination that it accepts its servitude as a normal if strenuous condition of life. All the external pressures of society encourage that belief. Since education has become a national emergency, it is a patriotic duty to do well in algebra. The student who gets an A in physics will not only advance to a successful career in space but will also defend his country against the Russians. The talented boy has replaced the athlete as the school hero, and the letter worth getting is no longer that on the sweater but that on the report card.

12   The process of subversion begins almost in the first year of the best high schools. The most highly motivated students know that they are engaged in a close race; only the fleetest will enter the desirable colleges. Ahead of them loom the great goals, the College Boards and the National Merit competition. Along the way are the lesser hurdles they must surmount, and their task is to train themselves to score well.

13   How can their high school education have any other meaning? Admission to college comes generally in the spring of their senior year and is based on performances on tests taken a good deal earlier. Everything that comes later is totally irrelevant. Furthermore, a variety of schemes for early admission and early appraisal have pushed some of the tests back into the middle of the third year of high school. For many students, therefore, almost half of their secondary school career becomes meaningless, since it does not prepare them for the examinations. It is a rare teacher who can resist the tendency to turn his classes into extended cram sessions.

14   Alas, the young people finally discover that entry into college solves no problems. It only reveals the new hurdles they could not earlier see. True, the place is strange and the conditions of life new, but the race is the same, only the pace is faster. Back in those innocent high school days, these boys and girls were a select group—the brightest and best. Now they are thrown into a mass in which everyone is select and everyone had been brightest and best. In this renewed competition some who had always been winners discover that they too will have to be losers. The cruelty of the contest is clearest in courses which establish grades on the basis of a statistical distribution curve. No matter how hard they work, or how able they are, one half of the class will fall below

the average. Each student, therefore, finds himself involved in a struggle with his neighbor, whose success will drag him down.

15   Any freshman can grasp the point of the explanation for his D on the question in Philosophy H. "No, there was nothing particularly *wrong* with the answer. But everyone else in the section did so well that the classifying apparatus sorted you out toward the lowest of the pigeonholes." He will learn thereafter to crowd his way to the top.

16   Meanwhile, the goal of college is the same as that of high school —the high score that will open the way to the next stage of competition. Now the students work for the grades that will admit them to the graduate or professional school. The intense haste with which they reach toward what they mistakenly believe to be narrowing opportunities shortens their vision. Tactics become preeminently important. These young people work hard, and they shun the snap course "which gets you nowhere." But they tiptoe gingerly through the curriculum, weighing all the angles. One will regularly carry an additional course all year, then at the last possible moment drop that in which the risk is greatest. Another sacrifices each summer vacation, not to shorten his studies, but because instructors are reputed to grow more pliable as the temperature rises. And only the reckless will dare not to know the right answers as the grader expects them, or allow questions to draw their thinking in unexpected directions.

17   Many students now feel unbearable pressure from their parents. The strain is not consciously applied, but it is none the less real. It is the product of a situation that leads young people to wonder whether their careers in college will jeopardize the love and affection of their parents.

18   Each family has hopefully groomed its own aspirants for the race. Mom and Dad often have made genuine sacrifices of time and energy to be sure their hopeful was adequately prepared. They must not be disappointed. The boy who does well advances to scholarships and jobs that will immediately have an effect upon the income of the whole family. The one who does not becomes a drag, reducing his father's chances for a new car, his little sister's prospects for an expensive education.

19   The solicitous letters and the regular telephone calls impress upon the student the fact that it is not he alone who is being tested, but the whole family. How proud they are when the stock rises, how concerned when it falls! The A shows the virtue of the home and school that produced the good performer. The C is not

only a blow to the ego of the recipient; it is a reflection upon the adequacy of his training. Unless they rebel entirely, the young people carry to class the anxiety, lest they let down those who had invested in them. So much hangs on the outcome.

20   The proliferation of rewards has, paradoxically, stimulated this destructive competition. The National Science Foundation and the Woodrow Wilson fellowships have done immense good. But, at the same time, they have put undesirable pressure on the aspirants. Those who make it are free (they think); they see themselves firmly planted on the academic escalator with a regular income, security, and marriage just within reach. The attractiveness of these immediate goals obscures every other consideration.

21   It is in vain to point out that success in tests is not necessarily the way to achievement, that the careers of great men do not always begin with a ranking in the upper tenth percentile, that places are available, and that there are other than competitive values to education. Their whole experience points in the other direction.

22   The losses to the students and to society are tremendous. The distorted emphasis nullifies much of what the colleges aim to do.

23   I speak now not of the reconciled mass who somehow make their peace with the system, but of the ablest, among whom the qualities of excellence might be found. These young people secure an admirable training in the techniques of the correct answer. They learn to remember; to be accurate, neat, and cautious. But they are rarely called on to use their ability autonomously or speculatively, to deal with situations in which the answers are not known but must be discovered.

24   They cannot afford the sense of the tentativeness of knowledge, of the imperfection of existing formulations. Writing against the clock, they must always put the cross in the right box and round out the essay with an affirmative conclusion. With what pain, if ever at all, will they learn how to know what they do not know, how to probe alone beyond the limits of what is handed to them, how to be creative original thinkers! By the time they carry their diplomas away, they will have missed an education—that experience which, by the exposure of one mind to the thinking of others, creates not answers but a lifetime of questions.

25   We are all sufferers by the losses sustained by this generation of students. An open society like our own depends in large measure upon the educational system to evaluate those who pass through

it and to channel them into the proper places in life. If the colleges
fail in the process of selection, the young people with the appropriate talents will not become the doctors and teachers, the diplo-
mats and businessmen, the physicists and engineers they should
be. When the pegs do not fit the holes, the structure creaks.

26   Undue emphasis upon performance measured by college may
have precisely that effect. These scores have only a slight predictive
value and are unlikely to furnish reliable indications of future
achievement. I do not mean that high-ranking students do worse
than low-ranking ones. As a group, they do better. But, in the
long run, not all A students do as well as they should, and not
all do better than all B students; there are enough dramatic re-
versals of form to raise doubts about excessive reliance upon these
standards. Every teacher has seen the slow starter work at his
own pace, then suddenly discover himself and out-distance the
front-runners.

27   We organize the boys and girls in classes and treat them as
anonymous integers in an elaborate record system. Yet we know
that each is an individual different from every other. Each has
his own way of learning. To pretend that all can be classified and
graded on the identical scale denies those differences and does
violence to reality. Above all, it puts a premium on malleability,
upon accommodation to existing expectations, upon the qualities
of getting along. The good boy is he who matches up to his teachers' previously formed standards. But is he the one likely to grow
into the man of achievement?

28   Unless he learns somehow to locate himself by his own standards,
a blast of awareness, in school or later, will blow him off his course.
My roommate, said the boy who was my tutee, was good at everything; there was not a blemish on the record at commencement.
In his senior year, my roommate took the aptitude tests in business, medicine, and law, did well in all, and as a matter of course
entered the law school, having done best in that subject. No doubt
he would have been at the head of the pack in that race also, but
in an unguarded moment my roommate allowed himself to wonder
what being a lawyer would mean to him. He did not know how to
go about finding the answer.

29   In the past, the looseness and inefficiency of the educational
system provided the means for rescuing talent in danger of being
wasted. The boy whose interests matured late or changed as he
grew up could jog along at his own rate and make up for lost time
when he was ready. But the more rigid the system becomes, the

less room it leaves for the variant patterns of the maverick. The species, indeed, becomes ever less likely to appear, as the habit or desire for nonconformity is stifled. The student totally absorbed in the race loses confidence in himself and accepts the premature rating as a valid measure of his ability. Then the evaluation becomes self-fulfilling. Placidly the young man tells me he would like to be a historian, and will if he earns a *magna*. If he gets only a *cum* he will go into his father's laundry business. Life becomes a play in which the first act determines the outcome of the plot.

30   As a result, many of the most sensitive youngsters simply throw up their hands. They turn their backs on the whole process and all too often reject all the values attached to the college. They hasten into marriage, seeking in life the reality and personal security school does not afford them. Or they simply refuse to finish; increasingly, the able students are among those who leave before graduation. The stronger or more stubborn ones stick it out for the sheepskin; the weaker or more reflective ones break down or pull out—in either case, a tragic waste of talent. For they were all good when they got to college (otherwise they would not have been admitted), and the failure is not altogether theirs.

31   There was a boy who had been at Harvard only one year. As a freshman in a smaller college he had done so well, and his high school record had been so good, that he had been encouraged to transfer, and a scholarship had enabled him to do so. After two semesters he was defeated and refused to go on. In the interminable calculation of pluses and minuses, he felt he was in danger of losing sight of what he had come for, and he wished to leave college to be educated. This is the stuff beats are made of. Such people do better to preserve their authenticity as persons by going away or by abstracting themselves from the routine rather than by yielding to the pressures. Yet the college loses by the inability to influence—and be influenced by—them.

32   She is a junior of about twenty, neat and not bad-looking; nothing distinguishes her in the rows of notetakers in the lecture hall. Now she has found the excuse for a conference in some question about the reading. She talks nervously about what is not on her mind and then blurts out what is. She will not be back to finish next year. She has taken a librarian's job in Georgia, in a small town, where she will be useful. Why? Nothing here seems worth doing; the courses she takes are all right, but she gets only B's in them. She has studied bits of philosophy and bits of government, and she is interested in the relation of ethics to politics. As

she talks, life comes back to her voice and the words tumble out fluently. Well, why not go on with the subject next year? It will not make a manageable thesis. It had not occurred to her that one could learn outside the framework of the requirements.

33   The system favors certain character types over others, and not always the most desirable ones. For the young man who knows when he enters that he will be an actuary or a geologist or a patent attorney, the learning track runs clearly to his destination and all the stations are plainly marked. He will make few mistakes and run few risks. Even if he is not altogether docile, he operates within a limited framework and wastes no time. His schooling is likely to be uneventful; it may also be unadventurous and unimproving.

34   By contrast, those who come to college without specifically defined goals or who change as they learn are at a competitive disadvantage. They must make choices along the whole route, and therefore face the hazard of mistaken decisions. They are prone to turn into dead ends and to need second chances. Since what is relevant to their needs is not already marked out for them, they may gain more from looking out of the window than from taking notes. Their records will look spotty and erratic. Yet they may be growing at every stage and may, in the end, be the better for their mistakes than their fellows who never faltered. Society may be the loser by the failure to make room for the recovery of such talents. We need not only men who can get the job done, but also those who can wonder why it needs to be done.

35   Under the pressure of unremitting competition, a valuable sector of the educational enterprise shows signs of contraction. Since the measured blocks and units of formal instruction have clearly defined weight, it is foolhardy to expend precious energies upon activities to which no immediate reward is attached. Those who waste time by the way will lose ground in the race to the "bookers" who concentrate on the assignments. The tendency to shy away from distractions is recent and has not gone far, but it is already ominous.

36   Not all learning in the college community of the past was confined to the classroom. Often the students taught each other more effectively than the teachers could, gained more from extracurricular activities than from formal classwork. The experience of writing for the paper, or of managing a team, or of singing or playing, and, most of all, the undirected talk that swirled formlessly through the night have a value that cannot be recognized in grades

or credits. There will be ever less time for them as the shadow of the examination falls across the college. Boys made rivals by competition will be less ready to help one another, and the immensely variegated activities of the college as it was may dry up.

37   Finally, the whole process thrusts an uncongenial role upon the instructor. His function as a teacher becomes subsidiary to that of the grader; he is judge rather than counselor, impartial arbiter rather than ally of the student. That, too, distorts the meaning of education. It destroys the intimacy of a relationship in which the older person conceives his role as that of helping the younger, in which the younger can turn to the older for aid and advice without fear of being evaluated in the process.

38   There is no simple corrective to this disorder, even were its nature clearly perceived. Much of the difficulty springs from the unprecedented demands a democratic society places upon the colleges. We cannot and should not halt the increasing size of student bodies. We need more rather than fewer fellowships. And the college should continue to play a part in career selection. These are conditions of the value we place upon equality of opportunity. Only thus can we locate ability wherever it may be found and compensate for the inequalities of family background. Yet, to the degree that we encourage these desirable trends, our institutions will become more formal, more bureaucratic, and more rigidly organized.

39   But we need not, in consequence, continue to encumber ourselves with outmoded methods of evaluation which frustrate the larger goals of education. It will be a long, difficult task to get away from them.

40   I tease myself sometimes with daydreams of how we might break out of the present situation. A few institutions have already separated the teaching and the marking functions. That is as it should be, and the result is to clarify the relationship of the teacher to his students. It would be gratifying to appear in a classroom where everyone was on the same side, where there was not one to police and the others to be policed, but all were to work toward the same end. Evidence points to the merits of a divorce between the essentially incompatible tasks of instructor and grader.

41   That separation of tasks would, of course, make it impossible to administer examinations and award marks for every segment of instruction. So much the better. No other system of higher education subjects its students to the endlessly badgering tests of the

American college. The examinations of French and English universities are difficult, but they come where they belong, at the terminus of a stage in education. And they probe not fragments of courses, but the mastery of a whole field of knowledge, however and whenever acquired. These methods cannot be simply transferred to our own situation. But they indicate that we can safely do without the recurrent, meaningless hurdles we now set in the way of our students. We can aim at a mode of evaluation that will judge the whole man as he leaves the campus, not the bits and pieces of him we glimpse as he passes through it.

42   Above all, we can take the heat off by leaving these people alone. Most college freshmen are now eighteen years old. They are men and women who are, or should be, above all concerned with discovering themselves. All those prescriptions and requirements, all those efforts at surveillance and discipline, obscure the true nature of their tasks. They must learn after their own fashion, even at the cost of false starts, errors, and lost time. The college can help them, if they wish to be helped, mostly by creating an environment for discovery. The faculty can help them, if they wish to be helped, mostly through establishing the contacts, fruitful when free, of the more, with the less, experienced minds. But the stifling competitive atmosphere of the race for position, which the college itself generates by anachronistic grading methods, has no place in that environment.

QUESTIONS FOR STUDY

1. In what way (or ways) are the terms *unity* and *coherence* superficially similar? How might we effectively differentiate between these terms?

2. What is the "unifying" thread that runs through the Brooks and Warren essay? Comment on the *coherence* of the essay. Is the *emphasis* of the essay apparent and effective? Explain. Have the authors effectively fitted this "threefold" set of organizational concepts into the larger framework of introduction, body, and conclusion? Justify your answer, pointing to specific portions of the essay.

3. Are unity, coherence, and emphasis "things" that a student finds after the essay is completed? How might the student incorporate these "things" into the actual writing process itself?

4. Define the term *local transition*. Point out examples used by the authors in the section dealing with local transitions. Explain the function of the transitional devices used in paragraph 16 and between paragraphs 12-21 of Handlin's essay "Are Colleges Killing Education?"

5. What elements should be included in an effective introduction? How many of these do you find in the introduction to "Are Colleges Killing Education?" What makes an effective conclusion? Is Handlin's conclusion effective?

6. Has Handlin written a coherent essay? Is it unified? Are there any extraneous elements that you might want to delete? How does the metaphor of "the race" operate in the essay?

7. Point out various devices that Handlin uses to achieve emphasis. Which are most effective? Does your interest flag at any point? Explain.

8. What is the reason for the grading system existing as it does in its present form? What effect does the competition for grades have on the approach a student must take toward his subject matter? What types of students seem better fitted for the "race" for grades? Why? What types become victims of this system? Discuss the effects of outside (parental, etc.) pressures that accrue because of a competitive grading system. What are some of the remedies the author suggests?

WRITING TOPICS

1. Write an essay in which you criticize a college lecture, paying particular attention to those elements in the lecture corresponding to unity, coherence, and emphasis in writing (do not overlook these elements in your own writing). You might consider what information you would include if you were delivering the lecture. What information might you omit? How might the introduction and conclusion be made more effective?

2. Analyze a group or organization that you have knowledge of, showing how they operate when they have to arrive at a decision. (A word about analysis — when we analyze something, we are taking it apart.) Basically, there are two ways to analyze something, by partition or by classification. For example: when we decide to examine a car, we can either examine it piece by piece, or we can divide it into various systems—hydraulic system, electrical system, fuel system, etc. *Partition*, therefore, consists of separating the item under examination into its component elements, dividing the original item into as many pieces as is necessary to insure comprehension. *Classification*, on the other hand, consists of dividing the item under examination into a number of previously assigned categories or systems. Keep in mind what you have learned from reading the Brooks and Warren essay.

3. Do you feel the grading system should be changed from its present form? Using the essay by Handlin as a departure point, write an essay arguing for or against a change.

4. Write an essay analyzing the Handlin essay or any other essay for the elements of organization—unity, coherence, emphasis, introduction, and conclusion. Be sure you employ these elements in your paper.

Descriptive writing, like any other, has as its most fundamental purpose persuasion. Whether the writer is attempting to render objectively the significant facts about the object under consideration or to sway the reader to react to it as he does, his larger goal is always the same: to persuade his reader to visualize that object as he does. Description of any sort requires a clear and distinct knowledge of both the object and the writer's intention. With these established, precise observation, selectivity in detail, and vividness in expression must all combine to create either a verbal replica or an accurate representation of the writer's response to his object (the term "object" is to be understood here in its very broadest sense). In this chapter from their text, *Rhetoric, Principles and Usage*, Richard Hughes and P. Albert Duhamel differentiate between the two basic categories of descriptive prose and explain with examples the techniques inherent in the successful writing of each.

Description

Richard Hughes, P. Albert Duhamel

1 Most writing involves description of someone or something. A personal letter to a friend frequently calls for a description of a new acquaintance, a new acquisition, or some place recently visited. Business and professional reports commonly involve the description of problems which must be acted upon. Editorials and magazine articles often require the description of situations for which some remedy is being proposed.

2 Description, like all other forms of writing, is organized about a single integrating purpose. The writer of a travel book may want to describe the places he has visited as accurately, or as colorfully, as possible. A novelist may want to describe his characters and settings as realistically as possible, a journalist may want to describe something in a way which will make the course of action he is advocating seem like the right, indeed the only, one. But in every case, the purpose of description is allied to the larger purpose of persuasion. The travel book writer wants to "persuade" his readers to visit the places he writes about; the novelist wants to "persuade" his audience that the characters are real; the journalist wants to "persuade" his readers to an opinion or a course of action.

3 The use of descriptive passages as part of the purpose of persuasion can be illustrated from Daniel Webster's speech in the trial of John Knapp for the murder of Captain White. Webster's purpose in the following passage was not to render an objective description of the condition of Captain White's home the morning after the murder. It was to persuade the jury that those conditions

indicated a murder had been committed not by a chance intruder but by a group of conspirators who had planned very carefully.

Let me ask your attention, then, in the first place, to those appearances, on the morning after the murder, which have a tendency to show that it was done in pursuance of a preconcerted plan of operation. What are they? A man was found murdered in his bed. No stranger had done the deed, no one unacquainted with the house had done it. It was apparent that somebody within had opened, and somebody without had entered. There had obviously and certainly been concert and cooperation. The inmates of the house were not alarmed when the murder was perpetrated. The assassin had entered without any riot or any violence. He had found the way prepared for him. The house had been previously opened. The window was unbarred from within, and its fastening unscrewed. There was a lock on the door of the chamber in which Mr. White slept, but the key was gone. It had been taken away and secreted. The footsteps of the murderer were visible, outdoors, tending toward the window. The plank by which he entered the window still remained. The road he pursued had been thus prepared for him. The victim was slain, and the murderer had escaped. Every thing indicated that somebody within had cooperated with somebody without. Every thing proclaimed that some of the inmates, or somebody having access to the house, had had a hand in the murder. On the face of the circumstances, it was apparent, therefore that this was premeditated, concerted murder; that there had been a conspiracy to commit it.

Webster's description is not a model of the vividness for which a novelist strives, nor has it the objectivity expected of a report writer. It is, however, well adapted to the achieving of his purpose for it picks out those few details which tend to confirm his proposition, that "somebody within had opened and somebody without had entered," and neglects those details which might have tended to support the opposite view.

KINDS OF DESCRIPTION

4   Description tends to be either objective or impressionistic. It is objective if it attempts to portray its subject as it actually exists, with as little distortion as possible. It is impressionistic when it attempts to present an interpretation of its subject.

5   Descriptions can more accurately be defined as "tending" rather than as achieving either extreme. Although a completely objective description of some objects is theoretically possible, it would probably become only a confusing and colorless enumeration of details.

6   All descriptions are based on a core of fact, and they use words
and details with which readers are familiar. An impressionistic
description may exaggerate the poverty and bleakness of a setting
if this is the way a writer wants to make his readers see it. But
there is a core of reality around which he builds his description
and which makes it possible for him to communicate his perceptions to others.

OBSERVATION

7   Whether a description tends to be objective or impressionistic,
if it is to be vivid and effective, it must be based upon precise,
detailed, intelligent observation. Many writers keep journals in
order to train themselves to observe closely and to preserve a
record of their observations for later reference.

8   John Burroughs, who is famous for his descriptions of nature,
had this to say about the need for close observation.

> Thoreau, as revealed in his journal, was for years trying to settle
> in his own mind what was the first thing that stirred in spring, after
> the severe New England winter,—in what was the first sign or pulse
> of returning life manifest. . . . He dug into the swamps, he peered into
> the water, he felt with benumbed hands for the radical leaves of the
> plants under the snow; he inspected the buds on the willows, the cat-
> kins on the alders; he went out before daylight of a March morning
> and remained out after dark; he watched the lichens and mosses on
> the rocks; he listened for the birds; he was on the alert for the first
> frog ("Can you be absolutely sure," he says, "that you have heard the
> first frog that croaked in the township?") . . . .

Burroughs' own journal is an interesting record of his precise
observations and his reflections on these observations.

> . . . Old fox-hunters will tell you, on the evidence of their own eyes, that
> there is a black fox and a silver-gray fox, two species, but there are not;
> the black fox is black when coming toward you or running from you
> and silver-gray at point-blank view, when the eye penetrates the fur;
> each separate hair is gray the first half and black the last.

9   The writer who starts out to describe something with which he
is not sufficiently familiar naturally encounters mounting difficulties. He is usually forced into skirting the subject or, at best, merely
suggesting it.

DOMINANT IMPRESSION

10   Omission of detail is not serious when the subject is a common
one or when its description is only incidental to the discussion

as a whole. But when the subject is one which is probably unknown
to most of the readers and when its description is the core around
which the passage is built, the omission of any significant descriptive details may undermine the writer's basic purpose. A writer
should ask himself, "What, precisely, am I trying to describe? What
do I hope to achieve by means of this description?" For if the
description is to have unity, and if it is to be integrated into the
larger unity of the passage, then both the object to be described
and the purpose in describing it must be very clear in the writer's
mind.

11   A case in point would be the following passage, the author of
which is describing his reaction to the call of the wood thrush.

> As a child born and reared in the city, that wild, ringing call was
> perfectly new and strange to me when, one early dawn, I first heard it
> during a visit to the Delaware Water Gap. To me whose ears had grown
> familiar only with the rumble of paved streets, the sound was like a
> reiterated unearthly summons inviting me from my narrow prison
> existence out into a wide and unexplored world of impulse and adven-
> ture. Long afterwards I learned the name of the songster whose note
> had made so strong an impression on my childish senses, but still I
> associate the song with the grandiose scenery of the Water Gap.

The effect of the bird's call is loftily described as a "reiterated
unearthly summons inviting me from my narrow prison existence
out into a wide and unexplored world of impulse and adventure."
Of the call itself the writer says only that it was "wild" and "ringing." The writer then goes on with an explanation of the next time
he heard the same call.

> I was indeed almost a man—though the confession may sound in-
> credible in these days—before I again heard the wood thrush's notes,
> and my second adventure impressed me almost as profoundly as the
> first. In the outer suburbs of the city where my home had always been,
> I was walking one day with a brother, when suddenly out of a grove of
> laurel oaks sounded, clear and triumphant, the note which I remem-
> bered well, but which had come to have to my imagination the unreality
> and mystery of a dream of long ago. Instantly my heart leapt within
> me. "It is the fateful summons once more!" I cried, and, with my com-
> panion who was equally ignorant of birdlore, I ran into the grove to
> discover the wild trumpeter. That was a strange chase in the fading
> twilight, while the unknown songster led us from tree to tree, ever
> deeper into the woods. Many times we saw him on one of the lower
> boughs, but could not for a long while bring ourselves to believe that
> so wondrous a melody should proceed from so plain a minstrel. And
> at last, when we had satisfied ourselves of his identity, and the night
> had fallen, we came into the road with a strange solemnity hanging

over us. Our ears had opened to the unceasing harmonies of creation, and our eyes had been made aware of the endless drama of natural life. We had been initiated into the lesser mysteries; and if the sacred pageantry was not then, and never was to be, perfectly clear to our understanding, the imagination was nevertheless awed and purified.[1]

12   The writer is obviously trying to convey what must clearly have been a very deep and enduring emotional experience and to draw the reader into a vicarious participation or at least sympathetic appreciation of that experience. But participation is impossible when the cause of the experience is not clearly defined. Although the effect of the bird's call on the writer is stressed again and again, there is only passing mention of the call itself. And the slight mention is made in such sweepingly general terms as "wild" and "ringing" which evoke almost no response from the reader's imagination.

13   Every description involves selection, and it is essential that the writer carefully control this selection by focussing upon the dominant impression he wants to create in his reader's mind much as a scientist might think of an hypothesis he wanted to prove or a lawyer of a case he wanted to win. The writer must convey this dominant impression to his readers. If he is trying to write an objective description, he must check his work constantly to make sure his details are accurate. If he is writing impressionistic description, he must make certain that every element he has chosen to include contributes to the creation of his intended impression.

14   The following passage sets out to emphasize the relentless and almost unimaginable hardships in the life of the Eskimo woman.

> Their women were robust, for their life and work were so difficult as to mark them completely. They did their cooking by heather and twigs. This was not so bad in summer, when the ground was free of snow and they could collect their fuel in big bundles, carry it down to the tents, and make festive cooking fires. But in winter it was worse; then the women had to go out and scrape aside the snow to get to the heather, and since they did not have many skins and had to save their mittens, they pulled the heather loose with their bare hands. Imagine what that meant at a temperature of forty below! Their hands were completely malformed, black, hard to the feel as if made of wood, and full of frost scars. Besides, they let their nails grow very long, so that the general impression was that of sinister bird claws. When they came home in winter with their fuel, they couldn't burn it under the open sky, for that would use it up too quickly. Cooking wasn't possible in the snow

---

[1]Paul Elmer More, "A Hermit's Note on Thoreau," *Shelburne Essays* (1904).

house either as the snow would melt, and, also, the smoke would bother the master of the house. So adjoining the house they would build a small, low hut with a hole in the roof, and in there the woman would lie down to do the cooking. She had to blow on the fire continually to keep it going, ashes would fly around her face, hair, and shoulders, and her eyes were always red and watering, so that the tears made deep grooves of bare skin down over the otherwise dirt-covered face. You can easily understand that such a woman looked old and decrepit before she was thirty.[2]

15 The writer explicitly states his intended dominant impression in the first sentence. But it is the careful selection of supporting details, and the exclusion of any factors which might serve to disprove or offset it which maintain that dominant impression in the mind of the reader.

OBJECTIVE DESCRIPTION

16 The most nearly objective descriptions are usually to be found in scientific writing. The purpose of scientific description is to convey a clear, detailed picture of its subject. Scientists must report their observations, experiments, and results in precise, detailed, and unbiased terms. The descriptive scientists, especially the botanists, biologists, and zoologists must record their observations in detailed, objective terms so that others can benefit from their work and obtain the same results. Some descriptive scientists have become famous for reports which were not only scientifically significant but also remarkable for their literary qualities. The French entomologist Henri Fabre made insect life interesting for many lay readers without sacrificing scientific objectivity. In the following passage he tries to give the general reader a clear impression of the size and strength of the *Scoliae* or worker wasps. In the first paragraph he succeeds in conveying a clear idea of their size by comparing them with other insects and birds with which his readers might be expected to be more familiar.

Were strength to take precedence over the other zoological attributes, the Scoliae would hold a predominant place in the front rank of the wasps. Some of them may be compared in size with the little bird from the north, the Golden-crested Wren, who comes to us at the time of the first autumn mists and visits the rotten buds. The largest and most

[2]Reprinted by permission of The World Publishing Company from *Peter Freuchen's Book of the Eskimos,* edited by Dagmar Freuchen. Copyright © 1961 by Peter Freuchen Estate.

imposing of our sting-bearers, the Carpenter-bee, the Bumble-bee, the Hornet, cut a poor figure beside certain of the Scoliae.

A black livery, with broad yellow patches; leathery wings, amber-colored, like the skin of an onion, and watered with purple reflections; thick, knotted legs, covered with sharp hairs; a massive frame; a powerful head, encased in a hard cranium; a still, clumsy gait; a low, short, silent flight; this gives you a concise description of the female, who is strongly equipped for her arduous task. The male, being a mere philanderer, sports a more elegant pair of horns, is more daintily clad and has a more graceful figure, without altogether losing the quality of robustness which is his cohort's leading characteristic.[3]

17   One reason for Fabre's success as a reporter of the natural world was his refusal to be distracted by the deluding ideal of completeness. He focussed each passage to achieve one purpose, and did not try to make any single passage into a catch-all for a mass of irrelevant detail.

18   The test of the objectivity of a description is not its exhaustiveness, but its verifiability. Fabre's descriptions are objective not because they are total reproductions of reality but because they tend to reproduce reality as it is. They can be tested by comparing them with the originals.

IMPRESSIONISTIC DESCRIPTION

19   Impressionistic description is description which has been slanted, not necessarily to deceive the reader but to make him see reality as the author wants him to see it. The impressionist writer adds or omits details in order to present reality as he wants it to be envisioned.

20   Impressionistic description is also known as "suggestive," or "artistic," or "imaginative." All of these terms are intended to imply that the writer of impressionistic description is functioning more as an artist or creative writer than a reporter. He is comparable to a stage manager who suggests, by skillful manipulation of lights and shadows, more than is actually presented on the stage. The test of an impressionistic description is not to compare it with reality, but to ask whether it is likely to evoke the desired response in the readers.

21   The following paragraph was written by Somerset Maugham to make his readers see the beauty of the old fort at Mandalay as he

---

[3]Reprinted by permission of Dodd, Mead & Company, Inc. from *More Hunting Wasps,* by J. Henri Fabre. Copyright 1921 by Dodd, Mead & Company, Inc.

saw it. Maugham is not intent upon picturing the fort as it was, or as it might have seemed to a native. On the contrary, he announces the dominant impressions he wants to create as that of a "beauty that batters you and stuns you and leaves you breathless." Note how he omits unpleasant details—the physical surroundings of the fort, the dust, the heat, the debris of daily life—which would have made the actual scene far less romantic.

In the broad water of the moat (of the fort) the rosy wall and thick foliage of the trees and the Burmese in their bright clothes are sharply reflected. The water is still but not stagnant, and peace rests upon it like a swan with a golden crown. Its colors, in the early morning and toward sunset, have the soft, fatigued tenderness of pastel; they have the translucency, without the stubborn definiteness, of oils. It is as though light were a prestidigitator and in play laid on colors that he had just created and were about with a careless hand to wash them out again. You hold your breath, for you cannot believe that such an effect can be anything but evanescent. You watch it with the same expectancy with which you read a poem in some complicated metre when your ear awaits the long delayed rhyme that will fulfill the harmony. But at sunset, when the clouds in the west are red and splendid so that the wall, the trees, and the moat are drenched in radiance, and at night under the full moon when the white gateways drip with silver and the belvederes above them are shot with silhouetted glimpses of the sky, the assault on your senses is shattering. You try to guard yourself by saying it is not real. This is not a beauty that steals upon you unawares, that flatters and soothes your bruised spirit; this is not a beauty that you can hold in your hand and call your own and put in its place among familiar beauties that you know: it is a beauty that batters you and stuns you and leaves you breathless; there is no calmness in it nor control; it is like a fire that on a sudden consumes you, and you are left shaken and bare and yet by a strange miracle alive.[4]

22   Neither objective description nor impressionistic description can be considered as essentially better than the other. Both have their uses and both are to be judged on the basis of whether or not they fulfill their uses. Impressionistic description is well adapted to communicating a mood, establishing a feeling. Objective description is intended to convey information. To show how each kind of description has its appropriate function and how each differs from the other, two selections, both describing the American prairie,

[4]From *The Gentleman in the Parlour*. Copyright 1930 by Doubleday & Company, Inc. Reprinted by permission of Doubleday & Company, William Heinemann Ltd., and W. Somerset Maugham.

are presented together. The first is from an article in an encyclopedia. The details given in this description are very generalized because the writer is intent upon defining what is typical of all prairies.

PRAIRIE, a treeless region in the Mississippi Valley, adjacent to the forested area, so called since the time of the early French explorers. The eastern border of the prairie region is an irregular line crossing Minnesota and Wisconsin in a southeasterly direction and extending into western Indiana, thence crossing Illinois and Missouri southwesterly to the borders of Oklahoma and eastern Texas. From this forest line the prairies extend westward from 200 to 600 miles to the Great Plains, into which they merge quite imperceptibly. In general we may say that the characteristics of the prairies are intermediate between those of the adjacent forests on the east and the plains on the west. The soil, climate, rainfall, etc., of the prairies are much like those of the western edge of the forests. As we go westward the soil becomes more sandy, the climate more "continental" and the rainfall less, approaching the conditions which prevail on the plains.

The soil of the prairies is usually dark in color and rich in organic matter. It is composed of very fine particles, and when dried after wetting becomes very hard. It contains much finely divided sand, and is generally somewhat deficient in clay. While very rich and often of great depth, it is by no means inexhaustible, and the better classes of farmers have found it profitable to use fertilizers from time to time.

The climate of the prairies is somewhat more severe than that of the adjacent forest areas, on account of the free sweep of the winds which intensify the cold of winter as well as the heat of summer. The annual rainfall is about 30 inches, diminishing somewhat as we go westward, and this is so distributed that by far the greater portion falls in the spring and summer.

Although the prairies are usually spoken of as treeless, this is not strictly true, since the streams are always fringed with trees, the treeless areas extending over the higher lands from stream to stream. Yet since these forest fringes are often confined to the deep narrow valleys in which the streams flow, they are often scarcely noticeable as one looks over the landscape. The vegetation of the prairies naturally divides itself into that of the open country and that of the woodlands. In the open country the grasses constitute the dominant vegetation, since they are mostly perennial, and very tenacious of life.[5]

23   The second description of the prairie is taken from a novel. The writer's intention is to convey a sense of the vastness of the prairie and the feeling of isolation which it engendered among the early

[5]Quoted from the 1960 edition of the *Encyclopedia Americana,* by permission of the publishers, Grolier Incorporated, New York.

settlers. A comparison of this account with the encyclopedia article will reveal that the novelist exaggerated the emptiness of the scene. The trees and the breaks in the monotony of the land mentioned by the encyclopedia disappear in the novel. The heroine gazes "aimlessly" about because there is nothing for her to fix her eyes upon. The land stretches in a "broad expanse" away "endlessly" in every direction. It reminds her of the ocean, but is emptier than the ocean for here there is no life at all.

> With a common impulse, they went toward the hill; when they had reached the summit, Beret sat down and let her gaze wander aimlessly around. . . . In a certain sense, she had to admit to herself, it was lovely up here. The broad expanse stretching away endlessly in every direction, seemed almost like the ocean—especially now, when darkness was falling. It reminded her strongly of the sea, and yet it was very different . . . This formless prairie had no heart beat, no waves that sang, no soul that could be touched or cared . . . .
>
> The infinitude surrounding her on every hand might not have been so oppressive, might even have brought her a measure of peace, if it had not been for the deep silence, which lay heavier here than in a church. Indeed what was there to break it? She had passed beyond the outposts of civilization; the nearest dwelling places of men were far away. Here no warbling of birds rose in the air, no buzzing of insects sounded; even the wind had died away, the waving blades of grass that trembled to the faintest breath now stood erect and quiet, as if listening, in the great hush of the evening. . . . All along the way, coming out, she had noticed this strange thing: the stillness had grown deeper, the silence more depressing, the farther west they journeyed; it must have been over two weeks now since she had heard a bird sing! Had they travelled into some nameless, abandoned region? Could no living thing exist out here, in the empty, desolate, endless wastes of green and blue? How could existence go on she thought desperately? If life is to thrive and endure, it must at least have something to hide behind! . . . As her eyes darted nervously here and there, flitting from object to object and trying to pierce the purple dimness that was steadily closing in, a sense of desolation so profound settled upon her that she seemed unable to think at all.[6]

24 The novelist has been successful in creating the impression he intended, for by the time the reader reaches this last sentence he shares the heroine's feelings. He has been told that there are no birds, no insects. Even the wind, which the encyclopedia description emphasized blew summer and winter, has been painted out. Truly nothing exists in this vast, silent emptiness.

---

[6]*Giants in the Earth,* by O. E. Rolvaag. Reprinted by permission of Harper & Brothers.

POINT OF VIEW

25   If the unity of a descriptive passage is controlled by the dominant impression the writer wants to establish, its coherence is
governed by a clear and consistently maintained point of view—
the real or imagined physical vantage point from which the reader
is asked to view the object being described.

26   The point of view orients the reader in relationship to the details
of the description. Without a point of view the details of a descriptive passage can easily become confused. Not only must the reader
be provided with enough details so that he can visualize the object
being described, but these details must be presented in an order
that will permit him to absorb them in an orderly fashion. To
prevent the sequence of details in a description from becoming
scrambled, the writer should select a point of view from which he
imagines himself as viewing the scene which he is describing.

27   The point of view must be chosen with an eye to its appropri-
ateness to the dominant impression which the writer intends to
create. If the writer intends to describe the general shape of a large
building, his vantage point must necessarily be some distance away
from the building itself. On the other hand, if he proposes to
describe the changing patterns of sunlight on an old rug, he must
be "in" the room and fairly close to the spot of sunlight on the floor.

28   Most writers feel the need to change their point of view in order
to describe a setting from all sides. The writer must be careful to
let his reader know of any such change. If he does not, the reader
may keep on trying to fit the details into the original point of
view, and lose all sense of perspective.

29   The following passage was written to convey the excitement
attending the annual running of the Kentucky Derby. To give the
reader an unusual point of view on the Derby, to take him right
into the middle of things, William Faulkner decided to describe the
preparations for the Derby from a spot right on the track.

> And we ourselves are on the track now, but carefully and discreetly
> back against the rail out of the way: now we are no longer a handful
> clotting in a murmur of furlongs and poles and tenths of a second, but
> there are a hundred of us now and more still coming, all craning to
> look in one direction into the mouth of the chute. Then it is as if the
> gray, over-cast, slightly moist, post-dawn air itself had spoken above
> our heads. This time the exercise boy is a Negro, moving his mount at
> no schooled or calculated gait at all, just moving it rapidly, getting it
> off the track and out of the way, speaking not to us but to all cir-
> cumambience: man and beast either within hearing: "Y'awl can git out
> of the way too now; here's the big horse coming."

And now we can all see him as he enters the chute on a lead in the hand of a groom. The groom unsnaps the lead and now the two horses come on down the empty chute toward the empty track, out of which the final end of the waiting and the expectation has risen almost like an audible sound, a suspiration, a sigh.

Now he passes us (there are two of them, two horses, two riders, but we see only one), not just the Big Horse of the professional race argot because he does look big, bigger than we know him to be, so that most of the other horses we have watched this morning appear dwarfed by him, with the small, almost gentle, head and the neat small feet and the trim and delicate pasterns which the ancient Arab blood has brought to him, the man who will ride him Saturday hunched like a fly or a cricket on the big withers. He is not even walking. He is strolling. Because he is looking around. Not at us. He has seen people; the sycophant adulant roar has faded behind his drumming feet too many times for us to hold his attention. And not at track either because he has seen track before and it usually looks like this one does from his point (just entering the backstretch): empty.[7]

FUNDAMENTAL IMAGE

30   Describing something with words imposes some essential limitations on the writer. He can only "feed" his readers a word or a detail at a time. The reader takes in one bit of information at a time until he has enough to organize it into a meaningful whole.

31   One way of helping a reader organize such details is to use a fundamental image. A fundamental image is any familiar frame of reference, introduced early in a description, and then used as an outline, diagram or mould to locate all the details which follow. In the early days of printing, a line of type was set by using a grooved stick long enough to hold only the amount of type needed to make one line. A fundamental image serves as a kind of typestick into which a reader fits one word at a time until he has completed enough to read the line. The following paragraphs, taken from Victor Hugo's description of the Battle of Waterloo, illustrate the use of a fundamental image—in this case, the capital letter A.

Those who wish to form a clear idea of the battle of Waterloo need only imagine a capital A laid on the ground. The left stroke of the A is the Nivelles road, the right one the Genappe road, while the cross of the A is the sunken road from Onain to Braine l'Alleud. The top of the A is Mont Saint-Jean; Wellington is there; the left-hand lower

[7]From "Kentucky; May; Saturday," by William Faulkner. © Copyright 1955 by Estelle Faulkner and Jill Faulkner Summers. Reprinted from *Essays, Speeches and Public Letters,* by William Faulkner, edited by James B. Meriwether, by permission of Random House, Inc.

point is Hougemont; Reille is there with Jerome Bonaparte; the right-hand lower point is La Belle Alliance; Napoleon is there. A little below the point where the cross of the A meets the right stroke, is La Haye Sainte; in the center of this cross is the precise point where the final battle-word was spoken. It is here that the lion is placed, the involuntary symbol of the supreme heroism of the Imperial Guard.

The triangle contained at the top of the A between the two strokes and the cross is the plateau of Mont Saint-Jean. The dispute for this plateau was the whole battle.

32   A writer can, as Hugo has, give details in constant relation to his fundamental image, or he can present them in some kind of order beginning from an established point. The writer can move from top to bottom, from bottom to top; clockwise and counterclockwise; from right to left, or left to right. The choice of presentation is not as important as the necessity of adhering to it. Again, the fundamental image must not be altered without informing the reader.

VIVIDNESS IN DESCRIPTION

33   Of equal importance with the structure of a description is its content. Many descriptions fail to achieve their purpose because they lack detail. Sometimes this lack arises from the failure of the writer to observe carefully. A more common fault, however, is to include visual detail to the exclusion of everything else.

34   Much of our knowledge does come to us through the sense of sight, and visual detail cannot properly be omitted from any description without making it that much less effective. But the writer who is organizing his material should ask himself whether there are not details to be perceived by senses other than the sense of sight. He should ask himself not only how did the place look but also how it smelled, sounded, felt. Whether the description is intended to be objective or impressionistic, it will be the more vivid for this approach.

35   Thomas Wolfe, one of the most vivid recorders of the American scene, in his novel *Of Time and The River*, describes a long train ride taken by the hero, Eugene Gant, from his home in Virginia to Boston. Wolfe seeks to convey the grayness and drabness of a Pullman car in the early morning light—qualities normally perceived by the eye. Consequently, most of the detail in the following excerpt is visual: the whiteness of the dawn light and the linen in the berth, the scuffled and rumpled bed-clothes.

At day-break suddenly, he awoke. The first light of the day, faint, gray-white, shone through the windows of his berth. The faint gray light fell on the stiff white linen, feverishly scuffed and rumpled in the distressful visions of the night, on the hot pillows and on the long cramped figure of the boy, where the dim reflection already could be seen on the polished surface of the berth above his head. Outside, that smoky-gray light had stolen almost imperceptibly through the darkness. The air now shone gray-blue and faintly luminous with day, and the old brown earth was just beginning to emerge in that faint light.[8]

36 Next to the sense of sight, the sense of sound seems to provide us with the most information about our world. Sight requires light to function; but the sense of hearing can function in the dark. Notice how Wolfe, in describing the passage of the train through the night, has based his account upon details absorbed by the sense of sound.

The train had halted for a moment at one of the Virginia towns. . . . A trainman was coming swiftly down the station platform beneath the windows of the train, pausing from time to time to hammer on the car-wheels of each truck. A Negro toiled past below them with a heavy rattling truck in tow, piled high with baggage.

And elsewhere there were the casual voices of the train men—conductors, porters, baggage masters, station men—greeting each other with friendly words, without surprise, speaking of weather, work, plans for the future, saying farewell in the same way. Then the bell tolled, the whistle blew, the slow panting of the engine came back to them, the train was again in motion.

37 Descriptions based upon details interpreted through senses other than sight and hearing are relatively rare. In the following paragraphs, Robert Benchley is trying to recall for his readers the smells which he associates with the week end. In a sense, he is describing what the week end meant to him in terms of its smells.

But, sure as the smells of Sunday were, those of Saturday were none the less distinctive and a great deal more cheery. In our house we began getting whiffs of Saturday as early as Friday evening, when the bread was "set" on the kitchen table and the beans "put to soak" nearby. The smell of the cold bread-dough when the napkins were lifted from the pans always meant "no school tomorrow," and was a preliminary to the "no school today" smells of Saturday, which are at the basis of my present trouble.

---

[8]This and succeeding passages from *Of Time and The River,* by Thomas Wolfe, are reprinted with the permission of Charles Scribner's Sons. Copyright 1935, by Charles Scribner's Sons.

In New England, of course, the *leit motif* among the Saturday smells was the one of beans baking, but the bread and pies ran it a close second. A good cake in the oven could hold its own, too. Then, along about eleven-thirty the Saturday noon dinner began to loom up, being more plebeian than the Sunday noon dinner, it usually took the combined form of cabbage, turnips, beets and corned beef, all working together in one pot, with the potatoes, to make what is known as the "New England boiled dinner." That put a stop to any other smells that thought they were something earlier in the morning.[9]

38   Some of the rarest descriptions are those addressed solely, or mainly, to the sense of touch. Perhaps it is because the sense of touch is not developed as a source of information by those who have the gift of sight. But Helen Keller, who was deaf and blind, had to learn everything through the touch of her fingers. The following paragraphs are taken from her autobiography.

What a joy it is to feel the soft, springy earth under my feet once more, to follow grassy roads that lead to ferny brooks where I can bathe my fingers in a cataract of rippling notes, or to clamber over a stone wall into green fields that tumble and roll and climb in riotous gladness!

Next to a leisurely walk I enjoy a "spin" on my tandem bicycle. It is splendid to feel the wind blowing in my face and the springy motion of my iron steed. The rapid rush through the air gives me a delicious sense of strength and buoyancy, and the exercise makes my pulse dance and my heart sing.[10]

39   One final passage from Wolfe will reveal how he could combine details derived from the various senses into a very vivid description of the moment before Eugene Gant boarded the train.

He could feel, taste, smell, and see everything with an instant still intensity, the animate fixation of a vision seen instantly, fixed forever in the mind of him who sees it, and sense the clumped dusty autumn masses of trees that bordered the tracks upon the left, and smell the thick exciting hot tarred caulking of the tracks, the dry warmth and good worn wooden smell of the powerful railway ties, and see the dull dusty red, the gaping emptiness and joy of a freight car, its rough floor whitened with soft siltings of thick flour, drawn in upon a spur of rusty track behind a warehouse of raw concrete blocks, and see the sudden desolation, the warehouse flung down rawly, newly, there among the hot, humid, spermy, nameless, thick-leaved field-growth of the South.

---

[9]From "Saturday's Smells" by Robert Benchley from *The Benchley Roundup,* edited by Nathaniel Benchley.
[10]From *Story of My Life,* by Helen Keller. Copyright 1905 by Doubleday & Co., Inc. Reprinted by permission of the publisher.

SUMMARY

40   Descriptive passages, like all forms of writing, must have unity, coherence, and, of course, content. The content of a descriptive passage is dependent upon the writer's skill in observing. He must train himself to notice, to question himself on what he is perceiving, to make sure that all the senses which can report on a scene are being put to work.

41   The writer achieves unity by including in his description only such details as lead toward the dominant impression he wishes to create. Coherence is maintained by the establishment of, and adherence to, a physical point of view or fundamental image.

42   Objective description is more commonly found in writing intended to explain, to clarify, or to inform. Impressionistic description more commonly serves as the basis of what might be called a larger argument. It serves as part of a larger dominant impression toward which the writer is striving—whether it be a novelist who is trying to establish the reality of a setting, or the journalist who, through an effective description of slum areas, hopes to bring about civic reform.

In this chapter taken from *The Sea Around Us*, Rachel Carson traces the process of man's evolution from the sea. Her material is based strictly on scientific fact, but she infuses it with vivid description to create a tone of awe. This tone is achieved partly through the careful and detailed cataloguing, in chronological order, of the various stages of development. Thus the essay dramatically demonstrates the absolute dependence of one stage on all those preceding, and describes in fascinating terms the ultimate emergence of the human species.

The Gray Beginnings

Rachel Carson

And the earth was without form, and void;
and darkness was upon the face of the deep.   GENESIS

1   Beginnings are apt to be shadowy, and so it is with the beginnings
of that great mother of life, the sea. Many people have debated how
and when the earth got its ocean, and it is not surprising that their
explanations do not always agree. For the plain and inescapable
truth is that no one was there to see, and in the absence of eye-
witness accounts there is bound to be a certain amount of disagreement. So if I tell here the story of how the young planet Earth
acquired an ocean, it must be a story pieced together from many
sources and containing whole chapters the details of which we can
only imagine. The story is founded on the testimony of the earth's
most ancient rocks, which were young when the earth was young;
on other evidence written on the face of the earth's satellite, the
moon; and on hints contained in the history of the sun and the
whole universe of star-filled space. For although no man was there
to witness this cosmic birth, the stars and the moon and the rocks
were there, and, indeed, had much to do with the fact that there is
an ocean.

2   The events of which I write must have occurred somewhat more
than 2 billion years ago.[1] As nearly as science can tell that is the
approximate age of the earth, and the ocean must be very nearly
as old. It is possible now to discover the age of the rocks that compose the crust of the earth by measuring the rate of decay of the

[1]Scientists now think that the earth is at least 4½ billion years old. [eds.]

radioactive materials they contain. The oldest rocks found anywhere on earth—in Manitoba—are about 2.3 billion years old.
Allowing 100 million years or so for the cooling of the earth's
materials to form a rocky crust, we arrive at the supposition that
the tempestuous and violent events connected with our planet's
birth occurred nearly 2½ billion years ago. But this is only a
minimum estimate, for rocks indicating an even greater age may
be found at any time.

3   The new earth, freshly torn from its parent sun, was a ball of
whirling gases, intensely hot, rushing through the black spaces of
the universe on a path and at a speed controlled by immense forces.
Gradually the ball of flaming gases cooled. The gases began to
liquefy, and Earth became a molten mass. The materials of this
mass eventually became sorted out in a definite pattern: the
heaviest in the center, the less heavy surrounding them, and the
least heavy forming the outer rim. This is the pattern which
persists today — a central sphere of molten iron, very nearly as
hot as it was 2 billion years ago, an intermediate sphere of semi-
plastic basalt, and a hard outer shell, relatively quite thin and
composed of solid basalt and granite.

4   The outer shell of the young earth must have been a good many
millions of years changing from the liquid to the solid state, and
it is believed that, before this change was completed, an event of
the greatest importance took place — the formation of the moon.
The next time you stand on a beach at night, watching the moon's
bright path across the water, and conscious of the moon-drawn
tides, remember that the moon itself may have been born of a great
tidal wave of earthly substance, torn off into space. And remember
that if the moon was formed in this fashion, the event may have
had much to do with shaping the ocean basins and the continents
as we know them.

5   There were tides in the new earth, long before there was an
ocean. In response to the pull of the sun the molten liquids of the
earth's whole surface rose in tides that rolled unhindered around
the globe and only gradually slackened and diminished as the
earthly shell cooled, congealed, and hardened. Those who believe
that the moon is a child of earth say that during an early stage
of the earth's development something happened that caused this
rolling, viscid tide to gather speed and momentum and to rise to
unimaginable heights. Apparently the force that created these
greatest tides the earth has ever known was the force of resonance,

for at this time the period of the solar tides had come to approach, then equal, the period of the free oscillation of the liquid earth. And so every sun tide was given increased momentum by the push of the earth's oscillation, and each of the twice-daily tides was larger than the one before it. Physicists have calculated that, after 500 years of such monstrous, steadily increasing tides, those on the side toward the sun became too high for stability, and a great wave was torn away and hurled into space. But immediately, of course, the newly created satellite became subject to physical laws that sent it spinning in an orbit of its own about the earth.

6   There are reasons for believing that this event took place after the earth's crust had become slightly hardened, instead of during its partly liquid state. There is to this day a great scar on the surface of the globe. This scar or depression holds the Pacific Ocean. According to some geophysicists, the floor of the Pacific is composed of basalt, the substance of the earth's middle layer, while all other oceans are floored with a thin layer of granite. We immediately wonder what became of the Pacific's granite covering and the most convenient assumption is that it was torn away when the moon was formed. There is supporting evidence. The mean density of the moon is much less than that of the earth (3.3 compared with 5.5), suggesting that the moon took away none of the earth's heavy iron core, but that it is composed only of the granite and some of the basalt of the outer layers.

7   The birth of the moon probably helped shape other regions of the world ocean besides the Pacific. When part of the crust was torn away, strains must have been set up in the remaining granite envelope. Perhaps the granite mass cracked open on the side opposite the moon scar. Perhaps, as the earth spun on its axis and rushed on its orbit through space, the cracks widened and the masses of granite began to drift apart, moving over a tarry, slowly hardening layer of basalt. Gradually the outer portions of the basalt layer became solid and the wandering continents came to rest, frozen into place with oceans between them. In spite of theories to the contrary, the weight of geologic evidence seems to be that the locations of the major ocean basins and the major continental land masses are today much the same as they have been since a very early period of the earth's history.

8   But this is to anticipate the story, for when the moon was born there was no ocean. The gradually cooling earth was enveloped in heavy layers of cloud, which contained much of the water of the

new planet. For a long time its surface was so hot that no moisture could fall without immediately being reconverted to steam. This dense, perpetually renewed cloud covering must have been thick enough that no rays of sunlight could penetrate it. And so the rough outlines of the continents and the empty ocean basins were sculptured out of the surface of the earth in darkness, in a Stygian world of heated rock and swirling clouds and gloom.

9   As soon as the earth's crust cooled enough, the rains began to fall. Never have there been such rains since that time. They fell continuously, day and night, days passing into months, into years, into centuries. They poured into the waiting ocean basins, or, falling upon the continental masses, drained away to become sea.

10   That primeval ocean, growing in bulk as the rains slowly filled its basins, must have been only faintly salt. But the falling rains were the symbol of the dissolution of the continents. From the moment the rains began to fall, the lands began to be worn away and carried to the sea. It is an endless, inexorable process that has never stopped — the dissolving of the rocks, the leaching out of their contained minerals, the carrying of the rock fragments and dissolved minerals to the ocean. And over the eons of time, the sea has grown ever more bitter with the salt of the continents.

11   In what manner the sea produced the mysterious and wonderful stuff called protoplasm we cannot say. In its warm, dimly lit waters the unknown conditions of temperature and pressure and saltiness must have been the critical ones for the creation of life from non-life. At any rate they produced the result that neither the alchemists with their crucibles nor modern scientists in their laboratories have been able to achieve.

12   Before the first living cell was created, there may have been many trials and failures. It seems probable that, within the warm saltiness of the primeval sea, certain organic substances were fashioned from carbon dioxide, sulphur, phosphorus, potassium, and calcium. Perhaps these were transition steps from which the complex molecules of protoplasm arose — molecules that somehow acquired the ability to reproduce themselves and begin the endless stream of life. But at present no one is wise enough to be sure.

13   Those first living things may have been simple microorganisms rather like some of the bacteria we know today—mysterious borderline forms that were not quite plants, not quite animals, barely over the intangible line that separates the non-living from the living.

It is doubtful that this first life possessed the substance chlorophyll, with which plants in sunlight transform lifeless chemicals into the living stuff of their tissues. Little sunshine could enter their dim world, penetrating the cloud banks from which fell the endless rains. Probably the sea's first children lived on the organic substances then present in the ocean waters, or, like the iron and sulphur bacteria that exist today, lived directly on inorganic food.

14   All the while the cloud cover was thinning, the darkness of the nights alternated with palely illumined days, and finally the sun for the first time shone through upon the sea. By this time some of the living things that floated in the sea must have developed the magic of chlorophyll. Now they were able to take the carbon dioxide of the air and the water of the sea and of these elements, in sunlight, build the organic substances they needed for life. So the first true plants came into being.

15   Another group of organisms, lacking the chlorophyll but needing organic food, found they could make a way of life for themselves by devouring the plants. So the first animals arose, and from that day to this, every animal in the world has followed the habit it learned in the ancient seas and depends, directly or through complex food chains, on the plants for food and life.

16   As the years passed, and the centuries, and the millions of years, the stream of life grew more and more complex. From simple, one-celled creatures, others that were aggregations of specialized cells arose, and then creatures with organs for feeding, digesting, breathing, reproducing. Sponges grew on the rocky bottom of the sea's edge and coral animals built their habitations in warm, clear waters. Jellyfish swam and drifted in the sea. Worms evolved, and starfish, and hard-shelled creatures with many-jointed legs. The plants, too, progressed, from the microscopic algae to branched and curiously fruiting seaweeds that swayed with the tides and were plucked from the coastal rocks by the surf and cast adrift.

17   During all this time the continents had no life. There was little to induce living things to come ashore, forsaking their all-providing, all-embracing mother sea. The lands must have been bleak and hostile beyond the power of words to describe. Imagine a whole continent of naked rock, across which no covering mantle of green had been drawn — a continent without soil, for there were no land plants to aid in its formation and bind it to the rocks with their roots. Imagine a land of stone, a silent land, except for the

sound of the rains and winds that swept across it. For there was no living voice, and no living thing moved over its surface except the shadows of the clouds.

18   Meanwhile, the gradual cooling of the planet, which had first given the earth its hard granite crust, was progressing into its deeper layers; and as the interior slowly cooled and contracted, it drew away from the outer shell. This shell, accommodating itself to the shrinking sphere within it, fell into folds and wrinkles — the earth's first mountain ranges.

19   Geologists tell us that there must have been at least two periods of mountain building (often called "revolutions") in that dim period, so long ago that rocks have no record of it, so long ago that the mountains themselves have long since been worn away. Then there came a third great period of upheaval and readjustment of the earth's crust, about a billion years ago, but of all its majestic mountains the only reminders today are the Laurentian hills of eastern Canada, and a great shield of granite over the flat country around Hudson Bay.

20   The epochs of mountain building only served to speed up the processes of erosion by which the continents were worn down and their crumbling rock and contained minerals returned to the sea. The uplifted masses of the mountains were prey to the bitter cold of the upper atmosphere and under the attacks of frost and snow and ice the rocks cracked and crumbled away. The rains beat with greater violence upon the slopes of the hills and carried away the substance of the mountains in torrential streams. There was still no plant covering to modify and resist the power of the rains.

21   And in the sea, life continued to evolve. The earliest forms have left no fossils by which we can identify them. Probably they were soft-bodied, with no hard parts that could be preserved. Then, too, the rock layers formed in those early days have since been so altered by enormous heat and pressure, under the foldings of the earth's crust, that any fossils they might have contained would have been destroyed.

22   For the past 500 million years, however, the rocks have preserved the fossil record. By the dawn of the Cambrian period, when the history of living things was first inscribed on rock pages, life in the sea had progressed so far that all the main groups of back-boneless or invertebrate animals had been developed. But there were no animals with backbones, no insects or spiders, and still no plant or animal had been evolved that was capable of venturing

onto the forbidding land. So for more than three-fourths of geologic time the continents were desolate and uninhabited, while the sea prepared the life that was later to invade them and make them habitable. Meanwhile, with violent tremblings of the earth and with the fire and smoke of roaring volcanoes, mountains rose and wore away, glaciers moved to and fro over the earth, and the sea crept over the continents and again receded.

23   It was not until Silurian time, some 350 million years ago, that the first pioneer of land life crept out on the shore. It was an arthropod, one of the great tribe that later produced crabs and lobsters and insects. It must have been something like a modern scorpion, but, unlike its descendants, it never wholly severed the ties that united it to the sea. It lived a strange life, half-terrestrial, half-aquatic, something like that of the ghost crabs that speed along the beaches today, now and then dashing into the surf to moisten their gills.

24   Fish, tapered of body and stream-molded by the press of running waters, were evolving in Silurian rivers. In times of drought, in the drying pools and lagoons, the shortage of oxygen forced them to develop swim bladders for the storage of air. One form that developed an air-breathing lung was able to survive the dry periods by burying itself in mud, leaving a passage to the surface through which it breathed.

25   It is very doubtful that the animals alone would have succeeded in colonizing the land, for only the plants had the power to bring about the first amelioration of its harsh conditions. They helped make soil of the crumbling rocks, they held back the soil from the rains that would have swept it away, and little by little they softened and subdued the bare rock, the lifeless desert. We know very little about the first land plants, but they must have been closely related to some of the larger seaweeds that had learned to live in the coastal shallows, developing strengthened stems and grasping, rootlike holdfasts to resist the drag and pull of the waves. Perhaps it was in some coastal lowlands, periodically drained and flooded, that some such plants found it possible to survive, though separated from the sea. This also seems to have taken place in the Silurian period.

26   The mountains that had been thrown up by the Laurentian revolution gradually wore away, and as the sediments were washed from their summits and deposited on the lowlands, great areas of the continents sank under the load. The seas crept out of their

basins and spread over the lands. Life fared well and was exceedingly abundant in those shallow, sunlit seas. But with the later retreat of the ocean water into the deeper basins, many creatures must have been left stranded in shallow, land-locked bays. Some of these animals found means to survive on land. The lakes, the shores of the rivers, and the coastal swamps of those days were the testing grounds in which plants and animals either became adapted to the new conditions or perished.

27   As the lands rose and the seas receded, a strange fishlike creature emerged on the land, and over the thousands of years its fins became legs, and instead of gills it developed lungs. In the Devonian sandstone this first amphibian left its footprint.

28   On land and sea the stream of life poured on. New forms evolved; some old ones declined and disappeared. On land the mosses and the ferns and the seed plants developed. The reptiles for a time dominated the earth, gigantic, grotesque, and terrifying. Birds learned to live and move in the ocean of air. The first small mammals lurked inconspicuously in hidden crannies of the earth as though in fear of the reptiles.

29   When they went ashore the animals that took up a land life carried with them a part of the sea in their bodies, a heritage which they passed on to their children and which even today links each land animal with its origin in the ancient sea. Fish, amphibian, and reptile, warm-blooded bird and mammal—each of us carries in our veins a salty stream in which the elements sodium, potassium, and calcium are combined in almost the same proportions as in sea water. This is our inheritance from the day untold millions of years ago, when a remote ancestor, having progressed from the one-celled to the many-celled stage, first developed a circulatory system in which the fluid was merely the water of the sea. In the same way, our lime-hardened skeletons are a heritage from the calcium-rich ocean of Cambrian time. Even the protoplasm that streams within each cell of our bodies has the chemical structure impressed upon all living matter when the first simple creatures were brought forth in the ancient sea. And as life itself began in the sea, so each of us begins his individual life in a miniature ocean within his mother's womb, and in the stages of his embryonic development repeats the steps by which his race evolved, from gill-breathing inhabitants of a water world to creatures able to live on land.

30   Some of the land animals later returned to the ocean. After perhaps 50 million years of land life, a number of reptiles entered the

sea in Mesozoic time. They were huge and formidable creatures. Some had oarlike limbs by which they rowed through the water; some were web-footed, with long, serpentine necks. These grotesque monsters disappeared millions of years ago, but we remember them when we come upon a large sea turtle swimming many miles at sea, its barnacle-encrusted shell eloquent of its marine life. Much later, perhaps no more than 50 million years ago, some of the mammals, too, abandoned a land life for the ocean. Their descendants are the sea lions, seals, sea elephants, and whales of today.

31   Among the land mammals there was a race of creatures that took to an arboreal existence. Their hands underwent remarkable development, becoming skilled in manipulating and examining objects, and along with this skill came a superior brain power that compensated for what these comparatively small mammals lacked in strength. At last, perhaps somewhere in the vast interior of Asia, they descended from the trees and became again terrestrial. The past million years have seen their transformation into beings with the body and brain and spirit of man.

32   Eventually man, too, found his way back to the sea. Standing on its shores, he must have looked out upon it with wonder and curiosity, compounded with an unconscious recognition of his lineage. He could not physically re-enter the ocean as the seals and whales had done. But over the centuries, with all the skill and ingenuity and reasoning powers of his mind, he has sought to explore and investigate even its most remote parts, so that he might re-enter it mentally and imaginatively.

33   He fashioned boats to venture out on its surface. Later he found ways to descend to the shallow parts of its floor, carrying with him the air that, as a land mammal long unaccustomed to aquatic life, he needed to breathe. Moving in fascination over the deep sea he could not enter, he found ways to probe its depths, he let down nets to capture its life, he invented mechanical eyes and ears that could re-create for his senses a world long lost, but a world that, in the deepest part of his subconscious mind, he had never wholly forgotten.

34   And yet he has returned to his mother sea only on her own terms. He cannot control or change the ocean as, in his brief tenancy of earth, he has subdued and plundered the continents. In the artificial world of his cities and towns, he often forgets the true nature of his planet and the long vistas of its history, in which the existence of the race of men has occupied a mere moment of time. The sense of all these things comes to him most clearly in

the course of a long ocean voyage, when he watches day after day the receding rim of the horizon, ridged and furrowed by waves; when at night he becomes aware of the earth's rotation as the stars pass overhead; or when, alone in this world of water and sky, he feels the loneliness of his earth in space. And then, as never on land, he knows the truth that his world is a water world, a planet dominated by its covering mantle of ocean, in which the continents are but transient intrusions of land above the surface of the all-encircling sea.

QUESTIONS FOR STUDY

1. According to the authors of "Description," why must the process of description serve some other purpose beyond itself? Why might the term *disinterested description* be a contradiction in terms?

2. Explain the two basic types of description. Toward what sort of ends might each type be employed? Illustrate from your own experiences.

3. What is the role of observation in the descriptive process? How is observation related to dominant impression?

4. How can we test a given sample of descriptive prose for objectivity? How can a writer be selective and objective at the same time?

5. What are the characteristics of prose that *tend* toward impressionism? How important is observation in this type of description? Support your answer by referring to the selection by Rolvaag.

6. According to the authors of "Description," what is the function of *point of view?* Is there any basic disagreement between these authors and Brooks and Warren?

7. Are the authors merely calling "observation" by another name when they refer to "vividness in description"? Explain.

8. Which of the two basic types of description does Rachel Carson use? Support your contention by referring to pertinent passages.

9. Indicate how Rachel Carson's point of view is consistent with the integrating principle of her description.

10. One of the most important aspects of description is the selection of details. How does the author's selection of details help set the tone of her essay? What might the author have included that could have detracted from the essay's tone?

11. What is the central impression the author wishes to communicate? Select several passages from the essay that support your contention. How does the author's use of selective detail within these passages help strengthen this central impression?

12. Consider paragraph no. 3 in Rachel Carson's essay. How does the author order her descriptive elements? Point out evocative language that supports the more explicit purposes of this

essay. Is the language of the various sentences straightforward, or has the author varied word order and sentence patterns? Be specific. How might these sentence patterns be rearranged so as to be *less* effective?

13. Consider paragraph no. 22 in Rachel Carson's essay. Point out nouns and verbs that, so to speak, do double-duty; that is, they do more than name a thing or action — they also evoke an emotional response. Look for descriptive adjectives and adverbs. How many do you find? Do you think this is intentional on the author's part? Explain. Relate your answer to the need for accurate observation.

14. Often the use of figurative language — particularly simile and metaphor — is an important element in description. Consider paragraph no. 25. Point out some of Rachel Carson's figures of speech and comment on their effectiveness.

WRITING TOPICS

1. The scene is your classroom. You enter and look down at your desk, an ordinary, scarred classroom desk. But this time the desk holds a sheet of paper with unexpected questions — you have blundered into an unannounced quiz. And even worse — you do not know the answers to the questions. Now the desk begins to look somewhat different, as you pay close attention to each scratch and scrawl. But the answers refuse to come. Your writing assignment: describe that "ordinary, scarred classroom desk," as you stare at it, while time passes and the questions remain unanswered. Try to communicate your sense of desperation through a close description of the desk while you cudgel your brains for the evasive answers.

2. Complete the following sentence; then use it as the integrating principle of your description. "The room was in keeping with his personality:_____"
Choose only those observable details that emphasize the personality of the occupant. Make your objective description support one impression.

3. Attend a public lecture or sermon. Then write an essay in which you describe the manner in which the listening public is "set up" so that it will be receptive to the speaker. You

may care to note if there is music or if there are any preliminary ceremonies. What sort of introduction does the speaker rate? What are the physical surroundings like? If you wish, you may deal fleetingly with the effect the speaker actually has on his listeners.

4. Think back to the time when you were younger and watched an older sister or brother (with whom you were much too familiar) prepare for an important social event. Describe the changes that take place as the person puts on the new clothes, the new manners, and the new personality. Describe your own feelings as you witness this metamorphosis.

Definition and description are so intrinsically related it is not always easy to distinguish between them. One part of the difficulty lies in the difference between an object and a class; another is the difference between real and nominal definition. In this chapter from his book *Modes of Rhetoric* Leo Rockas explains how such distinctions are made and cites the several methods of approach to the intricate problem of definition.

Definition

Leo Rockas

1   Definition is abstract description, just as description is concrete definition. If you have a thing before you, the first in a new universe, and you tell all you can about it, you will not know whether you have described or defined it. Only by comparisons and contrasts with like things in the universe everybody knows can you tell whether you have preferred the unique, distinctive qualities in your account, resulting in description, or the common, typical ones, resulting in definition.

2   Description is of a thing, definition of a class. In actual practice description may require a rarer, poetic perception of the unique qualities of a thing, but definition would seem theoretically the more difficult mode. For if the unique qualities of a thing can be isolated, its description is simply composed of their total. But definition requires a judicious sifting of things and qualities to find which of the thing's membership in various classes is the most real or useful. And once a class is decided upon, the job is not finished. For an elegant definition is not composed of all the qualities common to the class, but only of those common qualities distinctive of the class. The class of all sports cars has many qualities common to all other cars, but they should be excluded or else you are defining cars in general. The traditional analysis of definition as genus plus differentia suggests two halves of equal importance; but the genus is ordinarily a mere passing mention, an apologetic location of the given class in one of the larger classes it belongs to; the definition actually occurs in the sometimes lengthy total of common qualities distinctive of the class under examination, which are the differentiae. Properties, as Aristotle defines

From *Modes of Rhetoric* by Leo Rockas. Reprinted by permission of St. Martin's Press, New York, © 1964.

them ("which belong only to that thing" — *Topics* I, 5) are rarer than he suggests. Qualities often belong to many things, and it is the exact combination of qualities which differentiates the class.

3   There are general classes of things, sharing a majority of their qualities, such as men, and abstract classes of things, sharing a minority of their qualities, such as the class of virtuous actions. Both are subject to definition. An abstract class may seem further removed from things, and so more abstract than a general class, but definitions of either are arrived at through abstraction, through sifting and arranging of things and qualities into the most equitable classes. Nor are general and abstract classes always clearly differentiable. If virtue is my subject for more than a few sentences, I must use classes of both men and actions. For that matter, neither are descriptions and definitions always clearly differentiable. All the most concrete words in the dictionary (toad, forsythia, butterscotch) can after all be defined; apparently their definitions must be less abstract than those of recognized abstractions, such as virtue and truth. Then there may be literary techniques and types which are founded on a mixture of description and definition, such as Theophrastan "characters" which seek to define a general class of men, using various concrete agencies ("Boorishness," "News-making," "Late-learning," "Friendship and Rascals"). Such a definition including concrete particulars wittily suggests that, however novel these particulars seem, you will find them duly repeated in every case.

4   The two modes can be distinguished, but they have much in common. Both description and definition read as a static enumeration of qualities, a telling of beads on a string. You take up the beads one at a time, and possibly in the best order, but the important thing is that you have the string of beads in your hand all at once. If I am defining the ranks of English nobility I may begin with the lowest and proceed to the highest, but this sequence is not temporal, nor, except metaphorically, even spatial. I may also begin with the highest. Both static modes are, however, remotely spatial. Just as description may often be spatially rendered in a picture, so definition may often be schematized by lines and boxes, like a family tree. Both modes are relatively free of time, but a skillful writer, even though no sequence is demanded, will strive to find the most convenient or graceful sequence, as if he were under an obligation to time all along.

5   Logicians have contrived various intricate rules for definition, but rhetorically all abstract, static discourse is definition. Pascal

quarrels with Plato's definition of man as a biped without feathers (since you can't make a man by plucking a chicken), but a rhetorician must accept not only Plato's definition but attempts even further afield: "a man is a two-face, a worrisome thing that leads you to sing the blues in the night." This already appears a violation of one of the rules, that a definition "should not be expressed in obscure or figurative language." But these traditional rules are probably too constricted, not only for rhetoric, but for logic as well. Definition is too often regarded merely as a tool of lexicography, or of persuasion. "Define your terms" is a rule anticipatory to debate. But however brief or extended, definition has an interest in its own right. An author may set forth his static perceptions of a class, and stop there; if he has taught you the secrets of heaven and earth in the attempt, you will not complain that he has been occasionally figurative, or even obscure.

6   Like description, definition is based on a pattern of static equations simply added to each other: $a = b$ *and* $c = d$. In this formula for definition, $=$ represents *to be* or any other static verb, usually in the present tense, a and c are classes or parts of classes, and b and d are the qualities which differentiate those classes. Any statement, or series of statements, filling this formula with abstract terms may be said to define the terms in positions a and c. The chief "rules" for definition (but they are not rules at all) is that no temporal sequence be engaged in the progression of verbs; and that no particular or concrete things sit for subjects. If these rules are disobeyed, the rules for some other mode of rhetoric will be obeyed. So long as discourse remains abstract, and static, it will define something.

7   Clearly this view of definition is broader than is usual, including most of what is called exposition. Whatever it is called, this mode is probably the commonest of the modes of rhetoric. Any answers to the questions "What is it like?" or simply "What is it?" will be definitions. The conveying of simple information, or the most sophisticated exchange of wisdom, will make large use of definition. If no material rhetorical differences can be found between the various types and styles of definition and exposition, there is no need to clutter the board with distinctions.

8   Some philosophers have distinguished between real and nominal definition. The statement a *is* b conceals an ambiguity, and may be taken to mean either "I assert a to be really b," or "I take a nominally to be b." The first defines a thing, the second a word. It is one of the achievements of Robinson's book (*Definition*, ch. VI)

to have shown that only nominal definition is an activity clear and simple enough to pass under one name; and that what has been called real definition had better be known by other names, such as abstraction or analysis or naming. Perhaps an easier, if less accurate, means of distinguishing between the two so-called kinds of definition is to say that real definition is what passes in the writer's thoughts and researches before writing; nominal definition is what he writes. However neatly Robinson would like us to separate the two, clearly read definition must somehow precede nominal definition.

9   If you begin with one thing, and aim to derive from it one of its classes, you will regard the thing as illustrative of the class. Perhaps this is how most abstraction takes place. You perceive the thing not for its particularity but for its generality — still it is only one thing. Illustration also serves in the nominal result both of definition and of persuasion. One of the means of clarification recommended by the handbooks is by concrete example or illustration. But a concrete example is a contradiction in terms, or at least a paradox. As an example or illustration actually exemplifies or illustrates something, some general type or principle, it presents only the qualities common to the class, and lacks any concrete integrity of its own. Minneapolis as illustrative of American cities of its size is the total of its qualities shared with other cities, rather than any of those unique to itself. From this point of view an illustration is nothing other than a static, abstract equation, an enumeration of the qualities common to a class — or a definition.

10   Analysis and synthesis are means of illustration. It may be that the handiest means of understanding, or of presenting, the thing illustrative of the class will be to separate the thing into its parts, and see how they are related. If you begin with the whole and isolate the parts you analyze it; if you begin with the parts and form the whole you synthesize them. But sequence is a matter of time, and the mode of definition is static. Consequently the sequence of a definition, whether real or nominal, is of little importance; the finished result will show no difference between an analysis and a synthesis. A violin is a whole, and it has separate, organically related parts. If you know your subject you may begin either with the whole or the parts; any sequence will define the violin, or the class of all violins. Sequence will only prove crucial if you are tracing a temporal process — how to make a violin, or how to play one — but those will not be definitions at all, if you take definition to be a static enumeration of the qualities of a class.

11   If you begin with two things instead of one, and aim to derive one or several classes from them, both become illustrations. Perhaps you will be most interested in the qualities shared by the two things, and so derive a single class to be defined. Or perhaps you will be interested in both the similarities and differences between them, and so partly define the class of qualities shared by the two things, and partly the separate classes of which each is a member. This procedure is called comparison and contrast, and it is unavoidable in even the simplest act of abstraction. Even illustration must introduce other like things into the reckoning; otherwise there is no sign of what the thing illustrates. In more intricate abstractions the ranking of similarities between things, or comparison, and of differences between them, or contrast, may become a more necessary procedure. Think of how many ways city and country businessmen resemble each other, and differ from each other, and you see the use of comparison and contrast. But note that you have only ended up with three classes, one of qualities common to the two, and the two of qualities peculiar to each — or three definitions.

12   Analogy is a special form of comparison and contrast, a comparison between the relations of things or classes otherwise contrasting. As an accompaniment of description analogy will usually prove particular or concrete; as an accompaniment of definition ideal or abstract. Often the most elevated abstractions cannot be talked about handily in their own terms, and so you must come down a notch or two to a place more spatially perceptible, and then superimpose the clearer pattern found there on the abstraction. Socrates' fondness for analogy is well known. In order to define justice in the individual or in the state, it may help to understand what harmony in the lyre amounts to. (*Republic* 443D) And, as the temporal extension of analysis is process, so the temporal extension of analogy is allegory, a story duplicating an abstract process on a lower level. Socrates' fondness for allegory is even better known. In order to understand how the philosopher feels who has perceived reality and tries to define it to the world, consider how a man must feel who has escaped from a cave of shadows to the light of day, and returns to tell his old companions what the light is like. (*Republic* 514 ff.)

13   If you begin with many or all possible things, and aim to derive numerous classes from them, you will carry comparison and contrast to even greater lengths. You may find that two or three classes of things fit into one larger class and that the new class bears interesting comparison and contrast with another like class

containing two or three classes of its own; and that the two larger
classes together form one even larger class. Perhaps you will limit
yourself to one area of experience and try to separate all its classes,
and find their interrelationships. Perhaps you will try, as Aristotle
did, to define the classes of all human experience. However limited
or grand, this procedure is called classification, and it is unavoidable in some measure in even the simpler forms of abstraction
above. You cannot tell whether a thing is illustrative of a class
unless you have somehow classified many separate things or classes;
you cannot compare and contrast things and classes without knowing more of their possible classification than you include in the
nominal result. But sometimes the nominal result may prove more
intricate than a scheme of three definitions. The laws of taxation
according to classification of taxpayers show how intricacies of
classification may prove convenient or necessary. But each class
along the way must be separately presented for its own sake, and
so you ended up with nothing other than an intricate scheme of
separate classes, or of classes within classes—or of many definitions.

14   Division is an alternate form of classification. Sometimes you
may begin, not with separate things and the classes they immediately form, but with a large class, and try to find what its divisions
are. This procedure may also be carried into the nominal result,
in which case the sequence of presentation would be from large to
smaller classes, or from up down, instead of the other way around.
But as between analysis and synthesis there is no static difference,
only temporal; so here the finished result will show no difference
between classification and division. Only one variety of division
proves of special interest. Aristotle offers a means of complete
division of a class, called a dichotomous division, by isolating one
quality of a class to make a smaller class, and forming another,
remaining class of the negative of the quality. When a painter puts
black marks on white paper he gets two configurations, one black,
one white, each formed by the exclusions of the other. If you try
to divide all human discourse into English and French you will have
a great deal left over; but if you divide it into English and non-
English you will have a complete, dichotomous division. Often, as
perhaps here, the result will be trivial; and this may explain
another of the traditional rules, that a definition "must not be in
negative when it can be in positive terms." Or you may come up
with a negative which is well recognized, as M. Jourdain did when
he found that all discourse not verse is prose, and that he'd been
talking it all his life.

15   Doubtless, these, then, are the varieties of abstraction or of real definition which must precede nominal definition. They are also the so-called methods of exposition, which as shown above result simply in one or many, or more or less highly abstract, definitions. None of these varieties are so abstruse that they could be missed by someone full of his subject. Unfortunately no adherence to these varieties, in part or in whole, insures the discovery of truth, which may sometimes come about haphazardly and then be rationalized by one or several of these varieties. A thinker's or a writer's obligation is to his material, not to ideal procedures of abstraction, and he had better let the material dictate his technique, however lopsided the result.

16   The members of the Pickwick Club are definers not quite but almost as irresponsible as Humpty Dumpty. "When *I* use a word," Humpty Dumpty says, in rather a scornful tone, "it means just what I choose it to mean — neither more nor less." The word "glory" he defines as "a nice knock-down argument." Mr. Blotton calls Mr. Pickwick a humbug, and refuses to withdraw the expression, but when the chairman asks whether he has used the expression in a common sense, Mr. Blotton "had no hesitation in saying he had not — he had used the word in its Pickwickian sense." Whereupon Mr. Pickwick generously responds that "his own observations had been merely intended to bear a Pickwickian construction."

17   Dictionaries are made to prevent such irresponsibility, which is not always so entertaining as here. Robinson differentiates two varieties of nominal definition: lexical, a report of how men in a given time and place have used a word; and stipulative, an announcement of how a given writer is about to use a word. The first variety is bound by usage, the second is perfectly free. But while you may permit a writer to use a word however he likes for purposes of his own discussion, the dictionary provides one convenient set of bounds for ordinary discussion. Modern dictionaries define, not reality, but usage. A dictionary is worth consulting, but never worth quoting, for ideally it tells no more about a word than you already know, if you know the word at all. If you seek to refine upon the meanings of a word, the dictionary provides only the vaguest assistance, as vague, that is, as the combined uses of all the users. Webster is at best a stenographer, no oracle.

18   According to the traditional rules, definitions should not be circular — should not, that is, repeat the term or terms to be defined in the remainder of the statement. But all human know-

ledge forms an invincible circularity of relatedness; if I define enough words I must begin repeating myself. And not only are all definitions finally circular, but also Pickwickian — if you read the scene above, that is, as an attempt to reinterpret the word or the thing so as to provide a more comfortable and convenient disposition of reality. No word or idea can ever be definitively defined, not even "liberty" when Milton and Mill have finished with it.

19   For verbal discourse is not mathematical discourse, as Pascal insists, nor is mathematical discourse perfect. You can imagine, he says, an ideal discourse in which all terms are defined and all propositions proved, but even in geometry there remain some basic terms which cannot themselves be defined by simpler terms. How far from ever being settled, then, must be discourse in the ordinary talk of men.

20   Still there must always be some uncertainty about which words or ideas stand at present in need of further definition. Anybody may consult his dictionary; if you have nothing more to say than the dictionary, you may let the word rest. But a dictionary is only a crude repository of information. If a subject really interests you, you had better see what the best authorities have to say on the subject; you may have been anticipated or contradicted. But if you have really thought about the subject yourself, you will usually find that no one has thought about it exactly as you have.

21   You may also feel that if a definition is composed of the qualities common to a class of things, those qualities must already be common, or well known, to anyone who has bothered to think about the subject. But may I insist on a progressive view of human knowledge. Fresh evidence occurs every day; and if there is nothing but the old evidence to consider on certain subjects, it is forever subject to fresh interpretations. Your sifting of things and qualities will come up with classes different from mine. If knowledge may be metaphorically regarded as existing along a scale of abstraction, there are always new strata of the scale to be examined, which have different qualities from those already examined.

22   And when you make your discoveries, you may, like Adam, name them. But if you give old names they may already mean something different to most people. If you give new names they may be ugly and properly called jargon. If you give new names based on old names they may have the familiarity of old ones, and the accuracy of new ones. Robinson seems to prefer the third of these alternatives, and suggests that the second might be chosen in the interests of accuracy oftener than the first.

23   Lexicographers, or nominal definers, try to find many or all the contexts for a word before setting out to define it. The contexts they find dictate the definitions they compose — for a meaning can exist only in relation to other meanings. Similarly, real definers must sift their experience to think of all the contexts in which they have observed the thing which interests them — for a thing can exist only in relation to other things. Since nobody's contexts, and nobody's equipment for distinguishing them, are the same as yours, truth is forever just on the verge of being stated. Even Aristotle and Kant oversimplified, if you stop and think about it.

In the essay "Liberals and Conservatives" Laurence Sears sets out to define the elusive abstract terms of the title. His method is comparison and contrast, and he strives for objectivity through the use of an historical approach. He finds the fundamental distinction between the two views to lie in their attitudes toward human nature: the liberal has an implicit faith in the rational powers of man whereas the conservative's view is skeptical. Both, Sears feels, play a necessary role in a democratic government, and the distinction he draws suggests the vital balancing qualities of a conjunction of the two concepts.

Liberals and Conservatives

Laurence Sears

1   It is one of the significant facts of our time that there is a growing concern with the meaning of political conservatism, and a dissatisfaction with the way that the term is popularly used. To a large degree both "liberal" and "conservative" are today little more than honorific terms used to give a comfortable glow of satisfaction, or else epithets designed to destroy the influence of those with whom we disagree. But even though the concepts are blurred, nonetheless one assumption is held in common, that *either* one *or* the other is the true belief, and that, although we may tolerate the opposite and mistaken view, *we* hold the truth and must be ready to do battle for it. It is the right versus the wrong. But there is another position which holds: (1) that it is one of the urgent tasks of our time to get these terms sharply defined; and (2) that when we do so, we will find that each position holds both a profound and a partial truth. That view needs reexamination today.

2   One of the difficulties that lie in the path of clear definition arises from the fact that we have largely forgotten our own political tradition. The picture often drawn of the conservative does not correspond with the features of men like Burke in England or James Madison or John Adams in this country. This is not surprising in the light of the fact that there have been so few clear-headed and consistent conservatives in this country in the last century that we have forgotten what they look like, grown contemptuous of their contribution, and identified them with the reactionary (as fatal a blunder as to identify the liberal with the radical). We are continually faced with this danger of identifying the conservative with men of our own time who are striving to get back to the good old

From the *Antioch Review* (Fall, 1953). Reprinted with permission of the *Antioch Review* and the author.

days, who are worshiping at the shrine of the economic gods of
the things as they were, and who would formulate a program entirely around such policies as the reduction of taxes, the removal of
economic controls, and the cessation of any attempt to break up
monopolies. But this is a travesty of our tradition and confirms
Reinhold Niebuhr's contention that contemporary American conservatism is little more than a decayed form of nineteenth-century
liberalism. It is time that we rescued this word "conservative," and
gave to it something of the meaning and dignity that it once had.

3   By way of comparison and contrast, it might be well to look
briefly at the tradition of liberalism, of which Jefferson is the outstanding example among the founding fathers. All political philosophies rest back ultimately upon an assumption about human
nature. Madison recognized this when he wrote: "What is government itself, but the greatest of all reflections on human nature?"
Jefferson was perfectly explicit at this point — he believed profoundly in the potential rationality of man. Hence the appeal to
reason by facts was his answer to all political problems. "Enlighten
the people generally, and tyranny and oppressions of body and
mind will vanish like evil spirits at the dawn of day." Here is the
faith of the liberal; men can be appealed to through their intelligence, and in the light of what is wise, they can in the long run be
trusted to act not solely in terms of their narrow self-interest, but
on behalf of that which is good for all.

4   It is worth noting that it is because of this belief in the reason-
ableness of man that liberals have to a large extent rejected the
necessity of force. L. T. Hobhouse saw this when he declared that
it was of the essence of liberalism to oppose the use of force since
it was the basis of tyranny.

5   A second characteristic of Jefferson was his deep concern with
the rights of man. It was not an accident that it was he who wrote
the Declaration of Independence with its insistence upon the fact
that all men are endowed by their creator with the inalienable
rights of life and liberty and the pursuit of happiness. As time went
on he stressed freedom of speech as the central right in any
democracy. Here again was his faith that men could be trusted
with such freedom and that the state would be the stronger for it.
"If there be any among us who would wish to dissolve this union
or to change its republican form, let them stand undisturbed as
monuments of the safety with which error of opinion may be tolerated where reason is left free to combat it." Finally, there was a
commitment on Jefferson's part to the belief that old ways were

never good enough. He sometimes loosely phrased this attitude so as to make it seem that he was advocating revolution, when in effect he was stressing the necessity of continually altering the political and social patterns in such a way as to meet the demands of a new day. Like all liberals, he seemed continually to be saying: "Hurry; the hour is very late and our work has just begun."

6   When one turns to the tradition of political conservatism, one inevitably examines the philosophy of John Adams and James Madison, and the first discovery is that, contrary to contemporary notions, theirs is not the position of reactionaries seeking merely to cling to their privilege, property, and power. These men are concerned with the achievement of positive values.

7   As regards their view of human nature, one finds a startling contrast with that of Jefferson. John Adams gives a classic statement:

> It is weakness rather than wickedness which renders men unfit to be trusted with unlimited power. The passions are all unlimited; nature has left them so; if they could be bounded, they would be extinct. . . . The love of gold grows faster than the heap of acquisition; the love of praise increases by every gratification, till it stings like an adder, and bites like a serpent; till the man is miserable every moment when he does not snuff the incense. Ambition strengthens at every advance, and at last takes possession of the whole soul so absolutely that a man sees nothing in the world of importance to others or himself but in his object.

Nor is this lack of faith in the rationality of men confined to those who are uneducated. The élite are mistrusted as much as the masses. Education is no answer to irrationality and greed. John Adams was suspicious of both groups alike—

> The more knowledge is diffused, the more the passions are extended, and the more furious they grow. . . . The increase and dissemination of knowledge, instead of rendering unnecessary the checks of emulation and the balances of rivalry in the orders of society and constitution of government, augment the necessity of both. . . . Bad men increase in knowledge as fast as good men; and science, arts, taste, sense, and letters are employed for the purposes of injustice and tyranny as well as those of law and liberty; for corruption as well as virtue.

8   Because of his lack of faith in the possibility of a rational appeal to the disinterested behavior of men, his primary concern was with the fact of power. Here is the core of the conservative philosophy, as true in England and on the Continent as it has been in this country. Though it is possible to define power in terms either of

coercion or of persuasion, the distinction remains. It is a matter of emphasis. Both sides would agree that the ideal situation is where power is delegated under maximum conditions of persuasion and with a minimum of pressure and force. But the liberal believes that his ends can be largely achieved through persuasion, while the conservative believes that persuasion is inadequate and coercion is inevitable. The play of contending groups seeking power for the achievement of their ends has always been the dominant concern of men like Adams, and they sought to understand not only its source but also its effect. Adams would whole-heartedly have agreed with Lord Acton in his insistence that power always corrupts and absolute power corrupts absolutely. Because of his conviction that this was the effect of power, he was concerned to find the means of distributing and balancing it so that no group or man should hold an inordinate amount. Since we cannot depend upon rational and disinterested behavior, the balance of power is the only answer to the selfishness of men. As John Randolph phrased it, "You may cover whole skins of parchment with limitations, but power alone can limit power."

9   It was James Madison, the man who had more influence in the drafting of our Constitution than anyone else, who formulated the patterns which have become an integral part of our political life, even though we are scarcely conscious of the philosophy which lies behind them. He started with a recognition of the existence of factions within society which he believed were based upon economic interests. The most common and durable source of factions has always been the various and unequal distribution of property. "Those who hold and those who are without property have ever formed distinct interests in society." It is startling to realize that at this point he was not far from the position of Marx as to the economic basis of politics; in his conviction that men are motivated primarily by their economic interests. But from then on he broke drastically with the Marxian philosophy. Whereas Marx believed that the history of the world lay in the struggle between classes, where one class must inevitably destroy the other, Madison did not believe that it was possible to give to all men the same economic interests, no matter what the economic structure might be, and insisted that any such attempt to remove factions would inevitably destroy liberty. And liberty was always his supreme value. Since, therefore, you cannot remove the causes, you must control the effects, and that can only be done in one of two ways.

10   In the first place, by a check upon the people's direct control over their government. It was because of this that he sought so

strenuously for the system of checks and balances which lies at the heart of our Constitution. In the second place, he believed in extending the sphere of interests, of expanding the number of factions and thereby taking in a greater variety of interests, thus giving an effective voice to all.

11   In summarizing this conservative philosophy in order to see more clearly its relevance in our own time, it is redundant to do more than mention the lack of faith in man, which was at its heart. There was little faith in men, either the common people or the aristocracy. Most men are seen as selfish when their interests are involved and many are potentially corrupt. One is reminded of the closing lines of the ballad "Frankie and Johnnie":

> This story has no moral
> This story has no end
> This story only goes to show
> That there ain't no good in men.

Viereck, to whom we are indebted for reminding us of the conservative tradition, has emphasized this fact of human frailty; of the extent to which men are prone to sin and selfishness, and has recognized that this was the foundation of the conservative position.

12   In the second place, because of this mistrust, the conservative has been determined to distribute and balance power. John Adams said, ". . . every project has been found to be no better than committing the lamb to the custody of the wolf, except the one which is called the balance of power. . . ." Power naturally grows because human passions are insatiable, but that power alone can grow which is unchecked, which has no equal power to control it.

13   Contemporary psychology has made an interesting contribution to this analysis of the meaning of power and its relation to democracy. James Marshall has written recently a brilliant article[1] exploring the meaning of power for a theory of democracy. He starts with an insistence that one cannot understand democracy without reducing it to the various elements of power. He goes on to point out that to "exercise power of any nature over people is to that extent to deny or relieve them of responsibility and that such denial limits their personalities, their opportunities for growth, and is the source of immaturity." Hence for him "the measure of a people's democracy is the extent of its freedom from dependence," for dependence has as its corollaries submissiveness and apathy, which are the denial of the whole spirit of democracy. "Freedom

---

[1]*Democracy in a World of Tension:* A Symposium prepared by UNESCO, pp. 214-227.

from dependence is requisite to maturity." His test of political democracy, therefore, is the freedom from dependence of its people, and its necessary condition is the diffusion of power.

14   In the third place, this conservative philosophy means an acceptance in bluntest terms of pressure politics. In fact, the question is raised as to what other politics there are. The definition of politics as the art of who gets what, when and how is widely accepted. Again it is worth reminding ourselves that the differences between the conservative and the liberal are matters of emphasis; each recognizes the need for persuasion as well as the facing of power by power. Perhaps an illustration will make clearer the distinction. We have in this country many hundreds of thousands of migrant workers who are, politically speaking, the forgotten men. As we face this obvious injustice, the liberal would seem more likely to depend upon an appeal to those who do have political power to share it with those without, trusting to the reason and decency of men to see how grossly unfair this situation is. I suspect that the genuine conservative would spend little time in such an appeal— rather he would try to see the migrants organized so that they could make an effective demand upon the body politic.

15   Such a philosophy implies that the basic economic conflicts of society must always remain. Any political kingdom of heaven where the lions and the lambs lie down together is not likely to transpire, and the philosophy of the Marxian that it is possible to remove these tensions by the destruction of one class is seen to be obvious nonsense, if, of course, one places any value whatever on liberty. This is a hard fact to face. We would like to get rid of the tensions of society. In some cases we will, but essentially any vital society is one which will contain multiple tensions, differences, and interests. As Tannenbaum has put it,[2] "Conflict, strife, divergence, difference of interest and opinion over many things for many reasons, and in varying degrees of intensity, are the conditions of social peace. The conflicting processes of democracy are consistent with and essentially a part of the stresses and strains of life itself." The emphasis lies upon the democratic *process* rather than upon any specific goals. Once again we must remind ourselves that the conservative is not uninterested in justice or in equality, but rather

---

[2]"Balance of Power in Society," in *Political Science Quarterly,* December, 1947.

that every achievement is but one step in an endless process which is itself the condition of growth, vitality, and hope.

16   A fourth characteristic of the conservative faith is its emphasis upon expediency rather than upon ultimate rights or principles. An illustration might be drawn from the career of Woodrow Wilson. When he faced the close of World War I, he formulated his famous Fourteen Points, among which was the self-determination of small nations. This was an appealing principle but many came to question whether it did not do more harm than good. The conservative would have been suspicious of any such principle and would certainly have been more likely to seek for adjustments which were at least possible, even though something less than ideal. There is less of a glorious vision held out by the conservative than by the liberal, but there is a sturdy insistence that starting with where we are we may achieve something better even though it falls far short of the dreams of men. There is the belief that although we may never achieve the day when all men may have life and liberty and be free to seek their happiness, yet we will make progress toward this achievement.

17   No specific economic system is necessarily assumed but there is a general approach to our economic problems. The liberal tends to look for that system which will give a maximum of equality and justice based upon deliberate adjustments of means to ends. The conservative tends to trust much more the invisible hand operating through the play of economic forces upon each other than he does to any conscious planning or centralized control. Once again it is the process rather than the results which are important. Galbraith, in *American Capitalism*, has approached the economic problem in such a spirit. He starts with a concern about the extent of governmental power and defends, as an alternative, a system where private economic power is held in check by the countervailing power of those who are subject to it. Politically, this means that the primary rule of the state is to give assistance in the development of such balances of power. Controls, in other words, would be largely automatic, the result of the balancing of forces rather than the deliberate and conscious control by those in power.

18   Finally, it needs to be said that the conservative, although he tends to move more slowly, is not committed to the preservation of a *status quo*. He is not, as was said before, a reactionary, and the distinction needs to be kept clear. He too would move ahead,

though more slowly. The great English conservative, Burke, characterized the role of the statesman as "the disposition to preserve and the ability to improve," and any genuine conservative would agree.

19   The contribution of, and commitment to, democracy on the part of the liberal is widely recognized, but we must understand clearly what the liberal means. Henry L. Stimson, himself one of the few consistent conservatives we have had in America in modern times, defined the liberal position acutely, even though he disagreed with it. Speaking of the dominant philosophy of the early years of the twentieth century, he said:

> The theoretically easy and emotionally satisfactory solution to the failures of democracy lay in "more democracy." If government was inefficient or subservient to powerful private interests, turn it back to the people. This solution, which was in direct line with the traditions of Jeffersonian democracy, found its expression in the movement for the direct election of senators and the direct primary and more exuberantly in the campaigns for the initiative, the referendum, and the recall. . . . The people had lost control of their government because its complexities provided a smoke screen for the manipulation of bosses and private interests; then let the people themselves take charge.[3]

Give information to the people, put into their hands direct control of their government, and ultimately our problems will be solved. The liberal would define democracy in other words, as that system of government where freely elected representatives are directly responsible to an informed and participating citizenry.

20   The conservative definition is different, though only in emphasis. Since the primary function of government lies in the maintenance of balance between influences, democracy will mean the distribution and therefore the minimization of power. It is not the mere tossing of direct and unlimited power into the hands of individual citizens, but a balance between competing groups which is the condition of political health, and compromise between varying interests becomes the condition of liberty. In fact a conservative might very well define democracy as that system of government where no one gets all he wants.

21   But if there are differences of definition, there is certainly as great a commitment to democracy on the part of the conservative as there is with the liberal. However, here again the reason differs. It is less his faith in the goodness of human nature than it is his conviction of the depravity of man which lies behind his devotion

---

[3]*On Active Service in Peace and War,* by Henry L. Stimson and McGeorge Bundy, Harper and Brothers.

to democracy. Niebuhr has said that "Man's capacity for justice makes democracy possible but man's inclination to injustice makes democracy necessary." Thus, by profoundly different roads the liberal and the conservative come to the democratic conclusion that sovereignty must be vested in all the people. In this conviction that we the people hold the ultimate authority, the two philosophies unite.

22   It is not difficult to see the strength of the liberal position. Throughout the entire tradition there has been a deep concern with human rights, with justice and equality, with a recognition of the need for change. Old ways have never been good enough. What is difficult for the liberal is to recognize that there have been weaknesses associated with his faith, that all too often people operating as groups cannot be depended upon to be disinterested, that only under specific conditions are they rational in their decisions. And most of all, the liberal has tended to forget that politics is always power politics and to ignore not merely the source of power but its effect. There were not many liberals who thought Hitler could be met with reason, but there have been many who thought that Stalin could be dealt with on a basis of reasonable compromise. They would have been wiser to have listened more carefully to the warning of Lord Acton.

23   To a liberal, the weaknesses within the conservative's position seem equally obvious. Conservatives forget that man can, under certain conditions, act rationally. There is the tendency for them to be comtemptuous of what they call "the masses"; to ignore the fact that there is more than coercive power involved in politics, that men have been and will be moved by the power of ideas and ideals. In their concern with the immediate, they have tended to forget that without a vision the people perish, and all too often they have been complacent in the face of the denial of the rights of man, and smugly timid in the presence of injustice. To be sure, John Morley spoke as a liberal with little respect for the Tory position, but there was truth in his criticism of the Conservative—

> . . . with his inexhaustible patience of abuses that only torment others; his apologetic words for beliefs that may not be so precisely true as one might wish, and institutions that are not altogether so useful as some might think possible; his cordiality towards progress and improvement in a general way, and his coldness or antipathy to each progressive proposal in particular; his pygmy hope that life will one day become somewhat better, punily shivering by the side of his gigantic conviction that it might well be infinitely worse.[4]

---

[4]Quoted by Randall in *The Making of the Modern Mind,* Chapter 7.

24   So much for the weakness of the conservative position, but its strength should be equally clear. Based on a recognition of the fact that men do not often act as wisely as the situations demand— that always groups are in conflict as they strive to further separate interests, they know that any effective democracy will be based upon an adequate dividing and balancing of strength. Such a philosophy must recognize the obvious fact that, as John Adams said, "power follows property" and that therefore if power is to be distributed, property must be more equitably held. Such an honest and consistent conservatism would be far more than a façade behind which are to be protected the property, privilege and power of a minority.

25   To one who thinks of himself as a liberal, the value of such a political philosophy committed to the preservation and extension of democracy and consistently and honestly devoted to the balancing of pressures through effective organization of all interest groups would seem to be obvious. It would certainly be a profoundly constructive force in American political history.

26   The reaction from the liberalism of recent years is obvious. In part it is due to the loss of confidence in human nature that has accompanied the spectacle of the past decade. In part it is a recognition of the fact that persuasion has seemed relatively impotent during these years, and that power could only be challenged by power. Whatever the reasons, the swing of the pendulum is carrying us away from the liberal faith. The danger is that this may not bring us a genuine conservative movement. Instead we may not only destroy the profound contributions of the liberal; we may mistake a decadent reactionism for a constructive conservatism. The radical and the reactionary should have little place in our society, but the liberal *and* the conservative we desperately need.

QUESTIONS FOR STUDY

1. In the first sentence of his essay Rockas writes: "Definition is abstract description, just as description is concrete definition." Explain, showing how this first sentence, in effect, summarizes the entire essay.

2. According to Rockas, why is the traditional analysis of definition—that is, genus plus differentia—inadequate?

3. What does Rockas mean when he says that ". . . definition is based on a pattern of static equations simply added to each other"?

4. Why does Rockas feel that, except for sequence, there is no difference in final result between an analysis and a synthesis?

5. Why does Rockas feel that "Analogy is a special form of comparison and contrast . . ."?

6. What is the function of classification in achieving a worthwhile definition? Why is division "an alternate form of classification"?

7. Rockas states: "Modern dictionaries define, not reality, but usage." Explain, showing why a dictionary is of little value in settling disputes calling for agreement on definitions.

8. Which of the approaches to definition does Sears employ in his essay "Liberals and Conservatives"? In the first paragraph of the essay what indicates the main approach that Sears will take in developing his thesis?

9. How does the method used in the third paragraph of Sears' essay establish the procedure that will be used in the following paragraphs? Point to paragraphs throughout the rest of the essay where the author follows through with this procedure.

10. Sears makes use of some methods of extended definition. Cite some examples of the following: comparison, contrast, analogy, classification, division, historical tracing, example.

11. In paragraphs 3 through 5 the author analyzes the liberal tradition. What, according to the author, are the central elements of this movement? What method of definition does he use to present these concepts? In paragraphs 6 through 8 he explores the conservative tradition. What method of definition does he use to present these concepts? What are the key aspects of the conservative tradition?

12. What is the difference between the two points of view in regard to "human nature," "power," and "economic structure"? According to Sears? According to you? Do you find people who claim to be liberals (or, for that matter, conservatives) who take positions that are at odds with the positions ascribed to them by Sears? Can you think of any reasons for the possible present-day confusion over labels?

13. What do you think the author intends in the summary of the conservative philosophy in paragraph 11? Do you find any similar treatment of the liberal position? Explain.

14. What are the strengths and weaknesses of the two positions as Sears views them? What is the "profound and a partial truth" held by the two positions of liberal and conservative?

15. To what is the basis of the "reaction from the liberalism of recent years" attributed? What is the relationship of the liberal and conservative to the "radical" and the "reactionary"?

16. Do the author's feelings intrude into the essay at all? Can we surmise what his personal position is? Why do you think the author, in view of the title of his essay (and the method of organization he has chosen), has devoted so little space to the liberal position?

WRITING TOPICS

1. Using one of the methods of definition treated by Rockas, develop an essay showing why there may possibly exist some confusion because of a lack of proper definition. For example, you may care to differentiate between the campus personality and the campus leader. (Note: avoid topics which cannot be handled properly in a reasonable amount of space: for example, the differences between socialism and communism.)

2. Using the concept of liberalism (which, of course, you will take pains to define) as you understand it, write an essay showing how this concept affects your outlook in terms of one of the following areas of concern: education, ethics, earning a living, personal relationships, etc. (Narrow your topic sufficiently.)

3. Using the definition of conservatism developed by Sears, write an essay showing that a policy maintained by a group presently in power is not truly indicative of a conservative frame of mind.

For instance, you may show that the college administration acts, in regard to a certain matter, out of a misunderstanding of the nature of conservatism.

4. Write an essay in which you show that the meaning of a given concept to your generation has changed in such a manner that a member of the older generation, although professing to hold the same beliefs, can no longer understand your position.

The rhetorical technique of comparison and contrast is one of the most effective means of establishing points of similarity and difference between separate objects. It is an especially significant technique because, in the process of recording likenesses and unlikenesses, the essential natures of both objects are more fully clarified. Thus, comparison and contrast is closely related to several other areas of rhetoric, including definition, analogy, classification and logic. In this chapter from his book *Logic and Rhetoric* James Johnson discusses several of the forms comparison and contrast may take and explains how they may be falsely extended or distorted.

Logical Order: Comparison and Contrast

James Johnson

"Why is a raven like a writing desk?"
LEWIS CARROLL, *Alice in Wonderland*

1　When the Mad Hatter asked Alice his famous riddle about the similarity between ravens and writing desks in the Tea Party scene of *Alice in Wonderland,* he was indirectly pointing out the limitations of classification as a logical method. How *is* a raven like a writing desk? One is an organism, animate, feathered, carnivorous, and capable of flight; the other is inanimate, vegetable (wood), manufactured, stationary, and a container. Both are things, or structured objects, but this categorical principle tells us very little. As Lewis Carroll, a brilliant logician and mathematician, well knew, ravens and writing desks simply cannot be dealt with effectively by the methods of classification.

2　There *are* ways of dealing with highly dissimilar objects, however. One is to compare them through a clever verbal twist on similar sounding words, or *homonyms.* This is the technique of the riddle: unlike objects are equated through a pun. Ingenious though they may be, puns are more revealing of the nature of words than the objects words represent; the logical method of *comparison and contrast* is a somewhat more significant and helpful way of treating unlike things. As its name denotes, comparison and contrast is *a systematic way of establishing points of resemblance and difference.*

3　Superficially, comparison and contrast may not differ very much from classification, which is used to separate objects on the basis of likeness and unlikeness. There are important differences between the two, however. Classification emphasizes common characteristics of groups of things, usually tangible; comparison and contrast emphasizes dissimilarities between individual things, often intangible, to distinguish the individual. Classification is concerned with surface, or physical, resemblances. Comparison and contrast is concerned with essential distinctions and thus is a more penetrating method of understanding the qualities of objects.

4   If the technique of classification were applied to rats, hamsters, and squirrels, for example, all of them would be lumped together in the family of *rodents:* furry mammals that nibble or gnaw. Such a grouping tells us very little about the nature of a hamster as opposed to a rat or a squirrel. A systematic comparison of a hamster and a squirrel, on the other hand, if methodically carried out, will provide a fuller and more accurate knowledge of both squirrels and hamsters.

5   It would be difficult to over-emphasize the importance of comparison and contrast in human thought, since it underlies our system of values, our conception of intangible qualities, the methods of scientific investigation — even our idea of progress. Our practice of evaluating one thing as "better" or "smaller" or "more (anything)" than something else depends on an arbitrary scale of measurement based on comparison and contrast. Such commonly used words as "hot," "dry," "sweet," and "solid" reflect the logical patterns of thought which seek to determine the *degree* or *extent* to which a quality is present in a combination of things. Scientific *data* are observed phenomena which are judged or evaluated by some comparative scale and then used as the basis for establishing a hypothesis, a process, or a classification. Our belief in progress or improvement depends on a value system determined by a comparison and contrast of present and past conditions. Even our language, with its use of comparative adjectives and adverbs (good, better, best; slowly, more slowly, very slowly) is permeated with comparisons and contrasts.*

6   Inevitably, since it plays such an important part in thinking, comparison and contrast appears often in written rhetoric. This technique can be employed to advantage when writing about

---

*It should be noted here that many people make errors in language usage by illogically trying to compare words that have no comparative or superlative degrees of comparison. Any adjective which indicates a supreme or unique state cannot logically be compared, e.g., "one," "square," "dead," "unique." Often people say "very unique," which is redundant at best and foolish at worst. "Unique" means *sui generis,* in a class alone, and thus, incomparable.

actions, people or ideas. The Greek biographers—Xenophon among them—discovered long ago that one of the best ways to depict a man's character is to show how he is like and unlike men of comparable positions. The contemporary journalist Richard Rovere uses the same technique in his portrait of the late Senator McCarthy. The ancient historian Herodotus compared and contrasted the customs and behavior of far-flung peoples of the Mediterranean world. Margaret Mead, a modern anthropologist, employs the same principles in her treatment of the Balinese and Samoans.

7   If you wish to use the principles of comparison and contrast in developing your ideas and expressing them in literary form, first select the objects, persons, actions, cultures, or ideas you want to treat, and define the major categories to which each belongs. Enumerate to yourself the characteristics the *sui generis* object shows by its inclusion in larger classes, and then compare, or correlate, the common qualities between the objects of your investigation. Alexander the Great and Julius Caesar were both ancient generals, warriors, adventurers, and rulers of empires, for instance. Then go on to point out the chief points of disparity: e.g., Alexander was a Macedonian, Hellenic in temperament, a monomaniac, the son of a militarist, trained in logic by Aristotle, and a mystic; whereas Caesar was a Roman, thoroughly Latin in disposition, widespread in interests, a patrician and not royal, educated in the arts, and a pragmatic administrator. Choose the points of major likeness and unlikeness for special emphasis, remembering always that you wish to emphasize the distinctive nature of the individual. It is your purpose to convey certain factual information about the objects of your discourse and to develop a clearer understanding of the nature of these objects collectively and singly.

8   In writing a comparison and contrast, you are likely to use some of the specialized versions of the method, which have been developed through the centuries. Some of these uses are primarily verbal; others are intellectual or logical. Both are subject to misuse at times. Let us see some of the chief forms of comparison and contrast in rhetoric.

FIGURATIVE LANGUAGE

9   You have already learned from reading some essays on Thought and Language that language is symbolic and abstract by nature. At times, it is difficult to state in words exactly what you mean, especially if your meaning concerns something intangible like an

emotion or an abstract concept (truth, justice). At other times, you may have difficulty in conveying an idea about something tangible that holds for you a quality not immediately apparent to other people. *Figurative language* is *those words and phrases which compare objects as possessing a like characteristic*. Tropes, or figures of speech, are thus a precise way of designating otherwise elusive qualities.

10   One of the chief kinds of figurative language is the *simile*. A simile is the direct comparison of two objects, qualities, or concepts for the sake of attributing a characteristic of one to the other. A simile is an open or obvious comparison; it always uses the word "like" or "as." (The Latin word, *similis, simile*, means "like" or "as.") Thus, "My love is like a red, red rose" is a simile; so are "sly as a fox," "slow as Christmas," and "quick as a wink." In every simile, some reasonably tangible action or object (a rose, a fox, Christmas, a wink) is cited for an outstanding quality (beauty, slyness, slowness, quickness), and any object directly compared with one of these (e.g., "my love") is assumed to share that quality. Poets are fond of such comparisons, because they permit an extensive comparison in a few words. Burns's tribute to his sweetheart asserts that she is beautiful, fresh, young, and sweet-smelling, simply by comparing her to a "red, red rose," which presumably has all these qualities. Properly used, a simile can make many positive comparisons in a few words.

11   The *metaphor* is a form of comparison, like the simile, but the comparison is covert or unstated. The words "like" and "as" do not appear; so metaphors tend to be more subtle than similes. A metaphoric comparison may be of several kinds. Two things, one concrete and the other abstract, may be linked together as in "a cloak of silence" or "a stream of traffic." (The similes would be "a cloak-like silence" or "traffic like a stream.") A metaphor may be a combination of a noun and a verb: "the sneeze erupted" or "the trees curtseyed." (The sneeze becomes a volcano and the trees polite ladies.) Or the metaphor may substitute one word in place of another: a political candidate is a "standard-bearer" or money becomes "lettuce." Dr. Johnson's well-known discussion of the poets Dryden and Pope shows how metaphoric language can convey a critical evaluation while making implicit comparisons.

12   Still another sort of figurative comparison is the *personification* of a non-human thing by attributing to it human qualities; e.g., "the wind sighed" or "the sun is smiling." The inherent comparison of a non-human thing to a person is the kind of thinking called

anthropomorphism; we try to understand something better by seeing it in terms of human emotion. Personification in rhetoric ranges from Aesop's *Fables* to Pogo and Mickey Mouse, and even John Ruskin's attack on the error of personification in his essay on the pathetic fallacy (i.e., attributing feelings to that which cannot feel) has not been successful in destroying the popularity of this type of figurative comparison.

13   There are other tropes which involve a comparative principle: *metonymy* is an assumed comparison between an object and something to which it is logically related: e.g., "the pen (literature) is mightier than the sword (warfare)." A *synecdoche* uses a part of something to refer to the entire thing: "to ask for a girl's hand (her entire person) in marriage." Like similes and metaphors, these lesser rhetorical figures are ways of expressing somewhat tenuous qualities in a concrete fashion through comparison.

14   As invaluable as they are to poets and prose writers alike, figures of speech lend themselves to exploitation by those who use words to persuade or to sell rather than to inform or enlighten. Advertising writers try to be as adept as poets in the use of figurative language. . . . an advertisement which proclaims that "Atoll Cigarettes Are Fresh as a Mountain Flower" or "Guzzler's Gin—the Mother's Milk of Alcoholic Beverages" is using a simile and a metaphor to *impute* a quality to a product which may not have it. Similarly, the newspaper which reports that "Senator Cato rasped or bellowed his proposals for a new Tax Law" is deliberately making an uncomplimentary comparison between the Senator and a file or a fire bellows.

THE ANALOGY

15   An *analogy* is an extended comparison for the sake of explanation or illustration. It is *the establishment of a point-by-point correspondence between two situations or objects for explanatory purposes.* If we wish to understand or to explain to others the arrangement and structure of the atom, for example, we may compare it to the structure of our solar system: the sun is like the nucleus, the planets are like electrons, and various other moons, comets, and planetary dust are like neutrinos, mesons, and so forth. An analogy in its simplest form could be stated as a simile—an atom is like the solar system—but it differs from a simile in that there is similarity or correspondence between several aspects of the compared objects rather than in a single aspect.

16   As a way to convey some idea of what things are or how they
work, the analogy is enormously helpful. The human heart may be
compared to a pump or the brain to a switchboard, so that these
highly complicated organs and their general principle of operation
can be grasped. But the comparison, however clever or illuminating,
is *not* complete: there are great differences between a brain and a
switchboard and we must not assume or assert that the similarities
are more than partial. When we overemphasize the comparative
aspects of the analogy and disregard the contrasts between the
analogous objects, we are susceptible to the error of the *False
Analogy*.

17   A false analogy may be of several kinds. It may be an extension
of a limited analogy to cover *all* circumstances under which a
comparison is made, the wrongful exaggeration of several points of
similarity to a total correspondence. This kind of false analogy
may be seen in the time-honored comparison of a government (the
body politic) with human anatomy. The head is the chief of state;
the arms are the military forces; the legs are the workers; and
so on and on, until the stomach becomes the Treasury Department,
or some such nonsense. These forced comparisons are a form of
confusion rather than clarification. Another kind of false analogy
is the comparison of two things with essentially unlike or irreconcilable natures. Communistic societies are sometimes compared
with a beehive: mechanistic class structure, rigidly designated
worker functions, the sharing of common goods. But people are
not bees, and it is doubtful that an analogy between them sheds
much true light.

18   Another kind of error, both in drawing mental comparisons or
putting them down in prose, is the *Argument by Analogy*. Here
the assumption is that limited points of similarity between analogous phenomena may be used to "prove" that what is true in
the case of one must also be true in the case of the second. Children are like puppies, so the argument by analogy runs; the way
to housebreak a puppy is to whip it; thus the way to "housebreak"
a child is to whip him. Examples of argument by analogy surround
us in our everyday lives; possibly even you and I are guilty of
them. American civilization is doomed because it is materialistic
as Rome was, and Rome fell. The atom bomb does not mean the
end of the human race, because people said the same thing about
the invention of gun powder, and gun powder has not ended the

human race. Use Rosebud Soap, as the glamorous stars of Broadway do, and you too will be glamorous.

19   Analogies are perfectly legitimate and very useful forms of comparison so long as they clarify the complex or help to explain the intangible. The parables of Jesus in the New Testament or the allegories of Socrates in the writings of Plato show how splendid a device the analogy is in the hands of a fine teacher. Because it necessarily simplifies, however, the analogy is a limited intellectual tool, and it must be used with care. To use an analogy to argue a point of view, or as a substitute for a complete comprehension of a complex situation, is dubious thinking and specious writing.

ANTITHESIS

20   *Antithesis* is a combination of two Greek words—*anti*, "against"; *thesis*, "proposition"—and it is a way of thinking or writing in which one thing is pitted against another to show their basic dissimilarities. The systematic contrast of ravens and writing desks at the start of the chapter was an example of antithesis. We might make a similar list of contrasting points about soul and body, Classicism and Romanticism, or culture and anarchy. The antithesis is the reverse of the analogy, which stresses points of resemblance.

21   Antithetical thinking is not only the basis for understanding the differences between two phenomena; it also underlies the spoken and written techniques of objective analysis. We speak of "weighing the pro's and con's" of a situation, by which we mean we try to reach some conception of the degree of truth in a case by considering opposite points of view. The very premises of law and trial by jury depend on an antithetical process conducted by a prosecuting and defense attorney. A formal debate, with affirmative and negative sides, is another instance of antithesis. And even an account book, with its credits and debits, uses the contrasting technique of antithetical thinking.

22   Rhetorically, antithetical statements of ideas or opinions may be indicated by a number of single words: "but," "nevertheless," "versus," "against," "opposing," and "contrariwise" among them. Or a more fully developed antithesis may use a balanced structure of phrases indicating opposition: "on the one hand this, on the other hand that," or "positively this but negatively that." So long

as antithesis is used to give information or explain by presenting opposing facts, it is a valuable aid to understanding. Sometimes, however, antithesis as a general type of logical order becomes a means of argument or persuasion, in which case it is called disjunction.

DISJUNCTION

23   *Disjunction* means separation; the meaning of the Latin root phrase ("to unyoke") indicates something of the nature of disjunctive thinking and disjunctive rhetoric. In disjunction, alternative assertions are made, of which only one is supposedly true. The sign of a disjunctive statement is the words "either ... or ...," as in the sentence, "Either Semiramis founded Babylon, or Ninus founded it." This statement not only denies any principle of similarity (such as "Like Ninus, Semiramis founded Babylon," or "Semiramis and Ninus founded Babylon"); it emphasizes antithesis to the extent that contradiction is implied ("It is impossible that both Semiramis and Ninus founded Babylon"), and that one alternative is true and the other is not. Thus the disjunctive statement indicates that, of two opposing ideas, only *one* can be valid.

24   In its use as a kind of deductive thinking, the disjunction can become very perplexing, as we shall see, but so long as it simply asserts alternatives and does not declare one of them false, it remains a type of exposition (or factual discourse). Even in this use, it may take one of several forms of expression; for instance:

> Either Hitler was a sadist or he was a masochist.
> If Hitler was not a masochist, then he was a sadist.
> Unless he was a masochist, Hitler was a sadist.

Any of these statements can be reduced to the "either ... or ..." format, where the choice is more obvious and the disjunction more apparent.

25   Since a disjunction is an assertion of alternatives (or two choices), it may become the wrong form of thinking or the erroneous sort of statement called the *False Dilemma*. This familiar phrase refers to such statements as:

> Either a piranha eats human flesh or it starves to death.
> Either Christopher Marlowe wrote *King Lear* or Thomas Ford did.
> Either you hate Khrushchev or you are a Communist.

In these statements, only a choice of two possibilities is given when other possibilities exist: a piranha eats other things when hapless swimmers are not available; neither Marlowe nor Ford wrote *King*

Lear; and many people who are non-Communists do not hate Khrushchev. If a disjunction states only two choices when more exist, it is a false dilemma.

THE NO DEGREE FALLACY

26   Since comparison and contrast is the basis for our ideas of *degree*, sometimes in our thinking we exaggerate the contrasts between two things to such a point that we view them as irreconcilable, diametrical extremes, and thus forget that they actually may simply be two points separated by a matter of extent or degree. None of us would be silly enough to declare that water must either be hot or else cold; it can be chilly, cool, tepid, or warm, and to assume that these graduations of heat do not exist is to simplify thought to a harmfully inaccurate extent. The illustration of hot or cold water may seem silly, but otherwise sensible people think and utter equally wrong examples of *No Degree* when they let their emotional urges conquer their logical ability.

27   "Set up Medical Care for the Aged, and America will soon have Socialized Medicine!" "Take that first drink, and you'll wind up an alcoholic!" "Let Alaska and Hawaii into the Union, and then Puerto Rico, Panama, and finally Tasmania will want in, too!" "Let the Russians hear one soft word from us, and they'll start bombing New York!" All of these commit the error of thinking there is no difference between one, limited action and an all-out process, or that one change cannot be admitted without admitting a large additional number of changes. Often the no degree fallacy is stated as a dilemma ("Either we keep Alaska out of the Union or *everybody* will want in"); but it is detectable in any form as a refusal to admit compromise or to seek for similarities where similarities exist.

28   In summary of all the techniques of comparison and contrast, we may say that they enable us to understand one thing more clearly by likening it to or differentiating it from some other thing. So long as figures of speech present accurate comparisons, and analogies illustrate properly, they aid understanding. So long as antitheses and disjunction merely distinguish differences or point out alternatives, we may accept them as valid. If tropes are slanted to convince us of an untruth, however, or an analogy misrepresents to "prove" a contention; if antithesis is exaggerated until a choice is unduly limited or degrees of likeness are not admitted; then comparison and contrast is used to muddle thinking and to obfuscate rhetoric rather than to improve the one and guide the other.

Recently there has been a great deal of concern voiced in several quarters over the changing role of the male in American society. In "The Crisis of American Masculinity" Arthur Schlesinger explores some of the factors that have contributed to this change. Like Laurence Sears, he employs the technique of comparison and contrast, setting the modern American male alongside his nineteenth century counterpart. The theatre, music, and psychology are cited as reflections of "an age of sexual ambiguity" that has manifested itself in a loss of masculine identity. However, Schlesinger feels the situation can be remedied through satire, art, and politics.

The Crisis of American Masculinity

Arthur Schlesinger, Jr.

1 What has happened to the American male? For a long time, he seemed utterly confident in his manhood, sure of his masculine role in society, easy and definite in his sense of sexual identity. The frontiersmen of James Fenimore Cooper, for example, never had any concern about masculinity; they were men, and it did not occur to them to think twice about it. Even well into the twentieth century, the heroes of Dreiser, of Fitzgerald, of Hemingway remain men. But one begins to detect a new theme emerging in some of these authors, especially in Hemingway: the theme of the male hero increasingly preoccupied with proving his virility to himself. And by mid-century, the male role had plainly lost its rugged clarity of outline. Today men are more and more conscious of maleness not as a fact but as a problem. The ways by which American men affirm their masculinity are uncertain and obscure. There are multiplying signs, indeed, that something has gone badly wrong with the American male's conception of himself.

2 On the most superficial level, the roles of male and female are increasingly merged in the American household. The American man is found as never before as a substitute for wife and mother— changing diapers, washing dishes, cooking meals and performing a whole series of what once were considered female duties. The American woman meanwhile takes over more and more of the big decisions, controlling them indirectly when she cannot do so directly. Outside the home, one sees a similar blurring of function. While men design dresses and brew up cosmetics, women become doctors, lawyers, bank cashiers and executives. "Women now fill many 'masculine' roles," writes the psychologist, Dr. Bruno Bettel-

heim, "and expect their husbands to assume many of the tasks once reserved for their own sex." Women seem an expanding, aggressive force, seizing new domains like a conquering army, while men, more and more on the defensive, are hardly able to hold their own and gratefully accept assignments from their new rulers. A recent book bears the stark and melancholy title *The Decline of the American Male*.

3   Some of this evidence, it should be quickly said, has been pushed too far. The willingness of a man to help his wife around the house may as well be evidence of confidence in masculinity as the opposite; such a man obviously does not have to cling to masculine symbols in order to keep demonstrating his maleness to himself. But there is more impressive evidence than the helpful husband that this is an age of sexual ambiguity. It appears no accident, for example, that the changing of sex—the Christine Jorgensen phenomenon—so fascinates our newspaper editors and readers; or that homosexuality, that incarnation of sexual ambiguity, should be enjoying a cultural boom new in our history. Such developments surely express a deeper tension about the problem of sexual identity.

4   Consider the theatre, that faithful mirror of a society's preoccupations. There have been, of course, popular overt inquiries into sexual ambiguities, like *Compulsion* or *Tea and Sympathy*. But in a sense these plays prove the case too easily. Let us take rather two uncommonly successful plays by the most discussed young playwrights of the United States and Great Britain—Tennessee Williams's *Cat On A Hot Tin Roof* and John Osborne's *Look Back in Anger*. Both deal with the young male in a singular state of confusion and desperation. In *Cat On A Hot Tin Roof*, Brick Pollitt, the professional football player, refuses to sleep with his wife because of guilty memories of his relations with a dead team mate. In *Look Back in Anger*, Jimmy Porter, the embittered young intellectual who can sustain a relationship with his wife only by pretending they are furry animals together, explodes with hatred of women and finds his moments of happiness rough-housing around the stage with a male pal.

5   Brick Pollitt and Jimmy Porter are all too characteristic modern heroes. They are, in a sense, castrated; one is stymied by fear of homosexuality, the other is an unconscious homosexual. Neither is capable of dealing with the woman in his life: Brick surrenders to a strong woman, Jimmy destroys a weak one. Both reject the normal female desire for full and reciprocal love as an unconscion-

able demand and an intolerable burden. Now not many American males have been reduced to quite the Pollitt-Porter condition. Still the intentness with which audiences have watched these plays suggests that exposed nerves are being plucked—that the Pollitt-Porter dilemma expresses in vivid and heightened form something that many spectators themselves feel or fear.

6   Or consider the movies. In some ways, the most brilliant and influential American film since the war is *High Noon*. That remarkable movie, which invested the Western with the classic economy of myth, can be viewed in several ways: as an existentialist drama, for example, or as a parable of McCarthyism. It can also be viewed as a mordant comment on the effort of the American woman to emasculate the American man. The sheriff plainly did not suffer from Brick Pollitt's disease. But a large part of the story dealt with the attempt of his girl to persuade him not to use force—to deny him the use of his pistol. The pistol is an obvious masculine symbol, and, in the end, it was the girl herself, in the modern American manner, who used the pistol and killed a villain. (In this connection, one can pause and note why the Gary Coopers, Cary Grants, Clark Gables and Spencer Tracys continue to play romantic leads opposite girls young enough to be their daughters; it is obviously because so few of the younger male stars can project a convincing sense of masculinity.)

7   Psychoanalysis backs up the theatre and the movies in emphasizing the obsession of the American male with his manhood. "Every psychoanalyst knows," writes one of them, "how many emotional difficulties are due to those fears and insecurities of neurotic men who are unconsciously doubting their masculinity." "In our civilization," Dr. Theodor Reik says, "men are afraid that they will not be men enough." Reik adds significantly: "And women are afraid that they might be considered only women." Why is it that women worry, not over whether they can fill the feminine role, but whether filling that role is enough, while men worry whether they can fill the masculine role at all? How to account for this rising tide of male anxiety? What has unmanned the American man?

8   There is currently a fashionable answer to this question. Male anxiety, many observers have declared, is simply the result of female aggression: what has unmanned the American man is the American woman. The present male confusion and desperation, it is contended, are the inevitable consequence of the threatened feminization of American society. The victory of women is the culmination of a long process of masculine retreat, beginning when

Puritanism made men feel guilty about sex and the frontier gave women the added value of scarcity. Fleeing from the reality of femininity, the American man, while denying the American women juridical equality, transformed her into an ideal of remote and transcendent purity with overriding authority over the family, the home, the school and culture. This habit of obeisance left the male psychologically disarmed and vulnerable when the goddess stepped off the pedestal and demanded in addition equal economic, political and legal rights. In the last part of the nineteenth century, women won their battle for equality. They gained the right of entry into one occupation after another previously reserved for males. Today they hold the key positions of personal power in our society and use this power relentlessly to consolidate their mastery. As mothers, they undermine masculinity through the use of love as a technique of reward and punishment. As teachers, they prepare male children for their role of submission in an increasingly feminine world. As wives, they complete the work of subjugation. Their strategy of conquest is deliberately to emasculate men — to turn them into Brick Pollitts and Jimmy Porters.

9   Or so a standard indictment runs; and no doubt there is something in it. American women have unquestionably gained through the years a place in our society which American men have not been psychologically prepared to accept. Whether because of Puritanism or the frontier, there has been something immature in the traditional American male attitude toward women—a sense of alarm, at times amounting to panic. Almost none of the classic American novels, for example, presents the theme of mature and passionate love. Our nineteenth-century novelists saw women either as unassailable virgins or abandoned temptresses—never simply as women. One looks in vain through *Moby Dick* and *The Adventures of Huckleberry Finn*, through Cooper and Poe and Whitman, for an adult portrayal of relations between men and women. "Where," Leslie Fiedler has asked, "is the American *Madame Bovary, Anna Karenina, Wuthering Heights,* or *Vanity Fair?*"

10   Yet the implication of the argument that the American man has been unmanned by the emancipation of the American woman is that the American man was incapable of growing up. For the nineteenth-century sense of masculinity was based on the psychological idealization and the legal subjection of women; masculinity so spuriously derived could never—and should never—have endured. The male had to learn to live at some point with the free and equal female. Current attempts to blame "the decline of the

American male" on the aggressiveness of the American female amount to a confession that, under conditions of free competition, the female was bound to win. Simple observation refutes this supposition. In a world of equal rights, some women rise; so too do some men; and no pat generalization is possible about the sexual future of society. Women have gained power in certain ways; in others, they have made little progress. It is safe to predict, for example, that we will have a Roman Catholic, perhaps even a Jew, for President before we have a woman. Those amiable prophets of an impending American matriarchy (all men, by the way) are too pessimistic.

11   Something more fundamental is involved in the unmanning of American men than simply the onward rush of American women. Why is the American man so unsure today about his masculine identity? The basic answer to this is surely because he is so unsure about his identity in general. Nothing is harder in the whole human condition than to achieve a full sense of identity—than to know who you are, where you are going, and what you mean to live and die for. From the most primitive myths of the most contemporary novels—from Oedipus making the horrified discovery that he had married his mother, to Leopold Bloom and Stephen Dedalus searching their souls in Joyce's Dublin and the haunted characters of Kafka trying to make desperate sense out of an incomprehensible universe—the search for identity has been the most compelling human problem. That search has always been ridden with trouble and terror. And it can be plausibly argued that the conditions of modern life make the quest for identity more difficult than it has ever been before.

12   The pre-democratic world was characteristically a world of status in which people were provided with ready-made identities. But modern western society—free, equalitarian, democratic—has swept away all the old niches in which people for so many centuries found safe refuge. Only a few people at any time in human history have enjoyed the challenge of "making" themselves; most have fled from the unendurable burden of freedom into the womblike security of the group. The new age of social mobility may be fine for those strong enough to discover and develop their own roles. But for the timid and the frightened, who constitute the majority in any age, the great vacant spaces of equalitarian society can become a nightmare filled with nameless horrors. Thus mass democracy, in the very act of offering the individual new freedom and opportunity, offers new moral authority to the group and thereby sets off a new

assault on individual identity. Over a century ago Alexis de Tocqueville, the perceptive Frenchman who ruminated on the contradictions of equality as he toured the United States in the Eighteen Thirties, pointed to the "tyranny of the majority" as a central problem of democracy. John Stuart Mill, lamenting the decline of individualism in Great Britain, wrote: "That so few now dare to be eccentric marks the chief danger of the time." How much greater that danger seems a century later!

13   For our own time has aggravated the assault on identity by adding economic and technological pressures to the political and social pressures of the 19th century. Modern science has brought about the growing centralization of the economy. We work and think and live and even dream in larger and larger units. William H. Whyte, Jr., has described the rise of "the organization man," working by day in immense business concerns, sleeping by night in immense suburban developments, deriving his fantasy life from mass-produced entertainments, spending his existence, not as an individual, but as a member of a group and coming in the end to feel guilty and lost when he deviates from his fellows. Adjustment rather than achievement becomes the social ideal. Men no longer fulfill an inner sense of what they *must* be; indeed, with the cult of the group, that inner sense itself begins to evaporate. Identity consists, not of self-realization, but of smooth absorption into the group. Nor is this just a matter of passive acquiescence. The group is aggressive, imperialistic, even vengeful, forever developing new weapons with which to overwhelm and crush the recalcitrant individual. Not content with disciplining the conscious mind, the group today is even experimenting with means of violating the subconscious. The subliminal invasion represents the climax of the assault on individual identity.

14   It may seem a long way from the loss of the sense of self to the question of masculinity. But if people do not know *who* they are, it is hardly surprising that they are no longer sure what sex they are. Nigel Dennis's exuberant novel, *Cards of Identity*, consists of a series of brilliant variations on the quest for identity in contemporary life. It reaches one of its climaxes in the tale of a person who was brought up by enlightened parents to believe that there was no such thing as pure male or female—everyone had elements of both—and who accepted this proposition so rigorously that he (she) could not decide what his (her) own sex was. "In what identity do you intend to face the future?" someone asks. "It seems that nowadays," comes the plaintive reply, "one must choose

between being a woman who behaves like a man, and a man who behaves like a woman. In short, I must choose to be one in order to behave like the other." If most of us have not yet quite reached that condition of sexual chaos, yet the loss of a sense of identity is obviously a fundamental step in the decay of masculinity. And the gratification with which some American males contemplate their own decline should not obscure the fact that women, for all their recent legal and economic triumphs, are suffering from a loss of identity too. It is not accidental that the authors of one recent book described modern woman as the "lost sex."

15   If this is true, then the key to the recovery of masculinity does not lie in any wistful hope of humiliating the aggressive female and restoring the old masculine supremacy. Masculine supremacy, like white supremacy, was the neurosis of an immature society. It is good for men as well as for women that women have been set free. In any case, the process is irreversible; that particular genie can never be put back into the bottle. The key to the recovery of masculinity lies rather in the problem of identity. When a person begins to find out *who* he is, he is likely to find out rather soon what sex he is.

16   For men to become men again, in short, their first task is to recover a sense of individual spontaneity. And to do this a man must visualize himself as an individual apart from the group, whatever it is, which defines his values and commands his loyalty. There is no reason to suppose that the group is always wrong: to oppose the group automatically is nearly as conformist as to surrender to it automatically. But there is every necessity to recognize that the group is one thing and the individual—oneself—is another. One of the most sinister of present-day doctrines is that of *togetherness*. The recovery of identity means, first of all, a new belief in apartness. It means a determination to resist the overpowering conspiracy of blandness, which seeks to conceal all tension and conflict in American life under a blanket of locker-room affability. And the rebirth of spontaneity depends, at bottom, on changes of attitude *within* people—changes which can perhaps be described, without undue solemnity, as moral changes. These changes will no doubt come about in as many ways as there are individuals involved. But there are some general suggestions that can be made about the techniques of liberation. I should like to mention three such techniques: satire, art, and politics.

17   Satire means essentially the belief that nothing is sacred — that there is no person or institution or idea which cannot but benefit

from the exposure of comedy. Our nation in the past has reveled in satire; it is, after all, the nation of Abraham Lincoln, of Mark Twain, of Finley Peter Dunne, of H. L. Mencken, of Ring Lardner. Indeed, the whole spirit of democracy is that of satire; as Montaigne succinctly summed up the democratic faith: "Sit he on never so high a throne, a man still sits on his own bottom." Yet today American society can only be described as a pompous society, at least in its official manifestations. Early in 1958 Mort Sahl, the night-club comedian, made headlines in New York because he dared make a joke about J. Edgar Hoover! It was not an especially good joke, but the fact that he made it at all was an encouraging sign. One begins to feel that the American people can only stand so much reverence—that in the end our native skepticism will break through, sweep aside the stuffed shirts and the stuffed heads and insist that platitudes are platitudinous and the great are made, among other things, to be laughed at. Irony is good for our rulers; and it is even better for ourselves because it is a means of dissolving the pomposity of society and giving the individual a chance to emerge.

18   If irony is one source of spontaneity, art is another. Very little can so refresh our vision and develop our vision and develop our values as the liberating experience of art. The mass media have cast a spell on us: the popular addiction to prefabricated emotional clichés threatens to erode our capacity for fresh and direct aesthetic experience. Individual identity vanishes in the welter of machine-made reactions. But thoughtful exposure to music, to painting, to poetry, to the beauties of nature, can do much to restore the inwardness, and thereby the identity, of man. There is thus great hope in the immense cultural underground of our age—the paper-bound books, the long-playing records, the drama societies, the art festivals, the new interest in painting and sculpture. All this represents a disdain for existing values and goals, a reaching out for something more exacting and more personal, an intensified questing for identity.

19   And politics in a true sense can be a means of liberation—not the banal politics of rhetoric and self-congratulation, which aims at burying all real issues under a mass of piety and platitude; but the politics of responsibility, which tries to define the real issues and present them to the people for decision. Our national politics have become boring in recent years because our leaders have offered neither candid and clear-cut formulations of the problems nor the

facts necessary for intelligent choice. A virile political life will be definite and hard-hitting, respecting debate and dissent, seeking clarity and decision.

20   As the American male develops himself by developing his comic sense, his aesthetic sense and his moral and political sense, the lineaments of personality will at last begin to emerge. The achievement of identity, the conquest of a sense of self—these will do infinitely more to restore American masculinity than all the hormones in the test tubes of our scientists. "Whoso would be a *man*," said Emerson, "must be a nonconformist"; and, if it is the present writer who adds the italics, nonetheless one feels that no injustice is done to Emerson's intention. How can masculinity, femininity, or anything else survive in a homogenized society, which seeks steadily and benignly to eradicate all differences between the individuals who compose it? If we want to have *men* again in our theatres and our films and our novels—not to speak of in our classrooms, our business offices and our homes—we must first have a society which encourages each of its members to have a distinct identity.

QUESTIONS FOR STUDY

1. Explain the following terms from Johnson's essay: figurative language (give several examples), analogy, antithesis, disjunction. What are the principal applications of comparison and contrast?

2. What techniques of contrast does Schlesinger use in his essay, "The Crisis of American Masculinity"? Be certain to consider his implied contrasts as well.

3. What is the basis of proof for Schlesinger's assertions? Does he take anything for granted?

4. Notice that Schlesinger also uses description and certain forms of logical argument for the development of his ideas. Point out examples of both and discuss their effectiveness.

5. Is there any evidence in the course of the essay to indicate that Schlesinger is trained in the field of history? If so, indicate the specific passages.

6. What is the central purpose of Schlesinger's essay? Where is that purpose stated?

7. What, in Schlesinger's opinion, is the role of man in today's society? How does he arrive at this assumption?

8. What is the "currently fashionable answer" to the problem of man's masculinity?

9. What is it in our modern society that is assaulting our identity? What does "the group" hold for man today?

10. Schlesinger suggests several sources of spontaneity that might help man achieve his identity. What are these sources and how, precisely, could they affect masculine identity?

WRITING TOPICS

1. Write an analysis of "The Crisis of American Masculinity" emphasizing the author's use of the rhetorical principle of comparison and contrast. If the essay can be divided into four categories—statement of problem, definition of current solution to problem, explanation of why current solution is false, alternative solution — consider any special techniques of the principle employed in each category.

2. Take one area of personal interest for you (baseball, theatre, politics, etc.) and compare and contrast it with another.

3. Read the essay in Part Three by Matthew Arnold entitled "Literature and Science" and analyze it for methods of comparison and contrast (as in topic one above).

By itself, a mastery of the techniques of logical argument and analysis will not necessarily improve one's writing ability. Such mastery will, however, enable one to spot flaws in his own and others' reasoning, and will sharpen his skill at persuasion, the first aim of rhetoric. In this chapter taken from their book *Understanding and Using English*, Newman and Genevieve Birk outline certain fundamentals of logic essential to every prose writer. Their own first premise is "argument . . . assumes opposition," and they explain the two principal means by which convincing arguments are developed and the possible fallacies which may result from the misuse of either.

Persuasion by Logical Argument

Newman and Genevieve Birk

1   The closely organized logical argument usually follows a basic plan of this kind: (1) The writer or speaker states the question clearly and fairly, defining any terms that might be ambiguous, and limiting the argument to the specific issues which he regards as important; he may in this preliminary step of his argument consider the history of the question and its present significance. (2) He states his position and supports that position by citing facts and authorities, and by reasoning from the evidence he presents. (3) He recognizes and refutes any outstanding arguments against his ideas. (4) He summarizes his argument and emphasizes the merits of his position or his proposal. Less formal arguments are likely to include these four steps too, but to follow a more personal, less orderly plan.

2   The writer of convincing argument must have studied his subject thoroughly. He must know exactly what the major issues are, so that he will not waste words in arguing trivial side issues or points on which there is general agreement. He must have not merely facts and authorities to support his position, but trustworthy, representative, up-to-date facts and reputable authorities. He must know his subject well enough to know more than one side of it. Argument, unlike some other kinds of persuasion, assumes opposition; understanding that opposition, being able to concede its strength on some points, but also to demonstrate its weakness on vital points, may be a large part of successful argumentation. In order to see weaknesses in the opposition, and in order to evaluate his own evidence and to arrive at sound conclusions, the writer needs, in addition to knowledge, skill in logical reasoning.

3   The reader of argument also needs this skill. If he is a critical reader, he will ask two questions about a piece of argumentative prose: Is the evidence good? Is the reasoning sound? In answering the first question he will be helped immeasurably, of course, if he has read and thought about the subject, if he himself has some command of the facts and some acquaintance with the recognized authorities in the field. But without this knowledge he still can make valid judgments about the evidence on which the writer's conclusions are based. He can see how well the writer's statements are substantiated. Some of them may be unsubstantiated, or practically so: "leading scientists agree," or "as psychologists tell us," or "the facts are well known," or "experiments have proved" is not equivalent to quoting scientists, psychologists, facts, or results of specific experiments. Some statements may have unreliable substantiation because the sources are unauthoritative or prejudiced: "the Podunk *Post-Examiner* of April 10, 1958, says . . ."; "the last issue of *Popular Reading* contains an article which settles this issue for all time"; "John Smith's authoritative study [written in 1935] says the last word on college football"; "the *Democratic Digest* gives an impartial account of the political situation." The reader can also recognize the citing of irrelevant authority — Thomas Jefferson, for example, quoted to support an argument against national health insurance; or a famous chemist quoted on old age pensions, or a prominent businessman on modern art. Persons competent in one field are not necessarily authorities in another. Finally, a reader can make some judgment of the evidence by asking himself how much of it there is, and whether the writer seems to have minimized or ignored evidence on the other side.

4   In answering the second question—Is the reasoning sound?—the reader is aided by a knowledge of logic. Frequently, while reading or listening to argument, one has an elusive sense of illogic in the thinking, a feeling of something's-wrong-but-I-can't-put-my-finger-on-it. A knowledge of the two kinds of logical thinking called *induction* and *deduction*, and of the common errors in logic, called *fallacies*, makes it easier to detect weaknesses in reasoning and also to recognize and to practice sound reasoning.

A. INDUCTION

5   Induction is the kind of reasoning by which we examine a number of particulars or specific instances and on the basis of them arrive at a conclusion. The scientific method is inductive when the

scientist observes a recurrent phenomenon and arrives at the conclusion or hypothesis that under certain conditions this phenomenon will always take place; if in the course of time further observation supports his hypothesis and if no exceptions are observed, his conclusion is generally accepted as truth and is sometimes called a law. In everyday living, too, we arrive at conclusions by induction. Every cat we encounter has claws; we conclude that all cats have claws. Every rose we smell is fragrant; we conclude that all roses are fragrant. An acquaintance has, on various occasions, paid back money he has borrowed; we conclude that he is frequently out of funds but that he pays his debts. Every Saturday morning for six weeks the new paper boy is late in delivering the paper; we conclude that he sleeps on Saturday mornings and we no longer look for the paper before nine o'clock. In each case we have reasoned inductively from a number of instances; we have moved from an observation of some things to a generalization about all things in the same category.

6   Occasionally, in restricted situations, it is possible to examine every instance. For example, a teacher may note that student A is present in class today, student B is present, C is present, and so on through the whole class list; by simple counting, the teacher can conclude that all members of the class are present today. Ordinarily, though, it is impossible to examine every instance—the claws of every cat, for example, or the nervous system of every cockroach, or every case of diphtheria, or every ruptured appendix, or the opinion of every voter. One must make an inductive jump from the instances he can know to a conclusion embracing things of the same sort that he cannot know. Inductive reasoning arrives, therefore, not at "truth" or "law," but at probability. The probability grows stronger and the induction becomes sounder when a substantial number of instances are examined, when the instances examined are typical, and when the exceptions, if any, are infrequent and explainable.

7   A conclusion based on too few instances or on untypical instances is called a *hasty generalization*. It is the most common fallacy in inductive reasoning, and is responsible for much misinformation and prejudice: "Negroes are lazy" "Why do you say that?" "Well, we had a Negro cook who was the laziest mortal I ever saw, and look at Bob Jones—he doesn't even try to get a job." The speaker is, of course, generalizing on the basis of only two examples, assuming that these examples are typical, and ignoring the countless exceptions. The hasty generalization may also occur in scientific

research; further research may reveal exceptions which modify or invalidate the earlier conclusion.

8   *Cause-effect induction* is reasoning about why things happened and about the relationship between them. We observe effects and arrive at a conclusion about their cause; or we observe a set of circumstances (causes) and draw a conclusion about their effects; or we observe some effects and reason from them that there will be other effects. A doctor examines a patient, learns his symptoms, and from the data makes a diagnosis; he has started with the effects of the illness and reasoned to the cause of them. In cause-to-effect thinking the process is reversed because we can see the causes and, usually with the help of past inductions, can predict the effects. A student visits football practice two days before the opening game; he observes that two players are fighting on the field, that the captain and the coach are on bad terms, that the team's best passer is on the bench with a broken arm, and that the backfield is slow; seeing these causes, he predicts that this will not be a successful team. Effect-to-effect thinking is chain reasoning which also usually relies on past inductions: "That little accident [cause] smashed the right front fender [observed effect]; Father will be angry and will make me pay for a new fender [further effect reasoned on the basis of past instances]; I won't be able to take Jane to the prom [ultimate effect]."

9   A great deal of scientific investigation deals with casual relationships; that is, with observing and describing those orderly connections between elements and events in the universe, on the basis of which causes can be assigned and effects predicted with accuracy. In our daily thinking, too, we make numerous cause-effect inductions, many of which, however, lack scientific exactitude; they need to be verified before they can be held as logical conclusions. The following effect-to-cause inductions are fairly typical of the kind of reasoning we hear and perhaps do every day. During a storm, the back door slams with such force that the glass breaks; we assume that the wind blew the door. A friend is obviously depressed on the day grades come out; we say that he is badly disappointed in his grades. An engagement is broken a month after the engaged girl's family loses its money; we conclude that the engagement was broken for that reason. All these inductions need further verification, for the cause in each case may well be different from the one assigned; the door may have been slammed by a member of the family who is happy to have the storm blamed for it; the friend may be depressed and the engagement may have been broken for any number of reasons.

10   These examples illustrate two common fallacies in cause-effect induction. The first fallacy is oversimplifying, and attributing to a single cause effects which actually have complex causes. "I failed the course because the teacher was unreasonably hard" is sometimes an example of this oversimplification. Other familiar examples are: "The atomic bomb won World War II"; "The Hoover administration was responsible for the depression of the nineteen thirties"; "The reason for the high cost of living is the high wages paid to labor."

11   Often closely related to oversimplification of the cause is the logical fallacy of seeing a cause-effect relationship between events which have only an accidental time relationship. This fallacy is called *post hoc ergo propter hoc*, Latin for "after that therefore because of that." A common instance of this reasoning is a statement like "I won't vote for the Democrats again. Six months after they got into office the city taxes went up two dollars." It is possible, of course, that the Democrats were responsible for the tax increase; but it is also possible that any administration would have found higher taxes necessary. Asserting without proof a cause-effect relationship simply because one event follows another is as illogical as asserting that breakfast causes lunch. Many superstitions are maintained by this *post hoc ergo propter hoc* thinking. A superstitious person walks under a ladder, and an hour later, for reasons entirely unrelated to that incident, has a quarrel with a good friend; he forgets or ignores the real causes of the quarrel, falls into the logical confusion of after-I-walked-under-the-ladder-therefore-because-I-walked-under-the-ladder, and is confirmed in his original faulty induction that walking under ladders brings bad luck.

12   *Induction by analogy* occurs when one observes that two things are similar in some ways, and then reasons, from the observed likenesses, that they are also similar in other ways. For example, Sir Isaac Newton observed that certain combustible substances— oils, turpentine, camphor, etc.—had refractive power two or three times greater than might be expected from their densities. He reasoned by analogy that the diamond, with its very high refractive powers, was also combustible. This inference was correct.

13   Reasoning from analogy is dangerous, however, and argument by analogy alone is seldom convincing, because analogous situations or objects have differences as well as similarities and the differences may outweigh the similarities. Sir David Brewster, a nineteenth-century physicist and biographer of Sir Isaac Newton, pointed out that if Newton had reasoned from analogy the com-

bustibility of greenockite and octahedrite, which also have high refractive powers, he would have been wrong. His reasoning about the diamond simply happened to be right. Long observation of Mars has given astronomers a body of data from which they have arrived inductively at a number of conclusions about that planet. Some people have reasoned by analogy that since Mars has atmosphere, temperatures, and seasonal changes comparable to earth's, it must also have life like ours. This conclusion is questionable; it disregards the observed differences between the two planets.

14   Analogy is not logical proof. In informative writing it is, as we have said earlier, a useful method of clarifying a difficult subject. Skillful analogy also has great persuasive power. But it should be used in conjunction with, not as a substitute for, more strictly logical reasoning; and it is effective only when the similarities are striking and the differences slight between the things being compared. The following induction by analogy is weak because the comparison is far-fetched and the differences are glaring:

> Even the most durable machines break down if they are worked constantly for long periods of time. Their parts wear out; they become inefficient. Are students supposed to be stronger than machines? Do they deserve less attention and care? We should have shorter assignments and longer vacations.

The following famous passage illustrates effective analogy. The comparison is used not to prove, but to describe and to persuade:

> In the field of world policy I would dedicate this Nation to the policy of the good neighbor—the neighbor who resolutely respects himself and because he does so, respects the rights of others—the neighbor who respects his obligations and respects the sanctity of his agreements in and with a world of neighbors.—Franklin D. Roosevelt, *First Inaugural Address*.

B. DEDUCTION

15   Inductive reasoning, as we have seen, moves from individual circumstances or instances to a conclusion; this conclusion, unless every possible instance has been examined, expresses probability; the probability is as strong as the weight of evidence which supports it. Deduction is reasoning from stated propositions or premises to a conclusion. If the conclusion follows logically from the premises and if the premises are true, deduction arrives at proof or certainty.

All men are mortal.
John is a man.
Therefore John is mortal.

The statement above is a syllogism, the pattern in which, in formal logic, a deductive argument is expressed. The syllogism consists of three statements—two premises and a conclusion. It contains three and only three main terms, each of which appears twice, but not twice in the same statement. The terms are given these names: the *major term* is the predicate of the conclusion; the *minor term* is the subject of the conclusion; and the *middle term* appears in both premises. The major term in the syllogism above is "mortal," and the premise in which it appears is called the *major premise.* The minor term is "John," and the premise in which it appears is called the *minor premise.* The middle term, "man/men," appears in both premises.

16   Diagraming the syllogism sometimes makes the relationship of statements clearer:

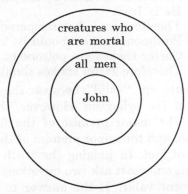

If all men are included in the larger group of mortal things (major premise), and if John is included in the group of all men (minor premise), then John is inevitably included in the group of those who are mortal (conclusion).

17   There are four patterns of the syllogism, in which the terms have different positions. In the following examples, the middle term (the term which appears in both premises) is printed in capital letters to show its position in the four patterns or "figures" of the syllogism:

Figure 1: All DOGS are carnivorous.
My cocker is a DOG.
Therefore my cocker is carnivorous.

Figure 2: No thief CAN BE TRUSTED.
All good men CAN BE TRUSTED.
Therefore no good men are thieves.

Figure 3: Every COLLEGE STUDENT has great opportunities.
Some COLLEGE STUDENTS are poor.
Therefore some poor people have great opportunities.

Figure 4: Most people devote themselves to MATERIAL GAIN.
MATERIAL GAIN is not a worthy goal in life.
Therefore most people do not devote themselves to
a worthy goal in life.

18   When a syllogism has any of these four relationships between terms and between premises and conclusion, its argument is said to be *valid*. It is worth noting here that a "valid" argument is not necessarily *factually true*. For example, for some readers, the conclusions in the second and fourth syllogism above will seem untrue because one or both of the two premises seem untrue. Perhaps the point will be clearer if we look at more obvious examples:

Major premise: All Irishmen have hot tempers.
Minor premise: He is Irish.
Conclusion: Therefore he is hot-tempered.
Major premise: Poisonous snakes should be killed.
Minor premise: Garter snakes are poisonous.
Conclusion: Therefore garter snakes should be killed.

These two arguments are "valid" because they have the logical form of Figure 1 of the syllogism. However, the conclusions are unreliable because the major premise of the first syllogism is a hasty generalization, and the minor premise of the second syllogism is a misstatement of fact. In judging the truth or reliability of a deductive argument, one must ask two questions: Are the premises true? Is the argument valid? If the answer to both questions is "yes," the deduction can be accepted as true.[1]

C. FALLACIES

19   We have mentioned earlier the common fallacies in inductive reasoning: hasty generalization, oversimplification of complex causes, *post hoc ergo propter hoc* argument, and faulty analogy.

---

[1]True premises and a valid argument can produce only a true conclusion. Untrue premises, as we have seen, can produce questionable or untrue conclusions. But it may be worth noting that a conclusion may happen to be true even though it is drawn from false premises: All cats are birds; all pigeons are cats; therefore all pigeons are birds. The conclusion here is true for reasons other than those stated in the premises.

The most common fallacies in deductive argument come from the faulty relationship of parts of the syllogism. Such fallacies sometimes produce a slippery illogic in the reasoning, difficult to detect. For example, in the first figure of the syllogism illustrated on page 321, the subject of the major premise is the predicate of the minor premise; the form of the syllogism is *All X is Y; Z is X; therefore Z is Y.* In the following syllogism of the same pattern, the terms are shifted:

> All tigers are felines. (X is Y)
> My cat is a feline (Z is Y)
> Therefore my cat is a tiger. (∴ Z is X)

The illogic here is made apparent by the absurdity of the conclusion; but it may not be so apparent in a similarly constructed syllogism:

> All communists say Russia doesn't want war.
> He says Russia doesn't want war.
> Therefore he is a communist.

Diagraming such arguments is a good way of seeing why they are invalid:

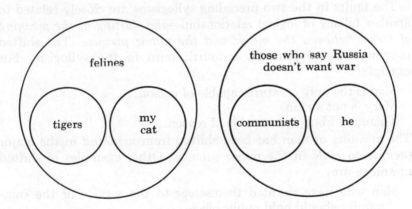

My cat and *he* are in the large circles of *felines* and *those who say Russia doesn't want war,* but not necessarily in the smaller circles of *tigers* and *communists.* There is no established relationship between the terms (tigers and my cat; communists and he) except the fact that they are both members of a larger group.

Another fallacy is in conclusions drawn from negative premises. If one premise is negative, the conclusion must be negative in a valid argument; if both premises are negative, no conclusion can be drawn.

Valid: All those attending the meeting are freshmen.
            John is not a freshman.
            Therefore John is not attending the meeting.
Invalid: No freshmen are attending the meeting.
            John is not a freshman.
            Therefore John is attending the meeting.

No conclusion can be drawn from the last two negative premises; John may or may not be attending the meeting.

21   In a valid argument, the conclusion follows inevitably from the premises. *Non-sequitur* (Latin for "it does not follow") is the fallacy of leaping to a conclusion not warranted by the premises. Drawing a conclusion from negative premises is one form of *non-sequitur*. Other examples are:

Anyone who works hard deserves a vacation now and then.
I work hard.
Therefore my parents should give me a trip to Bermuda.

Men who have made sacrifices for their country should be honored.
I have made sacrifices for my country.
Therefore I should be President.

22   The faults in the two preceding syllogisms are closely related to another fallacy of logical relationship—*the shifting of the meaning of terms between the major and the minor premise*. The shifted meaning is equivalent to a fourth term in the syllogism. For example:

Man is the only creature capable of reason.
Mary is not a man.
Therefore Mary is incapable of reason.

The meaning of man has been shifted from *mankind* in the major premise to *male* in the minor premise. Other examples of shifted meanings are:

Men who have devoted themselves to the service of the community should hold public office.
I have devoted myself to the service of the community by running a bakery for fifteen years.
Therefore I should hold public office.

Government employees who are sympathetic with Russian policy should be discharged.
This government employee belonged in 1943 to an organization which was friendly toward Russia.
Therefore he should be discharged.

23   We seldom encounter the complete syllogism except in discussions of logic and in very formal argument. More usual is a reduced

form of the syllogism in which one or two of the three parts, though implied, are not stated. The reduced syllogism is called an *enthymeme*. Sometimes in the enthymeme the conclusion of the syllogism is omitted because it is obvious: *Students who are found cheating on examinations fail the course; Clarence has been found cheating on an examination;* [the obvious omitted conclusion: therefore Clarence will fail the course]. Sometimes the minor premise is omitted for the same reason: *I like candidates who speak their minds; I'm going to vote for you* [omitted premise: you speak your mind]. Sometimes both the minor premise and the conclusion are omitted because the major premise adequately communicates them: *I date only men who have cars;* [omitted: you don't have a car; therefore I won't have a date with you]. Most frequently the major premise is omitted because the communicator assumes (often wrongly) that it is universally accepted and so does not require proof or even statement. One of the most useful skills of the hearer or reader of argument, therefore, is the ability to supply the omitted major premise. By recognizing that premise and examining it critically, he can better judge the reliability of the argument. The enthymemes below are familiar informal arguments; the major premise on which each one is based is put in brackets.

Jim must have been in a fight; he has a black eye. [Major premise. All black eyes are the result of fights.]

So he forgot he made the appointment. What can you expect? He's a college professor. [Major premise: College professors usually forget appointments. *Or,* College professors are absent-minded.]

He must be a grind! He got all A's last semester. [Students who get A records are grinds.]

He can't be a good doctor. He's in favor of socialized medicine. [No good doctor is in favor of socialized medicine.]

You're crazy, saying the meat tastes spoiled. I got it at the store just an hour ago. [Meat is always fresh when it is bought at stores.]

What a coward. He's a conscientious objector, you know. [All conscientious objectors are cowards.]

Naturally he's a delinquent. He reads ten comic books a week. [Reading comics always produces delinquency.]

Of course it's true. I read it in the paper. [Everything printed in the newspapers is true.]

They won't be happy together; he's two years younger than she. [Marriages are always unhappy if the man is younger than the woman.]

I think they'll be very nice neighbors. They have a new Cadillac. [People are nice neighbors if they have a new Cadillac.]

We're not talking about the same girl. The one I knew last summer had blonde hair. [Once a blonde always a blonde.]

His mother has trained him to be neat around the house; he'll make a wonderful husband. [Any man who is neat around the house is a wonderful husband; also, a man trained by his mother to be neat around the house will continue to be neat when he is married.]

24   Two other logical fallacies, not peculiar to induction or to deduction, but involving the quality of the whole argument, are *begging the question* and *ignoring the question.*

25   *Begging the question* is assuming, without proof, the truth of a proposition which actually needs proof. If an arguer says, "This senseless language requirement should be abolished," he is, with the word *senseless,* begging the question; the question is whether or not the language requirement is senseless; if it is, it should of course be abolished; simply calling it senseless is not a logical argument in its disfavor. "This corrupt political machine should be replaced by good government" is another example of begging the question. No proof is offered that the government under attack is a "corrupt political machine," or that the government supported by the speaker will be "good." Both propositions are simply assumed. *Arguing in a circle* is one form of begging the question:

People who are poor lack ambition because if they didn't lack ambition they wouldn't be poor.

The study of literature is worthwhile because literature is a worthwhile subject.

Such argument in a circle is sometimes baffling, particularly when the argument is long and the circular motion is therefore difficult to detect. What the arguer in a circle does, technically, is offer as proof of his first proposition a second proposition which can be proved only by proving the first.

26   *Ignoring the question* is diverting attention from the real issues, or shifting the argument to some other ground. It has many forms. Name-calling, introducing irrelevant facts, and using other devices of charged language may be means of ignoring the real question.

Sometimes a new argument is introduced in an effort to obscure the original issue: "I don't see why not. Susan Jones has a new coat. I should think you'd want me to be well dressed. It's a good thing someone in this family takes some pride in appearance. You haven't even shaved today." Arguing that an accused murderess should be acquitted because she is the mother of three children, and that a candidate should be mayor because he is a veteran of two wars are examples of ignoring the question by shifting from the central issues; the questions here are "Did she commit the murder?" and "Will he make a good mayor?" What is called argument *ad hominem* (to the man) is a way of ignoring the question by a shift from reasonable consideration of a measure to an attack on the character of the opponent; his ancestry, his religion, the fact that his first wife divorced him, that his son was arrested for speeding, etc. may be introduced to appeal to prejudice while the real question—the merits and defects of the measure itself—is ignored.

D. THE TEXTURE OF LOGICAL THOUGHT

27   Although we have separated induction and deduction for purposes of discussion, the two processes work together in most acts of reasoning. A simple illustration of the interplay between them is this: A friend asks you one afternoon to go with him to a movie at the neighborhood theatre. You say, "No; it's Saturday." Behind your refusal lies an induction, based on instances in your own experience, that on Saturday afternoons many school children attend this theatre and are very noisy. You make a quick deduction: Every Saturday afternoon this theatre is full of noisy school children; this is Saturday; therefore the theatre will be full of noisy school children. Another inductive-deductive process also takes place. You have arrived at the generalization that you do not enjoy a movie if you cannot hear all of it. You reason: I do not want to go to a movie if I cannot hear all of it; I will not be able to hear all of it today (because of the noise of the children); therefore I do not want to go to this movie on this day. Still another reasoning process about your relationship with the friend who has asked you to go to the movie may occur. From your past experience with him you may have induced: Jack is not offended if for some good reason I refuse his invitations. Now you may deduce: I am refusing this invitation for a good reason; therefore Jack will not be offended. In this kind of thinking, the inductions

and deductions are almost automatic. In more complex reasoning they are formulated only after conscious and disciplined thought.

28   We have said earlier that induction is important in scientific thinking; it enables human beings to arrive at generalizations and hypotheses about the world they live in, to see cause-effect relationships, and, on the basis of established probabilities, to make predictions and produce effects by controlling causes. As a science advances and its inductive hypotheses are further substantiated, the substantiated hypotheses supply premises from which deductive conclusions are drawn. One kind of reasoning leads to, supports, and leads back to the other. In the same way, in a logical argument, observed instances have perhaps led the speaker or writer inductively to the position he takes in the argument. From his inductions he may reason deductively about what should be done in a particular situation.

29   Closely interwoven though the two kinds of reasoning are, it is useful to have some knowledge of their differences, of the different kinds of reliability they can arrive at, and of the common fallacies in each kind of thinking. Being able to reduce a confusing argument to syllogistic form will enable one to see more clearly its premises and its validity. Being alert to hasty generalization, to faulty cause-effect reasoning, to conclusions which do not follow the premises, to question-begging and to ignoring of the question will help one judge the soundness of an argument. A knowledge of the processes of reasoning, in short, provides instruments of analysis with which one can better examine the texture of his own argument and the arguments of others.

E. TONE

30   In persuasion by logical argument, the writer may be formal or informal in his attitude toward his audience; but he is usually less concerned with getting their liking than with winning their respect. For this respect, he depends largely on the quality of the argument itself. If he presents the issues fairly; if he is reasonable in considering opposing points of view; if his evidence is good and his thinking clear and sound; if he respects the intelligence of his audience and assumes that they will not be convinced by slippery illogic and devices like arguments *ad hominem*, he will almost certainly gain a respectful hearing for what he has to say.

31   As a rule, the most skillful argument is reasonable in tone as well as in thought; it gives the impression of trying to arrive at truth,

not merely to win a case; it is good tempered, and free from dogmatism and conceit. Fighting-mad arguments and dogmatic statements do sometimes affect already-sympathetic or prejudiced audiences; but they are likely to alienate and offend an impartial audience. Benjamin Franklin, wise in argument and diplomacy, wrote in his autobiography:

I made it a rule to forbear all direct contradiction to the sentiments of others, and all positive assertion of my own. I even forbade myself . . . the use of every word or expression in the language that imported a fix'd opinion, such as *certainly, undoubtedly,* etc., and I adopted, instead of them, *I conceive, I apprehend,* or *I imagine* a thing to be so or so; or it *so appears to me at present.* When another asserted something that I thought an error, I deny'd myself the pleasure of contradicting him abruptly, and of showing immediately some absurdity in his proposition; and in answering I began by observing that in certain cases of circumstances his opinion would be right but in the present case there *appear'd* or *seem'd* to me some difference, etc. I soon found the advantage of this change in my manner; the conversations I engag'd in went on more pleasantly. The modest way in which I propos'd my opinions procur'd them a readier reception and less contradiction; I had less mortification when I was found to be in the wrong, and I more easily prevail'd with others to give up their mistakes and join with me when I happened to be in the right.

And this mode, which I at first put on with some violence to natural inclination, became at length so easy, and so habitual to me, that perhaps for these fifty years past no one has ever heard a dogmatical expression escape me. And to this habit (after my character of integrity) I think it principally owing that I had early so much weight with my fellow-citizens when I proposed new institutions, or alterations in the old, and so much influence in public councils when I became a member; for I was but a bad speaker, never eloquent, subject to much hesitation in my choice of words, hardly correct in language, and yet I generally carried my points.

With the rising crime rate in the United States today, arguments for and against the abolition of capital punishment are receiving increasing attention by the general reading public. In the essay "In Favor of Capital Punishment" Jacques Barzun first summarizes the arguments against capital punishment, then builds his own case on the premise of "sanctity of life"—the usual argument employed by the "against" group. Much of his case rests on his view of imprisonment, a punishment he considers worse than death because of its "defilement of human life."

In Favor of Capital Punishment

Jacques Barzun

1   A passing remark of mine in the Mid-Century magazine has brought me a number of letters and a sheaf of pamphlets against capital punishment. The letters, sad and reproachful, offer me the choice of pleading ignorance or being proved insensitive. I am asked whether I know that there exists a worldwide movement for the abolition of capital punishment which has everywhere enlisted able men of every profession, including the law. I am told that the death penalty is not only inhuman but also unscientific, for rapists and murderers are really sick people who should be cured, not killed. I am invited to use my imagination and acknowledge the unbearable horror of every form of execution.

2   I am indeed aware that the movement for abolition is widespread and articulate, especially in England. It is headed there by my old friend and publisher, Mr. Victor Gollancz, and it numbers such well-known writers as Arthur Koestler, C. H. Rolph, James Avery Joyce and Sir John Barry. Abroad as at home the profession of psychiatry tends to support the cure principle, and many liberal newspapers, such as the *Observer*, are committed to abolition. In the United States there are at least twenty-five state leagues working to the same end, plus a national league and several church councils, notably the Quaker and the Episcopal.

3   The assemblage of so much talent and enlightened goodwill behind a single proposal must give pause to anyone who supports the other side, and in the attempt to make clear my views, which are now close to unpopular, I start out by granting that my conclusion is arguable; that is, I am still open to conviction, *provided*

Reprinted from *The American Scholar*, Volume 31, Number 2, Spring, 1962. Copyright © 1962 by the United Chapters of Phi Beta Kappa. By permission of the publishers.

some fallacies and frivolities in the abolitionist argument are first disposed of and the difficulties not ignored but overcome. I should be glad to see this happen, not only because there is pleasure in the spectacle of an airtight case, but also because I am not more sanguinary than my neighbor and I should welcome the discovery of safeguards—for society *and* the criminal—other than killing. But I say it again, these safeguards must really meet, not evade or postpone, the difficulties I am about to describe. Let me add before I begin that I shall probably not answer any more letters on this arousing subject. If this printed exposition does not do justice to my cause, it is not likely that I can do better in the hurry of private correspondence.

4   I readily concede at the outset that present ways of dealing out capital punishment are as revolting as Mr. Koestler says in his harrowing volume, *Hanged by the Neck*. Like many of our prisons, our modes of execution should change. But this objection to barbarity does not mean that capital punishment—or rather, judicial homicide—should not go on. The illicit jump we find here, on the threshold of the inquiry, is characteristic of the abolitionist and must be disallowed at every point. Let us bear in mind the possibility of devising a painless, sudden and dignified death, and see whether its administration is justifiable.

5   The four main arguments advanced against the death penalty are: *1.* punishment for crime is a primitive idea rooted in revenge; *2.* capital punishment does not deter; *3.* judicial error being possible, taking life is an appalling risk; *4.* a civilized state, to deserve its name, must uphold, not violate, the sanctity of human life.

6   I entirely agree with the first pair of propositions, which is why, a moment ago, I replaced the term capital punishment with "judicial homicide." The uncontrollable brute whom I want put out of the way is not to be punished for his misdeeds, nor used as an example or a warning; he is to be killed for the protection of others, like the wolf that escaped not long ago in a Connecticut suburb. No anger, vindictiveness or moral conceit need preside over the removal of such dangers. But a man's inability to control his violent impulses or to imagine the fatal consequences of his acts should be a presumptive reason for his elimination from society. This generality covers drunken driving and teen-age racing on public highways, as well as incurable obsessive violence; it might be extended (as I shall suggest later) to other acts that destroy, precisely, the moral basis of civilization.

7   But why kill? I am ready to believe the statistics tending to show that the prospect of his own death does not stop the murderer. For one thing he is often a blind egotist, who cannot conceive the possibility of his own death. For another, detection would have to be infallible to deter the more imaginative who, although afraid, think they can escape discovery. Lastly, as Shaw long ago pointed out, hanging the wrong man will deter as effectively as hanging the right one. So, once again, why kill? If I agree that moral progress means an increasing respect for human life, how can I oppose abolition?

8   I do so because on this subject of human life, which is to me the heart of the controversy, I find the abolitionist inconsistent, narrow or blind. The propaganda for abolition speaks in hushed tones of the sanctity of human life, as if the mere statement of it as an absolute should silence all opponents who have any moral sense. But most of the abolitionists belong to nations that spend half their annual income on weapons of war and that honor research to perfect means of killing. These good people vote without a qualm for the political parties that quite sensibly arm their country to the teeth. The West today does not seem to be the time or place to invoke the absolute sanctity of human life. As for the clergymen in the movement, we may be sure from the experience of two previous world wars that they will bless our arms and pray for victory when called upon, the sixth commandment notwithstanding.

9   "Oh, but we mean the sanctity of life *within* the nation!" Very well: is the movement then campaigning also against the principle of self-defense? Absolute sanctity means letting the cutthroat have his sweet will of you, even if you have a poker handy to bash him with, for you might kill. And again, do we hear any protest against the police firing at criminals on the street—mere bank robbers usually—and doing this, often enough, with an excited marksmanship that misses the artist and hits the bystander? The absolute sanctity of human life is, for the abolitionist, a slogan rather than a considered proposition.

10   Yet it deserves examination, for upon our acceptance or rejection of it depend such other highly civilized possibilities as euthanasia and seemly suicide. The inquiring mind also wants to know, why the sanctity of *human* life alone? My tastes do not run to household pets, but I find something less than admirable in the uses to which we put animals—in zoos, laboratories and space

machines—without the excuse of the ancient law, "Eat or be eaten."

11   It should moreover be borne in mind that this argument about sanctity applies—or would apply—to about ten persons a year in Great Britain and to between fifty and seventy-five in the United States. These are the average numbers of those executed in recent years. The count by itself should not, of course, affect our judgment of the principle: one life spared or forfeited is as important, morally, as a hundred thousand. But it should inspire a comparative judgment: there are hundreds and indeed thousands whom, in our concern with the horrors of execution, we forget: on the one hand, the victims of violence; on the other, the prisoners in our jails.

12   The victims are easy to forget. Social science tends steadily to mark a preference for the troubled, the abnormal, the problem case. Whether it is poverty, mental disorder, delinquency or crime, the "patient material" monopolizes the interest of increasing groups of people among the most generous and learned. Psychiatry and moral liberalism go together; the application of law as we have known it is thus coming to be regarded as an historic prelude to social work, which may replace it entirely. Modern literature makes the most of this same outlook, caring only for the disturbed spirit, scorning as bourgeois those who pay their way and do *not* stab their friends. All the while the determinism of natural science reinforces the assumption that society causes its own evils. A French jurist, for example, says that in order to understand crime we must first brush aside all ideas of Responsibility. He means the criminal's and takes for granted that of society. The murderer kills because reared in a broken home or, conversely, because at an early age he witnessed his parents making love. Out of such cases, which make pathetic reading in the literature of modern criminology, is born the abolitionist's state of mind: we dare not kill those we are beginning to understand so well.

13   If, moreover, we turn to the accounts of the crimes committed by these unfortunates, who are the victims? Only dull ordinary people going about their business. We are sorry, of course, but they do not interest science on its march. Balancing, for example, the sixty to seventy criminals executed annually in the United States, there were the seventy to eighty housewives whom George Cvek robbed, raped and usually killed during the months of a career devoted to proving his virility. "It is too bad." Cvek alone

seems instructive, even though one of the law officers who helped
track him down quietly remarks: "As to the extent that his villain-
ies disturbed family relationships, or how many women are still
haunted by the specter of an experience they have never disclosed
to another living soul, these questions can only lend themselves to
sterile conjecture."

14   The remote results are beyond our ken, but it is not idle to
speculate about those whose death by violence fills the daily two
inches at the back of respectable newspapers—the old man sunning
himself on a park bench and beaten to death by four hoodlums,
the small children abused and strangled, the middle-aged ladies on
a hike assaulted and killed, the family terrorized by a released or
escaped lunatic, the half-dozen working people massacred by the
sudden maniac, the boatload of persons dispatched by the skipper,
the mindless assaults upon schoolteachers and shopkeepers by the
increasing horde of dedicated killers in our great cities. Where
does the sanctity of life begin?

15   It is all very well to say that many of these killers are themselves "children," that is, minors. Doubtless a nine-year-old mind
is housed in that 150 pounds of unguided muscle. Grant, for argument's sake, that the misdeed is "the fault of society," trot out the
broken home and the slum environment. The question then is,
What shall we do, not in the Utopian city of tomorrow, but here
and now? The "scientific" means of cure are more than uncertain.
The apparatus of detention only increases the killer's antisocial
animus. Reformatories and mental hospitals are full and have an
understandable bias toward discharging their inmates. Some of
these are indeed "cured"—so long as they stay under a rule. The
stress of the social free-for-all throws them back on their violent
modes of self-expression. At that point I agree that society has
failed—twice: it has twice failed the victims, whatever may be its
guilt toward the killer.

16   As in all great questions, the moralist must choose, and choosing has a price. I happen to think that if a person of adult body
has not been endowed with adequate controls against irrationally
taking the life of another, that person must be judicially, painlessly, regretfully killed before that mindless body's horrible auto-
mation repeats.

17   I say "irrationally" taking life, because it is often possible to
feel great sympathy with a murderer. Certain *crimes passionnels*
can be forgiven without being condoned. Blackmailers invite direct
retribution. Long provocation can be an excuse, as in that engag-

ing case of some years ago, in which a respectable carpenter of seventy found he could no longer stand the incessant nagging of his wife. While she excoriated him from her throne in the kitchen— a daily exercise for fifty years—the husband went to his bench and came back with a hammer in each hand to settle the score. The testimony to his character, coupled with the sincerity implied by the two hammers, was enough to have him sent into quiet and brief seclusion.

18   But what are we to say of the type of motive disclosed in a journal published by the inmates of one of our Federal penitentiaries? The author is a bank robber who confesses that money is not his object:

> My mania for power, socially, sexually, and otherwise can feel no degree of satisfaction until I feel sure I have struck the ultimate of submission and terror in the minds and bodies of my victims. . . . It's very difficult to explain all the queer fascinating sensations pounding and surging through me while I'm holding a gun on a victim, watching his body tremble and sweat. . . . This is the moment when all the rationalized hypocrisies of civilization are suddenly swept away and two men stand there facing each other morally and ethically naked, and right and wrong are the absolute commands of the man behind the gun.

19   This confused echo of modern literature and modern science defines the choice before us. Anything deserving the name of cure for such a man presupposes not only a laborious individual psychoanalysis, with the means to conduct and to sustain it, socially and economically, but also a re-education of the mind, so as to throw into correct perspective the garbled ideas of Freud and Nietzsche, Gide and Dostoevski, which this power-seeker and his fellows have derived from the culture and temper of our times. Ideas are tenacious and give continuity to emotion. Failing a second birth of heart and mind, we must ask: How soon will this sufferer sacrifice a bank clerk in the interests of making civilization less hypocritical? And we must certainly question the wisdom of affording him more than one chance. The abolitionists' advocacy of an unconditional "let live" is in truth part of the same cultural tendency that animates the killer. The Western peoples' revulsion from power in domestic and foreign policy has made of the state a sort of counterpart of the bank robber: both having power and neither knowing how to use it. Both waste lives because they are hypnotized by irrelevant ideas and crippled by contradictory emotions. If psychiatry were sure of its ground in diagnosing the

individual case, a philosopher might consider whether such dangerous obsessions should not be guarded against by judicial homicide
before the shooting starts.

20   I raise the question not indeed to recommend the prophylactic
execution of potential murderers, but to introduce the last two
perplexities that the abolitionists dwarf or obscure by their concentration on changing an isolated penalty. One of these is the
scale by which to judge the offenses society wants to repress. I can
for example imagine a truly democratic state in which it would
be deemed a form of treason punishable by death to create a disturbance in any court or deliberative assembly. The aim would be
to recognize the sanctity of orderly discourse in arriving at justice,
assessing criticism and defining policy. Under such a law, a natural
selection would operate to remove permanently from the scene
persons who, let us say, neglect argument in favor of banging
on the desk with their shoe. Similarly, a bullying minority in a
diet, parliament or skupshtina would be prosecuted for treason to
the most sacred institutions when fists or flying inkwells replace
rhetoric. That the mere suggestion of such a law sounds ludicrous
shows how remote we are from civilized institutions, and hence
how gradual should be our departure from the severity of judicial
homicide.

21   I say gradual and I do not mean standing still. For there is one
form of barbarity in our law that I want to see mitigated before
any other. I mean imprisonment. The enemies of capital punishment—and liberals generally—seem to be satisfied with any legal
outcome so long as they themselves avoid the vicarious guilt of
shedding blood. They speak of the sanctity of life, but have no concern with its quality. They give no impression of ever having read
what it is certain they have read, from Wilde's *De Profundis* to the
latest account of prison life by a convicted homosexual. Despite the
infamy of concentration camps, despite Mr. Charles Burney's remarkable work, *Solitary Confinement*, despite riots in prisons,
despite the round of escape, recapture and return in chains, the
abolitionists' imagination tells them nothing about the reality of
being caged. They read without a qualm, indeed they read with
rejoicing, the hideous irony of "Killer Gets Life"; they sigh with
relief instead of horror. They do not see and suffer the cell, the
drill, the clothes, the stench, the food; they do not feel the sexual
racking of young and old bodies, the hateful promiscuity, the
insane monotony, the mass degradation, the impotent hatred. They

do not remember from Silvio Pellico that only a strong political faith, with a hope of final victory, can steel a man to endure long detention. They forget that Joan of Arc, when offered "life," preferred burning at the stake. Quite of another mind, the abolitionists point with pride to the "model prisoners" that murderers often turn out to be. As if a model prisoner were not, first, a contradiction in terms, and second, an exemplar of what a free society should not want.

22   I said a moment ago that the happy advocates of the life sentence appear not to have understood what we know they have read. No more do they appear to read what they themselves write. In the preface to his useful volume of cases, *Hanged in Error*, Mr. Leslie Hale, M.P., refers to the tardy recognition of a minor miscarriage of justice—one year in jail: "The prisoner emerged to find that his wife had died and that his children and his aged parents had been removed to the workhouse. By the time a small payment had been assessed as 'compensation' the victim was incurably insane." So far we are as indignant with the law as Mr. Hale. But what comes next? He cites the famous Evans case, in which it is very probable that the wrong man was hanged, and he exclaims: "While such mistakes are possible, should society impose an irrevocable sentence?" Does Mr. Hale really ask us to believe that the sentence passed on the first man, whose wife died and who went insane, was in any sense *revocable?* Would not any man rather be Evans dead than that other wretch "emerging" with his small compensation and his reasons for living gone?

23   Nothing is revocable here below, imprisonment least of all. The agony of a trial itself is punishment, and acquittal wipes out nothing. Read the heart-rending diary of William Wallace, accused quite implausibly of having murdered his wife and "saved" by the Court of Criminal Appeals—but saved for what? Brutish ostracism by everyone and a few years of solitary despair. The cases of Adolf Beck, of Oscar Slater, of the unhappy Brooklyn bank teller who vaguely resembled a forger and spent eight years in Sing Sing only to "emerge" a broken, friendless, useless, "compensated" man—all these, if the dignity of the individual has any meaning, had better have been dead before the prison door ever opened for them. This is what counsel always says to the jury in the course of a murder trial and counsel is right: far better hang this man than "give him life." For my part, I would choose death without hesitation. If that option is abolished, a demand will one day be heard to claim it as

a privilege in the name of human dignity. I shall believe in the abolitionist's present views only after he has emerged from twelve months in a convict cell.

24   The detached observer may want to interrupt here and say that the argument has now passed from reasoning to emotional preference. Whereas the objector to capital punishment *feels* that death is the greatest of evils, I *feel* that imprisonment is worse than death. A moment's thought will show that feeling is the appropriate arbiter. All reasoning about what is right, civilized and moral rests upon sentiment, like mathematics. Only, in trying to persuade others, it is important to single out the fundamental feeling, the prime intuition, and from it to reason justly. In my view, to profess respect for human life and be willing to see it spent in a penitentiary is to entertain liberal feelings frivolously. To oppose the death penalty because, unlike a prison term, it is irrevocable is to argue fallaciously.

25   In the propaganda for abolishing the death sentence the recital of numerous miscarriages of justice commits the same error and implies the same callousness: what is at fault in our present system is not the sentence but the fallible procedure. Capital cases being one in a thousand or more, who can be cheerful at the thought of all the "revocable" errors? What the miscarriages point to is the need for reforming the jury system, the rules of evidence, the customs of prosecution, the machinery of appeal. The failure to see that this is the great task reflects the sentimentality I spoke of earlier, that which responds chiefly to the excitement of the unusual. A writer on Death and the Supreme Court is at pains to point out that when that tribunal reviews a capital case, the judges are particularly anxious and careful. What a left-handed compliment to the highest judicial conscience of the country! Fortunately, some of the champions of the misjudged see the issue more clearly. Many of those who are thought wrongly convicted now languish in jail because the jury was uncertain or because a doubting governor commuted the death sentence. Thus Dr. Samuel H. Sheppard, Jr., convicted of his wife's murder in the second degree is serving a sentence that is supposed to run for the term of his natural life. The story of his numerous trials, as told by Mr. Paul Holmes, suggests that police incompetence, newspaper demagogy, public envy of affluence and the mischances of legal procedure fashioned the result. But Dr. Sheppard's vindicator is under no illusion as to the conditions that this "lucky" evader of the electric

chair will face if he is granted parole after ten years: "It will carry with it no right to resume his life as a physician. His privilege to practice medicine was blotted out with his conviction. He must all his life bear the stigma of a parolee, subject to unceremonious return to confinement for life for the slightest misstep. More than this, he must live out his life as a convicted murderer."

26   What does the moral conscience of today think it is doing? If such a man is a dangerous repeater of violent acts, what right has the state to let him loose after ten years? What is, in fact, the meaning of a "life sentence" that peters out long before life? Paroling looks suspiciously like an expression of social remorse for the pain of incarceration, coupled with a wish to avoid "unfavorable publicity" by freeing a suspect. The man is let out when the fuss has died down; which would mean that he was not under lock and key for our protection at all. He *was* being punished, just a little —for so prison seems in the abolitionist's distorted view, and in the jury's and the prosecutor's, whose "second-degree" murder suggests killing someone "just a little."*

27   If, on the other hand, execution and life imprisonment are judged too severe and the accused is expected to be harmless hereafter—punishment being ruled out as illiberal—what has society gained by wrecking his life and damaging that of his family?

28   What we accept, and what the abolitionist will clamp upon us all the more firmly if he succeeds, is an incoherence which is not remedied by the belief that second-degree murder merits a kind of second-degree death; that a doubt as to the identity of a killer is resolved by commuting real death into intolerable life; and that our ignorance whether a maniac will strike again can be hedged against by measuring "good behavior" within the gates and then releasing the subject upon the public in the true spirit of experimentation.

29   These are some of the thoughts I find I cannot escape when I read and reflect upon this grave subject. If, as I think, they are relevant to any discussion of change and reform, resting as they do on the direct and concrete perception of what happens, then the simple meliorists who expect to breathe a purer air by abolishing the death penalty are deceiving themselves and us. The issue is for the public to judge; but I for one shall not sleep easier for

---

*The British Homicide Act of 1957, Section 2, implies the same reasoning in its definition of "diminished responsibility" for certain forms of mental abnormality. The whole question of irrationality and crime is in utter confusion, on both sides of the Atlantic.

knowing that in England and America and the West generally a hundred more human beings are kept alive in degrading conditions to face a hopeless future; while others—possibly less conscious, certainly less controlled—benefit from a premature freedom dangerous alike to themselves and society. In short, I derive no comfort from the illusion that in giving up one manifest protection of the law-abiding, we who might well be in any of these three roles—victim, prisoner, licensed killer—have struck a blow for the sanctity of human life.

QUESTIONS FOR STUDY

1. Describe the basic plan characteristic of a "closely organized logical argument." What else must a writer of convincing argument do besides follow this plan?

2. Explain induction as a type of logical thinking. What is meant by "probability"? "Hasty generalization"? Cause-effect induction? "Post hoc ergo propter hoc"? Induction by analogy? Describe the strong points as well as the weak points of each.

3. Explain deduction as a type of logical argument. How can we know when a syllogistic argument is valid? What are some of the common fallacies? Give some examples from your own experiences.

4. Why is it difficult—in "closely organized logical argument"— to separate the inductive and deductive modes of logic? Illustrate from your own experiences. What is the significance of tone? Give examples.

5. Does Barzun, in his essay "In Favor of Capital Punishment," adhere to the basic plan of a logical argument? If so, show exactly where these four basic divisions occur in the essay.

6. Why, at the outset, does Barzun state that the barbarity of the present form of capital punishment should not be considered as argument against abolition of the death penalty? Why does he prefer to use the term"judicial homicide" rather than capital punishment? How has Barzun proposed to extend the scope of "judicial homicide"?

7. What is his purpose in citing the four main arguments against the death penalty? Are these the real arguments against the death penalty, or has the author misstated the opposition's case?

8. What is the "moral sense" the author mentions in relation to the abolitionist point of view? How do euthanasia and suicide fit into this argument for the "sanctity of human life"?

9. Why does Barzun feel that the criminal gets more attention than the victim?

10. Much of this essay seems to be devoted to an attack on either the current state of prison management or the debilitating effects of life imprisonment. Is this a logical way of advocating the retaining of the death penalty? Explain. Has Barzun been indulging in any logical fallacies? If so, point them out.

11. In paragraph 21 of the Barzun essay the tone and language

become emotionally intensified. Analyze this paragraph to determine how the author achieves this intensity. Does this intensity weaken his logical approach to the subject? Explain.

12. In paragraph 22 does Barzun seem to be suggesting that executing an innocent man would have been preferable to sending him to jail? What is the purpose of including this example?

13. Have Barzun's arguments convinced you that the death penalty should be retained? If so, explain why his arguments have been effective. If not, explain why he has failed.

WRITING TOPICS

1. Using the elements of the basic plan suggested by the Birks, select a topic of campus interest (such as the fraternity-sorority system) and write an essay in which you attack the views of the opposition.

2. Imagine that you are a spokesman for the college administration and have been chosen to reply to certain demands made by an ad hoc student group. Using Barzun's technique (argument via concession), develop an essay in which you gradually shift the focus of the argument until you are arguing against something the students never asked for. Remember to buttress your position with arguments that even the students would have to agree with—the more emotional, the better.

3. Develop an essay in which you identify a local problem and then propose solutions. Keep in mind the elements of the basic plan suggested by the Birks. Also, avoid grandiose solutions.

4. Write an essay using syllogistic reasoning incorrectly. For instance, you might choose a syllogism similar to the following:
   a. If schools persist in treating students as if they were machines, the students will become dehumanized.
   b. Schools are treating students as if they were machines. (Evidence: IBM scored tests, large lecture sections, etc.)
   c. Students will become dehumanized.

In the above example the major premise, among other things, begs the question; that is, it assumes what should be proven. Terms—in both premises—are never defined. And the conclusion is assumed but never proven. Still, if care is taken and highly emotional language is employed, a person could write a rousing speech using this "syllogism" as his outline.

In this brief essay from his book *Logic and Effective Argument*, Manuel Bilsky's stated purpose is the understanding of logic rather than its application for rhetorical effectiveness. Nonetheless, his explanation of the uses of analogy implies an application which is relevant to the goals of rhetoric. He discusses three uses: vividness in description, clarity in explanation, and proof in argument. It should be noted that the first two frequently contribute to the third and so fall within the province of the subject of rhetoric. It may be profitable to compare Bilsky's observation on analogy with that of the Birks' in the preceding essay.

Analogy: This Is Like That

Manuel Bilsky

THE IMPORTANCE, NATURE, AND USES OF ANALOGY

1   How often have you heard remarks like these:

"Kankakee at last. Where'll we go to have the car serviced?"

"That Greaso Oil Company in Kalamazoo took good care of us. Why don't we look around for a Greaso station here?"

"Doctor, I guess being captain of the football team, editor of the *Daily*, chairman of the J-Hop, and trying to keep up my all-A record is a little too much for me. Lately, I've been feeling jittery most of the time."

"Looks to me as though you're sitting on a keg of dynamite with a burning match in your hand. You'd better do something about it in a hurry."

"What do you mean, we don't have enough words for all the feelings we're capable of experiencing? I just don't understand that kind of talk."

"It's like this. Suppose there was a stream flowing by and you put a big wooden board across it, big enough so that it stopped the water from flowing. Suppose now you cut holes in the board so that the water could get through the holes and only through the holes. The holes would stand for the feeling words we have, like 'anger,' 'sadness,' 'hope,' and the water for the feelings themselves. Do you see, then, how our vocabulary is limited? We have only a fixed number of holes. But the water, the range of feelings we can experience, is unlimited."

2   All these are instances of analogy. It is the most common form, certainly, of the kind of reasoning we hear every day in which people make certain judgments on the basis of other judgments. You

don't have to be very alert to spot analogies in newspaper editorials, for example. Every one you read is likely to contain one or two. Advertisements are full of them, scientists frequently use them; the barber in his attempts to convince you that you should try to keep that shock of hair, and the traffic cop in his efforts to make you slow down are both likely to resort to analogies. There is a play, written during the early days of the formation of auto worker's unions, in which an organizer says to a prospective member, "The top crowd's pressin' down! The bottom crowd's pressin' up! Whaddaya wanna be, a hamburger?" This analogy was enough to galvanize the worker into action.

3   The big reason why analogies are so important and so common is that they are effective and persuasive. You may use the cool processes of deduction and induction all day long trying in vain to prove something to somebody, but as soon as you employ an analogy, the story is entirely different. Why? Well, what do you do when you make analogies? For one thing you help the other person form a picture in his mind of what you're trying to say. Think of the example with the keg of dynamite. That student could visualize, could see the danger he was in much more readily than if the doctor had given him an hour-long discourse on the symptoms and dangers of mental fatigue. The old Chinese adage about the comparative effectiveness of pictures and words is appropriate here. And the transfer of feelings is also important. That jittery student feels alarm at the threatening picture of the keg of dynamite. He transfers this feeling to his own condition of nervous exhaustion. This as a result speeds up the action that he takes. He is more familiar with the effects of an exploding keg of dynamite—I am assuming that he goes to the movies occasionally—than he is with the effects of a nervous breakdown, so he transfers the feelings he has toward the one to the other.

4   Along more theoretical lines, there are people who say that the importance of analogy is due to other reasons. One person, for example, claims that analogy is the basis of both deductive and inductive reasoning, that neither of these could get started without the initial use of analogy. Another claims that analogy is the basis of all thought and all learning, that without the ability to make comparisons, a man could not survive for very long. The details of these assertions we don't need to go into here. But one thing we must remember: the primary concern in here is not rhetorical effectiveness, that is, how quickly and effectively we can get a person to do something; our interest is rather in logic. Translated into

the terms of this particular discussion, that means: what makes an analogy strong? What increases the probability that the statement argued for by an analogy is a true one?

5   What, exactly, is an analogy? The three examples at the beginning of the chapter seem to be alike in some ways and different in others. If we focus on the similarities, we can get a general idea of what analogy is. The obvious similarity is that they all make comparisons. The first compares one service station to another, the second compares a student's state of mind to dynamite, and the third compares words to the holes in a board. And this is actually the significant thing about analogy: it makes comparisons. When a person analogizes, he shows how two things are similar. Analogy-making, then, is comparison-making. Some people might carp at this definition on the ground that it is not sufficiently precise. But it will do well enough so that we can go on to make the kinds of distinctions which will take us to the analogy we are particularly interested in, namely, the argumentative analogy.

6   Examine the same examples carefully and you will see that there are some differences, differences which turn out to be rather important. The one with the board and the water doesn't seem to be functioning in exactly the same way as the doctor and his dynamite. In the latter the doctor seems to be pressing for a certain course of action. He is attempting to persuade the harassed student to quit some of his activities, drop out of school for a while, or something else of the sort. The doctor is drawing certain conclusions; he is presenting an argument. But the board and the water don't prove anything; they don't argue for anything. They simply clarify an idea. Obviously, then, analogy has different uses. There are a great many of these different uses, but if we look at three of them, we will get a fairly good idea of how analogy works. These three are the descriptive use, the explanatory use, and the argumentative use.

7   In describing something, you will, by using analogy, heighten the vividness of your writing. And this is the chief function that analogy serves in description. When you compare an abstract idea with something that is concrete and familiar to your reader, you enable him to see more clearly what you are talking about, actually to see, since you present him with a picture. Suppose you say "Hector is a pig." The person who hears you immediately gets in his mind the image or picture of the animal. The comparison also serves to communicate feelings. When you make a statement like this, you show pretty clearly how you feel toward Hector, and the person

who hears you shares these feelings, at least for the moment. Whether he continues to have such feelings depends among other things on what else you say about Hector.

8   Many figures of speech are analogies. The most familiar ones are similes and metaphors. Both of these make comparisons, the former expressed and the latter implied. When you say "Love is like the measles" or "Henry is as strong as an ox," you are using similes, expressed comparisons. And when you refer to life as a tragedy or to a sharp tongue, you are using metaphors; you are again making comparisons, analogizing. Poets, naturally enough, use this method of communicating ideas and feelings. Indeed someone has said that the "supreme agent" in poetry is "the command of metaphor." To describe effectively, then, is to make abundant use of analogies.

9   In explanation, analogy serves a somewhat different purpose. Not vividness but clarity is here the chief end. In various fields people are constantly using analogies to make to their readers a little clearer what would ordinarily be perhaps impossible to understand. The eminent geneticist of England, J. B. S. Haldane, in trying to describe the size of a gene, asked his listeners to imagine a hen's egg raised to the size of the earth, and a gene increased in volume on the same scale. The individual gene he said would then be large enough to place on a table. Einstein, in trying to make his theories somewhat intelligible to the general public, was fond of using analogies. When someone once asked him to describe relativity, his answer was, "Suppose a pretty girl were sitting on your lap for ten minutes. The time would seem like no time at all. On the other hand suppose you were sitting on a hot stove for one minute. That one minute would seem like eternity. That's what it means to say time is relative." Or to try to make clear some of his conceptions concerning the four-dimensional space-time continuum, he would say things like this: "Think of space that curves and has bumps. Or better yet, think of the surface of a potato." In these cases he was using analogies to make his ideas clear. Another interesting instance, this time in philosophy, occurred once when an instructor was trying to make clear the problem involved in the so-called interaction of mind and body when both are supposed to be entirely different kinds of stuff. The question was, "How could thought-stuff and body-stuff have any effect on each other?" He suggested that his listeners think of an angel trying to operate a slot machine.

10   These two uses of analogy, for description and for explanation, are expository, that is, their main job is to develop an idea, to help

in the effective communication of the idea. They contribute to the vividness and the clarity with which you present certain concepts. But they do not contribute any new knowledge or ideas; they do not try to prove anything; they do not pretend to show that a statement is true or false; they make no predictions. All they do is take old ideas and make them clearer and more vivid. But when someone does use an analogy to prove something, to make a prediction, to get to new knowledge, he is making a quite different use of analogy. He is using it as an argument. The first example in the chapter shows this. One of the travelers is in effect predicting that the Greaso station in Kankakee will be a source of good service. He makes this prediction on the basis of certain evidence, namely, his experience in the past with a similar oil station. The second example is also an argument. The doctor is trying to prove what is in this case a normative statement: "You ought to make certain changes in your way of living." The evidence here is that—as in the case of a parallel instance, the dynamite—if no changes take place, disaster will result. Hence these are two main uses of analogy: first, the non-argumentative, or expository, which is used mainly in description and explanation, and second, the argumentative. One word of caution: don't expect these three types to be pure. Every time you find an example of analogy, you will possibly be able to discern all three elements in it; that is, it will consist of descriptive, explanatory, and argumentative aspects. When you say therefore that this is an analogy used for argumentative purposes, you mean that the predominant use in this is argumentative.

Using the metaphor of a horse with blinkers to illustrate the
Western concept of history, Arnold J. Toynbee in *Civilization on
Trial* urges the necessity of abandoning the "synoptic view" in
favor of one that demonstrates the historical relationship of all
civilizations. Since the twentieth century appears to be fraught
with contradiction, the historian must "break out of the prison
walls of the local and short-lived histories of our own countries"
and see civilization as a unity.

Civilization on Trial

Arnold J. Toynbee

I

1 Our present Western outlook on history is an extraordinarily contradictory one. While our historical horizon has been expanding
vastly in both the space dimension and the time dimension, our
historical vision—what we actually do see, in contrast to what we
now could see if we chose—has been contracting rapidly to the
narrow field of what a horse sees between its blinkers or what a
U-boat commander sees through his periscope.

2 This is certainly extraordinary; yet it is only one of a number of
contradictions of this kind that seem to be characteristic of the
times in which we are living. There are other examples that probably loom larger in the minds of most of us. For instance, our world
has risen to an unprecedented degree of humanitarian feeling.
There is now a recognition of the human rights of people of all
classes, nations, and races; yet at the same time we have sunk to
perhaps unheard-of depths of class warfare, nationalism, and
racialism. These bad passions find vent in cold-blooded, scientifically planned cruelties; and the two incompatible states of mind
and standards of conduct are to be seen to-day, side by side, not
merely in the same world, but sometimes in the same country and
even in the same soul.

3 Again, we now have an unprecedented power of production side
by side with unprecedented shortages. We have invented machines
to work for us, but have less spare labour than ever before for
human service—even for such an essential and elementary service
as helping mothers to look after their babies. We have persistent

alternations of widespread unemployment with famines of man-power. Undoubtedly, the contrast between our expanding historical horizon and our contracting historical vision is something charac-teristic of our age. Yet, looked at in itself, what an astonishing contradiction it is!

4   Let us remind ourselves first of the recent expansion of our hori-zon. In space, our Western field of vision has expanded to take in the whole of mankind over all the habitable and traversable surface of this planet, and the whole stellar universe in which this planet is an infinitesimally small speck of dust. In time, our Western field of vision has expanded to take in all the civilizations that have risen and fallen during these last 6000 years; the previous history of the human race back to its genesis between 600,000 and a mil-lion years ago; the history of life on this planet back to perhaps 800 million years ago. What a marvellous widening of our historical horizon! Yet, at the same time, our field of historical vision has been contracting; it has been tending to shrink within the narrow limits in time and space of the particular republic or kingdom of which each of us happens to be a citizen. The oldest surviving Western states—say France or England—have so far had no more than a thousand years of continuous political existence; the largest existing Western state—say Brazil or the United States—embraces only a very small fraction of the total inhabited surface of the Earth.

5   Before the widening of our horizon began—before our Western seamen circumnavigated the globe, and before our Western cos-mogonists and geologists pushed out the bounds of our universe in both time and space—our pre-nationalist mediaeval ancestors had a broader and juster historical vision than we have to-day. For them, history did not mean the history of one's own parochial community; it meant the history of Israel, Greece, and Rome. And, even if they were mistaken in believing that the world was created in 4004 B.C., it is at any rate better to look as far back as 4004 B.C. than to look back no farther than the Declaration of Independence or the voyages of the *Mayflower* or Columbus or Hengist and Horsa. (As a matter of fact, 4004 B.C. happens, though our ances-tors did not know this, to be a quite important date: it approx-imately marks the first appearance of representatives of the species of human society called civilizations.)

6   Again, for our ancestors, Rome and Jerusalem meant much more than their own home towns. When our Anglo-Saxon ancestors were converted to Roman Christianity at the end of the sixth century

of the Christian era, they learned Latin, studied the treasures of sacred and profane literature to which a knowledge of the Latin language gives access, and went on pilgrimages to Rome and Jerusalem—and this in an age when the difficulties and dangers of travelling were such as to make modern war-time travelling seem child's play. Our ancestors seem to have been big-minded, and this is a great intellectual virtue as well as a great moral one, for national histories are unintelligible within their own time limits and space limits.

II

7   In the time dimension, you cannot understand the history of England if you begin only at the coming of the English to Britain, any better than you can understand the history of the United States if you begin only at the coming of the English to North America. In the space dimension, likewise, you cannot understand the history of a country if you cut its outlines out of the map of the world and rule out of consideration anything that has originated outside that particular country's frontiers.

8   What are the epoch-making events in the national histories of the United States and the United Kingdom? Working back from the present towards the past, I should say they were the two world wars, the Industrial Revolution, the Reformation, the Western voyages of discovery, the Renaissance, the conversion to Christianity. Now I defy anyone to tell the history of either the United States or the United Kingdom without making these events the cardinal ones, or to explain these events as local American or local English affairs. To explain these major events in the history of any Western country, the smallest unit that one can take into account is the whole of Western Christendom. By Western Christendom I mean the Roman Catholic and Protestant world—the adherents of the Patriarchate of Rome who have maintained their allegiance to the Papacy, together with the former adherents who have repudiated it.

9   But the history of Western Christendom, too, is unintelligible within its own time limits and space limits. While Western Christendom is a much better unit than the United States or the United Kingdom or France for a historian to operate with, it too turns out, on inspection, to be inadequate. In the time dimension, it goes back only to the close of the Dark Ages following the collapse of the western part of the Roman Empire; that is, it goes back less than 1300 years, and 1300 years is less than a quarter of the 6000

years during which the species of society represented by Western
Christendom has been in existence. Western Christendom is a civilization belonging to the third of the three generations of civilizations that there have been so far.

10   In the space dimension, the narrowness of the limits of Western
Christendom is still more striking. If you look at the physical map
of the world as a whole, you will see that the small part of it which
is dry land consists of a single continent—Asia—which has a number of peninsulas and off-lying islands. Now, what are the farthest
limits to which Western Christendom has managed to expand? You
will find them at Alaska and Chile on the west and at Finland and
Dalmatia on the east. What lies between those four points is
Western Christendom's domain at its widest. And what does that
domain amount to? Just the tip of Asia's European peninsula,
together with a couple of large islands. (By these two large islands,
I mean, of course, North and South America.) Even if you add in
the outlying and precarious footholds of the Western world in
South Africa, Australia, and New Zealand, its total habitable present area amounts to only a very minor part of the total habitable
area of the surface of the planet. And you cannot understand the
history of Western Christendom within its own geographical limits.

11   Western Christendom is a product of Christianity, but Christianity did not arise in the Western world; it arose outside the
bounds of Western Christendom, in a district that lies today within
the domain of a different civilization: Islam. We Western Christians did once try to capture from the Muslims the cradle of our
religion in Palestine. If the Crusades had succeeded, Western
Christendom would have slightly broadened its footing on the all-
important Asiatic mainland. But the Crusades ended in failure.

12   Western Christendom is merely one of five civilizations that survive in the world to-day; and these are merely five out of about
nineteen that one can identify as having come into existence since
the first appearance of representatives of this species of society
about 6000 years ago.

III

13   To take the four other surviving civilizations first: if the firmness
of a civilization's foothold on the continent—by which I mean the
solid land-mass of Asia—may be taken as giving a rough indication
of that civilization's relative expectation of life, then the other four
surviving civilizations are 'better lives'—in the jargon of the life
insurance business—than our own Western Christendom.

14   Our sister civilization, Orthodox Christendom, straddles the con-

tinent from the Baltic to the Pacific and from the Mediterranean to the Arctic Ocean: it occupies the northern half of Asia and the eastern half of Asia's European peninsula. Russia overlooks the back doors of all the other civilizations; from White Russia and North-Eastern Siberia she overlooks the Polish and Alaskan back doors of our own Western world; from the Caucasus and Central Asia she overlooks the back doors of the Islamic and Hindu worlds; from Central and Eastern Siberia she overlooks the back door of the Far Eastern world.

15   Our half-sister civilization, Islam, also has a firm footing on the continent. The domain of Islam stretches from the heart of the Asiatic continent in North-Western China all the way to the west coast of Asia's African peninsula. At Dakar, the Islamic world commands the continental approaches to the straits that divide Asia's African peninsula from the island of South America. Islam also has a firm footing in Asia's Indian peninsula.

16   As for the Hindu society and the Far Eastern society, it needs no demonstration to show that the 400 million Hindus and the 400 or 500 million Chinese have a firm foothold on the continent.

17   But we must not exaggerate the importance of any of these surviving civilizations just because, at this moment, they happen to be survivors. If, instead of thinking in terms of 'expectation of life,' we think in terms of achievement, a rough indication of relative achievement may be found in the giving of birth to individual souls that have conferred lasting blessings on the human race.

18   Now who are the individuals who are the greatest benefactors of the living generation of mankind? I should say: Confucius and Lao-tse; the Buddha; the Prophets of Israel and Judah; Zoroaster, Jesus, and Muhammad; and Socrates. And not one of these lasting benefactors of mankind happens to be a child of any of the five living civilizations. Confucius and Lao-tse were children of a now extinct Far Eastern civilization of an earlier generation; the Buddha was the child of a now extinct Indian civilization of an earlier generation. Hosea, Zoroaster, Jesus, and Muhammad were children of a now extinct Syrian civilization. Socrates was the child of a now extinct Greek civilization.

19   Within the last 400 years, all the five surviving civilizations have been brought into contact with each other as a result of the enterprise of two of them: the expansion of Western Christendom from the tip of Asia's European peninsula over the ocean, and the expansion of Orthodox Christendom overland across the whole breadth of the Asiatic continent.

20   The expansion of Western Christendom displays two special

features: being oceanic, it is the only expansion of a civilization to date that has been literally world-wide in the sense of extending over the whole habitable portion of the Earth's surface; and, owing to the 'conquest of space and time' by modern mechanical means, the spread of the network of Western material civilization has brought the different parts of the world into far closer physical contact than ever before. But, even in these points, the expansion of the Western civilization differs in degree only, and not in kind, from the contemporary overland expansion of Russian Orthodox Christendom, and from similar expansions of other civilizations at earlier dates.

21   There are earlier expansions that have made important contributions towards the present unification of mankind—with its corollary, the unification of our vision of human history. The now extinct Syrian civilization was propagated to the Atlantic coasts of Asia's European and African peninsulas westward by the Phoenicians, to the tip of Asia's Indian peninsula south-eastwards by the Himyarites and Nestorians, and to the Pacific north-eastwards by the Manichaeans and Nestorians. It expanded in two directions overseas and in a third direction overland. Any visitor to Peking will have seen a striking monument of the Syrian civilization's overland cultural conquests. In the trilingual inscriptions of the Manchu Dynasty of China at Peking, the Manchu and Mongol texts are inscribed in the Syriac form of our alphabet, not in Chinese characters.

22   Other examples of the expansion of now extinct civilizations are the propagation of the Greek civilization overseas westwards to Marseilles by the Greeks themselves, overland northwards to the Rhine and Danube by the Romans, and overland eastwards to the interiors of India and China by the Macedonians; and the expansion of the Sumerian civilization in all directions overland from its cradle in 'Iraq.

IV

23   As a result of these successive expansions of particular civilizations, the whole habitable world has now been unified into a single great society. The movement through which this process has been finally consummated is the modern expansion of Western Christendom. But we have to bear in mind, first, that this expansion of Western Christendom has merely completed the unification of the world and has not been the agency that has produced more than the last stage of the process; and, second, that, though the unifica-

tion of the world has been finally achieved within a Western framework, the present Western ascendency in the world is certain not
to last.

24　　In a unified world, the eighteen non-Western civilizations—four
of them living, fourteen of them extinct—will assuredly reassert
their influence. And as, in the course of generations and centuries,
a unified world gradually works its way toward an equilibrium
between its diverse component cultures, the Western component
will gradually be relegated to the modest place which is all that it
can expect to retain in virtue of its intrinsic worth by comparison
with those other cultures—surviving and extinct—which the Western society, through its modern expansion, has brought into association with itself and with one another.

25　　History, seen in this perspective, makes, I feel, the following call
upon historians of our generation and of the generations that will
come after ours. If we are to perform the full service that we have
the power to perform for our fellow human beings—the important
service of helping them to find their bearings in a unified world—
we must make the necessary effort of imagination and effort of will
to break our way out of the prison walls of the local and short-
lived histories of our own countries and our own cultures, and we
must accustom ourselves to taking a synoptic view of history as a
whole.

26　　Our first task is to perceive, and to present to other people, the
history of all the known civilizations, surviving and extinct, as a
unity. There are, I believe, two ways in which this can be done.

27　　One way is to study the encounters between civilizations, of
which I have mentioned four outstanding examples. These encounters between civilizations are historically illuminating, not only
because they bring a number of civilizations into a single focus of
vision, but also because, out of encounters between civilizations,
the higher religions have been born—the worship, perhaps originally Sumerian, of the Great Mother and her Son who suffers and
dies and rises again; Judaism and Zoroastrianism, which sprang
from an encounter between the Syrian and Babylonian civilizations; Christianity and Islam, which sprang from an encounter
between the Syrian and Greek civilizations; the Mahayana form
of Buddhism and Hinduism, which sprang from an encounter between the Indian and Greek civilizations. The future of mankind
in this world—if mankind is going to have a future in this world—
lies, I believe, with these higher religions that have appeared within
the last 4000 years (and all but the first within the last 3000

years), and not with the civilizations whose encounters have provided opportunities for the higher religions to come to birth.

28   A second way of studying the history of all the known civilizations as a unity is to make a comparative study of their individual histories, looking at them as so many representatives of one particular species of the genus Human Society. If we map out the principal phases in the histories of civilizations—their births, growths, breakdowns, and declines—we can compare their experiences phase by phase; and by this method of study we shall perhaps be able to sort out their common experiences, which are specific, from their unique experiences, which are individual. In this way we may be able to work out a morphology of the species of society called civilizations.

29   If, by the use of these two methods of study, we can arrive at a unified vision of history, we shall probably find that we need to make very far-going adjustments of the perspective in which the histories of diverse civilizations and people appear when looked at through our peculiar present-day Western spectacles.

30   In setting out to adjust our perspective, we shall be wise, I suggest, to proceed simultaneously on two alternative assumptions. One of these alternatives is that the future of mankind may not, after all, be going to be catastrophic and that, even if the Second World War prove not to have been the last, we shall survive the rest of this batch of world wars as we survived the first two bouts, and shall eventually win our way out into calmer waters. The other possibility is that these first two world wars may be merely overtures to some supreme catastrophe that we are going to bring on ourselves.

31   This second, more unpleasant, alternative has been made a very practical possibility by mankind's unfortunately having discovered how to tap atomic energy before we have succeeded in abolishing the institution of war. Those contradictions and paradoxes in the life of the world in our time, which I took as my starting point, also look like symptoms of serious social and spiritual sickness, and their existence—which is one of the portentous features in the landscape of contemporary history—is another indication that we ought to take the more unpleasant of our alternatives as a serious possibility, and not just as a bad joke.

32   On either alternative, I suggest that we historians ought to concentrate our own attention—and direct the attention of our listeners and readers—upon the histories of those civilizations and peoples which, in the light of their past performances, seem likely,

in a unified world, to come to the front in the long run in one or other of the alternative futures that may be lying in wait for mankind.

V

33   If the future of mankind in a unified world is going to be on the whole a happy one, then I would prophesy that there is a future in the Old World for the Chinese, and in the island of North American for the *Canadiens*. Whatever the future of mankind in North America, I feel pretty confident that these French-speaking Canadians, at any rate, will be there at the end of the story.

34   On the assumption that the future of mankind is to be very catastrophic, I should have prophesied, even as lately as a few years ago, that whatever future we might be going to have would lie with the Tibetans and the Eskimos, because each of these peoples occupied, till quite lately, an unusually sheltered position. 'Sheltered' means, of course, sheltered from the dangers arising from human folly and wickedness, not sheltered from the rigors of the physical environment. Mankind has been master of its physical environment, sufficiently for practical purposes, since the middle palaeolithic age; since that time, man's only dangers—but these have been deadly dangers—have come from man himself. But the homes of the Tibetans and the Eskimos are sheltered no longer, because we are on the point of managing to fly over the North Pole and over the Himalayas, and both Northern Canada and Tibet would (I think) be likely to be theatres of a future Russo-American war.

35   If mankind is going to run amok with atom bombs, I personally should look to the Negrito Pygmies of Central Africa to salvage some fraction of the present heritage of mankind. (Their eastern cousins in the Phillippines and in the Malay Peninsula would probably perish with the rest of us, as they both live in what have now come to be dangerously exposed positions.)

36   The African Negritos are said by our anthropologists to have an unexpectedly pure and lofty conception of the nature of God and of God's relation to man. They might be able to give mankind a fresh start; and, though we should then have lost the achievements of the last 6000 to 10,000 years, what are 10,000 years compared to the 600,000 or a million years for which the human race has already been in existence?

37   The extreme possibility of catastrophe is that we might succeed in exterminating the whole human race, African Negritos and all.

38   On the evidence of the past history of life on this planet, even
that is not entirely unlikely. After all, the reign of man on the
Earth, if we are right in thinking that man established his present
ascendency in the middle palaeolithic age, is so far only about
100,000 years old, and what is that compared to the 500 million
or 800 million years during which life has been in existence on the
surface of this planet? In the past, other forms of life have enjoyed
reigns which have lasted for almost inconceivably longer periods—
and which yet at last have come to an end. There was a reign of
the giant armored reptiles which may have lasted about 80 million
years; say from about the year 130 million to the year 50 million
before the present day. But the reptiles' reign came to an end.
Long before that—perhaps 300 million years ago—there was a
reign of giant armoured fishes—creatures that had already accomplished the tremendous achievement of growing a movable lower
jaw. But the reign of the fishes came to an end.

39   The winged insects are believed to have come into existence
about 250 million years ago. Perhaps the higher winged insects—
the social insects that have anticipated mankind in creating an
institutional life—are still waiting for their reign on Earth to come.
If the ants and bees were one day to acquire even that glimmer
of intellectual understanding that man has possessed in his day,
and if they were then to make their own shot at seeing history in
perspective, they might see the advent of the mammals, and the
brief reign of the human mammal, as almost irrelevant episodes,
'full of sound and fury, signifying nothing.'

40   The challenge to us, in our generation, is to see to it that this
interpretation of history shall not become the true one.

QUESTIONS FOR STUDY

1. What, according to Bilsky, is analogy? What accounts for the effectiveness and widespread use of analogy?

2. What is the descriptive use of analogy? The explanatory use? The argumentative use? Give examples of each from your own experience.

3. What difficulties might a person encounter if he uses analogy in argumentation (that is, to defend or prove something)?

4. When we compare two similar concrete objects (such as in the example of the Greaso Oil Company in Kalamazoo) we are using a literal analogy; that is, both items actually exist, and we are comparing them on the basis of ascertainable similarities and differences. What different patterns of thought do we have to adjust to when we use a figurative analogy (that is, comparing some abstract quality to a concrete object, as was done in the examples of the dynamite keg and the board with holes in it)?

5. What is the analogy used in Toynbee's title? Is it a valid analogy? Who is putting civilization on trial? Who is judging civilization? Who is the jury? Can you think of any other questions about this title that might be raised, in reference to the basic analogy?

6. In the first paragraph Toynbee uses two analogies: the horse seeing between its blinkers and the U-boat commander looking through his periscope. Both are intended to convey the same feeling—a narrowness of vision. What might have been the effect if Toynbee had used not the analogy of the U-boat commander looking through his periscope, but the analogy of a miner peering down a long, dimly-lit tunnel? Why do you think he uses the U-boat analogy?

7. When Toynbee speaks of civilizations have "births, growths, breakdowns, declines," [page 358] what analogy is he using? Is this a valid analogy? Explain.

8. When Toynbee speaks of "symptoms of serious social and spiritual sickness," [page 358] what analogy is he using? Is this a valid analogy? Explain.

9. Where does Toynbee offer proof for any of his analogies? Is the proof sufficient? Explain.

10. Toynbee speaks of some contradictions that seem to be characteristic of our times. How relevant are these contradictions for his central purpose? Has he proved to your satisfaction that our ancestors had a wider view of history? Explain.

11. How much proof has Toynbee offered that Western Christendom is one of the five remaining civilizations? What are the other four surviving civilizations? When Toynbee speaks of these four surviving civilizations as having "better lives," what analogy is he using? Is this a valid analogy? Explain.

12. Who are the individuals who are the greatest benefactors of the living generation of mankind? What do they all have in common?

WRITING TOPICS

1. Using either a literal or figurative analogy, write an essay in which you explain one of the following aphorisms by Eric Hoffer.* (see below)

   a. "We lie loudest when we lie to ourselves."
   b. "There is always a chance that he who sets himself up as his brother's keeper will end up by being his jailkeeper."
   c. "Sometimes the means we use to hide a thing serve only to advertise it."
   d. "Rudeness is the weak man's imitation of strength."
   e. "That which serves as a substitute for self-seeking may eventually serve as its camouflage."
   f. "A man by himself is in bad company."

2. Describe a campus activity in terms of an extended metaphor. For example, you may choose to describe the way certain people eat in terms of feeding time at the zoo or barnyard. When you extend the metaphor, remember to ask yourself the type of questions asked in question #5 in Questions For Study.

3. In a carefully written essay, use analogy to argue a given position. For instance, you might argue that college is like a warehouse. Students are stored for certain periods of time, under certain serial numbers, at certain costs, etc. Remember to avoid mixing metaphors; use only one main analogy in your essay.

---

*The quotations in question #1 are taken from *The Passionate State of Mind,* Harper & Brothers, New York, 1954.

4. Using analogy, write an essay in which you describe a less dignified event in terms of a more dignified one. This is a common source of humor. For instance, you might want to ascribe to a flock of chickens the characteristics of a legislative body. There would be various official positions to fill (the status of various chickens), committees to go into deliberation (subgroupings of chickens), and various parliamentary maneuverings (pecking at one another).

It is important to recognize that sentence patterns are controlled largely by the emphasis the writer chooses to make. These patterns are significant rhetorically because they contribute to the tone and purpose of the essay as a whole through the smaller segment of the sentence. Three principles are at work in the development of what Mr. Jordan calls the "character of sentences": separation, relationship and emphasis (the former two being partly subsumed by the third). This chapter, taken from *Using Rhetoric*, defines these principles and in the process explains from the point of view of the writer the demands and requirements of a well-turned, persuasive sentence.

Rhetoric and Emphasis:
Differences in Sentences

John E. Jordan

> There are nine and twenty ways
> Of writing tribal lays
> And every single one of them is right.

1   The key to writing is the recognition and exploitation of differences.
No two formulations of words are quite the same, each may be right
in its place, and for any specific purpose one is never just as good as
another. The differences are likely to be matters of emphasis—a
little more weight here, a shading of color there. Although these
differences are cumulative and ultimately make themselves felt—
like everything else in the writing process—in the shape of the
whole, they operate most fundamentally and conspicuously in the
arena of the sentence. Three concepts are necessary to an understanding of the character of sentences: the principle of separation,
the principle of relationship, and the principle of emphasis. Emphasis partly subsumes the others, for separation produces emphasis,
and relationships control emphasis. Let us, however, look at them
one at a time.

THE PRINCIPLE OF SEPARATION

2   Few activities are as hazardous as attempting to define a sentence. Consider, for example, the conventional formulation: "A
sentence is a group of words which conveys a complete thought
and has a subject and predicate." Obviously, a sentence does *not*
have to be a group of words, or have a subject and predicate:

> Fire!
> Coming?
> Yes.

And if "He fell down" is a complete thought, what is, "He fell down and hurt himself"? A more complete thought? Putting aside the metaphysical question of whether there is such a thing as a complete thought, it is doubtful whether a sentence can hold one. About the only thing that can be asserted positively about a sentence is its separateness. It is a segment of human discourse capable of standing alone. It makes sense by itself. In spoken utterances it is set off by pauses more marked and of longer duration than normally occur elsewhere—called open junctures—and by terminal intonation patterns—a falling inflection for statements and a rising inflection for questions. When we learn our language we learn the meanings of these pauses and inflections, for they are suprasegmental phonemes, signs of meaning added to the grosser phonemic pattern. We learn to know by these signs that the speaker is intentionally separating an element of his thought, that he wants us to receive it as a unit. If these signs set off elements which are not capable of standing alone because they do not make sense by themselves, we are confused, or we think the speaker is.

3   In written discourse the same situation obtains, except that the signs are visual instead of audible. We start a sentence with a capital letter and end it with a mark of terminal punctuation: a period, a question mark, or an exclamation point. If we find these signs separating material which does not make sense by itself, which is left up in the air and does not come to the kind of conclusion we expect from a terminal mark of punctuation, we are puzzled and dissatisfied.

4   Here, then, are two important aspects of the concept of separateness. It depends upon both the intention of the writer and the acceptance of the reader. The writer intends to cut out a piece of his thought, but he must cut a piece that his reader can perceive as having a kind of wholeness. He must present a unit, not a fragment. That is why a real "sentence fragment" is a criminal offence. A real sentence fragment is one that leaves the reader dissatisfied, not one that merely lacks a complete subject or predicate. Objectionable fragments usually, indeed, violate both requirements of separateness: they are not a result of the writer's deliberate intention; they are careless lapses which are the more insulting because they seem to overlook the reader's needs. They generally result from a writer's losing control of an ambitious sentence, forgetting where he is in it, and producing something like this: "Although Shakespeare's imagery is characteristically profuse and various, when an image cluster strikes a symbolic note, as often happens."

The following passage also contains three constructions which could be considered sentence fragments. See whether you would defend them.

> A man's home may be his castle. If he can meet the monthly payments. Moats have gone out of style, however, and wire-tapping has come in. You have to be careful with sunbathing in the back yard if there are neighbors with second-story windows and twenty-twenty curiosity. Laws prescribe how high your ceiling may be, how many windows, how much floor space, what kind of plumbing you can have. But you can still lock the front door, take off your shoes, and yell at the children. Provided you don't violate the anti-noise ordinance. Yes, a castle all right, a real stronghold.

5 The author of this passage is affecting a "double-take" style, and for that reason has separated two elements which are not logically separable: "If he can meet the monthly payments" and "Provided you don't violate the anti-noise ordinance." Since they follow elements which they qualify, they do not really bother the reader a great deal. But the punctuation is unconventional; these elements might better be connected to the preceding sentences by dashes. The last sentence, however, while technically a fragment, is entirely acceptable and more effective than it would have been had it been cast in conventional form.

6 These references to unconventional punctuation and conventional form remind us of something else important about the sentence. It is the ground on which rhetoric and grammar meet. In most of our discussion so far we have been able to think in terms of the unique demands of a particular situation, to consider what structure of ideas and forms best suits our potentialities and our readers' needs and interests. We can arrange sentences into a paragraph in any way that seems to us most effective; conceivably we can construct a paragraph fundamentally different from any other ever written. With sentences, however, we cannot be so original because part of the pattern of relationships of words in a sentence is determined by the grammar of our language.

THE PRINCIPLE OF RELATIONSHIP

7 In Latin, *Canis puerum mordet* is translated "The dog bit the boy," no matter in what order the words are arranged. *Canis* is in the nominative case, and must be the subject; *puerum* is in the accusative case, and must be the object. Such certainty is one of the advantages of an inflected language. English, of course, has by now

lost most of its inflections, a condition which also has its advantages, but which imposes a relatively strict word order. Obviously we cannot say "Bit the boy the dog"; our meaning would also not be clear if we said, "The boy the dog bit," or "The dog the boy bit"; and it makes a great deal of difference whether we say "The dog bit the boy" or "The boy bit the dog." Thus part of the pattern of relationship in sentence structure is grammatical. It also makes considerable difference whether we say "Money is the root of all evil" or "Money is of all evil the root." But the difference is rhetorical, not grammatical. Most of our concern as writers is with the finer nuances of rhetoric, but these in turn depend upon a knowledge of what is grammatically possible in the language and what can be accomplished by variations on it.

8   The normal word order in declarative sentences is:

Subject	*Verb*	*Object*	*or*	*Complement*
I	saw	him.		
I	came			home.

9   We have to be careful about sentence order, or we have the boy biting the dog. Neither can the verb stand at the beginning of the sentence except in questions or commands. In older English this pattern was common:

Verb	*Subject*
Came	he?
Come	ye.

Now it is almost restricted to the verbs "will," "shall," "can," "need," "must," "may," and split formulations with "do":

Will you?   Do you know the answer?

10   By putting other elements into the simple pattern, however, we can shift the order considerably without changing the basic relationship. A verb may come before the subject in a declarative sentence, provided it is initially modified:

Finally came the order to retreat.
After an overwhelming series of preliminary delicacies appeared the main course.

An emphatic object may come before the subject:

That aspect she refused to discuss.

11   Obviously the force of an inversion depends upon the recognized normalcy of the standard word order. Rhetoric is partly a structure of controlled violence against routine grammatical patterns; it has to operate, however, within grammatical limits, or it ceases to be

language. The inversion above does not affect the fundamental relationship of the grammatical pattern: "aspect" is still the object. The subtler relationships are, nevertheless, modified: "aspect," although grammatically the object, is rhetorically the subject of the sentence—it is the most important element.

12   It appears, then, that there are two kinds of relationships which a sentence must handle: grammatical and rhetorical. The first kind puts some restraints upon the writer, yet at the same time offers patterns which are both conveniences and opportunities for significant variation.

13   Our considerations might, therefore, lead to a definition of a sentence something like the one below. It will certainly not suit formal grammarians, but it might be helpful in suggesting to the writer the requirements and potentialities of the sentence. Here, then, is a writer's definition:

> A sentence is a grammatical and rhetorical device for expressing relationships among the elements of that segment of an idea which the writer wants to separate and present as a unit and which the reader can accept as capable of standing alone.

14   This definition makes explicit in the primary constructs of writing those principles we have held out from the beginning of this book: the choice of the writer to fit the demands of the reader. It emphasizes that a sentence is both a collection of parts and a whole, and is essentially a device for shaping and showing the complex relationships among these. The concept of a "device" may seem demeaning. We may feel that our sentences are organic structures, that if we cut them they will bleed. Granted a great sentence takes on life, but it does so, I suspect, because the writer knew very well what he wanted to do with it. If we think of our sentences as devices we can tinker with, we are less likely to become infatuated with premature formulations. For only by persistent tinkering are we likely to express precisely the intended relationship among the elements of the sentence.

THE PRINCIPLE OF EMPHASIS

15   The principle of emphasis does not amount to an injunction to strain and intensity, any more than yelling is the only way of being emphatic. The point is that *some* emphasis is inevitable. A perfectly level human utterance is impossible, because we have at least to put our words in some sequence, and this order is inescapably meaningful. It is not a question of whether or not to have emphasis,

but of what emphasis to have. Control of emphasis is simply the means by which we make a group of words say what we want them to say. Emphasis does not merely enhance or underline meaning, it defines meaning. Much inept writing results from writers' insensitivity to the devices of emphasis. Not having worked out precisely what they want to say, and not knowing how to say it precisely, they produce a rough approximation—often without realizing how far off they are.

16   Emphasis, of course, is a way of calling attention to something. We pay attention to whatever "sticks out," whatever is conspicuous because of a difference in appearance or location. Difference, it is important to recognize, is highly relative. In a context of great variety, where no two structures are alike, any pattern of repetition stands out. In a context of similarity, where everything fits and balances, any discordant uniqueness is conspicuous. Difference for its own sake has value: "variety is the spice of life." Meaningless variety, however, soon ceases to be spicy. It becomes irritating, frustrating, and frenetic. Since the point of difference is the point of emphasis, it should be meaningful.

17   A difference may be blatant or subtle, it may be on the surface or profoundly essential, it may be external or internal. Just as in spoken language the signs of emphasis may be volume, pitch, or gesture—the lift of an eyebrow, the purse of a lip, or any of the supplementary devices of meaning called kinesics—so in written discourse the signs may also be external, something added to the flow of words.

External Devices of Emphasis

18   External emphasis is like a woman's make-up, which when applied with discretion can be effective but cannot work wonders and is easily overdone. Too much superficial emphasis marks a "school girl" style, where we find a theatrical gush of superfluous and self-defeating underlining, double underlining, wavy underlining, small capitals, gothic script and combinations thereof, sprinkled with exclamation points, singly, in pairs, or in battalions.

19   Such physical features have a legitimate but limited place. Exclamation points are proper to mark a real exclamation—and then generally one is sufficient. Underlining, or italics in print, can be used to call attention to a word that would be stressed in oral discourse, particularly to distinguish between possible degrees of emphasis without revising the simple and straightforward utterance. Consider for example the sentence

I never said that.

Any of the four words might be stressed, and at least one probably would be in spoken language. The above written form, however, is so flat, so normal, that one cannot be sure of the emphasis. Alternative versions could make the emphatic element quite clear:

I, of all persons, never said that.
Never did I say that.
I never made the statement.
I never said such a ridiculous thing.

All of these would go fairly well in informal English except the second. If "never" is the point of emphasis, the more natural sentence would probably be the original with an underscore:

I *never* said that.

20   Italics can also be used effectively to point up parallel relationships, especially when the key words are prepositions or are otherwise inconspicuous; but they should be used sparsely:

It is not that Blake's Prophetic Books are impenetrable: the difficulty is not so much how to get *in* them as how to bring something *out*.

21   The more clamorous devices, such as small caps, can sometimes be used in newspaper columns to break up expanses of gray type, or in headings to mark sections and subdivisions in long essays and chapters; they have no place as designators of emphasis in serious writing. Such writing depends chiefly on the more basic internal emphasis.

Internal Devices of Emphasis

22   Internal emphasis, ultimately, is the result of a pattern produced by the writer's shuffling words around. For all we do when we write is to arrange words in patterns of relationships which give preeminence to certain elements. A sentence is a sort of verbal kaleidoscope. Turn it and watch the words fall into different patterns. Some of them will be ungrammatical, outside of the language, or on those fringes occupied by writers like James Joyce, Gertrude Stein and E. E. Cummings. Many— and their number and variety are amazing—will be beautifully and richly meaningful. The patterns are wrought by such concrete and manipulable things as coordination, subordination, predication, intensification, qualification, repetition, parallelism, position, length, rhythm, and euphony.

23 *Coordination* Coordination is a means of putting equal elements side by side in such a way as to emphasize their equality. The most natural way to do this is by using coordinating conjunctions:

and   but   for   nor   or   yet

An especially obvious kind of coordination can be produced by pairs of correlative conjunctions:

both . . . and
either . . . or
neither . . . nor
not only . . . but also
whether . . . or

24 The coordinated elements may be words, phrases, or clauses; they may be in pairs, triplets, or greater numbers; they must, however, be rhetorically and grammatically equal. Coordination is easy and natural: The preceding sentence, for example, contains two sets of coordinated nouns ("words, phrases, . . . clauses"; "pairs, triplets, . . . numbers"), one set of coordinated adverbs ("rhetorically . . . grammatically"), and a set of coordinated clauses ("the coordinated elements may be . . .; they may be . . .; they must . . . be").

25 One of the most comforting of logical exercises is finding similarities. The mind rejoices in the process of pairing things off—like the animals entering the Ark. Coordination is the structural device for emphasizing similarity, and it is important for the writer to recognize that the element of *parity* is essential in the coordinating process. Even when the relationship is one of opposition or contrast, the items must be on the same level so that they can be contrasted. You can write,

I got up early, but I missed the train.

You cannot say,

Getting up early, but I missed the train.

The coordinating conjunction *but* is improper because the ideas are not put on the same plane or in the same grammatical form. You could conceivably say,

Getting up early, I still missed the train.

But now the elements are not expressed coordinately. The idea of "getting up early" has been reduced from the status of a separate clause with an independent verb to that of a participial phrase; the two actions are not considered as equal and sequential, but are more intimately and subtly related.

26   Since coordination is so natural and consoling, we tend to overdo it. You probably remember a childhood experience of giving a report in class and stringing everything together with "and" 's. A more sophisticated awareness recognizes that everything is not logically parallel, that some things are more important than others, and that a variety of complicated relationships exists between ideas. A more sophisticated syntax copes with various emphases by different patterns of subordination.

27   Let us take a pair of ideas and consider some of the changes that can be rung upon them.

Life is a struggle.
Life is worthwhile.

When these ideas are put as above in parallel, similar, yet grammatically discrete units, they are coordinated, but in such a way as to emphasize their separateness. The impression this presentation creates is that here are two distinct ideas which have been manhandled together by rhetorical parallels. This form says to the reader, "Look, here are two ideas which may seem entirely unrelated, but which can be put side by side. What do you make of this relationship?" Other kinds of coordination say more to the reader about the character of the relationship:

Life is a struggle; life is worthwhile.

By putting the two ideas in one sentence the writer implies that there is an intimate connection between them. He does not yet say what he thinks that connection to be. The absence of any conjunction stresses abruptly the back to back relationship. Less terse and more natural is

Life is a struggle, and life is worthwhile.

28   The conjunction "and" puts ideas together on a dead level. Since no reason for the relationship is advanced, there is a vague implication of "that's the way it is." Still coordinated, but with a clear expression of one aspect of the character of the relationship is

Life is a struggle, but it is worthwhile.

Up until now the writer had allowed the paradoxical nature of the juxtaposition of the two ideas to stand without comment; the "but" emphasizes it, although simply and easily. More pointed, and more formal, are

Life is a struggle, but it is nonetheless worthwhile.
Life is a struggle; nevertheless it is worthwhile.

29   Since the version using the conjunctive adverb "nevertheless" requires a semicolon, it does not make as smooth a coordination; the reader is hauled up abruptly and the paradox exploded at him.

30   *Subordination*   A writer may not be content simply to place these
      ideas side by side in a compound sentence. He may wish to sub-
      ordinate one to another in any of a number of different ways. The
      most emphatic is by a subordinate clause in a complex sentence.
      Suppose that the relationship between these ideas is considered
      to be causal:

        Because life is a struggle, life is worthwhile.

      This same basic relationship may be implied by an overtly temporal
      or spatial formulation which invites the reader to draw the cause
      and effect conclusion from experience:

        When life becomes a struggle, it becomes worthwhile.
        Where (wherever) life is a struggle, it is worthwhile.

      Or the connection between the ideas may be concessive:

        Although life is a struggle, it is worthwhile.

      This relationship may be made somewhat stronger if expressed
      negatively:

        Unless life is a struggle, it is not worthwhile.

      Or it may be put in correlative form:

        Either life is a struggle, or it is not worthwhile.

31   It is worth noting that the concept of subordination here is pri-
      marily grammatical: the dependent clause cannot stand alone; it
      needs to be completed by the attached independent clause, and in
      that sense it is subordinate. Rhetorically, however, the subordinate
      clause may contain the most important ideas. In the following sen-
      tence other devices of emphasis overrule rhetorically the gram-
      matical subordination and place the stress upon the first clause:

        Just because life *is* a struggle, it is worthwhile.

32   All of the above versions of our chameleon sentence have two
      complete predicates, two finite verbs and their complements. A pos-
      sible modification which will change the emphasis is to reduce the
      predication. One of the clauses can easily be turned into a phrase:

        Life is a struggle, but worthwhile.
        Although a struggle, life is worthwhile.
        Being a struggle, life is worthwhile.

      Reduced predication usually results in less elaborate, less formal
      syntax and in further subordination of the elements deprived of
      their full verbs. It also brings brevity and economy and sometimes
      produces a neatly emphatic formulation:

        Life is a struggle worth making.

This version is probably better than the full relative clause:

Life is a struggle which is worth making.

33 Possibly the most effective way of stating this idea is the simple construction,

Life is a worthwhile struggle.

Here the content of what could be an independent clause has been reduced to one word, "worthwhile." But the very fact that this idea is reduced grammatically to an adjective and made to qualify ironically the other pole of the complex points up the basic incongruity of the concept. The tensions are made immediate and intimate, as in St. Chrysostom's famous dictum on the same pattern:

Woman is a desirable calamity.

34 *Intensification* Most blatant of the internal means of emphasis is intensification. This is produced by the use of superlative adjectives and adverbs, compounds of "-self," and words like "very" and "remarkably." Because intensification is obvious, and because it is easy, it is easily overdone:

Life itself is the bitterest of struggles, but it is nonetheless very much worthwhile.

The trouble with such lavish use of intensives is that it defeats itself because it arouses the reader's incredulity. His reaction is likely to be, "It isn't so," followed by anger or contempt or laughter, depending upon how seriously he takes the whole thing. That life is a struggle most people will admit; that it is a bitter struggle some may concede; that it is the bitterest of struggles raises the question of from where outside of life the standards for comparison are coming.

35 The stripped, bare statement is sometimes the strongest—"bare, as the mountains are bare," said Hazlitt of Wordsworth's poetry. Yet the bareness of a mountain is a relative thing: it may be intensified by rocks, or snow, or even a cloud cap. Used judiciously, devices of intensity give color and texture to style. Some words, however, designed as intensives, are actually weakening, either because they are so much used as to have become routine or because they are ambiguous. "Measurably," "significantly," "considerably," and "appreciably" are often used as if they meant "importantly," yet they carry a connotation, and often clearly mean, "just enough to measure or signify or consider or appreciate." Overused intensives include "colossal," "stupendous," "tremen-

dous"—adjectives of Hollywood press agents, and "super," "neat," "keen," and "tight"—vocabulary of teen-age slang. "Very" can be considered in the overused category. A well-known story has a distinguished city editor exorcising the word from his paper by telling his reporters to use "damn" instead of "very," and instructing his copy editors to cut out all profanity. Personally, I think that is going a little far: "very" does very well when a moderate and comfortable degree of intensification is desired. The use of "perfectly" as in "perfectly acceptable," is a cliché of intensity that is weakening, partly because it is routine, partly because it is not supportable, perfection usually being out of range.

36   Intensives, we should make clear, emphasize certain aspects of a statement; they do not, therefore, necessarily strengthen the whole statement, since the aspect selected may be weakening. Take the sentence in the above paragraph, for instance: "Personally, I think that is going a little far. . . ." "Personally" intensifies "I," and is actually depreciatory in effect, for it suggests possible differences of opinion. The selective character of intensification is apparent in the following alternatives; each is acceptable, but where the intensive is put makes a big difference:

Life is certainly a struggle, but it is worthwhile.
Life is a struggle, but it is certainly worthwhile.

37   *Qualification*   Most of the techniques of intensification discussed are methods of qualification. Qualification is a device of emphasis which depends upon giving the reader something and then taking part of it back. The writer qualifies the simple statement by limiting or elaborating it. He tells the reader a dog is red, and then adds "a sort of reddish brown with a high gloss." The psychological effect of this process is to make the statement more complicated and, therefore, to attract attention to it. This system works quite well, enhancing the precision, clarity, and effectiveness of the statement—provided the complexity does not get too involved. If it does, the process is self-defeating, for the qualification takes away so much that the reader is frustrated and confused. Try to test any qualification to see whether it does make for precision and clarity by adding something valid and important. Qualification is bad when it is no more than a sort of decoration, a product of that impulse which makes some writers act as if a noun without an adjective were indecently exposed.

38   In the previous section we were dubious about the intensive qualifier "bitterest" in "Life itself is the bitterest of struggles. . . ." What sort of qualification would be helpful? In the two basic pre-

dications, that life is a struggle and life is worthwhile, the concept "worthwhile" is logically close to an absolute. We may feel that life is *sometimes* worthwhile, but we cannot turn it off and on. We have to strike a balance and conclude that on the whole it either is or isn't. All we can do is indicate our sense of the preponderance in that balance:

Life is overwhelmingly worthwhile.
Life is by and large worthwhile.

Our previous sentences have treated "life" as if it also were an absolute, taking it to be synonymous with all human life. It can, of course, be qualified temporally, geographically, and socially:

Life in the twentieth century is a struggle.
Life in the desert is a struggle.
A share-cropper's life is a struggle.

39   Notice that these qualifications change the meaning of the statement much more fundamentally than do most of the alternative forms we have considered: the difference is a matter of substance as well as emphasis. The limitations provide more precision and clarity, but at the cost of making the utterance less proverbial, less gnomic. If the broader scope is desired, no limitation is appropriate. Indeed, the qualifier may emphasize the inclusiveness:

All life is a struggle.

Although one could imagine a context in which the "all" might seem natural, it does not appear to contribute much here; it seems redundant—"life" includes "all life," and the simpler statement is more effective. Never embroider when the plain stitch will serve the purpose better.

40   A case can be made, then, for the simplest form, which carries a connotation of flat inevitability: "Life is a struggle." Most minds, however, will resist the general proposition that life is always and only a struggle; and that fact accounts for the successful combination of "worthwhile struggle." A skillful and accurate writer might anticipate this union by the right qualification of the "life is a struggle" part of the combination. What can we try?

Life is partly a struggle.
Life is more or less a struggle.

These are accurate, but rather dull. Perhaps, exploiting an echo from Shakespeare, "Life is a fitful struggle."

41   *Repetition*   Even as the patterns of a kaleidoscope rely for their effects upon repetition produced by mirrors, so sentence patterns

can use repetition of form and diction for emphasis. Verbal repetition, as we have seen, is more likely to be employed to tie a paragraph together. Compare, however, these two versions:

Although life is a struggle, life is still worthwhile.
Although life is a struggle, it still seems worthwhile.

Much of the strength of the first sentence results from the repetition of "life" and "is."

42 Repetition is, however, like most rhetorical instruments, double-edged. It should never be allowed to result in redundance or to suggest a poverty of vocabulary. "Beauty is as beauty does" is a deliberate and effective use of patterned repetition. "A beautiful girl is beautiful not so much because of her physical beauty as because of the beauty of her conduct" is an inept and probably unintentional use of repetition that actually appears repetitious, which the proverbial version does not.

43 Does the duplication make the first of the following versions better than the second?

Life is a struggle, but it is a worthwhile struggle.
Life is a struggle but worthwhile.

Probably not, but the line is a narrow one. Change the rhythm slightly and the same device takes on power:

Life is a struggle—a worthwhile struggle.

The only safe way with verbal repetition is to read the sentence aloud, hear how it sounds, and try to analyze its effects. Unconscious repetition is likely to be bad, at least until the writer's intuitive ear has been well trained.

44 *Parallelism* Repetition of form is generally called parallelism, and is in fact only a detailed sort of coordination. Parallelism is a mark of an organized style; it imparts to a sentence an ordered solidity and achieves an emphasis through deliberate statements, as in the prelude to the Declaration of Independence:

When, in the course of human events, it becomes necessary for one people
to dissolve the political bands which have connected them with
another, and
to assume, among the powers of the earth,
the separate and
equal station to which
the laws of nature and
nature's God entitle them,
a decent respect to the opinions of mankind requires that they should declare the causes which impel them to the separation.

45   Notice, incidentally, how the interpolated phrases "in the course of human events" and "among the powers of the earth" loosen the rhythm and moderate the pace of the parallelism.

46   Parallelism does the same thing in writing that repetition of forms does in a painting—calls attention to the blocking. Items which are paralleled should, therefore, have some structural importance. In the above example "to dissolve" and "to assume," "separate" and "equal," "the laws of nature" and "nature's God" are crucial. Parallelism need not, however, be elaborate, or reserved for such important occasions as the Declaration of Independence. It can be used simply and naturally in the kind of writing college students do. Several of the versions of our "Life is a struggle" sentence employ simple parallelism. If the device is used excessively, it produces a mannered style, which can even become cloying and unclear when the patterns pile up. Ruskin sometimes overdoes it, as in this passage from his famous description of St. Mark's in *The Stones of Venice:*

And so, taking care not to tread on the grass, we will
  go along the straight walk to the west front, and there
  stand for a time, looking up at its
    deep-pointed porches and
    the dark places between their pillars
      where there were statues once, and
      where the fragments,
        here and
        there of a stately figure are still left, which has in it the
          likeness of
            a king, perhaps indeed
            a king on earth, perhaps
            a saintly king long ago in heaven;
and so
  higher and
  higher up to the great mouldering wall of
    rugged sculpture and
    confused arcades,
      shattered, and
      grey, and
      grisly with heads of
        dragons and
        mocking fiends,
          worn by the rain and
              swirling winds into unseemlier shape, and
          coloured on their stony scales by the deep russet-orange
              lichen, melancholy gold;

and so,
    higher still, to the bleak towers, so far above that the eye
        loses itself among the bosses of their traceries, though they are
            rude and
            strong, and only
        sees like a drift of eddying black points,
          now closing,
          now scattering, and
          now setting suddenly into invisible places among the
            bosses and
            flowers,
              the crowd of restless birds that fill the whole square
              with that strange clangour of theirs,
                so harsh and yet
                so soothing, like the cries of birds on a
                    solitary coast between the cliffs and
                        sea.

47   Few writers are now tempted to try anything as elaborate as
this. College writers are likely, however, to have two sorts of difficulty with parallelism. First, they may fail to complete a parallelism
which they have promised the reader. Note in the example below,
borrowed from Ruskin, how the parallelism is broken by the word
"scattering."

    Thousands of birds eddied about, now closing, now scattering, and now
    settling suddenly into invisible places among the bosses and flowers.

48   The other difficulty, which plagues particularly the writer who
lacks a sensuous awareness of the patterns of his words, comes from
suggesting to the reader unintended and false parallels. This is
especially likely to happen with homonyms:
    As the meeting was important, and *as* I was late, I drove *as* fast
    as I could.

Much better here to use "because" in the first two clauses.

49   *Position*   Parallelism is partly a matter of the physical relationships between the parallel elements in a piece of writing, including
their position within the sentence. The physical position of words
in the sentence, as we have already noted, is in our uninflected
language important in establishing basic relationships of subject
and object. That it is likewise important in determining lesser
shifts of meaning is sometimes overlooked by writers who are careless with the location of their words. Try moving "only" from position to position in the following variation on Robert Browning's
"Ah, did you once see Shelley plain" (*Memorabilia*):

He claimed that he saw Shelley plain.
  Only he claimed that he saw Shelley plain.
    (He alone made the claim.)
  He only claimed that he saw Shelley plain.
    (He claimed, but could be mistaken.)
  He claimed only that he saw Shelley plain.
    (That was all he claimed.)
  He claimed that only he saw Shelley plain.
    (He claimed no one else saw.)
  He claimed that he only saw Shelley plain.
    (He didn't hear him speak.)
  He claimed that he saw only Shelley plain.
    (He saw no one else.)

50   In more subtle ways the relative position of elements within a sentence also controls emphasis. From one point of view a sentence is a display case, in which some items are prominently exhibited and others inconspicuously tucked away. What are the emphatic positions? The most prominent positions in a sentence are normally the beginning and the end. Another way of looking at these strategic points, however, is as opening and closing curtains. Since the dramatic moment of the dimming of the houselights and the raising of the curtain is likely to be marred by noisy late comers, playwrights sometimes count on repeating anything important that is said in the first five minutes. Similarly, anticipatory constructions like "there is" and "it is" are frequent enough in English that we do not always expect something important at the outset.

51   The beginning of a sentence is nonetheless of potential strategic value: it is set off from the preceding sentence by a pause, so that the reader's attention is drawn anew; and the very fact that our syntactical patterns permit weak beginnings makes a bold start more prominent. By avoiding anticipatory constructions and using devices to dramatize the first words, we can make the opening strong when we want to. Always to do so would make for a monotonous and wearing style. Compare the following:

  There is conclusive evidence that life is a struggle.
  Conclusive evidence proves that life is a struggle.
  Life, conclusive evidence proves, is a struggle.

The second sentence would be generally preferable to the first, except perhaps in response to a sceptic who had denied the existence of such evidence. Between the second and the third sentences the choice would depend upon the context and the author's intentions. Unless these made an emphasis upon "conclusive evidence" appropriate (e.g., if it had been charged that the evidence were weak) the last version would be better. Its punctuation and rhythm set off "Life" in such a way as to give it particular emphasis and focus attention upon the central assertion.

52   The end of the sentence is naturally the strongest position. If readers are conditioned to accept a slow beginning, they usually expect a climactic ending, and they are likely to be impressed by what comes last. It is recognition of this principle that prompts women in their traditional insistence upon "having the last word." Notice the difference between

> Life is a struggle, but worthwhile.
> Life is worthwhile, but a struggle.

53   By the same principle, the last word or phrase before a semicolon or other strong stop within a sentence is in a potentially emphatic position. If these terminal positions are not used for key words, the effect is weakening. Unintentional weak use of strong points produces the flabbiness and ambiguity of an uncontrolled style. Purposeful failure to put the expected words in the terminal spots may, however, result in an ironic undercutting of the primary statement. Out of context it is hard to tell which this is:

> Life is a struggle more or less; but it is worthwhile generally.

54   *Periodic and Loose Sentences*   A special exploitation of the value of the final word is the periodic sentence, which cannot be grammatically satisfying until the period. It is like the trajectory of a projectile, a sustained flight of words with the bang at the end. A loose sentence, on the other hand, contains at least one independent unit with which the sense could stop before the period, for example:

> In fact, a loose sentence is so constructed that it can be brought to an earlier end simply by moving up the period, sometimes to any one of several possible terminations, each of which would make different but satisfying sense.

The preceding loose sentence could have stopped at "end," "period," or "terminations." Rephrase it as follows, and it becomes a periodic sentence:

> In fact, a loose sentence is so constructed that simply by moving up the period, sometimes to any one of several possible terminations, each of which would make different but satisfying sense, it can be brought to an earlier end.

In the above construction the meaning does not come to any resolution until the last word, which thereby takes on a special importance. This effect is achieved here, however, at the cost of moving "it" far from its referent.

55   Loose sentences and all but the simplest periodic sentences are *cumulative*. They grow by accretions similar in kind but placed at different points in the sentence. If we suppose that a primitive core sentence generates additions of complicating and qualifying elements, as shown in the diagrams, we can see easily the distinction between these two kinds of sentences. The additions to a periodic sentence are syntactical elements less complete than an independent clause which *precede* and look forward to or *intrude in* and expand the core sentence. Clauses, noun clusters, verb clusters, adjectives, and adverbs can be prefaced or interpolated to produce a great variety of periodic effects. Try experimenting with what other elements you can add to the core sentence in the diagram.

PERIODIC SENTENCES

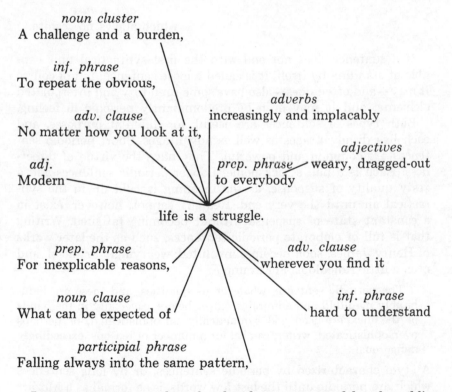

noun cluster
A challenge and a burden,

inf. phrase
To repeat the obvious,

                                        adverbs
adv. clause   increasingly and implacably
No matter how you look at it,

                                              adjectives
adj.   *prep. phrase* — weary, dragged-out
Modern   to everybody

                    life is a struggle.

prep. phrase   *adv. clause*
For inexplicable reasons,   wherever you find it

noun clause   *inf. phrase*
What can be expected of   hard to understand

participial phrase
Falling always into the same pattern,

56   Loose sentences, on the other hand, are generated by the additions of *independent clauses before* the core sentences, or *any attachable elements after* the grammatically complete core and looking back at it.

LOOSE SENTENCES

part. phrase
demanding our best.
adv. clause
whatever else it may be.

ind. clause   *ind. clause*
Still, time drags on, and   and man has to conquer it.

life is a struggle

adv.
unceasingly.
appositive
an exhilarating struggle.
prep. phrase
for all mankind.
adj. clause
which allows no respite.

57   If a sentence does not end with the first syntactical unit capable of standing by itself, it is called a loose sentence; but of course
it may—and often does—also have some prefatory and interpolated
elements, and it may even be predominantly periodic in feeling.

58   Both types of sentences are useful, for different purposes, and
each has disadvantages as well as advantages. Short periodic sentences are common and powerful. They have the virtue of directness. Each is a nail struck home. Longer periodic sentences add a
zesty quality of suspense, as the meaning is held up in the syntactical air until the very end. Readers cannot, however, exist in
a constant state of suspense without becoming fatigued. Writing
that is full of elaborate periodic sentences, such as the later works
of Henry James, soon becomes involuted, wearyingly artificial, and
even a little ridiculous. For example:

> The periodic sentence, whatever its qualities, and these are indu-
> bitably manifold and admirable, nevertheless, especially in the hands
> of the inexperienced and syntactically unsophisticated, or perhaps
> oversophisticated, writer, can be, for a number of reasons, exceedingly
> dangerous.

A style characterized by periodic sentences, or by long sentences
which are periodic until the last few words, is as formal as a Mozart
quartet. The reader cannot relax, but must sustain his attention to
the end of the sentence. He feels a certain deliberation and pre-
meditation on the part of the writer who can hardly ever indulge
in afterthoughts or tack on anything, but must give each utterance
a precious orbicularity.

59   Loose sentences are easy and natural. They are like wandering paths provided with a number of comfortable seats where the traveler may stop, rest, and survey the vista. They have the virtues of apparent intimacy and sincerity, for they suggest that the writer is working out his idea, piece by piece, before the reader's eyes. The cumulative effect can even give a special power to the end of the sentence, different from that of the periodic sentence, yet emphatic in its way. But wandering paths are not the shortest distances between two points, and a style made up exclusively of loose sentences may seem lax, uncontrolled, and indecisive.

60   A good writer inserts periodic elements in loose sentences and mixes up loose and periodic sentences, just as a good quarterback mixes up plays, to provide variety and surprise and thereby make points. He is not trying to trick his reader, but neither does he want him to know always what to expect. The writer, like the quarterback, selects plays not just because they are different but because he hopes they will gain ground. In a context of loose sentences, one conspicuous periodic sentence will break through. Such a periodic sentence should, of course, be used to carry an important idea.

61   *Sentence Length*   Another syntactic variation which controls emphasis is the length of sentences. A sentence may be almost any length, from one word up; the only criterion for any particular sentence is its function in its context. The general limitations on sentence length in any piece of writing depend, as does everything else, on the subject, the reader, and the writer. Seventeenth-century writers, such as Milton, sometimes constructed sentences over a hundred words long, partly because they used semicolons where we would use periods. Nineteenth-century writers, such as Ruskin, sometimes built elaborate long sentences for the musical effect. Twentieth-century writers, such as Joyce and Faulkner, sometimes string sentences out to produce the quality of stream of consciousness: the last chapter of *Ulysses*, some forty-five pages, is all one sentence. Such "sentences," however, are somewhat difficult to read because they violate the "principle of separation" which we saw to be fundamental to the sentence. Perhaps they ought not to be called "sentences."

62   On directions for lighting hot water heaters and in textbooks, newspaper stories, and most informal writing, propriety requires predominantly short sentences. In more formal writing, lofty in subject and pretentious in style, propriety allows longer and more complex sentences; ultimately the boundary is the reader's endurance. Few writers nowadays, however, are willing to push that very

far in any kind of expository writing. The first six sentences of a lead article in yesterday's newspaper had this pattern of sentence length based on number of words: 21, 51, 27, 44, 20, 10. The opening of an essay in the last issue of *The Saturday Review* runs 43, 17, 5, 6, 10, 7, 14, 29, 9, 31, 30, 37. The first paragraph of a recent book on Moliere's comedy is more even: 24, 34, 25, 22, 23, 22, 19, 32, 31. A paragraph from the work of a contemporary historian runs 22, 11, 17, 17, 13, 22, 24, 25, 59, 36, 36; one from a philosophizing modern scientist, 52, 20, 54, 25, 33, 34, 25, 12, 25, 23, 12.

63   Short sentences are strong sentences. They are crisp and clear. They hit hard. Long sentences wind their way "in linked sweetness long drawn out" around and about a subject, wrapping "the concernancy," as Hamlet says, in a rich cocoon of words, and sometimes pleasing the reader with their all-inclusiveness, sometimes losing him hopelessly in the intricacies of their endless coils. But absolute sentence length is of little importance. "No absolute," said D. H. Lawrence, "is going to make the lion lie down with the lamb." Relative length is what matters. In a context of sixty-word sentences, one of twenty-five words will appear powerfully laconic. Among sentences of six to ten words, the same twenty-five word sentence will seem elaborately long. A writer must tune his eye and his ear to the patterns of sentences, and use the difference of length— as he does every other difference—to mark emphasis and define meaning.

64   *Rhythm and Euphony*   Length is but one element in the vastly complex business of sentence rhythm and euphony. Listen to this passage from Thomas De Quincey's "Levana and Our Ladies of Sorrow":

> The second sister is called *Mater Suspiriorum*—Our Lady of Sighs. She never scales the clouds, nor walks abroad upon the winds. She wears no diadem. And her eyes, if they were ever seen, would be neither sweet nor subtle; no man could read their story; they would be found filled with perishing dreams, and with wrecks of forgotten delirium. But she raises not her eyes; her head, on which sits a dilapidated turban, droops for ever, for ever fastens on the dust. She weeps not. But she sighs inaudibly at intervals. Her sister, Madonna, is oftentimes stormy and frantic, raging in the highest against heaven, and demanding back her darlings. But Our Lady of Sighs never clamours, never defies, dreams not of rebellious aspirations. She is humble to abjectness. Hers is the meekness that belongs to the hopeless. Murmur she may, but it is in her sleep. Whisper she may, but it is to herself in the twilight. Mutter she does at times, but it is in solitary places that are desolate as she is desolate, in ruined cities, and when the sun has gone down to his rest.

Here is skillful variation of sentence length: 11, 11, 4, 34, 23, 3, 3, 6, 19, 14, 5, 9, 9, 11, 31. Notice the impact of the short sentences in their context. Observe the build-up to the climactic last sentence, which trails off in a manner appropriate to the sense. Listen to the effect of the turns like "droops *for ever, for ever* fastens" and "never clamours, never defies, dreams not," when the expectation of a third "never" is surprised. Hear the incremental parallelism of the end: "Murmur she may, but" followed by 5 words, "Whisper she may, but" followed by 7 words, "Mutter she does at times, but" followed by 25 words. Note the alliteration patterns in "*f*ound *f*illed with perishing *d*reams, and with wrecks of *f*orgotten *d*elirium."

65   Such skillful manipulation of sound requires an ear more delicate than most of us possess. It requires an ear like that of De Quincey, who could not abide to have on his shelf a book cacophonously entitled "Burke's Works." His compulsion to perfect sentence rhythms is apparent in his quotation, in a letter to the Wordsworths, of a remark an Oxford acquaintance made about Coleridge's periodical, *The Friend:*

"He" (i.e. Mr. Coleridge) "will have to repel equally the arrow of criticism — the dagger of envy — the bludgeon of calamity — and the (broad-) — sword of literary persecution." I confess to have added the word *broad;* as it seemed to be necessary to the climax — and the music; but the rest is correct. (Oct. 9, 1809)

66   If you, reader, can see why he thought "broad" was necessary, there is some hope for your ear. Still, the writer who has not felt on the pulse many and many a sentence had better not strive for the fine effects of euphony, but simply content himself with attempting to avoid cacophony. Sentence music is the last and the highest of the devices of emphasis.

Patriotism is a virtue that has long gone unquestioned by the American citizen. In "The Hard Kind of Patriotism" Adlai Stevenson suggests that this word needs reevaluation, that Americans need "to learn to love their country in a new way." In the shrinking world of the twentieth century a narrowly nationalistic patriotism is not only misguided but foolhardy as well. The safeguarding of those fundamental propositions upon which the United States was founded is more than ever the responsibility of each American.

The Hard Kind of Patriotism

Adlai E. Stevenson

1   It is not easy to be a patriot these days—not because it is difficult to love one's country. The difficulty lies with loving one's country in the right way.

2   The love itself is profound and instinctive, rooted in our childhood discovery of all the infinite delights of being alive—for me, the vast skies, the spring green of the corn, the fall colors and winter snow of the Illinois prairie; for all of us, the shining Christmas trees, the colored mesas and bright flowers of the desert, the rocky shores and pounding seas "way down East," the aspens showering autumn gold on the slopes of the Rockies.

3   It doesn't matter what your picture is. For all of us, it is "home," the place where we spent the endless, dream-filled days of childhood, the place that still nourishes our secret, life-giving imagination, the place we love as we love bread, as we love the earliest image of maternal care, as we love life itself. In doing so, we love what has largely made us what we are. The difficulty is, as I have said, to love it in the right way.

4   I think the complexity of modern technological society makes the loving difficult for everybody, but here in America we have some quite special problems, which come not from our complex present but from our historical inheritance.

5   Some states emerge from some pre-existing tribal unity, some grow up within an already established culture, and some are forged by conquest, with victor and vanquished settling down to a new synthesis.

6   None of these routes was followed by America. Our people have
come from every "tribal" group; they have largely had to create
their own civilization as they went along to absorb a continent.
They have never been conquered or had any sort of synthesis imposed upon them. Their community had, in fact, a unique beginning—it was from the moment of its birth a land "dedicated to a
proposition"—that men are born equal, that government is a
government of laws, not men, and exists to serve them, that "life,
liberty, and the pursuit of happiness" are man's inalienable right.

7   But consider the consequences of this astonishing start. We are
Americans because we belong to a certain ideal, visionary type of
political and social order. We can't point back to a long, shared
civilization. It is true, most of us have Europe and the West behind
us. But not all—and, anyway, it is a concept of the West that we
create rather than inherit. And no one is standing on our necks
keeping us down and together.

8   The result is a community, surely, whose instinctive, rooted,
taken-for-granted unity has to be all the more dynamic. If we are
not dedicated to our fundamental propositions, then the natural
cement in our society may not be enough to take the strain.

9   I would agree that there are substitutes. When a President said
that "the business of America is business," he told us something
about the degree to which a standard of living can do stand-in
duty for a way of life. But the question, "What manner of people
are we?" cannot be everlastingly answered in terms of two-car
families or split-level homes.

WILL THE FABRIC HOLD?

10   America is much more than an economic or geographical fact.
It is a political and moral fact—the first community in which men
set out in principle to institutionalize freedom, responsible government, and human equality. And we love it for this audacity! How
easy it is, contemplating this vision, to see in it—as Jefferson or
Lincoln saw in it—"The last, best hope of man." To be a nation
founded on an ideal in one sense makes our love of country a more
vital force than any instinctive pieties of blood and soil.

11   But it also demands a more complex and discriminating love.
Will the fabric hold if the ideal fades? If the effort to realize our
citizens' birthright of freedom and equality is not constantly
renewed, on what can we fall back? As a going concern, we can no
doubt survive many shocks and shames. It was Adam Smith who

remarked that "There is a great deal of ruin in every state." But can we survive, as a confident and growing community, if the essentially liberal thrust of our origins is forgotten, if we equate liberty with passive noninterference, if we exclude large minorities from our standards of equality, if income becomes a substitute for idealism, consumption for dedication, privilege for neighborly good will?

12   Well, you may say, "Why be so concerned; after all, one of the most forceful elements of our free society is precisely our discontent with our own shortcomings. Because we are free, because we are not the victims of censorship and manipulated news, because no dictatorial government imposes on us its version of the truth, we are at liberty to speak up against our shortcomings. We don't confuse silence with success. We know that 'between the idea and the reality . . . falls the shadow,' and we are determined to chase away that shadow in the uncompromising light of truth."

13   But *are we?* It is at this point that our patriotism, our love of country, has to be a discriminating, not a blind force. All too often, voices are raised, in the name of some superpatriotism, to still all criticism and to denounce honest divergencies as the next thing to treason. We have risen up from the pit of McCarthy's time, when honest men could lose their jobs for questioning whether there were 381 known Communists in the State Department. But the intolerant spirit which equates responsible criticisms with "selling the country short" or "being soft on communism" or "undermining the American way of life" is still abroad.

14   I can give you no comfort in suggesting there is an easy way around this type of criticism. Our position today *is* equivocal. We *are* in one sense a very conservative people—for no nation in history has had so much to conserve. Suggestions that everything is not perfect and that things must be changed *do* arouse the suspicion that something *I* cherish and *I* value may be modified. Even Aristotle complained that "everyone thinks chiefly of his own, hardly ever of the public interest." And our instinct is to preserve what we have, and then to give the instinct a colored wrapping of patriotism.

15   This is in part what the great Dr. Johnson meant when he said: "Patriotism is the last refuge of a scoundrel." To defend every abuse, every self-interest, every encrusted position of privilege in the name of love of country—when in fact it is only love of the status quo—that indeed is the lie in the soul to which any conservative society is prone.

16   We do not escape it—but with us, an extra edge of hypocrisy attaches to the confusion. For our basic reason for being a state is our attempt to build a dynamic and equal society of free men. Societies based on blood ties can perhaps safely confuse conservatism and patriotism. People with long backward-looking traditions can perhaps do so. Countries under the heel of dictators must do so. But if the world's first experiment in the open society uses patriotism as a cloak for inaction or reaction, then it will cease to be open—and then, as a social organism, it will lose its fundamental reason for existence.

17   Do not, therefore, regard the critics as questionable patriots. What were Washington and Jefferson and Adams but profound critics of the colonial status quo? Our society can stand a large dose of constructive criticism just because it is so solid and has so much to conserve. It is only if keen and lively minds constantly compare the ideal and the reality and see the shadow—the shadow of self-righteousness, of suburban sprawl, of racial discrimination, of interminable strikes—it is only then that the shadow can be dispelled and the unique brightness of our national experiment can be seen and loved.

18   The patriots are those who love America enough to wish to see her as a model to mankind. This is not treachery. This—as every parent, every teacher, every friend must know—is the truest and noblest affection. No patriots so defaced America as those who, in the name of Americanism, launched a witch-hunt which became a byword around the world. We have survived it. We shall survive John Birchism and all the rest of the superpatriots—but only at the price of perpetual and truly patriotic vigilance.

19   This discriminating and vigilant patriotism is all the more necessary because the world at large is one in which a simple, direct, inward-looking nationalism is not enough.

20   We face in Communist hostility and expansionism a formidable force, whether Mr. Khrushchev and Mr. Mao Tse-tung pull together or apart. They disagree so far only on whether capitalism should be peacefully or violently buried. They are both for the funeral. So long as this fundamental objective remains, we must regard the Communist Bloc as a whole with extreme wariness.

21   Even if the Communists are divided and confused everywhere— even if they have scored of late none of the victories in Africa, East Asia, and the Middle East our doomsayers predicted—still the Communist Bloc is aggressive and powerful and determined

to grow more so. Taken individually, the European states are all out-numbered. Even America has only a margin of superiority over the tough, austere Soviet Union. Even if the Russian forces in Cuba are not going to conquer the Americas, still their presence in this hemisphere endangers the peace.

22   So we have sensibly concluded in the NATO Alliance that our separate sovereignties and nationalisms must be transcended in a common, overwhelming union of deterrent strength. Together our weight keeps the balance of power firmly down on our side, and it removes from each state the temptation of playing óff one state against another and weakening the overall power in order to strengthen its own. This is the first reason for transcending narrow nationalism.

23   The second follows from our economic interdependence. The Atlantic world has taken 70 per cent of world trade and absorbed 70 per cent of its own investments for the last seventy years. We are an interwoven international economy. Bank rates in Britain affect investments in New York. Restrictions here affect carpet makers in Belgium. French farmers affect everybody. We can only avoid the mismanagement of this community if we pursue joint policies. My friend Jean Monnet has outlined the essential list: expansion of demand, currency stability, investment overseas, trade with the developing nations, reserves for world trade. Without joint policies here, we could easily slip back to the debacle of the period between the great civil wars of Europe of 1914 and 1939.

AFTER MANY TRIBAL WARS

24   In this context, separate, divisive nationalism is not patriotism. It cannot be patriotism to enlarge a country's illusory sense of potency and influence, and reduce its security and economic viability. True patriotism demands that, in some essential categories, purely national solutions be left behind in the interest of the nation itself. It is this effort to transcend narrow nationalism that marked the supremely successful Marshall Plan. It marks the great enterprise of European unification—after so many tribal wars. It could mark the building of an Atlantic partnership as a secure nucleus of world order.

25   So our vision must be of the open society fulfilling itself in an open world. This we can love. This gives our country its universal validity. This is a patriotism which sets no limits to the capacity

of our country to act as the organizing principle of wider and wider associations, until in some way not yet foreseen we can embrace the family of man.

26   And here our patriotism encounters its last ambiguity. There are misguided patriots who feel we pay too much attention to other nations, that we are somehow enfeebled by respecting world opinion. Well, "a decent respect for the opinions of mankind" was the very first order of business when the Republic was created; the Declaration of Independence was written, not to proclaim our separation, but to explain it and win other nations to our cause. The founding fathers did not think it was "soft" or "un-American" to respect the opinions of others, and today for a man to love his country truly, he must also know how to love mankind. The change springs from many causes. The two appalling wars of this century, culminating in the atom bomb, have taught all men the impossibility of war. Horace may have said: "It is sweet and fitting to die for one's country." But to be snuffed out in the one brief blast of an atomic explosion bears no relation to the courage and clarity of the old limited ideal.

27   Nor is this a simple shrinking from annihilation. It is something much deeper—a growing sense of our solidarity as a human species on a planet made one and vulnerable by our science and technology.

28   For, on this shrunken globe, men can no longer live as strangers. Men can war against each other as hostile neighbors, as we are determined not to do; or they can coexist in frigid isolation, as we are doing. But our prayer is that men everywhere will learn, finally, to live as brothers, to respect each other's differences, to heal each other's wounds, to promote each other's progress, and to benefit from each other's knowledge. If the evangelical virtue of charity can be translated into political terms, aren't these our goals?

29   Aristotle said that the end of politics must be the good of man. Man's greatest good and greatest present need is, then, to establish world peace. Without it, the democratic enterprise—one might even say the human enterprise—will be utterly, fatally doomed. War under modern conditions is bereft of even that dubious logic it may have had in the past. With the development of modern technology, "victory" in war has become a mockery. What victory —victory for what or for whom?

30   Perhaps younger people are especially sensitive to this growing conviction that nowadays all wars are civil wars and all killing is fratricide. The movement takes many forms—multilateral diplo-

macy through the United Nations, the search for world peace through world law, the universal desire for nuclear disarmament, the sense of sacrifice and service of the Peace Corps, the growing revulsion against Jim Crowism, the belief that dignity rests in man as such and that all must be treated as ends, not means.

31   But whatever its form, I believe that, far from being in any sense an enemy to patriotism, it is a new expression of the respect for life from which all true love springs. We can truly begin to perceive the meaning of our great propositions—of liberty and equality—if we see them as part of the patrimony of all men. We shall not love our corner of the planet less for loving the planet too, and resisting with all our skill and passion the dangers that would reduce it to smoldering ashes.

32   I can, therefore, wish no more for the profound patriotism of Americans than that they add to it a new dedication to the world-wide brotherhood of which they are a part and that, together with their love of America, there will grow a wider love which seeks to transform our earthly city, with all its races and peoples, all its creeds and aspirations, into Saint Augustine's "Heavenly city where truth reigns, love is the law, and whose extent is eternity."

QUESTIONS FOR STUDY

1. Explain the following principles from Jordan's essay: separation, relationship, emphasis.

2. Why should Jordan say (par. #1) that "Emphasis partly subsumes the others"? What are some of the devices for achieving emphasis? Which are more likely to be effective in student writing? Illustrate from your own essays. (You might also note which devices you avoid.)

3. What is the difference between the loose sentence and the periodic sentence? Give examples from your own writing. Have they been used in those situations that Jordan suggests?

4. What claim does Jordan make for varying sentence length? Check the word count of the sentences in the first paragraph of Jordan's essay to determine whether the author achieves this purpose.

5. Explain what the author means by "sentence music." Can you locate any passages in which Jordan makes use of this device? Can you point to any examples in your own writing?

6. Point out within the Stevenson essay devices for achieving emphasis. How does he intensify his statements? Does he qualify any of his remarks? Is there meaningful repetition? Has the position of any of Stevenson's syntactical elements affected the author's emphasis? Is he more prone to use the loose or periodic sentence?

7. Does Stevenson use any "sentence music"? Point out effective passages. Can you point to any passage in the Stevenson essay in which you might feel inclined to make the same type of insertion as Jordan refers to in his next-to-last paragraph?

8. What does Stevenson mean by loving one's country the right way? How does the modern technological society in which Americans live contribute to the problem? What is the significance of the "historical inheritance" for most Americans?

9. What does Stevenson mean by the statement, "compare the ideal and real to see the shadow"? Who are the "superpatriots" and how is their patriotism expressed?

10. What does Stevenson mean by an "inward-looking nationalism"? What does he finally suggest to be "true patriotism"?

WRITING TOPICS

1. Write an essay parodying the style of someone you have read this semester. Follow the procedure that Stevenson employs of going from the part to the whole and use some of the rhetorical techniques outlined in Jordan's essay.

2. Write an essay dealing with the role of the arts on your college campus. You can deal with "official" art condoned and supported by the administration, or you might choose to deal with any off-campus or "underground movements" if they exist. If you choose to deal with both, you might discuss their relation to each other and to the student body at large.

3. Write an essay exploring the role of "radical" groups either far "right" or "left" in a democracy.

4. Reread paragraph 30 in Stevenson's essay and write a paper exploring one of the movements he suggests there.

Style is a highly individual matter, developing in part out of the manner in which the writer views his material. It is difficult to discuss style except in terms of metaphor; that is, styles may be described as "weighty," "light," "flowing," "leisurely." In this chapter from their book *Principles of Writing* John Halverson and Mason Cooley describe these and other varieties of style through the use of detailed analyses of examples, and they suggest that sentence structure is the key to determining any particular style.

Structure in Style

John Halverson, Mason Cooley

1   A writer's style arises in great part from the structure of his sentences. What we call metaphorically a "crisp" or "weighty" or "flowing" or "crabbed" style is as much a matter of syntax as of vocabulary. A prose with many subordinate clauses, parenthetic qualifications, and suspended predications makes a very different impression from a prose of simpler structure. There is a wide range in which stylistic excellence can be, and has been, attained. There are also dangerous extremes, which require considerable virtuosity to bring off successfully: at one pole, the kind of long and involuted structures that flirt with unintelligibility; at the other, the "news-flash" manner, which often seems merely simple-minded. Brilliant stylistic victories have been won at both extremes, but they are tours de force.

      The first bull was Belmonte's. Belmonte was very good. But because he got thirty thousand pesetas and people had stayed in line all night to buy tickets to see him, the crowd demanded that he should be more than very good. Belmonte's great attraction is working close to the bull. In bull fighting they speak of the terrain of the bull and the terrain of the bull-fighter. As long as a bull-fighter stays in his own terrain he is comparatively safe. Each time he enters into the terrain of the bull he is in great danger. Belmonte, in his best days, worked always in the terrain of the bull. This way he gave the sensation of coming tragedy. People went to the corrida to see Belmonte, to be given tragic sensations, and perhaps to see the death of Belmonte. [HEMINGWAY]

2   In this passage the norm is short sentences without elaborate subordination, heavy adjectival modification, or parenthetical qual-

Reprinted with the permission of The Macmillan Company from *Principles of Writing* by John Halverson & Mason Cooley. © Copyright The Macmillan Company 1965.

ification. They suggest a clear-eyed, unemotional, rather laconic observer setting down matters just as they stood. Only in the infinitive series of the last sentence do feeling and complexity of tone enter when Hemingway evokes the image of a crowd gathered to experience tragic sensations and perhaps witness a death. Even then, the evocation is very restrained, controlled by the stylized simplicity of the writing.

3   Here, in contrast, is Henry James:

> It is very true that Fielding's hero in *Tom Jones* is but as "finely," that is but as intimately, bewildered as a young man of great health and spirits may be when he hasn't a grain of imagination: the point to be made is, at all events, that his sense of bewilderment obtains altogether on the comic, never on the tragic plane. He has so much "life" that it amounts, for the effect of comedy and application of satire, almost to his having a mind, that is to his having reactions and a full consciousness; besides which his author — *he* handsomely possessed of a mind — has such an amplitude of reflection for him and round him that we see him through the mellow air of Fielding's fine old moralism, fine old humor, and fine old style, which somehow enlarge, make every one and every thing important.

These two Jamesian sentences, weighted with subordination and qualification, make a subtle critical point about *Tom Jones;* they also express the richness and subtle modifications of James's sensibility. Both the Hemingway and the James passages are good, indeed eloquent, English prose, delicately controlled instruments of their authors' purposes. But both stand at, or beyond, the extreme limits of "normal" English prose. In weaker hands the stylized simplicity of Hemingway might well suggest empty-headedness or affected toughness; without James's richness of mind, the elaborations of his prose would seem only pompous spluttering. Any inexperienced writer who ventures into James's or Hemingway's stylistic territory is on dangerous ground. But in the territory between these two extremes there is room for great variation of effective style.

4   The use of heavily subordinated, complex sentences leads to a slow-moving, comparatively "heavy" style that is a suitable vehicle for a thoughtful, reflective attitude. It is a style suitable to complex ideas which the writer feels must be stated with qualifications if they are to be stated accurately. In the following passage the writer is discussing the function of literary criticism.

> When I say critisism, I mean of course in this place the commentation and exposition of works of art by means of written words; for of the general use of the word "criticism" to mean such writings, as

Matthew Arnold uses it in his essay, I shall presently make several qualifications. No exponent of criticism (in this limited sense) has, I presume, ever made the preposterous assumption that criticism is an autotelic activity. I do not deny that art may be affirmed to serve ends beyond itself; but art is not required to be aware of these ends, and indeed performs its function, whatever that may be, according to various theories of value, much better by indifference to them. Criticism, on the other hand, must always profess an end in view, which, roughly speaking, appears to be the elucidation of works of art and the correction of taste. The critic's task, therefore, appears to be quite clearly cut out for him; and it ought to be comparatively easy to decide whether he performs it satisfactorily, and in general, what kinds of criticism are useful and what are otiose. [T. S. ELIOT]

The syntax is dominated by devices of qualification, much of it in parenthetical constructions: "of course," "in this place," "(in this limited sense)," "I presume," "whatever that may be," "according to various theories of value," "in general." There are many subordinate clauses: "When I say . . .," "as Matthew Arnold uses . . .," "that criticism is . . .," "that art may be affirmed . . .," "whatever that may be," "which appears to be . . .," "whether he performs . . .," "What kinds of criticism are . . .," "what are. . . ." In fact there are no simple sentences in the passage. Contributing to the heavy atmosphere of qualification are also such noncommittal verb forms as "appears to be" (twice) and such circumlocutions as "I do not deny that art may be affirmed to" (equivalent to "Art may"). There is almost no structural repetition; and almost no sentence proceeds to its period without some kind of interruption.

5   Certainly this prose does not race or drive to a conclusion; it is a series of careful, gingerly steps. Its complexity and its twitchy rhythms prohibit hasty reading, thus forcing the reader to proceed as cautiously as the writer. The style, then, suits the context, where great (perhaps excessive) care is being given to the statement of a position, for it solicits the reader's careful attention. However, it is not a style to everyone's taste; for some it will suggest more pedantry than thoughtfulness and more complexity than the material warrants. The rather fancy vocabulary ("commentation," "autotelic," "otiose") does nothing to discourage such a reaction. It is a style with potential pitfalls, certainly. Yet it is Eliot's *own* style; it is to a considerable extent determined by his personality, which Eliot himself has, in a pleasant mood, written of thus:

> How unpleasant to meet Mr. Eliot!
> With his features of clerical cut,
> And his brow so grim
> And his mouth so prim

> And his conversation, so nicely
> Restricted to What Precisely
> And If and Perhaps and But.
> How unpleasant to meet Mr. Eliot!

Needless to say, many readers, including the Nobel Prize Com-
mittee, have found it pleasant enough to meet Mr. Eliot in both his
poetry and his prose.

6   Here is another example, from an earlier generation, of the same
general kind of style:

> One has often wondered whether upon the whole earth there is any-
> thing so unintelligent, so unapt to perceive how the world is really
> going, as an ordinary young Englishman of our upper class. Ideas he
> has not, and neither has he that seriousness of our middle class which
> is, as I have often said, the great strength of this class, and may
> become its salvation. Why, a man may hear a young Dives of the
> aristocratic class, when the whim takes him to sing the praises of
> wealth and material comfort, sing them with a cynicism from which
> the conscience of the veriest Philistine of our industrial middle class
> would recoil in affright. And when, with the natural sympathy of aris-
> tocracies for firm dealing with the multitude, and his uneasiness at
> our feeble dealing with it at home, an unvarnished young Englishman
> of our aristocratic class applauds the absolute rulers on the Continent,
> he in general manages completely to miss the grounds of reason and
> intelligence which alone give any colour of justification, any possibil-
> ity of existence, to those rulers, and applauds them on grounds which
> it would make their own hair stand on end to listen to. [MATTHEW
> ARNOLD]

Even more than the passage by Eliot, this quotation exemplifies
what is sometimes called the Mandarin style. It assumes that both
writer and reader are highly cultivated persons with enough leisure
and free play of mind to explore all the (frequently ironic) ramifi-
cations of the topic at hand. The choice of words—particularly such
ironic expressions as "young Dives," "whim," "sing the praises,"
and "firm dealing" and the colloquial flavor of "Why," and "make
their own hair stand on end"—gives the passage a somewhat
lighter tone than the Eliot quotation, but the general effect is still
distinctly heavy. There are many subordinate clauses: "whether
there is . . .," "how the world is really going," "which is . . .," "as
I have often said," "when the whim . . .," "from which . . .," "and
when . . .," "which alone . . .," "which it would make. . . ." The
sentences are long and complex and use suspended predication
(especially the last sentence). The frequent modifying clauses
interrupt the rhythm and slow down the pace. They are not used,
however, as in Eliot, to subtract anything from the principal idea,

but rather to amplify the circumstances. The style suggests a rich and reflective mind. For example, in the last sentence there is no absolute necessity for the long phrase "with the natural sympathy . . . at home" that interrupts the course of the *when*-clause it appears in. But we should not want to do without it; it is a side observation that palpably enriches the statement.

7   Again, this style has the vices of its virtues. Its complexity smacks somewhat of the schoolmaster. Its richness detracts from its strength. Though essentially Arnold is making a very strong statement indeed about young Englishmen of the upper class, it doesn't *sound* very strong; the force of the condemnation is somewhat dissipated by structural complexity.

8   The principal rhetorical danger of the style represented here by Eliot and Arnold is that of being too demanding on the reader. It is a style that requires more than a minimum effort on the reader's part. Now the writer has every right to expect an effort, and any intelligent reader is willing to make it. But self-evidently, there should also be a reward for his effort. If the ideas are not in themselves complex, it is a great mistake to couch them in very complicated language. For if the reader makes the effort to grasp your pearl of wisdom and finds only a clod, he will, quite justly, dismiss your writing as bloated.

9   Another problem is the use of humor in this style. Arnold's relatively quiet ironies sit well on his style, but a more obvious wit combined with this heavy style may produce a curious result. For example, in speaking of Nathaniel Hawthorne's early career, Henry James says:

> Certain of his tales found their way into one of the annuals of the time, a publication endowed with the brilliant title of *The Boston Token and Atlantic Souvenir*. The editor of this graceful repository was S. G. Goodrich, a gentleman who, I suppose, may be called one of the pioneers of American periodical literature.

The phrases "endowed with the brilliant title" and "graceful repository" have a nice ironic wit (at least *we* think so), but the final effect is a unique combination of the airy and elephantine. There is nothing wrong with this at all, but it is very special. If the wit is not genuine, the effect can be heavy-handed or grotesque.

10   A quite different style is achieved by shunning heavy subordination, suspended predication, and parenthetic phrases and depending instead on relatively simple sentences and the repetition of structures. Here is C. S. Lewis saying how, as we read English literature of the sixteenth century.

[1]we come to dread a certain ruthless emphasis; bludgeon-work. [2]Nothing is light, or tender, or fresh. [3]All the authors write like elderly men. [4]The mid-century is an earnest, heavy-handed, commonplace age: a drab age. [5]Then, in the last quarter of the century, the unpredictable happens. [6]With startling suddenness we ascend. [7]Fantasy, conceit, paradox, colour, incantation, return. [8]Youth returns. [9]The fine frenzies of ideal love and ideal war are readmitted.

This prose is terse and crisp; it reads quickly; it strikes directly at its subject. The effect is gained from the kind of syntax Lewis uses. Only simple sentences appear. There are no subordinate clauses in the passage, no interruptors to slow it down. The importance of the syntax can be seen if we consider how another writer might have written the fifth and sixth sentences:

Then in the last quarter of the century, the unpredictable happens, when, with startling suddenness, we ascend.

This is good English, but how much better the original syntax reflects "startling suddenness." We feel as well as read what Lewis is talking about. The effect is enhanced by the series constructions, particularly those without connectives. Finally, the constructions echo one another to produce a lightly hammering rhythm. Consider the fifth and sixth sentences again, where the same sentence pattern is repeated: an adverbial prepositional phrase followed by a simple subject-verb clause. Observe, too, how the structure of the seventh and eighth sentences echoes that of the fourth:

[4]The mid-century is an earnest, heavy-handed, commonplace age: a drab age.

[7]Fantasy, conceit, paradox, colour, incantation, return. [8]Youth returns.

The emphasis of reiteration heightens the contrast and the lyrical quality of "Youth returns." Lewis's style here corresponds to the content, just as Eliot's and Arnold's do in their very different way.

11   The dangers of this style are almost the reverse of those attaching to the heavy style. As the sentences move forward with such briskness and sparkle, such directness and lack of qualification, the reader may be led to ask himself whether something, possibly the inherent complexity of the subject, has been sacrificed to a rather tinselly effect. Lewis's syntax gratifies the dramatic instinct, but it can also arouse the suspicion that one is being offered an arbitrarily simplified map of a complicated intellectual terrain.

12   The following quotation from Henri Bergson catches in its syntax some of the compulsive quality of passionate love.

Analyse the passion of love, particularly in its early stages; is pleasure its aim? Could we not as well say it is pain? Perhaps a tragedy lies ahead, a whole life wrecked, wasted, ruined, we know it, we feel it, no matter, we must because we must. [Tr. by R. A. AUDRA and C. BRERETON]

Again the constructions are simple and serial; conjunctions are avoided: "wrecked, wasted, ruined," "we know . . . we feel . . . we must . . . we must." The jabbing intensity of the style, achieved mainly by the manipulation of syntax, again helps us *feel* the content and the writer's attitude.

13   A similar style can be attained with much more complex sentence structure, as this galloping prose attests:

How easy it is now to understand the prodigious success of *The Innocents Abroad,* appearing as it did at the psychological moment, at the close of the Civil War, at the opening of the epoch of industrial pioneering, at the hour when the life of business had become obligatory upon almost every American! How easy it is to understand why it was so generally used as a guidebook by Americans traveling in Europe! Setting out only to ridicule the sentimental pretentions of the author's pseudo-cultivated fellow-countrymen, it ridiculed in fact everything of which the author's totally uncultivated fellow-countrymen were ignorant, everything for which they wished just such an excuse to be ignorant where knowledge would have involved an expenditure in thought and feeling altogether too costly for the mind that was fixed upon the main chance. It attacked not only the illegitimate pretensions of the human spirit but the legitimate pretentions also. It expressly made the American business man as good as Titian and a little better: it made him feel that art and history and all the great, elevated, admirable, painful discoveries of human kind were not worth wasting one's emotions over. [VAN WYCK BROOKS]

Here there are many subordinate clauses, but they do not slow the pace very much, if at all, because they never suspend the predication; they never interrupt the invariable sequence of subject-verb-complement. This repeated sentence pattern carries the reader's attention forward in a straight line, without pause or backtracking, to a concluding statement that seems inevitable because of the energetic syntactical thrust that leads up to it. There is an abundance of structural repetition and a minimal use of conjunctions: "How easy it is now to understand . . . How easy it is to understand . . .", " at the psychological moment . . . at the close . . . at the opening . . . at the hour . . .", "pseudo-cultivated fellow-countrymen . . . totally uncultivated fellow-countrymen . . ."; "everything of which . . . everything for which . . .", "not only the illegitimate pretensions . . . but the legitimate pretensions . . ."; "It attacked . . . It expressly made . . . it made . . ."; etc. It is particularly

these structural and verbal repetitions that produce the hammering rhythm of the passage, a rhythm that sweeps the reader along
with it.

14   All three of these illustrations exhibit the velocity and intensity
and exclamatory quality characteristic of this style. The words rush
along. It is the antithesis of the slow and meditative style of Eliot
and Arnold. Its dangers are also the opposite of those inherent in
the heavier manner. While Arnold's style may tend to be stuffy,
Brooks's may become glib and even a trifle hysterical. And while
the one style may expect too much effort from the reader, the other
may not ask enough. The two styles seem to be, by nature, primarily suitable for different modes of thought and feeling; one
lends itself to reflection and amplification, the other to a more
emotional and dramatic approach. It is, for example, very hard
(though not impossible) to infuse Eliot's prose style with lyricism;
it is a style that cannot easily be taught to sing. Conversely, it is
hard to seem dispassionate or aloof in the style of Brooks. Injudi-
ciously used, both styles can easily be unconvincing. (In philosophy
John Dewey and Bertrand Russell are fairly representative of the
two styles, and one student of philosophy has observed that he can
hardly help thinking that the writing of Dewey is too dull to be
credible, that of Russell too clever.) Judiciously used, however,
both styles can provide the strongest support for effective communication because they can add a dimension of feeling to the
communication.

15   Not many accomplished writers employ one style or the other
exclusively. When they do, it is probably because of very strong
and relatively inflexible personalities or because they have evolved
such a characteristic manner that they cannot convey their thought
apart from it. D. H. Lawrence, for example, was a man of great
personal passion, and especially his non-fictional writing is generally in a passionate style, sometimes almost apocalyptic. Some
political writers, too, normally write in a passionate, sometimes
almost apoplectic manner. Conversely, T. S. Eliot, who praises objectivity and has deplored emotionalism, rarely departs from the
prose style that suits his temper and beliefs. But probably the bulk
of good writers find a middle way, usually a combination or alterna-
tion of the styles just discussed. When they are themselves reflective or wish the reader to reflect, they will use the syntax that is
most conducive to the desired effect. When they are themselves
excited or wish to excite the reader, they use the kind of syntax
most suitable to that end. Most of their sentences are neither

stuffed nor starved and follow normal sentence patterns. Here is an illustration from an eminent historian and accomplished writer:

> In the Middle Ages men thought and acted corporately. The status of every man was fixed by his place in some community — manor, borough, guild, learned University or convent. The villein and the monk scarcely existed in the eye of the law except through the lord of the manor and the Abbot of the monastery. As a human being, or as an English subject, no man had "rights" either to employment or to the vote, or indeed to anything very much beyond a little Christian charity. The unit of mediaeval society was neither the nation nor the individual but something between the two, — the corporation.
>
> By thus strictly formulating on the group principle the relation of every man to his fellows, civilization emerged out of the Dark Ages into the mediaeval twilight. Only in the later age of the Renaissance and Reformation, after the emancipation of the villeins had shattered the economic system on which the feudal world rested, was it possible to take another step forward towards personal freedom. Then indeed many of the mediaeval corporations went down before the omnipotent State on the one hand and the self-assertive individual on the other. [G. M. TREVELYAN]

The style is lucid, easy to read, lively, and authoritative. The thesis is stated briefly and economically in a simple sentence. The rest of the sentences being longer and more complicated, the first statement gains force from its succinctness. Normal word order prevails throughout. The first paragraph has no interrupters, no suspensions. The second paragraph begins with a rather long participial phrase, preparing the way for the more lengthily postponed predication of the next sentence, which has a long prepositional phrase and a long qualifying complex subordinate clause ("after the emancipation . . . had shattered the . . . system on which . . .") before the principal predication ("was it possible"), which itself leads on the rest of the complement ("to take . . ."). This rather complicated sentence is followed by another forcefully simple sentence. Like Brooks and Lewis, Trevelyan depends much more on coordination than on subordination; unlike them he also uses the normal series construction (a, b, *and* c) and the coordinating conjunctions.

16 The middleness of the middle way can be illustrated from the fourth sentence. Trevelyan writes:

> As a human being, or as an English subject, no man had "rights" either to employment or to the vote, or indeed to anything very much beyond a little Christian charity.

To play at reconstruction, we might, from a writer in another style, expect something like this:

No man, even though he were an English citizen and a human being, had "rights" either to employment or to the vote or indeed, besides a little Christian charity, to anything very much.

And from a stylist of another school, we might read:

As a human being, as an Englishman, no man had "rights" — to employment, to the vote, to anything beyond a little Christian charity.

Between the two possibilities of expression—the one leisurely and parenthetical in its syntax, the other terse and abrupt—Trevelyan has found a very readable middle way.

17   Here is another example from a contemporary prize-winning historian, writing of economic and moral changes in the age of Jackson:

[1]But industrialism brought the growing depersonalization of economic life. [2]With the increase in size of the labor force, the master was further and further removed from his workmen, till the head of a factory could have only the most tenuous community of feeling with his men. [3]With the development of manufacturing and improved means of distribution, the seller lost all contact with the buyer and feelings of responsibility to the consumer inevitably diminished. [4]The expansion of investment tended to bring on absentee ownership, with the divorce of ownership and management; and the rise of cities enfeebled the paternal sentiments with which many capitalists had regarded their works in towns and villages. [5]Slowly the vital economic relationships were becoming impersonal, passing out of the control of a personal moral code. [6]Slowly private morality and business morality grew apart. [7]Slowly the commercial community developed a collection of devices and ceremonials which enabled businessmen to set aside the ethic which ruled their private life and personal relations.

[8]Of these devices the most dramatic and generally intelligible was the corporation. [9]For a people still yearning for an economy dominated by individual responsibility, still under the spell of Jeffersonian dream, the corporation had one outstanding characteristic: its moral irresponsibility. [10]"Corporations have neither bodies to be kicked, nor souls to be damned," went a favorite aphorism. [11]Beyond good and evil, insensible to argument or appeal, they symbolized the mounting independence of the new economy from the restraints and scruples of personal life. [A. M. SCHLESINGER, JR.]

Again, the topic sentence is stated briefly and precisely in a simple sentence, of which every principal word will be developed in what follows. Complex sentences there are, but predication is never interrupted by extended modifiers. Several sentences postpone the predication, though not very elaborately; they alternate with sentences beginning with the subject (or single adverb followed by the subject). Thus sentences 2, 3, 9, and 11 postpone predication by phrases of varying length; of these only the ninth has an unusually long postponement. One sentence is moderately inverted, the eighth, where the phrase "Of these devices," appearing at the beginning instead of in its more usual position after "intelligible," is used as a transition from the first to the second paragraph. Regular word order of subject-verb-complement is invariable; most often the subject and verb are contiguous and are never separated by parentheses.

18   Though there is no series, there is abundant coordination, usually with the conjunction *and*. There is also a good deal of structural and verbal repetition: "With the increase . . . With the development . . ." (2 and 3), "Slowly . . . Slowly . . . Slowly . . ." (5, 6, 7), "still yearning . . . still under the spell . . ." (9), and the parallel adjectival phrases "Beyond good and evil, insensible to argument and appeal" (11). There are relatively few subordinate clauses, and these are all in the first paragraph. Observe here the difference between the sixth and seventh sentences: the one compact, the other, with its two adjective clauses ("which enabled . . . which ruled . . .," *not* parallel), long and stringy.

19   The general effect of the coordination and repetition is that of balance and cohesion; the whole passage is carefully knit together. Everything follows from the opening sentence. The transition between paragraphs is neatly accomplished by picking up the word "devices" of sentence 7 and giving it a prominent place in sentence 8; similarly the words "economy" and "personal" of the last sentence echo "economic" and "depersonalization" in the first. By such means an impression of unity emerges from the passage. From the extensive use of coordination, a sense of balance arises. Together they suggest rationality and objectivity, precisely the qualities most historians strive for.

20   Yet the writing is not cold and completely dispassionate; there is some sense of the writer's involvement. The passage increases in intensity as it goes along; there is a quiet but discernible movement, a growth to a climax. This development is, in the first place, lexical; that is, the vocabulary gradually changes from the mildness of such expressions as "depersonalization," "tenuous community of feeling," and "diminished" to such strong expressions as "moral irresponsibility," "kicked," "damned," and "Beyond good and evil." In the second place, the structure and rhythm of the sentences contribute to the same development. The first paragraph ends

almost languidly. Not only has the repetition of "slowly" had its effect, but the complex seventh sentence is leisurely. But this is followed by attention-getting variations of syntax: the inversion of sentence 8 and the lehgthily postponed predication of sentence 9. The suspense of this sentence is enhanced by the further semantic postponement of the critical phrase "moral irresponsibility," which gains much emphasis from the structure of the sentence. The subtle intensity of the second paragraph is enhanced further by the elimination of the coordinating conjunction twice ("still yearning . . ., still under . . ."; "Beyond good and evil, insensible . . .") and the avoidance of subordinate clauses. Notice how the force of sentence 9 is vitiated if we write:

> For a people who were still yearning for an economy which was dominated by individual responsibility and who were still under the spell of the Jeffersonian dream, the corporation had one outstanding characteristic, which was its moral irresponsibility.

This would not have the incisiveness demanded by the content. Conversely, consider the effect of eliminating the last *and* from the closing sentence and writing, ". . . from the restraints, the scruples of personal life." This would be more forceful than the present syntax. But would it be more desirable? From Schlesinger's viewpoint, probably not. He has so modulated the passage that it rises to a climax in the ninth sentence and returns to a comparatively restrained tone at the end, in keeping with the general style. He has made his point and yet avoided any hint of being carried away with it.

Joseph Wood Krutch is troubled over the enormous amounts of money and time being spent to send a man to the moon. He questions the rationale behind this expenditure and suggests that science and technology turn their resources toward more "important" problems, such as the population explosion. Krutch's essay is an excellent example of the application of the principles of rhetoric for the very basic purpose of persuasion.

Why I am not Going to the Moon

Joseph Wood Krutch

1   It was, I believe, a mountain climber who invented the phrase "because it is there" to explain why he wanted to climb a particular peak. Because ours is an age devoted to all sorts of unexamined enterprises his phrase has passed into popular speech and the very frequency with which it is invoked is a striking indication of the fact that many of the things we do, many of the ends we pursue, cannot be justified except by saying that, after all, these things can be done and these ends can be pursued.

2   Yet we cannot, after all, study everything that could be studied or do everything that could be done. Wisdom would seem to suggest that we ask, not only what can be done, but what is most worth doing—but that is exactly what the "because it is there" philosophy refuses to recognize. As Thoreau said, it is not worthwhile to go half way round the world to count the cats in Zanzibar. But there are, I presume, cats in Zanzibar and they could be counted. Better yet, the number could be pretty accurately estimated by a scientifically planned sampling. But before approving such an enterprise as one we ought to undertake, I would want some sounder reason than simply the fact that the cats are, presumably, there.

3   When President Kennedy was asked why our government was so eager to get someone to the moon, even he could think of no better answer than the catch-phrase "because it is there." Now, I am willing to believe that there may be better reasons. They may be military, and if there are sound military reasons I somewhat reluctantly yield to them. But I dismiss as mere foolish excuses most of the others I have heard—such as the prestige value of beat-

From the *Saturday Review* (Nov. 20, 1965). Reprinted by permission of the author and the *Saturday Review*.

ing the Russians or, most farfetched of all, von Braun's suggestion that colonization of the bodies in outer space is the best solution to the population problem.

4   At the risk of provoking the scorn of all the proponents of pure science, fundamental research, and so forth (as well as of all the "because it is there" boys), I would like to say that I have not yet heard any argument that seemed to me to justify the enormous expenditure of time, money, and brains upon this particular enterprise. Henry Adams said that the Middle Ages believed building cathedrals the thing most worth doing, just as the mid-nineteenth century in the United States gave the same sort of priority to railroad building. In our own time, exploration of space seems to have won a similar priority. We seem to regard it as not only worth doing but even more worth doing than anything else and, therefore, worth anything it may cost. But there is, it seems to me, no doubt that this inevitably means less time, less money, and less available brainpower to be spent on other things that, in addition to being there, seem to have stronger claims upon our attention.

5   That we should be dazzled by the sheer wonder of what man has been able to do is not surprising. The technical problems solved are surely the most difficult ever attacked by science. Out of nowhere has suddenly appeared a whole new race of experts who seem to move easily in a realm of thought and of practice that most of us cannot even enter. Within a few years they have accomplished what the most extravagant follower of Jules Verne would not have dared imagine except for some distant future. Yet the very wonder of it makes it difficult for us to maintain in any sense of proportion. To question its value is likely to seem mere impudence. Yet it ought to be, at least, questioned.

6   I am not thinking exclusively in terms of the argument that the money spent might be better used to relieve the sufferings of the poor, although that is itself an argument not quite so easily disposed of as Philip Morrison, professor of physics at Cornell and formerly a group leader at Los Alamos, assumed when he wrote recently in *The New Leader:* "The claim of each act we carry out in common must rest on its merit and not on the general thesis that no rich, strange, useless thing can justly be bought while some men lack necessities. . . . Those who built the Acropolis forgot the Helots; those who sailed the Indies thought nothing of the landless peasants."

7   The poor we have always with us and those who cite that text do not always seem to remember the context—which might seem

to make it support Professor Morrison's thesis. The comment was made as a reply to those of the disciples who had rebuked a stranger woman for pouring upon the head of Jesus a rich ointment which, they pointed out, might have been sold and the proceeds given to the poor. "The poor ye have always with you but me you have not always with you." But the question is not merely whether *any* rich, interesting, or beautiful thing can justifiably be bought while some men lack necessities. It is whether, in this particular case, the enormous expenditure is justified when it means neglecting, not only many men, but many other things with at least as much claim to being "rich, strange and (possibly) useful" as well.

8   Like the poor, this problem has always been with us and in one form or another probably always will be. But in times past men did have one guide in deciding *which* rich and strange thing was worth spending time and brains and money to create or do: They believed (as we do not) that one thing was intrinsically and absolutely better, wiser, or more to be admired than something else. They did not have to fall back on any "because it is there" argument because they had not, like us, been reduced by moral and cultural relativism to a sort of impotence that leaves us powerless to defend one choice as opposed to another and that therefore encourages us to do whatever can be done and to offer no reason more persuasive than the simple "because it is there to be done."

9   If we do indeed do some things that should have been left undone and do others less worth doing than those we neglect, none of that can be blamed on science itself. The great but limited field of its competence is knowing (pure science) and doing (technology). It cannot—as the wiser of its practitioners admit—evaluate. Though it can teach us how to get to the moon, we need something else to tell us whether or not we ought to go there.

10   Hence it is that if science is not to blame, some scientists are— just insofar as they encourage the now almost universal belief that science is omnicompetent and that any problems that cannot be solved by the scientific method (and that means all questions involving evaluation) are simply unsolvable or, essentially, meaningless. The tendency to fall back upon "because it is there" as the only answer to the question why a certain thing should be done is simply a demonstration of the inadequacy of science alone as a guide for either society or for the life of an individual.

11   Three centuries and a half ago Francis Bacon wrote in *The Advancement of Learning:* "We are much beholden to Machiavelli and others, that write what men do, and not what they ought to

do." This was perhaps a useful observation at the time; but the situation in the intellectual world is now by no means what it was in Bacon's day. And of all the threats to civilization perhaps none is greater than that which leads sociology to ask only what men do do and technology only what can be done, or, to use again the popular phrase, "what is there." By banishing "ought" from the vocabulary of our sociology, and by asking of our technologists only what they can do rather than what is worth doing, we are making ourselves passengers in a vehicle over which no critical intelligence pretends to exercise any control and which may, indeed, take us not only to the moon but to destinations even less desirable.

12   Some will no doubt answer that many of the advances of science are due to boundless curiosity concerning things that seem to have no possible application. But such curiosity is much safer when it leads us to know whatever we can know rather than to do whatever we can do. We have a tendency to rush from knowing to doing without pausing for reflection. Technology, if not science, has sometimes entailed penalties when it has taught us how to do things better left undone. This fact was seldom noted even by a few until quite recently when even a minority began to wonder whether or not it would have been better for everybody if the secret of the atom had never been penetrated. Curiosity, even scientific curiosity, can open a Pandora's box as well as a treasure chest. And one should use a certain amount of caution in lifting the lid of any box whose contents are unknown.

13   Primitive man suffered from both a lack of knowledge and a lack of know-how. He believed a great many absurd and often troublesome things that were not true. He had a very limited knowledge of how to do what he wanted to do. But this last limitation was also something of a safeguard, even if a rather unsatisfactory one. He could not destroy his environment as disastrously as we can destroy ours, and he could not kill as many of his neighbors as he would have been glad to kill if he had known how. Perhaps his intentions and desires were even worse than ours, but he didn't know as well as we how to implement them. We know only too well. Know-how continues to leave know-what and know-whether further and further behind.

14   I do not know just how military expenditures compare with those incurred in connection with the exploration of space. But except for defense, no other single enterprise of the government is financed on so lavish a scale. This surely suggests that those responsible for giving it this unquestioned priority assume that of all the

achievements possible in our generation this is the one most important. But does anyone seriously believe that this is true? That if a good fairy should grant us one wish we should say, "Let me get to the moon, and beyond"?

15   Consider, for example, the population explosion and not only what it has already done to make life difficult and ugly but also what it threatens to do in the future. In the minds of many thoughtful people it is a danger to mankind that may be as great as that of atomic warfare—the one threatening us with too many people, the other with a world in which there will be none at all. One could easily fill a book full of statements by responsible persons that say just this in one way or another. One moderate comment from Dr. Walter Hoagland, president of the American Academy of Arts and Sciences, will suffice. In a recent *Bulletin of the Atomic Scientist* he described experiments that demonstrate to his satisfaction that in animal populations overcrowding produces various pathological conditions including a fatal adrenal malfunction called the "Stress Syndrome." He believes that the same thing will happen to human beings under similar circumstances, and this seems to dispose of the assurance that the feeding of a monstrously overgrown population will present no serious problems to an ever-advancing technology.

16   Dr. Hoagland went on to suggest that we can "do nothing and just wait for the Stress Syndrome or a new virus to do its work," or we can "leave the solution to some trigger-happy dictator with a suitable stockpile of atomic weapons." On the other hand, so he suggests, we might just possibly "decide on an optimum population for the world and by education and social pressure try to see that it is not exceeded."

17   Admittedly, that last suggestion, though the only sensible one, involves problems to which the solutions are not at the moment by any means obvious. But it is to President Johnson's credit that he has given, more clearly than any other high government official ever has, recognition to the fact that the population explosion should be reckoned with somehow, sometime. Not long after his inauguration the foreign aid bill contained this sentence: "Funds available to carry out this provision may be used to conduct research into the problems of population growth." True, the implication seems to be that no such problems exist in our own country. And the very fact that so timid a statement should mark an epoch is itself enough to demonstrate how casually, almost as a parenthetical afterthought, we approach what is, in actual fact, the

second if not the first greatest threat to the future of mankind. Suppose that we had got no further in our plans to explore space than the provision in an omnibus bill for funds "to conduct research into the problem of space travel." Would that not suggest that we didn't think it very important — just something that might be looked into some day and at leisure?

18   Historians of ancient Egypt say that what we would call its "national income" was, during its days of greatness, very high. But the standard of living endured by the majority of its population was very low indeed because all of the income above what was essential to the barest existence went into the pyramids and other extravagances.

19   Now, no one could say that such a situation exists today in the United States. A good deal of our national income goes, not only into welfare, but into the pockets of citizens who buy with it what they like—whether that be education for their children, books and pictures and music for themselves, or (in somewhat more numerous instances) the most expensive automobiles their income (plus available credit) will get them. But future historians (if there are any) may wonder that we put into our rocket motors and all that goes into the making of them so large a slice of the national income.

20   Once, for several centuries, the Western world was united in the belief that the most important task it could possibly accomplish would be the recovery of the Holy Sepulcher. It sacrificed thousands of lives, to say nothing of vast wealth and a large part of its manpower, in the attempt to achieve something that few of us today can regard as having been more than an irrational obsession. Yet to a large section of the intelligent men of that time the enterprise must have seemed as obviously important as landing on the moon seems to us. But is not the moon, like the Holy Sepulcher, a mere symbol? It is not even in the hands of the infidel—though I suppose that if the Russians get there first it will be considered to be. And I wonder if, at some not too distant date, our crusade will not have come to seem no less incomprehensible than that of our forefathers.

21   Why don't we devote to the problem of overpopulation an effort as determined as that we are making to get to the moon before the Russians? Why, even at long last, do we do no more than to say that a small part of a large fund may be used to "conduct research into the problem" but not even to take any action?

22   The most important of the answers to this question is not the opposition of moralists or the indifference of those who see in what

they call a "bumper crop of babies" an ever-increasing market for the baby foods it will eat and, a little later, for the cigarettes it will smoke. The most important reasons are, first, the fact that this problem is far more difficult than the problem (stupendous though it is) of how to get to the moon; and, second, that the solution, if there is one, cannot be reached by the methods that have yielded such astonishingly successful results when applied to all the problems that do not involve human nature and that therefore yield to mechanical solutions. That the technological problem of birth control has been solved, that our so triumphant know-how includes the know-how of contraception, is quite typical of our age's greatest strength. That we do not know how our know-how can be applied to promote a good life is equally so. If a Cousteau suggests that we build undersea cities and a von Braun gives the even more preposterous suggestion that we colonize the planets; if, moreover, these are taken seriously by some, it can only be because these are purely technological solutions and it is upon technology that most of us rest whatever hopes we may have for a decent future.

23   I remember having read, some fifteen or more years ago, a book by Willy Ley in which was discussed the conditions that would have to be created before a rocket could break away from the earth's gravity and proceed indefinitely toward whatever object in space it had been pointed at. To do that, if I remember correctly, the rocket would have to be capable of a speed twice what it had been possible to achieve up to that time. This critical speed was named "the escape velocity." And though the ironic implications of the term did not strike me then, they do strike me now. Perhaps one of the reasons we are so attracted by the problems of space exploration is that absorption in them helps us forget the more difficult problems lying right at our feet and that an "escape velocity" is precisely what we have achieved.

24   A good many science fiction stories have been written about the survivors, sometimes the last surviving couple, on a depopulated earth. If I were to try my hand at that kind of fiction I should imagine a pair of astronauts who had escaped to the moon and who looked back at an earth where the Stress Syndrome produced by overcrowding had at last involved, not only the exchange of the Russian and American overkill stockpile, but also the smaller but effective contributions from what are now called — but by then wouldn't be — the undeveloped countries. Our astronauts had brought along the equipment necessary for the return journey. But it did not take them long to decide not to use it.

QUESTIONS FOR STUDY

1. Explain what Halverson and Cooley mean by "crisp," "weighty," "flowing," and "crabbed" styles.

2. How would you describe the style of Joseph W. Krutch in his essay, "Why I am not Going to the Moon"?

3. Analyze one of the paragraphs (22 for example) in "Why I am not Going to the Moon" for the elements of sentence structure. First analyze each sentence from the grammatical point of view, then from the rhetorical. From this analysis give a characterization of the author's style. Does he prefer simple sentences to complex or compound? Does he employ parallelism? Is his attitude restrained or intense?

4. What sort of paragraph transitions does Krutch frequently employ? Point out the topic sentences in the first three paragraphs.

5. What is the dominant tone of the essay? Select passages that help to establish this tone.

6. According to Krutch, why does man want to go to the moon? What are the arguments for going to the moon and how does Krutch refute them?

7. What is Krutch's attitude toward the two aspects of science (knowing and doing) in relation to the past as well as the present?

8. What is Krutch's final argument for not going to the moon? In your opinion, how sound is that argument?

WRITING TOPICS

1. Write an essay comparing and contrasting the styles of Stevenson and Krutch.

2. Read the Clarke essay in Section Three and write an analysis demonstrating the differences in his arguments as opposed to Krutch's.

3. In a brief essay analyze your own style in other essays written for the course. Try to determine as objectively as possible both its weaknesses and strengths.

PART THREE

PART THREE

Part Three

Contents

Essays for Further Analysis

The Uses of the Moon   *Arthur C. Clarke* 424

Of the Limits to the Authority of
   Society over the Individual   *John Stuart Mill* 436

Civil Disobedience   *Henry David Thoreau* 454

Inviting Communists to Speak
   at Colleges   *William F. Buckley, Jr.* 474

Learning vs. Invention   *Samuel Johnson* 481

The American Scholar   *Ralph Waldo Emerson* 485

Literature and Science   *Matthew Arnold* 502

An Argument Against Abolishing
   Christianity   *Jonathan Swift* 520

Man Against Darkness   *Walter T. Stace* 531

Aes Triplex   *Robert Louis Stevenson* 543

The Uses of the Moon

Arthur C. Clarke

> *Putting a colony there may be practical,*
> *cold-cash sense—which has nothing to do with*
> *propaganda or military operations.*

1   The two greatest nations in the world have now given notice that they will land men on the Moon within the next decade. This will be one of the central facts of political life in the years to come; indeed, it may soon dominate human affairs even more dramatically than was suggested in the novel *Advise and Consent*. It is essential, therefore, that we understand the importance of the Moon in our future; if we do not, we will be going there for the wrong reasons, and will not know what to do when we arrive.

2   Many people imagine that the whole project of lunar exploration is merely a race with the Russians—a contest in conspicuous consumption of brains and material, designed to impress the remainder of mankind. No one can deny the strong element of competition and national prestige involved, but in the long run, this will be the least important aspect of the matter. If the race to the Moon were nothing more than a race, it would make good sense to let the Russians bankrupt themselves in the strain of winning it, in the calm confidence that their efforts would collapse in recriminations and purges sometime during the 1970s.

3   There are some shortsighted people (including a few elderly, but unfortunately still influential, scientists) who would adopt just such a policy. Why spend tens of billions of dollars, they ask, to land a few men on a barren, airless lump of rock, nothing more

than a cosmic slag heap, baked by the Sun during the daytime and frozen to subarctic temperatures in the long night? The polar regions of this Earth are far more hospitable; indeed, the deep oceans could probably be exploited and even colonized for a fraction of the sum needed to conquer the Moon.

4   All this is true; it is also totally irrelevant. The Moon *is* a barren, airless wasteland, blasted by intolerable radiations. Yet a century from now it may be an asset more valuable than the wheat fields of Kansas or the oil wells of Oklahoma. And an asset in terms of actual hard cash—not the vast imponderables of adventure, romance, artistic inspiration, and scientific knowledge. Though, ultimately, these are the only things of real value, they can never be measured. The conquest of the Moon, however, can be justified to the cost accountants, not only to the scientists and the poets.

5   Let me first demolish, with considerable pleasure, one common argument for going to the Moon—the military one. Some ballistic generals have maintained that the Moon is "high ground" that could be used for reconnaissance and bombardment of the Earth. Though I hesitate to say that this is complete nonsense, it is so near to it as to make very little practical difference.

6   You cannot hope to see as much from 250,000 miles away as from a TV-satellite just above the atmosphere, and the use of the Moon as a launching site makes even less sense. For the effort required to set up one lunar military base with all its supporting facilities, at least a hundred times as many bases could be established on Earth. It is also far easier to intercept a missile coming from the Moon—taking many hours for the trip in full view of telescopes and radar—than one sneaking round the curve of the Earth in twenty minutes. Only if, which Heaven forbid, we extend our present tribal conflicts to the other planets will the Moon become of military importance.

7   Before we discuss the civilized uses of our one natural satellite, let us summarize the main facts about it. They may be set down quite briefly:

Area: The Moon's radius is just over a thousand miles — one quarter of the Earth's. Thus its area is one-sixteenth of our planet's —more than that of Africa, and almost as much as that of both the Americas combined. Such a territory will take many years (and many lives) to explore in detail.

Material: The amount of material in the Moon (if you would like it in tons) comes to 750,000,000,000,000,000,000,000. This is millions of millions times more than all the coal, iron, minerals, and ores that man has shifted in the whole of history. It is not enough mass, however, to give the Moon much of a gravitational pull; as everyone now knows, a visitor to the Moon has only a fraction (actually one-sixth) of his terrestrial weight.

Gravity: This low gravity has several consequences, almost all of them good. The most important is that the Moon has been unable to retain an atmosphere; if it ever had one, it long ago escaped from the Moon's feeble clutch and leaked off into space. For all practical purposes, therefore, the lunar surface is in a perfect vacuum. (*This* is an advantage? Yes: we'll see why in a moment.)

Atmosphere: Because there is no atmosphere to weaken the Sun's rays or to act as a reservoir of heat at night, the Moon is a world of very great temperature extremes. On our Earth, in any one spot, the thermometer seldom ranges over as much as a hundred degrees even during the course of a year. Though the temperature can exceed 100 degrees in the tropics, and drop to 125 *below* zero in the Antarctic, these figures are quite exceptional. But every point on the Moon undergoes twice this range during the lunar day; indeed, an explorer could encounter such changes within seconds, merely by stepping from sunlight into shadow. This obviously presents problems, but the very absence of atmosphere which causes such extremes also makes it easy to deal with them—for a vacuum is one of the best heat insulators, a fact familiar to anyone who has ever taken hot drinks on a picnic.

Weather: No air means no weather. It is hard for us, accustomed to wind and rain, cloud and fog, hail and snow, to imagine the complete absence of all these things. None of the meteorological variations which make life interesting, unpredictable, and occasionally impossible on the surface of this planet takes place on the Moon; the only change there is the utterly unvarying cycle of day and night. Such a situation may be monotonous—but it simplifies to an unbelievable extent the problems facing architects, engineers, explorers, and indeed everyone who will ever conduct operations of any kind on the Moon.

Day: The Moon turns rather slowly on its axis, so that its day (and its night) are almost thirty times longer than ours. As a result, the sharp-edged frontier between night and day, which moves at a thousand miles an hour on the Earth's equator, has a maximum speed of less than ten miles an hour on the Moon. In high lunar latitudes, a walking man could keep in perpetual daylight with little exertion. And because the Moon turns on its axis in the same time as it revolves around the Earth, it always keeps the same hemisphere turned toward us. Until the advent of Lunik III, this was extremely frustrating to astronomers; in another generation, as we shall see, they will be very thankful for it.

COLONISTS AT WORK

8   So much for the main facts; now for a few assumptions which most people would accept as reasonable in 1961, though they would have laughed at them before 1957.

9   The first is that suitably protected men can work and carry out engineering operations on the face of the Moon, either directly or by remote control through robots.

10   The second is that the Moon consists of the same elements as the Earth, though doubtless in different proportions and combinations. Most of our familiar minerals will be missing: there will be no coal or limestone, since these are the products of life. But there will be carbon and hydrogen and oxygen and calcium in other forms, and we can evolve a technology to extract them from whatever sources are available. It is even possible that there may be large quantities of free (though frozen) water not too far below the Moon's surface; if this is the case, one of the chief problems of the lunar colonists will be solved.

11   In any event—without going into details of mining, ore processing, and chemical engineering—it will be possible to obtain all the materials needed for maintaining life. The first pioneers will be content with mere survival, but at a later stage they will build up a self-supporting industry based almost entirely on lunar resources. Only instruments, specialized equipment, and men will come from Earth; the Moon will supply all the rest—ultimately, of course, even the men.

12   There have been many studies and books on the subject of lunar colonization (I have written one myself), and all those who have been into the subject are agreed on the general picture, though the details vary. It may take as little as fifty years (the interval between the Wright biplane and the B-52) to establish a viable lunar colony; it may take a hundred. But if we wish, it can be done; on the Moon, to borrow the words of William Faulkner's Nobel Prize speech, man will not merely survive—he will prevail.

13   Now for the reasons why it is worth the expense, risk, and difficulty of prevailing on the inhospitable Moon. They are implicit in the question: what can the Moon offer that we cannot find on Earth?

14   One immediate but paradoxical answer is Nothing—millions of cubic miles of it. Many of the key industries in the modern world are based on vacuum techniques; electric lighting and its offspring, radio and electronics, could never have begun without the vacuum tube, and the invention of the transistor has done little to diminish its importance. (The initial steps of transistor manufacture have themselves to be carried out in vacuum.) A great many metallurgical and chemical processes and key stages in the production of such drugs as penicillin are possible only in a partial or virtually complete vacuum; but it is expensive to make a very good vacuum, and impossible to make a very large one.

15   On the Moon, there will be a "hard" vacuum of unlimited extent outside the door of every air lock. I do not suggest that it will be worthwhile switching much terrestrial industry to the Moon, even if the freight charges allowed it. But the whole history of science makes it certain that new processes and discoveries of fundamental importance will evolve as soon as men start to carry out operations in the lunar vacuum. Low-pressure physics and technology will proceed from rags to riches overnight; industries which today are unimagined will spring up on the Moon and ship their products back to Earth. For in that direction, the freight charges will be relatively low.

LAUNCH WITHOUT BOOSTERS

16   This leads us to a major role that the Moon will play in the development of the solar system: it is no exaggeration to say that this little world, so small and close at hand (the very first rocket to reach it took only thirty-five hours on the journey) will be the steppingstone to all the planets. The reason for this is its low gravity; it requires twenty times as much energy to escape from the Earth as from the Moon. As a supply base for all interplanetary operations, therefore, the Moon has an enormous advantage over the Earth—assuming, of course, that we can find the materials we need there. This is one of the reasons why the development of lunar technology and industry is so important.

17   From the gravitational point of view, the Moon is indeed high ground, while we on the Earth are like dwellers at the bottom of an immensely deep pit out of which we have to climb every time we wish to conduct any cosmic explorations. No wonder that we must burn a hundred tons of rocket fuel for every ton of payload

we launch into space—and on a one-way trip at that. For return journeys by rocket, thousands of tons would be needed.

18 This is why all *Earth-based* plans for space travel are so hopelessly uneconomic, involving gigantic boosters with tiny payloads. It is as if, in order to carry a dozen passengers across the Atlantic, we had to construct a ship weighing as much as the *Queen Elizabeth* but costing very much more. (The development costs for a large space vehicle are in the range of a billion dollars.) And, to make the whole thing completely fantastic, the vehicle can be used only once, *for it will be destroyed in flight.* Of the tens of thousands of tons that leave the Earth, only a small capsule will return. The rest will consist of boosters dropped in the ocean or discarded in space.

19 When nuclear power is harnessed for rocket propulsion, the position will be improved from the preposterous to the merely absurd. For even nuclear rockets must carry hundreds of thousands of tons of reaction mass, to provide a thrust when it is ejected. Every rocket, nuclear or chemical, has to have something to push against; that something is not the surrounding air, as many people once believed, but the rocket's own fuel. However, the nuclear rocket will use the very simplest of fuels—plain hydrogen. There must be plenty of this on the Moon, combined in water (which is 11 per cent hydrogen) or in some other form. The first order of business in lunar exploration will be to locate sources from which hydrogen may be obtained; when this has been done, and it is possible for ships to refuel on the Moon, the cost, difficulty, and complexity of all space operations will be reduced at least tenfold.

20 Since space craft need not carry fuel for the return trip (imagine where transatlantic flying would be today, if it operated on this basis!) it will no longer be necessary to build and jettison ten-thousand-ton vehicles to deliver ten-ton payloads. Instead of monstrous, multistaged boosters, we can use relatively small rockets that can be refueled and flown over and over again. Space flight would emerge from its present status as a fantastically expensive stunt, and would start to make economic—perhaps even commercial—sense.

21 This, however, would be only a beginning. The big breakthrough toward really efficient space operations may depend upon the fortunate fact that the Moon has no atmosphere. The peculiar conditions (peculiar by our standards—they are normal by those of the universe) prevailing there permit a launching technique much more

economical than rocket propulsion. This is the old idea of the "space-gun," made famous by Jules Verne almost a hundred years ago. It would probably not be a gun in the literal sense, powered by chemical explosives, but a horizontal launching track like those used on aircraft carriers, along which space vehicles could be accelerated electrically until they reached sufficient speed to escape from the Moon.

22   It is easy to see why such a device is completely impractical on Earth. To escape from the Earth, a body must reach the now-familiar speed of 25,000 miles an hour. At the fierce acceleration of ten gravities, which astronauts have already withstood for very short periods of time, it would take two minutes to attain this speed—and the launching track would have to be *four hundred miles* long. If the acceleration were halved to make it more endurable, the length of the track would have to be doubled. And, of course, any object traveling at such a speed in the lower atmosphere would be instantly burned up by friction. We can forget all about space-guns on Earth.

23   The situation is completely different on the Moon. Because of the almost perfect vacuum, the lunar escape speed of a mere 5,200 mph can be achieved at ground level without any danger from air resistance. And at an acceleration of ten gravities, the launching track need be only nineteen miles long—not four hundred, as on the Earth. It would be a massive piece of engineering, but a perfectly practical one, and it would wholly transform the economics of space flight.

24   Vehicles could leave the Moon *without burning any fuel at all;* all the work of take-off would be done by fixed power plants on the ground, which could be as large and massive as required. The only fuel that a space vehicle returning to Earth need carry would be a very small amount for maneuvering and navigating. As a result, the size of vehicle needed for a mission from Moon to Earth would be reduced tenfold; a hundred-ton space ship could do what had previously required a thousand-tonner.

FUEL BY CATAPULT

25   This kind of space travel would be a spectacular enough improvement; the next stage, however, would be the really decisive one. This is the use of a Moon-based launcher or catapult to place supplies of fuel where they are needed, in orbit round the Earth or indeed near or on any other planet in the solar system.

26   It is generally agreed that long-range space flight—particularly voyages beyond the Moon—will become possible only when we can refuel our vehicles in orbit. Plans have been drawn up in great detail for operations involving fleets of tanker-rockets which, perhaps over a period of years, could establish what are virtually filling stations in space. Such schemes will, of course, be fantastically expensive, for it requires about fifty tons of rocket fuel to put a single ton of payload into orbit round the Earth, only a couple of hundred miles up.

27   Yet a Moon-based launcher could do the same job—from a distance of 250,000 miles!—for a twentieth of the energy and without consuming any rocket fuel whatsoever. It would launch tanks of propellants "down" toward Earth, and suitable guidance systems would steer them into stable orbits where they would swing around endlessly until required. This would have as great an effect on the logistics of space flight as the dropping of supplies by air has already had upon polar exploration; indeed, the parallel is a very close one.

28   Though enormous amounts of power would be required to operate such lunar catapults, this will be no problem in the twenty-first century. A single hydrogen bomb, weighing only a few tons, *already* liberates enough energy to lift a hundred million tons completely away from the Moon. That energy will be available for useful purposes when our grandchildren need it; if it is not, we will have no grandchildren.

29   There is one other application of the lunar catapult that may be very important, though it may seem even more farfetched at the present time. It could launch the products of the Moon's technology all the way down to the surface of the Earth. A rugged, freight-carrying capsule, like a more refined version of today's nose cones and re-entry vehicles, could be projected from the Moon to make an automatic landing on the Earth at any assigned spot. Once again, no rocket fuel would be needed for the trip, except a few pounds for maneuvering. All the energy of launching would be provided by the fixed power plant on the Moon; all the slowing down would be done by the Earth's atmosphere. When such a system is perfected, it may be no more expensive to ship freight from Moon to Earth than it is now to fly it from one continent to another by jet. Moreover, the launching catapult could be quite short, since it would not have to deal with fragile human passengers. If it operated at fifty-gravities acceleration, a four-mile-long track would be sufficient.

30   I have discussed this idea at some length for two reasons. The
first is that it demonstrates how, by taking advantage of the
Moon's low gravity, its airlessness, and the raw materials that must
certainly be there, we can conduct space exploration far more
economically than by basing our operations on Earth. In fact,
until some revolutionary new method of propulsion is invented, it
is hard to see any other way in which space travel will be practical
on the large scale.

31   The second reason is the slightly more personal one that, to the
best of my knowledge, I was the first to develop this idea in a 1950
issue of the *Journal* of the British Interplanetary Society. Five
years earlier I had proposed the use of satellites for radio and TV
communications; I did not expect to see either scheme materialize
in my lifetime, but one has already happened and now I wonder
if I may see both.

LIGHT TO REPLACE SOUND

32   The subject of communications leads us to another extremely
important use of the Moon. As civilization spreads throughout the
solar system, it will provide the main link between Earth and her
scattered children. For though it is just as far to the other planets
from the Moon as from the Earth, sheer distance is not the only
factor involved. The Moon's surface is already in space, while the
surface of the Earth—luckily for us—is shielded from space by a
whole series of barriers through which we have to drive our signals.
The best known of these barriers is, of course, the ionosphere,
which reflects all but the shorter radio waves back to Earth. The
shortest waves of all, however, go through it with little difficulty,
so the ionosphere is no hindrance to space communications.

33   What *is* a serious barrier—and this has been realized only during
the past year—is the atmosphere itself. Thanks to the development of an extraordinary new optical device called the laser, which
I must ask you to take for granted, it now appears that the best
agent for long-distance communications is not radio, but light. A
light beam can carry millions of times as many messages as a radio
wave, and can be focused with infinitely greater accuracy. Indeed,
a laser-produced light beam could produce a spot on the Moon only
a few hundred feet across, where the beam from a searchlight
would be thousands of miles in diameter. Thus colossal ranges
could be obtained with very little power; calculations show that
with lasers we can think of signaling to the stars, not merely to the
planets.

34   But we cannot use light beams to send messages through the Earth's erratic atmosphere; a passing cloud could block a signal that had traveled across a billion miles of space. On the airless Moon, however, this would be no problem, for the sky is perpetually clear to waves of all frequencies, from the longest radio waves, through visible light, past the ultraviolet, and even down to the short X-rays which are blocked by a few inches of air. This whole immense range of electromagnetic waves will be available for communications or any other use—perhaps such applications as the broadcasting of power, which have never been practical on Earth. There will be enough "band-width" (or ether space) for all the radio and TV services we can ever imagine, no matter how densely populated the planets become and however many messages the men of the future wish to flash back and forth across the solar system.

35   We can thus imagine the Moon as a sort of central clearinghouse for interplanetary communications, aiming its tightly focused light beams to the other planets and to ships in space. Any messages that concerned Earth would be radioed across the trivial 250,000-mile gulf on those wave lengths that penetrate our atmosphere.

36   There are several other reasons why the Moon might almost have been designed as a base for interplanetary communications. Everyone is now familiar with the enormous radio telescopes which have been built to reach out into space and to maintain contact with such distant probes as our Pioneers and Explorers (and the Rangers, Mariners, and Prospectors that will follow them). The most ambitious of these instruments is the gigantic radio telescope (six hundred feet in diameter) to be built near Sugar Grove, West Virginia. This, the largest mobile structure on Earth, contains 20,000 tons of metal and will cost over $100 million.

37   On the Moon, both the cost and weight of this huge structure might be slashed to a few per cent. Thanks to the low gravity, a very much lighter construction could be used than is necessary on Earth. And the Moon's airlessness pays another dividend, for a terrestrial telescope has to be designed with a substantial safety factor so that it can withstand the worst that the weather can do. There is no need to worry about gales on the Moon, where there is not the slightest breeze to disturb the most gossamer structures.

38   Nor have we yet finished with the Moon's advantages from the view of those who want to send (and receive) signals across space. It turns so slowly on its axis that the problem of tracking is much simplified; *and it is a quiet place.* Or, to be more accurate, the far side of the Moon is a quiet place—probably the quietest that now

exists within millions of miles of the Earth. I am speaking, of course, in the radio sense; for the last sixty years, our planet has been pouring an ever-increasing racket into space. This has already seriously inconvenienced the radio astronomers, whose observations can be ruined by an electric shaver a hundred miles away.

39   But the land first glimpsed by Lunik III is beyond the reach of this electronic tumult; it is shielded from the din of Earth by two thousand miles of solid rock—a far better protection than a million miles of empty space. Here, where the earthlight never shines, will be the communications centers of the future, linking together with radio and light beams all the inhabited planets. And one day, perhaps, they will reach out beyond the solar system to make contact with those other intelligences for whom the first search has already begun. That search can hardly hope for success until we have succeeded in escaping from the braying of all the radio and TV stations of our own planet.

40   What has already been said should be more than enough to convince any imaginative person—anyone who does not believe that the future will be a carbon copy of the past—that the Moon will be a priceless possession and its exploration far more than the expensive scientific stunt that some foolish people have called it. At the same time it should be emphasized that the most important and valuable uses of the Moon will be ones that nobody has thought of today. I will merely hint at a few possibilities here.

WHO DESERVES IT?

41   In a recent discussion of space exploration, Professor Harold Urey made the point that the Moon is one of the most interesting places in the solar system—in some ways more so than Mars or Venus, even though there may be life on these planets. For the face of the Moon may have carried down the ages, virtually untouched by time, a record of the conditions that existed billions of years ago, when the universe itself was young. On Earth, all such records have long ago been erased by the winds and the rains and other geological forces. When we reach the Moon, it will be as if an entire library of lost volumes, a million times older than the library destroyed at Alexandria, will be suddenly thrown open to us.

42   Quite beyond price will be the skills we will acquire during the exploration—and ultimately, colonization—of this new land in the

sky. I suspect, though only time will tell whether this is true, that we will learn more about unorthodox methods of food production on the Moon within a few years than we could in decades on Earth. Can we, in an almost literal sense of the phrase, turn rocks into food? We must master this art (as the plants did, aeons ago) if we hope to conquer space. Perhaps most exciting of all are the possibilities opened up by low-gravity medicine and the enormous question: "Will men live longer on a world where they do not wear out their hearts fighting against gravity?" Upon the answer to this will depend the future of many worlds, and of nations yet unnamed.

43   Much of politics, as of life, consists of the administration of the unforeseen. We can foresee only a minute fraction of the Moon's potentialities, and the Moon itself is only a tiny part of the universe. The fact that the Soviet Union is making an all-out effort to get there has far deeper implications than have been generally faced.

44   The Russians, whatever else they may be, are realists. And as Sir Charles Snow has pointed out in his highly influential book, *Science and Government*, between 35 and 45 per cent of their top men have some technical and scientific training. (It is doubtful if the proportion is a quarter of this in the West.) As a result, they have often made correct choices—for example, the decision to develop the lithium bomb and giant rocket boosters—when the United States wasted its energies in such technological dead ends as tritium bombs and air-breathing missiles.

45   They may have done so again in the most important field of all. I wonder if any of the "Leave it to the Russians" school of anti-space-flight critics seriously imagines that Soviet science is outward bound merely to impress the uncommitted nations. That could be achieved in a dozen less expensive ways. No, the Russians know exactly what they are doing. Perhaps they are already laughing at the shortsighted prophets who have said: "Anyone who owns the Moon can dominate the Earth." They may no longer be concerned with such trivialities. They realize that if any nation has mastery of the Moon, it will dominate not merely the Earth, but the whole accessible universe.

46   If, in November 1967, there are only Russians on the Moon to drink a toast to the fiftieth anniversary of the Revolution, they will have won the solar system, and theirs will be the voice of the future.

47   As it will deserve to be.

Of the Limits to the Authority of Society over the Individual

John Stuart Mill

1   What, then, is the rightful limit to the sovereignty of the individual over himself? Where does the authority of society begin? How much of human life should be assigned to individuality, and how much to society?

2   Each will receive its proper share, if each has that which more particularly concerns it. To individuality should belong the part of life in which it is chiefly the individual that is interested; to society, the part which chiefly interests society.

3   Though society is not founded on a contract, and though no good purpose is answered by inventing a contract in order to deduce social obligations from it, every one who receives the protection of society owes a return for the benefit, and the fact of living in society renders it indispensable that each should be bound to observe a certain line of conduct towards the rest. This conduct consists, first, in not injuring the interests of one another; or rather certain interests, which, either by express legal provision or by tacit understanding, ought to be considered as rights; and secondly, in each person's bearing his share (to be fixed on some equitable principle) of the labors and sacrifices incurred for defending the society or its members from injury and molestation. These conditions society is justified in enforcing, at all costs to those who endeavor to withhold fulfillment. Nor is this all that society may do. The acts of an individual may be hurtful to others, or wanting in due consideration for their welfare, without going the length of violating any of their constituted rights. The offender may then be justly punished by opinion, though not by law. As soon as any part of a person's conduct affects prejudicially the interests of others, society has jurisdiction over it, and the question whether the gen-

From *On Liberty*.

eral welfare will or will not be promoted by interfering with it, becomes open to discussion. But there is no room for entertaining any such question when a person's conduct affects the interests of no persons besides himself, or needs not affect them unless they like (all the persons concerned being of full age, and the ordinary amount of understanding). In all such cases there should be perfect freedom, legal and social, to do the action and stand the consequences.

4   It would be a great misunderstanding of this doctrine, to suppose that it is one of selfish indifference, which pretends that human beings have no business with each other's conduct in life, and that they should not concern themselves about the well-doing or well-being of one another, unless their own interest is involved. Instead of any diminution, there is need of a great increase of disinterested exertion to promote the good of others. But disinterested benevolence can find other instruments to persuade people to their good, than whips and scourges, either of the literal or the metaphorical sort. I am the last person to undervalue the self-regarding virtues; they are only second in importance, if even second, to the social. It is equally the business of education to cultivate both. But even education works by conviction and persuasion as well as by compulsion, and it is by the former only that, when the period of education is past, the self-regarding virtues should be inculcated. Human beings owe to each other help to distinguish the better from the worse, and encouragement to choose the former and avoid the latter. They should be forever stimulating each other to increased exercise of their higher faculties, and increased direction of their feelings and aims towards wise instead of foolish, elevating instead of degrading, objects and contemplations. But neither one person, nor any number of persons, is warranted in saying to another human creature of ripe years, that he shall not do with his life for his own benefit what he chooses to do with it. He is the person most interested in his own well-being; the interest which any other person, except in cases of strong personal attachment, can have in it, is trifling, compared with that which he himself has; the interest which society has in him individually (except as to his conduct to others) is fractional, and altogether indirect; while with respect to his own feelings and circumstances, the most ordinary man or woman has means of knowledge immeasurably surpassing those that can be possessed by any one else. The interference of society to overrule his judgment and purposes in what only regards himself, must be grounded on general presumptions; which may be

altogether wrong, and even if right, are as likely as not to be mis-applied to individual cases, by persons no better acquainted with the circumstances of such cases than those are who look at them merely from without. In this department, therefore, of human affairs, Individuality has its proper field of action. In the conduct of human beings towards one another, it is necessary that general rules should for the most part be observed, in order that people may know what they have to expect; but in each person's own concerns, his individual spontaneity is entitled to free exercise. Considerations to aid his judgment, exhortations to strengthen his will, may be offered to him, even obtruded on him, by others; but he, himself, is the final judge. All errors which he is likely to commit against advice and warning, are far outweighed by the evil of allowing others to constrain him to what they deem his good.

5   I do not mean that the feelings with which a person is regarded by others, ought not to be in any way affected by his self-regarding qualities or deficiencies. This is neither possible nor desirable. If he is eminent in any of the qualities which conduce to his own good, he is, so far, a proper object of admiration. He is so much the nearer to the ideal perfection of human nature. If he is grossly deficient in those qualities, a sentiment the opposite of admiration will follow. There is a degree of folly, and a degree of what may be called (though the phrase is not unobjectionable) lowness or depradation of taste, which, though it cannot justify doing harm to the person who manifests it, renders him necessarily and properly a subject of distaste, or, in extreme cases, even of contempt: a person could not have the opposite qualities in due strength without entertaining these feelings. Though doing no wrong to any one, a person may so act as to compel us to judge him, and feel to him, as a fool, or as a being of an inferior order: and since this judgment and feeling are a fact which he would prefer to avoid, it is doing him a service to warn him of it beforehand, as of any other disagreeable consequence to which he exposes himself. It would be well, indeed, if this good office were much more freely rendered than the common notions of politeness at present permit, and if one person could honestly point out to another that he thinks him in fault, without being considered unmannerly or presuming. We have a right, also, in various ways, to act upon our unfavorable opinion of any one, not to the oppression of his individuality, but in the exercise of ours. We are not bound, for example, to seek his society; we have a right to avoid it (though not to parade the avoidance), for we have a right to choose the society most acceptable to us. We have

a right, and it may be our duty to caution others against him, if we think his example or conversation likely to have a pernicious effect on those with whom he associates. We may give others a preference over him in optional good offices, except those which tend to his improvement. In these various modes a person may suffer very severe penalties at the hands of others, for faults which directly concern only himself; but he suffers these penalties only in so far as they are the natural, and, as it were, the spontaneous consequences of the faults themselves, not because they are purposely inflicted on him for the sake of punishment. A person who shows rashness, obstinacy, self-conceit—who cannot live within moderate means—who cannot restrain himself from hurtful indulgences—who pursues animal pleasures at the expense of those of feeling and intellect—must expect to be lowered in the opinion of others, and to have a less share of their favorable sentiments, but of this he has no right to complain, unless he has merited their favor by special excellence in his social relations, and has thus established a title to their good offices, which is not affected by his demerits towards himself.

6   What I contend for is, that the inconveniences which are strictly inseparable from the unfavorable judgment of others, are the only ones to which a person should ever be subjected for that portion of his conduct and character which concerns his own good, but which does not affect the interests of others in their relations with him. Acts injurious to others require a totally different treatment. Encroachment on their rights; infliction on them of any loss or damage not justified by his own rights; falsehood or duplicity in dealing with them; unfair or ungenerous use of advantages over them; even selfish abstinence from defending them against injury—these are fit objects of moral reprobation, and, in grave cases, of moral retribution and punishment. And not only these acts, but the dispositions which lead to them, are properly immoral, and fit subjects of disapprobation which may rise to abhorrence. Cruelty of disposition; malice and ill-nature, that most anti-social and odious of all passions, envy; dissimulation and insincerity; irascibility on insufficient cause, and resentment disproportioned to the provocation; the love of domineering over others; the desire to engross more than one's share of advantages (the πλεονεξια of the Greeks); the pride which derives gratification from the abasement of others; the egotism which thinks self and its concerns more important than everything else, and decides all doubtful questions in his own favor; — these are moral vices, and constitute a bad and odious

moral character: unlike the self-regarding faults previously mentioned, which are not properly immoralities, and to whatever pitch they may be carried, do not constitute wickedness. They may be proofs of any amount of folly, or want of personal dignity and self-respect; but they are only a subject of moral reprobation when they involve a breach of duty to others, for whose sake the individual is bound to have care for himself. What are called duties to ourselves are not socially obligatory, unless circumstances render them at the same time duties to others. The term duty to oneself, when it means anything more than prudence, means self-respect or self-development; and for none of these is any one accountable to his fellow-creatures, because for none of them is it for the good of mankind that he be held accountable to them.

7   The distinction between the loss of consideration which a person may rightly incur by defect of prudence or of personal dignity, and the reprobation which is due to him for an offence against the rights of others, is not a merely nominal distinction. It makes a vast difference both in our feelings and in our conduct towards him, whether he displeases us in things in which we think we have a right to control him, or in things in which we know that we have not. If he displeases us, we may express our distaste, and we may stand aloof from a person as well as from a thing that displeases us; but we shall not therefore feel called on to make his life uncomfortable. We shall reflect that he already bears, or will bear, the whole penalty of his error; if he spoils his life by mismanagement, we shall not, for that reason, desire to spoil it still further: instead of wishing to punish him, we shall rather endeavor to alleviate his punishment, by showing him how he may avoid or cure the evils his conduct tends to bring upon him. He may be to us an object of pity, perhaps of dislike, but not of anger or resentment; we shall not treat him like an enemy of society: the worst we shall think ourselves justified in doing is leaving him to himself, if we do not interfere benevolently by showing interest or concern for him. It is far otherwise if he has infringed the rules necessary for the protection of his fellow-creatures, individually or collectively. The evil consequences of his acts do not then fall on himself, but on others; and society, as the protector of all its members, must retaliate on him; must inflict pain on him for the express purpose of punishment, and must take care that it be sufficiently severe. In the one case he is an offender at our bar, and we are called on not only to sit in judgment on him, but, in one shape or another, to execute our own sentence: in the other

case, it is not our part to inflict any suffering on him, except what may incidentally follow from our using the same liberty in the regulation of our own affairs, which we allow to him in his.

8   The distinction here pointed out between the part of a person's life which concerns only himself, and that which concerns others, many persons will refuse to admit. How (it may be asked) can any part of the conduct of a member of society be a matter of indifference to the other members? No person is an entirely isolated being; it is impossible for a person to do anything seriously or permanently hurtful to himself, without mischief reaching at least to his near connections, and often far beyond them. If he injures his property, he does harm to those who directly or indirectly derived support from it, and usually diminishes, by a greater or less amount, the general resources of the community. If he deteriorates his bodily or mental faculties, he not only brings evil upon all who depended on him for any portion of their happiness, but disqualifies himself for rendering the services which he owes to his fellow-creatures generally; perhaps becomes a burden on their affection or benevolence; and if such conduct were very frequent, hardly any offence that is committed would detract more from the general sum of good. Finally, if by his vices or follies a person does no direct harm to others, he is nevertheless (it may be said) injurious by his example; and ought to be compelled to control himself, for the sake of those whom the sight or knowledge of his conduct might corrupt or mislead.

9   And even (it will be added) if the consequences of misconduct could be confined to the vicious or thoughtless individual, ought society to abandon to their own guidance those who are manifestly unfit for it? If protection against themselves is confessedly due to children and persons under age, is not society equally bound to afford it to persons of mature years who are equally incapable of self-government? If gambling, or drunkenness, or incontinence, or idleness, or uncleanliness, are as injurious to happiness, and as great a hindrance to improvement, as many or most of the acts prohibited by law, why (it may be asked) should not law, so far as is consistent with practicability and social convenience, endeavor to repress these also? And as a supplement to the unavoidable imperfections of law, ought not opinion at least to organize a powerful police against these vices, and visit rigidly with social penalties those who are known to practise them? There is no question here (it may be said) about restricting individuality, or impeding the trial of new and original experiments in living. The only things it

is sought to prevent are things which have been tried and condemned from the beginning of the world until now; things which
experience has shown not to be useful or suitable to any person's
individuality. There must be some length of time and amount of
experience, after which a moral or prudential truth may be regarded as established and it is merely desired to prevent generation
after generation from falling over the same precipice which has
been fatal to their predecessors.

10   I fully admit that the mischief which a person does to himself,
may seriously affect, both through their sympathies and their interests, those nearly connected with him, and in a minor degree,
society at large. When, by conduct of this sort, a person is led to
violate a distinct and assignable obligation to any other person or
persons, the case is taken out of the self-regarding class, and becomes amenable to moral disapprobation in the proper sense of
the term. If, for example, a man, through intemperance or extravagance, becomes unable to pay his debts, or, having undertaken
the moral responsibility of a family, becomes from the same cause
incapable of supporting or educating them, he is deservedly re-
probated, and might be justly punished; but it is for the breach
of duty to his family or creditors, not for the extravagance. If the
resources which ought to have been devoted to them, had been
diverted from them for the most prudent investment, the moral
culpability would have been the same. George Barnwell murdered
his uncle to get money for his mistress, but if he had done it to
set himself up in business, he would equally have been hanged.
Again, in the frequent case of a man who causes grief to his family
by addiction to bad habits, he deserves reproach for his unkindness
or ingratitude; but so he may for cultivating habits not in themselves vicious, if they are painful to those with whom he passes
his life, or who from personal ties are dependent on him for their
comfort. Whoever fails in the consideration generally due to the
interests and feelings of others, not being compelled by some more
imperative duty, or justified by allowable self-preference, is a subject of moral disapprobation for that failure, but not for the cause
of it, nor for the errors, merely personal to himself, which may
have remotely led to it. In like manner, when a person disables
himself, by conduct purely self-regarding, from the performance
of some definite duty incumbent on him to the public, he is guilty
of a social offence. No person ought to be punished simply for being
drunk; but a soldier or a policeman should be punished for being
drunk on duty. Whenever, in short, there is a definite damage, or

a definite risk of damage, either to an individual or to the public, the case is taken out of the province of liberty, and placed in that of morality or law.

11   But with regard to the merely contingent or, as it may be called, constructive injury which a person causes to society, by conduct which neither violates any specific duty to the public, nor occasions perceptible hurt to any assignable individual except himself; the inconvenience is one which society can afford to bear, for the sake of the greater good of human freedom. If grown persons are to be punished for not taking proper care of themselves, I would rather it were for their own sake, than under pretence of preventing them from impairing their capacity of rendering to society benefits which society does not pretend it has a right to exact. But I cannot consent to argue the point as if society had no means of bringing its weaker members up to its ordinary standard of rational conduct, except waiting till they do something irrational, and then punishing them, legally or morally, for it. Society has had absolute power over them during all the early portion of their existence: it has had the whole period of childhood and nonage in which to try whether it could make them capable of rational conduct in life. The existing generation is master both of the training and the entire circumstances of the generation to come; it cannot indeed make them perfectly wise and good, because it is itself so lamentably deficient in goodness and wisdom; and its best efforts are not always, in individual cases, its most successful ones; but it is perfectly well able to make the rising generation, as a whole, as good as, and a little better than, itself. If society lets any considerable number of its members grow up mere children, incapable of being acted on by rational consideration of distant motives, society has itself to blame for the consequences. Armed not only with all the powers of education, but with the ascendency which the authority of a received opinion always exercises over the minds who are least fitted to judge for themselves; and aided by the *natural* penalties which cannot be prevented from falling on those who incur the distaste or the contempt of those who know them; let not society pretend that it needs, besides all this, the power to issue commands and enforce obedience in the personal concerns of individuals, in which, on all principles of justice and policy, the decision ought to rest with those who are to abide the consequences. Nor is there anything which tends more to discredit and frustrate the better means of influencing conduct, than a resort to the worse. If there be among those whom it is attempted to coerce into prudence or

temperance, any of the material of which vigorous and independent characters are made, they will infallibly rebel against the yoke. No such person will ever feel that others have a right to control him in his concerns, such as they have to prevent him from injuring them in theirs; and it easily comes to be considered a mark of spirit and courage to fly in the face of such usurped authority, and do with ostentation the exact opposite of what it enjoins; as in the fashion of grossness which succeeded, in the time of Charles II., to the fanatical moral intolerance of the Puritans. With respect to what is said of the necessity of protecting society from the bad example set to others by the vicious or the self-indulgent; it is true that bad example may have a pernicious effect, especially the example of doing wrong to others with impunity to the wrong-doer. But we are now speaking of conduct which, while it does no wrong to others, is supposed to do great harm to the agent himself: and I do not see how those who believe this, can think otherwise than that the example, on the whole, must be more salutary than hurtful, since, if it displays the misconduct, it displays also the painful or degrading consequences which, if the conduct is justly censured, must be supposed to be in all or most cases attendant on it.

12   But the strongest of all the arguments against the interference of the public with purely personal conduct, is that when it does interfere, the odds are that it interferes wrongly, and in the wrong place. On questions of social morality, of duty to others, the opinion of the public, that is, of an overruling majority, though often wrong, is likely to be still oftener right; because on such questions they are only required to judge of their own interests; of the manner in which some mode of conduct, if allowed to be practised, would affect themselves. But the opinion of a similar majority, imposed as a law on the minority, on questions of self-regarding conduct, is quite as likely to be wrong as right; for in these cases public opinion means, at the best, some people's opinion of what is good or bad for other people; while very often it does not even mean that; the public, with the most perfect indifference, passing over the pleasure or convenience of those whose conduct they censure, and considering only their own preference. There are many who consider as an injury to themselves any conduct which they have a distaste for, and resent it as an outrage to their feelings; as a religious bigot, when charged with disregarding the religious feelings of others, has been known to retort that they disregard his feelings, by persisting in their abominable worship

or creed. But there is no parity between the feeling of a person for his own opinion, and the feeling of another who is offended at his holding it; no more than between the desire of a thief to take a purse, and the desire of the right owner to keep it. And a person's taste is as much his own peculiar concern as his opinion or his purse. It is easy for any one to imagine an ideal public, which leaves the freedom and choice of individuals in all uncertain matters undisturbed, and only requires them to abstain from modes of conduct which universal experience has condemned. But where has there been seen a public which set any such limit to its censorship ? or when does the public trouble itself about universal experience? In its interferences with personal conduct it is seldom thinking of anything but the enormity of acting or feeling differently from itself; and this standard of judgment, thinly disguised, is held up to mankind as the dictate of religion and philosophy, by nine tenths of all moralists and speculative writers. These teach that things are right because they are right; because we feel them to be so. They tell us to search in our own minds and hearts for laws of conduct binding on ourselves and on all others. What can the poor public do but apply these instructions, and make their own personal feelings of good and evil, if they are tolerably unanimous in them, obligatory on all the world?

13   The evil here pointed out is not one which exists only in theory; and it may perhaps be expected that I should specify the instances in which the public of this age and country improperly invests its own preferences with the character of moral laws. I am not writing an essay on the aberrations of existing moral feeling. That is too weighty a subject to be discussed parenthetically, and by way of illustration. Yet examples are necessary, to show that the principle I maintain is of serious and practical moment, and that I am not endeavoring to erect a barrier against imaginary evils. And it is not difficult to show, by abundant instances, that to extend the bounds of what may be called moral police, until it encroaches on the most unquestionably legitimate liberty of the individual, is one of the most universal of all human propensities.

14   As a first instance, consider the antipathies which men cherish on no better grounds than that persons whose religious opinions are different from theirs, do not practise their religious observances, especially their religious abstinences. To cite a rather trivial example, nothing in the creed or practice of Christians does more to envenom the hatred of Mahomedans against them, than the fact of their eating pork. There are few acts which Christians and

Europeans regard with more unaffected disgust, than Mussulmans regard this particular mode of satisfying hunger. It is, in the first place, an offence against their religion; but this circumstance by no means explains either the degree or the kind of their repugnance; for wine also is forbidden by their religion, and to partake of it is by all Mussulmans accounted wrong, but not disgusting. Their aversion to the flesh of the "unclean beast" is, on the contrary, of that peculiar character, resembling an instinctive antipathy which the idea of uncleanness, when once it thoroughly sinks into the feelings, seems always to excite even in those whose persons, habits are anything but scrupulously cleanly and of which the sentiment of religious impurity, so intense in the Hindoos, is a remarkable example. Suppose now that in a people, of whom the majority were Mussulmans, that majority should insist upon not permitting pork to be eaten within the limits of the country. This would be nothing new in Mahomedan countries.* Would it be a legitimate exercise of the moral authority of public opinion? and if not, why not? The practice is really revolting to such a public. They also sincerely think that it is forbidden and abhorred by the Deity. Neither could the prohibition be censured as religious persecution. It might be religious in its origin, but it would not be persecution for religion, since nobody's religion makes it a duty to eat pork. The only tenable ground of condemnation would be, that with the personal tastes and self-regarding concerns of individuals the public has no business to interfere.

15   To come somewhat nearer home: the majority of Spaniards consider it a gross impiety, offensive in the highest degree to the Supreme Being, to worship him in any other manner than the Roman Catholic; and no other public worship is lawful on Spanish soil. The people of all Southern Europe look upon a married clergy as not only irreligious, but unchaste, indecent, gross, disgusting. What do Protestants think of these perfectly sincere feelings, and of the attempt to enforce them against non-Catholics? Yet, if man-

---

*The case of the Bombay Parsees is a curious instance in point. When this industrious and enterprising tribe, the descendants of the Persian fire-worshippers, flying from their native country before the Caliphs, arrived in Western India, they were admitted to toleration by the Hindoo sovereigns, on condition of not eating beef. When those regions afterwards fell under the dominion of Mahomedan conquerors, the Parsees obtained from them a continuance of indulgence, on condition of refraining from pork. What was at first obedience to authority became a second nature, and the Parsees to this day abstain both from beef and pork. Though not required by their religion, the double abstinence has had time to grow into a custom of their tribe; and custom, in the East, is a religion.

kind are justified in interfering with each other's liberty in things which do not concern the interests of others, on what principle is it possible consistently to exclude these cases? or who can blame people for desiring to suppress what they regard as a scandal in the sight of God and man? No stronger case can be shown for prohibiting anything which is regarded as a personal immorality, than is made out for suppressing these practices in the eyes of those who regard them as impieties; and unless we are willing to adopt the logic of persecutors, and to say that we may persecute others because we are right, and that they must not persecute us because they are wrong, we must beware of admitting a principle of which we should resent as a gross injustice the application to ourselves.

16   The preceding instances may be objected to, although unreasonably, as drawn from contingencies impossible among us: opinion, in this country, not being likely to enforce abstinence from meats, or to interfere with people for worshipping, and for either marrying or not marrying, according to their creed or inclination. The next example, however, shall be taken from an interference with liberty which we have by no means passed all danger of. Wherever the Puritans have been sufficiently powerful, as in New England, and in Great Britain at the time of the Commonwealth, they have endeavored, with considerable success, to put down all public, and nearly all private, amusements: especially music, dancing, public games, or other assemblages for purposes of diversion, and the theatre. There are still in this country large bodies of persons by whose notions of morality and religion these recreations are condemned; and those persons belonging chiefly to the middle class, who are the ascendant power in the present social and political condition of the kingdom, it is by no means impossible that persons of these sentiments may at some time or other command a majority in Parliament. How will the remaining portion of the community like to have the amusements that shall be permitted to them regulated by the religious and moral sentiments of the stricter Calvinists and Methodists? Would they not, with considerable peremptoriness, desire these intrusively pious members of society to mind their own business? This is precisely what should be said to every government and every public, who have the pretension that no person shall enjoy any pleasure which they think wrong. But if the principle of the pretension be admitted, no one can reasonably object to its being acted on in the sense of the majority, or other preponderating power in the country; and all

persons must be ready to conform to the idea of a Christian commonwealth, as understood by the early settlers in New England, if a religious profession similar to theirs should ever succeed in regaining its lost ground, as religions supposed to be declining have so often been known to do.

17   To imagine another contingency, perhaps more likely to be realized than the one last mentioned. There is confessedly a strong tendency in the modern world towards a democratic constitution of society, accompanied or not by popular political institutions. It is affirmed that in the country where this tendency is most completely realized—where both society and the government are most democratic—the United States—the feeling of the majority, to whom any appearance of a more showy or costly style of living than they can hope to rival is disagreeable, operates as a tolerably effectual sumptuary law, and that in many parts of the Union it is really difficult for a person possessing a very large income, to find any mode of spending it, which will not incur popular disapprobation. Though such statements as these are doubtless much exaggerated as a representation of existing facts, the state of things they describe is not only a conceivable and possible, but a probable result of democratic feeling, combined with the notion that the public has a right to a veto on the manner in which individuals shall spend their incomes. We have only further to suppose a considerable diffusion of Socialist opinions, and it may become infamous in the eyes of the majority to possess more property than some very small amount, or any income not earned by manual labor. Opinions similar in principle to these, already prevail widely among the artisan class, and weigh oppressively on those who are amenable to the opinion chiefly of that class, namely, its own members. It is known that the bad workmen who form the majority of the operatives in many branches of industry, are decidedly of opinion that bad workmen ought to receive the same wages as good, and that no one ought to be allowed, through piecework or otherwise, to earn by superior skill or industry more than others can without it. And they employ a moral police, which occasionally becomes a physical one, to deter skillful workmen from receiving, and employers from giving, a larger remuneration for a more useful service. If the public have any jurisdiction over private concerns, I cannot see that these people are in fault, or that any individual's particular public can be blamed for asserting the same authority over his individual conduct, which the general public asserts over people in general.

18   But, without dwelling upon supposititious cases, there are, in our own day, gross usurpations upon the liberty of private life actually practised, and still greater ones threatened with some expectation of success, and opinions proposed which assert an unlimited right in the public not only to prohibit by law everything which it thinks wrong, but in order to get at what it thinks wrong, to prohibit any number of things which it admits to be innocent.

19   Under the name of preventing intemperance, the people of one English colony, and of nearly half the United States, have been interdicted by law from making any use whatever of fermented drinks, except for medical purposes: for prohibition of their sale is in fact, as it is intended to be, prohibition of their use. And though the impracticability of executing the law has caused its repeal in several of the States which had adopted it, including the one from which it derives its name, an attempt has notwithstanding been commenced, and is prosecuted with considerable zeal by many of the professed philanthropists, to agitate for a similar law in this country. The association, or "Alliance" as it terms itself, which has been formed for this purpose, has acquired some notoriety through the publicity given to a correspondence between its Secretary and one of the very few English public men who hold that a politician's opinions ought to be founded on principles. Lord Stanley's share in this correspondence is calculated to strengthen the hopes already built on him, by those who know how rare such qualities as are manifested in some of his public appearances, unhappily are among those who figure in political life. The organ of the Alliance, who would "deeply deplore the recognition of any principle which could be wrested to justify bigotry and persecution," undertakes to point out the "broad and impassable barrier" which divides such principles from those of the association. "All matters relating to thought, opinion, conscience, appear to me," he says, "to be without the sphere of legislation; all pertaining to social act, habit, relation, subject only to a discretionary power vested in the State itself, and not in the individual, to be within it." No mention is made of a third class, different from either of these, viz., acts and habits which are not social, but individual; although it is to this class, surely, that the act of drinking fermented liquors belongs. Selling fermented liquors, however, is trading, and trading is a social act. But the infringement complained of is not on the liberty of the seller, but on that of the buyer and consumer; since the State might just as well forbid him to drink wine, as purposely make it impossible for him to

obtain it. The Secretary, however, says, "I claim, as a citizen, a right to legislate whenever my social rights are invaded by the social act of another." And now for the definition of these "social rights." "If anything invades my social rights, certainly the traffic in strong drink does. It destroys my primary right of security, by constantly creating and stimulating social disorder. It invades my right of equality, by deriving a profit from the creation of a misery, I am taxed to support. It impedes my right to free moral and intellectual development, by surrounding my path with dangers, and by weakening and demoralizing society, from which I have a right to claim mutual aid and intercourse." A theory of "social rights," the like of which probably never before found its way into distinct language — being nothing short of this — that it is the absolute social right of every individual, that every other individual shall act in every respect exactly as he ought; that whosoever fails thereof in the smallest particular, violates my social right, and entitles me to demand from the legislature the removal of the grievance. So monstrous a principle is far more dangerous than any single interference with liberty; there is no violation of liberty which it would not justify; it acknowledges no right to any freedom whatever, except perhaps to that of holding opinions in secret, without ever disclosing them for the moment an opinion which I consider noxious, passes any one's lips, it invades all the "social rights" attributed to me by the Alliance. The doctrine ascribes to all mankind a vested interest in each other's moral, intellectual, and even physical perfection, to be defined by each claimant according to his own standard.

20   Another important example of illegitimate interference with the rightful liberty of the individual, not simply threatened, but long since carried into triumphant effect, is Sabbatarian legislation. Without doubt, abstinence on one day in the week, so far as the exigencies of life permit, from the usual daily occupation, though in no respect religiously binding on any except Jews, is a highly beneficial custom. And inasmuch as this custom cannot be observed without a general consent to that effect among the industrious classes, therefore, in so far as some persons by working may impose the same necessity on others, it may be allowable and right that the law should guarantee to each, the observance by others of the custom, by suspending the greater operations of industry on a particular day. But this justification, grounded on the direct interest which others have in each individual's observance of the practice, does not apply to the self-chosen occupations in which a person

may think fit to employ his leisure; nor does it hold good, in the smallest degree, for legal restrictions on amusements. It is true that the amusement of some is the day's work of others; but the pleasure, not to say the useful recreation, of many, is worth the labor of a few, provided the occupation is freely chosen, and can be freely resigned. The operatives are perfectly right in thinking that if all worked on Sunday seven days' work would have to be given for six days' wages: but so long as the great mass of employments are suspended, the small number who for the enjoyment of others must still work, obtain a proportional increase of earnings; and they are not obliged to follow those occupations, if they prefer leisure to emolument. If a further remedy is sought, it might be found in the establishment by custom of a holiday on some other day of the week for those particular classes of persons. The only ground, therefore, on which restrictions on Sunday amusements can be defended, must be that they are religiously wrong; a motive of legislation which never can be too earnestly protested against. "Deorum injuriæ Diis curæ." It remains to be proved that society or any of its officers holds a commission from on high to avenge any supposed offence to Omnipotence, which is not also a wrong to our fellow-creatures. The notion that it is one man's duty that another should be religious, was the foundation of all the religious persecutions ever perpetrated, and if admitted, would fully justify them. Though the feeling which breaks out in the repeated attempts to stop railway travelling on Sunday, in the resistance to the opening of Museums, and the like, has not the cruelty of the old persecutors the state of mind indicated by it is fundamentally the same. It is a determination not to tolerate others in doing what is permitted by their religion, because it is not permitted by the persecutor's religion. It is a belief that God not only abominates the act of the misbeliever, but will not hold us guiltless if we leave him unmolested.

21   I cannot refrain from adding to these examples of the little account commonly made of human liberty, the language of downright persecution which breaks out from the press of this country, whenever it feels called on to notice the remarkable phenomenon of Mormonism. Much might be said on the unexpected and instructive fact, that an alleged new revelation, and a religion founded on it, the product of palpable imposture, not even supported by the *prestige* of extraordinary qualities in its founder, is believed by hundreds of thousands, and has been made the foundation of a society, in the age of newspapers, railways, and the electric tele-

graph. What here concerns us is, that this religion, like other and better religions, has its martyrs; that its prophet and founder was, for his teaching, put to death by a mob; that others of its adherents lost their lives by the same lawless violence; that they were forcibly expelled, in body, from the country in which they first grew up; while, now that they have been chased into a solitary recess in the midst of a desert, many in this country openly declare that it would be right (only that it is not convenient) to send an expedition against them and compel them by force to conform to the opinions of other people. The article of the Mormonite doctrine which is the chief provocative to the antipathy which thus breaks through the ordinary restraints of religious tolerance is its sanction of polygamy; which, though permitted to Mahomedans, and Hindoos, and Chinese, seem to excite unquenchable animosity when practiced by persons who speak English, and profess to be a kind of Christians. No one has a deeper disapprobation than I have of this Mormon institution; both for other reasons, and because, far from being in any way countenanced by the principle of liberty, it is a direct infraction of that principle, being a mere riveting of the chains of one half of the community, and an emancipation of the other from reciprocity of obligation towards them. Still, it must be remembered that this relation is as much voluntary on the part of the women concerned in it, and who may be deemed the sufferers by it, as is the case with any other form of the marriage institution; and however surprising this fact may appear, it has its explanation in the common ideas and customs of the world, which teaching women to think marriage the one thing needful, make it intelligible that many a woman should prefer being one of several wives, to not being a wife at all. Other countries are not asked to recognize such unions, or release any portion of their inhabitants from their own laws on the score of Mormonite opinions. But when the dissentients have conceded to the hostile sentiments of others, far more than could justly be demanded; when they have left the countries to which their doctrines were unacceptable, and established themselves in a remote corner of the earth, which they have been the first to render habitable to human beings; it is difficult to see on what principles but those of tyranny they can be prevented from living there under what laws they please, provided they commit no aggression on other nations, and allow perfect freedom of departure to those who are dissatisfied with their ways. A recent writer, in some respects of considerable merit, proposes (to use his own words,) not a crusade, but a *civilizade*, against this polygamous community, to put an end to what seems to him a retrograde step in civilization. It also appears so to me, but I am not aware that any community has a right to force another to be civilized. So long as the sufferers by the bad law do not invoke assistance from other communities, I cannot admit that persons entirely unconnected with them ought to step in and require that a condition of things with which all who are directly interested appear to be satisfied, should be put an end to because it is a scandal to persons some thousands of miles distant, who have no part or concern in it. Let them send missionaries, if they please, to preach against it; and let them, by any fair means (of which silencing the teachers is not one,) oppose the progress of similar doctrines among their own people. If civilization has got the better of barbarism when barbarism had the world to itself, it is too much to profess to be afraid lest barbarism, after having been fairly got under, should revive and conquer civilization. A civilization that can thus succumb to its vanquished enemy must first have become so degenerate, that neither its appointed priests and teachers, nor anybody else, has the capacity, or will take the trouble, to stand up for it. If this be so, the sooner such a civilization receives notice to quit, the better. It can only go on from bad to worse, until destroyed and regenerated (like the Western Empire) by energetic barbarians.

Civil Disobedience

Henry David Thoreau

1   I heartily accept the motto, — "That government is best which governs least;" and I should like to see it acted up to more rapidly and systematically. Carried out, it finally amounts to this, which also I believe,—"That government is best which governs not at all;" and when men are prepared for it, that will be the kind of government which they will have. Government is at best but an expedient; but most governments are usually, and all governments are sometimes, inexpedient. The objections which have been brought against a standing army, and they are many and weighty, and deserve to prevail, may also at last be brought against a standing government. The standing army is only an arm of the standing government. The government itself, which is only the mode which the people have chosen to execute their will, is equally liable to be abused and perverted before the people can act through it. Witness the present Mexican war, the work of comparatively a few individuals using the standing government as their tool; for, in the outset, the people would not have consented to this measure.

2   This American government,—what is it but a tradition, though a recent one, endeavoring to transmit itself unimpaired to posterity, but each instant losing some of its integrity? It has not the vitality and force of a single living man; for a single man can bend it to his will. It is a sort of wooden gun to the people themselves. But it is not the less necessary for this; for the people must have some complicated machinery or other, and hear its din, to satisfy that idea of government which they have. Governments show thus how successfully men can be imposed on, even impose on themselves, for their own advantage. It is excellent, we must all allow. Yet this government never of itself furthered any enterprise, but by the

alacrity with which it got out of its way. *It* does not keep the country free. *It* does not settle the West. *It* does not educate. The character inherent in the American people has done all that has been accomplished; and it would have done somewhat more, if the government had not sometimes got in its way. For government is an expedient by which men would fain succeed in letting one another alone; and, as has been said, when it is most expedient, the governed are most let alone by it. Trade and commerce, if they were not made of India-rubber, would never manage to bounce over the obstacles which legislators are continually putting in their way; and, if one were to judge these men wholly by the effects of their actions and not partly by their intentions, they would deserve to be classed and punished with those mischievous persons who put obstructions on the railroads.

3   But, to speak practically and as a citizen, unlike those who call themselves no-government men, I ask for, not at once no government, but *at once* a better government. Let every man make known what kind of government would command his respect, and that will be one step toward obtaining it.

4   After all, the practical reason why, when the power is once in the hands of the people, a majority are permitted, and for a long period continue, to rule is not because they are most likely to be in the right, nor because this seems fairest to the minority, but because they are physically the strongest. But a government in which the majority rule in all cases cannot be based on justice, even as far as men understand it. Can there not be a government in which majorities do not virtually decide right and wrong, but conscience?—in which majorities decide only those questions to which the rule of expediency is applicable? Must the citizen ever for a moment, or in the least degree, resign his conscience to the legislator? Why has every man a conscience, then? I think that we should be men first, and subjects afterward. It is not desirable to cultivate a respect for the law, so much as for the right. The only obligation which I have a right to assume is to do at any time what I think right. It is truly enough said, that a corporation has no conscience; but a corporation of conscientious men is a corporation *with* a conscience. Law never made men a whit more just; and, by means of their respect for it, even the well-disposed are daily made the agents of injustice. A common and natural result of an undue respect for law is, that you may see a file of soldiers, colonel, captain, corporal, privates, powder-monkeys, and all, marching in admirable order over hill and dale to the wars, against their

wills, ay, against their common sense and consciences, which makes it very steep marching indeed, and produces a palpitation of the heart. They have no doubt that it is a damnable business in which they are concerned; they are all peaceably inclined. Now, what are they? Men at all? or small movable forts and magazines, at the service of some unscrupulous man in power? Visit the Navy-Yard, and behold a marine, such a man as an American government can make, or such as it can make a man with its black arts,—a mere shadow and reminiscence of humanity, a man laid out alive and standing, and already, as one may say, buried under arms with funeral accompaniments, though it may be,

> "Not a drum was heard, not a funeral note,
>   As his corse to the rampart we hurried;
> Not a soldier discharged his farewell shot
>   O'er the grave where our hero we buried."

5   The mass of men serve the state thus, not as men mainly, but as machines, with their bodies. They are the standing army, and the militia, jailers, constables, posse comitatus, etc. In most cases there is no free exercise whatever of the judgment or of the moral sense; but they put themselves on a level with wood and earth and stones; and wooden men can perhaps be manufactured that will serve the purpose as well. Such command no more respect than men of straw or a lump of dirt. They have the same sort of worth only as horses and dogs. Yet such as these even are commonly esteemed good citizens. Others — as most legislators, politicians, lawyers, ministers, and office-holders—serve the state chiefly with their heads; and, as they rarely make any moral distinctions, they are as likely to serve the Devil, without *intending* it, as God. A very few, as heroes, patriots, martyrs, reformers in the great sense, and *men*, serve the state with their consciences also, and so necessarily resist it for the most part: and they are commonly treated as enemies by it. A wise man will only be useful as a man, and will not submit to be "clay," and "stop a hole to keep the wind away," but leave that office to his dust at least:

> "I am too high-born to be propertied,
>   To be a secondary at control,
>   Or useful serving-man and instrument
> To any sovereign state throughout the world."

6   He who gives himself entirely to his fellowmen appears to them useless and selfish; but he who gives himself partially to them is pronounced a benefactor and philanthropist.

7   How does it become a man to behave toward this American government today? I answer, that he cannot without disgrace be associated with it. I cannot for an instant recognize that political organization as *my* government which is the *slave's* government also.

8   All men recognize the right of revolution; that is, the right to refuse allegiance to, and to resist, the government, when its tyranny or its inefficiency are great and unendurable. But almost all say that such is not the case now. But such was the case, they think, in the Revolution of '75. If one were to tell me that this was a bad government because it taxed certain foreign commodities brought to its ports, it is most probable that I should not make an ado about it, for I can do without them. All machines have their friction; and possibly this does enough good to counterbalance the evil. At any rate, it is a great evil to make a stir about it. But when the friction comes to have its machine, and oppression and robbery are organized, I say, let us not have such a machine any longer. In other words, when a sixth of the population of a nation which has undertaken to be the refuge of liberty are slaves, and a whole country is unjustly overrun and conquered by a foreign army, and subjected to military law, I think that it is not too soon for honest men to rebel and revolutionize. What makes this duty the more urgent is the fact that the country so overrun is not our own, but ours is the invading army.

9   Paley, a common authority with many on moral questions, in his chapter on the "Duty of Submission to Civil Government," resolves all civil obligation into expediency; and he proceeds to say, "that so long as the interest of the whole society requires it, that is, so long as the established government cannot be resisted or changed without public inconveniency, it is the will of God that the established government be obeyed, and no longer. . . . This principle being admitted, the justice of every particular case of resistance is reduced to a computation of the quantity of the danger and grievance on the one side, and of the probability and expense of redressing it on the other." Of this, he says, every man shall judge for himself. But Paley appears never to have contemplated those cases to which the rule of expediency does not apply, in which a people, as well as an individual, must do justice, cost what it may. If I have unjustly wrested a plank from a drowning man, I must restore it to him though I drown myself. This, according to Paley, would be inconvenient. But he that would save his life, in such a case, shall lose it. This people must cease to hold

slaves, and to make war on Mexico, though it cost them their existence as a people.

10   In their practice, nations agree with Paley; but does any one
think that Massachusetts does exactly what is right at the present
crisis?

> "A drab of state, a cloth-o'-silver slut,
> To have her train borne up, and her soul trail in the dirt."

Practically speaking, the opponents to a reform in Massachusetts
are not a hundred thousand politicians at the South, but a hundred
thousand merchants and farmers here, who are more interested in
commerce and agriculture than they are in humanity, and are not
prepared to do justice to the slave and to Mexico, *cost what it may*.
I quarrel not with far-off foes, but with those who, near at home,
co-operate with, and do the bidding of, those far away, and without
whom the latter would be harmless. We are accustomed to say, that
the mass of men are unprepared; but improvement is slow, because
the few are not materially wiser or better than the many. It is not
so important that many should be as good as you, as that there
be some absolute goodness somewhere; for that will leaven the
whole lump. There are thousands who are *in opinion* opposed to
slavery and to the war, who yet in effect do nothing to put an end
to them; who, esteeming themselves children of Washington and
Franklin, sit down with their hands in their pockets, and say that
they know not what to do, and do nothing; who even postpone the
question of freedom to the question of free-trade, and quietly read
the prices-current along with the latest advices from Mexico, after
dinner, and, it may be, fall asleep over them both. What is the
price-current of an honest man and patriot to-day? They hesitate,
and they regret, and sometimes they petition; but they do nothing
in earnest and with effect. They will wait, well disposed, for others
to remedy the evil, that they may no longer have it to regret. At
most, they give only a cheap vote, and a feeble countenance and
God-speed, to the right, as it goes by them. There are nine hundred
and ninety-nine patrons of virtue to one virtuous man. But it is
easier to deal with the real possessor of a thing than with the temporary guardian of it.

11   All voting is a sort of gaming, like checkers or backgammon, with
a slight moral tinge to it, a playing with right and wrong, with
moral questions; and betting naturally accompanies it. The character of the voters is not staked. I cast my vote, perchance, as I
think right; but I am not vitally concerned that that right should
prevail. I am willing to leave it to the majority. Its obligation,

therefore, never exceeds that of expediency. Even voting *for the right* is *doing* nothing for it. It is only expressing to men feebly your desire that it should prevail. A wise man will not leave the right to the mercy of chance nor wish it to prevail through the power of the majority. There is but little virtue in the action of masses of men. When the majority shall at length vote for the abolition of slavery, it will be because they are indifferent to slavery, or because there is but little slavery left to be abolished by their vote. *They* will then be the only slaves. Only *his* vote can hasten the abolition of slavery who asserts his own freedom by his vote.

12   I hear of a convention to be held at Baltimore, or elsewhere, for the selection of a candidate for the Presidency, made up chiefly of editors, and men who are politicians by profession; but I think, what is it to any independent, intelligent, and respectable man what decision they may come to? Shall we not have the advantage of his wisdom and honesty, nevertheless? Can we not count upon some independent votes? Are there not many individuals in the country who do not attend conventions? But no: I find that the respectable man, so called, has immediately drifted from his position, and despairs of his country, when his country has more reason to despair of him. He forthwith adopts one of the candidates thus selected as the only *available* one, thus proving that he is himself *available* for any purposes of the demagogue. His vote is of no more worth than that of any unprincipled foreigner or hireling native, who may have been bought. O for a man who is a *man*, and, as my neighbor says, has a bone in his back which you cannot pass your hand through! Our statistics are at fault: the population has been returned too large. How many *men* are there to a square thousand miles in this country? Hardly one. Does not America offer any inducement for men to settle here? The American has dwindled into an Odd Fellow,—one who may be known by the development of his organ of gregariousness, and a manifest lack of intellect and cheerful self-reliance; whose first and chief concern, on coming into the world, is to see that the Almshouses are in good repair; and, before yet he has lawfully donned the virile garb, to collect a fund for the support of the widows and orphans that may be; who, in short, ventures to live only by the aid of the Mutual Insurance company, which has promised to bury him decently.

13   It is not a man's duty, as a matter of course, to devote himself to the eradication of any, even the most enormous wrong; he may still properly have other concerns to engage him; but it is his duty,

at least, to wash his hands of it, and, if he gives it no thought longer, not to give it practically his support. If I devote myself to other pursuits and contemplations, I must first see, at least, that I do not pursue them sitting upon another man's shoulders. I must get off him first, that he may pursue his contemplations too. See what gross inconsistency is tolerated. I have heard some of my townsmen say, "I should like to have them order me out to help put down an insurrection of the slaves, or to march to Mexico;— see if I would go;" and yet these very men have each, directly by their allegiance, and so indirectly, at least, by their money, furnished a substitute. The soldier is applauded who refuses to serve in an unjust war by those who do not refuse to sustain the unjust government which makes the war; is applauded by those whose own act and authority he disregards and sets at naught; as if the state were penitent to that degree that it hired one to scourge it while it sinned, but not to that degree that it left off sinning for a moment. Thus, under the name of Order and Civil Government, we are all made at last to pay homage to and support our own meanness. After the first blush of sin comes its indifference; and from immoral it becomes, as it were, *un*moral, and not quite unnecessary to that life which we have made.

14   The broadest and most prevalent error requires the most disinterested virtue to sustain it. The slight reproach to which the virtue of patriotism is commonly liable, the noble are most likely to incur. Those who, while they disapprove of the character and measures of a government, yield to it their allegiance and support are undoubtedly its most conscientious supporters, and so frequently the most serious obstacles to reform. Some are petitioning the state to dissolve the Union, to disregard the requisitions of the President. Why do they not dissolve it themselves,—the union between themselves and the state,—and refuse to pay their quota into its treasury? Do not they stand in the same relation to the state that the state does to the Union? And have not the same reasons prevented the state from resisting the Union which have prevented them from resisting the state?

15   How can a man be satisfied to entertain an opinion merely, and enjoy *it*? Is there any enjoyment in it, if his opinion is that he is aggrieved? If you are cheated out of a single dollar by your neighbor, you do not rest satisfied with knowing that you are cheated, or with saying that you are cheated, or even with petitioning him to pay you your due; but you take effectual steps at once to obtain the full amount, and see that you are never cheated again. Action

from principle, the perception and the performance of right, changes things and relations; it is essentially revolutionary, and does not consist wholly with anything which was. It not only divides states and churches, it divides families; ay, it divides the *individual*, separating the diabolical in him from the divine.

16   Unjust laws exist: shall we be content to obey them, or shall we endeavor to amend them, and obey them until we have succeeded, or shall we transgress them at once? Men generally, under such a government as this, think that they ought to wait until they have persuaded the majority to alter them. They think that, if they should resist, the remedy would be worse than the evil. But it is the fault of the government itself that the remedy *is* worse than the evil. *It* makes it worse. Why is it not more apt to anticipate and provide for reform? Why does it not cherish its wise minority? Why does it cry and resist before it is hurt? Why does it not encourage its citizens to be on the alert to point out its faults, and *do* better than it would have them? Why does it always crucify Christ, and excommunicate Copernicus and Luther, and pronounce Washington and Franklin rebels?

17   One would think, that a deliberate and practical denial of its authority was the only offense never contemplated by government; else, why has it not assigned its definite, its suitable and proportionate penalty? If a man who has no property refuses but once to earn nine shillings for the state, he is put in prison for a period unlimited by any law that I know, and determined only by the discretion of those who placed him there; but if he should steal ninety times nine shillings from the state, he is soon permitted to go at large again.

18   If the injustice is part of the necessary friction of the machine of government, let it go, let it go: perchance it will wear smooth,— certainly the machine will wear out. If the injustice has a spring, or a pulley, or a rope, or a crank, exclusively for itself, then perhaps you may consider whether the remedy will not be worse than the evil; but if it is of such a nature that it requires you to be the agent of injustice to another, then, I say, break the law. Let your life be a counter friction to stop the machine. What I have to do is to see, at any rate, that I do not lend myself to the wrong which I condemn.

19   As for adopting the ways which the state has provided for remedying the evil, I know not of such ways. They take too much time, and a man's life will be gone. I have other affairs to attend to. I came into this world, not chiefly to make this a good place

to live in, but to live in it, be it good or bad. A man has not everything to do, but something; and because he cannot do *everything*, it is not necessary that he should do *something* wrong. It is not my business to be petitioning the Governor or the Legislature any more than it is theirs to petition me; and if they should not hear my petition, what should I do then? But in this case the state has provided no way: its very Constitution is the evil. This may seem to be harsh and stubborn and unconciliatory; but it is to treat with the utmost kindness and consideration the only spirit that can appreciate or deserves it. So is all change for the better, like birth and death, which convulse the body.

20   I do not hesitate to say, that those who call themselves Abolitionists should at once effectually withdraw their support, both in person and property, from the government of Massachusetts, and not wait till they constitute a majority of one, before they suffer the right to prevail through them. I think that it is enough if they have God on their side, without waiting for that other one. Moreover, any man more right than his neighbors constitutes a majority of one already.

21   I meet this American government, or its representative, the state government, directly, and face to face, once a year—no more—in the person of its tax-gatherer; this is the only mode in which a man si⁺uated as I am necessarily meets it; and it then says distinctly, Recognize me; and the simplest, the most effectual, and, in the present posture of affairs, the indispensablest mode of treating with it on this head, of expressing your little satisfaction with and love for it is to deny it then. My civil neighbor, the tax-gatherer, is the very man I have to deal with,—for it is, after all, with men and not with parchment that I quarrel,—and he has voluntarily chosen to be an agent of the government. How shall he ever know well what he is and does as an officer of the government, or as a man, until he is obliged to consider whether he shall treat me, his neighbor, for whom he has respect, as a neighbor and well-disposed man, or as a maniac and disturber of the peace, and see if he can get over this obstruction to his neighborliness without a ruder and more impetuous thought or speech corresponding with his action. I know this well, that if one thousand, if one hundred, if ten men whom I could name,—if ten *honest* men only,—ay, if *one* HONEST man, in this State of Massachusetts, *ceasing to hold slaves*, were actually to withdraw from this copartnership, and be locked up in the county jail therefore, it would be the abolition of slavery in America. For it matters not how small the beginning may

seem to be: what is once well done is done forever. But we love better to talk about it: that we say is our mission. Reform keeps many scores of newspapers in its service, but not one man. If my esteemed neighbor, the State's ambassador, who will devote his days to the settlement of the question of human rights in the Council Chamber, instead of being threatened with the prisons of Carolina, were to sit down with the prisoner of Massachusetts, that State which is so anxious to foist the sin of slavery upon her sister, —though at present she can discover only an act of inhospitality to be the ground of a quarrel with her,—the Legislature would not wholly waive the subject the following winter.

22   Under a government which imprisons any unjustly, the true place for a just man is also a prison. The proper place today, the only place which Massachusetts has provided for her freer and less desponding spirits, is in her prisons, to be put out and locked out of the State by her own act, as they have already put themselves out by their principles. It is there that the fugitive slave, and the Mexican prisoner on parole, and the Indian come to plead the wrongs of his race should find them; on that separate, but more free and honorable ground, where the State places those who are not *with* her, but *against* her,—the only house in a slave State in which a free man can abide with honor. If any think that their influence would be lost there, and their voices no longer afflict the ear of the State, that they would not be as an enemy within its walls, they do not know by how much truth is stronger than error, nor how much more eloquently and effectively he can combat injustice who has experienced a little in his own person. Cast your whole vote, not a strip of paper merely, but your whole influence. A minority is powerless while it conforms to the majority; it is not even a minority then; but it is irresistible when it clogs by its whole weight. If the alternative is to keep all just men in prison, or give up war and slavery, the State will not hesitate which to choose. If a thousand men were not to pay their tax-bills this year, that would not be a violent and bloody measure, as it would be to pay them, and enable the State to commit violence and shed innocent blood. This is, in fact, the definition of a peaceable revolution, if any such is possible. If the tax-gatherer, or any other public officer, asks me, as one has done, "But what shall I do?" my answer is, "If you really wish to do anything, resign your office." When the subject has refused allegiance, and the officer has resigned his office, then the revolution is accomplished. But even suppose blood should flow. Is there not a sort of blood shed when the conscience

is wounded? Through this wound a man's real manhood and immortality flow out, and he bleeds to an everlasting death. I see this blood flowing now.

23   I have contemplated the imprisonment of the offender, rather than the seizure of his goods,—though both will serve the same purpose,—because they who assert the purest right, and consequently are most dangerous to a corrupt State, commonly have not spent much time in accumulating property. To such the State renders comparatively small service, and a slight tax is wont to appear exorbitant, particularly if they are obliged to earn it by special labor with their hands. If there were one who lived wholly without the use of money, the State itself would hesitate to demand it of him. But the rich man—not to make any invidious comparison—is always sold to the institution which makes him rich. Absolutely speaking, the more money, the less virtue; for money comes between a man and his objects, and obtains them for him; and it was certainly no great virtue to obtain it. It puts to rest many questions which he would otherwise be taxed to answer; while the only new question which it puts is the hard but superfluous one, how to spend it. Thus his moral ground is taken from under his feet. The opportunities of living are diminished in proportion as what are called the "means" are increased. The best thing a man can do for his culture when he is rich is to endeavor to carry out those schemes which he entertained when he was poor. Christ answered the Herodians according to their condition. "Show me the tribute-money," said he;—and one took a penny out of his pocket;—if you use money which has the image of Cæsar on it, and which he has made current and valuable, that is, *if you are men of the State*, and gladly enjoy the advantages of Cæsar's government, then pay him back some of his own when he demands it. "Render therefore to Cæsar that which is Cæsar's, and to God those things which are God's,"—leaving them no wiser than before as to which was which; for they did not wish to know.

24   When I converse with the freest of my neighbors, I perceive that, whatever they may say about the magnitude and seriousness of the question, and their regard for the public tranquillity, the long and the short of the matter is, that they cannot spare the protection of the existing government, and they dread the consequences to their property and families of disobedience to it. For my own part, I should not like to think that I rely on the protection of the State. But, if I deny the authority of the State when it presents its tax-bill, it will soon take and waste all my property, and so harass me and my children without end. This is hard. This

makes it impossible for a man to live honestly, and at the same
time comfortably, in outward respects. It will not be worth the
while to accumulate property; that would be sure to go again. You
must hire or squat somewhere, and raise but a small crop, and eat
that soon. You must live within yourself, and depend upon yourself always tucked up and ready for a start, and not have many
affairs. A man may grow rich in Turkey even, if he will be in all
respects a good subject of the Turkish government. Confucius
said: "If a state is governed by the principles of reason, poverty
and misery are subjects of shame; if a state is not governed by the
principles of reason, riches and honors are the subjects of shame."
No: until I want the protection of Massachusetts to be extended
to me in some distant Southern port, where my liberty is endan-
gered, or until I am bent solely on building up an estate at home
by peaceful enterprise, I can afford to refuse allegiance to Massachusetts, and her right to my property and life. It costs me less
in every sense to incur the penalty of disobedience to the State
than it would to obey. I should feel as if I were worth less in that
case.

25   Some years ago, the State met me in behalf of the Church, and
commanded me to pay a certain sum toward the support of a
clergyman whose preaching my father attended, but never I myself.
"Pay," it said, "or be locked up in the jail." I declined to pay.
But, unfortunately, another man saw fit to pay it. I did not see
why the schoolmaster should be taxed to support the priest, and
not the priest the schoolmaster; for I was not the State's schoolmaster, but I supported myself by voluntary subscription. I did
not see why the lyceum should not present its tax-bill, and have the
State to back its demand, as well as the Church. However, at the
request of the selectmen, I condescended to make some such statement as this in writing:—"Know all men by these presents, that
I, Henry Thoreau, do not wish to be regarded as a member of any
incorporated society which I have not joined." This I gave to the
town clerk; and he has it. The State, having thus learned that I
did not wish to be regarded as a member of that church, has never
made a like demand on me since; though it said that it must adhere
to its original presumption that time. If I had known how to name
them, I should then have signed off in detail from all the societies
which I never signed on to; but I did not know where to find a
complete list.

26   I have paid no poll-tax for six years. I was put into a jail once
on this account, for one night; and, as I stood considering the walls
of solid stone, two or three feet thick, the door of wood and iron,

a foot thick, and the iron grating which strained the light, I could not help being struck with the foolishness of that institution which treated me as if I were mere flesh and blood and bones, to be locked up. I wondered that it should have concluded at length that this was the best use it could put me to, and had never thought to avail itself of my services in some way. I saw that, if there was a wall of stone between me and my townsmen, there was a still more difficult one to climb or break through before they could get to be as free as I was. I did not for a moment feel confined, and the walls seemed a great waste of stone and mortar. I felt as if I alone of all my townsmen had paid my tax. They plainly did not know how to treat me, but behaved like persons who are underbred. In every threat and in every compliment there was a blunder; for they thought that my chief desire was to stand the other side of that stone wall. I could not but smile to see how industriously they locked the door on my meditations, which followed them out again without let or hindrance, and *they* were really all that was dangerous. As they could not reach me, they had resolved to punish my body; just as boys, if they cannot come at some person against whom they have a spite, will abuse his dog. I saw that the State was half-witted, that it was timid as a lone woman with her silver spoons, and that it did not know its friends from its foes, and I lost all my remaining respect for it, and pitied it.

27 Thus the State never intentionally confronts a man's sense, intellectual or moral, but only his body, his senses. It is not armed with superior wit or honesty, but with superior physical strength. I was not born to be forced. I will breathe after my own fashion. Let us see who is the strongest. What force has a multitude? They only can force me who obey a higher law than I. They force me to become like themselves. I do not hear of *men* being *forced* to live this way or that by masses of men. What sort of life were that to live? When I meet a government which says to me, "Your money or your life," why should I be in haste to give it my money? It may be in a great strait, and not know what to do: I cannot help that. It must help itself; do as I do. It is not worth the while to snivel about it. I am not responsible for the successful working of the machinery of society. I am not the son of the engineer. I perceive that, when an acorn and a chestnut fall side by side, the one does not remain inert to make way for the other, but both obey their own laws, and spring and grow and flourish as best they can, till one, perchance, over-shadows and destroys the other. If a plant cannot live according to its nature, it dies; and so a man.

28   The night in prison was novel and interesting enough. The prisoners in their shirt-sleeves were enjoying a chat and the evening air in the doorway, when I entered. But the jailer said, "Come, boys, it is time to lock up;" and so they dispersed, and I heard the sound of their steps returning into the hollow apartments. My room-mate was introduced to me by the jailer as "a first-rate fellow and a clever man." When the door was locked, he showed me where to hang my hat, and how he managed matters there. The rooms were whitewashed once a month; and this one, at least, was the whitest, most simply furnished, and probably the neatest apartment in the town. He naturally wanted to know where I came from, and what brought me there; and, when I had told him, I asked him in my turn how he came there, presuming him to be an honest man, of course; and, as the world goes, I believe he was. "Why," said he, "they accuse me of burning a barn; but I never did it." As near as I could discover, he had probably gone to bed in a barn when drunk, and smoked his pipe there; and so a barn was burnt. He had the reputation of being a clever man, had been there some three months waiting for his trial to come on, and would have to wait as much longer; but he was quite domesticated and contented, since he got his board for nothing, and thought that he was well treated.

29   He occupied one window, and I the other; and I saw that if one stayed there long, his principal business would be to look out the window. I had soon read all the tracts that were left there, and examined where former prisoners had broken out, and where a grate had been sawed off, and heard the history of the various occupants of that room; for I found that even here there was a history and a gossip which never circulated beyond the walls of the jail. Probably this is the only house in the town where verses are composed, which are afterward printed in a circular form, but not published. I was shown quite a long list of verses which were composed by some young men who had been detected in an attempt to escape, who avenged themselves by singing them.

30   I pumped my fellow-prisoner as dry as I could, for fear I should never see him again; but at length he showed me which was my bed, and left me to blow out the lamp.

31   It was like traveling into a far country, such as I had never expected to behold, to lie there for one night. It seemed to me that I never had heard the town-clock strike before, nor the evening sounds of the village; for we slept with the windows open, which were inside the grating. It was to see my native village in the light

of the Middle Ages, and our Concord was turned into a Rhine stream, and visions of knights and castles passed before me. They were the voices of old burghers that I heard in the streets. I was an involuntary spectator and auditor of whatever was done and said in the kitchen of the adjacent village-inn,—a wholly new and rare experience to me. It was a closer view of my native town. I was fairly inside of it. I never had seen its institutions before. This is one of its peculiar institutions; for it is a shire town. I began to comprehend what its inhabitants were about.

32   In the morning, our breakfasts were put through the hole in the door, in small oblong-square tin pans, made to fit, and holding a pint of chocolate, with brown bread, and an iron spoon. When they called for the vessels again, I was green enough to return what bread I had left; but my comrade seized it, and said that I should lay that up for lunch or dinner. Soon after he was let out to work at haying in a neighboring field, whither he went every day, and would not be back till noon; so he bade me good-day, saying that he doubted if he should see me again.

33   When I came out of prison,—for some one interfered, and paid that tax,—I did not perceive that great changes had taken place on the common, such as he observed who went in a youth and emerged a tottering and gray-headed man; and yet a change had to my eyes come over the scene,—the town, and State, and country,—greater than any that mere time could effect. I saw yet more distinctly the State in which I lived. I saw to what extent the people among whom I lived could be trusted as good neighbors and friends; that their friendship was for summer weather only; that they did not greatly propose to do right; that they were a distinct race from me by their prejudices and superstitions, as the Chinamen and Malays are; that in their sacrifices to humanity they ran no risks, not even to their property; that after all they were not so noble but they treated the thief as he had treated them, and hoped, by a certain outward observance and a few prayers, and by walking in a particular straight though useless path from time to time, to save their souls. This may be to judge my neighbors harshly; for I believe that many of them are not aware that they have such an institution as the jail in their village.

34   It was formerly the custom in our village, when a poor debtor came out of jail, for his acquaintances to salute him, looking through their fingers, which were crossed to represent the grating of a jail window, "How do ye do?" My neighbors did not thus salute me, but first looked at me, and then at one another, as if I

had returned from a long journey. I was put into jail as I was going to the shoemaker's to get a shoe which was mended. When I was let out the next morning, I proceeded to finish my errand, and, having put on my mended shoe, joined a huckleberry party, who were impatient to put themselves under my conduct; and in half an hour,—for the horse was soon tackled,—was in the midst of a huckleberry field, on one of our highest hills, two miles off, and then the State was nowhere to be seen.

35   This is the whole history of "My Prisons."

36   I have never declined paying the highway tax, because I am as desirous of being a good neighbor as I am of being a bad subject; and as for supporting schools, I am doing my part to educate my fellow-countrymen now. It is for no particular item in the tax-bill that I refuse to pay it. I simply wish to refuse allegiance to the State, to withdraw and stand aloof from it effectually. I do not care to trace the course of my dollar, if I could, till it buys a man or a musket to shoot one with,—the dollar is innocent,—but I am concerned to trace the effects of my allegiance. In fact, I quietly declare war with the State, after my fashion, though I will still make what use and get what advantage of her I can, as is usual in such cases.

37   If others pay the tax which is demanded of me, from a sympathy with the State, they do but what they have already done in their own case, or rather they abet injustice to a greater extent than the State requires. If they pay the tax from a mistaken interest in the individual taxed, to save his property, or prevent his going to jail, it is because they have not considered wisely how far they let their private feelings interfere with the public good.

38   This, then, is my position at present. But one cannot be too much on his guard in such a case, lest his action be biased by obstinacy or an undue regard for the opinions of men. Let him see that he does only what belongs to himself and to the hour.

39   I think sometimes, Why, this people mean well, they are only ignorant; they would do better if they knew how: why give your neighbors this pain to treat you as they are not inclined to? But I think again, This is no reason why I should do as they do, or permit others to suffer much greater pain of a different kind. Again, I sometimes say to myself, When many millions of men, without heat, without ill will, without personal feeling of any kind, demand of you a few shillings only, without the possibility, such is their constitution, of retracting or altering their present demand, and without the possibility, on your side, of appeal to any other mil-

lions, why expose yourself to this overwhelming brute force? You do not resist cold and hunger, the winds and the waves, thus obstinately; you quietly submit to a thousand similar necessities. You do not put your head into the fire. But just in proportion as I regard this as not wholly a brute force, but partly a human force, and consider that I have relations to those millions as to so many millions of men, and not of mere brute or inanimate things, I see that appeal is possible, first and instantaneously, from them to the Maker of them, and, secondly, from them to themselves. But if I put my head deliberately into the fire, there is no appeal to fire or to the Maker of fire, and I have only myself to blame. If I could convince myself that I have any right to be satisfied with men as they are, and to treat them accordingly, and not according, in some respects, to my requisitions and expectations of what they and I ought to be, then, like a good Mussulman and fatalist, I should endeavor to be satisfied with things as they are, and say it is the will of God. And, above all, there is this difference between resisting this and a purely brute or natural force, that I can resist this with some effect; but I cannot expect, like Orpheus, to change the nature of the rocks and trees and beasts.

40   I do not wish to quarrel with any man or nation. I do not wish to split hairs, to make fine distinctions, or set myself up as better than my neighbors. I seek rather, I may say, even an excuse for conforming to the laws of the land. I am but too ready to conform to them. Indeed, I have reason to suspect myself on this head; and each year, as the tax-gatherer comes round, I find myself disposed to review the acts and position of the general and State governments, and the spirit of the people, to discover a pretext for conformity.

> "We must affect our country as our parents,
>   And if at any time we alienate
>   Our love or industry from doing it honor,
>   We must respect effects and teach the soul
>   Matter of conscience and religion,
>   And not desire of rule or benefit."

I believe that the State will soon be able to take all my work of this sort out of my hands, and then I shall be no better a patriot than my fellow-countrymen. Seen from a lower point of view, the Constitution, with all its faults, is very good; the law and the courts are very respectable; even this State and this American government are, in many respects, very admirable, and rare things, to be thankful for, such as a great many have described them; but seen from a point of view a little higher, they are what I have described them; seen from a higher still, and the highest, who shall say what they are, or that they are worth looking at or thinking of at all?

41   However, the government does not concern me much, and I shall bestow the fewest possible thoughts on it. It is not many moments that I live under a government, even in this world. If a man is thought-free, fancy-free, imagination-free, that which *is not* never for a long time appearing *to be* to him, unwise rulers or reformers cannot fatally interrupt him.

42   I know that most men think differently from myself; but those whose lives are by profession devoted to the study of these or kindred subjects content me as little as any. Statesmen and legislators, standing so completely within the institution, never distinctly and nakedly behold it. They speak of moving society, but have no resting-place without it. They may be men of a certain experience and discrimination, and have no doubt invented ingenious and even useful systems, for which we sincerely thank them; but all their wit and usefulness lie within certain not very wide limits. They are wont to forget that the world is not governed by policy and expediency. Webster never goes behind government, and so cannot speak with authority about it. His words are wisdom to those legislators who contemplate no essential reform in the existing government; but for thinkers, and those who legislate for all time, he never once glances at the subject. I know of those whose serene and wise speculations on this theme would soon reveal the limits of his mind's range and hospitality. Yet, compared with the cheap professions of most reformers, and the still cheaper wisdom and eloquence of politicians in general, his are almost the only sensible and valuable words, and we thank Heaven for him. Comparatively, he is always strong, original, and, above all, practical. Still, his quality is not wisdom, but prudence. The lawyer's truth is not Truth, but consistency or a consistent expediency. Truth is always in harmony with herself, and is not concerned chiefly to reveal the justice that may consist with wrong-doing. He well deserves to be called, as he has been called, the Defender of the Constitution. There are really no blows to be given by him but defensive ones. He is not a leader, but a follower. His leaders are the men of '87. "I have never made an effort," he says, "and never propose to make an effort; I have never countenanced an effort, and never mean to countenance an effort, to disturb the arrangement as originally made, by which the various States came

into the Union." Still thinking of the sanction which the Constitution gives to slavery, he says, "Because it was a part of the original compact,—let it stand." Notwithstanding his special acuteness and ability, he is unable to take a fact out of its merely political relations, and behold it as it lies absolutely to be disposed of by the intellect,—what, for instance, it behooves a man to do here in America to-day with regard to slavery,—but ventures, or is driven, to make some such desperate answer as the following, while professing to speak absolutely, and as a private man,—from which what new and singular code of social duties might be inferred? "The manner," says he, "in which the governments of those States where slavery exists are to regulate it is for their own consideration, under their responsibility to their constituents, to the general laws of propriety, humanity, and justice, and to God. Associations formed elsewhere, springing from a feeling of humanity, or any other cause, have nothing whatever to do with it. They have never received any encouragement from me, and they never will."

43   They who know of no purer sources of truth, who have traced up its stream no higher, stand, and wisely stand, by the Bible and the Constitution, and drink at it there with reverence and humility; but they who behold where it comes trickling into this lake or that pool, gird up their loins once more, and continue their pilgrimage toward its fountain-head.

44   No man with a genius for legislation has appeared in America. They are rare in the history of the world. There are orators, politicians, and eloquent men, by the thousand; but the speaker has not yet opened his mouth to speak who is capable of settling the much-vexed questions of the day. We love eloquence for its own sake, and not for any truth which it may utter, or any heroism it may inspire. Our legislators have not yet learned the comparative value of free-trade and of freedom, of union, and of rectitude, to a nation. They have no genius or talent for comparatively humble questions of taxation and finance, commerce and manufactures and agriculture. If we were left solely to the wordy wit of legislators in Congress for our guidance, uncorrected by the seasonable experience and the effectual complaints of the people, America would not long retain her rank among the nations. For eighteen hundred years, though perchance I have no right to say it, the New Testament has been written; yet where is the legislator who has wisdom and practical talent enough to avail himself of the light which it sheds on the science of legislation?

45   The authority of government, even such as I am willing to submit to,—for I will cheerfully obey those who know and can do better than I, and in many things even those who neither know nor can do so well,—is still an impure one: to be strictly just, it must have the sanction and consent of the governed. It can have no pure right over my person and property but what I concede to it. The progress from an absolute to a limited monarchy, from a limited monarchy to a democracy, is a progress toward a true respect for the individual. Even the Chinese philosopher was wise enough to regard the individual as the basis of the empire. Is a democracy, such as we know it, the last improvement possible in government? Is it not possible to take a step further towards recognizing and organizing the rights of man? There will never be a really free and enlightened State until the State comes to recognize the individual as a higher and independent power, from which all its own power and authority are derived, and treats him accordingly. I please myself with imagining a State at last which can afford to be just to all men, and to treat the individual with respect as a neighbor; which even would not think it inconsistent with its own repose if a few were to live aloof from it, not meddling with it, nor embraced by it, who fulfilled all the duties of neighbors and fellow-men. A State which bore this kind of fruit, and suffered it to drop off as fast as it ripened, would prepare the way for a still more perfect and glorious State, which also I have imagined, but not yet anywhere seen.

Inviting Communists to Speak at Colleges

William F. Buckley Jr.

1   Last spring, Dr. John Meng addressed a letter to his faculty. Dr. Meng is the president of Hunter College, a political scientist by training, and a man well known for his Liberal views. "Ladies and gentlemen," he wrote, and I quote the letter almost in its entirety, "a properly chartered student organization . . . complying with all the requirements established by the Faculty Council and by the Office of the Dean of Students . . . has organized a series of . . . forums under the general title 'Out of the Mainstream.' The first two of these forums, scheduled for April 11 and May 2, are to be addressed by George Lincoln Rockwell, self-styled Commander of the American Nazi Party, and by Gus Hall, General Secretary of the Communist Party, U.S.A. . . . Student sentiment on the . . . campus with regard to the propriety of these invitations is sharply divided . . . Students on both sides of the controversy agree in expressing detestation for the doctrines professed by the . . . two invited speakers. What the students are arguing about is whether they have properly assumed the responsibility which is theirs as a result of the freedom accorded them by the College. . . . Those of us who remember the Second World War, the horrors of Nazism, and the cruelties of Communism on the march, tend to forget that these memories are not a part of the mental equipment of most of our present student body. Their knowledge of those events is largely knowledge transmitted by an older generation or through the medium of historical accounts. It is not surprising that many of them should evince some intellectual interest in listening to a living, avowed Nazi or to an openly-dedicated Communist speaking in the American idiom.

From the *National Review* (Oct. 22, 1963), 150 East 35th Street, New York. Reprinted by permission of the *National Review* and the author.

2   "This situation affords the teaching staff of the College an
opportunity to manifest true understanding of the intellectual
curiosity of some of our students and at the same time to drive
home to these students with more than ordinary effectiveness the
lessons so many of us learned through harsh experience about the
meaning of democracy and the individual responsibilities which
it entails.

3   "Certainly none of us welcomes the presence on our campus of
these disciples of discord. Neither does any one of us wish to foster
the spread of their iniquitous teachings. . . . I am completely confident that neither the staff nor the students of Hunter College will
permit the foul mouthings of a pipsqueak Hitler, or the delusive
dialectic of a Khrushchev in knee-pants to persuade them to
abandon their intellectual integrity. To accord these undistin-
guished visitors anything more demonstrative than a shudder of
polite disgust would be to attribute to their presence a totally
fictitious importance.

4   "Those of you," Dr. Meng concluded, "who prefer love to hate,
beauty to bestiality, and freedom to bondage may join with others
of us among the staff and students of the College in attending the
Passover Assembly at Park Avenue . . . at the time [the Fuehrer
and the Commissar are] scheduled to speak in the Bronx."

5   Dr. Meng thus expressed himself, movingly, on what he understands to be the moral question involved in inviting a Nazi or a
Communist to speak on a college campus: to do so, he is saying,
is to put curiosity above other values, communicating a kind of
callousness, a sense of aloofness from the suffering caused, and
still being caused, by those who practice their ideologies on whole
peoples all over the world. But moving though his words are, they
seem not to be at the center of Dr. Meng's analysis which is, as
it should be in any deliberation of this nature, intellectual and
analytical, rather than emotional. What Dr. Meng is saying to his
faculty is this: Those who issued these invitations are undergraduates. They do not know what Nazism was, and do not, apparently,
know what Communism is. Therefore they deem it necessary to
their intellectual experience to hear out a Nazi, and a Communist,
in—as he puts it—the American idiom. But Dr. Meng, by declining to examine more closely the unarticulated premises of this
summary, yielded that point which I most earnestly cherish, and
wish to stress, even beyond the moral or, if you wish, the human
point.

WHO BENEFITS?

6   Dr. Meng says in his remarks governing the forthcoming appearances of both the Nazi and the Communist speakers—he never distinguishes between the two — he says that the students of Hunter have not experienced Communism; more specifically, that they have not heard a defense of Communism in the American idiom, delivered by a Communist. Conceivably, Dr. Meng himself, and many members of his faculty, have never heard a live Communist defend Communism, or a live Nazi defend Nazism; but, he implies, it is not *necessary* that they should have this experience in order to permit them to know what they need to know as educated and responsible members of the academic and civil communities. He did not say to the faculty: "Those of you who have not heard a Communist should make it a point to attend this lecture, to fill out an otherwise uncompleted educational experience." He speaks on the assumption that the faculty know quite well enough what is the Communist position, and how it sounds articulated in the American idiom; that, by implication, the ends of education are not served by listening to a Communist who comes on campus to speak; but rather—but rather what?

7   What *is* served? other than extrinsic points?—An affirmation of the students' administrative right to invite whomsoever they please to address them? But Dr. Meng does not challenge that right—assuming it to be a right, any more than the authorities of Yale University: it was never in question. What then? What does one come to know, that one did not know before, on listening to an American Communist speak?

NO ENLIGHTENMENT

8   Nothing, presumably, that one did not know before, if one is ready to participate in a political union, concerning either Marxist analysis or Communist rhetoric. It is inconceivable, Dr. Meng would presumably say, that a thirty-minute address by an official of the Communist Party would add to an understanding of the theory or nature or strategy of the Communist Party. Every official of the Communist Party ruthlessly observes the discipline of his calling; and over four decades, when has it ever been reported that a Communist official, addressing a college gathering or any other non-Communist gathering, said something unexpected? When last did an official of the Party speaking to a college audience let himself improvise, speak ad libitum, vouchsafing us, for even one in-

stant, a sunburst, illuminating the dark mysteries of the Communist pathology? Communists do, sometimes, speak their minds; but never to bourgeois gatherings: here they are on duty, fighting men on the march; they come to recapitulate their dogmas, to press their drive to co-opt the moral slogans of the West, and to practice the science of confusion. Not that they succeed in confusing—they seek rather self-legitimization. They do not confuse the proletariat, for heaven's sake, in whose name their own slogans are forged; they are hardly likely to confuse an audience of college students: they are not likely, in Dr. Meng's phrase, to "persuade [the students] to abandon their intellectual integrity."

9   Might they, then, these Communist speakers, contribute as much factual, or even human knowledge about the current Communist program, about Communist apologetics, as a single copy of the *Worker?* Less, by far, one would think; considering that the average issue of the *Worker*, which takes no more than thirty minutes to read, covers a wider range of issues, giving the Communist view of the day on everything from Cuba to Ross Barnett to the New York Giants, and does so, moreover, without that encumbering self-consciousness which is the greatest barrier to human communication: though the difference in the version one gets from Gus Hall at Yale and Gus Hall in the *Worker* is even there not great enough in and of itself to justify a professional political curiosity about the disparity between the two renditions. And if it were, that curiosity is easily gratified by reading the *Worker*, where Mr. Hall's speeches to college audiences are often printed, in full.

10   Is this enough of an argument, one might ask? That an individual's views are well known, and that it is known that he adheres to these rigidly? No, that argument is not sufficient. If it alone were relevant it might be used by the protectionists among you to shield the Political Union from, say, a typical spokesman for the Democratic or the Republican parties, on the grounds that their lines of argument are at any given moment predictable, and that therefore the chances of hearing something new, something fresh, are if not as much against you as in the case of the Communist, they are nearly enough against you to permit you to argue analogically against their appearance.

MODERN MYTH

11   The argument broadens here in many directions, and one needs to draw a breath deeply, for to go from here, to there, we must tread on highly delicate ground, step right over one of the most

highly cherished dogmas of the modern age, namely, the notion that all ideas are created equal, that it is the responsibility of academic freedom to guard the gates of epistemological relativism. Even so, the reason why a Democratic bore might be acceptable while a Communist bore would not is not emotional, but intellectual. Fiercely though the archetypal Democrat or Republican will resist the opportunity to respond to the challenge of public debate as a human being, rather than as an automaton, there is in his heart and mind calcified though they may have become out of long and unthinking and unquestioning service to his party, there is at the root a disposition to think of himself as a member of our community, possessed of a point of view which is held by the community at large to be, within the widest limits of toleration, reasonable. Some views are unreasonable and tolerable. Some views are unreasonable and intolerable, especially insofar as they are systemic rather than merely personal. The Democrat and the Republican will regularly exaggerate in behalf of their causes; sometimes they will consciously lie, they will feign concern, where none is felt; they will decry the manners and morals of the opposition, knowing well that their own manners and morals are indistinguishable: but they remain, flesh and blood and heart, a part of America; they are as they are because American politics is as American politics is, and until we reform it, that is how they will continue to be, the men whom our institutions have nurtured.

DIALOGUE IMPOSSIBLE

12   The Communist has of course renounced our institutions, which is perhaps all right, but he has done something very much more; he has renounced the bond—whatever it is: but fragile though it is, it is there, make no mistake about it—that holds together Republicans and Democrats, socialists and Manchesterians, syndicalists and elitists, pacifists and warmongers, civil libertarians and McCarthyites, Townsendites and Coughlinites, Southerners, Westerners, Easterners, Northerners: the Communist has renounced the bond explicitly and intentionally — renunciation in the first degree—and for the duration of that renunciation he cannot speak to us, and we cannot speak to him, because however deep we reach, we cannot find a common vocabulary; we can no more collaborate with him to further the common understanding than Anne Frank could have collaborated with Goebbels in a dialogue on race relations. Until that trance is broken, formal communication is impossible—for he speaks to us in a language whose utter unrelation

to reality rules out any possibility of meaningful discourse. There is no idiom available to us for simultaneous usage. Certainly the American idiom will not do. We all abuse the instruments of discourse, but we seek, under the massive roccoco superstructure of point and counterpoint, to say things to each other that come truly out of our minds and our hearts, because we feel that in deeply significant ways, we are related by that highly elastic, but not infinitely elastic, bond, that binds us to each other.

13   Such a man, then, whose explicit message we know beforehand, which message he must deliver undeviatingly, cannot communicate to us orally anything of *political* interest, the subject with which the Political Union properly interests itself. He is a fit object of curiosity for students of certain other subjects than politics. A Communist might with good reason be called upon to address serious students of sociology, seeking some accidental insight into the social causes that might have led a man to ideological mania; or to serious students of psychology who seek to examine the reflexes of a man who, for the sake of his Truth, will utter and defend every necessary untruth, every necessary depravity. The court room at Tel Aviv was crowded with professors of the specialized social sciences: but they were not men who would have invited Adolf Eichmann to their college to defend the regime of Adolf Hitler.

14   The Communists are of concern to non-specialists, I am trying to say, *primarily as human beings* suffering from the most exotic and the most mortal illness of our times, that mania of ideology, which in one of its excrescences in our time, while you were living, blithely stoked the ovens of Germany with Jewish flesh, which without the quiver a normal man feels on running over a dog, committed millions to death by starvation in the very bread-basket of Soviet Russia; which, driven by ideological lust, this very day commits dozens of millions of Chinese to death in pursuit of a lunatic delusion in China: the servants of these ideologies are dislodged from the human situation and yet—

BEYOND THE POLITICAL

15   And yet they are human beings themselves, for no one has the power formally to renounce his membership in the human race. And it is over their plight as human beings that we must, it strikes me, pause; for that is the problem supremely that you face, above all others; certainly above the political problem, it being conceded you are immune to seductive passes at your intellectual and moral

integrity, and that the words, the wooden words, are words you knew before.

16   That problem is human. What will you do when Gus Hall, the human being, comes here to defend the cause of what you know ahead of time to be the cause of organized inhumanity? Will you show that "shudder of polite disgust"? Is this a new social skill we need to cultivate, in our time?—a part of the social equipment endowed upon us in virtue of our great good fortune as recipients of a Hunter or Yale education? Did *your* son learn at his college how to give off a shudder of polite disgust?

17   —Or will you applaud him when he is introduced? Yes, there will be applause—in recognition of his courage in facing a hostile audience. But the applause will be confused, will it not: because you know very well that objective courage is not necessarily admirable. The man who threw acid in the face of Victor Riesel in the middle of Times Square was courageous, as was Khrushchev when he ordered the tanks to run over your courageous counterparts in Budapest. Is it not likely that among those of you who applaud there will be those who are in fact applauding their own courage in applauding a real live apologist for human atrocity? But the applause is likely to be of that special metallic quality, no matter how frenetic it sounds, which issues uniquely out of that ambiguity that comes out of your unpossessed souls. Some of you may feel the obligation to externalize your knowledge that *you* know he is here to defend the indefensible. You may jeer him, as he has been jeered by those who wrestle for their livelihood with their hands, who especially despise him because he claims to speak for them; some of you may treat him with that terrible coldness that is the sign of the intellectual foreknowledge that you cannot, at your level of attainment, take seriously the man who speaks and works for a kingdom which it is the very purpose of your education to know to despise. Why then bring him here, if no purpose can be served, and if it can only result that you will humiliate yourselves, and him? Because you are *willing* to humiliate yourselves in order to humiliate him?

18   Fight him, fight the tyrants everywhere; but do not ask them to your quarters, merely to spit upon them: and do not ask them to your quarters if you cannot spit upon them: to do the one is to ambush a human being as one might a rabid dog; to do the other is to ambush oneself, to force oneself—in disregard of those who have *died* trying to make the point—to force oneself to break faith with humanity.

Learning vs. Invention

Samuel Johnson

—*Tibi res antiquæ laudis & artis*   VIRG. [*Georg.* II. 174.]
Aggredior, sanctos ausus recludere fontes.
For thee my tuneful accents will I raise,
And treat of arts disclos'd in ancient days;
Once more unlock for thee the sacred spring.   DRYDEN.

1   The direction of *Aristotle* to those that study politicks, is, first to examine and understand what has been written by the ancients upon government; then to cast their eyes round upon the world, and consider by what causes the prosperity of communities is visibly influenced, and why some are worse, and others better administered.

2   The same method must be pursued by him who hopes to become eminent in any other part of knowledge. The first task is to search books, the next to contemplate nature. He must first possess himself of the intellectual treasures which the diligence of former ages has accumulated, and then endeavour to encrease them by his own collections.

3   The mental disease of the present generation, is impatience of study, contempt of the great masters of ancient wisdom, and a disposition to rely wholly upon unassisted genius and natural sagacity. The wits of these happy days have discovered a way to fame, which the dull caution of our laborious ancestors durst never attempt; they cut the knots of sophistry which it was formerly the business of years to untie, solve difficulties by sudden irradiations of intelligence, and comprehend long processes of argument by immediate intuition.

4   Men who have flattered themselves into this opinion of their own abilities, look down on all who waste their lives over books,

From *The Rambler.*

as a race of inferior beings condemned by nature to perpetual pupillage, and fruitlessly endeavouring to remedy their barrenness by incessant cultivation, or succour their feebleness by subsidiary strength. They presume that none would be more industrious than they, if they were not more sensible of deficiencies, and readily conclude, that he who places no confidence in his own powers, owes his modesty only to his weakness.

5   It is however certain that no estimate is more in danger of erroneous calculations than those by which a man computes the force of his own genius. It generally happens at our entrance into the world, that by the natural attraction of similitude, we associate with men like ourselves young, sprightly, and ignorant, and rate our accomplishments by comparison with theirs; when we have once obtained an acknowledged superiority over our acquaintances, imagination and desire easily extend it over the rest of mankind, and if no accident forces us into new emulations, we grow old, and die in admiration of ourselves.

6   Vanity, thus confirmed in her dominion, readily listens to the voice of idleness, and soothes the slumber of life with continual dreams of excellence and greatness. A man elated by confidence in his natural vigour of fancy and sagacity of conjecture, soon concludes that he already possesses whatever toil and enquiry can confer. He then listens with eagerness to the wild objections which folly has raised against the common means of improvement; talks of the dark chaos of indigested knowledge; describes the mischievous effects of heterogeneous sciences fermenting in the mind; relates the blunders of lettered ignorance; expatiates on the heroick merit of those who deviate from prescription, or shake off authority; and gives vent to the inflations of his heart by declaring that he owes nothing to pedants and universities.

7   All these pretensions, however confident, are very often vain. The laurels which superficial acuteness gains in triumphs over ignorance unsupported by vivacity, are observed by *Locke* to be lost whenever real learning and rational diligence appear against her; the sallies of gaiety are soon repressed by calm confidence, and the artifices of subtilty are readily detected by those who having carefully studied the question, are not easily confounded or surprised.

8   But though the contemner of books had neither been deceived by others nor himself, and was really born with a genius surpassing the ordinary abilities of mankind; yet surely such gifts of prov-

idence may be more properly urged as incitements to labour, than encouragements to negligence. He that neglects the culture of ground, naturally fertile, is more shamefully culpable than he whose field would scarcely recompense his husbandry.

9   Cicero remarks, that not to know what has been transacted in former times is to continue always a child. If no use is made of the labours of past ages, the world must remain always in the infancy of knowledge. The discoveries of every man must terminate in his own advantage, and the studies of every age be employed on questions which the past generation had discussed and determined. We may with as little reproach borrow science as manufactures from our ancestors; and it is as rational to live in caves till our own hands have erected a palace, as to reject all knowledge of architecture, which our understandings will not supply.

10   To the strongest and quickest mind it is far easier to learn than to invent. The principles of arithmetick and geometry may be comprehended by a close attention in a few days; yet who can flatter himself that the study of a long life would have enabled him to discover them, when he sees them yet unknown to so many nations, whom he cannot suppose less liberally endowed with natural reason, than the *Grecians* or *Egyptians?*

11   Every science was thus far advanced towards perfection, by the emulous diligence of contemporary students, and the gradual discoveries of one age improving on another. Sometimes unexpected flashes of instruction were struck out by the fortuitous collision of happy incidents, or an involuntary concurrence of ideas, in which the philosopher to whom they happened had no other merit than that of knowing their value, and transmitting unclouded to posterity that light which had been kindled by causes out of his power. The happiness of these casual illuminations no man can promise to himself, because no endeavours can procure them; and therefore, whatever be our abilities or application, we must submit to learn from others what perhaps would have lain hid for ever from human penetration, had not some remote enquiry brought it to view; as treasures are thrown up by the ploughman and the digger in the rude exercise of their common occupations.

12   The man whose genius qualifies him for great undertakings, must at least be content to learn from books the present state of human knowledge; that he may not ascribe to himself the invention of arts generally known; weary his attention with experiments of which the event has been long registered; and waste, in attempts

which have already succeeded or miscarried, that time which might have been spent with usefulness and honour upon new undertakings.

13   But though the study of books is necessary, it is not sufficient to constitute literary eminence. He that wishes to be counted among the benefactors of posterity, must add by his own toil to the acquisitions of his ancestors, and secure his memory from neglect by some valuable improvement. This can only be effected by looking out upon the wastes of the intellectual world, and extending the power of learning over regions yet undisciplined and barbarous; or by surveying more exactly her antient dominions, and driving ignorance from the fortresses and retreats where she skulks undetected and undisturbed. Every science has its difficulties which yet call for solution before we attempt new systems of knowledge; as every country has its forests and marshes, which it would be wise to cultivate and drain, before distant colonies are projected as a necessary discharge of the exuberance of inhabitants.

14   No man ever yet became great by imitation. Whatever hopes for the veneration of mankind must have invention in the design or the execution; either the effect must itself be new, or the means by which it is produced. Either truths hitherto unknown must be discovered, or those which are already known enforced by stronger evidence, facilitated by clearer method, or ellucidated by brighter illustrations.

15   Fame cannot spread wide or endure long that is not rooted in nature, and manured by art. That which hopes to resist the blast of malignity, and stand firm against the attacks of time, must contain in itself some original principle of growth. The reputation which arises from the detail or transposition of borrowed sentiments, may spread for a while, like ivy on the rind of antiquity, but will be torn away by accident or contempt, and suffered to rot unheeded on the ground.

The American Scholar

Ralph Waldo Emerson

AN ORATION DELIVERED BEFORE THE PHI BETA KAPPA SOCIETY,
AT CAMBRIDGE, AUGUST 31, 1837

Mr. President and Gentlemen:

1 I greet you on the recommencement of our literary year. Our anniversary is one of hope, and, perhaps, not enough of labor. We do not meet for games of strength or skill, for the recitation of histories, tragedies, and odes, like the ancient Greeks; for parliaments of love and poesy, like the Troubadours; nor for the advancement of science, like our contemporaries in the British and European capitals. Thus far, our holiday has been simply a friendly sign of the survival of the love of letters amongst a people too busy to give to letters any more. As such it is precious as the sign of an indestructible instinct. Perhaps the time is already come when it ought to be, and will be, something else; when the sluggard intellect of this continent will look from under its iron lids and fill the postponed expectation of the world with something better than the exertions of mechanical skill. Our day of dependence, our long apprenticeship to the learning of other lands, draws to a close. The millions that around us are rushing into life, cannot always be fed on the sere remains of foreign harvests. Events, actions arise, that must be sung, that will sing themselves. Who can doubt that poetry will revive and lead in a new age, as the star in the constellation Harp, which now flames in our zenith, astronomers announce, shall one day be the pole-star for a thousand years?

2 In this hope I accept the topic which not only usage but the nature of our association seem to prescribe to this day, — the AMERICAN SCHOLAR. Year by year we come up hither to read one

485

more chapter of his biography. Let us inquire what light new days and events have thrown on his character and his hopes.

3   It is one of those fables which out of an unknown antiquity convey an unlooked-for wisdom, that the gods, in the beginning divided Man into men, that he might be more helpful to himself just as the hand was divided into fingers, the better to answer its end.

4   The old fable covers a doctrine ever new and sublime; that there is One Man, — present to all particular men only partially, or through one faculty; and that you must take the whole society to find the whole man. Man is not a farmer, or a professor, or an engineer, but he is all. Man is priest, and scholar, and statesman and producer, and soldier. In the *divided* or social state these functions are parcelled out to individuals, each of whom aims to do his stint of the joint work, whilst each other performs his. The fable implies that the individual, to possess himself, must sometime return from his own labor to embrace all the other laborers. But unfortunately, this original unit, this fountain of power, has been so distributed to multitudes, has been so minutely subdivided and peddled out, that it is spilled into drops, and cannot be gathered. The state of society is one in which the members have suffered amputation from the trunk, and strut about so many walking monsters,—a good finger, a neck, a stomach, an elbow, but never a man.

5   Man is thus metamorphosed into a thing, into many things. The planter, who is Man sent out into the field to gather food, is seldom cheered by any idea of the true dignity of his ministry. He sees his bushel and his cart, and nothing beyond, and sinks into the farmer, instead of Man on the farm. The tradesman scarcely even gives an ideal worth to his work, but is ridden by the routine of his craft, and the soul is subject to dollars. The priest becomes a form; the attorney a statute-book; the mechanic a machine; the sailor a rope of the ship.

6   In this distribution of functions the scholar is the delegated intellect. In the right state he is *Man Thinking*. In the degenerate state, when the victim of society, he tends to become a mere thinker, or still worse, the parrot of other men's thinking.

7   In this view of him, as Man Thinking, the theory of his office is contained. Him Nature solicits with all her placid, all her monitory pictures; him the past instructs; him the future invites. Is not indeed every man a student, and do not all things exist for the student's behoof? And finally, is not the true scholar the only true

master? But the old oracle said, "All things have two handles: beware of the wrong one." In life, too often, the scholar errs with mankind and forfeits his privilege. Let us see him in his school, and consider him in reference to the main influences he receives.

8   I. The first in time and the first in importance of the influences upon the mind is that of nature. Every day, the sun; and, after sunset, Night and her stars. Ever the winds blow; ever the grass grows. Every day, men and women, conversing—beholding and beholden. The scholar is he of all men whom this spectacle most engages. He must settle its value in his mind. What is nature to him? There is never a beginning, there is never an end, to the inexplicable continuity of this web of God, but always circular power returning into itself. Therein it resembles his own spirit, whose beginning, whose ending, he never can find,—so entire, so boundless. Far too as her splendors shine, system on system shooting like rays, upward, downward, without centre, without circumference,—in the mass and in the particle, Nature hastens to render account of herself to the mind. Classification begins. To the young mind every thing is individual, stands by itself. By and by, it finds how to join two things and see in them one nature; then three, then three thousand; and so, tyrannized over by its own unifying instinct, it goes on tying things together, diminishing anomalies, discovering roots running under ground whereby contrary and remote things cohere and flower out from one stem. It presently learns that since the dawn of history there has been a constant accumulation and classifying of facts. But what is classification but the perceiving that these objects are not chaotic and are not foreign, but have a law which is also a law of the human mind? The astronomer discovers that geometry, a pure abstraction of the human mind, is the measure of planetary motion. The chemist finds proportions and intelligible method throughout matter; and science is nothing but the finding of analogy, identity in the most remote parts. The ambitious soul sits down before each refractory fact; one after another reduces all strange constitutions, all new powers, to their class and their law, and goes on forever to animate the last fibre of organization, the outskirts of nature, by insight.

9   Thus to him, to this schoolboy under the bending dome of day is suggested that he and it proceed from one root; one is leaf and one is flower; relation, sympathy, stirring in every vein. And what is that root? Is not that the soul of his soul? A thought too bold, a dream too wild. Yet when this spiritual light shall have revealed the law of more earthly natures,—when he has learned to worship

the soul, and to see that the natural philosophy that now is only the first gropings of its gigantic hand, he shall look forward to an ever expanding knowledge as to a becoming creator. He shall see that nature is the opposite of the soul, answering to it part for part. One is seal and one is print. Its beauty is the beauty of his own mind. Its laws are the laws of his own mind. Nature then becomes to him the measure of his attainments. So much of nature as he is ignorant of, so much of his own mind does he not yet possess. And in fine, the ancient precept, "Know thyself," and the modern precept, "Study nature," become at last one maxim.

10   II. The next great influence into the spirit of the scholar is the mind of the Past,—in whatever form, whether of literature, of art, of institutions, that mind is inscribed. Books are the best type of the influence of the past, and perhaps we shall get at the truth,— learn the amount of this influence more conveniently,—by considering their value alone.

11   The theory of books is noble. The scholar of the first age received into him the world around; brooded thereon; gave it the new arrangement of his own mind, and uttered it again. It came into him life; it went out from him truth. It came to him short-lived actions; it went out from him immortal thoughts. It came to him business; it went from him poetry. It was dead fact; now, it is quick thought. It can stand, and it can go. It now endures, it now flies, it now inspires. Precisely in proportion to the depth of mind from which it issued, so high does it soar, so long does it sing.

12   Or, I might say, it depends on how far the process had gone, of transmuting life into truth. In proportion to the completeness of the distillation, so will the purity and imperishableness of the product be. But none is quite perfect. As no air-pump can by any means make a perfect vacuum, so neither can any artist entirely exclude the conventional, the local, the perishable from his book, or write a book of pure thought, that shall be as efficient, in all respects, to a remote posterity, as to contemporaries, or rather to the second age. Each age, it is found, must write its own books, or rather, each generation for the next succeeding. The books of an older period will not fit this.

13   Yet hence arises a grave mischief. The sacredness which attaches to the act of creation, the act of thought, is transferred to the record. The poet chanting was felt to be a divine man: henceforth the chant is divine also. The writer was a just and wise spirit: henceforward it is settled the book is perfect; as love of the hero

corrupts into worship of his statue. Instantly the book becomes noxious: the guide is a tyrant. The sluggish and perverted mind of the multitude, slow to open to the incursions of Reason, having once so opened, having once received this book, stands upon it, and makes an outcry if it is disparaged. Colleges are built on it. Books are written on it by thinkers, not by Man Thinking; by men of talent, that is, who start wrong, who set out from accepted dogmas, not from their own sight of principles. Meek young men grow up in libraries, believing it their duty to accept the views which Cicero, which Locke, which Bacon, have given; forgetful that Cicero, Locke, and Bacon were only young men in libraries when they wrote these books.

14   Hence, instead of Man Thinking, we have the bookworm. Hence the book-learned class, who value books, as such; not as related to nature and the human constitution, but as making a sort of Third Estate with the world and the soul. Hence the restorer of readings, the emendators, the bibliomaniacs of all degrees.

15   Books are the best of things, well used; abused, among the worst. What is the right use? What is the one end which all means go to effect? They are for nothing but to inspire. I had better never see a book than to be warped by its attraction clean out of my own orbit, and made a satellite instead of a system. The only thing in the world, of value, is the active soul. This every man is entitled to; this every man contains within him, although in almost all men obstructed and as yet unborn. The soul active sees absolute truth and utters truth, or creates. In this action it is genius not the privilege of here and there a favorite, but the sound estate of every man. In its essence it is progressive. The book, the college, the school of art, the institution of any kind, stop with some past utterance of genius. This is good, say they,—let us hold by this. They pin me down. They look backward and not forward. But genius looks forward: the eyes of man are set in his forehead, not in his hind-head: man hopes: genius creates. Whatever talent may be, if the man create not, the pure efflux of the Deity is not his;—cinders and smoke there may be, but not yet flame. There are creative manners, there are creative actions, and creative words, manners, actions, words, that is, indicative of no custom or authority, but springing spontaneous from the mind's own sense of good and fair.

16   On the other part, instead of being its own seer, let it receive from another mind its truth, though it were in torrents of light, without periods of solitude, inquest, and self-recovery, and a fatal

disservice is done. Genius is always sufficiently the enemy of genius by over-influence. The literature of every nation bears me witness. The English dramatic poets have Shakspearized now for two hundred years.

17   Undoubtedly there is a right way of reading, so it be sternly subordinated. Man Thinking must not be subdued by his instruments. Books are for the scholar's idle times. When he can read God directly, the hour is too precious to be wasted in other men's transcripts of their readings. But when the intervals of darkness come, as come they must,—when the sun is hid and the stars withdraw their shining,—we repair to the lamps which were kindled by their ray, to guide our steps to the East again, where the dawn is. We hear, that we may speak. The Arabian proverb says, "A fig tree, looking on a fig tree, becometh fruitful."

18   It is remarkable, the character of the pleasure we derive from the best books. They impress us with the conviction that one nature wrote and the same reads. We read the verses of one of the great English poets, of Chaucer, of Marvell, of Dryden, with the most modern joy,—with a pleasure, I mean, which is in great part caused by the abstraction of all *time* from their verses. There is some awe mixed with the joy of our surprise, when this poet, who lived in some past world, two or three hundred years ago, says that which lies close to my own soul, that which I also had well-nigh thought and said. But for the evidence thence afforded to the philosophical doctrine of the identity of all minds, we should suppose some preestablished harmony, some foresight of souls that were to be, and some preparation of stores for their future wants like the fact observed in insects, who lay up food before death for the young grub they shall never see.

19   I would not be hurried by any love of system, by any exaggeration of instincts, to underrate the Book. We all know, that as the human body can be nourished on any food, though it were boiled grass and the broth of shoes, so the human mind can be fed by any knowledge. And great and heroic men have existed who had almost no other information than by the printed page. I only would say that it needs a strong head to bear that diet. One must be an inventor to read well. As the proverb says, "He that would bring home the wealth of the Indies, must carry out the wealth of the Indies." There is then creative reading as well as creative writing. When the mind is braced by labor and invention, the page of whatever book we read becomes luminous with manifold allusion. Every sentence is doubly significant, and the sense of our

author is as broad as the world. We then see, what is always true, that as the seer's hour of vision is short and rare among heavy days and months, so is its record, perchance, the least part of his volume. The discerning will read, in his Plato or Shakspeare, only that least part,—only the authentic utterances of the oracle;—all the rest he rejects, were it never so many times Plato's and Shakspeare's.

20   Of course there is a portion of reading quite indispensable to a wise man. History and exact science he must learn by laborious reading. Colleges, in like manner, have their indispensable office,— to teach elements. But they can only highly serve us when they aim not to drill, but to create; when they gather from far every ray of various genius to their hospitable halls, and by the concentrated fires, set the hearts of their youth on flame. Thought and knowledge are natures in which apparatus and pretension avail nothing. Gowns and pecuniary foundations, though of towns of gold, can never countervail the least sentence or syllable of wit. Forget this, and our American colleges will recede in their public importance, whilst they grow richer every year.

21   III. There goes in the world a notion that the scholar should be a recluse, a valetudinarian,—as unfit for any handiwork or public labor as a penknife for an axe. The so-called "practical men" sneer at speculative men, as if, because they speculate or *see*, they could do nothing. I have heard it said that the clergy,—who are always, more universally than any other class, the scholars of their day,—are addressed as women; that the rough, spontaneous conversation of men they do not hear, but only a mincing and diluted speech. They are often virtually disfranchised; and indeed there are advocates for their celibacy. As far as this is true of the studious classes, it is not just and wise. Action is with the scholar subordinate, but it is essential. Without it he is not yet man. Without it thought can never ripen into truth. Whilst the world hangs before the eye as a cloud of beauty, we cannot even see its beauty. Inaction is cowardice, but there can be no scholar without the heroic mind. The preamble of thought, the transition through which it passes from the unconscious to the conscious, is action. Only so much do I know, as I have lived. Instantly we know whose words are loaded with life, and whose not.

22   The world,—this shadow of the soul, or *other me*,—lies wide around. Its attractions are the keys which unlock my thoughts and make me acquainted with myself. I run eagerly into this resounding tumult. I grasp the hands of those next me, and take

my place in the ring to suffer and to work, taught by an instinct that so shall the dumb abyss be vocal with speech. I pierce its order; I dissipate its fear; I dispose of it within the circuit of my expanding life. So much only of life as I know by experience, so much of the wilderness have I vanquished and planted, or so far have I extended by being, my dominion. I do not see how any man can afford, for the sake of his nerves and his nap, to spare any action in which he can partake. It is pearls and rubies to his discourse. Drudgery, calamity, exasperation, want, are instructors in eloquence and wisdom. The true scholar grudges every opportunity of action past by, as a loss of power. It is the raw material out of which the intellect moulds her splendid products. A strange process too, this by which experience is converted into thought as a mulberry leaf is converted into satin. The manufacture goes forward at all hours.

23   The actions and events of our childhood and youth are now matters of calmest observation. They lie like fair pictures in the air. Not so with our recent actions,—with the business which we now have in hand. On this we are quite unable to speculate. Our affections as yet circulate through it. We no more feel or know it than we feel the feet, or the hand, or the brain of our body. The new deed is yet a part of life,—remains for a time immersed in our unconscious life. In some contemplative hour it detaches itself from the life like a ripe fruit, to become a thought of the mind. Instantly it is raised, transfigured; the corruptible has put on incorruption. Henceforth it is an object of beauty, however base its origin and neighborhood. Observe too the impossibility of antedating this act. In its grub state, it cannot fly, it cannot shine, it is a dull grub. But suddenly, without observation, the selfsame thing unfurls beautiful wings, and is an angel of wisdom. So is there no fact, no event, in our private history, which shall not sooner or later, lose its adhesive, inert form, and astonish us by soaring from our body into the empyrean. Cradle and infancy, school and playground, the fear of boys, and dogs, and ferules, the love of little maids and berries, and many another fact that once filled the whole sky, are gone already; friend and relative, profession and party, town and country, nation and world, must also soar and sing.

24   Of course, he who has put forth his total strength in fit actions has the richest return of wisdom. I will not shut myself out of this globe of action, and transplant an oak into a flowerpot, there to hunger and pine; nor trust the revenue of some single faculty, and

exhaust one vein of thought, much like those Savoyards, who, getting their livelihood by carving shepherds, shepherdesses, and smoking Dutchmen, for all Europe, went out one day to the mountain to find stock, and discovered that they had whittled up the last of their pine trees. Authors we have, in numbers, who have written out their vein, and who, moved by a commendable prudence, sail for Greece or Palestine, follow the trapper into the prairie, or ramble round Algiers, to replenish their merchantable stock.

25   If it were only for a vocabulary, the scholar would be covetous of action. Life is our dictionary. Years are well spent in country labors; in town; in the insight into trades and manufactures; in frank intercourse with many men and women; in science; in art; to the one end of mastering in all their facts a language by which to illustrate and embody our perceptions. I learn immediately from any speaker how much he has already lived, through the poverty or the splendor of his speech. Life lies behind us as the quarry from whence we get tiles and copestones for the masonry of to-day. This is the way to learn grammar. Colleges and books only copy the language which the field and the work-yard made.

26   But the final value of action, like that of books, and better than books, is that it is a resource. That great principle of Undulation in nature, that shows itself in the inspiring and expiring of the breath; in desire and satiety; in the ebb and flow of the sea; in day and night; in heat and cold; and, as yet more deeply ingrained in every atom and every fluid, is known to us under the name of Polarity,—these "fits of easy transmission and reflection," as Newton called them, are the law of nature because they are the law of spirit.

27   The mind now thinks, now acts, and each fit reproduces the other. When the artist has exhausted his materials, when the fancy no longer paints, when thoughts are no longer apprehended and books are a weariness,—he has always the resource *to live.* Character is higher than intellect. Thinking is the function. Living is the functionary. The stream retreats to its source. A great soul will be strong to live, as well as strong to think. Does he lack organ or medium to impart his truths? He can still fall back on this elemental force of living them. This is a total act. Thinking is a partial act. Let the grandeur of justice shine in his affairs. Let the beauty of affection cheer his lowly roof. Those "far from fame," who dwell and act with him, will feel the force of his constitution in the doings and passages of the day better

than it can be measured by any public and designed display. Time shall teach him that the scholar loses no hour which the man lives. Herein he unfolds the sacred germ of his instinct screened from influence. What is lost in seemliness is gained in strength. Not out of those on whom systems of education have exhausted their culture, comes the helpful giant to destroy the old or to build the new, but out of unhandselled savage nature out of terrible Druids and Berserkers come at last Alfred and Shakspeare.

28   I hear therefore with joy whatever is beginning to be said of the dignity and necessity of labor to every citizen. There is virtue yet in the hoe and the spade, for learned as well as for unlearned hands. And labor is everywhere welcome; always we are invited to work; only be this limitation observed, that a man shall not for the sake of wider activity sacrifice any opinion to the popular judgments and modes of action.

29   I have now spoken of the education of the scholar by nature, by books, and by action. It remains to say somewhat of his duties.

30   They are such as become Man Thinking. They may all be comprised in self-trust. The office of the scholar is to cheer, to raise, and to guide men by showing them facts amidst appearances. He plies the slow, unhonored, and unpaid task of observation. Flamsteed and Herschel, in their glazed observatories, may catalogue the stars with the praise of all men, and the results being splendid and useful, honor is sure. But he, in his private observatory, cataloguing obscure and nebulous stars of the human mind, which as yet no man has thought of as such,—watching days and months sometimes for a few facts; correcting still his old records;—must relinquish display and immediate fame. In the long period of his preparation he must betray often an ignorance and shiftlessness in popular arts, incurring the disdain of the able who shoulder him aside. Long he must stammer in his speech; often forego the living for the dead. Worse yet, he must accept— how often!—poverty and solitude. For the ease and pleasure of treading the old road, accepting the fashions, the education, the religion of society, he takes the cross of making his own, and, of course, the self-accusation, the faint heart, the frequent uncertainty and loss of time, which are the nettles and tangling vines in the way of the self-relying and self-directed; and the state of virtual hostility in which he seems to stand to society, and especially to educated society. For all this loss and scorn, what offset?

He is to find consolation in exercising the highest functions of human nature. He is one who raises himself from private considerations and breathes and lives on public and illustrious thoughts. He is the world's eye. He is the world's heart. He is to resist the vulgar prosperity that retrogrades ever to barbarism, by preserving and communicating heroic sentiments, noble biographies, melodious verse, and the conclusions of history. Whatsoever oracles the human heart, in all emergencies, in all solemn hours, has uttered as its commentary on the world of actions,—these he shall receive and impart. And whatsoever new verdict Reason from her inviolable seat pronounces on the passing men and events of to-day, —this he shall hear and promulgate.

31   These being his functions, it becomes him to feel all confidence in himself, and to defer never to the popular cry. He and he only knows the world. The world of any moment is the merest appearance. Some great decorum, some fetish of a government, some ephemeral trade, or war, or man, is cried up by half mankind and cried down by the other half, as if all depended on this particular up or down. The odds are that the whole question is not worth the poorest thought which the scholar has lost in listening to the controversy. Let him not quit his belief that a popgun is a popgun, though the ancient and honorable of the earth affirm it to be the crack of doom. In silence, in steadiness, in severe abstraction, let him hold by himself; add observation to observation, patient of neglect, patient of reproach, and bide his own time,—happy enough if he can satisfy himself alone that this day he has seen something truly. Success treads on every right step. For the instinct is sure, that prompts him to tell his brother what he thinks. He then learns that in going down into the secrets of his own mind he has descended into the secrets of all minds. He learns that he who has mastered any law in his private thought is master to that extent of all men whose language he speaks, and of all into whose language his own can be translated. The poet in utter solitude remembering his spontaneous thoughts and recording them, is found to have recorded that which men in crowded cities find true for them also. The orator distrusts first the fitness of his frank confessions, his want of knowledge of the persons he addresses, until he finds that he is the complement of his hearers;—that they drink his words because he fulfills for them their own nature; the deeper he dives into his privatest secretest presentiment, to his wonder he finds this is the most

acceptable, most public, and universally true. The people delight
in it; the better part of every man feels, This is my music; this
is myself.

32   In self-trust all the virtues are comprehended. Free should the
scholar be,—free and brave. Free even to the definition of freedom
"without any hindrance that does not arise out of his own constitution." Brave; for fear is a thing which a scholar by his very
function puts behind him. Fear always springs from ignorance.
It is a shame to him if his tranquillity, amid dangerous times,
arise from the presumption that like children and women his is
a protected class; or if he seek a temporary peace by the diversion
of his thoughts from politics or vexed questions, hiding his head
like an ostrich in the flowering bushes, peeping into microscopes,
and turning rhymes, as a boy whistles to keep his courage up.
So is the danger a danger still; so is the fear worse. Manlike let
him turn and face it. Let him look into its eye and search its
nature, inspect its origin,—see the whelping of this lion,—which
lies no great way back; he will then find in himself a perfect
comprehension of its nature and extent; he will have made his
hands meet on the other side, and can henceforth defy it and pass
on superior. The world is his who can see through its pretension.
What deafness, what stone-blind custom, what overgrown error
you behold is there only by sufferance,—by your sufferance. See
it to be a lie, and you have already dealt it its mortal blow.

33   Yes, we are the cowed,—we the trustless. It is a mischievous
notion that we are come late into nature; that the world was finished a long time ago. As the world was plastic and fluid in the
hands of God, so it is ever to so much of his attributes as we
bring to it. To ignorance and sin, it is flint. They adapt themselves to it as they may; but in proportion as a man has any thing
in him divine, the firmament flows before him and takes his
signet and form. Not he is great who can alter matter, but he who
can alter my state of mind. They are the kings of the world who
give the color of their present thought to all nature and all art, and
persuade men by the cheerful serenity of their carrying the matter,
that this thing which they do is the apple which the ages have
desired to pluck, now at last ripe, and inviting nations to the
harvest. The great man makes the great thing. Wherever Mac-
donald sits, there is the head of the table. Linnaeus makes botany
the most alluring of studies, and wins it from the farmer and the
herb-woman; Davy, chemistry; and Cuvier, fossils. The day is always his who works in it with serenity and great aims. The unstable

estimates of men crowd to him whose mind is filled with a truth, as the heaped waves of the Atlantic follow the moon.

34   For this self-trust, the reason is deeper than can be fathomed, —darker than can be enlightened. I might not carry with me the feeling of my audience in stating my own belief. But I have already shown the ground of my hope, in adverting to the doctrine that man is one. I believe man has been wronged; he has wronged himself. He has almost lost the light that can lead him back to his prerogatives. Men are become of no account. Men in history, men in the world of to-day, are bugs, are spawn, and are called "the mass" and "the herd." In a century, in a millennium, one or two men; that is to say, one or two approximations to the right state of every man. All the rest behold in the hero or the poet their own green and crude being,—ripened; yes, and are content to be less, so *that* may attain to its full stature. What a testimony, full of grandeur, full of pity, is borne to the demands of his own nature, by the poor clansman, the poor partisan, who rejoices in the glory of his chief. The poor and the low find some amends to their immense moral capacity, for their acquiescence in a political and social inferiority. They are content to be brushed like flies from the path of a great person, so that justice shall be done by him to that common nature which it is the dearest desire of all to see enlarged and glorified. They sun themselves in the great man's light, and feel it to be their own element. They cast the dignity of man from their downtrod selves upon the shoulders of a hero, and will perish to add one drop of blood to make that great heart beat, those giant sinews combat and conquer. He lives for us, and we live in him.

35   Men, such as they are, very naturally seek money or power and power because it is as good as money,—the "spoils," so called "of office." And why not? for they aspire to the highest, and this, in their sleep-walking, they dream is highest. Wake them and they shall quit the false good and leap to the true, and leave governments to clerks and desks. This revolution is to be wrought by the gradual domestication of the idea of Culture. The main enterprise of the world for splendor, for extent, is the upbuilding of a man. Here are the materials strewn along the ground. The private life of one man shall be a more illustrious monarchy, more formidable to its enemy, more sweet and serene in its influence to its friend, than any kingdom in history. For a man, rightly viewed, comprehendeth the particular natures of all men. Each philosopher, each bard, each actor has only done for me, as by a delegate, what

one day I can do for myself. The books which once we valued more than the apple of the eye, we have quite exhausted. What is that but saying that we have come up with the point of view which the universal mind took through the eyes of one scribe; we have been that man, and have passed on. First, one, then another, we drain all cisterns, and waxing greater by all these supplies, we crave a better and more abundant food. The man has never lived that can feed us ever. The human mind cannot be enshrined in a person who shall set a barrier on any one side to this unbounded, unboundable empire. It is one central fire, which, flaming now out of the lips of Etna, lightens the capes of Sicily, and now out of the throat of Vesuvius, illuminates the towers and vineyards of Naples. It is one light which beams out of a thousand stars. It is one soul which animates all men.

36   But I have dwelt perhaps tediously upon this abstraction of the Scholar. I ought not to delay longer to add what I have to say of nearer reference to the time and to this country.

37   Historically, there is thought to be a difference in the ideas which predominate over successive epochs, and there are data for marking the genius of the Classic, of the Romantic, and now of the Reflective or Philosophical age. With the views I have intimated of the oneness or the identity of the mind through all individuals, I do not much dwell on these differences. In fact, I believe each individual passes through all three. The boy is a Greek; the youth, romantic; the adult, reflective. I deny not, however, that a revolution in the leading idea may be distinctly enough traced.

38   Our age is bewailed as the age of Introversion. Must that needs be evil? We, it seems, are critical; we are embarrassed with second thoughts; we cannot enjoy any thing for hankering to know whereof the pleasures consists; we are lined with eyes; we see with our feet; the time is infected with Hamlet's unhappiness,—

"Sicklied o'er with the pale cast of thought."

It is so bad then? Sight is the last thing to be pitied. Would we be blind? Do we fear lest we should outsee nature and God, and drink truth dry? I look upon the discontent of the literary class as a mere announcement of the fact that they find themselves not in the state of mind of their fathers, and regret the coming state as untried; as a boy dreads the water before he has learned that he can swim. If there is any period one would desire to be born in, is it not the age of Revolution; when the old and the new stand side by side and admit of being compared; when the energies of all men are searched by fear and by hope; when the historic glories of the old can be compensated by the rich possibilities of the new era? This time, like all times, is a very good one, if we but know what to do with it.

39   I read with some joy of the auspicious signs of the coming days, as they glimmer already through poetry and art, through philosophy and science, through church and state.

40   One of these signs is the fact that the same movement which effected the elevation of what was called the lowest class in the state, assumed in literature a very marked and as benign an aspect. Instead of the sublime and beautiful, the near, the low, the common, was explored and poetized. That which had been negligently trodden under foot by those who were harnessing and provisioning themselves for long journeys into far countries, is suddenly found to be richer than all foreign parts. The literature of the poor, the feelings of the child, the philosophy of the street, the meaning of the household life, are the topics of the time. It is a great stride. It is a sign—is it not?—of new vigor when the extremities are made active, when currents of warm life run into the hands and the feet. I ask not for the great, the remote, the romantic; what is doing in Italy or Arabia; what is Greek art, or Provençal minstrelsy; I embrace the common, I explore and sit at the feet of the familiar, the low. Give me insight into to-day, and you may have the antique and future worlds. What would we really know the meaning of? The meal in the firkin; the milk in the pan; the ballad in the street; the news of the boat; the glance of the eye; the form and the gait of the body;—show me the ultimate reason of these matters; show me the sublime presence of the highest spiritual cause lurking, as always it does lurk, in these suburbs and extremities of nature; let me see every trifle bristling with the polarity that ranges it instantly on an eternal law; and the shop, the plough, and the ledger referred to the like cause by which light undulates and poets sing;—and the world lies no longer a dull miscellany and lumber-room, but has form and order; there is no trifle, there is no puzzle, but one design unites and animates the farthest pinnacle and the lowest trench.

41   This idea has inspired the genius of Goldsmith, Burns, Cowper, and, in a newer time, of Goethe, Wordsworth, and Carlyle. This idea they have differently followed and with various success. In contrast with their writing, the style of Pope, of Johnson, of Gibbon, looks cold and pedantic. This writing is blood-warm.

Man is surprised to find that things near are not less beautiful and wondrous than things remote. The near explains the far. The drop is a small ocean. A man is related to all nature. This perception of the worth of the vulgar is fruitful in discoveries. Goethe, in this very thing the most modern of the moderns, has shown us, as none ever did, the genius of the ancients.

42   There is one man of genius who has done much for this philosophy of life, whose literary value has never yet been rightly estimated;—I mean Emanuel Swedenborg. The most imaginative of men, yet writing with the precision of a mathematician, he endeavored to engraft a purely philosophical Ethics on the popular Christianity of his time. Such an attempt of course must have difficulty which no genius could surmount. But he saw and showed the connection between nature and the affections of the soul. He pierced the emblematic or spiritual character of the visible, audible, tangible world. Especially did his shade-loving muse hover over and interpret the lower parts of nature; he showed the mysterious bond that allies moral evil to the foul material forms, and has given in epical parables a theory of insanity, of beasts, of unclean and fearful things.

43   Another sign of our times, also marked by an analogous political movement, is the new importance given to the single person. Every thing that tends to insulate the individual,—to surround him with barriers of natural respect, so that each man shall feel the world is his, and man shall treat with man as a sovereign state with a sovereign state,—tends to true union as well as greatness. "I learned," said the melancholy Pestalozzi, "that no man in God's wide earth is either willing or able to help any other man." Help must come from the bosom alone. The scholar is that man who must take up into himself all the ability of the time, all the contributions of the past, all the hopes of the future. He must be an university of knowledges. If there be one lesson more than another which should pierce his ear, it is, The world is nothing, the man is all; in yourself is the law of all nature, and you know not yet how a globule of sap ascends; in yourself slumbers the whole of Reason; it is for you to know all; it is for you to dare all. Mr. President and Gentlemen, this confidence in the unsearched might of man belongs, by all motives, by all prophecy, by all preparation, to the American Scholar. We have listened too long to the courtly muses of Europe. The spirit of the American freeman is already suspected to be timid, imitative, tame. Public and private avarice make the air we breathe thick and fat. The

scholar is decent, indolent, complaisant. See already the tragic consequence. The mind of this country, taught to aim at low objects, eats upon itself. There is no work for any but the decorous and the complaisant. Young men of the fairest promise, who begin life upon our shores, inflated by the mountain winds, shined upon by all the stars of God, find the earth below not in unison with these, but are hindered from action by the disgust which the principles on which business is managed inspire, and turn drudges, or die of disgust, some of them suicides. What is the remedy? They did not yet see, and thousands of young men as hopeful now crowding to the barriers for the career do not yet see, that if the single man plant himself indomitably on his instincts, and there abide, the huge world will come round to him. Patience,—patience; with the shades of all the good and great for company; and for solace the perspective of your own infinite life; and for work the study and the communication of principles, the making those instincts prevalent, the conversion of the world. Is it not the chief disgrace in the world, not to be an unit;—not to be reckoned one character;—not to yield that peculiar fruit which each man was created to bear, but to be reckoned in the gross, in the hundred, or the thousand, of the party, the section, to which we belong; and our opinion predicted geographically, as the north, or the south? Not so, brothers and friends—please God, ours shall not be so. We will walk on our own feet; we will work with our own hands; we will speak our own minds. The study of letters shall be no longer a name for pity, for doubt, and for sensual indulgence. The dread of man and the love of man shall be a wall of defence and a wreath of joy around all. A nation of men will for the first time exist, because each believes himself inspired by the Divine Soul which also inspires all men.

Literature and Science

Matthew Arnold

1   Practical people talk with a smile of Plato and of his absolute ideas; and it is impossible to deny that Plato's ideas do often seem unpractical and impracticable, and especially when one views them in connection with the life of a great work-a-day world like the United States. The necessary staple of the life of such a world Plato regards with disdain; handicraft and trade and the working professions he regards with disdain; but what becomes of the life of an industrial modern community if you take handicraft and trade and the working professions out of it? The base mechanic arts and handicrafts, says Plato, bring about a natural weakness in the principle of excellence in a man, so that he cannot govern the ignoble growths in him, but nurses them, and cannot understand fostering any other. Those who exercise such arts and trades, as they have their bodies, he says, marred by their vulgar businesses, so they have their souls, too, bowed and broken by them. And if one of these uncomely people has a mind to seek self-culture and philosophy, Plato compares him to a bald little tinker, who has scraped together money, and has got his release from service, and has had a bath, and bought a new coat, and is rigged out like a bridegroom about to marry the daughter of his master who has fallen into poor and helpless estate.

2   Nor do the working professions fare any better than trade at the hands of Plato. He draws for us an inimitable picture of the working lawyer, and of his life of bondage; he shows how this bondage from his youth up has stunted and warped him, and made him small and crooked of soul, encompassing him with difficulties which he is not man enough to rely on justice and truth as means

From *Discourses in America*.

to encounter, but has recourse, for help out of them, to falsehood and wrong. And so, says Plato, this poor creature is bent and broken, and grows up from boy to man without a particle of soundness in him, although exceedingly smart and clever in his own esteem.

3   One cannot refuse to admire the artist who draws these pictures. But we say to ourselves that his ideas show the influence of a primitive and obsolete order of things, when the warrior caste and the priestly caste were alone in honour, and the humble work of the world was done by slaves. We have now changed all that; the modern majority consists in work, as Emerson declares; and in work, we may add, principally of such plain and dusty kind as the work of cultivators of the ground, handicraftsmen, men of trade and business, men of the working professions. Above all is this true in a great industrious community such as that of the United States.

4   Now education, many people go on to say, is still mainly governed by the ideas of men like Plato, who lived when the warrior caste and the priestly or philosophical class were alone in honour, and the really useful part of the community were slaves. It is an education fitted for persons of leisure in such a community. This education passed from Greece and Rome to the feudal communities of Europe, where also the warrior caste and the priestly caste were alone held in honour, and where the really useful and working part of the community, though not nominally slaves as in the pagan world, were practically not much better off than slaves, and not more seriously regarded. And how absurd it is, people end by saying, to inflict this education upon an industrious modern community, where very few indeed are persons of leisure, and the mass to be considered has not leisure, but is bound, for its own great good, and for the great good of the world at large, to plain labour and to industrial pursuits, and the education in question tends necessarily to make men dissatisfied with these pursuits and unfitted for them!

5   That is what is said. So far I must defend Plato, as to plead that his view of education and studies is in the general, as it seems to me, sound enough, and fitted for all sorts and conditions of men, whatever their pursuits may be. "An intelligent man," says Plato, "will prize those studies which result in his soul getting soberness, righteousness, and wisdom, and will less value the others." I cannot consider *that* a bad description of the aim of education, and of the motives which should govern us in the choice of studies,

whether we are preparing ourselves for a hereditary seat in the English House of Lords or for the pork trade in Chicago.

6   Still I admit that Plato's world was not ours, that his scorn of trade and handicraft is fantastic, that he had no conception of a great industrial community such as that of the United States, and that such a community must and will shape its education to suit its own needs. If the usual education handed down to it from the past does not suit it, it will certainly before long drop this and try another. The usual education in the past has been mainly literary. The question is whether the studies which were long supposed to be the best for all of us are practically the best now; whether others are not better. The tyranny of the past, many think, weighs on us injuriously in the predominance given to letters in education. The question is raised whether, to meet the needs of our modern life, the predominance ought not now to pass from letters to science; and naturally the question is nowhere raised with more energy than here in the United States. The design of abasing what is called "mere literary instruction and education," and of exalting what is called "sound, extensive, and practical scientific knowledge," is, in this intensely modern world of the United States, even more perhaps than in Europe, a very popular design, and makes great and rapid progress.

7   I am going to ask whether the present movement for ousting letters from their old predominance in education, and for transferring the predominance in education to the natural sciences, whether this brisk and flourishing movement ought to prevail, and whether it is likely that in the end it really will prevail. An objection may be raised which I will anticipate. My own studies have been almost wholly in letters, and my visits to the field of the natural sciences have been very slight and inadequate, although those sciences have always strongly moved my curiosity. A man of letters, it will perhaps be said, is not competent to discuss the comparative merits of letters and natural science as means of education. To this objection I reply, first of all, that his incompetence, if he attempts the discussion but is really incompetent for it, will be abundantly visible; nobody will be taken in; he will have plenty of sharp observers and critics to save mankind from that danger. But the line I am going to follow is, as you will soon discover, so extremely simple, that perhaps it may be followed without failure even by one who for a more ambitious line of discussion would be quite incompetent.

8   Some of you may possibly remember a phrase of mine which has been the object of a good deal of comment; an observation to the effect that in our culture, the aim being *to know ourselves and the world*, we have, as the means to this end, *to know the best which has been thought and said in the world*. A man of science, who is also an excellent writer and the very prince of debaters, Professor Huxley, in a discourse at the opening of Sir Josiah Mason's college at Birmingham, laying hold of this phrase, expanded it by quoting some more words of mine, which are these: "The civilized world is to be regarded as now being, for intellectual and spiritual purposes, one great confederation, bound to a joint action and working to a common result; and whose members have for their proper outfit a knowledge of Greek, Roman, and Eastern antiquity, and of one another. Special local and temporary advantages being put out of account, that modern nation will in the intellectual and spiritual sphere make most progress, which most thoroughly carries out this programme."

9   Now on my phrase, thus enlarged, Professor Huxley remarks that when I speak of the above-mentioned knowledge as enabling us to know ourselves and the world, I assert *literature* to contain the materials which suffice for thus making us know ourselves and the world. But it is not by any means clear, says he, that after having learnt all which ancient and modern literatures have to tell us, we have laid a sufficiently broad and deep foundation for that criticism of life, that knowledge of ourselves and the world, which constitutes culture. On the contrary, Professor Huxley declares that he finds himself "wholly unable to admit that either nations or individuals will really advance, if their outfit draws nothing from the stores of physical science. An army without weapons of precision, and with no particular base of operations, might more hopefully enter upon a campaign on the Rhine, than a man, devoid of a knowledge of what physical science has done in the last century, upon a criticism of life."

10   This shows how needful it is for those who are to discuss any matter together, to have a common understanding as to the sense of the terms they employ,—how needful, and how difficult. What Professor Huxley says, implies just the reproach which is so often brought against the study of *belles lettres*, as they are called: that the study is an elegant one, but slight and ineffectual; a smattering of Greek and Latin and other ornamental things, of little use for anyone whose object is to get at truth, and to be a practical man.

So, too, M. Renan talks of the "superficial humanism" of a school-course which treats us as if we were all going to be poets, writers, preachers, orators, and he opposes this humanism to positive science, or the critical search after truth. And there is always a tendency in those who are remonstrating against the predominance of letters in education, to understand by letters *belles lettres*, and by *belles lettres* a superficial humanism, the opposite of science or true knowledge.

11   But when we talk of knowing Greek and Roman antiquity, for instance, which is the knowledge people have called the humanities, I for my part mean a knowledge which is something more than a superficial humanism, mainly decorative. "I call all teaching *scientific*," says Wolf, the critic of Homer, "which is systematically laid out and followed up to its original sources. For example: a knowledge of classical antiquity is scientific when the remains of classical antiquity are correctly studied in the original languages." There can be no doubt that Wolf is perfectly right; that all learning is scientific which is systematically laid out and followed up to its original sources, and that a genuine humanism is scientific.

12   When I speak of knowing Greek and Roman antiquity, therefore, as a help to knowing ourselves and the world, I mean more than a knowledge of so much vocabulary, so much grammar, so many portions of authors in the Greek and Latin languages, I mean knowing the Greeks and Romans, and their life and genius, and what they were and did in the world; what we get from them, and what is its value. That, at least, is the ideal; and when we talk of endeavouring to know Greek and Roman antiquity, as a help to knowing ourselves and the world, we mean endeavouring so to know them as to satisfy this ideal, however much we may still fall short of it.

13   The same also as to knowing our own and other modern nations, with the like aim of getting to understand ourselves and the world. To know the best that has been thought and said by the modern nations, is to know, says Professor Huxley, "only what modern *literatures* have to tell us; it is the criticism of life contained in modern literature." And yet "the distinctive character of our times," he urges, "lies in the vast and constantly increasing part which is played by natural knowledge." And how, therefore, can a man, devoid of knowledge of what physical science has done in the last century, enter hopefully upon a criticism of modern life?

14   Let us, I say, be agreed about the meaning of the terms we are using. I talk of knowing the best which has been thought and

uttered in the world; Professor Huxley says this means knowing *literature*. Literature is a large word; it may mean everything written with letters or printed in a book. Euclid's *Elements* and Newton's *Principia* are thus literature. All knowledge that reaches us through books is literature. But by literature Professor Huxley means *belles lettres*. He means to make me say, that knowing the best which has been thought and said by the modern nations is knowing their *belles lettres* and no more. And this is no sufficient equipment, he argues, for a criticism of modern life. But as I do not mean, by knowing ancient Rome, knowing merely more or less of Latin *belles lettres*, and taking no account of Rome's military, and political, and legal, and administrative work in the world; and as, by knowing ancient Greece, I understand knowing her as the giver of Greek art, and the guide to a free and right use of reason and to scientific method, and the founder of our mathematics and physics and astronomy and biology,—I understand knowing her as all this, and not merely knowing certain Greek poems, and histories, and treatises, and speeches,—so as to the knowledge of modern nations also. By knowing modern nations, I mean not merely knowing their *belles lettres*, but knowing also what has been done by such men as Copernicus, Galileo, Newton, Darwin. "Our ancestors learned," says Professor Huxley, "that the earth is the center of the visible universe, and that man is the cynosure of things terrestrial; and more especially was it inculcated that the course of nature had no fixed order, but that it could be, and constantly was, altered." But for us now, continues Professor Huxley, "the notions of the beginning and the end of the world entertained by our forefathers are no longer credible. It is very certain that the earth is not the chief body in the material universe, and that the world is not subordinated to man's use. It is even more certain that nature is the expression of a definite order, with which nothing interferes." "And yet," he cries, "the purely classical education advocated by the representatives of the humanists in our day gives no inkling of all this!"

15   In due place and time I will just touch upon that vexed question of classical education; but at present the question is as to what is meant by knowing the best which modern nations have thought and said. It is not knowing their *belles lettres* merely which is meant. To know Italian *belles lettres* is not to know Italy, and to know English *belles lettres* is not to know England. Into knowing Italy and England there comes a great deal more, Galileo and Newton amongst it. The reproach of being a superficial humanism,

a tincture of *belles lettres*, may attach rightly enough to some
other disciplines; but to the particular discipline recommended
when I proposed knowing the best that has been thought and said
in the world, it does not apply. In that best I certainly include
what in modern times has been thought and said by the great
observers and knowers of nature.

16   There is, therefore, really no question between Professor Huxley
and me as to whether knowing the great results of the modern
scientific study of nature is not required as a part of our culture,
as well as knowing the products of literature and art. But to follow
the processes by which those results are reached, ought, say the
friends of physical science, to be made the staple of education for
the bulk of mankind. And here there does arise a question between
those whom Professor Huxley calls with playful sarcasm "the
Levites of culture," and those whom the poor humanist is sometimes apt to regard as its Nebuchadnezzars.

17   The great results of the scientific investigation of nature we are
agreed upon knowing, but how much of our study are we bound
to give to the processes by which those results are reached? The
results have their visible bearing on human life. But all the processes, too, all the items of fact, by which those results are reached
and established, are interesting. All knowledge is interesting to a
wise man, and the knowledge of nature is interesting to all men.
It is very interesting to know, that, from the albuminous white
of the egg, the chick in the egg gets the materials for its flesh,
bones, blood, and feathers; while, from the fatty yolk of the egg,
it gets the heat and energy which enable it at length to break its
shell and begin the world. It is less interesting, perhaps, but still
it is interesting, to know that when a taper burns, the wax is
converted into carbonic acid and water. Moreover, it is quite true
that the habit of dealing with facts, which is given by the study
of nature, is, as the friends of physical science praise it for being,
an excellent discipline. The appeal, in the study of nature, is constantly to observation and experiment; not only is it said that the
thing is so, but we can be made to see that it is so. Not only does
a man tell us that when a taper burns the wax is converted into
carbonic acid and water, as a man may tell us, if he likes, that
Charon is punting his ferry-boat on the river Styx, or that Victor
Hugo is a sublime poet, or Mr. Gladstone the most admirable of
statesmen; but we are made to see that the conversion into carbonic acid and water does actually happen. This reality of natural
knowledge it is, which makes the friends of physical science con-

trast it, as a knowledge of things, with the humanist's knowledge, which is, say they, a knowledge of words. And hence Professor Huxley is moved to lay it down that, "for the purpose of attaining real culture, an exclusively scientific education is at least as effectual as an exclusively literary education." And a certain President of the Section for Mechanical Science in the British Association is, in Scripture phrase, "very bold," and declares that if a man, in his mental training, "has substituted literature and history for natural science, he has chosen the less useful alternative." But whether we go these lengths or not, we must all admit that in natural science the habit gained of dealing with facts is a most valuable discipline, and that every one should have some experience of it.

18   More than this, however, is demanded by the reformers. It is proposed to make the training in natural science the main part of education, for the great majority of mankind at any rate. And here, I confess, I part company with the friends of physical science, with whom up to this point I have been agreeing. In differing from them, however, I wish to proceed with the utmost caution and diffidence. The smallness of my own acquaintance with the disciplines of natural science is ever before my mind, and I am fearful of doing these disciplines an injustice. The ability and pugnacity of the partisans of natural science make them formidable persons to contradict. The tone of tentative inquiry, which befits a being of dim faculties and bounded knowledge, is the tone I would wish to take and not to depart from. At present it seems to me, that those who are for giving to natural knowledge, as they call it, the chief place in the education of the majority of mankind, leave one important thing out of their account: the constitution of human nature. But I put this forward on the strength of some facts not at all recondite, very far from it; facts capable of being stated in the simplest possible fashion, and to which, if I so state them, the man of science will, I am sure, be willing to allow their due weight.

19   Deny the facts altogether, I think, he hardly can. He can hardly deny, that when we set ourselves to enumerate the powers which go to the building up of human life, and say that they are the power of conduct, the power of intellect and knowledge, the power of beauty, and the power of social life and manners,—he can hardly deny that this scheme, though drawn in rough and plain lines enough, and not pretending to scientific exactness, does yet give a fairly true representation of the matter. Human nature is built up by these powers; we have the need for them all. When we have rightly met and adjusted the claims of them all, we shall then be

in a fair way for getting soberness and righteousness, with wisdom. This is evident enough, and the friends of physical science would admit it.

20   But perhaps they may not have sufficiently observed another thing; namely, that the several powers just mentioned are not isolated, but there is, in the generality of mankind, a perpetual tendency to relate them one to another in divers ways. With one such way of relating them I am particularly concerned now. Following our instinct for intellect and knowledge, we acquire pieces of knowledge; and presently, in the generality of men, there arises the desire to relate these pieces of knowledge to our sense for conduct, to our sense for beauty,—and there is weariness and dissatisfaction if the desire is balked. Now in this desire lies, I think, the strength of that hold which letters have upon us.

21   All knowledge is, as I said just now, interesting; and even items of knowledge which from the nature of the case cannot well be related, but must stand isolated in our thoughts, have their interest. Even lists of exceptions have their interest. If we are studying Greek accents, it is interesting to know that *pais* and *pas*, and some other monosyllables of the same form of declension, do not take the circumflex upon the last syllable of the genitive plural, but vary, in this respect, from the common rule. If we are studying physiology, it is interesting to know that the pulmonary artery carries dark blood and the pulmonary vein carries bright blood, departing in this respect from the common rule for the division of labour between the veins and the arteries. But every one knows how we seek naturally to combine the pieces of our knowledge together, to bring them under general rules, to relate them to principles; and how unsatisfactory and tiresome it would be to go on forever learning lists of exceptions, or accumulating items of fact which must stand isolated.

22   Well, that same need of relating our knowledge, which operates here within the sphere of our knowledge itself, we shall find operating, also, outside that sphere. We experience, as we go on learning and knowing,—the vast majority of us experience,—the need of relating what we have learned and known to the sense which we have in us for conduct, to the sense which we have in us for beauty.

23   A certain Greek prophetess of Mantineia in Arcadia, Diotima by name, once explained to the philosopher Socrates that love, and impulse, and bent of all kinds, is, in fact, nothing else but the desire in men that good should forever be present to them.

This desire for good, Diotima assured Socrates, is our fundamental desire, of which fundamental desire every impulse in us is only some one particular form. And therefore this fundamental desire it is, I suppose,—this desire in men that good should be forever present to them,—which acts in us when we feel the impulse for relating our knowledge to our sense for conduct and to our sense for beauty. At any rate, with men in general the instinct exists. Such is human nature. And the instinct, it will be admitted, is innocent, and human nature is preserved by our following the lead of its innocent instincts. Therefore, in seeking to gratify this instinct in question, we are following the instinct of self-preservation in humanity.

24 But, no doubt, some kinds of knowledge cannot be made to directly serve the instinct in question, cannot be directly related to the sense for beauty, to the sense for conduct. These are instrument-knowledges; they lead on to other knowledges, which can. A man who passes his life in instrument-knowledges is a specialist. They may be invaluable as instruments to something beyond, for those who have the gift thus to employ them; and they may be disciplines in themselves wherein it is useful for every one to have some schooling. But it is inconceivable that the generality of men should pass all their mental life with Greek accents or with formal logic. My friend Professor Sylvester, who is one of the first mathematicians in the world, holds transcendental doctrines as to the virtue of mathematics, but those doctrines are not for common men. In the very Senate House and heart of our English Cambridge I once ventured, though not without an apology for my profaneness, to hazard the opinion that for the majority of mankind a little of mathematics, even, goes a long way. Of course this is quite consistent with their being of immense importance as an instrument to something else; but it is the few who have the aptitude for thus using them, not the bulk of mankind.

25 The natural sciences do not, however, stand on the same footing with these instrument-knowledges. Experience shows us that the generality of men will find more interest in learning that, when a taper burns, the wax is converted into carbonic acid and water, or in learning the explanation of the phenomenon of dew, or in learning how the circulation of the blood is carried on, than they find in learning that the genitive plural of *pais* and *pas* does not take the circumflex on the termination. And one piece of natural knowledge is added to another, and others are added to that, and at last we come to propositions so interesting as Mr. Darwin's

famous proposition that "our ancestor was a hairy quadruped furnished with a tail and pointed ears, probably arboreal in his habits." Or we come to propositions of such reach and magnitude as those which Professor Huxley delivers, when he says that the notions of our forefathers about the beginning and the end of the world were all wrong, and that nature is the expression of a definite order with which nothing interferes.

26   Interesting, indeed, these results of science are, important they are, and we should all of us be acquainted with them. But what I now wish you to mark is, that we are still, when they are propounded to us and we receive them, we are still in the sphere of intellect and knowledge. And for the generality of men there will be found, I say, to arise, when they have duly taken in the proposition that their ancestor was "a hairy quadruped furnished with a tail and pointed ears, probably arboreal in his habits," there will be found to arise an invincible desire to relate this proposition to the sense in us for conduct, and to the sense in us for beauty. But this the men of science will not do for us, and will hardly even profess to do. They will give us other pieces of knowledge, other facts, about other animals and their ancestors, or about plants, or about stones, or about stars; and they may finally bring us to those great "general conceptions of the universe, which are forced upon us all," says Professor Huxley, "by the progress of physical science." But still it will be *knowledge* only which they give us; knowledge not put for us into relation with our sense for conduct, our sense for beauty, and touched with emotion by being so put; not thus put for us, and therefore, to the majority of mankind, after a certain while, unsatisfying, wearying.

27   Not to the born naturalist, I admit. But what do we mean by a born naturalist? We mean a man in whom the zeal for observing nature is so uncommonly strong and eminent, that it marks him off from the bulk of mankind. Such a man will pass his life happily in collecting natural knowledge and reasoning upon it, and will ask for nothing, or hardly anything, more. I have heard it said that the sagacious and admirable naturalist whom we lost not very long ago, Mr. Darwin, once owned to a friend that for his part he did not experience the necessity for two things which most men find so necessary to them,—religion and poetry; science and the domestic affections, he thought, were enough. To a born naturalist, I can well understand that this should seem so. So absorbing is his occupation with nature, so strong his love for his occupation, that he goes on acquiring natural knowledge and reasoning upon it, and

has little time or inclination for thinking about getting it related to the desire in man for conduct, the desire in man for beauty. He relates it to them for himself as he goes along, so far as he feels the need; and he draws from the domestic affections all the additional solace necessary. But then Darwins are extremely rare. Another great and admirable master of natural knowledge, Faraday, was a Sandemanian. That is to say, he related his knowledge to his instinct for conduct and to his instinct for beauty, by the aid of that respectable Scottish sectary, Robert Sandeman. And so strong, in general, is the demand of religion and poetry to have their share in a man, to associate themselves with his knowing, and to relieve and rejoice it, that, probably, for one man amongst us with the disposition to do as Darwin did in this respect, there are at least fifty with the disposition to do as Faraday.

28   Education lays hold upon us, in fact, by satisfying this demand. Professor Huxley holds up to scorn mediaeval education, with its neglect of the knowledge of nature, its poverty even of literary studies, its formal logic devoted to "showing how and why that which the Church said was true must be true." But the great mediaeval Universities were not brought into being, we may be sure, by the zeal for giving a jejune and contemptible education. Kings have been their nursing fathers, and queens have been their nursing mothers, but not for this. The mediaeval Universities came into being, because the supposed knowledge, delivered by Scripture and the Church, so deeply engaged men's hearts, by so simply, easily, and powerfully relating itself to their desire for conduct, their desire for beauty. All other knowledge was dominated by this supposed knowledge and was subordinated to it, because of the surpassing strength of the hold which it gained upon the affections of men, by allying itself profoundly with their sense for conduct, their sense for beauty.

29   But now, says Professor Huxley, conceptions of the universe fatal to the notions held by our forefathers have been forced upon us by physical science. Grant to him that they are thus fatal, that the new conceptions must and will soon become current everywhere, and that every one will finally perceive them to be fatal to the beliefs of our forefathers. The need of humane letters, as they are truly called, because they serve the paramount desire in men that good should be forever present to them,—the need of humane letters, to establish a relation between the new conceptions, and our instinct for beauty, our instinct for conduct, is only the more visible. The Middle Age could do without humane letters,

as it could do without the study of nature, because its supposed
knowledge was made to engage its emotions so powerfully. Grant
that the supposed knowledge disappears, its power of being made
to engage the emotions will of course disappear along with it,—but
the emotions themselves, and their claim to be engaged and satisfied, will remain. Now if we find by experience that humane letters
have an undeniable power of engaging the emotions, the importance
of humane letters in a man's training becomes not less, but greater,
in proportion to the success of modern science, in extirpating what
it calls "mediaeval thinking."

30   Have humane letters, then, have poetry and eloquence, the
power here attributed to them of engaging the emotions, and do
they exercise it? And if they have it and exercise it, *how* do they
exercise it, so as to exert an influence upon man's sense for conduct, his sense for beauty? Finally, even if they both can and do
exert an influence upon the senses in question, how are they to
relate to them the results, — the modern results, — of natural
science? All these questions may be asked. First, have poetry and
eloquence the power of calling out the emotions? The appeal is to
experience. Experience shows that for the vast majority of men,
for mankind in general, they have the power. Next, do they exercise it? They do. But then, *how* do they exercise it so as to affect
man's sense for conduct, his sense for beauty? And this is perhaps
a case for applying the Preacher's words: "Though a man labor to
seek it out, yet he shall not find it; yea, farther, though a wise
man think to know it, yet shall he not be able to find it." Why
should it be one thing, in its effect upon the emotions, to say,
"Patience is a virtue," and quite another thing, in its effect upon
the emotions, to say with Homer,

τλητὸν γὰο Μοῖραι θυμὸν θέσαν ἀνθρώποισιν—

"for an enduring heart have the destinies appointed to the children of men"? Why should it be one thing, in its effect upon the
emotions, to say with the philosopher Spinoza, *Felicitas in eo
consistit quod homo suum esse conservare potest*—"Man's happiness consists in his being able to preserve his own essence," and
quite another thing, in its effect upon the emotions, to say with
the Gospel, "What is a man advantaged, if he gain the whole
world, and lose himself, forfeit himself?" How does this difference
of effect arise? I cannot tell, and I am not much concerned to
know; the important thing is that it does arise, and that we can
profit by it. But how, finally, are poetry and eloquence to exercise

the power of relating the modern results of natural science to man's instinct for conduct, his instinct for beauty? And here again I answer that I do not know *how* they will exercise it, but that they can and will exercise it I am sure. I do not mean that modern philosophical poets and modern philosophical moralists are to come and relate for us, in express terms, the results of modern scientific research to our instinct for conduct, our instinct for beauty. But I mean that we shall find, as a matter of experience, if we know the best that has been thought and uttered in the world, we shall find that the art and poetry and eloquence of men who lived, perhaps, long ago, who had the most limited natural knowledge, who had the most erroneous conceptions about many important matters, we shall find that this art, and poetry, and eloquence, have in fact not only the power of refreshing and delighting us, they have also the power, — such is the strength and worth, in essentials, of their authors' criticism of life,—they have a fortifying, and elevating, and quickening, and suggestive power, capable of wonderfully helping us to relate the results of modern science to our need for conduct, our need for beauty. Homer's conceptions of the physical universe were, I imagine, grotesque; but really, under the shock of hearing from modern science that "the world is not subordinated to man's use, and that man is not the cynosure of things terrestrial," I could, for my own part, desire no better comfort than Homer's line which I quoted just now, "for an endur-

$$\tau\lambda\eta\tau\grave{o}\nu \ \gamma\grave{\alpha}o \ \text{Mo}\tilde{\iota}\varrho\alpha\iota \ \theta\upsilon\mu\grave{o}\nu \ \theta\acute{\epsilon}\sigma\alpha\nu \ \grave{\alpha}\nu\theta\varrho\acute{\omega}\pi\omicron\iota\sigma\iota\nu—$$

ing heart have the destinies appointed to the children of men"!

31   And the more that men's minds are cleared, the more that the results of science are frankly accepted, the more that poetry and eloquence come to be received and studied as what in truth they really are,—the criticism of life by gifted men, alive and active with extraordinary power at an unusual number of points;—so much the more will the value of humane letters, and of art also, which is an utterance having a like kind of power with theirs, be felt and acknowledged, and their place in education be secured.

32   Let us therefore, all of us, avoid indeed as much as possible any invidious comparison between the merits of humane letters, as means of education, and the merits of the natural sciences. But when some President of a Section for Mechanical Science insists on making the comparison, and tells us that "he who in his training has substituted literature and history for natural science has chosen the less useful alternative," let us make answer to him that

the student of humane letters only, will, at least, know also the great general conceptions brought in by modern physical science; for science, as Professor Huxley says, forces them upon us all. But the student of the natural sciences only, will, by our very hypothesis, know nothing of humane letters; not to mention that in setting himself to be perpetually accumulating natural knowledge, he sets himself to do what only specialists have in general the gift for doing genially. And so he will probably be unsatisfied, or at any rate incomplete, and even more incomplete than the student of humane letters only.

33   I once mentioned in a school-report, how a young man in one of our English training colleges having to paraphrase the passage in *Macbeth* beginning,

Can'st thou not minister to a mind diseased?

turned this line into, "Can you not wait upon the lunatic?" And I remarked what a curious state of things it would be, if every pupil of our national schools knew, let us say, that the moon is two thousand one hundred and sixty miles in diameter, and thought at the same time that a good paraphrase for

Can'st thou not minister to a mind diseased?

was, "Can you not wait upon the lunatic?" If one is driven to choose, I think I would rather have a young person ignorant about the moon's diameter, but aware that "Can you not wait upon the lunatic?" is bad, than a young person whose education had been such as to manage things the other way.

34   Or to go higher than the pupils of our national schools. I have in my mind's eye a member of our British Parliament who comes to travel here in America, who afterwards relates his travels, and who shows a really masterly knowledge of the geology of this great country and of its mining capabilities, but who ends by gravely suggesting that the United States should borrow a prince from our Royal Family, and should make him their king, and should create a House of Lords of great landed proprietors after the pattern of ours; and then America, he thinks, would have her future happily and perfectly secured. Surely, in this case, the President of the Section for Mechanical Science would himself hardly say that our member of Parliament, by concentrating himself upon geology and mineralogy, and so on, and not attending to literature and history, had "chosen the more useful alternative."

35   If then there is to be separation and option between humane letters on the one hand, and the natural sciences on the other, the

great majority of mankind, all who have not exceptional and over-powering aptitudes for the study of nature, would do well, I cannot but think, to choose to be educated in humane letters rather than in the natural sciences. Letters will call out their being at more points, will make them live more.

36   I said that before I ended I would just touch on the question of classical education, and I will keep my word. Even if literature is to retain a large place in our education, yet Latin and Greek, say the friends of progress, will certainly have to go. Greek is the grand offender in the eyes of these gentlemen. The attackers of the established course of study think that against Greek, at any rate, they have irresistible arguments. Literature may perhaps be needed in education, they say; but why on earth should it be Greek literature? Why not French or German? Nay, "has not an English-man models in his own literature of every kind of excellence?" As before, it is not on any weak pleadings of my own that I rely for convincing the gainsayers; it is on the constitution of human nature itself, and on the instinct of self-preservation in humanity. The instinct for beauty is set in human nature, as surely as the instinct for knowledge is set there, or the instinct for conduct. If the instinct for beauty is served by Greek literature and art as it is served by no other literature and art, we may trust to the instinct of self-preservation in humanity for keeping Greek as part of our culture. We may trust to it for even making the study of Greek more prevalent than it is now. Greek will come, I hope, some day to be studied more rationally than at present; but it will be in-creasingly studied as men increasingly feel the need in them for beauty, and how powerfully Greek art and Greek literature can serve this need. Women will again study Greek, as Lady Jane Grey did; I believe that in that chain of forts, with which the fair host of the Amazons are now engirdling our English universities, I find that here in America, in colleges like Smith in Massachusetts, and Vassar College in the State of New York, and in the happy families of the mixed universities out West, they are studying it already.

37   *Defuit una mihi symmetria prisca,* — "The antique symmetry was the one thing wanting to me," said Leonardo da Vinci; and he was an Italian. I will not presume to speak for the Americans, but I am sure that, in the Englishman, the want of this admirable symmetry of the Greeks is a thousand times more great and crying than in any Italian. The results of the want show themselves most glaringly, perhaps, in our architecture, but they show themselves,

also, in all our art. *Fit details strictly combined, in view of a large general result nobly conceived;* that is just the beautiful *symmetria prisca* of the Greeks, and it is just where we English fail, where all our art fails. Striking ideas we have, and well-executed details we have; but that high symmetry which, with satisfying and delightful effect, combines them, we seldom or never have. The glorious beauty of the Acropolis at Athens did not come from single fine things stuck about on that hill, a statue here, a gateway there;— no, it arose from all things being perfectly combined for a supreme total effect. What must not an Englishman feel about our deficiencies in this respect, as the sense for beauty, whereof this symmetry is an essential element, awakens and strengthens within him! what will not one day be his respect and desire for Greece and its *symmetria prisca*, when the scales drop from his eyes as he walks the London streets, and he sees such a lesson in meanness as the Strand, for instance, in its true deformity! But here we are coming to our friend Mr. Ruskin's province, and I will not intrude upon it, for he is its very sufficient guardian.

38   And so we at last find, it seems, we find flowing in favour of the humanities the natural and necessary stream of things, which seemed against them when we started. The "hairy quadruped furnished with a tail and pointed ears, probably arboreal in his habits," this good fellow carried hidden in his nature, apparently, something destined to develop into a necessity for humane letters. Nay, more; we seem finally to be even led to the further conclusion that our hairy ancestor carried in his nature, also, a necessity for Greek.

39   And therefore, to say the truth, I cannot really think that humane letters are in much actual danger of being thrust out from their leading place in education, in spite of the array of authorities against them at this moment. So long as human nature is what it is, their attractions will remain irresistible. As with Greek, so with letters generally: they will some day come, we may hope, to be studied more rationally, but they will not lose their place. What will happen will rather be that there will be crowded into education other matters besides, far too many; there will be, perhaps, a period of unsettlement and confusion and false tendency; but letters will not in the end lose their leading place. If they lose it for a time, they will get it back again. We shall be brought back to them by our wants and aspirations. And a poor humanist may possess his soul in patience, neither strive nor cry, admit the energy and brilliancy of the partisans of physical science, and their present favour

with the public, to be far greater than his own, and still have a happy faith that the nature of things works silently on behalf of the studies which he loves, and that, while we shall all have to acquaint ourselves with the great results reached by modern science, and to give ourselves as much training in its disciplines as we can conveniently carry, yet the majority of men will always require humane letters; and so much the more, as they have the more and the greater results of science to relate to the need in man for conduct, and to the need in him for beauty.

An Argument Against
Abolishing Christianity

Jonathan Swift

1   I am very sensible what a weakness and presumption it is, to reason against the general humour and disposition of the world. I remember it was with great justice, and a due regard to the freedom both of the public and the press, forbidden upon several penalties to write, or discourse, or lay wagers against the Union, even before it was confirmed by parliament, because that was looked upon as a design, to oppose the current of the people, which, besides the folly of it, is a manifest breach of the fundamental law that makes this majority of opinion the voice of God. In like manner and for the very same reasons, it may perhaps be neither safe nor prudent to argue against the abolishing of Christianity, at a juncture when all parties appear so unanimously determined upon the point, as we cannot but allow from their actions, their discourses, and their writings. However, I know not how, whether from the affectation of singularity, or the perverseness of human nature, but so it unhappily falls out, that I cannot be entirely of this opinion. Nay, though I were sure an order were issued for my immediate prosecution by the Attorney-General, I should still confess that in the present posture of our affairs at home or abroad, I do not yet see the absolute necessity of extirpating the Christian religion from among us.

2   This perhaps may appear too great a paradox even for your wise and paradoxical age to endure; therefore I shall handle it with all tenderness, and with the utmost deference to that great and profound majority which is of another sentiment.

3   And yet the curious may please to observe, how much the genius of a nation is liable to alter in half an age. I have heard it affirmed for certain by some very old people, that the contrary opinion was even in their memories as much in vogue as the other is now; and,

that a project for the abolishing of Christianity would then have appeared as singular, and been thought as absurd, as it would be at this time to write or discourse in its defence.

4   Therefore I freely own that all appearances are against me. The system of the Gospel, after the fate of other systems is generally antiquated and exploded; and the mass or body of the common people, among whom it seems to have had its latest credit, are now grown as much ashamed of it as their betters; opinions, like fashions, always descending from those of quality to the middle sort, and thence to the vulgar, where at length they are dropped and vanish.

5   But here I would not be mistaken, and must therefore be so bold as to borrow a distinction from the writers on the other side, when they made a difference between nominal and real Trinitarians. I hope no reader imagines me so weak to stand up in the defence of real Christianity, such as used in primitive times (if we may believe the authors of those ages) to have an influence upon men's belief and actions: To offer at the restoring of that would indeed be a wild project; it would be to dig up foundations; to destroy at one blow all the wit, and half the learning of the kingdom; to break the entire frame and constitution of things; to ruin trade, extinguish arts and sciences with the professors of them; in short, to turn our courts, exchanges, and shops into deserts; and would be full as absurd as the proposal of Horace, where he advises the Romans all in a body to leave their city, and seek a new seat in some remote part of the world, by way of cure for the corruption of their manners.

6   Therefore I think this caution was in itself altogether unnecessary, (which I have inserted only to prevent all possibility of cavilling) since every candid reader will easily understand my discourse to be intended only in defence of nominal Christianity; the other having been for some time wholly laid aside by general consent, as utterly inconsistent with our present schemes of wealth and power.

7   But why we should therefore cast off the name and title of Christians, although the general opinion and resolution be so violent for it, I confess I cannot (with submission) apprehend the consequence necessary. However, since the undertakers propose such wonderful advantages to the nation by this project, and advance many plausible objections against the system of Christianity, I shall briefly consider the strength of both, fairly allow them their greatest weight, and offer such answers as I think most reasonable.

After which I will beg leave to shew what inconveniences may possibly happen by such an innovation, in the present posture of our affairs.

8   *First,* One great advantage proposed by the abolishing of Christianity is, that it would very much enlarge and establish liberty of conscience, that great bulwark of our nation, and of the Protestant Religion, which is still too much limited by priestcraft, notwithstanding all the good intentions of the legislature, as we have lately found by a severe instance. For it is confidently reported, that two young gentlemen of real hopes, bright wit, and profound judgment, who upon a thorough examination of causes and effects, and by the mere force of natural abilities, without the least tincture for learning, having made a discovery, that there was no God, and generously communicating their thoughts for the good of the public, were some time ago, by an unparalleled severity, and upon I know not what obsolete law, broke for blasphemy. And as it hath been wisely observed, if persecution once begins, no man alive knows how far it may reach, or where it will end.

9   In answer to all which, with deference to wiser judgments, I think this rather shews the necessity of a nominal religion among us. Great wits love to be free with the highest objects; and if they cannot be allowed a God to revile or renounce, they will speak evil of dignities, abuse the government, and reflect upon the ministry; which I am sure few will deny to be of much more pernicious consequence, according to the saying of Tiberius, *Deorum offensa diis curæ.* As to the particular fact related, I think it is not fair to argue from one instance, perhaps another cannot be produced; yet (to the comfort of all those who may be apprehensive of persecution) blasphemy we know is freely spoken a million of times in every coffeehouse and tavern, or wherever else good company meet. It must be allowed indeed, that to break an English free-born officer only for blasphemy, was, to speak the gentlest of such an action, a very high strain of absolute power. Little can be said in excuse for the general; perhaps he was afraid it might give offence to the allies, among whom, for aught we know, it may be the custom of the country to believe a God. But if he argued, as some have done, upon a mistaken principle, that an officer who is guilty of speaking blasphemy, may some time or other proceed so far as to raise a mutiny, the consequence is by no means to be admitted; for, surely the commander of an English army is likely to be but ill obeyed, whose soldiers fear and reverence him as little as they do a Deity.

10   It is further objected against the Gospel System, that it obliges men to the belief of things too difficult for free-thinkers, and such who have shaken off the prejudices that usually cling to a confined education. To which I answer, that men should be cautious how they raise objections which reflect upon the wisdom of the nation. Is not every body freely allowed to believe whatever he pleases, and to publish his belief to the world whenever he thinks fit, especially if it serves to strengthen the party which is in the right? Would any indifferent foreigner, who should read the trumpery lately written by Asgil, Tindal, Toland, Coward, and forty more, imagine the Gospel to be our rule of faith, and confirmed by parliaments? Does any man either believe, or say he believes, or desire to have it thought that he says he believes one syllable of the matter? And is any man worse received upon that score, or does he find his want of nominal faith a disadvantage to him in the pursuit of any civil or military employment? What if there be an old dormant statute or two against him, are they not now obsolete, to a degree, that Empsom and Dudley themselves if they were now alive, would find it impossible to put them in execution?

11   It is likewise urged, that there are, by computation, in this kingdom, above ten thousand parsons, whose revenues added to those of my lords the bishops, would suffice to maintain at least two hundred young gentlemen of wit and pleasure, and freethinking, enemies to priestcraft, narrow principles, pedantry, and prejudices; who might be an ornament to the Court and Town; And then, again, so great a number of able divines might be a recruit to our fleet and armies. This indeed appears to be a consideration of some weight: But then, on the other side, several things deserve to be considered likewise: As, first, whether it may not be thought necessary that in certain tracts or country, like what we call parishes, there shall be one man at least of abilities to read and write. Then it seems a wrong computation, that the revenues of the Church throughout this island would be large enough to maintain two hundred young gentlemen, or even half that number, after the present refined way of living; that is, to allow each of them such a rent, as in the modern form of speech, would make them easy. But still there is in this project a greater mischief behind; and we ought to beware of the woman's folly, who killed the hen that every morning laid her a golden egg. For, pray what would become of the race of men in the next age, if we had nothing to trust to beside the scrofulous, consumptive productions, furnished by our men of wit and pleasure, when, having

squandered away their vigour, health and estates, they are forced by some disagreeable marriage to piece up their broken fortunes, and entail rottenness and politeness on their posterity? Now, here are ten thousand persons reduced by the wise regulations of Henry the Eighth, to the necessity of a low diet, and moderate exercise, who are the only great restorers of our breed, without which the nation would in an age or two become one great hospital.

12   Another advantage proposed by the abolishing of Christianity, is the clear gain of one day in seven, which is now entirely lost, and consequently the kingdom one seventh less considerable in trade, business, and pleasure; besides the loss to the public of so many stately structures now in the hands of the Clergy, which might be converted into playhouses, exchanges, market-houses, common dormitories, and other public edifices.

13   I hope I shall be forgiven a hard word, if I call this a perfect *cavil*. I readily own there has been an old custom time out of mind, for people to assemble in the churches every Sunday, and that shops are still frequently shut, in order as it is conceived, to preserve the memory of that ancient practice, but how this can prove a hindrance to business or pleasure, is hard to imagine. What if the men of pleasure are forced one day in the week, to game at home instead of the chocolate-houses? Are not the taverns and coffeehouses open? Can there be a more convenient season for taking a dose of physic? Are fewer claps got upon Sundays than other days? Is not that the chief day for traders to sum up the accounts of the week, and for lawyers to prepare their briefs? But I would fain know how it can be pretended that the churches are misapplied? Where are more appointments and rendezvouzes of gallantry? Where more care to appear in the foremost box with greater advantage of dress? Where more meetings for business? Where more bargains driven of all sorts? And where so many conveniences or enticements to sleep?

14   There is one advantage greater than any of the foregoing, proposed by the abolishing of Christianity: that it will utterly extinguish parties among us, by removing those factious distinctions of High and Low Church, of Whig and Tory, Presbyterian and Church of England, which are now so many mutual clogs upon public proceedings, and are apt to prefer the gratifying themselves, or depressing their adversaries, before the most important interest of the state.

I confess, if it were certain that so great an advantage would redound to the nation by this expedient, I would submit and be silent: But will any man say, that if the words *whoring, drinking, cheating, lying, stealing*, were by act of parliament ejected out of the English tongue and dictionaries, we should all awake next morning chaste and temperate, honest and just, and lovers of truth? Is this a fair consequence? Or, if the physicians would forbid us to pronounce the words *pox, gout, rheumatism* and *stone*, would that expedient serve like so many talismans to destroy the diseases themselves? Are party and faction rooted in men's hearts no deeper than phrases borrowed from religion, or founded upon no firmer principles? And is our language so poor that we cannot find other terms to express them? Are *envy, pride, avarice* and *ambition* such ill nomenclators, that they cannot furnish appellations for their owners? Will not *heydukes* and *mamalukes, mandarins* and *patshaws*, or any other words formed at pleasure, serve to distinguish those who are in the ministry from others who would be in it if they could? What, for instance, is easier than to vary the form of speech, and instead of the word church, make it a question in politics, whether the Monument be in danger? Because religion was nearest at hand to furnish a few convenient phrases, is our invention so barren, we can find no other? Suppose, for argument sake, that the Tories favoured Margarita, the Whigs Mrs. Tofts, and the Trimmers Valentini, would not *Margaritians, Toftians*, and *Valentinians* be very tolerable marks of distinction? The *Prasini* and *Veniti*, two most virulent factions in Italy, began (if I remember right) by a distinction of colours in ribbons, which we might do with as good a grace about the dignity of the blue and the green, and would serve as properly to divide the Court, the Parliament, and the Kingdom between them, as any terms of art whatsoever, borrowed from religion. And therefore I think, there is little force in this objection against Christianity, or prospect of so great an advantage as is proposed in the abolishing of it.

16   'Tis again objected, as a very absurd ridiculous custom, that a set of men should be suffered, much less employed and hired, to bawl one day in seven against the lawfulness of those methods most in use toward the pursuit of greatness, riches and pleasure, which are the constant practice of all men alive on the other six. But this objection is, I think, a little unworthy so refined an age as ours. Let us argue this matter calmly: I appeal to the breast of any polite free-thinker, whether in the pursuit of gratifying a predominant passion, he hath not always felt a wonderful incitement, by reflecting it was a thing forbidden; and therefore we see, in order to cultivate this taste, the wisdom of the nation hath

taken special care, that the ladies should be furnished with prohibited silks, and the men with prohibited wine. And indeed it were to be wished, that some other prohibitions were promoted, in order to improve the pleasures of the town; which, for want of such expedients begin already, as I am told, to flag and grow languid, giving way daily to cruel inroads from the spleen.

17   'Tis likewise proposed as a great advantage to the public, that if we once discard the system of the Gospel, all religion will of course be banished for ever; and consequently, along with it, those grievous prejudices of education, which under the names of *virtue, conscience, honour, justice*, and the like, are so apt to disturb the peace of human minds, and the notions whereof are so hard to be eradicated by right reason or freethinking, sometimes during the whole course of our lives.

18   Here first, I observe how difficult it is to get rid of a phrase, which the world is once grown fond of, though the occasion that first produced it, be entirely taken away. For several years past, if a man had but an ill-favoured nose, the deep-thinkers of the age would some way or other contrive to impute the cause to the prejudice of his education. From this fountain were said to be derived all our foolish notions of justice, piety, love of our country, all our opinions of God, or a future state, Heaven, Hell, and the like: And there might formerly perhaps have been some pretence for this charge. But so effectual care has been taken to remove those prejudices, by an entire change in the methods of education, that (with honour I mention it to our polite innovators) the young gentlemen who are now on the scene, seem to have not the least tincture of those infusions, or string of those weeds; and, by consequence, the reason for abolishing nominal Christianity upon that pretext, is wholly ceased.

19   For the rest, it may perhaps admit a controversy, whether the banishing of all notions of religion whatsoever, would be convenient for the vulgar. Not that I am in the least of opinion with those who hold religion to have been the invention of politicians, to keep the lower part of the world in awe by the fear of invisible powers; unless mankind were then very different to what it is now: For I look upon the mass or body of our people here in England, to be as free-thinkers, that is to say, as staunch unbelievers, as any of the highest rank. But I conceive some scattered notions about a superior power to be of singular use for the common people, as furnishing excellent materials to keep children quiet when they grow peevish, and providing topics of amusement in a tedious winter-night.

20   Lastly, 'tis proposed as a singular advantage, that the abolishing of Christianity will very much contribute to the uniting of Protestants, by enlarging the terms of communion so as to take in all sorts of dissenters, who are now shut out of the pale upon account of a few ceremonies which all sides confess to be things indifferent: That this alone will effectually answer the great ends of a scheme for comprehension, by opening a large noble gate, at which all bodies may enter; whereas the chaffering with dissenters, and dodging about this or t'other ceremony, is but like opening a few wickets, and leaving them at jar, by which no more than one can get in at a time, and that, not without stooping, and sideling, and squeezing his body.

21   To all this I answer; that there is one darling inclination of mankind, which usually affects to be a retainer to religion, though she be neither its parent, its godmother, or its friend; I mean the spirit of opposition, that lived long before Christianity, and can easily subsist without it. Let us, for instance, examine wherein the opposition of sectaries among us consists, we shall find Christianity to have no share in it at all. Does the Gospel any where prescribe a starched, squeezed countenance, a stiff, formal gait, a singularity of manners and habit, or any affected modes of speech different from the reasonable part of mankind? Yet, if Christianity did not lend its name to stand in the gap, and to employ or divert these humours, they must of necessity be spent in contraventions to the laws of the land, and disturbance of the public peace. There is a portion of enthusiasm assigned to every nation, which, if it hath not proper objects to work on, will burst out, and set all into a flame. If the quiet of a state can be bought by only flinging men a few ceremonies to devour, it is a purchase no wise man would refuse. Let the mastiffs amuse themselves about a sheep's skin stuffed with hay, provided it will keep them from worrying the flock. The institution of convents abroad, seems in one point a strain of great wisdom, there being few irregularities in human passions, which may not have recourse to vent themselves in some of those orders, which are so many retreats for the speculative, the melancholy, the proud, the silent, the politic and the morose, to spend themselves, and evaporate the noxious particles; for each of whom we in this island are forced to provide a several sect of religion, to keep them quiet: And whenever Christianity shall be abolished, the legislature must find some other expedient to employ and entertain them. For what imports it how large a gate you open, if there will be always left a number who place a pride and a merit in not coming in?

22   Having thus considered the most important objections against Christianity, and the chief advantages proposed by the abolishing thereof; I shall now with equal deference and submission to wiser judgments as before, proceed to mention a few inconveniences that may happen, if the Gospel should be repealed; which perhaps the projectors may not have sufficiently considered.

23   And first, I am very sensible how much the gentlemen of wit and pleasure are apt to murmur, and be choqued at the sight of so many draggled-tail parsons, that happen to fall in their way, and offend their eyes; but at the same time, these wise reformers do not consider what an advantage and felicity it is, for great wits to be always provided with objects of scorn and contempt, in order to exercise and improve their talents, and divert their spleen from falling on each other or on themselves; especially when all this may be done without the least imaginable danger to their persons.

24   And to urge another argument of a parallel nature: If Christianity were once abolished, how could the freethinkers, the strong reasoners, and the men of profound learning, be able to find another subject so calculated in all points whereon to display their abilities? What wonderful productions of wit should we be deprived of, from those whose genius by continual practice hath been wholly turned upon raillery and invectives against religion, and would therefore never be able to shine or distinguish themselves upon any other subject! We are daily complaining of the great decline of wit among us, and would we take away the greatest, perhaps the only topic we have left? Who would ever have suspected Asgil for a wit, or Toland for a philosopher, if the inexhaustible stock of Christianity had not been at hand to provide them with materials? What other subject, through all art or nature, could have produced Tindal for a profound author, or furnished him with readers? It is the wise choice of the subject that alone adorns and distinguishes the writer. For, had a hundred such pens as these been employed on the side of religion, they would have immediately sunk into silence and oblivion.

25   Nor do I think it wholly groundless, or my fears altogether imaginary, that the abolishing of Christianity may perhaps bring the Church into danger, or at least put the senate to the trouble of another securing vote. I desire I may not be mistaken; I am far from presuming to affirm or think that the Church is in danger at present, or as things now stand; but we know not how soon it may be so when the Christian religion is repealed. As plausible as this project seems, there may a dangerous design lurk under

it: Nothing can be more notorious, than that the Atheists, Deists, Socinians, Anti-trinitarians, and other subdivisions of free-thinkers, are persons of little zeal for the present ecclesiastical establishment: Their declared opinion is for repealing the Sacramental Test; they are very indifferent with regard to ceremonies; nor do they hold the *jus divinum* of Episcopacy. Therefore this may be intended as one politic step toward altering the constitution of the Church established, and setting up Presbytery in the stead, which I leave to be further considered by those at the helm.

26   In the last place, I think nothing can be more plain, than that by this expedient, we shall run into the evil we chiefly pretend to avoid; and that the abolishment of the Christian religion will be the readiest course we can take to introduce popery. And I am the more inclined to this opinion, because we know it has been the constant practice of the Jesuits to send over emissaries, with instructions to personate themselves members of the several prevailing sects among us. So it is recorded, that they have at sundry times appeared in the guise of Presbyterians, Anabaptists, Independents and Quakers, according as any of these were most in credit; so, since the fashion hath been taken up of exploding religion, the popish missionaries have not been wanting to mix with the freethinkers; among whom, Toland the great oracle of the Antichristians is an Irish priest, the son of an Irish priest; and the most learned and ingenious author of a book called "The Rights of the Christian Church," was in a proper juncture reconciled to the Romish faith, whose true son, as appears by a hundred passages in his treatise, he still continues. Perhaps I could add some others to the number; but the fact is beyond dispute, and the reasoning they proceed by is right: For, supposing Christianity to be extinguished, the people will never be at ease till they find out some other method of worship; which will as infallibly produce superstition, as this will end in popery.

27   And therefore, if notwithstanding all I have said, it still be thought necessary to have a bill brought in for repealing Christianity, I would humbly offer an amendment; that instead of the word, Christianity, may be put religion in general; which I conceive will much better answer all the good ends proposed by the projectors of it. For, as long as we leave in being a God and his providence, with all the necessary consequences which curious and inquisitive men will be apt to draw from such premises, we do not strike at the root of the evil, though we should ever so effectually annihilate the present scheme of the Gospel: For, of what use is freedom of

thought, if it will not produce freedom of action, which is the sole end, how remote soever in appearance, of all objections against Christianity? And therefore, the freethinkers consider it as a sort of edifice, wherein all the parts have such a mutual dependence on each other, that if you happen to pull out one single nail, the whole fabric must fall to the ground. This was happily expressed by him who had heard of a text brought for proof of the Trinity, which in an ancient manuscript was differently read; he thereupon immediately took the hint, and by a sudden deduction of a long *sorites*, most logically concluded; "Why, if it be as you say, I may safely whore and drink on, and defy the parson." From which, and many the like instances easy to be produced, I think nothing can be more manifest, than that the quarrel is not against any particular points of hard digestion in the Christian system, but against religion in general; which, by laying restraints on human nature, is supposed the great enemy to the freedom of thought and action.

28   Upon the whole, if it shall still be thought for the benefit of Church and State, that Christianity be abolished; I conceive however, it may be more convenient to defer the execution to a time of peace, and not venture in this conjuncture to disoblige our allies, who, as it falls out, are all Christians, and many of them, by the prejudices of their education, so bigoted, as to place a sort of pride in the appellation. If upon being rejected by them, we are to trust an alliance with the Turk, we shall find ourselves much deceived: For, as he is too remote, and generally engaged in war with the Persian emperor, so his people would be more scandalized at our infidelity, than our Christian neighbours. For they [the Turks] are not only strict observers of religious worship, but what is worse, believe a God; which is more than required of us even while we preserve the name of Christians.

29   To conclude: Whatever some may think of the great advantages to trade by this favourite scheme, I do very much apprehend, that in six months time after the act is passed for the extirpation of the Gospel, the Bank, and East-India Stock, may fall at least one *per cent*. And since that is fifty times more than ever the wisdom of our age thought fit to venture for the preservation of Christianity, there is no reason we should be at so great a loss, merely for the sake of destroying it.

Man Against Darkness

W. T. Stace

1

1   The Catholic bishops of America recently issued a statement in which they said that the chaotic and bewildered state of the modern world is due to man's loss of faith, his abandonment of God and religion. For my part I believe in no religion at all. Yet I entirely agree with the bishops. It is no doubt an oversimplification to speak of *the* cause of so complex a state of affairs as the tortured condition of the world today. Its causes are doubtless multitudinous. Yet allowing for some element of oversimplification, I say that the bishops' assertion is substantially true.

2   M. Jean-Paul Sartre, the French existentialist philosopher, labels himself an atheist. Yet his views seem to me plainly to support the statement of the bishops. So long as there was believed to be a God in the sky, he says, men could regard him as the source of their moral ideals. The universe, created and governed by a fatherly God, was a friendly habitation for man. We could be sure that, however great the evil in the world, good in the end would triumph and the forces of evil would be routed. With the disappearance of God from the sky all this has changed. Since the world is not ruled by a spiritual being, but rather by blind forces, there cannot be any ideals, moral or otherwise, in the universe outside us. Our ideals, therefore, must proceed only from our own minds; they are our own inventions. Thus the world which surrounds us is nothing but an immense spiritual emptiness. It is a dead universe. We do not live in a universe which is on the side of our values. It is completely indifferent to them.

3   Years ago Mr. Bertrand Russell, in his essay *Free Man's Wor-ship*, said much the same thing.

> Such in outline, but even more purposeless, more void of meaning, is the world which Science presents for our belief. Amid such a world, if anywhere, our ideals henceforward must find a home. . . . Blind to good and evil, reckless of destruction, omnipotent matter rolls on its relentless way; for man, condemned today to lose his dearest, tomorrow himself to pass through the gate of darkness, it remains only to cherish, ere yet the blow falls, the lofty thoughts that ennoble his little day; . . . to worship at the shrine his own hands have built; . . . to sustain alone, a weary but unyielding Atlas, the world that his own ideals have fashioned despite the trampling march of unconscious power.

4   It is true that Mr. Russell's personal attitude to the disappearance of religion is quite different from either that of M. Sartre or the bishops or myself. The bishops think it a calamity. So do I. M. Sartre finds it "very distressing." And he berates as shallow the attitude of those who think that without God the world can go on just the same as before, as if nothing had happened. This creates for mankind, he thinks, a terrible crisis. And in this I agree with him. Mr. Russell, on the other hand, seems to believe that religion has done more harm than good in the world, and that its disappearance will be a blessing. But his picture of the world, and of the modern mind, is the same as that of M. Sartre. He stresses the *purposelessness* of the universe, the facts that man's ideals are his own creations, that the universe outside him in no way supports them, that man is alone and friendless in the world.

5   Mr. Russell notes that it is science which has produced this situation. There is no doubt that this is correct. But the way in which it has come about is not generally understoood. There is a popular belief that some particular scientific discoveries or theories, such as the Darwinian theory of evolution, or the views of geologists about the age of the earth, or a series of such discoveries, have done the damage. It would be foolish to deny that these discoveries have had a great effect in undermining religious dogmas. But this account does not at all go to the root of the matter. Religion can probably outlive any scientific discoveries which could be made. It can accommodate itself to them. The root cause of the decay of faith has not been any particular discovery of science, but rather the general spirit of science and certain basic assumptions upon which modern science, from the seventeenth century onwards, has proceeded.

2

6   It was Galileo and Newton—notwithstanding that Newton himself was a deeply religious man—who destroyed the old comfortable picture of a friendly universe governed by spiritual values. And this was effected, not by Newton's discovery of the law of gravitation nor by any of Galileo's brilliant investigations, but by the general picture of the world which these men and others of their time made the basis of the science, not only of their own day, but of all succeeding generations down to the present. That is why the century immediately following Newton, the eighteenth century, was notoriously an age of religious skepticism. Skepticism did not have to wait for the discoveries of Darwin and the geologists in the nineteenth century. It flooded the world immediately after the age of the rise of science.

7   Neither the Copernican hypothesis nor any of Newton's or Galileo's particular discoveries were the real causes. Religious faith might well have accommodated itself to the new astronomy. The real turning point between the medieval age of faith and the modern age of unfaith came when the scientists of the seventeenth century turned their backs upon what used to be called "final causes." The final cause of a thing or event meant the purpose which it was supposed to serve in the universe, its cosmic purpose. What lay back of this was the presupposition that there is a cosmic order or plan and that everything which exists could in the last analysis be explained in terms of its place in this cosmic plan, that is, in terms of its purpose.

8   Plato and Aristotle believed this, and so did the whole medieval Christian world. For instance, if it were true that the sun and the moon were created and exist for the purpose of giving light to man, then this fact would explain why the sun and the moon exist. We might not be able to discover the purpose of everything, but everything must have a purpose. Belief in final causes thus amounted to a belief that the world is governed by purposes, presumably the purposes of some overruling mind. This belief was not the invention of Christianity. It was basic to the whole of Western civilization, whether in the ancient pagan world or in Christendom, from the time of Socrates to the rise of science in the seventeenth century.

9   The founders of modern science—for instance, Galileo, Kepler, and Newton—were mostly pious men who did not doubt God's purposes. Nevertheless they took the revolutionary step of consciously and deliberately expelling the idea of purpose as control-

ling nature from their new science of nature. They did this on the ground that inquiry into purposes is useless for what science aims at: namely, the prediction and control of events. To predict an eclipse, what you have to know is not its purpose but its causes. Hence science from the seventeenth century onwards became exclusively an inquiry into causes. The conception of purpose in the world was ignored and frowned on. This, though silent and almost unnoticed, was the greatest revolution in human history, far outweighing in importance any of the political revolutions whose thunder has reverberated through the world.

10   For it came about in this way that for the past three hundred years there has been growing up in men's minds, dominated as they are by science, a new imaginative picture of the world. The world, according to this new picture, is purposeless, senseless, meaningless. Nature is nothing but matter in motion. The motions of matter are governed, not by any purpose, but by blind forces and laws. Nature on this view, says Whitehead—to whose writings I am indebted in this part of my paper—is "merely the hurrying of material, endlessly, meaninglessly." You can draw a sharp line across the history of Europe dividing it into two epochs of very unequal length. The line passes through the lifetime of Galileo. European man before Galileo—whether ancient pagan or more recent Christian—thought of the world as controlled by plan and purpose. After Galileo European man thinks of it as utterly purposeless. This is the great revolution of which I spoke.

11   It is this which has killed religion. Religion could survive the discoveries that the sun, not the earth, is the center; that men are descended from simian ancestors; that the earth is hundreds of millions of years old. These discoveries may render out of date some of the details of older theological dogmas, may force their restatement in new intellectual frameworks. But they do not touch the essence of the religious vision itself, which is the faith that there is plan and purpose in the world, that the world is a moral order, that in the end all things are for the best. This faith may express itself through many different intellectual dogmas, those of Christianity, of Hinduism, of Islam. All and any of these intellectual dogmas may be destroyed without destroying the essential religious spirit. But that spirit cannot survive destruction of belief in a plan and purpose of the world, for that is the very heart of it. Religion can get on with any sort of astronomy, geology, biology, physics. But it cannot get on with a purposeless and meaningless universe.

12 If the scheme of things is purposeless and meaningless, then the life of man is purposeless and meaningless too. Everything is futile, all effort is in the end worthless. A man may, of course, still pursue disconnected ends, money, fame, art, science, and may gain pleasure from them. But his life is hollow at the center. Hence the dissatisfied, disillusioned, restless, spirit of modern man.

13 The picture of a meaningless world, and a meaningless human life, is, I think, the basic theme of much modern art and literature. Certainly it is the basic theme of modern philosophy. According to the most characteristic philosophies of the modern period from Hume in the eighteenth century to the so-called positivists of today, the world is just what it is, and that is the end of all inquiry. There is no reason for its being what it is. Everything might just as well have been quite different, and there would have been no reason for that either. When you have stated what things are, what things the world contains, there is nothing more which could be said, even by an omniscient being. To ask any question about *why* things are thus, or what purpose their being so serves, is to ask a senseless question, because they serve no purpose at all. For instance, there is for modern philosophy no such thing as the ancient problem of evil. For this once famous question presupposes that pain and misery, though they seem so inexplicable and irrational to us, must ultimately subserve some rational purpose, must have their places in the cosmic plan. But this is nonsense. There is no such overruling rationality in the universe. Belief in the ultimate irrationality of everything is the quintessence of what is called the modern mind.

14 It is true that, parallel with these philosophies which are typical of the modern mind, preaching the meaninglessness of the world, there has run a line of idealistic philosophies whose contention is that the world is after all spiritual in nature and that moral ideals and values are inherent in its structure. But most of these idealisms were simply philosophical expressions of romanticism, which was itself no more than an unsuccessful counterattack of the religious against the scientific view of things. They perished, along with romanticism in literature and art, about the beginning of the present century, though of course they still have a few adherents.

15 At the bottom these idealistic systems of thought were rationalizations of man's wishful thinking. They were born of the refusal of men to admit the cosmic darkness. They were comforting illusions within the warm glow of which the more tender-minded

intellectuals sought to shelter themselves from the icy winds of the universe. They lasted a little while. But they are shattered now, and we return once more to the vision of a purposeless world.

3

16   Along with the ruin of the religious vision there went the ruin of moral principles and indeed of all values. If there is a cosmic purpose, if there is in the nature of things a drive towards goodness, then our moral systems will derive their validity from this. But if our moral rules do not proceed from something outside us in the nature of the universe—whether we say it is God or simply the universe itself—then they must be our own inventions. Thus it came to be believed that moral rules must be merely an expression of our own likes and dislikes. But likes and dislikes are notoriously variable. What pleases one man, people, or culture displeases another. Therefore morals are wholly relative.

17   This obvious conclusion from the idea of a purposeless world made its appearance in Europe immediately after the rise of science, for instance in the philosophy of Hobbes. Hobbes saw at once that if there is no purpose in the world there are no values either. "Good and evil," he writes, "are names that signify our appetites and aversions; which in different tempers, customs, and doctrines of men are different. . . . Every man calleth that which pleaseth him, good; and that which displeaseth him, evil."

18   This doctrine of the relativity of morals, though it has recently received an impetus from the studies of anthropologists, was thus really implicit in the whole scientific mentality. It is disastrous for morals because it destroys their entire traditional foundation. That is why philosophers who see the danger signals, from the time at least of Kant, have been trying to give to morals a new foundation, that is, a secular or nonreligious foundation. This attempt may very well be intellectually successful. Such a foundation, independent of the religious view of the world, might well be found. But the question is whether it can ever be a *practical* success, that is, whether apart from its logical validity and its influence with intellectuals, it can ever replace among the masses of men the lost religious foundation. On that question hangs perhaps the future of civilization. But meanwhile disaster is overtaking us.

19   The widespread belief in "ethical relativity" among philosophers, psychologists, ethnologists, and sociologists is the theoretical

counterpart of the repudiation of principle which we see all around us, especially in international affairs, the field in which morals have always had the weakest foothold. No one any longer effectively believes in moral principles except as the private prejudices either of individual men or of nations or cultures. This is the inevitable consequence of the doctrine of ethical relativity, which in turn is the inevitable consequence of believing in a purposeless world.

20   Another characteristic of our spiritual state is loss of belief in the freedom of the will. This also is a fruit of the scientific spirit, though not of any particular scientific discovery. Science has been built up on the basis of determinism, which is the belief that every event is completely determined by a chain of causes and is therefore theoretically predictable beforehand. It is true that recent physics seems to challenge this. But so far as its practical consequences are concerned, the damage has long ago been done. A man's actions, it was argued, are as much events in the natural world as is an eclipse of the sun. It follows that men's actions are as theoretically predictable as an eclipse. But if it is certain now that John Smith will murder Joseph Jones at 2.15 P.M. on January 1, 1963, what possible meaning can it have to say that when that time comes John Smith will be *free* to choose whether he will commit the murder or not? And if he is not free, how can he be held responsible?

21   It is true that the whole of this argument can be shown by a competent philosopher to be a tissue of fallacies—or at least I claim that it can. But the point is that the analysis required to show this is much too subtle to be understood by the average entirely unphilosophical man. Because of this, the argument against free will is generally swallowed whole by the unphilosophical. Hence the thought that man is not free, that he is the helpless plaything of forces over which he has no control, has deeply penetrated the modern mind. We hear of economic determinism, cultural determinism, historical determinism. We are not responsible for what we do because our glands control us, or because we are the products of environment or heredity. Not moral self-control, but the doctor, the psychiatrist, the educationist, must save us from doing evil. Pills and injections in the future are to do what Christ and the prophets have failed to do. Of course I do not mean to deny that doctors and educationists can and must help. And I do not mean in any way to belittle their efforts. But I do wish to draw

attention to the weakening of moral controls, the greater or less repudiation of personal responsibility which, in the popular thinking of the day, result from these tendencies of thought.

4

22   What, then, is to be done? Where are we to look for salvation from the evils of our time? All the remedies I have seen suggested so far are, in my opinion, useless. Let us look at some of them.

23   Philosophers and intellectuals generally can, I believe, genuinely do something to help. But it is extremely little. What philosophers can do is to show that neither the relativity of morals nor the denial of free will really follows from the grounds which have been supposed to support them. They can also try to discover a genuine secular basis for morals to replace the religious basis which has disappeared. Some of us are trying to do these things. But in the first place philosophers unfortunately are not agreed about these matters, and their disputes are utterly confusing to the non-philosophers. And in the second place their influence is practically negligible because their analyses necessarily take place on a level on which the masses are totally unable to follow them.

24   The bishops, of course, propose as remedy a return to belief in God and in the doctrines of the Christian religion. Others think that a new religion is what is needed. Those who make these proposals fail to realize that the crisis in man's spiritual condition is something unique in history for which there is no sort of analogy in the past. They are thinking perhaps of the collapse of the ancient Greek and Roman religions. The vacuum then created was easily filled by Christianity, and it might have been filled by Mithraism if Christianity had not appeared. By analogy they think that Christianity might now be replaced by a new religion, or even that Christianity itself, if revivified, might bring back health to men's lives.

25   But I believe that there is no analogy at all between our present state and that of the European peoples at the time of the fall of paganism. Men had at that time lost their belief only in particular dogmas, particular embodiments of the religious view of the world. It had no doubt become incredible that Zeus and the other gods were living on the top of Mount Olympus. You could go to the top and find no trace of them. But the imaginative picture of a world governed by purpose, a world driving towards the good— which is the inner spirit of religion—had at that time received no

serious shock. It had merely to re-embody itself in new dogmas, those of Christianity or some other religion. Religion itself was not dead in the world, only a particular form of it.

26 But now the situation is quite different. It is not merely that particular dogmas, like that of the virgin birth, are unacceptable to the modern mind. That is true, but it constitutes a very superficial diagnosis of the present situation of religion. Modern skepticism is of a wholly different order from that of the intellectuals of the ancient world. It has attacked and destroyed not merely the outward forms of the religious spirit, its particularized dogmas, but the very essence of that spirit itself, belief in a meaningful and purposeful world. For the founding of a new religion a new Jesus Christ or Buddha would have to appear, in itself a most unlikely event and one for which in any case we cannot afford to sit and wait. But even if a new prophet and a new religion did appear, we may predict that they would fail in the modern world. No one for long would believe in them, for modern men have lost the vision, basic to all religion, of an ordered plan and purpose of the world. They have before their minds the picture of a purposeless universe, and such a world-picture must be fatal to any religion at all, not merely to Christianity.

27 We must not be misled by occasional appearances of a revival of the religious spirit. Men, we are told, in their disgust and disillusionment at the emptiness of their lives, are turning once more to religion, or are searching for a new message. It may be so. We must expect such wistful yearnings of the spirit. We must expect men to wish back again the light that is gone, and to try to bring it back. But however they may wish and try, the light will not shine again,—not at least in the civilization to which we belong.

28 Another remedy commonly proposed is that we should turn to science itself, or the scientific spirit, for our salvation. Mr. Russell and Professor Dewey both make this proposal, though in somewhat different ways. Professor Dewey seems to believe that discoveries in sociology, the application of scientific method to social and political problems will rescue us. This seems to me to be utterly naïve. It is not likely that science, which is basically the cause of our spiritual troubles, is likely also to produce the cure for them. Also it lies in the nature of science that, though it can teach us the best means for achieving our ends, it can never tell us what ends to pursue. It cannot give us any ideals. And our trouble is about ideals and ends, not about the means for reaching them.

5

29   No civilization can live without ideals, or to put it in another
way, without a firm faith in moral ideas. Our ideals and moral
ideas have in the past been rooted in religion. But the religious
basis of our ideals has been undermined, and the superstructure
of ideals is plainly tottering. None of the commonly suggested
remedies on examination seems likely to succeed. It would therefore look as if the early death of our civilization were inevitable.

30   Of course we know that it is perfectly possible for individual
men, very highly educated men, philosophers, scientists, intellectuals in general, to live moral lives without any religious con-
victions. But the question is whether a whole civilization, a whole
family of peoples, composed almost entirely of relatively uneducated men and women, can do this.

31   It follows, of course, that if we could make the vast majority
of men as highly educated as the very few are now, we might save
the situation. And we are already moving slowly in that direction
through the techniques of mass education. But the critical question seems to concern the time-lag. Perhaps in a few hundred years
most of the population will, at the present rate, be sufficiently
highly educated and civilized to combine high ideals with an absence of religion. But long before we reach any such stage, the
collapse of our civilization may have come about. How are we to
live through the intervening period?

32   I am sure that the first thing we have to do is to face the truth,
however bleak it may be, and then next we have to learn to live
with it. Let me say a word about each of these two points. What
I am urging as regards the first is complete honesty. Those who
wish to resurrect Christian dogmas are not, of course, consciously
dishonest. But they have that kind of unconscious dishonesty which
consists in lulling oneself with opiates and dreams. Those who talk
of a new religion are merely hoping for a new opiate. Both alike
refuse to face the truth that there is, in the universe outside man,
no spirituality, no regard for values, no friend in the sky, no help
or comfort for man of any sort. To be perfectly honest in the
admission of this fact, not to seek shelter in new or old illusions,
not to indulge in wishful dreams about this matter, this is the first
thing we shall have to do.

33   I do not urge this course out of any special regard for the sanctity of truth in the abstract. It is not self-evident to me that truth
is the supreme value to which all else must be sacrificed. Might not
the discoverer of a truth which would be fatal to mankind be

justified in suppressing it, even in teaching men a falsehood? Is truth more valuable than goodness and beauty and happiness? To think so is to invent yet another absolute, another religious delusion in which Truth with a capital T is substituted for God. The reason why we must now boldly and honestly face the truth that the universe is non-spiritual and indifferent to goodness, beauty, happiness, or truth is not that it would be wicked to suppress it, but simply that it is too late to do so, so that in the end we cannot do anything else but face it. Yet we stand on the brink, dreading the icy plunge. We need courage. We need honesty.

34 Now about the other point, the necessity of learning to live with the truth. This means learning to live virtuously and happily, or at least contentedly, without illusions. And this is going to be extremely difficult because what we have now begun dimly to perceive is that human life in the past, or at least human happiness, has almost wholly depended upon illusions. It has been said that man lives by truth, and that the truth will make us free. Nearly the opposite seems to me to be the case. Mankind has managed to live only by means of lies, and the truth may very well destroy us. If one were a Bergsonian one might believe that nature deliberately puts illusions into our souls in order to induce us to go on living.

35 The illusions by which men have lived seem to be of two kinds. First, there is what one may perhaps call the Great Illusion—I mean the religious illusion that the universe is moral and good, that it follows a wise and noble plan, that it is gradually generating some supreme value, that goodness is bound to triumph in it. Secondly, there is a whole host of minor illusions on which human happiness nourishes itself. How much of human happiness notoriously comes from the illusions of the lover about his beloved? Then again we work and strive because of the illusions connected with fame, glory, power, or money. Banners of all kinds, flags, emblems, insignia, ceremonials, and rituals are invariably symbols of some illusion or other. The British Empire, the connection between mother country and dominions, is partly kept going by illusions surrounding the notion of kingship. Or think of the vast amount of human happiness which is derived from the illusion of supposing that if some nonsense syllable, such as "sir" or "count" or "lord" is pronounced in conjunction with our names, we belong to a superior order of people.

36 There is plenty of evidence that human happiness is almost wholly based upon illusions of one kind or another. But the scientific spirit, or the spirit of truth, is the enemy of illusions and

therefore the enemy of human happiness. That is why it is going to be so difficult to live with the truth.

37   There is no reason why we should have to give up the host of minor illusions which render life supportable. There is no reason why the lover should be scientific about the loved one. Even the illusions of fame and glory may persist. But without the Great Illusion, the illusion of a good, kindly, and purposeful universe, we shall *have* to learn to live. And to ask this is really no more than to ask that we become genuinely civilized beings and not merely sham civilized beings.

38   I can best explain the difference by a reminiscence. I remember a fellow student in my college days, an ardent Christian, who told me that if he did not believe in a future life, in heaven and hell, he would rape, murder, steal, and be a drunkard. That is what I call being a sham civilized being. On the other hand, not only could a Huxley, a John Stuart Mill, a David Hume, live great and fine lives without any religion, but a great many others of us, quite obscure persons, can at least live decent lives without it.

39   To be genuinely civilized means to be able to walk straightly and to live honorably without the props and crutches of one or another of the childish dreams which have so far supported men. That such a life is likely to be ecstatically happy I will not claim. But that it can be lived in quiet content, accepting resignedly what cannot be helped, not expecting the impossible, and thankful for small mercies, this I would maintain. That it will be difficult for men in general to learn this lesson I do not deny. But that it will be impossible I would not admit since so many have learned it already.

40   Man has not yet grown up. He is not adult. Like a child he cries for the moon and lives in a world of fantasies. And the race as a whole has perhaps reached the great crisis of its life. Can it grow up as a race in the same sense as individual men grow up? Can man put away childish things and adolescent dreams? Can he grasp the real world as it actually is, stark and bleak, without its romantic or religious halo, and still retain his ideals, striving for great ends and noble achievements? If he can, all may yet be well. If he cannot, he will probably sink back into the savagery and brutality from which he came, taking a humble place once more among the lower animals.

Aes Triplex

Robert Louis Stevenson

1   The changes wrought by death are in themselves so sharp and final, and so terrible and melancholy in their consequences, that the thing stands alone in man's experience, and has no parallel upon earth. It out-does all other accidents because it is the last of them. Sometimes it leaps suddenly upon its victims, like a Thug; sometimes it lays a regular siege and creeps upon their citadel during a score of years. And when the business is done, there is sore havoc made in other people's lives, and a pin knocked out by which many subsidiary friendships hung together. There are empty chairs, solitary walks, and single beds at night. Again, in taking away our friends, death does not take them away utterly, but leaves behind a mocking, tragical, and soon intolerable residue, which must be hurriedly concealed. Hence a whole chapter of sights and customs striking to the mind, from the pyramids of Egypt to the gibbets and dule trees of mediaeval Europe. The poorest persons have a bit of pageant going towards the tomb; memorial stones are set up over the least memorable; and, in order to preserve some show of respect for what remains of our old loves and friendships, we must accompany it with much grimly ludicrous ceremonial, and the hired undertaker parades before the door. All this, and much more of the same sort, accompanied by the eloquence of poets, has gone a great way to put humanity in error; nay, in many philosophies the error has been embodied and laid down with every circumstance of logic; although in real life the bustle and swiftness, in leaving people little time to think, have not left them time enough to go dangerously wrong in practice.

2   As a matter of fact, although few things are spoken of with more fearful whisperings than this prospect of death, few have less influence on conduct under healthy circumstances. We have all heard

of cities in South America built upon the side of fiery mountains, and how, even in this tremendous neighborhood, the inhabitants are not a jot more impressed by the solemnity of mortal conditions than if they were delving gardens in the greenest corner of England. There are serenades and suppers and much gallantry among the myrtles overhead; and meanwhile the foundation shudders underfoot, the bowels of the mountain growl, and at any moment living ruin may leap sky-high into the moonlight, and tumble man and his merry-making in the dust. In the eyes of very young people, and very dull old ones, there is something indescribably reckless and desperate in such a picture. It seems not credible that respectable married people, with umbrellas, should find appetite for a bit of supper within quite a long distance of a fiery mountain; ordinary life begins to smell of high-handed debauch when it is carried on so close to a catastrophe; and even cheese and salad, it seems, could hardly be relished in such circumstances without something like a defiance of the Creator. It should be a place for nobody but hermits dwelling in prayer and maceration or mere born-devils drowning care in a perpetual carouse.

3   And yet, when one comes to think upon it calmly, the situation of these South American citizens forms only a very pale figure for the state of ordinary mankind. This world itself, travelling blindly and swiftly in over-crowded space, among a million other worlds travelling blindly and swiftly in contrary directions, may very well come by a knock that would set it into explosion like a penny squib. And what, pathologically looked at, is the human body with all its organs, but a mere bagful of petards? The least of these is as dangerous to the whole economy as the ship's powder-magazine to the ship; and with every breath we breathe, and every meal we eat, we are putting one or more of them in peril. If we clung as devotedly as some philosophers pretend we do to the abstract idea of life, or were half as frightened as they make out we are, for the subversive accident that ends it all, the trumpets might sound by the hour and no one would follow them into battle —the blue-peter might fly at the truck, but who would climb into a sea-going ship? Think (if these philosophers were right) with what a preparation of spirit we should affront the daily peril of the dinner-table: a deadlier spot than any battle-field in history, where the far greater proportion of our ancestors have miserably left their bones! What woman would ever be lured into marriage, so much more dangerous than the wildest sea? And what would it be to grow old? For, after a certain distance, every step we take in life we find the ice growing thinner below our feet, and all

around us and behind us we see our contemporaries going through.
By the time a man gets well into the seventies, his continued
existence is a mere miracle; and when he lays his old bones in bed
for the night, there is an overwhelming probability that he will
never see the day. Do the old men mind it, as a matter of fact?
Why, no. They were never merrier; they have their grog at night,
and tell the raciest stories; they hear of the death of people about
their own age, or even younger, not as if it was a grisly warning,
but with a simple childlike pleasure at having outlived some one
else; and when a draught might puff them out like a. guttering
candle, or a bit of a stumble shatter them like so much glass, their
old hearts keep sound and unaffrighted, and they go on, bubbling
with laughter, through years of man's age compared to which the
valley at Balaclava was as safe and peaceful as a village cricket-
green on Sunday. It may fairly be questioned (if we look to the
peril only) whether it was a much more daring feat for Curtius
to plunge into the gulf, than for any old gentleman of ninety to
doff his clothes and clamber into bed.

4   Indeed, it is a memorable subject for consideration, with what
unconcern and gaiety mankind pricks on along the Valley of the
Shadow of Death. The whole way is one wilderness of snares, and
the end of it, for those who fear the last pinch, is irrevocable ruin.
And yet we go spinning through it all, like a party for the Derby.
Perhaps the reader remembers one of the humorous devices of the
deified Caligula: how he encouraged a vast concourse of holiday-
makers on to his bridge over Baiæ bay; and when they were in
the height of their enjoyment, turned loose the Prætorian guards
among the company, and had them tossed into the sea. This is
no bad miniature of the dealings of nature with the transitory race
of man. Only, what a chequered picnic we have of it, even while
it lasts! and into what great waters, not to be crossed by any
swimmer, God's pale Prætorian throws us over in the end!

5   We live the time that a match flickers; we pop the cork of a
ginger-beer bottle, and the earthquake swallows us on the instant.
Is it not odd, is it not incongruous, is it not, in the highest sense
of human speech, incredible, that we should think so highly of the
ginger-beer, and regard so little the devouring earthquake? The
love of Life and the fear of Death are two famous phrases that
grow harder to understand the more we think about them. It is
a well-known fact that an immense proportion of boat accidents
would never happen if people held the sheet in their hands instead
of making it fast; and yet, unless it be some martinet of a professional mariner or some landsman with shattered nerves, every

one of God's creatures makes it fast. A strange instance of man's unconcern and brazen boldness in the face of death!

6   We confound ourselves with metaphysical phrases, which we import into daily talk with noble inappropriateness. We have no idea of what death is, apart from its circumstances and some of its consequences to others; and although we have some experience of living, there is not a man on earth who has flown so high into abstraction as to have any practical guess at the meaning of the word *life*. All literature, from Job and Omar Khayyam to Thomas Carlyle or Walt Whitman, is but an attempt to look upon the human state with such largeness of view as shall enable us to rise from the consideration of living to the Definition of Life. And our sages give us about the best satisfaction in their power when they say that it is a vapour, or a show, or made out of the same stuff with dreams. Philosophy, in its more rigid sense, has been at the same work for ages; and after a myriad bald heads have wagged over the problem, and piles of words have been heaped one upon another into dry and cloudy volumes without end, philosophy has the honour of laying before us, with modest pride, her contribution towards the subject: that life is a Permanent Possibility of Sensation. Truly a fine result! A man may very well love beef, or hunting, or a woman; but surely, surely, not a Permanent Possibility of Sensation! He may be afraid of a precipice, or a dentist, or a large enemy with a club, or even an undertaker's man; but not certainly of abstract death. We may trick with the word life in its dozen senses until we are weary of tricking; we may argue in terms of all the philosophies on earth, but one fact remains true throughout— that we do not love life, in the sense that we are greatly pre-occupied about its conservation; that we do not, properly speaking, love life at all, but living. Into the views of the least careful there will enter some degree of providence; no man's eyes are fixed entirely on the passing hour; but although we have some anticipation of good health, good weather, wine, active employment, love, and self-approval, the sum of these anticipations does not amount to anything like a general view of life's possibilities and issues; nor are those who cherish them most vividly, at all the most scrupulous of their personal safety. To be deeply interested in the accidents of our existence, to enjoy keenly the mixed texture of human experience, rather leads a man to disregard precautions, and risk his neck against a straw. For surely the love of living is stronger in an Alpine climber roping over a peril, or a hunter riding merrily at a stiff fence, than in a creature who lives upon a diet and walks a measured distance in the interest of his constitution.

7   There is a great deal of very vile nonsense talked upon both sides of the matter: tearing divines reducing life to the dimensions of a mere funeral procession, so short as to be hardly decent; and melancholy unbelievers yearning for the tomb as if it were a world too far away. Both sides must feel a little ashamed of their performances now and again when they draw in their chairs to dinner. Indeed, a good meal and a bottle of wine is an answer to most standard works upon the question. When a man's heart warms to his viands, he forgets a great deal of sophistry, and soars into a rosy zone of contemplation. Death may be knocking at the door, like the Commander's statue; we have something else in hand, thank God, and let him knock. Passing bells are ringing all the world over. All the world over, and every hour, some one is parting company with all his aches and ecstasies. For us also the trap is laid. But we are so fond of life that we have no leisure to entertain the terror of death. It is a honeymoon with us all through, and none of the longest. Small blame to us if we give our whole hearts to this glowing bride of ours, to the appetites, to honour, to the hungry curiosity of the mind, to the pleasure of the eyes in nature, and the pride of our own nimble bodies.

8   We all of us appreciate the sensations; but as for caring about the Permanence of the Possibility, a man's head is generally very bald, and his senses very dull, before he comes to that. Whether we regard life as a lane leading to a dead wall—a mere bag's end, as the French say—or whether we think of it as a vestibule or gymnasium, where we wait our turn and prepare our faculties for some more noble destiny; whether we thunder in a pulpit, or pule in little atheistic poetrybooks, about its vanity and brevity; whether we look justly for years of health and vigour, or are about to mount into a bath-chair, as a step towards the hearse; in each and all of these views and situations there is but one conclusion possible: that a man should stop his ears against paralysing terror, and run the race that is set before him with a single mind. No one surely could have recoiled with more heartache and terror from the thought of death than our respected lexicographer; and yet we know how little it affected his conduct, how wisely and boldly he walked, and in what a fresh and lively vein he spoke of life. Already an old man, he ventured on his Highland tour; and his heart, bound with triple brass, did not recoil before twenty-seven individual cups of tea. As courage and intelligence are the two qualities best worth a good man's cultivation, so it is the first part of intelligence to recognize our precarious estate in life, and the first part of courage to be not at all abashed before the fact. A

frank and somewhat headlong carriage, not looking too anxiously before, not dallying in maudlin regret over the past, stamps the man who is well armoured for this world.

9   And not only well armoured for himself, but a good friend and a good citizen to boot. We do not go to cowards for tender dealing; there is nothing so cruel as panic; the man who has least fear for his own carcass has most time to consider others. That eminent chemist who took his walks abroad in tin shoes, and subsisted wholly upon tepid milk, had all his work cut out for him in considerate dealings with his own digestion. So soon as prudence has begun to grow up in the brain, like a dismal fungus, it finds its first expression in a paralysis of generous acts. The victim begins to shrink spiritually; he develops a fancy for parlours with a regulated temperature, and takes his morality on the principle of tin shoes and tepid milk. The care of one important body or soul becomes so engrossing, that all the noises of the outer world begin to come thin and faint into the parlour with the regulated temperature; and the tin shoes go equally forward over blood and rain. To be overwise is to ossify; and the scruple-monger ends by standing stockstill. Now the man who has his heart on his sleeve, and a good whirling weathercock of a brain, who reckons his life as a thing to be dashingly used and cheerfully hazarded, makes a very different acquaintance of the world, keeps all his pulses going true and fast, and gathers impetus as he runs, until, if he be running towards anything better than wildfire, he may shoot up and become a constellation in the end. Lord look after his health, Lord have a care of his soul, says he; and he has at the key of the position, and swashes through incongruity and peril towards his aim. Death is on all sides of him with pointed batteries, as he is on all sides of all of us; unfortunate surprises gird him round; mim-mouthed friends and relations hold up their hands in quite a little elegiacal synod about his path: and what cares he for all this? Being a true lover of living, a fellow with something pushing and spontaneous in his inside, he must, like any other soldier, in any other stirring, deadly warfare, push on at his best pace until he touch the goal. "A peerage or Westminster Abbey!" cried Nelson in his bright, boyish, heroic manner. These are great incentives; not for any of these, but for the plain satisfaction of living, of being about their business in some sort or other, do the brave, serviceable men of every nation tread down the nettle danger, and pass flyingly over all the stumbling-blocks of prudence. Think of the heroism of Johnson, think of that superb indifference to mortal limitation that set him upon his dictionary, and carried him

through triumphantly until the end! Who, if he were wisely considerate of things at large, would ever embark upon any work much more considerable than a halfpenny post card? Who would project a serial novel, after Thackeray and Dickens had each fallen in mid-course? Who would find heart enough to begin to live, if he dallied with the consideration of death?

10   And, after all, what sorry and pitiful quibbling all this is! To forego all the issues of living in a parlour with a regulated temperature—as if that were not to die a hundred times over, and for ten years at a stretch! As if it were not to die in one's own lifetime, and without even the sad immunities of death! As if it were not to die, and yet be the patient spectators of our own pitiable change! The Permanent Possibility is preserved, but the sensations carefully held at arm's length, as if one kept a photographic plate in a dark chamber. It is better to lose health like a spendthrift than to waste it like a miser. It is better to live and be done with it, than to die daily in the sickroom. By all means begin your folio; even if the doctor does not give you a year, even if he hesitates about a month, make one brave push and see what can be accomplished in a week. It is not only in finished undertakings that we ought to honour useful labour. A spirit goes out of the man who means execution, which outlives the most untimely ending. All who have meant good work with their whole hearts, have done good work, although they may die before they have the time to sign it. Every heart that has beat strong and cheerfully has left a hopeful impulse behind it in the world, and bettered the tradition of mankind. And even if death catch people, like an open pitfall, and in mid-career, laying out vast projects, and planning monstrous foundations, flushed with hope, and their mouths full of boastful language, they should be at once tripped up and silenced: is there not something brave and spirited in such a termination? and does not life go down with a better grace, foaming in full body over a precipice, than miserably straggling to an end in sandy deltas? When the Greeks made their fine saying that those whom the gods love die young, I cannot help believing they had this sort of death also in their eye. For surely, at whatever age it overtake the man, this is to die young. Death has not been suffered to take so much as an illusion from his heart. In the hot-fit of life, a-tiptoe on the highest point of being, he passes at a bound on to the other side. The noise of the mallet and chisel is scarcely quenched, the trumpets are hardly done blowing, when, trailing with him clouds of glory, this happy-starred, full-blooded spirit shoots into the spiritual land.